MENTAL RETARDATION

Second Edition

James R. Patton
University of Hawaii

James S. Payne
University of Mississippi

Mary Beirne-Smith
University of Alabama

Charles E. Merrill Publishing Company
A Bell & Howell Company
Columbus   Toronto   London   Sydney

Published by Charles E. Merrill Publishing Co.
A Bell & Howell Company
Columbus, Ohio 43216

This book was set in Palatino.
Production Editor and Text Designer: Jeffrey Putnam
Cover Design Coordination: Cathy Watterson
Cover Photo: Mary Hagler

Photo credits: p. 11, Andrew T. Scull, from *Museums of Madness*, New York: St. Martin's Press, 1979; p. 19, B. Blatt and F. Kaplan, from *Christmas in Purgatory: A Photographic Essay on Mental Retardation* (3rd ed.), Syracuse, NY: Human Policy Press, 1974; p. 31, Bruce Johnson; p. 71, Tom Hutchinson; p. 103, United Press International; p. 109, Institute of Human Learning, University of California; p. 113, The Archives of the History of American Psychology; p. 146, Eugene E. Doll; p. 152, Rich Bucurel; p. 157, Mary Hagler; p. 172, Jeremy Rowe; p. 204, U.S. Department of Housing and Urban Development; p. 215, Joan Bergstrom; p. 235, Jim Shaffer; p. 297, Randall D. Williams/© Sheryl Ewing; p. 302, Jeff Bates; p. 361, © Jean Greenwald; p. 370, Mike Davis; p. 403, Cuyahoga County Board of Mental Retardation; p. 420, Ohio Historical Society; p. 487, © Tom Myers; p. 497, v/DIA-Editorial Photo Archives.

Library of Congress Catalog Card Number: 85-72203
International Standard Book Number: 0-675-20483-6
Printed in the United States of America
2 3 4 5 6 7 8 9 — 91 90 89 88 87 86

PREFACE

Special education began with mentally retarded learners because they were recognizably "different" from their peers. Thus, for at least 200 years we have been compiling a considerable body of knowledge about how retarded people learn, about how and what to teach them, and about how we as a society treat our retarded citizens. Yet society is, of course, always changing. Recent events, such as the development of systematic instructional techniques and the passage of the Education for All Handicapped Children Act (P.L. 94-142), have accelerated the rate of change in our field and made critical the need for informed, educated teachers of the retarded. Our purpose in this book is to give up-to-date information on the characteristics of retarded learners, the causes of their retardation and its assessment, and available placement services and programming for retarded people of all ages. We've tried to digest the research and add what we've learned through our own experience. We present the results in a way that we hope is engaging, meaningful, and scholarly, without being overly technical.

Introductory students are sometimes unenthusiastic about the mental retardation course. To combat this attitude, we've designed this book to be more useful for future teachers and other professionals working with retarded people. When possible, we try to show how understanding a given topic relates to teaching. For example, we've tried to show why definitions and prevalence figures are important. We've also "decoded" many of the big words in the discussions of causes of retardation and related them to the reality of working in a classroom or residential setting. We've linked the learning characteristics of retarded students to suggested teaching strategies for them.

In addition, we've included short vignettes in each chapter that give a real-life picture of the retarded, their teachers, and their communities. Like the text, these vignettes cover all age ranges—from preschool through adulthood—and all levels of severity—from mild through profound. Finally, the book progresses from a basic understanding of definition and causes to assessment, teaching procedures, and considerations of the mentally retarded individual in family and society.

ACKNOWLEDGMENTS

We owe our appreciation to many people who helped with the development, research, and production of this book. A revision takes considerable time, so it is quite possible we have overlooked some people in this acknowledgment. To them we apologize. Nevertheless, there are several individuals to whom we are deeply indebted. We are especially grateful to

- ☐ Linda Wilberger, our typist, for diligently and patiently typing from our often illegible handwriting.
- ☐ the field reviewers—Dr. Reuben Altman, University of Missouri-Columbia; Dr. Harvey Switzky, Northern Illinois University; Dr. Tom Burton, University of Georgia; Dr. Eleanor Wright, University of North Carolina-Wilmington; Dr. Gabriel Nardi, West Virginia University; and Dr. Hank Bursani, Miami University—for their time and effort in reading and reviewing the revised and re-revised manuscript.
- ☐ Vicki Knight, Jan Hall, and Jeff Putnam, at Merrill, for their unending enthusiasm, support, patience, understanding, and dedication to this book.

We would also like to thank these people, whose efforts and cheerfulness helped make this book possible: Karen Emoto, Gayle Tsukada, Jill Takemoto, Tammy Kaneshiro, and Laure Takekawa.

J.R.P.
J.S.P.
M.B.S.

CONTENTS

PART THREE   *Major Concerns and Issues*

PART FOUR   *Programming Options*

PART FIVE   *Future*

In memory of
James E. Smith, Jr.,
Smitty

CHAPTER ONE

Historical Perspectives

Many significant events and people have influenced the development of the field of mental retardation, and a look at some of them seems an appropriate place to start. Historical reminiscing, while not seeming to be immediately practical, can be interesting and beneficial for at least two reasons: we can gain a better understanding of our present state, and we may knowledgeably plan for the future based on what we know from history (Mesibov, 1976).

While many of the gains in services for mentally retarded people have been due to the unending and devoted efforts of individuals, there have also been strong sociopolitical forces that most certainly have influenced the development of the field. Clearly, when studying history, we must appreciate the social climate of a given time. Simply stated, in the past, much of what has happened to mentally retarded individuals has been determined largely by sociopolitical forces. And it is no different today. Rappaport (1977), while referring to social sciences in general, captures the essence of these dynamics.

> All of man's quest for understanding . . . can be shown to be influenced by social forces, mediated through personal values

This chapter was contributed by James R. Patton.

> and beliefs . . . it is difficult for people to recognize the social forces influencing their behavior and beliefs because these forces are often diffused and are mixed with the commonsense beliefs of the time. We cannot easily become "unstuck" in time, and we pay little attention to the importance of when we live or how we think. (Rappaport, 1977, pp. 26–27)

Rappaport's idea of mediation can be extended one step further to include the ultimate conclusion about the influence of social forces—social forces affect the *actions* of people in history. Rappaport goes on to state that it is important to "recognize that applied social science and the human service professions are inherently *political*" (p. 26).

Thus the purpose of this chapter is to give you an appreciation of how social and political forces have affected our interactions with mentally retarded people, both in the past and today. In addition, we will attempt to establish a case for what we call a "recycling phenomenon." Many issues which have received our attention in recent years may not be as new as they seem.

> Many people also think that the issues facing special education today are new. But if you read the historical literature of special education, you will see that today's issues and problems are remarkably similar to those of long ago. Issues, problems, and ideas arise, flower, go to seed, and reappear when the conditions are again right for their growth. (Payne, Patton, Kauffman, Brown, & Payne, 1983, p. 164)

Throughout this chapter, we will mention issues which were discussed and debated long ago. You may feel dismayed by the fact that so much time has elapsed and these issues still remain just that—issues, with no final "solutions" in sight. Consequently, this chapter has three objectives. First, we will focus on the historical context of "mental retardation," giving you a glimpse of the sociopolitical influences that have determined where we are today and some recurrent themes expressed throughout the short documented history of the field. Second, we will present the "content" of history; that is, the names, dates, places, and events that are typically associated with history. Third, we hope to introduce you to the complexities of human services as they relate to programming for mentally retarded people.

A HISTORICAL OVERVIEW

While attitudes toward and treatment of mentally retarded persons can actually be traced back to ancient civilizations (including Egypt, Sparta, Rome, and China), for all practical purposes, the documented history relating to the mentally retarded is rather brief, approximately spanning the last 200 years.

Accordingly, we can divide the history of the attitudes toward and treatment of mentally retarded people into ten periods. The ten eras are

1. A state of confusion   prior to 1700
2. The awakening   1700–1800
3. Nascent optimism   1800–1860
4. Disillusionment   1860–1890
5. Sounding the alarm   1890–1920
6. Reconsideration   1920–1930
7. Ebb and flow   1930–1950
8. Turning point   1950–1960
9. Limelight   1960–1970
10. Action and introspection 1970–present

Before we proceed through the various periods, we must address the problem of terminology. Throughout this chapter, those who are called *mentally retarded* will be described in accordance with current systems of classification. While this terminology will help us maintain a consistent standard, we would be remiss not to mention that, historically, other terms have been used officially to describe retarded individuals. Today, however, many people find these terms such as *fool, idiot, imbecile, moron, feebleminded, mental defective,* and *retardate* (among others) to be offensive.

See chapter 2 for a more complete discussion of classification and labeling.

A STATE OF CONFUSION: PRIOR TO 1700

Before the 18th century, the concept of *mental retardation,* regardless of the name used to describe it, was enigmatic to a world that did not have a sophisticated knowledge base with which to understand it. As a result, people around the world held a wide variety of attitudes and perceptions toward the mentally retarded.

Basically, there was no consensus among Western societies as to who these deviant people were, why they acted the way they did, and how they should be treated. Different societies' responses to these questions ranged from treating mentally retarded individuals as buffoons and court jesters to perceiving them as demons or as capable of divine revelations. Evidently, throughout ancient history, different patterns of treatment developed, reflecting an overall confusion.

Throughout this early history and continuing until the early 1900s, when we refer to persons with mental limitations, we are specifically speaking of relatively severely handicapped individuals. "Mild" retardation as we perceive it today had not been defined and was not recognized in the true sense of the term. As Hewett and Forness (1977) mention, "the borderline retarded individual was not noticeably backward in a day when few could read and write" (p. 30). Most mildly retarded individuals blended into society without too much difficulty; it was not until the 20th century that mild retardation came to be recognized as a describable condition.

The Renaissance Before 1700, certain developments resulting from the Renaissance of the 14th, 15th, and 16th centuries created a new social climate that would eventually have direct implications for mentally retarded persons. Although the Renaissance was important to the world in many ways, Maloney and Ward (1978) suggest that two features were appreciably noteworthy.

> By the end of the Renaissance, it had become clear that the goal of a united European Christendom would never be realized. The dominance and centrality of the Catholic Church in medieval Europe's intellectual, cultural, and political affairs, which accounted for the all-encompassing "religious-other-worldly" outlook, came to an end with the rise of the modern nation-state. Thus, the dominance of religion and religious conceptualizations was broken. Man was free to think instead of this world and himself. The second factor was an even more important ideological change. Copernicus had shocked his contemporaries with his theory that the earth was not at the center of the universe, an idea that had fit in nicely with the religious views of the time. Galileo's invention of the telescope confirmed the correctness of Copernicus' "heretical" allegation. Man was no longer the center of the universe, but rather a mere cosmic speck. Modern man has great difficulty appreciating the tremendous, shocking impact of such a discovery on medieval thinking. This drastic change in world-view had immense theological implications and hastened the demise of religious domination. This discovery also increased man's willingness to look at himself and his environment more openly, naturally, and empirically (i.e., scientifically). (1978, pp. 21–22)

These forces tended to refocus man's concept of himself and of the world. The ultimate effects of these changes were reflected in the development of a climate which would be conducive to the philosophy of humanism and to the revolutionary fervor of the 18th century.

Before 1700, if any "service" (using the word loosely) was provided to handicapped individuals, it merely involved housing and sustenance, usually provided in monasteries. We do not have any evidence of systematic programs of training or service delivery. Although obvious changes were occurring in the world, not much was changing for the mentally retarded person of the 17th century.

In America at this time, the family unit was of prime importance, and accordingly much responsibility was placed on the family to take care of any exceptional member. As a carry-over from our European origins, the colonies enacted laws that "provided" for many of the needy by creating almshouses and workhouses. Although looked upon as financial burdens, those individuals who could not provide for themselves were taken care of by colonial societies.

THE AWAKENING: 1700–1800

Perhaps the two most significant features of the 18th century were the advent of "sensationalism" and the revolutionary changes in both Europe and America. Through the efforts of various philosophers, most notably Locke and Rousseau, new ideas that stressed the importance of the senses on development began to take hold. Their ideas provided new ways of perceiving the nature of the human mind and ultimately influenced educational reform.

As mentioned previously, Renaissance thinking encouraged a philosophy of humanism, principally concerned with man's worth as a human being and with the freedom to develop to a maximum level. Eventually, these ideas were seen as being in conflict with the existing philosophies and policies of some established nations. Consequently, both Europeans and Americans reacted to these needs for freedom through revolution, as Maloney and Ward relate (1978).

> The political culmination of this movement occurred during what historians call the Age-of-Revolution (1775 to 1795). This referred primarily to the American and French revolutions, although the revolutionary spirit was widespread across all of Europe. The essence of these revolutions was the declaration of individual human rights, as embodied in the American Bill of Rights and the French Declaration of Rights. All men were now deemed to be created equal and to have the inalienable rights of life, liberty, and the pursuit of happiness. A more specific humanitarian concern was expressed in the popular French revolutionary slogan: "Liberté, Égalité, Fraternité." (pp. 22–23)

We might wonder what effect these historical events had on mentally retarded people. We believe that they had two major implications. First, a new social attitude was established. It held that all "men," even those who were disabled, had rights. This attitude helped lead to a climate that would support efforts to help these individuals. Second, the times were right for idealistic young people to put the philosophy of humanism and the ideas of Locke and Rousseau into practice.

EARLY OPTIMISM: 1800–1860

The first part of the 19th century is best depicted as a time of enthusiasm toward working with handicapped people, as displayed by a number of young, devoted people. Nurtured by the events of the previous century, these "pioneers" were willing to try to do something that never had been tried previously; they attempted to help less fortunate people through bona fide service. The recognized birth of special education and systematic services for disabled individuals occurred in Europe in the early 1800s.

Without question, the field of special education was dramatically influenced by Jean Marc Itard (1774–1838). Early in his career, Itard, a medical doctor who initially was concerned with diseases of the ear and the needs of the deaf, became quite interested in a feral child who was found in a wooded area near Aveyron, France, in 1799. Intrigued by this boy, whom he named Victor, Itard thought that he could transform this *homme sauvage* from a state of savagery to a state of civilized behavior (Humphrey & Humphrey, 1962).

Believing that Victor's skill deficiencies were due to environmental limitations, Itard thought he could develop those skills which were lacking by implementing a systematic training program. His program included five major objectives.

1. To render social life more congenial to the boy by making it more like the wild life he had recently kept.
2. To excite his nervous sensibility with varied and energetic stimuli and supply his mind with the raw impression of ideas.
3. To extend the range of his ideas by creating new wants and expanding his relations with the world around him.
4. To lead him to the use of speech by making it necessary that he should imitate.
5. To apply himself to the satisfaction of his growing physical wants, and from this lead to the application of his intelligence to the objects of instruction. (Kanner, 1964, p. 14)

Although Itard worked with Victor for 5 years, Victor did not progress as well as Itard wished, and subsequently the program was terminated. From that point until 1828 Victor lived mostly in a purely custodial setting. Itard felt he was a near total failure with Victor, yet history documented his efforts and he was praised by the French Academy of Science. Itard's importance rests not so much in his success or failure with Victor, but rather in the precedent that he set by systematically working with a severely impaired child. The influence he had on other figures at that time clearly distinguishes Itard as one of the most significant pioneers in the field of special education.

One person who was profoundly affected by Itard's work was Edouard Seguin (1812–1880). Encouraged by Itard to get involved in the treatment of "idiocy," Seguin was also motivated to help the less fortunate by a strong religious influence. Like Itard, Seguin also chose to undertake the *education de son enfant idiot.* After 18 months of intensive work with this boy, Seguin was able to demonstrate that the boy had learned a number of skills. Seguin extended his methods to other chil-

"Homme sauvage" means wild boy.

dren, and in 1837 he established a program for "educating" the feeble-minded at the Salpetriere in Paris.

Seguin's methods and educational programs, which were even more systematic than Itard's, stressed physiological and moral education. This methodology, as Seguin developed it, incorporated a general training program that integrated muscular, imitative, nervous, and reflective physiological functions (Seguin, 1846). Many educational techniques which Seguin used in his programs, such as individualized instruction and behavior management, can be found in today's methodology.

Seguin emigrated to the United States in 1848, principally due to the political unrest in Paris at that time. While he lived in the United States, he often served as a consultant to those who sought his advice and expertise on programming for retarded residents of institutions. In 1866, Seguin published a book entitled *Idiocy and Its Treatment by Physiological Methods*, which became a major reference for educating mentally retarded individuals in the latter part of the 19th century. Seguin also served as the first president of the Association of Medical Officers of American Institutions for Idiotic and Feebleminded Persons. Hervey Wilbur, in his eulogy to Seguin, perhaps best summarized the impact this man had on the field.

> This association is now called the American Association on Mental Deficiency.

> He entered upon the work with enthusiasm. There he toiled, till there he grew, little by little, a system—principles and methods—which has been the guide of all later labors in the same direction, the world over. (Wilbur, 1880)

Another individual who figured significantly in providing services to the mentally retarded was Johann Guggenbühl (1816–1863). Guggenbühl has been credited with establishing the first residential facility designed to provide comprehensive treatment for mentally retarded individuals. This facility, called the Abendberg, which he founded in 1841, was located in the mountains of Switzerland.

Well publicized, principally through the efforts of Guggenbühl himself, the Abendberg drew the attention of many prominent people. As Payne, Patton, Kauffman, Brown & Payne (1983) mention, the real significance of Guggenbühl's facility rests in its impact on the visitors it attracted, many of whom were interested in establishing similar facilities. As Kanner notes, "The Abendberg became the destination of pilgrimages made by physicians, philanthropists, and writers from many lands, who promptly published glowing reports when they went back home" (1964, p. 25).

Unfortunately, the glowing reviews and accolades attributed to the Abendberg were short-lived, and eventually severe criticism of the facility prevailed. Although forced to close due to intolerable conditions, in its heyday the Abendberg nevertheless served as the model on which many other institutions were designed. It can also serve as an example of a program that achieved recognition but was unable to maintain it. Notwithstanding, Guggenbühl created a prototype for the institutional care of retarded persons, the effects of which can still be felt today.

Although it may seem that Europe conceived and gave birth to the field of special education, the United States was not without its own pioneers and important events during the mid-1800s. Three individuals who had much to do with securing services for mentally retarded persons in this country were Dorothea Dix, Samuel Howe, and Hervey Wilbur.

During the early 1840s, Dorothea Dix zealously campaigned for better treatment of the less fortunate, who were housed in facilities such as asylums, almshouses, poorhouses, and country homes (Cegelka & Prehm, 1982). At this time there were no other options. Her efforts are reflected in her own words, directed towards the Massachusetts Legislature in 1843.

> I come to present the strong claims of suffering humanity. I come to place before the Legislature of Massachusetts the condition of the miserable, the desolate, the outcast. I come as the advocate of helpless, forgotten, insane, and idiotic men and women; of beings sunk to a condition from which the most unconcerned would start with real horror; of being wretched in our prisons, and more wretched in our almshouses. And I cannot suppose it needful to employ earnest persuasion, or stubborn argument, in order to arrest and fix attention upon a subject only the more strongly pressing in its claims because it is revolting and disgusting in its details. (Dix, 1843)

See chapter 15 for a view of advocacy today.

Obviously, Dorothea Dix dramatized what advocacy is all about, and through her efforts she was able to focus much attention on those whom she called "suffering humanity."

Samuel Howe (1801–1876) contributed greatly to providing services for mentally retarded people through his efforts to establish the public's obligation to train these individuals. In 1848, after visiting Guggenbühl's Abendberg and convincing the Massachusetts Legislature to appropriate $2500 per year, Howe established the first *public* setting for training mentally retarded individuals. This new setting was a wing of Boston's Perkins Institution for the Blind, of which Howe was the director. A few months earlier in this same year, Hervey Wilbur (1820–1883) had founded the first *private* setting for treating mentally retarded individuals at his home in Barre, Massachusetts.

What then was the result of the work of pioneers such as Itard, Seguin, Guggenbühl, Howe, Dix, and Wilbur? First, an atmosphere of optimism developed, implying that many mentally retarded persons could be trained, "cured," and reintegrated into the community as productive citizens. Second, based upon this very same hope and enthusiasm, many promises were made and reflected in the lofty goals that were established. Ironically, it was precisely the uncontrolled enthusiasm prevalent at the time that would be partially responsible for the pessimism of the next period.

DISILLUSIONMENT: 1860–1890

As any student of United States history knows quite well, the 1860s were a time of national disharmony, enflamed by years of growing sectional conflict. Prior to the Civil War, America was basically an agrarian society, characterized by small farms and small towns. After the War, the country began to experience a dramatic change in the form of urbanization and industrialization. These changes and others had a strong effect on the treatment of mentally retarded persons.

This national metamorphosis precipitated many problems, some of which accompanied the increased growth of cities. Correlates of urban life such as crime, poverty, and disease were later to be associated with retarded persons. In addition, while industrialization provided vocational opportunities for many people, the skills required were often too demanding for many retarded persons.

Remember that the retarded who were recognizable at this time had moderate and severe limitations.

Specifically, what happened to the enthusiasm of the mid-1800s? There was a critical change in attitude toward the possibility of reintegrating the retarded into the community. Initially accepting the grandiose claims of many enthusiastic individuals, who stated that these less fortunate could be "cured," critics began to realize that these goals—while laudable—were unrealistic. A pronounced climate of pessimism developed. As we know well today, those individuals who were said to be capable of being cured in the 1800s (i.e., severely handicapped people) were indeed capable of skill acquisition, but for most of these individuals a complete return to "normalcy" was quite unrealistic. Therefore, in retrospect, we can easily imagine the problems encountered by those early advocates who earnestly tried to reintegrate these severely retarded individuals into the community.

There were many problems that contributed to the disillusionment of this era. However, four factors seem to be the most salient. First, as already mentioned, the population being addressed was not capable of being "cured" or "transformed into totally normal functioning members of society." Second, community reintegration demands more than merely providing training. If successful reintegration requires community preparation and development, as we think it does, then we should not be surprised to discover that this was a neglected concern in the 1800s. Sadly, even today, the provision of community services and support is glaringly inadequate. Third, after an atmosphere of hope and excitement had been created, many retarded individuals were pitied, resulting in two important developments: (*a*) services to individuals who needed systematic, intense programming were diluted, and (*b*) more institutions were formed (Maloney & Ward, 1978). These developments would have a tragic effect on retarded people in the late 1800s. Fourth was the previously mentioned demands of an increasingly more complex society created by postwar urbanization and industrialization.

Obviously, these were formidable obstacles to the fruition of the early goals championed by the idealistic pioneers of the early and mid-1800s. While it is easy now to reproach those enthusiasts for creating a "no-win" situation that ultimately resulted in many regressive developments for the mentally retarded people whom they wanted to help, we need to understand that these early advocates (however naive in not understanding the limitations of their claims) were most sincere in their zeal, hopes, and efforts. Unfortunately for those individuals on whom those great expectations were based, they were now being perceived as "incurable." It was unfortunate in itself that the early enthusiasm had waned, but even more unfortunate was the fact that the worst was yet to come.

SOUNDING THE ALARM: 1890–1920

As the 19th century came to a close, the disillusionment that resulted from the failure to reintegrate the mentally retarded into the community developed into a more reactionary attitude. The alarm was sounded! Institutions originally designed to serve as training facilities from which individuals would leave to return to community settings now began to assume a new role—custodial.

During this period of alarm, a dramatic change in social attitudes was piqued by a number of significant events, which were cumulatively very debilitating to any movement favorable to the needs of the mentally retarded population. Many citizens were now concerned that mentally retarded people were dangerous to society. Kanner captures the prevailing perceptions during this time.

> The mental defectives were viewed as a menace to civilization, incorrigible at home, burdens to the school, sexually promiscuous, breeders of feebleminded offspring, victims and spreaders of poverty, degeneracy, crime, and disease. Consequently, there was a cry for the segregation of all mental defectives, with the aim of purifying society, of erecting a solid wall between it and its contaminators. (1964, p. 85)

It did not take long for society to develop ways to control the number of mentally defective people; these means of social control included restricted marriages, sterilization, and institutionalization (Cegelka & Prehm, 1982).

This artist sketch of an institutional resident in England around 1815 was mass-produced and used by early reformers in a campaign to improve conditions.

Many contributing factors precipitated regressive events of the late 1800s and early 1900s. Three general trends seemed to have a pronounced effect on the creation of this state of alarm: the eugenics scare, the influx of immigrants to the United States, and the mental test movement. It will be helpful to explore each of these trends.

The Eugenics Scare Although the thrust of the eugenics movement was not felt until the late 1800s and early 1900s, its antecedents can be traced to earlier times. Simply stated, this movement was interested in controlling the number of "feebleminded" through selective breeding.

Influenced by the ideas of Charles Darwin, Sir Francis Galton extended Darwin's concept of evolution to humans. In 1869, Galton published *Hereditary Genius*, which espoused the idea that individual traits, most notably genius, were inherited. With time, Galton seemed to catalyze the eugenics movement that advocated the genetic control of mental defectives, and this idea would be nurtured by others. What Galton established was a theoretical basis for the inheritance of mental defectiveness. Gregor Mendel's discovery of the laws of inheritance at the turn of the 20th century was the scientific breakthrough that would lend much support to Galton's ideas.

Two publications reinforced society's attitude that mental retardation had genetic implications: *The Jukes, a Study in Crime, Pauperism, Disease and Heredity* (Dugdale, 1877) and *The Kallikak Family* (Goddard, 1913 as reprinted by Macmillan Publishing Co., 1972). Each of these books traced the genetic relationships of the members of one family. Dugdale's original work actually focused on criminality and its correlates, and only later was the added correlate of mental retardation inferred. Goddard's work, however, had as its central theme the notion that feeblemindedness was inherited; elaborate pedigree studies (through five generations) were presented as evidence.

These events fueled the movement to genetically control the menace of feeblemindedness. Strong evidence that eugenics was being taken seriously can be found in the enactment of sterilization laws during the early 1900s, Indiana having the dubious distinction of enacting the first such law in 1907. As added measures of control, the institutions strictly segregated men and women to eliminate the chance for possible feebleminded progeny.

Immigration During the second half of the 19th century, the United States experienced a great increase in the number of immigrants, mostly from southern and eastern Europe. As most of these immigrants flocked to the growing urban centers, many problems emerged. Americans of

Read the vignette below for one professional's view of mental retardation in 1912.

This immigrant situation did have one positive effect—it reaffirmed the need for compulsory education provided by the government.

MINDS MADE FEEBLE

In 1912 Henry Goddard reported the results of his study of the inheritance of feeblemindedness. His book, *The Kallikak Family: A Study in the Heredity of Feeble-Mindedness*, was very influential because it underscored the perceived threat which feeblemindedness could have on society and helped fuel the eugenics movement. The book was very popular and to this day the Kallikak story is regularly retold in discussions of mental retardation.

The effects of the study are described well by J. David Smith in his recent investigation, *Minds Made Feeble*.

> Goddard's book on the Kallikak family was received with acclaim by the public and by much of the scientific community. . . . Only gradually was criticism forthcoming which questioned the methods used in the study and the implications and conclusions drawn from the data collected. Even in the

light of substantive and knowledgeable criticism, however, the essential message of the Kallikak study persisted for years. Even today its influence, in convoluted forms, continues to have a social and political impact. That message is simple, yet powerful. Ignorance, poverty, and social pathology are in the blood—in the seed. It is not the environment in which people are born and develop that makes the critical difference in human lives. People are born either favored or beyond help.

It was this message and the social myth which accompanied it which compelled Smith to investigate and report the complete story of the Kallikak family and the study which was its genesis. A few highlights of Smith's findings are presented below.

☐ Questions as to whether Deborah Kallikak was actually feeble-

northern and western European origin looked upon these immigrants as inferior; this stance was supported by a study performed by Goddard which concluded that many of these foreigners were feebleminded.

The Testing Movement A third major trend contributing to the alarmist climate of the early 1900s was the introduction of the mental test. In 1905, Alfred Binet and Theodore Simon developed an instrument designed to be used in the French schools to screen those students who were not benefitting from regular classroom instruction. Their creation, the mental test, has had a lasting effect on the field of special education. In essence, in the mental scale of intelligence, Binet and Simon created a new definable category of retardation, known to us today as *mild retardation*; however, Goddard labeled this group "morons" in 1910. Prior to this time, those recognizable as mentally retarded were more severely involved, but now new "alarms" were being sounded about the size and magnitude of the problem created by this newly identified group of retarded persons.

minded arise. (Deborah Kallikak was the woman with whom Goddard came into contact and whose ancestors he studied.)

☐ Goddard's professional acquaintances seemed to have had a great influence on him.

☐ The methodology used to study the Kallikak family and the skills of those who collected the information are once again questioned.

☐ The "real" Kallikaks do not seem to have been as abhorrent as they were described by Goddard. Smith commented, "The truth of their lives was sacrificed to the effort to prove a point. The Kallikak study is fiction draped in the social science of its time."

☐ The implications of the study "proved to be a very potent indictment against the poor, the uneducated, racial minorities, the foreign born, and those classified as mentally retarded or mentally ill," resulting in a number of social policies such as compulsory sterilization, restricted immigration, and institutionalization which adversely affected these groups.

☐ Through painstaking investigation, Smith determined the real name of the family which Goddard studied (Kallikak was a pseudonym): However, the name is not revealed.

One of Smith's major contributions is his admonition to be aware of the significance and power of social myths: "Social myths are constantly in the making, compelling in their simplicity, and alluring because we want to believe them. Perhaps understanding the Kallikak story will help in recognizing and resisting them."

Although Binet and Simon introduced their test to French society, it did not take long for it to be brought to the United States. In 1911, Henry Goddard translated the Binet-Simon scales into English; and in 1916 Lewis Terman of Stanford University refined the mental scales into the instrument known as the Stanford-Binet. Terman is also given credit for introducing the concept of **IQ (intelligence quotient).**

Since significantly more individuals could be empirically identified as mentally retarded, special classes for mentally retarded students developed and grew in number. In 1896, the first special class for retarded students in the United States was established in Providence, Rhode Island. Another event of significance was New Jersey's enactment in 1911 of legislation mandating the education of mentally retarded students.

Special classes and programming for mentally retarded students in Europe had begun as early as 1859 in Germany.

RECONSIDERATION: 1920–1930

With the onset of World War I, the military services needed a way to obtain information relatively quickly from large groups of people for use in assigning personnel. Thus the first group intelligence scales (the alpha and beta tests) were developed. The results of this testing further cultivated a climate of alarm by suggesting that mild mental retardation was more widespread than anyone had previously believed.

The alarm was indeed sounded! Society was frightened by the menace of retardation. With mental retardation being more prevalent than once thought, with its seeming inheritability, and with its correlation with crime, poverty, incorrigibility, and disease, it is not difficult to understand how such an alarmist attitude could develop and prevail. While quite strong by the end of the second decade of the 20th century, this aura of fear would begin to fade in the ensuing years. However, the impact of this era would be long-lasting.

Although World War I was hardly a blessing, it did have some positive effects on social attitudes toward the handicapped. As with all wars, many veterans returned to their homes with war-caused disabilities. In 1920, the Vocational Rehabilitation Act (P.L. 66-236) was enacted to allow civilians to benefit from vocational rehabilitation. With the end of the war, the need for providing services to veterans was acknowledged, and now these services were being extended to other individuals who displayed need. In 1921, Yerkes published a work on the intellectual capacities of World War I soldiers. This study suggested that mild retardation was more widespread than previously thought and exacerbated feelings of extreme caution already ignited by earlier events.

The 1920s were a time of experimentation. Lifestyles changed quickly with the stock market crash of 1929 and the Great Depression that followed. Like war, the Great Depression did not have many pleasant effects; however, there were some. As far as exceptional individuals were concerned, the Depression caused the average person, who had been unaware of or not interested in the problems of human need, to be put into a position of appreciation. Everyone was needy.

Special education, as a bona fide field of professionals, took a tremendous step in 1922 when Elizabeth Farrell established the International Council for the Education of Exceptional Children. Prior to this time, the field had no unifying organizational structure on a national level. This new organization, which Farrell served as the first president, is now known as The Council for Exceptional Children (CEC), certainly a key institutional force in special education.

EBB AND FLOW: 1930–1950

Following a period of great concern about the social menace of mental retardation in the early part of the 20th century, the next 20 years can be depicted as a time of limited progress. Recovery from the setbacks of the previous era was certainly needed. The transition from alarm to "guarded enlightenment" was affected by a number of events, as Maloney and Ward (1978) state.

1. The view of mental retardation as a unitary, recessive, inherited trait began to fade as the science of genetics grew in scope and precision.
2. New clinical studies demonstrated the significance of other, nonhereditary, sources of mental retardation, such as trauma, infection, and endocrine disturbance.
3. The methodological flaws and biased interpretations of the pedigree studies were becoming more and more apparent.
4. Other surveys of institutional populations indicated that over one-half of them had intellectually normal parents, further weakening the singular heredity view and associated calls for eugenic solutions.
5. The older research studies that had linked mental retardation with every conceivable social ill were critically reanalyzed and found wanting.
6. Newer, better controlled, and more objective studies failed to reveal the dramatic links of the previous era. (p. 57)

Although the alarmist climate was fading, the years between 1930 and 1950 did not see much in the way of advances that directly affected the mentally retarded. Nevertheless, these 20 years did witness certain events that had either an indirect, immediate effect or a more direct, latent effect on mentally retarded people.

Sociopolitical influences During the early 1930s, the United States was trying to regain a certain stability, both economically and socially. One interesting event occurred when President Herbert Hoover convened the first White House Conference on Child Health and Protection in 1930. This conference drew national attention, however brief, to the needs of exceptional individuals. Certainly, at this point in history, most people were concerned with their existence and survival under uncomfortable circumstances. Nevertheless, the nation was attending to other issues also. Despite these problems, the number of classes for special students kept growing.

After the presidential elections of 1932, the United States went through many changes. The new president, Franklin D. Roosevelt, influenced this country's attitudes toward the welfare of all citizens. Roosevelt's "New Deal" philosophy was responsible for much social change through legislation and the formulation of new programs. One such piece of legislation that affected exceptional individuals was the Social Security Act of 1935. In a nutshell, there seemed to be two major trends in the treatment of exceptional individuals during the 1930s: (*a*) a new attitude supportive of a public welfare system was generated and (*b*) responsibility toward those in need was affirmed.

With the direct involvement of the United States in World War II, the attention and behavior of the nation were refocused once again. We can see certain similarities between World War I and World War II as they affected the mentally retarded population. As was the case in WWI, the general screening of soldiers in the 1940s reestablished the perceived extent of mild retardation. Likewise, when the war was over, many families, and the nation as a whole, felt the realities of disability. A heightened sensitivity to the needs of disabled veterans developed. WW II also created increased employment opportunities for retarded individuals in war-related industries.

Research and Programmatic Influences From 1930 to 1950, there were many relevant developments in both the social and physical sciences. In 1934, Fölling, a Norwegian physician, explained the biochemical mechanics related to the metabolic disturbance referred to as **PKU (phenylketonuria).** The importance of this discovery goes beyond the singularity of this event.

> A new era dawned in 1934 when Fölling in Norway discovered phenylpyruvic acid oliophrenia (phenylketonuria) as a metabolic disturbance which could eventually become reversible by means of proper dietary regulation. This contribution, termed "one of the great discoveries in medical history" by Clemens E. Bonda, at long last made the issue of mental deficiency appear respectable as a legitimate field of research in the biological sciences. Slowly and at first reluctantly, the medical profession began to take an interest. (Kanner, 1964, p. 141)

Two assessment instruments of major importance were developed during this period. In 1935, Edgar Doll published his Vineland Social Maturity Scale (VSMS). This scale allowed professionals to gain additional information about a mentally retarded person's behavior and level of functioning. In 1949, David Wechsler published another intelligence scale, entitled the Wechsler Intelligence Scale for Children (WISC). Like the VSMS, this device proved to be very useful for assessment. Although it may not be readily apparent, these instruments have had a pronounced effect on the identification and classification of many retarded individuals ever since their publication.

The VSMS has recently been revised and is now called the Vineland Adaptive Behavior Scales. For a more detailed explanation of the WISC, see chapter 4. For the VSMS, see chapter 5.

Another influence on the public perception of mental retardation was a number of studies that seemed to stress the importance of environment as causing mental retardation. As the "nature-nurture" controversy was debated, certain studies, most notably those performed by Skeels and his colleagues, questioned the notion that IQ was fixed or constant. Skeels and Dye (1939) inferred that environmental factors have a critical effect on IQ; or, if you will, on one's being classified as mentally retarded.

This controversy is still continuing; it is explored in depth in chapter 7.

A TURNING POINT: 1950–1960

As the decade of the fifties began, the field of special education went through changes that would have notable effects in following years. Foremost among these changes was a new national policy concerned with the problems of special people.

After the second world war, the United States experienced a period of renewed prosperity. This created a climate in which "the demands of parents, the enthusiasm of professionals, and federal, state and private funding gave new impetus to progress in the area of mental retardation" (Hewett & Forness, 1977). These three forces, augmented by other variables, highlighted this "turning point" in history. Although institutional changes were beginning to occur, at best these events would be classified as a "quiet revolution." Individuals were still being institutionalized at an alarming rate; tragically, too many persons who should not have been placed in these settings found themselves there. It is important to note that today there are many human service professionals who believe institutional care in any form is no longer defensible.

Parent Groups Certainly one of the most important events recorded to date was the formation in 1950 of the National Association for Retarded Children (NARC). This organization, composed mostly of parents of retarded children, became the supreme advocate for retarded children. Functioning as lobbyist, service provider, and promoter of research, NARC has had a profound impact on exceptional people. Most importantly, NARC was a coordinated effort of its members to express their attitudes, beliefs, concerns, and desires in politically effective ways.

NARC was renamed the National Association for Retarded Citizens in 1973. In 1982 the name was again changed to the Association for Retarded Citizens—United States

Sociopolitical Developments By the early 1950s, the United States was beginning to adopt a national policy committed to the needs of the mentally retarded, and a policy willing to financially support endeavors that addressed these needs. Over the years, social attitudes toward retarded people had changed from fear and repulsion to tolerance and compassion. Whether sparked by the troubled times of the 1930s and 1940s which the nation as a whole endured, or influenced by purely economic motives, during the 1950s financial backing required to develop more and better programs was provided. If only for economic reasons, the importance of maximizing the potential of handicapped people was acknowledged during this time as echoed by President Eisenhower in a 1954 message to Congress.

> We are spending three times as much in public assistance to care for nonproductive disabled people as it would cost to make them self-sufficient and taxpaying members of their communities. Rehabilitated people as a group pay back in federal income taxes many times the cost of their rehabilitation.

By 1952, 46 of the 48 states had enacted legislation for educating mentally retarded children. However, the education mandated by these state legislatures did not provide programming for *all* mentally retarded individuals. Most severely and moderately retarded children were still excluded from receiving educational services.

It was not until 1975 and passage of P.L. 94-142, The Education for All Handicapped Children Act, that the issue of "educating" *all* mentally retarded students was formally addressed. On the federal level, 1954 is notable because in that year Congress passed the Cooperative Research Act (P.L. 83-531), which provided money for research that would be directed toward mentally retarded persons. In 1958, P.L. 85-926 was passed. It provided incentives to various organizations (i.e., state educational agencies and institutions of higher education) in the form of grants to encourage the preparation of teachers of the mentally retarded. Thus, if federal legislation may be perceived as an index of national commitment to a cause, and it should be, then we can see that a policy supportive of the needs of special people was developing in the 1950s.

As the fifties came to a close, three forces were beginning to shape future events. First, the publication of *Mental Subnormality*, written by Masland, Sarason, and Gladwin in 1958, reflected the emergence of a new philosophical orientation. This school of thought stressed that certain social and cultural variables have a strong correlation with mental retardation. The influence of this point of view on the field can be observed in the 1959 definition of mental retardation proposed by the American Association on Mental Deficiency (Heber, 1959). This definition associated intellectual deficits with "impairment in one or more of the following: (1) maturation, (2) learning, and (3) social adjustment" (Heber, 1959, p. 3).

Chapter 2 discusses the question of definition of retardation in depth.

Even in 1965, American institutions for the mentally retarded were often dismal places. The deinstitutionalization movement aims to move residents from institutions like this back into their communities and improve conditions for those who remain in institutions. This photo is taken from Burton Blatt's book, *Christmas in Purgatory*, which was considered unpublishable until a parents' group donated the money to publish it. The pictures later became the largest photo spread in *Look* magazine up to that time. This episode dramatically shows Americans' changing attitudes during the 1960s.

Second, educators and advocates began to be concerned about the segregation of retarded students in special classes. Existing research tended to support the special class setting. Nevertheless, this issue would continue to be debated in the future, resulting in some major changes in the 1970s.

Third, when the Soviet Union launched Sputnik in 1958, the United States responded dramatically—at first with shock and then with a zeal for technological development unparalleled in history. In essence, the nation's uncontrollable desire to grow technologically would focus very sharply on the institution of education. Changes were evidently needed, and many changes did result. Both regular education and special education were affected by the vigor of the times. And so, the nation was primed for the tumultuous sixties.

LIMELIGHT: 1960–1970

If asked to reflect on the decade of the 1960s, most adults can recall many tragic episodes in a time of rather extreme social change. The violent deaths of national leaders and the widespread opposition and resulting reaction to the Vietnam War are vivid recollections of the 1960s. Paradoxically, the early part of this decade was characterized by generalized enthusiasm, and this enthusiasm was quite evident in the area of special education. There are many reasons why special education was on center stage during the sixties.

Sociopolitical Variables   When President Kennedy assumed office in 1961, he symbolized the energy of our country at that time. Kennedy, who had a retarded sister, once again brought national attention to the needs of those who are mentally retarded. In 1961, he established the President's Panel on Mental Retardation (PPMR), which was to serve as a guide and source for national policy. Under the direction of Leonard Mayo (1962), this panel published *A Proposed Program for National Action to Combat Mental Retardation,* which set the tone for policy decisions for the next decade. The principal recommendations found in the report were

1. Research in the causes of retardation and in methods of care, rehabilitation, and learning.
2. Preventive health measures, including (*a*) a greatly strengthened program of maternal and infant care directed first at the centers of population where prematurity and the rate of "damaged" children are high; (*b*) protection against such known hazards to pregnancy as radiation and harmful drugs, and (*c*) extended diagnostic and screening services.
3. Strengthened educational programs generally and extended and enriched programs of special education in public and private schools closely coordinated with vocational guidance, vocational rehabilitation, and specific training and preparation for employment; education for the adult mentally retarded, and workshops geared to their needs.
4. More comprehensive and improved clinical and social services.
5. Improved methods and facilities for care, with emphasis on the development of a wide range of local community facilities.
6. A new legal, as well as social, concept of the retarded, includ-

ing protection of their civil rights; life guardianship provisions when needed; and enlightened attitude on the part of the law and the courts; and clarification of the theory of responsibility in criminal acts.

7. Helping overcome the serious problems of manpower as they affect the entire field of science and every type of service through extended programs of recruiting with fellowships; and increased opportunities for graduate students, and those preparing for the professions to observe and learn at first hand about the phenomenon of retardation. Because there will never be a fully adequate supply of personnel in this field and for other cogent reasons, the panel has emphasized the need for more volunteers in health, recreation, and welfare activities, and for a domestic Peace Corps to stimulate voluntary service.

8. Programs of education and information to increase public awareness of the problem of mental retardation. (Mayo, 1962, pp. 14–15)

Other recommendations, with a very contemporary flavor, were also proposed.

1. That programs for the retarded, including modern day care, recreation, residential services, and ample educational and vocational opportunities, be comprehensive.

2. That they operate in or close to the communities where the retarded live—that is, that they be community centered.

3. That services be so organized as to provide a central or fixed point for the guidance, assistance, and protection of retarded persons if and when needed, and to assure a sufficient array or continuum of services to meet different types of need.

4. That private agencies as well as public agencies at the local, state, and federal levels continue to provide resources and to increase them for this worthy purpose. While the federal government can assist, the principal responsibility for financing and improving services for the mentally retarded must continue to be borne by states and local communities. (Mayo, 1962, pp. 14–15)

Federal legislation relevant to the needs of mentally retarded people continued to be enacted during the sixties. In 1963, Congress passed The Mental Retardation Facilities and Mental Health Centers Construction Act, which established monies for the construction of Mental Retardation Research Centers (MRRC). These centers conducted organized multidisciplinary research on various complex facets of mental retardation. In 1965, the Elementary and Secondary Education Act (ESEA) (P.L. 89-10), was passed. Part of this legislation focused attention on the needs of disadvantaged students. In 1966, ESEA was amended, and as a result the Bureau of Education for the Handicapped (BEH), a subcomponent of the Office of Education (OE), was created.

National policy on the needs of the disadvantaged reached its pinnacle with President Johnson's "War on Poverty." With the growing interest in social and cultural determinants of behavior, it is not surprising that much attention was given to environmental causes of retardation. Project Head Start did just that. The concept that early intervention might ameliorate some of the negative effects of unfavorable social or cultural situations was fashionable and encouraged during the mid-sixties.

If nothing else can be said of the 1960s, certainly we can state that it was a time responsive to personal and civil rights. The civil rights movement was consummated by passage into law of the Civil Rights Act of 1964; however, this law did not deal directly with exceptional people, per se. Nevertheless, the achievements and impetus provided by the civil rights movement and the resulting legislation would be realized and extended to handicapped people in the 1970s.

Trends in Service Delivery With continuing support provided by state and federal governments, the proliferation of programs and services for mentally retarded people grew almost exponentially. But the spotlight was soon to flicker, *if not dim!* Lloyd Dunn's 1968 challenge to the efficacy of special class placement symbolized some of the reexamination occurring in the late sixties and early seventies.

On a positive note, a new philosophical theme was beginning to take hold. The principle of normalization, which originated during the 1950s in Scandinavia, was finding much support in the United States. Bank-Mikkelsen and Nirje were eminently responsible for the development and dissemination of this principle in Scandinavia, while Wolf Wolfensberger was instrumental in championing the principle in the United States. To a great extent this was due to a single publication which had a great impact on professionals in the United States. Entitled *Changing Patterns in Residential Services for the Mentally Retarded,* this publication included a discussion of the principle of normalization by Bengt Nirje (1969), which sparked a movement in this country that epitomized the next decade. Nirje defined normalization as "making available to the mentally retarded patterns and conditions of everyday life which are as close as possible to the norms and patterns of the mainstream of society" (p. 181).

As the needs of retarded people were being recognized by more professionals, there was a new emphasis on community-based services. This trend has continued. To some degree this emphasis was catalyzed by the fact that many children of concerned parents had become adolescents and young adults. Their parents continued to be concerned.

During the 1960s, the nature/nurture issue, brewing for many years, seemed to be best answered by those espousing the interaction between heredity and environment. While supporters of this orientation acknowledged both hereditary and environmental determinants of mild mental retardation, the environmental factor was emphasized. In 1969, much attention was drawn to this issue by Arthur Jensen. Jensen (1969) published an article in the *Harvard Educational Review* entitled "How Much Can We Boost IQ and Scholastic Achievement?" Basically, Jensen argued that genetic factors are more important than environmental factors in determining IQ (i.e., the high inheritability of intelligence.) Where Jensen's article received the most criticism was in his inference that social class and racial variations in intelligence are attributable to genetic differences.

See chapter 7.

Similar to the social climate of the late 1960s, which involved many forms of reactionary behavior, services to and concepts of the mentally retarded population were also being challenged. For the nation as a whole, the revolutionary fervor of the sixties would wane as the seventies progressed; as a result, a decided acquiescence could be detected in the country. However, for exceptional individuals and those working with them, the early seventies were reminiscent of the turbulent sixties in many ways.

FROM ACTION TO INTROSPECTION: 1970–PRESENT

Throughout the history of services to persons who are mentally retarded, there has been no period of more demonstrable gains than the early 1970s. Without a doubt, the pioneers of the early 19th century made great gains in initiating services; however, events of the 1970s left them in the dust. At long last, it was formally established that mentally retarded Americans have certain personal and civil rights which guarantee service and protection. The number of mentally retarded students served (see Figure 1.1) greatly increased through the 1960s and continued to grow in the early 1970s. The number fell as dramatically in the late 1970s and early 1980s.

Most notably, the early 1970s were litigious times indeed. A new forum for ensuring services to the handicapped was beginning to emerge. While courts had been used previously, only now would they be used frequently and strategically. Many rights afforded the regular citizenry had been denied to many retarded individuals, and the courtroom now became the forum to secure these rights. Supported by parent groups and at least tolerated by a society responsive to human rights, many issues were brought to the courtroom. Chief among these issues were the rights to education and treatment.

The right to education issue was sparked in 1971 by a celebrated class action suit, *Pennsylvania Association for Retarded Children* (PARC) *v.*

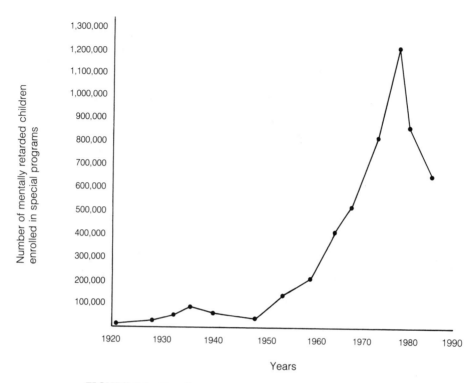

FIGURE 1.1   Enrollment of Mentally Retarded Children in Special Programs: 1922 to 1984

Source: Data from U.S. Department of the Census, 1975 and U.S. Department of Education, Office of Special Education

This issue is discussed more fully in chapter 7.

Commonwealth of Pennsylvania. This litigation resulted in a consent agreement which established a free, appropriate public school education for all mentally retarded children within the jurisdiction of this federal court district. The impact of this court-ordered agreement extended beyond Pennsylvania as similar suits dealing with this right to education issue were filed in many other states in the months following this decision.

Although *PARC v. Pennsylvania* was specifically concerned with the exclusion of retarded children from public education, other exceptional individuals were soon to enjoy the same right. In that same year, a suit on behalf of all exceptional individuals, regardless of type and severity, was filed in federal district court of Washington, D.C. This case, *Mills v. Board of Education of the District of Columbia,* decided in favor of the plaintiffs, extended the right of education to all handicapped people.

During this same period, many retarded individuals living in institutions were receiving very little in the way of services beyond custodial care. During 1971, in the case *Wyatt v. Stickney,* the lack of treatment being provided residents at a state institution for the mentally retarded was contested. Although aspects of this case are still being reviewed, the original decision handed down by the federal judge declared that the residents of Partlow State School and Hospital were entitled to treatment. The judge also enumerated the steps to be taken to comply with this decision.

As can be seen, the courts began to shape the events of the seventies. What may seem strange to the casual observer and eminently significant to the special education professional are the critical and influential roles that judges, lawyers, and expert witnesses played during the litigious period of the early '70s. To many professionals who were often the main service providers to the mentally retarded, it seemed that much of the policy was formed by professionals in other fields. Although to a certain extent this is true, knowledgeable parents and special educators at that time realized that rights had not been secured or guaranteed through committee or panel action; as a result, legal procedures seemed necessary.

The "activity" period of the early 1970s was highlighted by the enactment of much federal legislation concerning handicapped individuals. Two pieces of legislation stand unparalleled in history for what they mandated. In 1973, amendments to the Vocational Rehabilitation Act (P.L. 93-112) were passed. Serving as a "Bill of Rights" for exceptional people, Section 504 of this act ensured that "the handicapped of America *should* have access to education and jobs, and *should not* be denied anything that any other citizen is entitled to or already receives" (La Vor, 1977, p. 249). Two years later, the landmark Education for All Handicapped Children Act (P.L. 94-142) was signed into law. The major provisions of this legislation are:

- ☐ Every handicapped child between the ages of 3 and 21* is entitled to a free, appropriate public education in the least restrictive environment.
- ☐ Due process procedures are ensured to protect the rights of students and their parents.
- ☐ Students are entitled to special and related services which are determined as necessary.
- ☐ Every student will have a written individual education program (IEP), which is jointly agreed upon by parents and school personnel.

---

*Some state discretion is possible above and below these ages. In fact some states serve handicapped persons from birth through age 21.

☐ First priority is given to students previously excluded from educational services and second priority to those whose programs were inappropriate.

☐ No eligible child is to be rejected from receiving services.

Another federal law which has had an impact on mentally retarded persons was the Developmental Disabilities Assistance and Bill of Rights Act of 1978 (P.L. 95-602). This legislation provided a functional definition of developmental disabilities as well as funding to assist persons who demonstrate problems in major life function areas.

Ironically, with the passage of P.L. 94-142, it appears that the field of special education has assumed an air of philosophical caution. Perhaps relieved by the fact that there were now statutory provisions for educating exceptional people, professionals in the field seemed to reexamine what was occurring. To be sure, many exciting developments occurred in the late 1970s. The emergence of a definable group of professionals devoted to working with the severely/profoundly handicapped, emphasis on the development of community services, institutional reform, and deinstitutionalization are but a few of rather recent trends of professional interest. However, if we examine even these laudable efforts, we do not have to look too far to realize that they too have not been addressed with the blind optimism of the early to mid-19th century or even the enthusiastic vigor of the early 1960s. Perhaps we have learned from history to be a bit more cautious and not promise more than we can provide or achieve.

Through the 1970s, the field of special education and the provision of services to mentally retarded persons have made remarkable progress. Yet, as the 1980s began, a two-part philosophy emerged: on the one hand, there was an eagerness to increase services and to maximize the quality of these services; on the other hand was an understanding that it was necessary to constantly reevaluate all actions.

The 1980s have seen further developments in the field of mental retardation. The population is continuing to change as shown in Figure 1.1. Smith and Polloway (1983) have suggested several factors to account for this decrease: (a) definitional changes and changes in professional thinking which have encouraged caution and conservatism about identification and misdiagnosis, (b) the effects of early intervention efforts in preventing some cases of mild retardation.

In 1983, the American Association on Mental Deficiency issued its latest definition of mental retardation which is more consistent with definitions put forth by the American Psychiatric Association and the World Health Organization.

Notable legislative activity occurred in the early 1980s. In 1982 action was initiated to revise the rules and regulations of the Education

CURRENT ATTITUDES

The following editorial appeared in the *Rappahannock News* (Virginia) on March 1, 1979. It clearly shows that some attitudes have not changed very much from those of earlier times. Although we are distressed about the board members' feelings about special students, we share their concern for the needs of "average" students.

SPECIAL EDUCATION

"Many of these kids are going to amount to nothing."

That was the reaction from one of the school board members to provisions for expansion of the county's special education program contained in the six-year plan for Rappahannock schools.

The board members flew into a harangue against state mandates for special education at the close of Tuesday's budget meeting. Walter M., Arthlinda Q., Beverly M. and Alan S. joined together to bemoan the lack of attention paid to "average" children.

The jump in participation in special education programs from 19 students last year to 87 this year prompted the outcry. Mrs. Q. was particularly outraged against what she saw as a waste of money on children who would never be contributing members of society.

"The plain little average child needs help. With some extra attention, they can achieve above average . . . They're the ones who are going to earn their own living and support these others." she stated, in an apparent representation of the board's majority view.

Is this the truth as the school board sees it? Do the board members think that most of the 87 Rappahannock children in special education programs will end up as society's burdens?

The facts are that the overwhelming majority of Rappahannock's special education students are those same "plain little average" children the board is so concerned about ignoring.

Only 17 students in the programs are classified as retarded. Realistically, some of these 17 may need public assistance later in life. But some won't. Some will be able to support themselves, leading normal lives despite handicaps, thanks to the special education programs, mandated by the state, that seem so distasteful to the school board.

The rest of the 87 special education students in the speech and learning disabilities classes have average to slightly above-average intelligence. They go to special programs a few hours a week to enable them to learn how to overcome their handicaps. For the balance of the school week, they attend regular classes with "normal" students.

The parents of many of these students see their children going on to college instead of on welfare roles. Unlike some school board members, they don't expect their offspring to grow up and require support from their "average" classmates.

Certainly, the jump in participation from 19 to 87 in one year looks alarming. But these kids haven't been dug out of the woodwork to fill the seats in the special programs instituted this year. They've been in Rappahannock schools all along— just tucked away neatly into folders.

for All Handicapped Children Act (P.L. 94-142). The original changes proposed by the Office of Special Education and Rehabilitative Services were met with overwhelming public and professional opposition, resulting in no major substantive changes. P.L. 94-142 was amended in 1983 (P.L. 98-199). These new amendments reinforce the original act's provisions, establish several new or expanded demonstration programs, and contain modest increases in the authorization levels for various programs. As this book goes to press, two other pieces of legislation are working their way through Congress. The Community and Family Living Amendments of 1983 (S. 2053) encourage that more community-based services be established for severely disabled individuals by gradually phasing out all federal Medicaid dollars from institutions. The Civil Rights Act of 1984 (H.R. 5490, S. 2568) is intended to restore the federal government's jurisdiction in civil rights cases (including Section 504), which the Supreme Court severely limited in a recent court case.

Three important court cases took place in the early 1980s. The case of *Larry P. v. Riles* was recently heard in the 9th Circuit Court of Appeals. This court upheld a lower court ruling prohibiting California schools from using intelligence tests to place black students in classes for mentally retarded students. In *Pennhurst v. Halderman*, the Supreme Court reversed the 3rd Circuit Court of Appeals decision that affirmed that the residents of Pennhurst State School and Hospital were entitled to adequate habilitation under the Developmentally Disabled Assistance and Bill of Rights Act. The Supreme Court made it clear that this act does not create any substantive rights to adequate treatment. The third litigative action was the first case relating to P.L. 94-142 to be heard by the Supreme Court. At issue in this third case, *Board of Education v. Rowley*, was whether a hearing impaired girl was entitled to interpreter service to provide her with an appropriate education. Although acknowledging the procedural safeguards and need for individual education programs, the Supreme Court determined that states did not have to provide more than a minimal level of services designated appropriate.

As the 1980s progressed, other issues emerged which are still being debated today. Some of these include the educability of severe and profoundly retarded individuals, effectiveness of mainstreaming the mildly retarded into regular education, and bioethical issues of withholding treatment. These and other issues must still be resolved.

From a historical perspective, we must be careful that social and public attitudes toward exceptional people do not change drastically in a negative direction. Aggravated by economic problems or policy shifts, cutbacks and restrictions are possible. If a positive national policy supportive of the needs of special people is not carefully maintained, we may witness a historical déja vu of disillusionment and alarm. We must move through the 1980s with guarded optimism, because much of what can be done for exceptional people has been, and will continue to be, grounded in its sociopolitical and economic context.

SUMMARY

Throughout the development of the field of mental retardation, a number of identifiable trends have had a marked influence on where we are today. This chapter reviews many of the events, people, and sociopolitical factors that have been particularly noteworthy.

From the early optimism of the early 1800s, exemplified in the efforts of Itard, Seguin, and others, to the current state of the art as reflected by current economic and political constraints, the field has undergone many changes. It is important to be alert to what history has to say to us, for it is not unthinkable to see history repeating itself. Unquestionably we must resist a reemergence of the pejorative attitudes and distasteful treatment that prevailed toward the end of the 1800s. Most humbling is the fact that some features identifiable in the field today are not so different from features prevalent many years ago.

PART ONE
Background
Information

CHAPTER TWO

Definition and Prevalence

Mentally retarded people have been called *dumb, stupid, immature, defective, deficient, subnormal, feebleminded, incompetent,* and *dull,* as well as *idiot* and *fool* in earlier times. Although the word *fool* generally referred to the mentally ill and the word *idiot* was directed toward the mentally retarded, the terms were frequently used interchangeably (Hilliard & Kirman, 1965). Even today many nonprofessionals confuse the conditions. Mental illness, broadly speaking, is a confused state of thinking involving distorted perceptions of people and/or the environment. It may be accompanied by radical changes of mood. **Mental retardation** generally refers to delayed intellectual growth and is manifested in immature reactions to environmental input and below average social performance.

The history of mental retardation is further complicated when you consider that retardation has been confused with physical deformity, dwarfism, epilepsy, and deafness. The situation is made even more complex because a combination of these handicapping conditions does appear in some individuals.

One of the first steps in understanding a phenomenon is understanding the terms used to describe it, no matter how crude or limited they may be. This chapter looks at the evolving history of the term

---

This chapter was contributed by Eric D. Jones and James S. Payne.

"mental retardation" and how the definition affects estimates of the number of "retarded" people.

In the past, the term *idiot* was used to refer to people of all levels of mental retardation, from mild to profound. It is derived from the Greek word *idiotos*, meaning a person who does not take part in public life. The word used to apply to untrained or ignorant people, and it was used in this sense until the 17th century (Penrose, 1966).

According to Kolstoe (1972), the *de praerogative regis* (prerogative of the King) issued between 1255 and 1290 A.D. defined an idiot as one who "hath no understanding from his nativity" (p. 2). About 200 years later Sir Anthony Fitzherbert stated that an idiot was "such a person who cannot account or number, nor can tell who his father or mother, nor how old he is, etc., so as it may appear he has not understanding of reason what shall be his profit or his loss" (Guttmacher & Weihofen, 1952). The key factor in identification as an idiot appears to be lack of understanding.

Idiocy was believed to be inborn and incurable. As mentioned in chapter 1, one of the first accounts of attempts to cure or at least ameliorate mental retardation was reported by Itard ([1801]1962), who worked with a wild boy captured in a forest in 1799. The boy, whom Itard named Victor, did not speak or respond to the sound of gunfire, yet he startled at the sound of a cracking nut. He did not seem to feel the differences between hot and cold or smell differences between foul and pleasant odors. Pinel, a well-known physician of the time, diagnosed Victor as an incurable idiot. Itard believed that with proper education Victor could be cured. Seguin, a student of Itard, followed in Itard's footsteps by attempting to cure retarded people; Penrose (1966) reports that, "Esquirol referred to Seguin's mission as the removal of the mark of the beast from the forehead of the idiot" (pp. 4–5).

In essence, the word *idiot* was elusive, confusing and had no common meaning, although its primary use was to signify severe mental retardation. As time went on and new terms like *feeblemindedness* and *mental deficiency* came into vogue, the confusion remained. It has only been in the 20th century that professionals have attempted to systematize the terminology and definitions, although some negative repercussions of the MR label remain.

DEFINITION OF MENTAL RETARDATION

TRADITIONAL DEFINITIONS

There have been many definitions of *mental retardation*. During the first half of the 20th century, the two definitions that seem to be referred to repeatedly were developed by Tredgold and Doll. Tredgold (1937) defined mental deficiency as

> A state of incomplete mental development of such a kind and degree that the individual is incapable of adapting himself to the normal environment of his fellows in such a way to maintain existence independently of supervision, control, or external support. (p. 4)

Doll (1941) defined mental retardation when he stated

> We observe that six criteria by statement or implication have been generally considered essential to an adequate definition and concept. These are (1) social incompetence, (2) due to mental subnormality, (3) which has been developmentally arrested, (4) which obtains at maturity, (5) is of constitutional origin, and (6) is essentially incurable. (p. 215)

Both definitions incorporated several criteria which were characteristic of the times (e.g., intellectual deficits, developmental immaturity, deficits in adaptive behavior, and incurability). The importance of each criterion in the Tredgold and Doll definitions was significantly altered in subsequent definitions. The most notable alterations were made in the definitions developed by the American Association on Mental Deficiency (AAMD).

THE AAMD DEFINITIONS

In 1919, the American Association for the Study of the Feebleminded (later to become AAMD) appointed a committee on Classification and Uniform Statistics. This committee, in collaboration with the National Committee for Mental Hygiene, developed in 1921 the first manual defining the conditions of mental retardation. Subsequent revisions of the manual were printed in 1933, 1941, and 1957.

In 1959, a committee of professionals headed by Rick Heber developed the fifth AAMD definition of mental retardation. That definition was reprinted and slightly revised in 1961. The sixth revision was developed by a committee chaired by Herbert Grossman in 1973. Although the stated definition was similar to that developed by Heber's committee some 14 years earlier, the interpretation was significantly more conservative (i.e., fewer individuals could be identified as mentally retarded under the Grossman definition compared to the Heber definition). It is important to mention that the 1973 AAMD definition was incorporated in the Education for All Handicapped Children Act of 1975 (P.L. 94-142), as the legal definition of *mental retardation*. Grossman's definition was reaffirmed, with minor revisions, in 1977; the eighth and most current revision was published in 1983. The 1983 definition described important considerations related to interpretation and clinical judgment used to classify an individual as mentally retarded. The current AAMD definition, although somewhat criticized within the field, remains the most widely accepted and legal definition of mental retardation.

It is worthwhile to review the development of the AAMD definitions. The Heber (1959) definition of mental retardation and the subsequent revisions represent how the field has evolved and how thinking has changed regarding those identified as mentally retarded. The Heber (1959, revised in 1961) definition stated:

> Mental retardation refers to subaverage general intellectual functioning which originates during the developmental period and is associated with impairment in adaptive behavior.

Subaverage general intellectual functioning refers to performance on a standardized intelligence test which is at least one standard deviation below the mean. The **standard deviation** is a statistic used to describe the degree to which an individual's score varies from the average or mean score for the population. Figure 2.1 illustrates the concepts of the standard deviation, population mean, and normal curve.

In the 1961 AAMD *Manual,* the **developmental period** was recognized to be variable; but for purposes of definition, it was judged to range from birth through 16 years of age. **Adaptive behavior** referred to the individual's adaptation to the demands of his environment. Impaired adaptive behavior could be reflected in maturation, learning, and/or social adjustment. Impaired adaptive behavior was considered in terms of standards and norms of appropriate behavior for the individual's chronological age group. Although the concept of deficient adaptive behavior was loosely defined, its use in the Heber definition represented a major departure from the earlier definitions of Tredgold and Doll. It recognizes that an individual might be deficient in one or more aspects of adaptive behavior at one time in life, but not at another time. Favorable changes in social demands and conditions, or in the individual's increased ability to meet natural and social demands, could mean that a person would no longer be called "mentally retarded." According to Heber (1959, 1961), the definition refers to an individual's *current* functioning, not to an ultimate or permanent status. Unlike the earlier definitions, the Heber definitions did not consider mental retardation to be incurable.

Events Leading to Further Revisions The 1961 AAMD definition of mental retardation was viewed by many professionals as an improvement over previous definitions. However, it was not received without criticism. Perhaps the only aspect of the defintion which was accepted without notable controversy was the concept of mental retardation as an alterable or changeable status based on the individual's present level of functioning. There was, however, considerable debate over the concept of adaptive behavior. Clausen (1972a) argued that the procedures for evaluating adaptive behavior were not adequate for diagnosis. He contended that diagnoses of mental retardation should be based solely

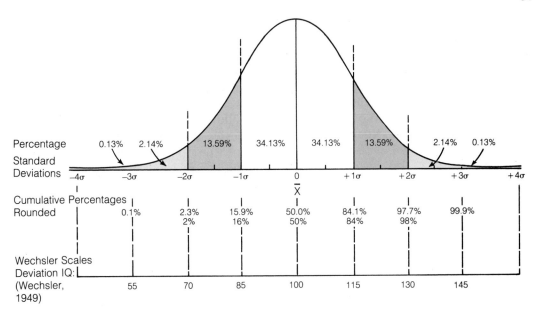

FIGURE 2.1 The Normal Curve

σ = standard deviation

$\overline{X}$ = population mean—the average score.

The Wechsler Intelligence Scales use a deviation IQ score with a mean of 100 and a standard deviation of 15. In a normal distribution, a person who scores 1σ above the mean receives a Wechsler score of 115. One who scores below 70 on a Wechsler scale (>2σ below the mean) may be classified as mentally retarded if impairments in adaptive behavior are also shown.

From "Methods of Expressing Test Scores." *Test Service Bulletin*, 1955, *48*, 8. Reprinted with permission.

upon the data from **psychometric** evaluations. From an earlier investigation, he revealed that, in spite of the AAMD's inclusion of the concept of adaptive behavior in the definition, diagnoses of mental retardation were frequently made solely on the basis of intelligence test data (Clausen, 1967). Clausen's proposed psychometric definition was highly controversial and apparently unpopular. There were two basic grounds for opposition to a definition based solely on psychometric criteria. First, such a definition could threaten the concept of mental retardation as an alterable or changeable condition. Intelligence test results are quite stable over time; hence, it would be possible that important changes in observable behavior would not be reflected by intelligence test scores. The second criticism of the psychometric definition was that, on the basis of tests standardized on members of the majority culture, too many children from minority cultures had been misdiagnosed as mentally retarded.

It was generally recognized that the 1961 Heber definition was overinclusive. With that definition as a guide for diagnosis, it was possible to identify almost 16% of the general population and perhaps greater proportions of the bilingual/multicultural populations as mentally retarded. Clausen (1972b) suggested that the definition be made more conservative by requiring that an individual IQ score be two or more (instead of one) standard deviations below the mean on an intelligence test. Other professionals suggested that the loose connection between adaptive behavior and intelligence be strengthened. Both positions have been consistently reflected in the later revisions of the AAMD definition.

The 1973 Definition In 1973, the AAMD committee headed by Grossman was assigned to review the Manual on Terminology and Classification in Mental Retardation. The definition which was developed stated:

> Mental retardation refers to significantly subaverage general intellectual functioning existing concurrently with deficits in adaptive behavior, and manifested during the development period.

In this version, *significantly subaverage intellectual functioning* meant performance two standard deviations below the mean on an intelligence test (that is, performance comparable to the lowest 2.14% of the norm population). *Adaptive behavior* was defined in terms of the degree and efficiency with which the individual meets "the standards of personal independence and social responsibility expected of his age and cultural group" (p.11). Adaptive behavior was thus considered to be relative to the individual's age and sociocultural group. An expanded set of criteria is provided for the assessment of adaptive behavior.

Figure 2.1 illustrates this point.

The 1961 Heber definition included both subaverage intellectual functioning and deficits in adaptive behavior as necessary qualifying conditions for diagnosis. However, the relationship between adaptive behavior and intellectual functioning was not sufficiently explicit. Children were consistently labeled mentally retarded on the basis of IQ alone. The two most important distinctions between the 1961 and the 1973 definitions were that (*a*) the relationship between adaptive behavior and intelligence was strengthened, and (*b*) subaverage intelligence was defined as *two* standard deviations below the mean. Instead of simply requiring intellectual functioning and adaptive behavior to be *associated*, Grossman stated that adaptive behavior deficits and subaverage intellectual functioning had to *exist concurrently*. In addition, the developmental period was extended from birth to 18 years of age. The new developmental period matched the age range of public education.

In spite of the extension of the developmental period, the 1973 revision was a much more conservative definition than those that preceded it. Table 2.1 illustrates this point. According to the 1961 AAMD definition, a total of almost 16% of the general population could have

TABLE 2.1 Comparison of Heber and Grossman AAMD Definitions of Mental Retardation

Phrase	Heber (1959, 1961)	Grossman (1973)	Grossman (1983)	Difference
General Definition	Subaverage general intellectual functioning which originates during the developmental period and is associated with impairment in adaptive behavior.	Significantly subaverage general intellectual functioning existing concurrently with deficits in adaptive behavior, and manifested during the developmental period.	Significantly subaverage general intellectual functioning resulting in or associated with concurrent impairments in adaptive behavior and manifested during the developmental period.	Adaptive behavior is associated with low IQ (Heber) versus concurrent with low IQ (Grossman).
Subaverage	Greater than one standard deviation below the mean.	Significantly subaverage: Two or more standard deviations below the mean.	Significantly subaverage: defined as an IQ of 70 or below on standardized measures of intelligence; could be extended upward through IQ 75 or more, depending on the reliability of the intelligence test used.	Heber includes one standard deviation more than Grossman. Hypothetically Heber's definition includes approximately 13.6% of the general population while Grossman includes 2.3%.
Assessment Procedure	General intellectual functioning: may be assessed by one or more of the standardized tests developed for that purpose.	Same as Heber.	Same as Heber for intellectual functioning. Adaptive behavior assessed by clinical assessment and standardized scales.	No difference.
Developmental Period	Approximately 16 years.	Upper age limit of 18 years.	Period of time between conception and the 18th birthday.	Grossman extended the developmental period from 16 to 18 years of age.

TABLE 2.1 (continued)

Phrase	Heber (1959, 1961)	Grossman (1973)	Grossman (1983)	Difference
Adaptive Behavior	*Impairment in adaptive behavior*: Refers to the effectiveness of the individual to adapt to the natural and social demands of his environment. May be reflected in: 1. Maturation 2. Learning 3. Social adjustment	Defined as effectiveness or degree with which the individual meets the standards of personal independence and social responsibility expected of his age and cultural group. May be reflected in the following areas: *During infancy and early childhood in:* 1. Sensory-motor skills development 2. Communication skills 3. Self-help skills 4. Socialization *During childhood and early adolescence in:* 5. Application of basic academics in daily life activities 6. Application of appropriate reasoning and judgment in mastery of the environment 7. Social skills *During late adolescence and adult life in:* 8. Vocational and social responsibilities and performances	Defined as significant limitations in an individual's effectiveness in meeting the standards of maturation, learning, personal independence, and/or social responsibility that are expected for his or her age level and cultural group.	Grossman's definition specifies more areas of adaptive behavior. He mentions that adaptive behavior is relative to the individual's cultural group.

TABLE 2.1 (continued)

Phrase	Heber (1959, 1961)	Grossman (1973)	Grossman (1983)	Difference
Levels of Severity	Borderline retardation IQ 68–84	—	Grossman does not include borderline	Grossman does not include borderline
	Mild retardation IQ 52–67	Mild retardation IQ 52–67	Mild retardation 50–55 to approx. 70	Same
	Moderate retardation IQ 36–51	Moderate retardation IQ 36–51	Moderate retardation 35–40 to 50–55	Same
	Severe retardation IQ 20–35	Severe retardation IQ 20–35	Severe retardation 20–25 to 35–40	Same
	Profound retardation IQ < 20	Profound retardation IQ < 20	Profound retardation below 20 or 25 unspecified	Same

From H. J. Grossman, *"Manual on Terminology and Classification in Mental Retardation."* Washington, D.C.: American Association of Mental Deficiency, 1983. Reprinted by permission.

been identified as mentally retarded from a purely psychometric perspective. According to the 1973 definition, less than 3% of the population could be considered mentally retarded from the same perspective. The 1973 revision of the definition resulted in a reduction by more than 85% of the number of individuals who could be identified as mentally retarded. Table 2.1 does not indicate the impact of the stronger connection between adaptive behavior and intelligence. However, the two are imperfectly correlated at all levels of performance. Presumably, a number of individuals who might score two or more standard deviations below the mean on an intelligence test would not be referred for evaluation if they demonstrate important adaptive skills.

Two of the most significant documents supporting a more conservative and cautious definition of the mentally retarded were "Special Education for the Mildly Retarded—Is Much of it Justifiable?" by Dunn (1968) and the Report of the President's Committee on Mental Retardation (PCMR) (1970), entitled *The Six-Hour Retarded Child*. Dunn, a respected authority in the field of mental retardation, reported that many culturally disadvantaged children were being incorrectly classified as mildly retarded and placed in special classes. The lack of adequate adaptive behavior scales, coupled with the convenient practice of identifying students as mentally retarded on the basis of IQ score alone, probably fostered the mislabeling of nonretarded children as retarded. Dunn stated:

> A better education than special class placement is needed for
> socioculturally deprived children with mild learning problems
> who have been labeled educable mentally retarded. Over the
> years, the status of these pupils who come from poverty, broken
> and inadequate homes, and low status ethnic groups has been a
> checkered one. . . .
>   I have loyally supported and promoted special classes for
> the educable mentally retarded for most of the last 20 years, but
> with growing disaffection. In my view, much of our past and
> present practices are morally and educationally wrong. We have
> been living at the mercy of general educators who have referred
> our problem children to us. And we have been generally ill pre-
> pared and ineffective in educating these children. Let us stop
> being pressured into continuing and expanding a special educa-
> tion program that we know now to be undesirable for many of
> the children we are dedicated to serve. (p. 5).

The Six-Hour Retarded Child (PCMR, 1970) agreed with Dunn's charge; that is, a significant number of culturally disadvantaged children, especially in urban areas, had been misclassified as mildly retarded and inappropriately placed in classes for the retarded. The "six-hour retarded children" are those who are classified as mentally retarded during the six hours they spend in an academic setting, but who function normally outside the school. It is important to note that reports by Dunn and the PCMR were emotional, and, while not based on rigorous empirical data, were, in fact, based on systematic observation and a strong philosophical commitment. Figure 2.2 illustrates how the 1973 AAMD definition attempted to accentuate the dual criteria—intellectual functioning and adaptive behavior.

Note that any given individual can now be labeled mentally retarded *only* if he or she exhibits retarded behavior in *both* adaptive behavior and intellectual functioning. Persons who fit the conditions of any other positions on the matrix are not considered mentally retarded. The definition of mental retardation required the concurrent existence of deficits in adaptive behavior and intellectual functioning.

AAMD 1977 Definition In 1977, the AAMD published its seventh manual on classification and terminology. The wording of the 1977 definition is identical to the 1973 version; however the 1977 manual made a few modifications in the interpretation of the definition. To begin with, *significantly subaverage* remained two standard deviations below the mean and *adaptive behavior* was essentially unchanged. The major change centered around **clinical judgment.** The manual explains in detail the problems related to measuring adaptive behavior. Yet its importance was highlighted in the sentence, "For a person to be diagnosed as being mentally retarded, impairments in intellectual functioning must co-exist with deficits in adaptive behavior" (p. 12). The manual goes on to state

> Individuals with (intelligence) scores slightly above these ceilings (two standard deviations below the mean) may be diagnosed as mildly retarded during a period when they manifest serious impairments of adaptive behavior. In such cases, the burden is on

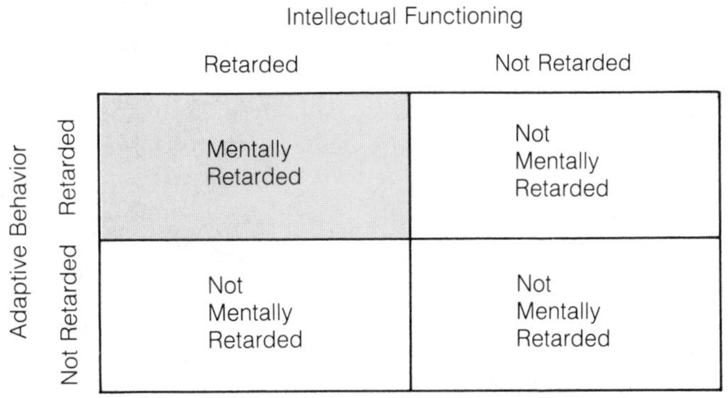

Intellectual Functioning

	Retarded	Not Retarded
Adaptive Behavior — Retarded	Mentally Retarded	Not Mentally Retarded
Adaptive Behavior — Not Retarded	Not Mentally Retarded	Not Mentally Retarded

FIGURE 2.2 Two-Fold Specification in the AAMD Definition of Mental Retardation

the examiner to avoid misdiagnosis with its potential stigmatizing effects. (p. 12)

Later Grossman illustrates clinical judgment, by stating

> A small minority of persons with IQ's up to 10 points above the guideline ceilings are so impaired in their adaptive behavior that they may be classified as having mild mental retardation. (pp. 19–20)

In conclusion, the 1977 definition, although worded identically to the 1973 definition, allows the diagnosis of mental retardation to be applied to individuals who, according to the previous definition, would not and could not have been so classified.

AAMD 1983 Definition   In 1983, the AAMD published its eighth manual on classification and terminology. Unfortunately, the out-of-date 1977 definition was reprinted mistakenly on page 1 as well as in the glossary of the manual; however, the correct definition was accurately stated on page 11:

> Mental retardation refers to significantly subaverage general intellectual functioning resulting in or associated with concurrent impairments in adaptive behavior and manifested during the developmental period. (p. 11)

Clinical judgment remained an important issue—so important that the appendix cited several examples of cases followed by how the decisions were derived based on the information presented in the cases.

The tone of the manual emphasizes that the contents were carefully researched and contemplated before publication and the decisions derived were logical, practical, and consistent with a need to explore a worldwide system of mental retardation. The authors collaborated with representatives of two other major classification systems so that the different systems would be as compatible as possible; the two systems are the World Health Organization's system of *International Classification of Diseases, Clinical Modification, Ninth Edition* (ICD-9) and the American Psychiatric Association's *Diagnostic and Statistical Manual of Mental Disorders, Third Edition* (DSM-III).

The manual straightforwardly interprets *significantly subaverage* as an IQ of 70 or below on standardized measures of intelligence. Yet this upper limit is intended as a guideline and could be extended to an IQ of 75 or more providing behavior is impaired and *clinically determined* to be due to deficits in reasoning and judgment. In this definition, the strict use of standard deviations is discouraged and the concept of standard error of measurement is emphasized.

Clinicians using the system should be well aware that in determining whether a person is retarded and at what level of intellectual functioning the individual is operating, it is important to understand the concept of standard error of measurement and use it when making a clinical determination of retardation and level of functioning. (p. 7)

No tests are perfectly *reliable* and some degree of random fluctuation in obtained scores is always expected. The standard error of measurement is an estimate of the degree to which the test scores would be expected to vary due to random error alone. For example, we know that the standard error of measurement on the Wechsler Intelligence Scale for Children—Revised is 3 IQ points. If a child received a score of 72 on that test, the examiner should report that the student's true IQ would probably be within the range of 69 to 75. The clinician would then decide whether other conditions, such as concurrent deficits in adaptive behavior or cultural difference, were present and associated with the level of performance on the IQ test. According to the 1983 AAMD manual, an individual with an IQ of 75 or higher would be classified as mentally retarded if deficits in adaptive behavior were also found to be present. On the other hand, an IQ of 70 to 67 or perhaps lower would not provide a *sufficient basis* for classifying a child from a minority culture as mentally retarded. The clinician would have to determine to what extent bias affected performance and whether deficits in adaptive behavior were present and associated with the attained level of performance. It is a simple fact that you cannot measure something precisely unless you can define it precisely. Intelligence, achievement, and adaptive behavior are ready examples of rather imprecisely defined concepts. Therefore, it is naive to arbitrarily treat scores obtained on those measures as precise measures; the standard error of measurement is a concept that allows flexibility in interpretation, yet at the same time provides reasonable structure.

The *adaptive behavior* component in the 1983 definition remained unchanged, but, again, clinical judgment was emphasized in borderline cases. The measurement of adaptive behavior may involve observation, informal interview, or the use of a standardized scale. Furthermore, adaptive behavior is compared to norms for the individual's age and cultural group. The manual emphasizes throughout that, because of the present state of affairs with adaptive behavior, clinical judgment must be used.

Although the meaning of *developmental period* did not change, the emphasis did. The new definition stresses that the developmental period *begins at conception* and extends through age 18.

Although the 1983 manual was as up-to-date and definitive as possible, and was supported by other prestigious organizations, the committee recognized that, as more data are collected and as times change, the definition of mental retardation will inevitably change:

> The 1983 definition, slightly modified for clarity, was introduced in the 1959 manual; it is intended to represent the current status of scientific knowledge in the field and the current thinking about social issues associated with mental retardation. One may anticipate that as both knowledge and philosophy change, there will be modifications reflecting such changes in future manuals. (p. 10)

ALTERNATIVE DEFINITIONAL PERSPECTIVES

The 1983 AAMD definition bears the distinction of being the legal definition of *mental retardation*. It is also the most frequently cited definition of mental retardation in the professional literature. But, in spite of their endorsement and popularity, the Grossman (1973, 1977, 1983) definitions have not met with universal approval among professionals. The AAMD definitions have been criticized because of their clear clinical overtones. We will examine some alternative perspectives: developmental disabilities, educational, sociological, psychometric, behavioral analysis, and social behavioral. None of these perspectives offers an alternative definition which is as comprehensive and extensive as the AAMD definition. Yet, each does present an orientation which those who are concerned with mental retardation should consider.

A DEVELOPMENTAL DISABILITIES PERSPECTIVE

During the last few years, the term *developmental disabilities* has been used more frequently. The meaning of this term overlaps with that of mental retardation. Defined in the Developmental Disabilities Assistance and Bill of Rights Act of 1978 (P.L. 95-602), the concept refers to

> a severe chronic disability of a person which: (a) is attributable to a mental or physical impairment or combination of mental or physical impairment; (b) is manifested before the person attains age twenty-two; (c) is likely to continue indefinitely; (d) results in substantial functional limitations in three or more of the following areas of major life activity (self-care, receptive and expressive language, learning, mobility, self-direction, capacity for independent living, economic self-sufficiency); and (e) reflects the person's need for a combination and sequence of special, interdisciplinary, or generic care, treatment, or other services which are of lifelong or extended duration and are individually planned and coordinated.

The definition accentuates functional limitations in major life activities, suggesting problems more associated with a moderately or severely retarded population. Notwithstanding, it may apply to some mildly retarded persons during some part or all of their lives. The implication of chronicity may not apply very well to many mildly retarded adults and for this reason differentiates this definition from the AAMD definition of mental retardation. Nevertheless, for most moderately, severely, and profoundly retarded individuals, the concept of developmental disabilities is appropriate and useful.

AN EDUCATIONAL PERSPECTIVE

John Kidd (1977) criticized the 1973 Grossman definition, contending that it did not adequately present the educational perspective. First of all, the 1973 definition implied that subaverage intellectual functioning and deficits in adaptive behavior are separable; Kidd objected to this concept of separation. Second, Kidd objected to the requirement that mental retardation be "manifested during the developmental period." He asserted that, since brain damage manifested during the developmental period is often indistinguishable from brain damage manifested after the developmental period, it is logically indefensible to preclude the later cases.

Note that the AAMD 1977 and 1983 definitions still consider intellectual functioning coexisting with deficits in adaptive behavior

Robinson and Robinson (1976) similarly noted that

> the specification that retardation be evident by age eighteen serves the conventional but *perhaps dubious purpose* of differentiating mental retardation from traumatic or deteriorative disorders originating in adulthood. (p. 31)

The 1977 and 1983 AAMD revisions have continued to reaffirm that the developmental period be defined as the period of time between birth and 18 years, even though P.L. 94-142 now requires the provision of educational services for all handicapped children between 3 and 21 years.

Kidd (1979), representing the Council for Exceptional Children—Mental Retardation (CEC-MR) on the Committee on Terminology and Classification, proposed the following working definition:

> Mental retardation refers to subaverage general human cognitive functioning irrespective of etiology(ies), typically manifested during the developmental period, which is of such severity as to markedly limit one's ability to (a) learn and consequently to (b) make logical decisions, choices, and judgments, and (c) cope with one's self and one's environment. (p. 76)

Kidd's educationally-oriented definition differed from Grossman's (1973, 1977) earlier definitions in that he proposed that the standard error of measurement be considered at each level of classification of mental retardation. Kidd (1979) also argued that a ceiling IQ of 70 was too low for use in educational settings. In this respect his definition was similar to the Heber (1959, 1961) definitions. He proposed that the ceiling level IQ be raised to 75 plus or minus the standard error of measurement. Thus, it would be possible, for example, to identify some individuals with Wechsler IQs as high as 78 as mentally retarded.

Many changes in the 1983 AAMD manual were similar to Kidd's suggestions and were acknowledged as such:

> While not adopting the CEC-MR recommendations verbatim, the 1983 manual does incorporate the essence of these four points:
> 1. the new "ceiling" IQ for mental retardation is "70 to 75 or more."
> 2. the standard deviation as formerly used was abandoned.
> 3. the deficits in adaptive behavior now must "result from or be associated with" subaverage intellectual functioning.
> 4. flexibility in IQ scores as classification units is provided, e.g., moderate mental retardation—IQ 35 to 40 to 50 to 55. (Kidd, 1983, p. 243)

Kidd's (1983) acknowledgment and criticism of the AAMD 1983 definition directs special attention toward the unequal representation of disciplines among members of the AAMD Committee on Terminology and Classification. Kidd challenged the organization to follow more closely its bylaws, which stipulate not more than two members from any one discipline are to be represented.

A SOCIOLOGICAL PERSPECTIVE

Jane Mercer (1973a, b) has rejected the traditional approaches to defining mental retardation. Traditional approaches (e.g., Heber, 1959, 1961; Grossman, 1973, 1983) to identifying abnormal behavior have taken a clinical perspective, which tends to define mental retardation on the basis of either a pathological model or a statistical model. The pathological (or medical) model regards mental retardation as a disease, recognized and defined by the presence of its symptoms, although it is also possible for the pathology to exist without a complete manifestation of its symptoms. The statistical model will always identify a certain portion of the population as abnormal. The distinction is made by comparing an individual's performance with the performance of a standardized norm group. Whether or not the individual is regarded as abnormal depends upon the degree to which he or she deviates from the average of the population on the performance of a particular task. Mercer (1973a, b) argued that neither the pathological nor the statistical approach is adequate for identifying cases of mild mental retardation. In her estimation, the AAMD definition was also unsatisfactory because it contained aspects of both approaches. As an alternative, she offered a social-system perspective, which defined mental retardation as "an achieved social status in a social system." She stated

> The status of mental retardate is associated with a role which persons occupying that status are expected to play. A person's career in acquiring the status of playing the role of mental retardate can be described in the same fashion as the career of a person who acquires any other status such as lawyer, bank president or teacher. (Mercer, 1973b)

Mercer's research findings (1973a, b) suggested that individuals are labeled *mentally retarded* as a function of their performance in social situations. She asserts that the social-system approach accounts for the disproportionate numbers of school-age children from lower socioeconomic groups and minority cultures who were labeled mildly mentally retarded. She advocated a more conservative definition of mental retardation, one that would operationalize the measurement of adaptive behavior. While the AAMD definitions have become more conservative and have improved the operationalization of the adaptive behavior, Mercer (1973a, b) contended that they were still inadequate. According to her view, multiple norm frameworks must be developed to adequately describe children from different sociocultural settings. That is, children must be described (and labeled if necessary) in relation to their own social and cultural background, without judging that background as "deviant" or "deficient." Mercer also recommended that the identification and diagnosis of mental retardation be based upon data which identify the children's competencies as well as their deficits. Children whose problems are school-specific should not be labeled mentally retarded. Because neither the AAMD definitions nor other traditional approaches incorporate her recommendations, Mercer considers them inadequate for labeling mild or borderline cases of mental retardation—especially among members of minority cultures.

A PSYCHOMETRIC PERSPECTIVE

The earliest definitions of *mental retardation* defined it in descriptive terms involving social incompetence of deficits in adaptive behavior. This approach has several serious shortcomings. First of all, cumbersome, imprecise descriptions of *mental retardation* made the definitions subjective in their application; moreover, they permitted only the most gross comparisons of the individuals who were identified as retarded. In short, these definitions did not provide for objective diagnoses and bases for comparison. However, with the advent of intelligence testing, begun by Binet in 1905, the problem of subjectivity was partially dispelled. IQ tests presume to offer three advantages when used to diagnose mental retardation: (*a*) they are fairly objective; (*b*) they are relatively simple to administer and score; and *(c)* because of standardization, they indicate the relative status of an individual within a group. Yet, despite these advantages, the use of conventional intelligence tests in the definition and diagnosis of mental retardation has been widely criticized. Opponents of IQ testing note that anxiety, poor health, and lack of motivation, for example, can detract from a person's performance on any test. When IQ test performance is so affected, children can be permanently labeled with an inaccurately low score. Furthermore, scant attention is given to the error inherent in any derived score. In addition, most standardized IQ tests are heavily verbal; a child whose linguistic background is not standard, edited American English (e.g., a Black ghetto child, an Asian, or a Chicano) is at a serious disadvantage. Furthermore, critics contend that traditional mental measures do not consider the demands of the individual's environment. Moreover, recent court cases (e.g., *Larry P. v Riles*) have articulated one of the most serious criticisms: IQ tests give a biased assessment of intelligence when administered to children from cultural minorities or lower socioeconomic groups. As a result, children from these groups are overrepresented among those labeled mentally retarded.

A BEHAVIOR ANALYSIS PERSPECTIVE

Sidney Bijou (1966) has taken the position that mental retardation should be dealt with from a behavioral perspective. He suggested that

> Developmental retardation be treated as observable, objectively defined stimulus-response relationships without recourse to hypothetical mental concepts such as "defective intelligence" and hypothetical biological abnormalities such as "clinically inferred brain injury." *From this point of view a retarded individual is one who has a limited repertory of behavior shaped by events that constitute his history.* (p. 2)

According to Bijou, research which concentrates upon "the processes that prevent, reduce, or delay the formation of stimulus/response functions will produce more adequate principles and techniques for dealing with retardation" (p. 2). He regarded the development of retarded behavior as a function of the individual's observable interactions like his social, physical, and biological environment.

Repp (1983) argued that Bijou's behavior analytic approach to mental retardation is the only approach that addresses the problem with a solution. Bijou's behavioral definition is based upon two important assumptions. First, all behaviors (adaptive and maladaptive) are acquired and maintained according to the same principles of learning. Mentally retarded persons are capable of learning; they may learn more slowly than nonretarded persons, but they do not learn by a different set of rules. The second basic assumption is that all behavior depends on environmental conditions. In support of that assumption are thousands of demonstrations that systematic manipulations of environmental conditions will produce predictable improvements in the behaviors of mentally retarded persons.

A PERSONAL VIEW OF RETARDATION

Very seldom do we attempt to consider retardation from the eyes and minds of those whom we so label. This approach, referred to as a phenomenological perspective (Taylor & Bogdan, 1977), provides another vantage point from which to understand retardation.

Katie Tager, 29, resides at a semi-independent living apartment building. She is mildly retarded, but that doesn't stop her from keeping her own apartment, contributing to the community, and being actively involved with other people.

She is putting together two books: *Accepting Me,* a collection of her poems and writings, and *Let Special People Be Free,* a collection of essays, poems, personal stories, and artwork by handicapped adults and children.

The following poem of Katie's was recently published in *Arts Access,* a newsletter of Very Special Arts Hawaii.

accepting me

accepting me for who
I am some people find
it hard to do
They don t see my disability
I tell them I am mildly
retarded but they don t
believe me
I tell them some disabilities
you can t see but its
in my head where it
happen to me
I think and do things
slower then you and
sometimes its hard for
me to understand what
you find easy to know
I try and learn the
best I can and accept
what I am not able to
do
Try accepting me you
will see how much it
means to me
Its not hard to under
stand and be my friend
then you'll accept me
for who I am

Source: This insert was taken from an item written by John Oh for *Arts Access.*

Like Mercer (1973a, b), Bijou rejected the notion that retardation is a symptom of an underlying condition or pathology. Bijou claimed that approaches which have conceptualized retardation as a symptom of more fundamental problems (e.g., subnormal mentality) have contributed relatively little knowledge to the field.

It is difficult to determine whether or not Bijou's behavior analysis approach to describing mental retardation has had a direct effect upon the AAMD or other formal definitions of mental retardation. Both the behavioral and the AAMD definitions of mental retardation apply only to current levels of functioning, and the condition of mental retardation is regarded as modifiable. Bijou, however, articulated the most logical basis for considering mental retardation a changeable and alterable condition. His definition has had an important impact on the development of educational and therapeutic interventions. Ullman and Krasner (1969) considered Bijou's behavioral analysis approach to have been largely responsible for a productive trend in the development of principles and techniques used to teach mentally retarded students.

A SOCIAL BEHAVIORAL PERSPECTIVE

Although quite similar in principle to Bijou's behavioral perspective, the social behavioral orientation extends beyond the basic behavioral tenets. Formulated and espoused by Staats (1975), social behaviorism includes a personality dimension made up of three basic behavioral repertoires: emotional-motivational, language-cognitive, and sensory-motor. Learning is explained as the cumulative-hierarchical development of complex systems of behaviors that are acquired as a function of an individual's interaction with environmental factors. All three of the behavioral repertoires are used in this process.

Mental retardation is best described as problems in the acquisition of these complex systems of behaviors and involves "*deficits* or *inappropriate* development largely of the language-cognitive personality repertoires, but also the other personality repertoires as well" (Staats & Burns, 1981, p. 290). Consequently, the primary focus of this orientation is on skill development, the conditions of learning (i.e., environmental factors and the reinforcing elements operating within), and the basic behavioral repertoires which are essential if learning is to occur.

CLASSIFICATION

Labeling a child mentally retarded is a serious undertaking and every attempt should be made to ensure accuracy. A fairly unsophisticated technique would be to compare retarded behaviors with average "normal" behaviors. The individual comparison is accomplished by observing a child and then deciding if he has behaved intelligently or not. For severe cases of mental retardation, this "eyeballing" technique may be almost adequate, but the technique is grossly inadequate when it is used to judge mild or less severe cases of mental retardation.

At a slightly higher degree of sophistication, classification may be accomplished with a standardized intelligence test; but by itself this method is inadequate. Because of the importance and complexity of classifying individuals as mentally retarded, the National Association for Retarded Children (1971) developed the following guidelines for case finding, screening, and evaluating school children suspected of being mentally retarded.

1. No child should be classified as mentally retarded until he or she has been evaluated by an evaluation team composed of qualified diagnosticians who bring to bear skills needed to assess medical, psychological, social, educational, and vocational factors, as applicable. The team should assume responsibility for proposing and interpreting an individual educational plan for the child in the school setting, with provisions for ongoing evaluation of the child's progress and/or needs. The team should also develop suggestions for assisting the child and his family to maximize his growth potentials within his out-of-school hours;

2. The classification of retardation should not be applied until the child's adaptive behavior has been assessed in relation to the community and family situation, taking into account the cultural norms of his natural milieu. Where adaptive behavior in any life situation is found to be significantly discrepant from intellectual expectations, the label retardation should not be used, at least until further observation has justified it;

3. The classification of retardation should be applied only to those children who continue to function at a significantly subnormal level even after various remediation attempts. Special attention should also be given to the identification and treatment of debilitating physical conditions such as auditory and visual impairments, malnutrition, epileptic seizures, or other sensory-motor impairments.

4. Psychological evaluation for the purpose of classification should always include the use of individual test procedures which measure a range of skills and which are appropriate to a child's cultural and linguistic background. Testing should assess specific learning disorders, if any, and the extent to which inferior performance is due to reversible environmental factors such as repeated failure, cultural dissonance, inappropriate expectations by teachers, situational anxieties, personality disorders, or inadequate motivation.

5. A child who is suspected of being mentally handicapped should be observed in his regular class setting. However,

classroom behavior alone should never be used as the criteria for labeling a child mentally retarded. Regular classroom teachers should be assisted to ascertain the wide variety of reasons other than retardation which may contribute to inappropriate responses to the school academic environment and to underachievement. They should be assisted to implement behavior modification procedures, when appropriate, both to enhance learning and to help the child develop behavior which is more acceptable to his peers; and

6. No assessment of a child should be considered complete unless the parents have been actively involved in the evaluation process as significant observers of the child and his performance. In addition, assistance to parents in the home management problems related to optimal child development should be offered through a trained home visitor, where appropriate. (pp. 13–15)*

The same document (National Association for Retarded Children, 1971) listed criteria for placement of retarded persons in educational programs designed exclusively for the mentally retarded. This segregation may be appropriate when

1. There is a documented history of retarded overall functioning which is substantiated through evaluation by a team of qualified diagnosticians;
2. There is consistent impairment of adaptive behavior in the child's home and community as well as in the school culture and environment;
3. There is no significant alleviation in the child's inferior performance and achievement after the modifications in school and home environments;
4. There is a significant continuing residual disability which cannot be expected to respond to environmental manipulation alone;
5. There is the considered opinion of an evaluation team that the curriculum of the regular class composed of age mates will not maximize the child's potential for learning and achievement as effectively as a modified curriculum individualized and directed by a teacher especially trained to teach children with impairment of learning potentials; and
6. There remain daily opportunities for the special class child to interact with regular class students in nonacademic situations. (pp. 15–16)**

Although the need for services to retarded people continues, authorities are in a state of flux, quandary, confusion, ambivalence, tur-

*Used with permission of Association for Retarded Citizens, National Headquarters.
**Used with permission of Association for Retarded Citizens, National Headquarters.

moil. . . . They're damned if they use the term *mental retardation*, and damned if they don't. Without any common terminology, the concept of mental retardation would become more hazy, and parents as well as professionals would have difficulties without a generic term to which to refer. In addition, funds would be more difficult to earmark. As we have seen, there have been periodic changes in terminology referring to the mentally retarded. Dunn (1973a) provided three reasons for the continuous search for new and more appropriate terms which designate persons with "intellectual inadequacies."

1. Sooner or later negative values are attached to any term used to describe retarded persons. Thus, the new terms, at least when they are first introduced, are socially acceptable; however, before long they, too, acquire negative connotations.
2. The condition of mental retardation is so complex and broad, with so many causes and levels, it may be virtually impossible to include its entire scope under one rubric.
3. Many different disciplines are involved and interested in the field of mental retardation, including education, psychology, sociology, medicine, speech pathology, and social science; and each develops a definition suited to its particular orientation.

Several systems of terminology used to refer to the mentally retarded population and corresponding levels of severity of retardation are presented in Table 2.2 Note that many of the same names represent different levels or even different concepts. For instance, *feeblemindedness* has been used as the generic name of mental retardation as well as a specific level of severity of mental retardation.

The definition of *mental retardation* has changed, is changing, and will continue to change. Dunn is often considered to be the most outspoken advocate for doing away with the term *mental retardation* for educational purposes. He reasons that the term should be abandoned by educators because it is irrelevant and stigmatizing (1973b). In place of *mental retardation*, he advocates the use of the term *general learning disabilities*.

Pupils with general learning disabilities are those who require special education because they score no higher than the second percentile for their ethnic or racial subgroup on both verbal and performance types of individual intelligence test batteries administered in their most facile language. (p. 68)

The continual searching for any different definitions and terms consistently yields diminishing returns. Any word can come to have a negative connotation. For example, one school district, aware of the detrimental effects of labeling children *mentally retarded*, began placing the retarded children in an educational program designed to teach lan-

TABLE 2.2 Terminology and Levels of Severity of Retardation

Proponents	Generic Term	95	90	85	80	75	70	65	60	55	50	45	40	35	30	25	20	15	10	5	0
American Association for the Study of the Feebleminded	Feebleminded						Moron					Imbecile				Idiot					
Tredgold & Soddy (Great Britain)	Mental deficiency						High grade; feeble-minded				Middle grade; imbecile				Low grade; idiot					
AAMD (Heber, 1961)	Mental retardation (adaptive behavior not included)			Borderline mentally retarded			Mild			Moderate			Severe		Profound					
AAMD (Grossman, 1973)	Mental retardation (adaptive behavior not included)						Mild			Moderate			Severe		Profound					
AAMD (Grossman, 1983)	Mental retardation (adaptive behavior not included)						Mild			Moderate			Severe		Profound					
American Psychiatric Assoc (1980) DSM III	Mental deficiency						Mild			Moderate			Severe		Profound					
World Health Organization	Mental subnormality						Mild			Moderate			Severe							
Wechsler (1949) (WISC)	Mental deficiency			Dull normal			Border-line	Mental defective													
Terman & Merrill (1960) (Stanford-Binet)	Mental deficiency						Border-line defective	Mental defective													
Amer. Educators (cited by Smith, 1971)	Mentally retarded or mentally handicapped			Dull normal			Educable				Trainable				Custodial dependent, or low grade						

Adapted from M. Gelof, "Comparison of Systems of Classification Relating Degree of Retardation to Measured Intelligence" (Table 1). *American Journal of Mental Deficiency*. 1963. *68*. 299–301. Used by permission.

guage, arithmetic, and reading directly. A series of commercial programs produced by Science Research Associates, DISTAR (Direct Instructional Systems for Teaching Arithmetic and Reading), was used. Before half the year was over, a group of concerned citizens asked that the program be abandoned because DISTAR was for "dumb" kids, and children not enrolled in DISTAR classes were making fun of the DISTAR children by yelling "DISTAR, DISTAR" at them at recess. It may be impossible to find acceptable terms and useful definitions without adult education and increased understanding of intellectually handicapped persons.

After navigating the maze of actual definitions and issues, and philosophies regarding definitions and definitional practices, one may be left with solving the task of determining who is "really" mentally retarded. However, the lesson is not that the emerging definitions are better or more accurate, but that the definition of mental retardation is totally a social/political one that rests with the powers that be, and not in the minds of the people who experience intellectual deficits.

INCIDENCE AND PREVALENCE

Prevention and treatment are the two of the most pressing issues in the field of mental retardation. In order to determine causal factors and to deliver services and treatment efficiently, professionals have used two estimates of the frequency of mental retardation: **incidence** and **prevalence.** Although the words incidence and prevalence are considered synonymous in some usages, they refer to different types of statistical frequencies when discussing handicapping conditions.

INCIDENCE

Incidence refers to the number of *new* cases identified within a population over a specific period of time. The data for most estimates of incidence are obtained from cases which were clinically identified when an individual entered a type of treatment (Stein & Susser, 1975). Incidence figures are valuable for investigating the causes of a handicap and developing possibilities for prevention. For example, researchers have found that maternal age at a child's birth and the incidence of the chromosomal aberration which results in Down syndrome in the child are related. That relationship was determined by comparing the incidence rates of Down syndrome births with populations of mothers from different age ranges. For instance, a child born to a mother between the ages of 20 and 30 has a 1 in 1500 chance of having Down syndrome; to a mother between 35 and 40, a 1 in 300 chance; to a mother between 40 and 45, a 1 in 70 chance; and to a mother over 45, a 1 in 40 chance of having Down syndrome (Bunker, Lambdin, Lynch, Mickey, Roderick, Van Pelt, &

See chapter 6.

Fosnot, 1972). While researchers have not determined *why* chromosomal aberrations are more frequent among older mothers than younger mothers, the relationship between maternal age and the incidence of Down syndrome has suggested possibilities for prevention.

PREVALENCE

Prevalence refers to the total number of cases of a disorder *existing* within a population at a particular place or at a particular time (Dorland, 1957). Prevalence rates are frequently represented as percentages. MacMillan (1982) uses the following equation to express prevalence of mental retardation as a percentage.

$$\text{Prevalence} = \frac{\text{The number of persons who are identified as mentally retarded within a given period of time}}{\text{The total number of persons within that population}} \times 100$$

Unlike incidence, prevalence is not concerned with the number of new cases. Therefore, it is not as useful in determining causal relationships. Prevalence statistics are, however, better than incidence statistics for determining community need for services at a particular time. Need is more accurately determined by directly surveying the population than by relying upon service use (Stein & Susser, 1975).

For several reasons, variations in estimates of the incidence and prevalence of mental retardation have been found between studies and between populations. Among the factors which can influence the incidence and prevalence of mental retardation are differences in defining criteria, methodologies, sex, age, community, race, and sociopolitical factors. We will look at each of these.

VARIATIONS DUE TO DEFINITIONAL PERSPECTIVE

The difficulty of defining retardation is reflected in the number of reviews on the prevalence of mental retardation that mention the imprecision in definition and the general haziness of the concept itself (e.g., Dunn 1963; Jastak, MacPhee, & Whiteman, 1963; Kirk, 1962; Masland, Sarason, & Gladwin, 1958; O'Connor, 1966; Osgood, Gorsuch, & McGrew, 1966; Penrose, 1966; Williams, 1963). The problem of defining the mentally retarded population was emphasized when Johnson (1959) criticized one of the most widely quoted surveys (Census of Referred Suspected Mental Retardation, conducted in Onondaga County, New York, in 1953). Johnson criticized the Onondaga study because it used an all-inclusive definition of mental retardation and, therefore, possibly reported more cases of mental retardation than actually existed according to generally accepted definitions.

At times, prevalence figures have been estimated without a survey being conducted. Hypothetical prevalence statistics can be projected from formal definitions of mental retardation which rely entirely upon psychometric data (e.g., Wechsler, 1949) or rely substantially upon such data (e.g., Heber, 1961; Grossman, 1973). In 1916, Terman introduced groupings of ability related to IQ scores obtained on the 1916 Binet intelligence test. These classifications were changed in the 1937 revision of the Binet test and continued in the 1960 revision (Terman & Merrill, 1960). Because these groupings were used so frequently, a standard classification system was developed from them. Wechsler (1949) included a similar classification system for the Wechsler Intelligence Scale for Children (WISC). Table 2.3 presents the intellectual classification systems of the Stanford-Binet and the WISC, along with percentages of the standardization samples falling within each classification. The Grossman and Heber classifications are also included, accompanied by representative percentages estimated by IQ data and based on the normal curve. It is apparent that changes in the definition of mental retardation can produce changes in the hypothetical prevalence.

TABLE 2.3 Heber and Grossman Definition of Mental Retardation with the Binet and WISC Classification Systems

Proponents	←	125	120	115	110	105	100	95	90	85	80	75	70	65	60	55	50	45	40	35	30	25	20	→
Binet		Superior 11.3[1]				High average 23.1	Normal or average 46.5				Low average 14.5	Borderline defective 5.6			Mentally defective 2.63										
WISC		Superior 6.7				Bright normal 16.1	Average 50.0				Dull normal 16.1	Borderline 6.7			Defective 2.2										
Heber Binet												Borderline retarded 13.59					Mild 2.14	Moderate 0.13			Severe	Profound		
Heber WISC												Borderline retarded 13.59					Mild 2.14	Moderate 0.13			Severe-profound			
Grossman Binet								[2]									Mild 2.14	Moderate 0.13			Severe	Profound		
Grossman WISC																	Mild 2.14	Moderate 0.13			Severe-profound			

1. Number in each section represents percentage.
2. Shaded areas represent possible additional retardation based on clinical judgment.

These classification levels and the characteristics of individuals falling into each level are discussed in depth in chapter 3.

With the exception of Heber's (1961) definition, however, 70 has been used as the approximate cutoff score used in all cases for differentiating retarded from nonretarded individuals. The classifications using specific IQ scores should not be considered discrete classes of intellect, but should be viewed as points on a continuum of mental ability. If IQ were the only criterion for defining mental retardation, the percentages in Table 2.3 would suggest that approximately 2.5% of the population may be mentally retarded (Binet, 2.63; WISC, 2.2; Heber, 15.86; and Grossman, 2.27). In 1971–1972 the United States Office of Education (USOE) prevalence figures reported 2.3% of the school-age population as mentally retarded (0.8%, moderate and severe; 1.5%, mildly retarded). The President's Committee on Mental Retardation estimated that approximately 3% of the population is mentally retarded. However, the validity of the commonly accepted figure of 3% prevalence has been seriously challenged. Mercer (1973a) conducted a prevalence survey in a California community that supported a 1% prevalence. Tarjan, Wright, Eyman, and Keeran (1973) had hypothesized a figure of 1%, feeling that the 3% model assumes

(*a*) The diagnosis of mental retardation is based essentially on an IQ below 70; (*b*) mental retardation is identified in infancy; (*c*) the diagnosis does not change; and (*d*) the mortality of retarded individuals is similar to that of the general population. (p. 370)

Tarjan, Wright, Eyman, and Keeran (1973) claimed these assumptions are not supported by clinical evidence. For example, they report

First, the commonly accepted criteria for the clinical diagnosis of mental retardation require that concurrently with a significant impairment in intelligence, as measured by psychometric tests, a similar impairment in adaptive behavior also be present, and that both of these symptoms manifest themselves during the developmental years (Heber, 1961). Many preschool children and adults, however, do not show major impairment in general adaptation even with relatively low IQs. As a consequence, the clinical diagnosis of mental retardation, particularly when it is of mild degree, is age-dependent. It is usually not established before school age and often disappears during late adolescence or young adulthood.

Second, mortality in retarded individuals is inversely related to IQ, with only the mildly retarded having life expectancies which approximate those of the general population. . . . Though 3% of the newborn population will be suspected and even diagnosed as mentally retarded some time during their life, probably during their school years, it is incorrect to assume that at any given time 3% of the population is so identified or is apt to be so diagnosed. (p. 370) Generally, most professionals regard a prevalence figure of 1% or less as the best indicator of reality.

VARIATIONS DUE TO METHODOLOGIES

Farber (1968) listed four commonly used techniques for estimating the number of mentally retarded individuals in a population: genealogical random-test, birth register, period method, and census method.

> The genealogical random-test method involves random sampling of a number of normal individuals to test relatives (usually siblings and parents) for possible mental retardation. The error usually made with this technique is using convenient, easily obtained samples. . . .
>
> The birth register technique involves random sampling from the birth register of a political unit. While it provides a complete sampling list, this method depends upon accuracy of the vital statistics and the residential stability of the persons born in the area. . . .
>
> The period method of estimating the number of mentally retarded individuals involves everyone born or living in a specific area during a certain period of time. This type of investigation is generally feasible in rural areas with low migration rates. . . .
>
> The census method is the most widely used means for estimating the prevalence of mental deficiency. It is independent of rates of migration, fertility, and mortality, but it usually results in underestimation of the rates of mental deficiency in the community. The usual procedure is to contact persons in institutions where the probability of finding mentally retarded individuals is high. For example, Akesson canvassed institutions, hospitals, and clinics who might have contact with the retarded; he consulted with local informants, including ministers, teachers, district nurses, representatives for social organizations, superintendents in homes for the aged and for children, and persons knowledgeable of local conditions. Akesson then examined referred individuals by (*a*) an interview, (*b*) a short screening test, (*c*) the revised Stanford-Binet test (Swedish version), (*d*) objective data concerning the individual's accomplishments and social environment, and finally (*e*) a medical examination. (pp. 56–57)*

Most prevalence surveys are conducted by reviewing case files, analyzing agency referral data, or counting tabulated census data. A few studies actually locate the subjects for testing or interviewing. As can be expected, prevalence figures differ markedly from study to study.

VARIATIONS DUE TO SEX

In general, males are more frequently identified as mentally retarded than females at all age levels. Three generally accepted explanations

---

*From Bernard Farber: MENTAL RETARDATION: ITS SOCIAL CONTEXT AND SOCIAL CONSEQUENCES. Copyright © 1968 by Houghton Mifflin Company. Used by permission.

See chapter 6 for
more on biological
causes of retardation.

account for sex differences in prevalence. First, biological defects associated with the X chromosome have a greater probability of being manifested by males than females. Second, it also appears that different child-rearing practices and different social demands are associated with sex differences in prevalence. For example, aggressive behavior for males is typically reinforced during child rearing. A mildly retarded aggressive boy may not perceive the differences between appropriate and inappropriate situations for being aggressive. And those mildly retarded individuals who exhibit behavior problems have greater chances of being identified as retarded than those who do not exhibit behavior problems (Masland, Sarason, & Gladwin, 1958). Finally, society's demands for self-sufficiency traditionally have been higher for males than females (Robinson & Robinson, 1976).

VARIATIONS DUE TO AGE

Prevalence figures vary considerably as a function of the age of the individuals identified as mentally retarded (Lewis, 1929; Penrose, 1966). As shown in Figure 2.3, more cases of mental retardation are identified during the school years than during the pre- and postschool years. The personal and social demands which a person must meet change with age. Failure to cope efficiently with social demands may lead to the individual being labeled mentally retarded. On the other hand, individuals who have been labeled as mentally deficient during their school years are able to shed that label by meeting many demands of adult life. Individuals who are identified as subnormal from early childhood through adulthood are more apt to be the more severely retarded (Gottlieb, 1975; Mercer, 1973b).

FIGURE 2.3   Identification and Visibility of Mental Retardation

MR Classification	Approximate Percentage of Total MR Population	Age(s) When Identification Typically Occurs	Individual(s) Who Typically First Recognizes Problems	Individual(s) Typically Confirming Diagnosis of MR	Visibility of Person as MR
Mild	70–75%	6 years +	teacher parent	school psychologist diagnostic team	Change with CA; tend to be identified upon entry to school and to lose label upon exit from school setting
Moderate	20%	1–5 years	parents physician	physician diagnostic team	For most part, tend to be recognized as MR throughout their lifetimes
Severe/ Profound	5%	0–1 years	physician	physician	Maintain MR distinction throughout their lifetimes

VARIATIONS DUE TO COMMUNITY DIFFERENCES

Communities vary in their ability to absorb individuals with limited talents. For example, retarded individuals are more apt to be identified in urban communities than in rural communities (MacMillan, 1982). That variation has been subject to different interpretations. First, urban communities are generally described as being more complex than rural communities. It is commonly believed that the social demands of urban communities are, therefore, more difficult to meet. MacMillan suggested that individuals with borderline retardation from urban districts are more likely to be identified as mentally retarded because urban districts tend to have better developed referral and diagnostic services. Some marginal cases may never be formally diagnosed in rural districts.

Socioeconomic conditions within communities are also related to differences in prevalence rates. Children who are born and reared in deprived, lower socioeconomic groups are 15 times more likely to be labeled *mentally retarded* than children from the suburbs (Tarjan et al., 1973). A number of interpretations have tried to account for the much higher rates of mental retardation among children from lower socioeconomic groups and deprived environments. Prevalence figures indicate that, as the severity of retardation increases, cultural and socioeconomic factors become less pronounced. In other words, just as many wealthy families as poor families have severely retarded children.

See chapter 4 for a more complete discussion.

VARIATIONS DUE TO SOCIOPOLITICAL FACTORS

There is evidence to suggest that the number of retarded individuals identified at a given time is influenced significantly by prevailing attitudes, policy, and practices. For instance, over the last eight years the number of students classified as mentally retarded by school systems throughout the United States has dropped dramatically. Smith and Polloway (1983) analyzed federal data concerning these changes for 1976 to 1981. They found that the number of students between the ages of 3 and 21 served under P.L. 94-142 and P.L. 89-313 dropped approximately 13%. Additional data have been made available that indicate a further reduction in the number of students classified as retarded. Further analysis of the change between 1976 and 1984 indicates a 32.7% decrease; Figure 2.4 presents these data. Why this dramatic change? In large part it is due to sociopolitical factors that have influenced how we identify and serve students who are decidedly below the norm. One of the most important reasons for this change is a more conservative posture on identifying students as mildly retarded, especially if they are from culturally diverse backgrounds. There is a noticeable caution in the field to avoid the misdiagnosis and misplacement of minority group students. Another factor is that a number of higher functioning mildly retarded children are now being served in classes for learning disabled students.

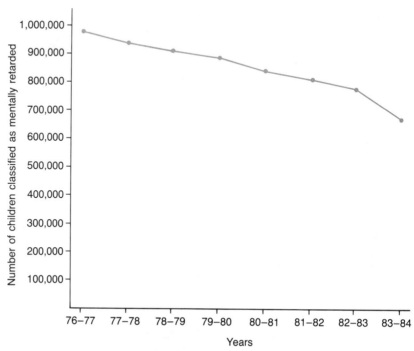

Reprinted by permission of the U.S. Department of Education, Office of Special Education, Washington, D.C.

FIGURE 2.4 Number of Children Classified as Mentally Retarded Between Ages 3–21 Years Served Under P.L. 89-313 and P.L. 94-142 Annually Since School Year 1976–1977

One explanation for this is that these settings are less stigmatizing than classes for the educable mentally retarded students. Other factors are playing a critical role in the changing numbers of retarded students, such as the positive effects of early intervention efforts. Nevertheless, it is important to remember that much of what happens to retarded people, including how many of them are so identified, is a function of prevailing thought of a given time.

CONDUCTING AN ACTUAL PREVALENCE STUDY

People who have never participated in a survey or census often think prevalence and incidence figures are mundane and menial as well as boring. Admittedly, it is difficult to keep in mind that the results may be important for the formulation and development of meaningful programs and services for people who may be in dire need. To understand some of the experiences encountered in conducting a survey and reflect on the importance of prevalence and incidence information, consider the following excerpts taken from various survey reports.

Dr. E. O. Lewis (1929) succinctly and precisely described the feelings of any surveyor in his *Report of the Mental Deficiency Committee*. In the prefacing letter to the chairman and members of the mental deficiency committee, he wrote:

> The report which is my privilege to submit for your consideration is a record indicating the extent to which my colleagues and I, to whom you intrusted the investigation of the incidence of mental defect, have been able to accomplish the task. We have spent almost three-and-a-half years in the investigation; two-and-a-half years were taken in collecting data in the six investigated areas, and about a year in analyzing the data and preparing the report. We realized at the outset that the task we had undertaken was a formidable one; but when we came to close grips with it, its magnitude and complexity, not to mention its delicacy, were even greater than we had anticipated (p. 82).

Lewis' (1929) study often is referred to as the England and Wales study. It is the most thorough large-scale investigation of the prevalence of mental defects. Goodman and Tizard (1962) reported that "it forms a baseline from which trends over the past twenty-five years can be measured" (p. 216). The Lewis study surveyed six areas which were classified as half-urban and half-rural. Each area contained about 100,000 persons. One of the most remarkable aspects of the study is that each individual was diagnosed by Lewis. He personally examined each one of the reported retardates. In general, a group test was given as a screening device. Then Lewis examined the individuals with low scores on the group tests, epileptic children, and paralyzed children. As you read the original report, you cannot help but be impressed with both its thoroughness and concern for individual people. Lewis provided a detailed account of the development and implementation of the study. Notice the exactness yet frustration reflected in the following two excerpts:

> It is not necessary to discuss in detail the relative helpfulness of the various sources of information. The source that proves most disappointing was the most helpful in another; for example, comparatively little help was received from the police authorities in some of the investigated areas, while in others most valuable and complete information was obtained from this quarter. . . .
>
> The general practitioner is naturally the person who knows most of the low grade mental defectives in the district in which he practices. We visited several general practitioners and in almost every case we were received kindly, but it must be admitted that the help given did not justify the time spent in arranging these visits. It cannot be denied that doctors are at present ex-

TABLE 2.4 School Age Retarded Children with IQs Below 50

Study	Age group	Prevalence	Incidence (per 1,000)
Middlesex, England (1960)[1]	5–9	417	3.02
	10–14	574	3.61
	7–13	738	3.45
England-Wales (1925–27)[2]	7–15	415	0.67
	7–13[1]	327	4.55
Onondaga County New York (1953)[3]	5–9	76	2.36
	10–14	79	3.39
	15–17	32	2.63
Eastern Health District Baltimore, Md. (1936)[4]	10–14	18	3.3
New York State (1955)[5]	7–15	7361	3.3
	5–15	8539	3.0
	7–18	9327	3.4
Wyandotte County Kansas (1971)[6]	5–9	111	5.16
	10–14	114	6.29
	7–13	161	5.83

1. Figures from Goodman and Tizard, Table 4, p. 218. (1962)
2. Figures from Lewis, Tables 6(A), 6(B), and 6(C), pp. 173 and 174. (1929)
3. Figures from Onondaga Study (unpublished), Indexes 3.32 and 4.1, pp. 22 and 35. (1953)
4. Figures from Lemkau, Tietze, and Cooper (third paper), Table 4, p. 282. (1962)
5. Figures from Bienenstok and Coxe, Tables 8 and 9, pp. 23 and 25. (1956)
6. Figures from Payne, Table 1, p. 226. (1971)

tremely cautious in giving any information concerning the mental condition of their patients (pp. 30–31).

Any person interested in conducting a prevalence survey dealing with the mentally retarded should definitely read this classic document. The original report is difficult to obtain, but a xerox copy may be purchased for $114.00 from the British Information Services, 845 Third Avenue, New York, New York 10022.

A less expensive study that is easier to obtain is *Mental Retardation, Its Nature and Incidence* by Jastak, MacPhee, and Whiteman (1963). It may be purchased from University Publishers, Inc., 239 Park Avenue, S., New York, New York, for $6.00. They described the problems, techniques, and procedures with such clarity that the information and ideas can be used in future prevalence studies. Examples of a few of their findings are as follows:

1. The arrangement of working in teams and weekly meetings was morale-sustaining.
2. On the basis of a pilot study, a manual describing interviewing procedures was developed.
3. Evening hours produced more contacts than day-time hours.
4. News media were exploited by developing a portfolio of endorsements and clippings from newspapers to show to hesitant subjects.
5. Information was gathered about persons who refused to cooperate, and suggestions were provided for working with persons who resisted.

Resistant subjects were classified into nine categories. The following three examples were the most commonly found:

> *Passive resistance:* In this category were a sizable number of respondents who, although they have no reason for not cooperating, were considered problems because of their passive resistance. The interviewers found it most difficult to convey to these people the real need for participation. Persuasion, endorsements, letters from community notables made no impression on them. Their indifference most often manifested itself by broken appointments. Indeed, the problem here was not in making appointments but in having them kept by the respondents. . . . With this type of resistance a surprise visit by the interviewer to complete his interview at the moment of encounter was often successful. . . .
>
> *Illness:* the respondent was sometimes unwilling to be interviewed because of "illness." In such instances the attending physician was reached whenever possible, to determine whether the illness was severe enough to exclude the patient from the study and whether the respondent might take part without injury to his health. If the latter were the case, this kind of approach was used: "We understand that you aren't feeling very well. However, we think you will find this an enjoyable experience. It might be just the sort of thing that you need to forget your troubles for a little while." . . .
>
> *Too busy:* When the reason for being busy was given, attempts were made to appeal to the respondent's sense of civic responsibility. If this failed, the plea would be as follows: "As a favor, do it for us. We realize how busy you may be, but give us a little of your time to complete this, and we'll not trouble you any more" (Jastak, MacPhee, & Whiteman, 1963, pp. 48–52)

Payne (1962) described factors to consider when hiring surveyors. He stated:

> One of the basic requirements of a surveyor was being physically fit, because a majority of the work was field work and required standing, walking, and on occasion some running. All surveyors were good healthy specimens, but all complained of sore feet and muscles. Also, complaints were issued pertaining to the heat and the cold. Even with these complaints, not one surveyor missed a day's work in the twenty-seven weeks of the survey. Female surveyors in the beginning were a little overly dressed and within three days were wearing flats rather than heels. The males at first wore suits and ties, but found in some areas of the county that persons would not answer the door because, upon later investigation, it was discovered that the surveyor was mistaken for a bill collector. To avoid the image of the bill collector, the male surveyors dressed more casually and did not wear ties. At one time all surveyors carried a clipboard and a briefcase, but because of the salesman image they found it best to leave the briefcase in the car and only carry the clipboard. When this was done, the problem of dogs became apparent. It seemed as though the surveyors felt more secure when carrying the briefcase and on a couple of occasions actually used the case to knock angry dogs away. Therefore, the surveyors returned to carrying briefcases but still dressed casually. Two surveyors were not familiar with the county and experienced difficulty in locating homes. The locating of homes became somewhat easier with the help issued from fire stations, local post offices, and Standard Oil stations (they lived up to their motto "When you travel, ask us"). The problem of locating homes should not be underestimated because of the extreme amount of time it can take to locate a family. The county was divided into eight geographical districts and a surveyor was assigned to two districts. The district assignments were developed to confine each surveyor to a small area, thus enabling the surveyor to familiarize himself with a particular area. Also, the problem of penmanship deserves mentioning. Several surveyors exhibited poor penmanship and this may seem trivial to the reader, but time needed to be allotted for each surveyor to review each case with the secretary so the information could be typed. A couple of surveyors complained of sore knuckles and, therefore, the "survey knock" was developed. The "survey knock" consisted of knocking on the door with the palm of the hand rather than the knuckles (pp. 69–70).

As with Jastak, MacPhee, and Whiteman (1963), Payne (1962) found that weekly meetings assisted in the development of new interviewing techniques and maintaining a high degree of *espirit de corps*. The following experiences have been extracted from protocols to show what the surveyors actually faced in the field:

I was told that _____ sits all day in front of a large picture window and as people go by they honk and wave at _____ and he waves back. I went to the home and found the boy sitting in front of the picture window; his parents were not at home. I went out and sat in the car to wait for the parents to come home. I was there about forty-five minutes before the parents arrived and during that time twenty-three people went by the house, honked, and waved, while _____ waved back, grinning from ear to ear.

I attempted several times to contact _____ but could never find anyone at home; therefore, I called the family on the phone. Mrs. _____ cussed a lot and seemed to be somewhat resistant as I talked with her on the phone. She mentioned several local agencies and schools that she would like to get her hands on; however, when I got to the home for the personal interview, she never raised her voice once. She asked if I would like to meet her little boy. She then took me into the next room where there was, according to her, a human adding machine. She said that her boy spent most of his time adding simple figures. I proceeded to give him a list of figures to add and noticed that when he was supposedly calculating, he made funny noises like a machine; however, he did not answer the problems correctly.

I was informed by Mr. _____ that his wife had run off and left him with four kids. He was a very unusual fellow, about 59 years of age. An old beat-up galvanized bucket was located in the corner of the front room and during the interview the kids would come in and urinate in the bucket. One youngster stood fairly far from the bucket and I would say his aim and accuracy were better than average.

I went to this one address in the early evening and found the house on an old dirt road setting back behind some trees. It looked as though no one was living in the home; however, I knocked on the door. As I stood on the porch knocking, I glanced down at my feet and noticed a snake come out of a crack in the porch. The snake went around my right foot and crossed over the top of my left foot and proceeded on its way off the end of the porch. I found no one at home at this address.

I went to call on _____ and didn't find the home until about 8:30 p.m. I knocked on the door and it was answered by a nice looking woman I would say around 26 years of age. She opened the door about eight to ten inches and before I could tell her my name and purpose, she whispered, "My husband is here now, could you come back later."

In conclusion, prevalence surveys (or surveyors) are quite conspicuous; the numbers and figures included in them represent real people living in communities. The importance of surveys today relates to how individuals, identified as mentally retarded, can best be provided relevant, effective, comprehensive services. This quest has exemplified itself through Child-Find programs throughout the nation.

CHILD-FIND

The enactment of P.L. 94-142 and the 1983 amendments (P.L. 98-199) have given official recognition to the importance of developing case registers of handicapped individuals. That law requires local education agencies to conduct and document their efforts to identify all at-risk children who reside within their jurisdiction. After they have been identified as being "at risk," those children must be evaluated to determine whether or not they are handicapped and thus qualify for educational and related services. This task is enormous.

The child-find procedures of some projects (e.g., Mazzullo, 1977; National Association of State Directors of Special Education, 1977; Turner, 1976) have been reported, along with some informal evaluations to help others conduct identification programs. Unfortunately, the relative effectiveness of these different procedures has not been determined. More formal evaluations and comparisons of various child-find procedures have been presented by Zehrbach (1975) and Kurtz, Neisworth, and Laub (1977).

Public Awareness Campaign   All of the reported child-find projects have relied initially at least in part upon media campaigns. Television, radio, and newspaper advertisements have frequently been used. Posters in public places such as buses and store windows are also used extensively. All of the reporting projects emphasize the importance of setting a positive tone and using a multilingual, multicultural approach to reach all members of the community. While media campaigns have been probably effective in creating public awareness, they are, admittedly, not believed to be responsible for the increased numbers of at-risk children who have been located. Zehrbach (1975) did not find media campaigns to be a very effective technique for sensitizing lower socioeconomic communities. Families which responded most frequently to these campaigns tend to be of higher socioeconomic status, more literate, and better organized.

Some communities use bilingual campaigns, including posters like this one, in their child-find programs.

Notices to Parents Some school districts have attempted to elicit responses from parents by sending notices home with children already in school. Zehrbach (1975) reported that sending notices to parents was a relatively effective approach for contacting parents. "Approximately 47% of the anticipated population in one district was located in this way." (p. 78).

Surveys House-to-house and telephone surveys have been found to be the most effective procedures for identifying at-risk children (Kurtz et al., 1977; Zehrbach, 1975). In the past there were usually enough handicapped individuals identified by the traditional referral process to fill existing programs. Identifying *every* handicapped child for special education was not the goal then. Only a limited number of children were serviced, and waiting lists were common. Now, P.L. 94-142 requires that educational agencies identify (and document their attempts to identify) *every* handicapped child who could qualify for services. Although direct contact surveys are the most reliable of available methodologies, their great expense prevents their widespread use.

PROBLEMS WITH CHILD-FIND PROGRAMS

While some child-find programs have been successful, it appears that school districts typically have been unable to identify all of the handicapped children in their districts. Kennedy and Danielson (1978) pointed out that, depending upon a state's population, the numbers of unidentified mentally retarded may be quite large. The newsletter *A Report on Education of the Handicapped* (1979) suggested that school districts have tended to identify handicapped children according to already existing services, rather than according to the individual needs of the children. The reported quoted a high school principal as saying, "It doesn't do any good to identify them [handicapped children] if we can't do a thing about their problem" (p. 5). Another school official acknowledged that the identification of handicapped children "had everything to do with what the evaluator knows the school will be able to do for the child" (p. 5). It appears that, while an increased number and variety of services have recently become available, the numbers and types of new cases identified depend in part upon existing service levels in the community. There are probably many children who are believed to have handicaps, but who currently are not identified by the schools. Parents may neglect to refer their children for several reasons. They may fear stigma. They may be aware of the problem and prepared to deal with the possible stigmatization of their child, but may not realize that, by law, the school is obligated to provide their handicapped child with an education and necessary related services. Some parents have also been intimidated by school officials who were not willing to provide the handicapped child with special education services. In many cases, teachers have become discouraged by the apparent inaction (or inappropriate action) taken on referrals. The teachers' discouragement possibly results in their making fewer referrals or making referrals only when they are fairly sure service will be provided. The National Association of State Directors of Special Education (1977) also suggested that, although the numbers of children identified for special education have increased, the numbers depend in part upon services already available.

In conclusion, prevalence surveys are quite conspicuous; the numbers and figures included in them represent real people living in communities. The importance of incidence rates may yet increase for there is a movement to define intellectual retardation by prevalence alone, that is, to say that a certain percentage of any population is by definition "retarded." IQ averages tend to differ among various cultural as well as economic populations. A child considered average in one area might be considered retarded or gifted in another. Martinson (1973) commented that there is a great responsibility for locating, identifying, and subsequently supplying appropriate educational services for the gifted among different cultures and minority groups. One alternative may be to desig-

CHILD-FIND PROCEDURES

Because extensive child find procedures are required by the Education for All Handicapped Children Act, many enterprising efforts have been undertaken to identify handicapped children who are in need of special education. Conventional techniques include census surveys, mass media, parent questionnaires, agency and physician contacts, and parent-teacher contacts. Many local education agencies have developed attractive and interesting 10- and 30-second television ads. In addition, other creative ideas have been used, including the distribution of child-find information with regular bills by General Telephone in the state of Washington.

In general, there seem to be two approaches to child-find: a referral approach and a screening approach. An example of a brochure used in the referral method is shown here, and the poster shown in the photograph on page 71 is another example. Basically, this approach uses the mass media or the mail and relies on public response to identify those individuals in need of services. The screening method, which is seemingly a more active approach and consequently more costly, looks at a large number of individuals in a given area and hopefully identifies those people at-risk. A relatively common example of a screening technique is yearly hearing examinations administered to elementary school students at the beginning of each school year. With both referral and screening, more thorough assessment follows the initial identification of the child.

Your Local School Division is Searching For Handicapped Children Who Are Not Getting Special Help - Ages 2 through 21.

Do You Have or Know of Any Child Who is Having Trouble Walking or Moving, Seeing or Speaking, Hearing or Listening or Other Problems.

Do you know of a child ages 2 through 21 who does not go to school because of any of the following reasons:	Put a check ☑ if this child is 2 or 3 years of age and cannot:	Put a check ☑ if this child is 4 or 5 and cannot:
☐ cannot walk	☐ walk	☐ walk, run, jump
☐ is not like others	☐ talk	☐ throw and catch ball
☐ is sick for a long time	☐ be alert - look at you when you speak	☐ talk in sentences and ask questions
☐ seems slow or different	☐ be warm and cuddly	☐ help and do things
☐ has trouble moving	☐ sit with you and listen or look at book	☐ listen well to stories or cartoons
☐ has toilet trouble	☐ sleep through night	☐ sleep well at night
☐ cannot see	☐ take a nap	☐ go to toilet by self
☐ has trouble seeing clearly	☐ start on toilet training	☐ feed and wash self
☐ cannot hear	☐ drink from cup	☐ play with others
☐ has trouble hearing	☐ feed self	☐ show interest in learning colors, numbers and letters
☐ cannot talk	☐ play with toys	☐ be still and quiet at some time during the day
☐ is very hard to understand	☐ sit still	☐ show curiosity toward new things

See chapter 4 for
more on culturally
biased tests.

nate the upper 3% of any cultural group as gifted. Thus, different IQ
cut-off limits could be selected for each cultural group. This method for
labeling gifted and retarded children temporarily allows us to skirt the
issue of culturally biased tests.

Most policy decisions result either directly or indirectly in allocations of resources to meet goals. Public policy makers include the President, members of federal and state legislatures, county commissioners,
school administrators, and special interest groups, such as the Council
for Exceptional Children. Most persons who make or affect policies related to the mentally retarded are not professionals. All of them, however, are involved in making decisions about the relative importance of
different goals and deciding the appropriate expenditures of resources
to meet each goal. It is important that policy makers identify the most
beneficial set of goals and provide the necessary allocations of resources.
The prudence and equity of policy decisions affecting the mentally retarded depend heavily on the decision-makers' understanding of the
demography of mentally retarded people. In 1978 the National Institute
of Handicapped Research funded a project to establish a means of providing national estimates of the incidence, prevalence, and other demographic characteristics of disabled Americans. The purpose of this effort
was to provide an adequate statistical base for policy. Roistacher,
Holstrom, Cantril, and Chase (1981) noted that by 1978 more than 80
federal agencies (plus many more state and local agencies) were providing services to the handicapped. Many of the agencies collected incidence, prevalence, and demographic data, but most agencies had different legislative mandates, which resulted in different purposes for
collecting data. Ultimately, the collected data lacked comparability
across agencies. Roistacher et al. (1981) noted that different definitions
and data collection methodologies made aggregation of data impossible.
While definitional and methodological problems can be reduced, Roistacher et al. (1981) stated that developing an adequate statistical base for
policy making would be beneficial. Furthermore, while knowing the
numbers of people identified as mentally retarded is important, we still
know relatively little about their demographic and clinical characteristics, attitudes and aspirations, and service experiences. Collecting such
information is important, but national level data are needed if policy
makers are to make informed decisions.

SUMMARY

To understand the term *mental retardation*, we must begin by establishing
a definition. Historically, a variety of attempts have been made to con-
cisely state the condition implied by this term and its precursors. The

AAMD definitions of Heber and Grossman have most recently reflected the essential dual dimensions of the concept of retardation, with the latter definition currently being the most widely accepted. Nevertheless, the definition has continued to be questioned and alternatives suggested, and further evolution is probable.

Classification involves delineating specific subgroups of retarded persons. This task has given rise to a variety of systems and a host of specific terms. The most commonly used approaches are categorization according to educability or to the AAMD psychological system. Although varied terms for retardation in general and levels of retardation in particular continue to be adopted and rejected, we must assume that this process eventually will be less and less fruitful.

Prevalence figures in mental retardation have proven to be difficult to establish; significantly wide ranges have been reported in the literature. Although 3% has been used by the government as an estimate of the prevalence of retardation, there remains little consistent support of this figure. Additional concerns in prevalence relate to variations based on age, sex, and community environment. Ultimately the accurate determination of incidence must be achieved along with intensive childfind campaigns.

Prevalence surveys may seem unimportant, but as efforts are made to plan programs, develop services, and allocate funds, it is highly probable that prevalence data will provide information to guide the magnitude and extensiveness of our efforts to combat and treat mental retardation.

CHAPTER THREE

Characteristics of Mentally Retarded Individuals

By definition, mentally retarded individuals are distinguished from the nonretarded on the basis of intellectual functioning and adaptive behavior. Significantly subaverage intellectual functioning is described as mild, moderate, severe, or profound, according to the degree to which a person's measured general intelligence deviates from the normal range. Adaptive behavior refers to the amount of personal independence and social responsibility the person demonstrates at various stages throughout life.

In both of these areas, the amount or degree of deficit is of prime importance. By naming various levels of retardation, we are emphasizing the wide range of behaviors and abilities found among those identified as "mentally retarded." Viewing retardation on a continuum, we might place the mildly retarded child who is having difficulty with the academic subjects within the regular classroom at one end, and the profoundly retarded youngster who is immobile and unresponsive to his surroundings at the other end. The first section of this chapter will look at the general characteristics of persons at each of these levels of retardation.

This chapter was contributed by Carol H. Thomas and James R. Patton.

While the "mentally retarded" are, indeed, a heterogeneous group, we can make certain generalizations based on research with individuals who exhibit deficits in intellectual and social functioning. These generalizations can serve as a framework to further our understanding of mentally retarded people. After we have looked at the four levels of retardation, therefore, we will discuss the behavior and abilities of all retarded individuals in three broad areas: social and emotional behavior, learning, and physical and health characteristics.

CHARACTERISTIC BEHAVIORS

Most current definitions of mental retardation recognize four levels of severity: mild, moderate, severe, and profound. While there are specific intellectual and adaptive behavior requirements differentiating these categories, we must emphasize that not only are there wide behavioral differences in persons identified as belonging to separate classifications, but also among individuals at the same level of severity. As with the nonretarded, a great many variables determine the physical and psychological make-up of an individual.

The characteristic behaviors discussed in this section are frequently observed among retarded people of various levels at different stages of life. As previously mentioned, many factors influence individual functioning and behavior among the retarded. Some of these variables are evidence of organic involvement; additional handicapping conditions such as sensory or orthopedic impairments; problems relating to health; concern and resources of the family; availability of services, both medical and educational; and how early the retardation was diagnosed and intervention begun.

MILDLY RETARDED

Mildly retarded individuals demonstrate adaptive behavior and intellectual functioning at the upper end of the retardation continuum. According to the most recent AAMD definition (Grossman, 1983), assessed intellectual functioning of the mildly retarded is within the IQ range of 50 to 55 to approximately 70 with concurrent deficits in adaptive behavior. This classification encompasses the majority of the mentally retarded.

The cause of most cases of mild retardation is unknown. While hereditary factors are an etiological consideration at any level, other variables such as nutrition, health care, and environmental stimulation appear to play an important role. Indeed, a disproportionate number of the mildly retarded are from lower socioeconomic status families.

While the slower rate at which these children develop motor, social, and language skills may be noticeably different from their peers,

See chapter 7 for a discussion of the interaction of genetic and environmental variables.

MENTALLY RETARDED PERSONS IN POPULAR LITERATURE

There have been and will continue to be many myths and misperceptions concerning mentally retarded people. For example, to many people, the visual image commonly conjured by the term "mentally retarded" is a person with Down syndrome. People's attitudes are often based on the popular media, including literature, films, and television. Unfortunately, there have been few laudable examples where popular media have accurately conveyed what it really is like to be mentally retarded.

In a specialized bibliography of 20th century American fiction, King (1975) reviewed a collection of works that included mentally retarded characters. He made one comment about one work that bears repeating. "It is possible that William Faulkner's *The Sound and the Fury* is the great 20th century American novel. If it is, and if Benjamin Compson is its chief protagonist, then the hero of the great American novel of the 20th century is a 33-year-old idiot. A curious anomaly" (p. 106). Few works of American fiction can rival Faulkner's classic work, but here is a list, adapted from King, of other noteworthy works that involve mentally retarded characters.

Baker, Elliot. *Pocock and Pitt.* New York: Putnam's, 1971.

Bellamann, Henry. *King's Row.* New York: Simon and Schuster, 1942.

Bellow, Saul. *The Adventures of Augie March.* New York: Random House, 1965.

Buck, Pearl. *A House Divided.* New York: John Day, 1931.

mild retardation is often not suspected until the children enter school. Often a combination of difficulty with academic subjects and behavioral problems focuses attention on the child. Learning problems may appear to be specific to one subject, such as reading, or generalized to all subjects. Children who do not have the verbal and communication skills of their age mates may withdraw from interpersonal relationships or seek attention in a variety of inappropriate ways. The child may misbehave because he or she cannot clearly distinguish between acceptable and unacceptable standards of behavior. Problem behavior might also result from the frustrations of scholastic failure or as an attempt to gain acceptance from other children, who might encourage deviant behavior. As we will see later in this chapter, much of the social behavior of retarded children appears as a result of repeated failures.

Children formally identified as mildly retarded and provided with special education and related services designed to meet their unique needs are often referred to as educable mentally retarded (EMR). This

Caldwell, Erskine. *Tobacco Road*. New York: Random House, 1940.

Capote, Truman. *A Christmas Memory*. New York: Random House, 1966.

Capote, Truman. *Breakfast at Tiffany's*. New York: Random House, 1958.

Carpenter, Don. *A Blade of Light*. New York: Harcourt, Brace & World, 1968.

Chappell, Fred. *The Inkling*. New York: Harcourt, Brace & World, 1965.

De Vries, Peter. "*The Cat's Pajamas*" in *The Cat's Pajamas and Witches' Milk*. Boston: Little, Brown, 1968.

Dickey, James. *Deliverance*. Boston: Houghton Mifflin, 1970.

Didion, Joan. *Play It As It Lays*. New York: Farrar, Straus, & Giroux, 1970.

Egan, Lesley. *Against the Evidence*. New York: Harper & Row, 1962.

Erno, Richard B. *The Catwalk*. New York: Crown Publishers, 1965.

Farrell, James T. *Invisible Swords*. New York: Doubleday, 1971.

Faulkner, William. "The Bear" in *Go Down Moses*. New York: Random House, 1955, 191–331.

Faulkner, William. *The Hamlet*. New York: Random House, 1956.

Greenberg, Joanne. *Monday Voices*. New York: Harper & Row, 1965.

McCullers, Carson. *Reflections in a Golden Eye*. New York: Bantam, 1967.

McMurtry, Larry. *The Last Picture Show*. New York: Dial Press, 1966.

Olsen, Paul. *Shadow of Me*. New York: Holt, Rinehart, Winston, 1968.

Smith, Lillian E. *Strange Fruit*. New York: New American Library, 1954.

Spencer, Elizabeth. *Light in the Piazza*. New York: McGraw Hill, 1960.

Steele, Max. *The Goblins Must Go Barefoot*. New York: Harper & Row, 1951.

Steinbeck, John. *Of Mice and Men*. New York: Random House, 1938.

Williams, Joan. *The Morning and the Evening*. New York: Atheneum, 1961.

Wolff, Ruth. *A Crack in the Sidewalk*. New York: John Day, 1965.

term, often used by educators, refers to the model of service delivery required by most mildly retarded students (MacMillan, Meyers, & Morrison, 1980). It reflects their ability to profit from academic instruction, as opposed to the moderately retarded or "trainable" child, who is generally placed into a nonacademic program. The educable child can, in many cases, be educated within the regular classroom by using materials and methods found to be effective with retarded learners. Many programs for mildly retarded children include a resource teacher or a special class for a portion of the day in order to provide specialized help in specific areas of instruction. Wherever possible, mildly retarded students remain in regular classes. During junior and senior high school, vocational training is generally emphasized in order to provide job skills which will be helpful in obtaining and maintaining later employment.

Educational placement alternatives are discussed in depth in chapter 12.

While there is some support for the contention that there are more personality disorders among mildly retarded adults than among the population as a whole (Chinn, Drew, & Logan, 1979), most are able to lead satisfying and productive lives as attested to in recent biographical works on retarded adults such as *Like Normal People* (Meyers, 1980). Many mildly retarded adults secure employment and become economically self-sufficient. With increased knowledge about how retarded individuals learn, we should be able to provide even more effectively for their social, emotional, and educational needs.

MODERATELY RETARDED

Children who function at any level below mild retardation are usually identified as retarded at birth or during the first few years of life. **Moderately retarded** individuals are those who display significant deficits in adaptive behavior and are functioning intellectually within the 35 to 40 to 50 to 55 IQ range (Grossman, 1983). Various clinical syndromes, notably Down syndrome, are often associated with moderate retardation and produce distinct physical characteristics. In addition, a higher percentage of moderately retarded children than mildly retarded have additional handicapping conditions.

Down syndrome is covered in more depth later in this chapter and in chapter 6.

Moderately retarded children will demonstrate developmental delays in such skills as sitting, crawling, walking, and language. Families of children with developmental problems often require support and assistance from such individuals as physicians, health care workers, nutritionists, social workers, teachers, and home trainers. This support helps them deal with the unique problems presented by an exceptional child and provides an optimum environment for the child's physical and psychosocial growth. In recent years there have been very encouraging results from programs employing infant stimulation as a means of enhancing developmental progress (Bricker & Dow, 1980; Strickland, 1971; Watson & Ramey, 1972).

See chapters 7 & 12.

See chapter 14.

Institutionalization is still an issue with regard to retarded individuals functioning at the moderate level and below. At one time, residential placement was a frequently used option. Many factors are necessarily involved in the decision to institutionalize a child. One is the specialized care and training felt to be needed for the child, which would place both a physical and an economic strain on the family. Because of the prevailing attitude that the moderately retarded could not benefit from being in public schools, relatively few communities provided educational services for them. In more recent years, however, advances in understanding of and methods for teaching retarded learners as well as legislation mandating the right of all children to a free appropriate public education (P.L. 94-142) have vastly increased educational opportunities for retarded students. While educational programs must be provided even for those individuals in residential placements, far fewer moderately retarded children are institutionalized than were in the past, and many remain at home or in the same community throughout their lives.

Educators generally refer to children at this level as trainable mentally retarded (TMR), emphasizing the training aspect of their education over the more academically oriented programs for the educable retarded. Even this aspect is currently being debated, however, as some moderately retarded youngsters have been able to benefit from academic experiences (Apffel, Kelleher, Lilly & Richardson, 1975; Fink & Sandall, 1980; Litton, 1978). For the most part, however, emphasis is placed on self-help skills such as self-feeding, self-dressing, cleanliness, grooming, and other aspects of daily living, which may include purchasing groceries, making change, simple food preparation, and recognizing signs and labels.

The last several years of school usually include a heavy emphasis on vocational training, either at the school itself or in specialized facilities within the community. Later, employment may be feasible in a sheltered workshop or similar environment where clients are trained to perform specific tasks in highly structured and well-supervised settings. While moderately retarded adults will always require a certain amount of supervision, many can achieve some independence and lead satisfying lives.

SEVERELY AND PROFOUNDLY RETARDED

Much of the special education literature treats all retarded individuals who function at a lower level than the moderate classification as one group. The justification for this practice is that the severity of the retardation, the high incidence of multiple handicaps, and the frequency of institutionalization of these individuals lead to similar methods of training and treatment for the two groups. Most commonly used definitions, however, make a distinction between the **severely retarded** and the **profoundly retarded** in terms of functioning. The AAMD distinguishes between the two groups in terms of IQ range by designating the scores of 20 to 25 to 35 to 40 for severe mental retardation and a score below 20 or 25 for profound retardation (Grossman, 1983). It is important to remember that individuals at the lower end of the retardation continuum are often nonverbal and extremely limited motorically, which makes precise assessment difficult. Of course, evaluation will also reveal severe deficits in adaptive behavior.

As we have mentioned, the more severe the retardation, the more likely it is that the child will be identified as retarded at birth or at an early age. Severe developmental lags and additional handicaps, which most frequently include sensory impairments, cerebral palsy, epilepsy, and emotional disturbances, increase the need for continuous care and supervision. It is estimated that approximately 30% of the severely retarded and 80 to 90% of the profoundly retarded reside in institutions (Eyman & Miller, 1978). For young children remaining in the home, center- or home-based programs provide direct services to the infant or preschooler and training and support to the parents to help them provide for the unique needs of their handicapped child.

Severely handicapped youngsters of school age generally develop some communication skills and are able to interact with the environment. While these children do not usually profit from academic training, programs designed to improve speech and to teach self-help skills such as toileting, dressing, feeding, and cleanliness have been successful. Task analysis is used to break each task down into small sequential steps. Each step is then trained separately using rewards as incentives for appropriate responses or approximations of responses. After much repetition each step learned is then chained to the next sequential step until the entire task is learned.

Profoundly retarded persons, while functioning below that of the severely retarded, are still capable of a wide range of behaviors. Some may be able to communicate through primitive speech, gestures, or simple signs, recognize familiar faces, respond to simple commands, and achieve some self-help skills. Others, however, may be bedridden, unaware, and unresponsive to the environment. Advances in equipment design for the physically handicapped, technical developments in electronic wheelchairs and communication systems employing synthetic speech, computerized instruction, prosthetic devices, and specially designed clothing have significantly contributed to the achievements made by this population. Recent reviews of the literature dealing with both severely and profoundly retarded persons conclude that these groups can learn meaningful behaviors (Stainback & Stainback, 1983) and that social responsiveness among the profoundly retarded is greater than had been assumed (Landesmann-Dwyer, 1978).

As might be expected, the life span of these retarded individuals is typically shorter than normal, with the nonambulatory profoundly retarded having the highest mortality rate. Those that survive into adulthood are still very dependent upon the care of others. Severely retarded individuals, however, will generally require less care than the profoundly retarded and have, in some cases, been trained to perform vocational tasks (Baroff & Tate, 1967; Gold, 1973; Hunter & Bellamy, 1977; O'Neill & Bellamy, 1978).

SOCIAL AND EMOTIONAL CHARACTERISTICS

All children are born with certain basic needs that must be satisfied before they can develop physically, socially, or intellectually. Growth in any one of these areas is necessarily related to and influenced by growth, or the lack of growth, in the others. One means of viewing social and emotional needs within this context has been formulated by

IDIOT SAVANT

There are individuals, though not many of them, who have significant limitations in their general cognitive abilities yet display unusual aptitude, ability, or talent in a specific area. Such an individual is commonly referred to as an *idiot savant*. This phenomenon has baffled professionals for centuries and continues to do so today. The unusual behaviors demonstrated by idiots savant are typically very specialized (e.g., memory skills, calendar calculation, mathematical abilities, artistic talents, mechanical abilities).

The following passage is part of an newspaper article written by Timothy Harper of the Associated Press that appeared in February, 1983. It describes the special talent of a man named Alonzo Clemens who exemplifies the inexplicable behavior of the idiot savant.

An IQ of 40 and the Talent of a Master

by Timothy Harper, *Associated Press*

Boulder, Colo.—Alonzo owes almost everything to his art.

If not for his talent at hand-sculpting lifelike miniature animals out of wax, Alonzo might not be able to partially provide for himself financially or dream of someday owning a horse.

Alonzo—his last name is Clemens but everyone simply calls him by his first name—is a 25-year-old retarded black man who lives here in a group home for the developmentally disabled. He also has an extraordinary talent for wax sculpture that amazes experts in both art and psychology.

With an IQ of about 40 and the social skills of a 6-year-old—his dark eyes are usually hooded and he often says "Yet" for "Yes"—Alonzo's remarkable sculpting skill classifies him as an "idiot savant."

From the French for "learned idiot," the phrase is disdained by mental health professionals because of the connotations of "idiot." But modern psychology has not come up with a more apt term for people who are severely retarded yet have some incredible abilities.

. . . while idiots savant are extremely rare, Alonzo is even more rare because his unusual skill is an art. More often, an idiot savant's special gift will be in some sort of uncanny mathematical ability, such as doing complicated equations very quickly or automatically naming the day of the week for any date in the last century.

An example is Leslie Lemke of Pewaukee, Wis. He was born blind and retarded and with cerebral palsy, but 10 years ago—when he was 18—Lemke's adoptive mother discovered he could listen to a piece of classical music and then play it back note for note on the piano.

Maslow (1954), who conceived of individual needs leading to psychological health as forming a hierarchy. According to this model, higher order needs such as belonging, love, self-esteem, and self-actualization can only be achieved once more potent physiological and safety needs have been met. Even in the higher order needs, achievement of each level leading towards self-actualization depends upon the satisfaction of the previous level's needs.

While the satisfaction of physical and health needs are essential to survival, emotional and social growth are vitally important for the overall development of the child. The child's psychosocial growth is fostered by feeling loved and accepted by the significant people in his or her life as well as by being stimulated and active. Physical and emotional security provides a basis for the development of trust, which allows the child to explore and examine aspects of the environment and to strive toward developing a sense of self (Erickson, 1968). Rogers (1951) sees an atmosphere of security and acceptance as essential for acquiring feelings of self-worth and self-esteem and for the development of the full potential of the individual.

Mentally retarded children have the same basic physiological, social, and emotional needs as nonretarded children. Because of their unique experiences in dealing with an environment with which they are less able to cope, however, they often develop patterns of behavior which are counterproductive to realizing their full potential.

SOCIAL LEARNING THEORY

Investigations of how people learn social behavior and the ways in which individuals interact with the environment are often referred to as **social learning theory** research. Cromwell (1963) has applied aspects of the social learning theory (SLT) developed by Rotter (1954) in an effort to further understand the behavior of the mentally retarded within a social context. In general, SLT assumes that an individual interacting with the environment has the capacity for either moving toward an object (approach behavior) or for moving away from it (avoidance behavior). Two variables that influence the individual's behavior are the expectation of a particular reinforcement and the value of that reinforcement or goal for the individual. SLT research has produced a number of implications for social learning among the retarded. We will discuss three of these: **locus of control, expectancy for failure,** and **outerdirectedness.**

Locus of Control Locus of control refers to how one perceives the consequences of his own behavior. An individual who is operating primarily from an *internal* locus of control sees events—both positive and negative—as a result of his own actions. On the other hand, one who sees positive and negative events as being primarily controlled by outside forces, such as fate, chance, or other people, is said to have an *external* locus of control (Lawrence & Winschel, 1975).

Young children tend to be externally oriented, perceiving many circumstances and events in their lives as being beyond their control. As the child matures, however, he becomes more aware of the influence of his own actions. As a result, he gradually shifts to a more internal locus of control (Lawrence & Winschel, 1975). External control, therefore, is considered to be a more debilitating orientation, as it keeps the child from accepting responsibility for his or her own successes and failures and impedes the development of self-reliance.

Mercer and Snell (1977) reviewed the results of locus of control studies which involved retarded subjects. The studies indicate that retarded subjects are more externally oriented than nonretarded subjects. Mercer and Snell conclude that "the consistent finding that mental retardates are external and that external orientation tends to be handicapping challenges us to explore techniques for promoting internal orientations" (p. 190).

Expectancy for Failure In social learning theory, *expectancy* refers to the reinforcement that is anticipated as a result of a given behavior. Rotter (1954) postulates two types of expectancies. The first is the expectation of a particular type of reinforcement, such as a tangible reward or social approval. The second involves expectations which are generalized from the results of past experiences with particular types of problem-solving activities. In other words, a new task is approached with either the expectation of success or the expectation of failure, based on what the individual has experienced in the past.

Studies by Cromwell (1963) which involved retarded subjects found these subjects to have a high expectancy for failure. Zigler (1973) noted that an individual who has accumulated failure experiences sets lower aspirations and goals in an effort to avoid additional failures. Heber (1964) pointed out that this fear of failure may become circular: the expectation of failure lowers the amount of effort put into a task, performance of the task is thus below what might be anticipated from the capabilities of the individual, and the expected failure becomes a reality.

Outerdirectedness Another result of attempts to avoid failure is a style of problem-solving called *outerdirectedness*. Instead of relying on one's self for solutions to problems, the outerdirected individual imitates the behavior of others or looks to others for cues or guidance.

While this type of behavior is not limited to the retarded, Zigler (1966) suggested that it is prevalent among retarded persons because they have learned to distrust their own abilities, again because of the frequency with which they have failed in the past. Efficient problem solving necessarily involves using both external cues and one's own cognitive resources. Relying too heavily on external cues could result in a dependence upon them, even when a task is well within one's own capabilities.

Implications of Social Learning Theory While we have only touched on the complex theoretical framework of social learning theory and the suggestions from certain studies which are relevant for retarded people, we do want to show the interrelatedness of social and intellectual functioning and the importance of social adaptation as a component of retardation. In addition, we can draw certain implications from social learning theory research for structuring the social environment of the retarded people with whom we work.

In the three characteristics discussed (locus of control, expectancy for failure, and outerdirectedness), one recurring factor is the detrimental effect of repeated failures. Perhaps the most important implication to be derived, then, is the necessity of providing retarded children with tasks in which they can succeed. This holds true for both social and academic settings. Allowing the child to be successful is an invaluable motivational tool. Yet all children, handicapped and otherwise, need to learn to deal with failure as well. A sensitive teacher can shape classroom experiences in such a way that the child gains enough self-confidence through repeated successes to be able to rebound from an occasional, inevitable failure. Another aspect of this same issue is that parents and teachers need to be sensitive to their own expectations for the child, so that they do not inadvertently reinforce the child's own expectation for failure. They must take care to avoid conveying to the child the idea that they think he or she is not competent to handle simple tasks. Rather, parents and teachers should require their retarded children and students to assume responsibilities that are within their grasp and should make it clear to the children exactly what is expected of them.

Other ways to increase the chances of success are setting specific as well as realistic goals, providing immediate feedback for specific behavior, and providing desirable rewards for accomplishments. If the child has repeatedly failed at a certain task, the situation should be restructured to present a novel approach to the problem, so that success may be achieved. Finally, while it is desirable to help retarded children become more innerdirected and self-reliant, their tendency to rely heavily on external cues should be used to advantage. Teachers and parents should provide children with appropriate behavior models (Kauffman & Payne, 1975; Mercer & Snell, 1977).

LEARNING CHARACTERISTICS

We may think of **learning** as the process whereby practice or experience results in a change in behavior which is not due to maturation, growth, or aging. The definition implies (*a*) that the changed behavior is relatively permanent, as distinguished from responses due to drugs or fatigue, and (*b*) that the learner is involved and participating, rather than changing because of body growth or deterioration (Bower, 1978). While the learning process is highly complex, research has determined certain principles which contribute to our understanding.

LEARNING AND PERFORMANCE

Learning is a hypothetical construct and, as such, cannot be measured directly. How much or how little learning has actually taken place can only be inferred from the performance of the individual. If a child points to the object the teacher has just named or spells a word correctly, we assume that learning has taken place. If the child performs the task incorrectly or does not attempt the task at all, we assume that learning has not occurred. Since learning can only be measured indirectly, we must be cautious in interpreting performance levels as direct indicators of the child's learning. There are a great many factors which influence if and how a child responds in any given situation. They include the physical and social setting, types and contents of materials, procedures being used, and incentives.

INFORMAL AND FORMAL LEARNING

Learning does not occur only in a formally structured situation. The environment provides unlimited opportunities for informal or **incidental learning** which result in new behaviors or attitudes. While we are very dependent upon incidental learning for acquiring skills and knowledge, it is difficult to control and may result in the acquisition of undesirable or unproductive behaviors. We have already mentioned the outer-directedness of retarded individuals. Their reliance upon others for cues and guidance may result in much incidental learning. If this learning is to be beneficial to the student, resulting in favorable changes in behavior, teachers must pay careful attention to the cues which are given.

LEARNING AND MATURATION

We have implied that physical maturity can result in behavior changes. The development of certain motor skills such as walking appears not to be influenced by training or experience until the child has the necessary physical maturity. However, delayed development is a characteristic of retarded people, and the degree of delay is generally related to the severity of the retardation and the presence of other handicapping conditions. If you expect the disabled person to acquire skills at the normal rate of development, therefore, you may end up frustrated and may fail in your attempts to teach new skills. However, while training and practice will not supplant the maturation process, studies of infant stimulation provide enough encouragement to justify training and practice in order to enhance development.

EXPERIMENTAL APPROACHES

A large body of research has been conducted on various aspects of retardation, including cognition. There are two major models or frameworks from which to view this research. The first of these is the **developmental model,** which assumes that cognitive development, at least for the mildly retarded youngster, is similar to that of the younger, nonretarded child. According to Zigler (1969), retarded children progress through the same developmental levels in the same sequence as do nonretarded children, but at a slower rate. And they do not achieve as high a level of cognitive development.

Proponents of this point of view believe that retarded children fail because they are presented with tasks which are beyond their current ability level. Educational programs based on a developmental model would, therefore, use traditional teaching strategies but be geared primarily to the mental age (MA) of the individual. The developmental view of cognitive growth can be thought of as a series of steps or stages in which new tasks are presented only when the child reaches the mental age appropriate to that task.

Proponents of the second model, the **difference or defect model,** view the cognitive development of retarded persons as qualitatively different from that of the nonretarded. Ellis (1969) contended that there are differences in the way in which retarded people process information and that the main task of research is to describe these areas of difference. The implications for teaching, therefore, are that unique teaching methods and materials are needed to overcome or lessen the effects of the deficiency.

PROCESSES INVOLVED IN LEARNING

Retarded individuals, by definition, perform below average on tests of intelligence and are characterized as slow and inefficient learners. Whether you subscribe to the developmental or difference model of the cognitive functioning of retarded people, the practical issue of providing the optimum learning environment remains. Toward this end, a vast amount of research has been conducted in the area of learning and applied to the retarded. Most theorists have concentrated their efforts on one aspect of learning, such as attention or memory. In generalizing the findings to educational programming, however, we must emphasize that implications from various theories relating to separate aspects of learning may be used in combination, to offer the retarded learners the best opportunities for realizing their potential.

To present information from theories concerning the separate aspects of learning while maintaining an awareness of the total learning process, we will use Ross's (1976) learning paradigm. The components of the learning process, as identified by Ross, are listed in Table 3.1, along with the major theorist involved in each area and the implications considered to be most relevant by Mercer and Snell (1977), in their comprehensive review of learning theory research.

Ross considers the expectations held by the learner to be the initial stage of the learning process. The learner then attends to the situation and selectively attends to the learning task. Information is organized and stored in order to be recalled at some point in time or transferred or generalized to a different situation. The next step in the learning process is **performance,** the observable behavior which is used as the basis for determining whether or not learning has occurred. As mentioned earlier, performance is an indirect measure of learning which may be influenced by motivation and other factors. Therefore, it must be interpreted

TABLE 3.1 Components of the Learning Process and Respective Theories and Implications

Learning Components	Proponents	Major Implication
Expectancy	Social Learning Theory	Provide continuous success.
Selective Attention	Zeaman and House Fisher and Zeaman Denny (Incidental)	Make cues of task stimuli distinctive.
Organizing Input for Storage	Spitz	Organize or group input.
		Pair material with meaningful event or object.
Memory and Recall	Ellis	Use verbal rehearsal.
Transfer		Train in a variety of settings. Use modeling.
Performance	Dependent measure of all the research Skinner	Develop appropriate tasks.
Feedback	Skinner	Provide systematic consequation.

From C.D. Mercer & M.E. Snell, *Learning Theory Research in Mental Retardation.* Columbus, Ohio: Charles E. Merrill, 1977. P. 321. Reprinted by permission.

cautiously. **Feedback,** the last component in Ross's learning paradigm, refers to information which is given to the learner following a specific response. These consequences of behavior may be viewed as a positive or negative reinforcement, as punishment, or as a feature of expectancy. We will now look at each of these components of the learning process, and their implications for teaching.

Expectancy The first component in the model is **expectancy,** the way in which an individual approaches a task or situation based on previous experiences with similar tasks or situations. As viewed by Ross (1976), expectancy is not only present at the beginning of a learning situation but remains throughout the process as an incentive for continuing the task.

We have already mentioned the expectation of failure that is a feature of social learning theory. In general, retarded learners exhibit a higher expectancy for failure than do nonretarded students, as a result of their experiences with past failures. In an effort to avoid further failure, the retarded child may lower his goals or aspirations below what he is actually capable of achieving. The main implication for teaching, therefore, is to minimize failure experiences and maximize success.

Selective Attention The second component of Ross's (1976) learning paradigm is focusing attention on the relevant dimensions of the learning task. More specifically, **selective attention** refers to scanning the stimulus field, locating the relevant stimuli, and then attending to those stimuli over a period of time. The representative theorists in this area identified by Mercer and Snell (1977) are Zeaman and House (1963), who used the Wisconsin General Test Apparatus (WGTA) illustrated in Figure 3.1 to present two-choice visual discrimination tasks to retarded children. In each trial, two stimuli were placed on the sliding tray of the WGTA and presented to the subject, who was asked to select one of the stimuli. If, for example, the stimuli consisted of shapes and the circle was the shape to which the subject was being taught to respond, a reward would be presented each time the subject chose the circle over the other stimulus. Once the subject consistently selected the circle, discrimination learning was said to have occurred.

Various groups of retarded children were examined using discrimination learning tasks, and their performances were then translated into learning curves, or graphs illustrating the percentage of correct responses corresponding to the number of trials. Figure 3.2 shows the type of learning curve obtained. Analysis of the curves reveals two distinct stages involved in learning the discrimination tasks. In stage 1, correct responses were made about 50% of the time, or at about chance level. During the second stage, however, correct responses increased

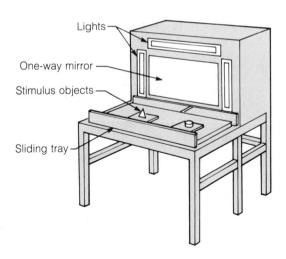

FIGURE 3.1 Discrimination Learning Apparatus

Adapted from D. Zeaman and B.J. House, ''The Role of Attention in Retardate Discrimination Learning.'' In N.R. Ellis (Ed.), *Handbook of Mental Deficiency*. New York: McGraw-Hill, 1963, p. 160. Reprinted by permission.

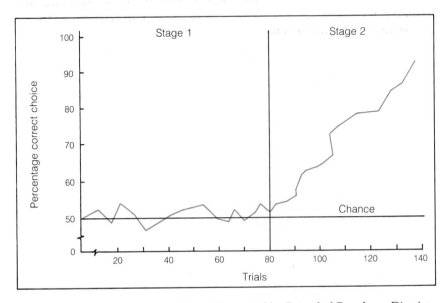

FIGURE 3.2 Typical Learning Curve Generated by Retarded People on Discrimination Tasks

dramatically, as illustrated by a sharp rise on the learning curve. Zeaman and House suggest that the first stage is an attention phase, where the subject randomly attends to various aspects of the task. Once the subject has focused on the key features of the task, or selectively attends to the relevant dimensions of the stimuli, the second, or learning, phase begins.

Comparisons were made of the learning curves obtained from the performances of nonretarded children and retarded children of varying mental ages. Zeaman and House found the two distinct stages in the curves of all groups, as well as the sharp rise in performance at the beginning of the second stage. The differences between the groups were in the number of trials in stage 1. Children with lower mental ages required more trials in the attention phase than did children with higher mental ages. One of their conclusions, therefore, was that it required more time for the retarded subjects to attend to the relevant dimensions of the stimuli. In a revision of the theory, Zeaman and House (1979) also noted a relationship between MA and the number of dimensions that could be attended to simultaneously. Retarded learners could not attend to as many dimensions simultaneously as could the nonretarded learners.

While the initial research by Zeaman and House continues to generate investigations into many aspects of attention, we can draw several implications from their work in selective attention for teaching retarded learners. Among them are that the teacher should (a) present stimuli which vary on only a few distinct dimensions, (b) direct the child's attention to these relevant dimensions, (c) remove extraneous stimuli which may distract the child from attention to the task at hand, and (d) reward the child for attending to the task (Mercer & Payne, 1975).

Input Organization According to Spitz (1966), once the child has attended to a specific stimulus, the information must be organized and stored so that it can be recalled when needed. This is called **input organization.** Spitz breaks down the learning process into the following steps:

> a. Arouse (person is alerted)
> b. Attend (attention is given to a specific stimulus)
> c. Input (file into appropriate hold area)
> d. Hold (hold for permanent storage)
> e. Recall (retrieve material from temporary file, if necessary)
> f. Storage (put into appropriate permanent file)
> g. Recall (retrieve material from permanent file if necessary)
>   (pp. 52–53)

Spitz' (1966) research led him to theorize that the input step in the learning process was more difficult for retarded subjects than for nonretarded subjects, noting a deficiency in retarded subjects' ability to organize the input stimuli for storage and recall. This finding has generated a great deal of research concerning strategies designed to enhance a student's ability to categorize incoming data. Two such methods are grouping and mediation.

Grouping, or clustering material prior to its presentation, is seen by Spitz (1973) as more beneficial to the retarded learner than presenting material in random order. Restructuring the perceptual field in some meaningful way for individuals who characteristically have difficulty at this stage of the learning process should facilitate memory and recall. Grouping is perhaps the simplest method of organizing information. Material may be grouped spatially, presented in different visual arrangements; temporally, by presenting the material with a pause or time lapse between items; perceptually, by enclosing certain items in a shape or configuration; or categorically, by content or commonality of items.

Stephens (1966) has further broken down this grouping by content into physical similarity (items of the same color), function (articles of clothing), concepts (plants, animals), and sequential equivalence (subjects and objects as used in grammatical arrangements). Work by Stephens (1972) in presenting stimuli according to types of grouping indicates that the most basic type of grouping is that of physical similarity. As a child increases in mental age, more advanced grouping strategies are used. This same progression was reported for both EMR and normal subjects.

A mediator is something that goes between or connects. In verbal learning, **mediation** refers to the process by which an individual connects a stimulus and a response. One approach to the study of verbal learning, *paired associate learning,* focuses on verbal mediation as a means of learning responses to stimulus words or elements. In this technique, the subject is generally presented with pairs of words. Then only the first word in each pair is presented, and the subject is to recall the second. Performance of this task appears to be enhanced by verbalizing the connection between the two stimulus words. Studies reviewed by Meyers and MacMillan (1976) note marked improvement in tasks of this type even by retarded subjects, when the subjects were instructed in mediation strategies or provided with mediators such as sentences relating the stimulus to the response. Also found to facilitate learning in paired associate tasks were the meaningfulness of the material and the use of stimulus words or objects familiar to the subject (Estes, 1970).

Several implications for teaching can be drawn from this research. First, materials presented to retarded learners should be familiar or have some relevance for them. Second, information should be grouped or organized into meaningful parts. Finally, retarded learners should be instructed in mediational strategies.

Memory **Memory,** the ability to retrieve information that has been stored, is one of the most heavily researched components of the learning process. A distinction is usually made between **short-term memory** (STM) and **long-term memory** (LTM). The distinction relates to the recency with which information has been processed. Information recalled after a period of days or months or longer is usually referred to as *long-term memory,* while data stored from a few seconds to a few hours may be thought of as *short-term memory* (Ellis, 1970). Most researchers contend that once learned, information is retained over the long term about as well by retarded individuals as by nonretarded individuals (Belmont, 1966; Ellis, 1963). In the area of short-term memory, however, retarded learners appear to have considerable difficulty (Ellis, 1963). In order to provide a theoretical framework for comparing the STM performance of retarded and nonretarded subjects, Ellis (1970) devised the multiprocess memory model illustrated in Figure 3.3.

According to this model, external stimulation enters via attention and is processed through one or more of the three storage mechanisms. The primary memory (PM) and the secondary memory (SM) are elements of short-term memory, with the PM being the most limited, capable of retaining only a few items at a time for very short intervals. The tertiary memory (TM) may be thought of as long-term memory, capable

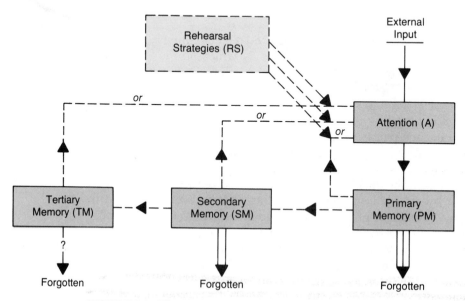

FIGURE 3.3 The Multiprocess Memory Model

Adapted from N.R. Ellis, "Memory Processes in Retardates and Normals." In N.R. Ellis (Ed.), *International Review of Research in Mental Retardation* (Vol. 4). New York: Academic Press, 1970. p. 6. Copyright © 1970 by Academic Press. Reprinted by permission.

of retaining information over long periods of time. Rehearsal strategies are the vehicles by which information is fed back through attention and PM and is transferred to various storage mechanisms. The area of rehearsal strategy, or refocusing of attention on information that might otherwise be lost, is the essence of Ellis' (1970) model.

Ellis (1970) and his associates consider the short-term memory problems characteristic of retarded learners to be due primarily to their inability to use rehearsal strategies or to use adequate rehearsal activities. Some success has been reported (Belmont & Butterfield, 1971; Brown, Campione, & Murphy, 1974) in efforts to improve short-term memory performance among retarded learners by direct teaching or rehearsal or practice procedures although the effects of the training appear to be specific to the training task and not readily transferred (Belmont & Butterfield, 1977). The major rehearsal strategies noted by Mercer and Snell (1977) in their review of studies concerning STM were verbal rehearsal and image rehearsal. *Verbal rehearsal* refers to labeling aspects of a task and verbalizing these labels aloud or silently while the task is being performed. For example, verbal rehearsal might be used to help a retarded worker learn the steps of a complex assembly task; e.g., "Pick up one nut; pick up one bolt; put the bolt into the nut," and so forth. In using *image rehearsal*, the child is taught to associate aspects of a task with pictures of events which will help him to recall them. For instance, a youngster might be taught to tie his shoes by making one "rabbit ear," making another and tying the two together. Other teaching implications to facilitate recall include (a) organizing material into meaningful segments, (b) using reinforcement and incentives for remembering, (c) using repetition and drill, and (d) reminding and encouraging the child to use rehearsal strategies.

Transfer After several trials on a particular task, a student will usually develop a learning set, which is knowledge of how to go about solving that particular kind of problem. Transfer is generally regarded as the ability to apply that knowledge to new tasks or problems. As with other aspects of the learning process, retarded students appear to demonstrate deficiencies in this area (Stephens, 1972).

While transfer is not a prime factor in the major learning theories, several teaching implications have evolved from the literature on transfer of learning reviewed by Drew and Espeseth (1969) and Smith (1974). Among these are

1. Select meaningful tasks in order to facilitate learning and ease of transfer,
2. Present easier material first and gradually increase difficulty,
3. Present facts and concepts in sequence,

4. Explain common characteristics of situations in order to facilitate the transfer of information from one setting or task to another, and

5. Reward correct responses.

The learning theories we have reviewed are related to specific aspects of the learning process and offer suggestions for working with retarded children in ways which might increase their performance on specific kinds of learning tasks. While some theories are more comprehensive than others, no one theory covers all aspects or types of learning. There are several major theoretical approaches, however, that provide a framework for viewing the development of cognitive abilities or learning in a particular setting or under certain conditions. By applying the principles outlined in these approaches to our knowledge of the learning characteristics of retarded students, we can gain additional insight into how to provide the optimum learning environment.

Cognitive-Developmental Theory The original tenets of **cognitive-developmental theory** were formulated by Jean Piaget, based on observations of his own ("normal") children. He viewed mental development as a result of continuous interaction with and adaptation to the environment or the child's perception of that environment. According to Piaget (1969), each child progresses through stages of development where various cognitive skills are acquired. The main stages of development, along with approximate age norms, are

1. Sensorimotor stage—Birth to 2 years
2. Preoperational stage—2 to 7 years
3. Concrete operations—7 to 11 years
4. Formal or abstract operations—11 years and older.

The **sensorimotor stage** is characterized by sensory experiences and motor activity. As the young child becomes more aware of the surrounding environment, he begins to distinguish between himself and other persons and objects in his world. The second stage, **preoperational,** involves more than purely physical operations. The child begins to use symbols for the people and objects around him, to assimilate customs, and to acquire new experiences by imitating the actions of others. During the **concrete operations** stage, the child develops further abilities to order and classify objects. While mental operations are more highly developed, the child is usually limited to solving problems with which he has had direct or concrete experience. The ability to perform abstract thinking and reason by hypothesis is said to develop around the age of 11 or 12, and characterizes the abstract or **formal operations** stage.

Piagetian theory has been related to mentally retarded children by Inhelder (1968) and Woodward (1963, 1979) who view the retarded as progressing through the same stages of cognitive development as do the nonretarded. The major differences, however, are in terms of rate and highest level achieved. The age at which a retarded child would reach each stage would be later. The more severe the retardation, the slower would be the progression through the stages. In addition, retarded individuals may not achieve all stages of development. According to Inhelder, the mildly retarded or EMR child may reach the concrete operations level, but moderately retarded individuals will achieve no farther than the preoperational stage. The severely and profoundly retarded person will remain at the sensorimotor level.

According to Piagetian theory, mental development progresses as a result of the child's own interactions with his surroundings. The role of the educator, therefore, is seen as providing materials and opportunities appropriate to the child's stage of development with which he can interact. Teachers of mentally handicapped students need to be aware of the developmental sequences in order to determine a child's readiness for a particular task, and to consider the slow rate and the expected optimal level of functioning when planning curricula for children with varying levels of retardation.

Operant Conditioning The modification of behavior through systematically arranging environmental events may be called **operant conditioning** (Wallace & Kauffman, 1978). The use of operant techniques has become widespread within the field of special education and has proven successful in both motivating and controlling the behavior of retarded individuals.

Based on the premise that behavior is primarily controlled by its consequences, the chance that a response will be repeated can be altered by manipulating the consequences that follow it. In other words, a behavior that leads to desirable or pleasurable consequences will be strengthened, while a behavior that leads to an undesirable consequence such as punishment will be weakened. For instance, a young child testing the response value of his first swear words will be more likely to repeat them if his audience laughs appreciatively than if the reply is a backhand to the backside and a bar of soap. To be effective, the consequence used must have some positive or negative value for the *individual learner* and be contingent upon, or paired with, a behavior offered by the learner.

Polloway, Payne, Patton and Payne (1985) list all three types of positive consequences readily available in the teaching situation—social reinforcers (praising; touching the child's hand, or hugging), tangibles (food, money, or tokens), and activities which would be highly regarded by a particular child (playing games, free time, listening to records, going to the library). Negative consequences for undesirable behavior might include "time out" (removing the child from the classroom setting for a specific amount of time), aversive stimuli (which may range from yelling at the child to some of the more extreme measures employed by clinicians to curtail self-destructive behaviors), and negative reinforcement.

In general, retarded individuals perform according to the principles of operant conditioning in much the same manner as do nonretarded persons (Mercer & Snell, 1977; Robinson & Robinson, 1976). In fact, there appears to be extensive research demonstrating the effectiveness of operant techniques even with the severely retarded (e.g., Azrin & Foxx, 1971; Barton, Guess, Garcia, & Baer, 1970; Mithaug, 1979; Schultz, Wehman, Renzaglia, & Karan, 1978). While only the most elementary principles of operant conditioning have been included in this discussion, some implications for teachers of the retarded are apparent. Some management techniques based on behavioral principles adapted from Wallace and Kauffman (1978) include *(a)* identify consequences or rewards that will be desirable to individual children, *(b)* increase desired behavior by reinforcing such behavior with praise or other rewards, *(c)* reinforce approximations or slight improvements toward desired behaviors, *(d)* reinforce appropriate behavior immediately, and *(e)* decrease undesirable behavior by removing consequences that reinforce it or by rewarding a behavior which is incompatible with the inappropriate behavior.

Observational Learning **Imitation, modeling,** and learning through observation are the terms most often associated with **observational learning,** which refers to learning that results from demonstrations by others. Much of the research in this area is attributed to Bandura and his associates (1969). It substantiates the important role that observational learning plays in acquiring social behaviors, sex roles, language, and religious and political practices. In addition, imitation and modeling are involved in the development of new behaviors and the modification of existing behavior, and may result in the learning of inappropriate as well as appropriate responses.

While there is not a great deal of research concerning the use of observational techniques with the retarded, certain characteristics of retarded learners would support the use of this tool. The tendency of retarded persons to be outerdirected or to look to others for cues or guidance in problem solving (Turnure & Zigler, 1964) and their suggestibility (Zigler, 1973) indicates that modeling could be effectively used for acquiring or changing behavior.

While Altman and Talkington (1971) emphasized what they consider to be the advantages of observational learning over operant techniques for the retarded, they conclude that effectiveness of learning may be enhanced by using one in conjunction with the other. The implications for working with the retarded then might include

1. Be aware that any behavior observed may serve as a model
2. Call attention to students exhibiting desirable behavior
3. Ignore or punish undesirable behavior so that it is not modeled by others in an attempt to gain attention
4. Reward modeling of appropriate behavior
5. Use audiovisual as well as live models to facilitate learning (MacMillan, 1977).

PHYSICAL AND HEALTH CHARACTERISTICS

The physical and health characteristics and corresponding needs of mildly retarded persons do not differ dramatically from those of nonretarded individuals. The more severe the retardation, however, the more pronounced the corresponding physical defects and health problems. The following discussion will highlight some of the health problems often found among retarded individuals, as well as general health considerations that have specific implications for them.

SPECIFIC HEALTH PROBLEMS

Mental retardation may be accompanied by one or more additional defects. In general, the more severe the retardation, the more likely that other handicapping conditions will be present as well. The extent to which motor development is delayed generally corresponds to the severity of the retardation and the existence of other medical problems. The growth rate is slower, and retarded individuals are generally deficient in both height and weight when compared to normal children (Mosier, Grossman, & Dingman, 1965). Motor deficiencies are often noted among retarded people; however, these difficulties may be due, in part, to lack of instruction and practice opportunities rather than a direct result of the retardation.

Sensory defects are also more common among the retarded, with visual and auditory problems frequently noted (Barlow, 1978). Even colorblindness appears to be more prevalent among moderately retarded individuals than among the mildly retarded or normal population (O'Connor, 1975). Early screening for sensory defects is essential in the event that correctional devices or surgery may be indicated. In fact, early identification of any health problems may be critical to the total development of the child. While the retardation itself may obscure or impede efforts to diagnose additional problems, early intervention and treatment may lessen the effects of the disability and influence the rate and level of development the child may attain.

Down Syndrome Some children with moderate or more severe retardation may be classified as a "clinical type." In order to be regarded as a specific clinical type, an individual must show certain facial, body, and disease characteristics relating to a particular syndrome associated with mental retardation. While there are a number of these syndromes, the one most frequently associated with mental retardation is Down syndrome, accounting for approximately 10% of the moderately and more severely retarded population.

Besides their distinct physical appearance, Down syndrome children frequently have specific health-related problems. A significant number of these children have structural defects of the heart which may threaten their survival. Surgical procedures are sometimes successful in correcting the defect. Lung abnormalities are also frequently seen in Down syndrome children, resulting in susceptibility to upper respiratory infections. The incidence of leukemia is also higher than in the normal population. Other health problems also found with frequency among Down syndrome children are eye and ear infections, obesity, skin problems primarily due to their characteristically rough and dry skin, problems of the teeth and gums, and hearing impairments.

Individuals working with Down syndrome children should be alert to signs of infection, particularly ear and upper respiratory infections, so that early medical treatment may prevent more serious problems. Physical education and exercise programs should also be provided, although the type and amount of activity required of a particular child should be planned with the guidance of medical personnel.

Cerebral Palsy While not all children with cerebral palsy (CP) are mentally retarded, the retarded child who does have this condition presents a number of health-related problems. Cerebral palsy is a neuromuscular disability that may result from damage to the brain at birth or during the early years of life. While the condition may include any number of intellectual, sensory, and behavioral disorders, the motor disability presents several potential problems. Limbs that are not exercised may lose their usefulness altogether. Some children may be on movement or exercise programs which will need to be implemented at certain intervals during the day. If a child wears a cast or a brace, those working with the child should be alert to signs of circulation problems such as swelling, coldness, change of color, and evidence of infection, as well as other skin problems.

Individuals working with the retarded, cerebral palsied youngster should be aware of a number of other problems which may accompany the disorder. Speech difficulties complicated by lack of muscle control are common, often requiring speech therapy or other special educational measures. Visual and auditory problems are also seen more frequently in the CP child, and corrective measures may be warranted to improve vision or hearing. Difficulties with chewing and swallowing may present real hazards if the child is given such foods as hard candy, popcorn, and chewing gum. Parents should be consulted for specific instructions regarding eating and drinking. As with other disabilities, upper respiratory infections are common, and early symptoms should be reported since the consequences of such infections may be severe.

Seizures Another health problem often associated with cerebral palsy, but also characteristic of other conditions which may accompany mental retardation, is seizures (Neisworth & Smith, 1978). Seizures vary from momentary disturbances which may go unnoticed **(petit mal)** to episodes involving jerking of the muscles and loss of consciousness **(grand mal)**. Some children experience an *aura* or sensation just before a seizure begins and may be able to give some indication that a seizure is imminent. In some children, the likelihood of a seizure is increased by certain events, such as flickering lights or loud sounds, or the physical condition of the child, as when he is highly excited, ill, or fatigued. By being aware of children who have a history of seizures, teachers can be alert to factors that might precede or precipitate them. Once a seizure occurs, it should not be interrupted. The major concern is to keep the child from injuring himself. During a grand mal seizure, the child should be eased to the floor, furniture and other objects pushed away from him, and if possible, restrictive clothing loosened and the child turned on his side to aid breathing. Someone should remain with the child until the seizure ends, and then allow him to rest.

GENERAL HEALTH CONSIDERATIONS

Nutrition Proper kinds and amounts of food are necessary for the general well-being of all children. Poor diet has been found not only to arrest biological development and resistance to disease and illness, but also to be a negative factor in social adjustment and academic learning (Paige, 1975). Among those labeled *mildly retarded*, inadequate diet may be a factor. Inadequate or unbalanced diets may be a result of insufficient food, poor supervision of meals and snacks, or lack of understanding of the importance of proper nutrition and how to provide it.

Among the more severely retarded, additional problems enter the picture. Many of these children become obese, often as a result of physical inactivity or improper diet. Other children require more calories than

COSMETIC INTERVENTION

The following article, which appeared in a local newspaper on July 13, 1979, captures the essence and philosophy behind the "therapeutic cosmetic intervention" movement. Although there are opponents to this concept, who stress that mentally retarded people should be accepted as they are without cosmetic alterations, we feel that efforts such as those described in this article are worth considering because of two possible benefits: gaining public acceptance and increasing a person's self-esteem.

Retarded Are Made Over

by Rosemary Armao

Their teeth are ragged. Their pants flap around their ankles. They wear red stripes with orange polka dots. In institutions and in the community, the retarded are—too frequently—easy to pick out.

Standing out like that makes them easier targets of fear and prejudice, says Robert D. Shushan, executive director of the Los Angeles-based Exceptional Children's Foundation.

Shushan says educators spend "a fortune getting the retarded to say vowels and consonants" but forget to teach them to match clothing colors and to tuck in their shirts.

To prove the power of what he calls "therapeutic cosmetic intervention," he has traveled across the country and into several other nations with a satchel of before-and-after slides, a box of eyeglass frames and a makeover program that takes high school hair stylists and amateur cosmetologists to retardation centers.

He recently visited the Columbus State Institute. Pointing to Richard, a middle-aged resident in his audience, Shushan asked permission to discuss the man's appearance.

Shushan told him the patterns on his pants and shirt clashed. He suggested Richard smile with his lips together to hide missing front teeth. His hair was cut and he was given eyeglasses in tortoise shell frames. Then he stood before the audience holding a book.

"Think of all the things we, so-called normal people, do to ourselves to look good," Shushan said. "It's all illusion. In this day and age there are things we can do to make a difference."

Too often, he added, these things are not done for the retarded and, "They look the way they do by default."

He said many dentists advise parents not to "waste money" on orthodontics for their retarded children.

Because they can't read, they aren't tested for glasses.

Hand-me-downs that other children would reject as too worn or ill-fitting, the retarded happily wear.

"Mother just turns up the cuffs. What does it matter."

"And what about facial expressions?" Shushan asks parents. "We don't give the retarded the proper models. When we talk to them, it's like we'd talk to a small child. With an extra big smile, right?"

Or else the retarded are underestimated, he said. He recalled a retarded 19-year-old, well-dressed and presentable except that he absent-mindedly dangled his tongue down his chin.

"His mother told me, 'Oh, he's always done that. I could never break it.' I told the boy 'Hey, you know, you look really good with your tongue in your mouth. You should do that all the time.' A year later, I ran into him and his mother again and he came running up to me pointing at his mouth and saying 'tongue, tongue.'"

Sharon, a moderately retarded woman with cerebral palsy who has spent 17 of her 23 years at Columbus State, stood up. Two rubber bands held her hair in bunches at the top and back. She wore a yellow shirt, bright blue shorts and black gym sneakers.

Thirty minutes later she looked in a mirror at blue eyes shaded with shadow, curly blonde hair cut loose and short and a scarf that framed her face. She clapped along with the admiring audience.

"That's my answer to people who ask me 'do they know what's happening to them?'" Shushan said. "If a person is motivated to feel good about himself, you've given him self-esteem, dignity."

He said many mental facilities he has visited don't even have mirrors, "Or they're the old, blotchy kind."

"If I went into any institution and even among the bedridden, and improved their appearances, the community would look at that institution differently. The staff would look at the residents differently."

Sometimes the bad looks of the retarded are deliberate, he said.

"I had one mother say to me, 'I don't want my daughter to look so pretty. I don't want boys chasing her.' Or some will say, 'I don't want my son to look so normal because then people will expect too much of him.'"

Then, Shushan turned to another retarded woman, Linda, and asked "Do you know what it means to be responsible for yourself? Would you like that?"

"Yes," Linda told him, "it means wash my own hair."

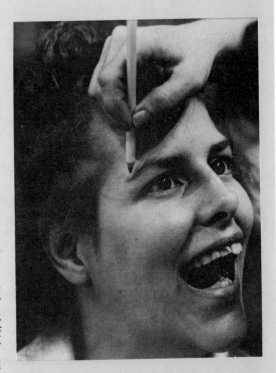

"Sharon reacts to her makeover."

normal, special diets, or nutritional supplements because of specific health concerns. Motor difficulties may present major problems in feeding. Assistance may be required in terms of providing the types of foods a child can best manage, arranging food and containers to facilitate eating, providing prosthetic devices to aid in feeding, and allowing adequate time for this task. Some children, of course, are so severely handicapped that they are unable to feed themselves and will require patient assistance to meet their nutritional needs.

Illness and Disease As might be expected, retarded individuals are more susceptible to disease and illness than are nonretarded people. Poor nutrition and lack of adequate health care which includes an immunization program would appear to be major factors among children from lower socioeconomic classes. Moderately and more severely retarded children often have additional handicapping conditions or health problems which account for their relatively poor health. The frequency of heart and lung disorders among Down syndrome children is but one example.

Several specific problems are commonly noted among retarded children. Cold symptoms and upper respiratory infections are frequent and often of longer duration than in nonretarded children. The seriousness of the symptoms is often compounded by the presence of other disorders such as cardiac conditions.

Skin difficulties are common. Down syndrome children characteristically have dry skin that readily becomes inflamed and infected. Children who are confined to beds or wheelchairs must be moved regularly so that sores do not develop. Casts and braces present the possibility of broken or irritated skin and, therefore, infection.

A relatively high incidence of dental problems is also found among retarded children. Among children from a lower socioeconomic environment, dental problems are often due to poor nutrition and failure to practice daily dental hygiene or have routine dental checkups. Malformations of the oral cavity and the resulting teeth and gum problems are common among the more severely retarded. Routine dental care often poses a major problem for those individuals caring for the severely retarded child.

Accidents and Injury Developmentally delayed children are likely to be poorly coordinated and awkward. Add to this the poor judgment and impaired reasoning which may be associated with subaverage intellectual ability, and a higher than average accident rate may be predicted. Conditions which accompany the retardation—such as limited vision, muscle weakness, motor disabilities, and seizures—may also contribute to increased injuries.

Physical Activity A certain amount of exercise and activity is necessary to the total well-being of any individual. For the child who is mentally retarded, a planned program of physical activity is essential for a number of reasons. Mildly retarded individuals may not differ appreciably from the nonretarded in physical and motor skills. Sports and other physical activities may provide an opportunity for expression and achievement as well as an outlet for releasing tension. Gains in physical strength and motor coordination as well as feelings of accomplishment often enhance social and personal adjustment.

With more severely retarded persons, planned physical education and recreation programs provide enjoyment and a productive use of leisure time, as well as the activity necessary to combat such typical problems as obesity. Improvement in gross motor and fine motor skills may contribute to physical independence and increase opportunities for social development as well. The use of adaptive equipment and materials enables individuals with many handicapping conditions to participate in a wide variety of games and activities.

While opportunities for physical education and recreation have represented an area of neglect with respect to the mentally retarded (Chinn et al., 1979), the future outlook is far more encouraging, as shown by recent studies on physical fitness and the retarded (Beasley, 1982; Halle, Silverman, & Regan, 1983). Provisions of P.L. 94-142 include not only physical education but recreation and leisure education as related services which are to be provided to handicapped children. Community agencies and citizen groups are becoming more actively involved in providing opportunities for recreation and competitive events such as the Special Olympics. Programs offered by colleges and universities designed to train professionals in techniques for working with the handicapped in the area of physical education and recreation are increasing in number and scope.

SUMMARY

We have presented a general overview of the major social/emotional, learning, and physical/health characteristics of mentally retarded people. While these general characteristics are useful in understanding mental retardation, they should not be regarded as universal truths. The range from mild to profound retardation is indeed a wide one—probably as wide as the range from borderline retardation to "genius." And the individuals we identify as "mentally retarded" are as different from each other as two "normal" people. Furthermore, a given person may be "mildly" academically retarded, but "severely" physically or socially delayed. We must remember that these labels are simply for our convenience in designing programs and obtaining funds.

CHAPTER FOUR

Intelligence and Intelligence Testing

THEORIES OF INTELLIGENCE

Intelligence can be called the ability to adapt, achieve, solve problems, interpret incoming stimuli to modify behavior, accumulate knowledge, or respond to items on an intelligence test. Diverse concepts of intelligence have been formulated by the many theorists in the field. Robinson and Robinson (1976) analyzed many theories of intelligence and found three themes common to most definitions of intelligence.

1. The capacity to learn,
2. The total body of acquired knowledge, and
3. Adaptability to environmental demands.

Capacity to learn refers to an individual's ability to benefit from education. *Acquired knowledge* includes all the concepts and information that the individual has learned up to this point, as well as his ability to learn. *Adaptive aspects of intelligence* are those which enable a person to fit himself into his environment and to adjust successfully to environmental changes. Theories that describe intelligence as a learning capacity or the

---

This chapter was contributed by Mary Beirne-Smith and Keith Hume.

ability to adapt assume that intelligence is an innate quality—an inborn aptitude or potential for intelligent behavior. On the other hand, equating intelligence with acquired knowledge emphasizes not potential but previous achievement. The difference then, between the instruments used to measure these two types of attributes, both called *intelligence*, is the difference between an aptitude test and an achievement test—a significant variation.

Early theorists posited several important definitions that influenced what we believe about intelligence today. Terman (1921) believed that intelligence varies directly with the ability to think abstractly. In his words

> It cannot be disputed . . . that in the long run [those who] . . . excel in abstract thinking . . . eat while others starve, survive epidemics, master new continents, conquer time and space, and substitute religion for magic, science for taboos and justice for revenge. [Those who] excel in conceptual thinking could, if they wished, quickly exterminate or enslave all [those] . . . notably their inferiors in this respect. (p. 128)

Most early definitions of intelligence described it as a unitary trait, that is, a single, indivisible factor. David Wechsler (1944), author of the four Wechsler intelligence scales (1955, 1966, 1974, 1981), diverged from this viewpoint when he described intelligence as an aggregate phenomenon, composed of many discrete mental abilities. Moreover, he proposed that certain other factors such as purposiveness, drive, and incentive influence a person's level of intellectual functioning and, therefore, his or her score on an intelligence test. Based on his particular view of the nature of the intellect, Wechsler's scales assess a variety of specific abilities and yield corresponding subtest scores as well as a global index.

In discussing theories of intelligence, it is important to mention that a theory has three functions: to make sense out of chaos, to assist in predicting outcomes, and to facilitate change. A theory about intelligence takes the complex behavior of man and tries to make some sense out of it, e.g., "He did that because he is not very intelligent." As the theory develops and solidifies, predictions may be made, e.g., "He is functioning in the dull normal range of intelligence, and he will probably experience difficulty learning through traditional instruction." A viable theory of intelligence not only helps to explain and predict behavior or events, but it also may suggest ways to change things, e.g., "If he is placed in a more stimulating yet controlled environment, he might acquire more knowledge and develop more skills than if he were left in a traditional learning environment."

Until research unearths additional information about cerebral functioning, we must realize that "intelligence" is only a hypothetical construct. It does not exist in any concrete form; it cannot be located by probing around in the body. The construct called *intelligence* is useful in that it gives theorists a conceptual framework within which to explain individual differences and measure them. It is, as Maloney and Ward (1978) explain, a "shorthand way of classifying or grouping a set of behaviors which may be broadly labeled 'intelligent'" (p. 88). Accordingly, intelligence tests sample a cluster of behaviors from which we infer the presence and level of intelligence, and the resulting IQ score is an index of how well these behaviors were performed. An IQ score is *neither* a brain cell count nor the measured amount of some wondrous substance embedded between layers of gray matter. Yet most persons would place IQ in the same class as birthdates and fingerprints—they regard it as a personal description that does not change. This is an unfortunate misinterpretation of a scientific theory with colloquial connotations. For one thing, the validity of IQ tests as measures of intelligence is questionable. For another, intelligence per se has never been adequately defined. Consequently, there is little reason to regard an IQ as anything more than a score on an IQ test.

Still, keeping in mind its limitations, the concept of intelligence is a valuable theoretical tool. Speaking directly to educators, Edwards and Scannel (1968) emphasize that it is important for teachers to understand that intelligence refers to two aspects—"the innate potential of the individual and the functional expression of the potential as usable and used ability" (p. 7). They further emphasize that innate potential is physiological, while the functional aspects are behavioral. Educators must concern themselves with the behavioral domain, since it is only in this arena that educational diagnosis and treatment occur. Regardless of the preponderance of definitions of intelligence, intelligence is still a hypothetical construct; it is inferred from tests and behavior. In other words, behavior reflects intelligence. An operationally defined theoretical construct of intelligence is useful to the extent that it is helpful in thinking about people (Spiker & McCandless, 1954). For teachers, the concept of intelligence is useful when it helps them constructively formulate teaching strategies and make placement decisions.

NATURE VS. NURTURE

If teachers view intelligence as biologically based, fixed, or predominantly inherited, they may see their job as a disseminator of material to be consumed by students. This position assigns learning and nonlearning predominantly to the child; i.e., if the child does not learn, it is his or her own fault. On the other hand, if teachers view intelligence as something which can be cultivated, altered, or facilitated, they may see their job as instrumental to the process. This position enables teachers to evaluate a child's learning and nonlearning as an indication of their effectiveness as teachers.

The varying concepts of intelligence and how children learn are directly related to the nature-nurture controversy; that is, either intelligence is innate or it is learned. Actually, few authorities claim that it is an either/or proposition. Rather, most concede that intellectual functioning is shaped by a combination of biological and environmental factors, and thus, it is partly fixed and partly malleable.

See chapters 6 and 7 for more on the nature vs. nurture issue.

The bulk of the continuing debate concerns the relative impact of the two major ingredients that combine to mold intelligence. It is generally agreed that the facts of a person's upbringing may nourish or starve his cognitive growth to any level within the constraints of his biologically endowed potential. But how rigid are those constraints? How powerful are environment forces? How mutable are the effects of this interaction? Ingalls (1978), for one, explains that it is useless to try to assign a percentage to the relative influence of heredity and environment. Even the most genetically promising mind can have its development retarded if the environment provides no stimulation. Ingalls illustrates with an analogy of plant growth.

> The height of a given plant is a result of the particular gene type of the seed, the quality of the soil, the amount of rain, and numerous other factors. If a given plant grows to be four feet tall, it makes no sense to say that it achieved this height because of the seed variety. It is equally nonsensical to say that 80% of the height was due to the genes. (p. 41)

Even though the logic of this approach seems irrefutable, Jensen (1966, 1969, 1980, 1981) has insisted that genes and prenatal develop-

Arthur Jensen is a leading advocate of the genetic view of intelligence.

ment account for 80% of the variance in intelligence, while only 20% of the variance can be accounted for by the environment. Citing research studies, growth figures, and models of intelligence, Jensen has presented a convincing case. Particularly, he objects to the philosophy that cites environmental deprivation and test bias as the reasons for IQ variance between cultural groups. He believes the major determinant to be genetic, not environmental, input. Based on his examination of such compensatory education programs as Head Start, Jensen has concluded that growing up in a severely impoverished environment can stunt a child's intellectual growth, but that no amount of enrichment can make him more intelligent than his potential allows. However, additional mental abilities other than those normally tapped by intelligence tests are malleable and deserve attention from those who wish to equalize educational opportunity.

Thus far, we know that environmental influences have a substantial impact on measured intelligence (Hunt, 1961). This finding, coupled with theories of intelligence like Feuerstein's (1979, 1981) theory of cognitive modifiability (which suggests ways of facilitating the behavioral change that is associated with intellectual growth), compels educators and social scientists to arrange environments which stimulate intellectual growth. Finally, if measured intelligence is sensitive to environmental influence, it is imperative that learners be tested and observed periodically, so that the educational program may allow for changes in their intellectual and adaptive growth.

INTELLIGENCE TESTING

The earliest attempts to measure cognitive functioning were tests of sensory abilities assumed to indicate the presence or absence of that single entity called *intelligence*. In the 1890s, for instance, Cattell devised a "mental test" which appraised such discrimination abilities as estimating the length of a 10-second interval and distinguishing tactile sensations. These early tests, though able to sort out certain measurable differences between individuals, failed to provide any meaningful measure of cognitive ability, largely because they lacked **validity.** That is, the results of these tests were poor predictors of school achievement, success in life, and other ostensible indices of intelligence.

BINET

The first effective test of intellectual ability was devised in the early 1900s by French psychologist Alfred Binet. In 1904 the Minister of Public Instruction in Paris appointed Binet to a commission to study the problem of educating subnormal children. It was believed that children who were failing in school and disrupting normal classrooms would profit more from slower-paced instruction in special classes. Binet and his colleague, Theodore Simon, set out to devise an instrument to sift mentally deficient children out of the school-age population. The first test, the 30-item Measuring Scale of Intelligence, was published in 1905, and then revised in 1908 and again in 1911. The Binet-Simon Scale far surpassed any of the earlier measures in predicting school achievement because, rather than assessing sensory functions, it tested mental abilities such as comprehension, memory, and reasoning, which are necessary for scholastic success. Binet's early work had been in the study of individual differences, and during this period he had criticized the use of sensory tests to discriminate between bright and dull persons. He did not agree with his predecessors that slow reflexes were sufficient ground on which to conclude that a person was intellectually slow. Nor did he find it necessary to examine all areas of interindividual differences. Consequently, the Binet-Simon Scale sampled those higher level, complex processes which the authors believed to be the essential elements of intelligence.

Initially, Binet considered memory and judgment to be these most essential elements. However, he later discovered that persons with good memories are not always the most intelligent. "One may have good sense and lack memory. The reverse is also common" (Binet & Simon, 1916/1961, p. 94). Therefore, the first Binet scale dealt heavily with the assessment of judgments. Poor judgment was considered to include not just simple response errors but also absurd errors.

Binet and Simon went to great lengths to differentiate between the concept of general or natural intelligence and that of acquired intelligence, the knowledge gained through instruction. Binet and Simon sought to measure raw intelligence or capacity to learn; they were not interested in measuring what had been learned, or the "degree of instruction which the subject possessed" (Binet & Simon, 1916/1961, p. 93). Reading and writing were considered to be learned skills; therefore, their test of intelligence was constructed so as not to measure reading and writing. The initial version, for example, instead tested the child's ability to identify pictured objects, repeat a three-digit series, reproduce geometric figure drawings, define abstract words, and perform similar nonacademic tasks. The following case study cited by Binet and Simon (1916/1961) illustrates their concern with tapping natural over acquired intelligence.

> One of the cases, to us a very striking one, was that of little Germaine, a child of 11 years who came from a Paris school. Her parents, having carried their Penates to Levallois-Perret, had sent their child to one of the schools for girls in that city. But the directress refused little Germaine under the pretext that her school was full; in reality, because the child was extremely back-

ward. In fact, the retardation was at least 3 years; her reading was hesitating, almost syllabic; faults of orthography spoiled her dictation exercise. She wrote the following phrase under our eyes: The pretly litl grils stude the flwr that the gathrd yesty (which signifies: "The pretty little girls studied the flowers that they gathered yesterday"). Her number work was equally poor. She was asked, "If I have 19 apples, and eat 6 of them, how many have I left?" The child, reckoning mentally, said "12" which is inexact but reasonable. Trying it on paper, she was lost; she made an addition instead of subtraction and found 25. In other calculations she showed that she had the power to reckon mentally, but not on paper; in the last case she made the addition correctly when she should have subtracted. It is, however, a frequent, not to say constant, rule that those backward in arithmetic do the operations better than the problems, and do more easily operations of addition and multiplication than those of subtraction and division. In short, this child had a retardation of 3 years; but knowledge of her scholarship was lacking. On the other hand her wide-awake and mischievous air and the vivacity of her speech made a favorable impression on us. We made the test of intelligence and that showed us that her intelligence was normal; she was backward scarcely a year. This is a characteristic example which shows the use of our measuring scale. (p. 110)

Mental Age The 1908 revision of Binet and Simon's scale introduced the notion that children gain in cognitive ability as they mature—hence, the concept of **mental age** (MA). Essentially, MA is a reading of the child's intellectual level (as gauged by his performance on a mental measurement test) recorded independently of chronological age. A child who passed on the Binet scale only those items that an average 5-year-old should pass earned a mental age of 5. A 7-year-old child with a mental age of 5 would be considered intellectually subaverage; a 3-year-old with the same MA would be regarded as bright. To arrive at this statistic, the revised Binet test items were arranged by age levels from 3 to 10, with five additional problems each for the ages of 12, 15, and adult. The computation of MA is simple; a basal level (level on test where all items are passed) and a ceiling level (level on test where all items are failed) are determined. The MA score is obtained by adding to the basal level a specified number of months credit for each item passed above the basal item. For instance, if an 8-year-old child solved all the problems through age 8, passed two out of five tests at age 9, one out of five tests at age 10, and failed all at age 12, the MA after all credits were assigned would be 8⅗ years, or 8 years and 7 months.

STANFORD-BINET

Today American teachers know of the Binet-Simon Scale as the Stanford-Binet Intelligence Scale (Terman & Merrill, 1973). Dr. Lewis Terman adapted the Binet scale for American use in 1916 while at Stanford University, and his version has since been revised in this country three times—in 1937 and 1960 by Terman and Maud Merrill, and in 1973 by R. L. Thorndike (Terman & Merrill, 1973). The current form of the Stanford-Binet includes materials such as toys and miniature objects (beads, balls, cars, and dolls, for example) which the examinee is instructed to manipulate in various ways, and booklets and pictures (of animals and household objects, and so on) about which he must answer questions. The examinee is also required to draw geometric figures and to respond to questions and problems presented orally. Test items are grouped by age from year II difficulty level to superior adult level questions. Items within each age grouping are equally difficult; that is, the test design ensures that about half the subjects of normal intelligence at a given age will fail items appropriate to that age and half will pass. In other words, a typical item at the VII level would be passed by 50% of the 7-year-olds and failed by 50%. A greater percentage of younger children would fail the same item; a smaller percentage of older subjects would find it too difficult.

Lewis Terman conceived of intelligence as a unitary factor and incorporated that concept into his Stanford-Binet Intelligence Tests. (Courtesy of The Archives of the History of American Psychology)

Intelligence Quotient (Ratio)   In the 1916 revision of the Binet test, Terman, influenced by Stern (1912), introduced the concept of an **intelligence quotient** (IQ) as a better scoring index than mental age. Binet had proposed that a 2-year lag in mental age, as defined by performance on his test, be the criterion for judging a child mentally retarded. However, Stern explained that the absolute difference between MA and CA meant a greater mental deficit for younger than for older children. In other words, a 1-year delay is much more serious for a 4-year-old than for a 15-year-old. To account for this, Stern suggested that the computation of a **ratio IQ score,** which Terman incorporated into his test. The intelligence quotient is found by dividing an individual's mental age by his chronological age and multiplying the quotient by 100. The formula is:

$$\frac{MA}{CA} \times 100 = IQ$$

In the previous example, the 8-year-old child with an MA of 8 years 7 months would have an IQ of 107.

$$\frac{96 + 7}{96} \times 100 = 107$$

The theoretical average child, whose MA equals his CA, will have an IQ of 100. Using this method, the absolute different between MA and CA has a diminishing influence on IQ as the child gets older. To return to our example of a 1-year deficit, the 5-year-old with an MA of 4 has earned an IQ score of 80 (20 points below average), whereas the 1-year deficit in the 15-year-old's MA gives him a score of 93 (only 7 points below average).

   The major advantage of ratio IQ over a simple MA is that it gives an index of a child's IQ test performance relative to others in his age group. As the child grows, he gains in cognitive ability; but as long as his gains are average for his age, his IQ score will not change. The problem with this statistic, as with any ratio using CA as the divisor, is that most persons' mental development slows to a halt at some time in their late teens; yet their chronological age continues to increase arithmetically. As a result, the ratio MA/CA progressively decreases as the average person ages past 18, and his intelligence quotient diminishes accordingly. Thus, to avoid implying that adults become more feebleminded with every passing day, CA must be held at some point between 16 and 18 when computing ratio IQ for adults; yet the fact that mental age plateaus at different times for different people makes choosing a universally valid cut-off CA impossible. Stern's ratio IQ is an appropriate tool for measuring intelligence test performances of children and early adolescents, but its use with adults is questionable. David Wechsler, author of the intelligence scales which have replaced the Stanford-Binet as favorites for school and psychological use, corrected this flaw by devising a new index—the **deviation IQ score.**

Derivation of the deviation IQ score is explained on p. 114.

WECHSLER

The Stanford-Binet Intelligence Scale views intelligence as a single, global entity. Another way to examine intelligence is to start with the idea that the global entity of intelligence is composed of many specific intellectual abilities. Wechsler incorporated this notion of a general intelligence consisting of specific intellectual abilities into the development of a series of intelligence scales, beginning in 1939 with the Wechsler-Bellvue scales for adults. In 1949, Wechsler published his Intelligence Scale for Children (WISC) age 6 through 16, which he revised to its present form (WISC-R) in 1974. The Wechsler Adult Intelligence Scale (WAIS) first appeared in 1959 to replace the original Bellvue Scale for use with individuals 16 years and older and was revised to its present form (WAIS-R) in 1981. For children between 4 and 6½ years old, Wechsler published the Preschool and Primary Scale of Intelligence (WPPSI) in 1966. These Weschler tests are the mental measurements most often encountered by school administrators and classroom teachers.

When they first appeared, the Wechsler scales were distinguished by several unique features, generally considered to be changes for the better (Ingalls, 1978). For one thing, every Wechsler scale is subdivided into smaller tests. The WISC, for example, consists of 10 subsets with two alternates, five verbal subtests with one alternate and five performance (nonverbal) subtests with one alternate. Each subtest is treated separately and is theoretically said to measure a different ability; yet, when combined, global intellectual capacity is assessed. Wechsler (1939) believed that the Binet test does not tap performance, an important facet of intelligence. He developed a performance scale with problem-solving items which require judgment, reasoning, foresight, and planning, but which depend on little verbal ability.

Generally speaking, the verbal portion of the Wechsler tests requires more communication and interaction between the person taking the test and the test administrator than the nonverbal portion. On the performance section, the examinee works more independently of the examiner, and relatively little social interaction is required. The WISC-R provides estimates of the individual's levels of functioning in verbal and nonverbal ability as well as an estimate of overall intelligence, in the form of a Verbal IQ, a Performance IQ, and a Full Scale IQ. The subtests of the WISC-R are listed and described in Table 7.1.

INTELLIGENCE QUOTIENT (DEVIATION)

Perhaps Wechsler's most significant innovation was his use of the **deviation IQ score** in place of Stern's ratio computation. Rather than applying a derived MA to a ratio formula, the Wechsler IQ is found by converting the raw scores on each subtest to standard scores which are normalized for the examinee's age group, and adding them for a total standard score, called the deviation IQ. Wechsler reasoned that intelligence is normally distributed; that is, the majority of people will score at or around the mean, and progressively fewer people will achieve scores that spread out in either direction from the mean. Thus, a group of IQ scores can be portrayed as a normal curve with an average (mean) of 100 and a standard deviation which is the same (15) at every age level. The normal curve is sometimes also referred to as the *bell-shaped* or the *Gaussian curve*.

See Figure 2.1 for an example of a normal curve showing deviation IQs for the WISC-R.

Terman and Merrill (1960) adopted the deviation IQ as a scoring standard for the 1960 revision of the Stanford-Binet, though they chose a standard deviation of 16 rather than 15 as on Wechsler's scales. The current Stanford-Binet manual includes tables for converting MA to deviation IQ. The WISC and the recent Stanford-Binet (Terman & Merrill, 1973) were mathematically constructed to fit the percentages indicated within the curve.

The advantage of the deviation IQ is that the standing of an individual child may be compared with the scores of children his own age, and the intervals from age to age remain the same. That is, the differences disclosed at each age level all fall under the percentages and percentiles shown under the normal curve. For instance, a child of age 5 who scored one standard deviation below the mean would earn an IQ on the WISC of 85 and would score roughly at the 16th percentile; therefore, approximately 84% of the 5-year-olds would score above him (34.13 + 34.13 + 13.49 + 2.14 + 0.13 = 84.12%). The same would hold true for a 7-year-old who scored one standard deviation below the mean.

COMPARISON OF STANFORD-BINET AND WISC-R

To review, intelligence is a hypothetical construct which has been conceived for the purpose of making descriptive, comparative, and predictive statements about people. This construct is evaluated through behavior; and the most frequently used individual tests of this behavior are the Stanford-Binet (Terman & Merrill, 1973) and the WISC-R (Wechsler, 1974).

It is worth noting that Binet never defined the construct *intelligence;* instead, he chose for his test a variety of items that tapped the common-sense notion of intelligent behavior. Wechsler, on the other hand, had very definite ideas about the nature of intellectual functioning (a general phenomenon composed of specific intellects), and he constructed his test accordingly.

Both the Stanford-Binet and the WISC-R purport to measure general mental ability, yet verbal abilities constitute the greater part of the

TABLE 4.1 WISC-R Subtests

Subtest	Content	Correlates or Performance Requirements
Information	Questions of fact; general knowledge	Rote memory; educational level; early experience
Similarities	Questions requiring grouping	Verbal reasoning; abstract thinking; concept formation
Arithmetic*	Questions requiring mental calculations	Recent memory; concentration; ability to calculate
Vocabulary	Defining words	Word knowledge; early experience and education
Comprehension	Questions requiring judgment and practical decision making concerning problems of everyday life; proverbs	Judgment or common sense; emotional control; socialization
Digit Span (Optional)	Repetition of numbers presented orally forward and backward	Immediate recall; passive attention
Picture Completion	Requires identifying missing parts in line drawings	Concentration; visual discrimination; logical thinking
Picture Arrangement*	Requires ordering of cartoon frames presented out of sequence	Visual organization; social awareness or competence
Block Design*	Requires reproduction of abstract	Visual organization; planning; visual-motor coordination
Object Assembly*	Requires assembling puzzles representing real objects	Visual organization; visual-motor coordination
Coding*	Requires copying symbols in order	Psychomotor speed; concentration; associative learning; visual-motor coordination
Mazes	Requires solution of maze puzzles	Planning; visual-motor coordination

*Asterisk indicates timed test.

tests. Even the performance tasks of the WISC-R require understanding of verbal directions. The Stanford-Binet and the Verbal Scale of the WISC are very similar, and both are good predictors of school success. Wechsler conceived intelligence in a somewhat broader sense than did Terman and Merrill. One reflection of the difference is the relative importance of speed, which is more important with the WISC-R than the Binet. The overly cautious child may be penalized on the Wechsler scale.

The Binet is administered by age levels. A basal age is found, and the child continues answering test items until he fails all items of a particular level. The WISC-R is administered by content structure. A content area is selected, and the child answers questions until he consecutively fails a specified number of items or until he completes all the items in that particular content area. Another content area is selected; after the child completes this content area, another area is selected; and so forth. As compared with the WISC-R, the administration of the Binet is more cumbersome. It is bulkier, and it takes longer. Children taking the Binet leave the test after a lengthy series of failures, since a ceiling must be determined, while children taking the WISC-R are allowed to proceed to a different subtest after failing a few items of any one type. Motivation seems to be higher on the WISC-R, yet Hutt (1947), in one well-known study, experimented with an adaptive procedure designed to eliminate frustration and encourage motivation on the Binet. He found only slight differences for his group as a whole.

Both the Binet and WISC-R were standardized on all-white populations and they have received a great deal of criticism for being culturally biased. Anastasi (1982) accurately describes how some children may perform poorly by virtue of the biases in language and cultural background which underlie the tests. The two tests, like most other intelligence tests, seem to favor urban children over rural children, children from better environments, and verbal over nonverbal children.

Within all tests there is a certain amount of variance or error. Scores may be inaccurate for any number of reasons, such as poor testing environment, fatigue of the examiner or the subject, or poor test construction. To account for these errors, test authors often report an index, called the **standard error of measurement,** indicating a range of probable error. Every individual score earned on the test can easily (approximately a ⅔ chance) vary within the standard error of measurement. For instance, a person earning an IQ of 70 on the Binet, with a standard error of measurement of 5, would have a 68% chance of having a "true" score between 65 to 75. Thus, most professionals concerned with psychological testing strongly discourage the reporting of single scores; rather, scores should be reported as a range. The difference between the Binet and the WISC-R in the standard error of measurement is negligible.

OTHER INTELLIGENCE TESTS

Although the WISC-R and Stanford-Binet individual tests of intelligence have become very popular within the schools, there are other individual tests of intelligence. Many of these other tests are readily available, easy to give, and require only 15 or 30 minutes to administer. These advantages increase their popularity and afford more people the opportunity to use them. However, test administrators and interpreters have a responsibility to remember such factors as the standard error of measurement, the standard deviation, the testing conditions, the socioeconomic level of the examinee, the standardization sample, and the purpose of testing. Those who use the results of intelligence tests must keep in mind the specific functions of the tests: to predict school performance, to classify individuals for instruction and research, or to discover patterns of abilities and disabilities which have *educational* relevance (Smith, 1968).

One of the most widely used individual intelligence tests other than the Binet and Wechsler scales is the Slosson Intelligence Test (Slosson, 1971). The SIT is a relatively quick screening test that requires little psychometric training to administer or score. It is similar in design and in content to the Stanford-Binet (many of the items are identical) and uses a comparable scoring procedure. A basal and a ceiling level are determined and correctly answered items in between are credited to the basal score. The age score that is obtained may be converted to a ratio IQ. As mentioned, the SIT is a popular instrument, and some states permit its use in placement decisions. The problem with this procedure is that its function as a screening device is to draw out of a larger group those who need a closer look—that is, it should *overselect* candidates for special attention. In contrast, instruments used for judging whether or not a child requires special class placement should tend to *underselect*. According to the prevailing educational philosophy today, any error that is made in the placement process should be in the direction of keeping the student in the regular class, the mainstream of services.

Inappropriate placement of minority children into classes for the mentally retarded is one very unfortunate outcome of basing placement decisions upon single scores from intelligence tests, particularly tests that require a great deal of knowledge derived from the white, middle-class American culture. Children who grow up in non-Anglo subcultures will naturally score lower on such tests than will children from the dominant cultural group. Concern with this type of test bias has sparked the development of a number of "culture-free" measures which attempt to eliminate all cultural factors that might favor one group over another (as opposed to Mercer's SOMPA [Mercer & Lewis, 1977a], which includes and adjusts for such factors). One such test is the Raven's Progressive Matrices (Raven, 1958). This device attempts to measure pure abstract reasoning ability uninfluenced by prior knowledge. The test items all follow the same format: the child is shown a matrix of abstract designs with one missing element, which he must supply. Raven's and tests like it (Catell's Culture-Fair Intelligence Test, Porteus Mazes) use no language, except for the instructions, in order to eliminate the cultural influences inherent in language.

This problem is further addressed in the next section of this chapter and in chapter 5.

Handicapping conditions present another set of influences which limit the usefulness of conventional intelligence scales. Adapting items from traditional tests to accommodate handicapped test-takers—for example, reading test questions to blind examinees—is only half the solution. The results will remain somewhat biased if the handicapped subject is compared to a nonhandicapped standardization sample, whose acculturation is different. Therefore, the most appropriate measures for special populations are those few that are designed for and normed on groups with specific handicaps. The Nebraska Test of Learning Aptitude (Hiskey, 1966) is designed to assess the learning capacity of both deaf and hearing children ages 3 to 16, and provides separate normative data for each group. The examiner pantomimes instructions to the deaf subjects and reads orally to the hearing children; he must take care to use the appropriate set of norms when administering the test. The Arthur Adaptation of the Leiter International Performance Scale (Arthur, 1950) is an untimed, entirely nonverbal device for assessing the intelligence of children 2 to 12 years old who are hearing-impaired, verbally handicapped, or not facile with English language.

While these scales have been used to evaluate older severely retarded children, this use is not recommended.

Several devices currently on the market attempt to appraise the mental capacity of infants or those functioning below a 2-year-old level. The Bayley Scales of Infant Development (Bayley, 1969) assess three ability areas for infants from birth to age 30 months. The mental scale tests sensory perception, language, and discrimination abilities, among others. The motor section measures the child's gross motor development. Each of these two scales yields a developmental quotient similar to a deviation IQ. The third part is a personality rating that yields a description of the infant's temperament instead of an overall index. Other commonly used infant scales are the Denver Developmental Screening Test (Frankenburg & Dodds, 1967) and the Catell Infant Intelligence Scale (Catell, 1947).

Thus far, infant assessment scales as a class have failed to provide any reliable measure of intelligence for children under age 2, mainly because the results do not correlate with IQ scores obtained as the child gets older. Because these children are too young to be tested through language, infant intelligence is inferred through achievement of psychomotor milestones. However, mental and motor abilities need not develop simultaneously; therefore, a test that presumes to measure one by observing the other cannot be valid. Physically handicapped youngsters who naturally perform poorly on infant motor tests run the risk of being labeled *mentally retarded* as a result, often to the detriment of any serious efforts toward their education. Developmental scales for this group should be administered and interpreted only by professionals well acquainted with their limitations.

SOME CRITICISMS OF GENERAL INTELLIGENCE TESTING

There is considerable controversy about the issue of intelligence testing in the schools. Some critics of intelligence testing find fault with the instruments themselves. These critics point out that experts disagree about how intelligence is defined and how it is best measured. They

ALTERNATIVE CONCEPTUALIZATION FOR MEASURING INTELLECTUAL FUNCTIONING: KAUFMAN ASSESSMENT BATTERY FOR CHILDREN

New ways of conceptualizing and assessing intellectual functioning are introduced from time to time. One of the most recent and popular is the Kaufman Assessment Battery for Children (K-ABC) (Kaufman & Kaufman, 1983). It is an individually administered norm-referenced assessment battery, measuring both intelligence and achievement of children between the chronological ages of 2.5 and 12.5.

The theoretical basis for this instrument is closely tied to certain concepts of information processing that have been derived from the work of various cognitive psychologists and neuropsychologists. Intellectual ability is considered to be composed of two different processing abilities: sequential processing and simultaneous processing. Sequential processing involves the ability to deal with information in a sequential fashion. Simultaneous processing requires the ability to process information at one time and as a whole. Based on this conceptualization, subtests have been developed to assess these different abilities. In addition to the two scales based on these abilities, there are two additional scales: an achievement scale and a nonverbal scale. The nonverbal scale provides an alternative way for assessing atypical children by combining certain subtests which can be administered nonverbally and require nonverbal responses from the child.

The three major scales and their corresponding subtests are:

Sequential Processing Scale:
  Hand Movements
  Number Recall
  Word Order

Simultaneous Processing Scale:
  Magic Window (partial picture is presented)
  Face Recognition
  Gestalt Closure (partially drawn figure)
  Triangles
  Matrix Analogies
  Spatial Memory
  Photo Series
Achievement Scale:
  Expressive Vocabulary
  Faces and Places
  Arithmetic
  Riddles
  Reading/Decoding
  Reading/Understanding

While the K-ABC has become popular with many psychometrists across the nation, it has required them to adjust their diagnostic and interpretive skills. Salvia and Ysseldyke (1985) provide some cautionary notes about the K-ABC:

> Simultaneous and sequential processing are proposed as measures of intelligence. However, such an orientation to intellectual assessment is quite revolutionary. For many diagnosticians, acceptance of the K-ABC's orientation will require a considerably larger base of research support. We believe that the way to cope with novel theoretical orientation is to defer acceptance until a firm base of research indicates their validity. Until such research is available, patience and skepticism may serve the tester well. (p. 458)

Readers are referred to the Fall 1984 issue of the *Journal of Special Education*, which is a symposium on the K-ABC.

further argue that test scores are subject to various forms of statistical and administrative error and that test scores can vary considerably from time to time. In a sense, this point is well taken. The concept of intelligence or IQ was introduced at a time (1916) when the prevailing belief held intelligence to be hereditary and, therefore, constant. Intelligence is generally thought by lay persons and professionals alike as a basic, enduring attribute of an individual. But if intelligence is a basic, constant quantity, why do IQ scores fluctuate? When a child scores a 95 IQ at age 6, an 89 IQ at age 13, and a 105 IQ at age 16, does this mean that he had average intelligence at the first testing, but that he lost intelligence between ages 6 and 12 and became brighter again by age 16? Not really. Most likely what happened was that the child was somewhat influenced on the repeated tests by emotional or motivational factors or variations in his experience at these different points in his life. Or perhaps the examiner's behavior and the test instrument itself were more or less appropriate to the youngster on these different occasions. The basic problem is that, although the word *intelligence* is used to refer to the totality of a person's ability and potential, no finite behavior sample can possibly demonstrate everything that is worth knowing about that person's capabilities. Therefore, there are no completely adequate measures of intelligence, but those in use do have a purpose. Some seem to do a better job than others, depending on the reasons for the administration of the test.

The standards by which tests, including intelligence tests, are judged include the related standards of validity and reliability. Test specialists distinguish several types of validity. **Construct validity** is how well a test measures the hypothetical construct (personality, intelligence, etc.) that it is designed to measure. Some critics of intelligence tests are taking issue at one point with the construct validity of these measures. However, the construct validity of intelligence tests is mainly a concern of test designers and those who theorize about the true nature of intelligence. The users of intelligence tests are more concerned with another type of validity, **predictive validity.** Predictive validity refers to how well test performance predicts some other behavior. As mentioned earlier, intelligence testing originated as an attempt to predict success in school. Most intelligence tests do this moderately to very well by current standards. Most reported correlations between tested intelligence and academic achievement range between .45 and .75, an average to good correlation. Other criteria presumably associated with intelligence such as occupational achievement and income correlate only fairly well with IQ test scores. Generally the relationship is not as strong as the relationship between intelligence test performance and performance in school.

Reliability is the extent to which a measuring device consistently yields the same or similar results upon repeated administrations. A test may be considered reliable if, assuming there has been no change in ability, the relative standing of the subjects' scores upon the second test administration is the same as it was on the first. The importance of reliability can be understood by considering the relationship between reliability and validity. Simply stated, reliability limits validity. An unreliable (nonrepeatable) test cannot be valid (although it is possible to have an invalid but reliable instrument—one that yields consistent scores but measures something other than what it purports to measure). Measures of emotions such as anxiety tend to be unreliable, since anxiety is a relatively temporary condition, and repeated measures of anxiety are likely to catch the individual at some times when he is anxious and at other times when he is calm.

See Amante, Van Houten, Grieve, Bader, & Margules, 1977, for a review.

While the validity and reliability of the Wechsler (1949, 1966, 1974, 1981) and Stanford-Binet (Terman & Merrill, 1973) tests approach the current "state of the art" of measurement, we may hope for improved tests with further research. Only by improving our tools for educational planning and decision making can we continue to try and optimize educational opportunities for each individual child.

In fact, recent litigation and P.L. 94-142 require schools to base placement decisions on more than one source of assessment data.

Other critics of the use of intelligence tests in the schools argue that the tests are culturally biased and thus discriminate against ethnic minority students. These critics point to the fact that ethnic minority groups and economically disadvantaged children tend to score lower on the Wechsler and Stanford-Binet tests than students drawn from middle and upper class homes in the dominant culture group (Jencks, 1972). Attempts to explain these group differences in IQ test performance take many directions. Some have argued that the differences are essentially genetic (Jensen, 1969, 1980), that they are attributable to different culturally conditioned cognitive styles (Golden & Berns, 1976), and that they reflect a multitude of environmental differences.

Regardless of the origin of group differences in IQ test scores, some argue that to continue basing placement decisions on measures with demonstrated cultural bias perpetuates inequities in the cultural and economic system by tracking ethnic minority and disadvantaged students into low-level employment. How the psychoeducational community and advocates of testing in the schools will respond to their critics' challenges is not yet clear. Of course, IQ test scores alone are not the only criteria used for making placement decisions or decisions concerning provision of special services. Usually, teacher ratings, achievement scores (which are open to some of the same criticisms as IQ scores), classroom performance, and social adjustment are considered also. Some have suggested decreased reliance on test scores and increased reliance on measures such as adaptive behavior ratings (Mercer, 1973a) and social competence. Another alternative is decreased emphasis on tracking and increased concentration on student-oriented pacing with **mastery learning** (Guskey, 1980). This approach involves presenting the material to the student at whatever rate he can incorporate it satisfactorily. Thus, there is less emphasis on forcing everyone to cover the subject matter at the same speed. This is not a new idea, but perhaps is one with new promise.

One thorough and innovative approach to equality of opportunity in testing is Mercer's proposed *System of Multicultural Pluralistic Assessment (SOMPA)*, (Mercer & Lewis, 1977a). Her approach starts with the assumption that a number of cultural groups are present in this country. She proposes to establish norms for several generally accepted psychological tests (including the WISC-R) for Blacks, Anglos, Chicanos, and Latinos. This will allow for comparisons of the individual's test performance with norms for persons with similar ethnocultural backgrounds. A 1977 civil rights mandate outlawing discriminatory testing in the

WHAT IT IS LIKE TO TAKE A CULTURALLY SPECIFIC TEST

In recent years, much has been written on the cultural bias and discriminatory nature of many assessment instruments (especially intelligence tests) used in making decisions relating to students who come from varying subcultural or ethnic backgrounds. The content of many of these devices is decisively biased in favor of students from Caucasian, middle-class backgrounds. While there are persuasive arguments both *for* and *against* maintaining this situation, we would like you to "experience" what it *may be like* for some people to be subjected to tests that demand experience in or knowledge of a specific cultural setting. We have taken examples from two sources, both associated with different ethnic or cultural settings.

We encourage you to read the sample items and try to answer each. If they appear difficult, confusing, foreign, or unanswerable, then you are beginning to understand how questions can be inexorably entwined with culture. Correct answers appear at the bottom of the page.

Examples 1–5 are taken from "People Ain't Dumb—It's Them Tests!" (compiled by the editors of the *Appalachian Review*—West Virginia University), based on Appalachian culture.

1. An air-tite is
   a. a trapeze costume
   b. rubber overshoes
   c. store bought coffin
   d. jar lid
2. The most successful method for catching catfish is
   a. gigging
   b. setting a trot line
   c. dynamiting
   d. creating electric shock with two pokers and a car battery
3. Never put new wood shingles on a roof
   a. by moonlight
   b. in April

schools has opened up the market for measures such as Mercer's; California and Louisiana already require its inclusion in the special-placement eligibility process.

As Hutt and Gibby (1979) point out, SOMPA will no doubt produce more valid test scores for members of the various subgroups. However, there are some problems raised by the assumption that subcultures are homogeneous—just as the original assumption of cultural homogeneity underlying the standardization of the WISC-R and Stanford-Binet results in test norms that place members of a subculture at a competitive disadvantage. Will four sets of norms be enough to provide equality of test opportunity for everyone? There are many more than four definable social, cultural, and economic groups in the population. SOMPA also sidesteps the question of predictive validity, where the criterion to be predicted is success in the prevailing culture.

---

   c. if you can help it
   d. at all
4. A gee-haw-whinny-diddle is a
   a. good time
   b. harness for a horse
   c. toy
   d. type of persimmon
5. An asafetida bag is a
   a. style of asafetida
   b. nostrum for colds
   c. strainer for blinky milk
   d. stocking cap

Examples 6–10 are taken from "The Hana-Butta Test," developed by Warren Gouveia of Maui, Hawaii, and are based on Hawaiian culture.

6. A "puka" is a
   a. fish
   b. star
   c. curve
   d. hole
   e. vine
7. If you live on the "mauka" side of the street, then your home is probably
   a. toward the mountains
   b. on the west side
   c. on the south side
   d. on the east side
   e. toward the ocean
8. "You get stink ear" means that you
   a. only listen to negative things
   b. have wax in your ear
   c. don't listen well
   d. try to hear all the gossip you can
   e. are capable of hearing the voices of spirits
9. Which word is most out of place here?
   a. haupia
   b. poi
   c. kalua pig
   d. loko
   e. hanai
10. "Hana-butta" is known statewide as
   a. high-fat butter made in Hana
   b. mucous running from the nose of a person with a bad cold
   c. margarine from the Hana Dairy
   d. a famous peanut butter shake
   e. a peanut butter sandwhich

Answers: (1) d (2) c (3) a (4) c (5) b (6) d (7) a (8) c (9) e (10) b

See Reitan & Davison, 1974, for an overview.

Another possible response to the criticisms of test fallibility and bias comes from the growing body of research in neuropsychological testing. Neuropsychologists are adding new dimensions to traditionally held views of intelligence. Monitoring the electrical activity of the brain is a technique long used by researchers to measure the extent of retardation in brain-injured children. Now, neurometric specialists are suggesting the use of electroencephalograph (EEG) readings as part of intelligence test batteries for children whose neuromotor handicaps rule out conventional forms of mental measurement. Specifically, scientists speak of measuring the brain's "evoked potential," the results of which are said to produce "a fingerprint of the brain" (Beck, 1979). This fingerprint is the EEG recording of the brain's characteristic response to interruption of a predictable sensory stimulus pattern. For example, the subject may be shown a series of lights flashed in a Morse code-type sequence and repeated until the brain becomes acclimated and ceases to attend. Once the pattern is broken, however, the brain snaps back to attention, and its recorded response to this interruption—its "evoked potential"—can be charted against the EEGs and IQ scores of a normal standardization group. Similarly, registering the rate of cardiac responses to stimulus pattern interruptions has been proposed as a cognitive ability index unbiased by handicapping conditions or cultural factors (Kearsley, 1979). Both of these methods were initially devised for use with handicapped subjects but have added potential for testing non-English speaking subjects and preliterate children.

There are, of course, drawbacks to modern neurometric techniques. Like the patriarchal, pre-Binet sensory tests of intellect, they tap only a limited number of mental functions. One may rightly wonder why reaction speed recorded by tracing brain waves should be any more a valid measure of overall intelligence than is reaction speed gauged by Catell's early "mental test." Furthermore, the validity of these tests is evaluated in terms of correlations with the results from IQ tests, the validity of which has also yet to be proven. Neurometric study represents a step in the right direction toward correcting traditional intelligence testing flaws, but such new approaches are as yet too experimental, costly, and lengthy for general use. Nonetheless, psychological research seems destined to change the way we think about intelligence.

INTELLIGENCE IN THE DEFINITION OF MENTAL RETARDATION

The stance which you take regarding the nature of intelligence will necessarily affect your notions about how mental retardation should be defined. To maintain that "intelligence" is a unitary characteristic is to assume that mental retardation results from a deficiency in that single trait. This deficit may presumably be recorded as a single score obtained from a test such as the Stanford-Binet (Terman & Merrill, 1973). If, however, you contend (as does Wechsler, 1939), that intelligence is an aggregate capacity composed of specific abilities, each of which can be assessed on a scale such as Wechsler's (1955, 1966, 1974, 1981) then mental retardation is somewhat harder to conceptualize. In the current swing of the pendulum, theorists today generally favor the multiple abilities approach to defining intelligence. Emerging empirical and scientific evidence supportive of the multiple abilities approach to defining intelligence has prompted a change in the definition of mental retardation used by the American Association on Mental Deficiency (AAMD). The recent revision of the AAMD *Classification in mental retardation* (Grossman, 1983) abandons the previously recommended (Grossman, 1977) use of 2 standard deviations below the mean (and thus, the upper limit Stanford-Binet IQ 68 and Wechsler IQ 69) as the ceiling for classification as mentally retarded. Instead, the obtained IQ is considered one probable score bound by the upper and lower limits of the standard error of measurement. Significantly subaverage general intellectual is defined as:

> IQ of 70 or below on standardized measures of intelligence. This upper limit is intended as a guideline; it could be extended upward through IQ 75 or more, depending on the reliability of the intelligence test used. This particularly applies in schools and similar settings if behavior is impaired and clinically determined to be due to deficits in reasoning and judgment. (p. 11)

In addition *developmental disabilities* are differentiated from less severe forms of mental retardation by both etiology and degree, and by permanence of the handicap. The developmentally disabled individual is defined as one with central nervous system pathology, an obtained IQ below approximately 55, and a "permanent and 'substantial'" handicap.

Further, while learning-disabled and mentally retarded children may exhibit similar learning problems, the level of measured intelligence remains the discriminating characteristic between the two groups. That is, the presumably average intelligence required for classification as learning disabled excludes the mentally retarded from that category of handicapping conditions. Therefore, while mentally retarded individuals may have learning disabilities, learning disabled individuals may not be mentally retarded.

Despite the fine distinctions required by legal and administrative constraints the opinion of most educators today is that "it is far more important to understand the particular pattern of strengths and weaknesses of a child than to know his or her general level of functioning" (Ingalls, 1978, p. 48).

EDUCATIONAL MALPRACTICE

The problems with misplacement of students based on the administration of intelligence tests are well documented. The recent decision in the *Larry P. v. Riles* (1979) lawsuit supports the position that these instruments are poignantly inappropriate for assessing students from minority racial and cultural backgrounds. Not long ago "educational malpractice" was nothing more than a concept, malpractice itself being much more identifiable with physicians.

However, times are changing, as reflected in the following excerpt, which appeared in a publication of the New York State Association for Retarded Children (1979). This excerpt illustrates the fact that the ugliness of "malpractice" has become a reality in the field of education, as well. It is no coincidence that this example highlights the vulnerability of intelligence testing to challenges of educational malpractice.

Award for "retarded" label

A Queens man, wrongly branded retarded for 12 years by the Board of Education, is entitled to $500,000 in damages, according to the Appellate Division in Brooklyn.

By a 3–2 vote, the court ruled that Daniel Hoffman, now 27, was entitled to the first "educational malpractice" award in the state because of the "awesome and devastating effect" the board's actions had on his life.

In the case, which will ultimately be decided by the Court of Appeals, the state's highest court, the majority did reduce the original jury award from $750,000.

The case began three months before his sixth birthday, when Hoffman was in kindergarden in 1957. He was placed in a school for retarded children after he scored 74, one point below the cutoff, on an IQ test administered by a board psychologist.

The negligence occurred when the Board did not re-evaluate Hoffman's intelligence "within a two-year period so that a more accurate estimation of his abilities

could be made," as the psychologist had recommended.

Instead, Hoffman was "closeted with mentally retarded children" until 1969 when a second IQ test found Hoffman had "good intelligence with above average intellectual abilities." The test correctly revealed that Hoffman was "so incapacitated by a speech defect that communication is very difficult for him."

The tragic result, according to psychiatric testimony, which Shapiro incorporated into his opinion, was that Hoffman's family and school personnel "did not provide the stimulation that would otherwise have been given the child" because of "the assumption of the correctness of the school's diagnosis."

This caused Hoffman to accept "his role as retarded," Shapiro said, "on the basis of his serious speech defect. Knowing that he could not speak as well as other children, his self-image was already deflated, making it more likely that he would accept the conclusion that he was retarded."

SUMMARY

This chapter introduces the major theoretical influences shaping our current notions of how intelligence is defined and assessed. The debate concerning the relative impact of heredity and upbringing on intellectual ability leads only to the tentative conclusion that there is no conclusion. Intelligence testing has evolved from early tests of sensory abilities through tests of intelligence as a single factor to tests of intelligence as comprising many different abilities. Today's educators use a variety of measures of intelligence, including infant scales, "culture-free" devices, tests for special populations, and pluralistic assessment. While all these tools can be useful, and new developments like neurometric research are promising for the future, educators must remember the ultimate goal of assessing any student—to gather information which can be used in planning instructional programs for individual children.

CHAPTER
FIVE

Adaptive Behavior

Before intelligence tests were developed, social incompetence was the main characteristic by which individuals were judged to be mentally retarded (Nihira, 1969). As we have seen, recent definitions of mental retardation emphasize, or at least consider, individuals' capabilities to adjust and function adequately within their environments. This concept of social competence or **adaptive behavior** can be thought of as a person's ability to "cope" with the social demands of his or her environment. The ability to deal effectively with social demands has been called "the reversible aspect of mental retardation, and it reflects primarily those behaviors which are most likely to be modified through appropriate treatment or training methods" (Leland, 1978, p. 28).

In highlighting impairment in social adaptation as an inherent dimension of mental retardation, Dunn (1973b) cites the 1944 amended Education Act of Great Britain. This act abolished scholastic inability as the basis for the use of the terms *mental deficiency* and *mental subnormality*, making only persons designated as socially incompetent, or destined to be socially incompetent, able to be legally classified as mentally subnormal. Intellectually inadequate children needing special academic

This chapter was contributed by James S. Payne, James R. Patton, and Frances E. Patton.

education may be more appropriately referred to as **educationally subnormal.** Dunn concludes, "Perhaps, more than 25 years later, it is time the United States and Canada followed the lead of Great Britain and divorced scholastic inability from mental retardation" (p. 67).

When individuals develop and function like their peers do, they are considered normal. It is only when a person's behavior lags behind that of his peers that mental retardation becomes a possible consideration. During infancy and early childhood, mental retardation is suspected when the child is slow in developing sensory motor skills, communication skills, self-help skills, and socialization skills. During childhood and early adolescence, mental retardation is suspected primarily when there is some deficiency in basic learning, that is, academic learning, reasoning, judgment, and social perception. It is during this period that the greatest incidence of mental retardation is reported. During late adolescence and adulthood, persons are looked upon as mentally subnormal when they repeatedly prove themselves to be incompetent in handling vocational and social responsibilities. However, social and occupational problems need not grow directly out of academic ineptitude. It is common to find adults who were identified during their school years as mentally retarded functioning satisfactorily and adjusting adequately in their postschool environments. In fact, most mildly retarded adults, and many lower functioning and multiply handicapped adults, moved from institutions make a relatively successful community adjustment (Edgerton, 1977; Seltzer & Seltzer, 1978).

We should note two important aspects of the assessment of mental deficiency. During infancy, early childhood, childhood, and early adolescence, cognitive deficits are suspected when a child's behaviors seem subnormal in comparison with norms for the age group. However, during late adolescence and adulthood, retardation is determined by comparing behaviors not with standards for a particular age group, but rather with broader community and social expectations. Remember that we are referring to *speculated* or *suspected* mental deficiency and not actual classification or diagnosis. Unless someone behaves subnormally in some way, retardation is never suspected. Moderate and severe to profound handicapping conditions are usually identified during infancy and early childhood, because these children differ to such a degree that something is obviously wrong. This is not the case with mild retardation. Mildly retarded children generally function on a par with their peer group during infancy and early childhood, in the absence of heavy intellectual demands. However, when they enter school, they are compared with their peers in an educational setting. Retardation is usually suspected when these children fail to keep pace academically with their schoolmates. A dilemma of classification develops because children may be regarded as retarded during the time they spend in school but may

This problem affects many bilingual and ethnic minority children. See the discussion of the ABIC system later in this chapter.

function normally with peers in the neighborhood. Such is the problem of the "six-hour retarded child" (President's Committee on Mental Retardation, 1970). Does academic slowness per se constitute mental retardation? If children score in the significantly subaverage range of a standardized intelligence test and fail to learn in school, yet perform competently in a nonscholastic environment, are they retarded? It would not be unusual for them to be classified and diagnosed as mentally subnormal. However, by most current definitions, including the one incorporated in P.L. 94-142, and more recently P.L. 98-149, they should not be classified as such because they have not demonstrated social incompetence in all settings. According to most definitions, for individuals to be labeled retarded, they must exhibit problems in social adaptation. Thus, in theory, adaptive behavior has emerged as an important index in the identification of mental retardation: however, in practice, its usage has been limited due to its imprecision (Frankenberger, 1984; Patrick & Reschly, 1982).

THE CONCEPT OF ADAPTIVE BEHAVIOR

See chapter 2.

The American Association on Mental Deficiency's definition of mental retardation developed by Heber (1959, 1961) and later revised by Grossman (1973, 1977, 1983) identifies two essential parameters: subaverage intelligence and impairment in adaptive behavior. Although the relationship between the two parameters is not completely clear (Reschly, 1982), the AAMD definition indicates that problems in adaptive behavior can result from or be associated with deficits in intelligence. Because both must exist concurrently, there must be impairment in adaptive behavior before a child can technically be classified as mentally retarded. While the current AAMD definition (Grossman, 1983) certainly accentuates the two criteria for a person to be classified as mentally retarded, *present practices* in the field do not reflect the same orientation (Smith & Polloway, 1983). As we will discuss later in this chapter, many definitions of mental retardation used by state agencies seem confused about adaptive behavior measurement. Moreover, in practice, the intellectual dimension is emphasized in determining whether an individual is mentally retarded.

In a sense, what has happened is that an understandable confusion has developed with regard to both the definition of mental retardation and the concept of adaptive behavior. Reflecting the attitudes of many professionals in the field, Baumeister and Muma (1975) commented on both of these problems.

> We cannot throw around such terms as "general intelligence" and "adaptive behavior" without encountering some disagree-

ment about their precise meaning and usage. . . .Adaptive behavior turns out to be a rather vague and ill-defined concept. (p. 299–302).

This confusion over definition extends to the terminology used to describe virtually the same idea. The term *adaptive behavior* as used by the American Association on Mental Deficiency (Grossman, 1983) has also been called *social competence* (Cain, Levine, & Elzey, 1963), *social maturity* (Doll, 1953), *adaptive capacity* (Fullan & Loubser, 1972), and *adaptive fitting* (Cassel, 1976).

Although the study and subsequent development of scales to assess adaptive behavior have been slow, adaptive behavior has emerged as an important factor in the classification of mental retardation. Whether it continues to be important remains to be seen.

When we talk about the prevention of mental retardation, we must look at this "different" individual and discover what behaviors and physical aspects make us describe him as different. Having determined which of his behaviors are different, which of his developmental patterns are anomalous, and so on, we are in a better position to determine the origin of these defects or these different behaviors, and we can set up models for prevention. We recognize that many of these defects are also related to improper nutrition, to improper disease control, to inappropriate child growth and development patterns, etc. These social ills certainly must be modified if the conditions are to be successfully prevented. But, in addition, since we are dealing with a child who is identified as different from the rest of his peers, who are also probably suffering from similar levels of malnutrition, poor disease control, etc., there is some additional element which has thus made this child "different." It is the recognition and delineation of this special element that will make the advent of appropriate preventive measures possible. (Leland, 1973, p. 98)

DEFINITIONS

The definition of adaptive behavior currently used by the AAMD has undergone several revisions. The current manual entitled *Classification in Mental Retardation* (Grossman, 1983) describes adaptive behavior as "the effectiveness or degree with which an individual meets the standards of personal independence and social responsibility expected for age and cultural group" (p. 157).

While this definition presents the concept in general terms, adaptive behavior can also be expressed as the sum of several components. A classic study of Sloan and Birch (1955) proposed three areas under which impairments in adaptive behavior could be measured: maturation, learning capacity, and social adjustment. These same areas are still associated with adaptive behavior (Grossman, 1983, p. 157). Table 5.1 de-

TWO VIEWS OF ADAPTIVE BEHAVIOR

In 1972, *The Journal of Special Education* presented a symposium consisting of a series of articles discussing the definition of mental retardation. Principal attention was given to the concept of adaptive behavior. Two contributors to this symposium, Henry Leland and John Clausen, expressed strikingly different views of adaptive behavior and its significance in the definition of mental retardation. Many of the issues that they raised remain controversial to this day, and their viewpoints are worth looking at. Here are excerpts from those articles, reflecting their opinions (in part).

CLAUSEN

The problem with "adaptive behavior" is that it is an ill-defined elusive concept, the inclusion of which results in added confusion, rather than increased clarity, regarding the condition of mental deficiency. (p. 52)

My position is that the concept's inclusion introduces an element of subjectivity which is detrimental to work in the field. (p. 52)

Scales must be adjusted to the demands of the community of which the individual is a member . . . None of the attempts to develop a scale for adaptive behavior . . . seems to include an assessment of the community in which a person lives. (pp. 53–54)

Let it be kept in mind that I am not arguing against the significance of adaptive behavior, only against the appropriateness of its inclusion in the definition of mental deficiency. (p. 53)

LELAND

Considerations of subaverage intellectual functioning and adaptive behavior should be based on the generalized impressions of what the child is doing in those specific activities essential to his survival in a particular setting, rather than on abstract estimations of his ability to do things in no way related to that survival. (p. 74)

The issue is not and cannot be whether the child is "really retarded," but rather how society has defined him and what particular behaviors led to that social definition. Once we know which of the child's behaviors is interfering with his ability to survive in his social unit and what types of behaviors are creating this unpleasant visibility, we are in a position to know which behaviors are most in need of modification, on a priority basis. . . . We can create an "invisibility" by reversing the elements about which society is most upset. ·. . . p. 75)

There are no generalized behaviors specific to mental retardation. There are, rather, behaviors that a specific social unit describes as retarded under specific demand situations. (p. 76)

scribes behavioral characteristics in each of the three age areas for four different levels of functioning which loosely correspond to the AAMD's designations of levels as mild, moderate, severe, and profound, reading from the bottom. This table is outdated in its claim that trainable retarded children are "generally unable to profit from training in self-help"—an assumption repeatedly dethroned in practice. It further states that TMR persons "cannot learn functional academic skills," which is true in many cases but certainly not in all. These fallacies aside,

TABLE 5.1 Degrees of Retardation as a Function of Adaptive Behavior

	Preschool age Birth–5 Maturation and development	School age 6–21 Training and education	Adult 21– Social and vocational adequacy
Level I	Gross retardation; minimal capacity for functioning in sensorimotor areas; needs nursing care.	Some motor development present; cannot profit from training in self-help; needs total care.	Some motor and speech development; totally incapable of self-maintenance; needs complete care and supervision.
Level II	Poor motor development; speech is minimal; generally unable to profit from training in self-help; little or no communication skills.	Can talk or learn to communicate; can be trained in elemental health habits; cannot learn functional academic skills; profits from systematic habit training ("trainable").	Can contribute partially to self-support under complete supervision; can develop self-protection skills to a minimal useful level in controlled environment.
Level III	Can talk or learn to communicate; poor social awareness; fair motor development; may profit from some training in self-help; can be managed with moderate supervision.	Can learn functional academic skills to approximately fourth grade level by late teens if given special education ("educable").	Capable of self-maintenance in unskilled or semiskilled occupations; needs supervision and guidance when under mild social or economic stress.
Level IV	Can develop social and communication skills, minimal retardation in sensorimotor areas; rarely distinguished from normal until later age.	Can learn academic skills to approximately sixth grade level by late teens; cannot learn general high school subjects; needs special education particularly at secondary school age levels ("educable").	Capable of social and vocational adequacy with proper education and training; frequently needs supervision and guidance under serious social and economic stress.

Adapted from W. Sloan & J. Birch, "A Rationale for Degrees of Retardation," *American Journal of Mental Deficiency*, 1955, *60*, p. 262. Reprinted by permission.

Sloan and Birch present an otherwise accurate breakdown of adaptive behavior components that characterize the four levels of severity.

Leland (1978) also looked at adaptive behavior in terms of discrete elements. In his attempts to develop a scale to measure it, he defined the construct as "the ability to adapt to environmental demands . . . represented by three behavioral formations," that is, independent functioning, personal responsibility, and social responsibility. Other research efforts have identified various dimensions of adaptive functioning by examining scales that purport to assess it. Studies by Nihira (1969) and Lambert and Nicoll (1976) analyzed the AAMD Adaptive Behavior Scale to isolate its components. Nihira's study of an institutional population using the scale extracted three facets: (a) personal independence, (b) social maladaptation, and (c) personal maladaptation. Lambert and Nicoll based their investigation on a public school population and derived four related dimensions: (a) functional autonomy, (b) social responsibility, (c) interpersonal adjustment, and (d) intrapersonal adjustment. Nihira's most recent definition of adaptive behavior acknowledges its multidimensional nature: "a composite of many aspects and a function of a wide range of specific abilities and disabilities" (1976).

Each of the factors which researchers claim to be components of adaptive functioning—personal independence, social responsibility, and so forth—are skills required for adjustment in society at large. However, when assessing adaptive ability, it is necessary to remember that very few people behave, or are expected to behave, in the same manner in all places at all times. Most individuals have a number of different roles they are expected to fulfill that vary according to the different social contexts in which they find themselves. For instance, when the president of a large investment bank is at home drinking beer and watching Monday night football with a gang of old fraternity brothers, he will probably exhibit behaviors that are suitable to that setting but would be inappropriate at an executive board meeting. Furthermore, the pluralism in a society such as ours, the diversity of ethnic, cultural, religious, and social groups that thrive autonomously within the confines of our common culture, creates endless possibilities for different values to dictate dissimilar degrees of acceptability for common behaviors. A Hawaiian who happened to bring Kalua pig to a pot luck supper at the local orthodox Jewish synagogue, would experience a different reaction to his choice of dishes than he might from relatives and friends at a family outing. Clearly, situational and cultural factors exert a great influence over a person's behaviors and thus compound the complexity of the adaptive behavior concept. Few researchers have been more concerned with this contextual aspect than have Mercer and her colleagues. Recognizing the notion of a pluralistic society, Mercer (1977) perceives adaptive behavior from the standpoint of how an individual performs in vari-

Observe the negative orientation of the terms used with the subjects perceived as deviant—the institutional population—as opposed to those describing the largely normal public school subjects.

ous social systems: the family, the peer group, the community, the school, and the economy. Every person must adopt different social roles in relation to each of these settings, and it is the performance in these contexts that determines adaptability. Although many definitions, dimensions, and interpretations of adaptive behavior have been recognized, a useful way to consider this concept merely might be to look at how a person *copes* with life.

From a review of the adaptive behavior sections of the Heber and Grossman manuals and from an analysis of recent developments, it appears that there have been four major influences in the formulation of our current thinking on adaptive behavior: Sloan and Birch's (1955) article, "A Rationale for Degrees of Retardation"; Doll's (1965) *Vineland Social Maturity Scale;* the Parsons State Hospital project from which the *AAMD Adaptive Behavior Scale* (Nihira, Foster, Shellhaas, & Leland, 1969) eventually evolved; and an extension of the Pacific State Hospital project from which the *System of Multicultural Pluralistic Assessment (SOMPA)* (Mercer & Lewis, 1977b) was developed. One subscale of the SOMPA is the *Adaptive Behavior Inventory for Children* (ABIC). The combined impact of all these forces has been most significant for both definition and assessment.

THE MEASUREMENT OF ADAPTIVE BEHAVIOR

All educational assessment can serve two primary functions: identification and placement, and intervention and educational programming (Coulter & Morrow, 1978). When reviewing adaptive behavior instruments, these two functions of assessment should be kept in mind.

The use of adaptive behavior measures has been, and most certainly will continue to be, controversial (Clausen, 1972b; Leland, 1978). Some of the debate focuses on conceptual issues, while other concerns center around practical matters. Many of the conceptual problems derive from the many dimensions of the concept, which we have already discussed, suggesting that maybe "the term 'adaptive behavior' actually encompasses more than one concept" (Coulter & Morrow, 1978, p. 216).

Grossman (1973) has acknowledged the difficulty of measuring adaptive behavior and emphasizes that

> Measures of adaptive behavior cannot be administered directly in offices, but must be determined on the basis of a series of observations in many places over considerable periods of time. For this reason, rating scales or interview data usually make up the data from which levels of adaptive behavior are inferred (p. 16).

In the most recent AAMD manual on definition, Grossman (1983) highlighted some of the major differences between the measure of intelligence and adaptive behavior. First, adaptive behavior measures attempt to obtain an index of persons' usual behavior patterns; intelligence measures are designed to obtain the highest levels of potential ability. Second, adaptive behavior measures tap a number of different everyday living areas while intelligence tests typically focus on language and reasoning abilities. Third, adaptive behavior information is obtained usually, but not always, through interviews of people who know the person being assessed; on the other hand, intelligence testing is regularly administered in a standardized way with a controlled testing setting.

Mindful of some of the problems, let us now examine some of those instruments currently being used to assess adaptive behavior. Table 5.2 presents a comprehensive overview of most of the devices of importance. We will also look at certain instruments, which demand further explanation, in the next sections.

TABLE 5.2 Adaptive Behavior Measures

Test of Scale Author(s), Publisher	Age Range	Measurement Reference	Domains, Chapters or Sections
Adaptive Behavior Inventory for Children (ABIC) (a part of SOMPA) Mercer & Lewis, 1977 The Psychological Corporation 757 Third Avenue New York, New York 10017	5–0 to 11–11	N*	7 subscales, 24 items (e.g., family role performance, peer-group role performance, student role performance)
Adaptive Behavior Scale Nihira, Foster, Shellhaas, & Leland, 1975	3–0 to 69	N & C	2 parts, 24 subscales (e.g., independent functioning, physical development, domestic activity, untrustworthy behavior)
Adaptive Behavior Scale School Version Lambert & Windmiller, 1981 McGraw-Hill	3–0 to 16	N & C	2 parts, 21 subscales (e.g., independent functioning, physical development, responsibility, violent, & destructive behavior)
Balthazar Scales of Adaptive Behavior I. Scales of Functional Independence II. Scales of Social Adaptation Balthazar, 1973 Consulting Psychologists Press 577 College Ave. Palo Alto, California 94306	5 to 57	C	More than 8 major areas, 16 + subscales (e.g., toileting, eating, unadaptive self-directed behaviors, verbal communication, play activities)

TABLE 5.2 (continued)

Test of Scale Author(s), Publisher	Age Range	Measurement Reference	Domains, Chapters or Sections
Behavior Characteristics Progression Chart (BCP) Santa Cruz County Office of Education Vort Corporation Box 11132 Palo Alto, California 94306	0 to adult	C	More than 50 domains or strands covering a wide range of development
Cain-Levine Social Competency Scale Cain, Levine, & Elzey, 1963 Consulting Psychologists Press 577 College Avenue Palo Alto, California 94306	5–0 to 13–11	N	2 parts, 4 subscales (self-help, initiative, social skills, communication)
Callier-Azusa Scale Stillman (Ed.), 1975 Callier Center for Communication Disorders The University of Texas/Dallas 1966 Inwood Road Dallas, Texas 75235	0 to 8	N	5 subscales (perceptual abilities, daily living skills, language development, motor development, socialization)
Cambridge Assessment, Developmental Rating & Evaluation Welch, O'Brien, & Ayers, 1974 Cambridge Area Developmental Rehabilitation and Education Center Cambridge Independent School District Cambridge, Minnesota 55008	0 to adult	C	16 domains (e.g., gross-motor development, dressing, fine-motor development, self-concept)
Camelot Behavioral Checklist Foster, 1974 Edmark Associates 1329 Northup Way Bellevue, Washington 98005	not speci-fied	N & C	10 domains (e.g., self-help, physical development, home duties, vocational behaviors, economic behaviors, independent travel)
Developmental Evaluation Scale Dallas County MHMR Center, 1973 Dallas County MHMR Center 2710 Stemmons Freeway Dallas, Texas 75207	0 to adult	C	6 major domains, 16 subsections (e.g., physical, self-help maladaptive behavior, communication, social independence)
Fairview Behavior Evaluation Battery Fairview State Hospital, 1970 Research Department 2501 Harbor Boulevard Costa Mesa, California 92626	0 to 10	C	5 scales (developmental, self-help, social skills, language evaluation, problem behavior record)
Learning Accomplishment Profile Sanford, 1974 Kapplan School Supply Corporation 600 Jonestown Road Winston-Salem, North Carolina 27103	0 to 7	N	6 major areas (gross motor, fine motor, self-help, social, cognitive, language)

TABLE 5.2   (continued)

Test of Scale Author(s), Publisher	Age Range	Measurement Reference	Domains, Chapters or Sections
Oakwood Resident Movement Scale and Curriculum Berdine, Murphy, & Roller, 1976 (in press) by Berdine	0 to adult	C	77 adaptive behavior areas, 8 subscales (e.g., independent functioning, physical development, economic activity)
Preschool Attainment Record American Guidance Services, 1966 American Guidance Services Publishers Building Circle Pines, Minnesota 55014	6 mos to 7 yrs	N	4 domains, 8 subtests (e.g., ambulation, manipulation, rapport, creativity, communication, responsibility, information, ideation)
Social and Prevocational Information Battery Halpern, Raffield, Irvin, & Link, 1975 CTB/McGraw-Hill Del Monte Research Park Monterey, California 93940	EMR adoles-cents	N	9 tests (e.g., purchasing habits, budgeting, job-related behavior, home management, hygiene, grooming)
The TARC Assessment System Sailor & Mix, 1975 H & H Enterprises P.O. Box 3342 Lawrence, Kansas 66044	3 to 16	N	Four major domains with specific subscales within each (self-help, motor, communication, social skills)
T.M.R. Performance Profile for the Severely and Moderately Retarded DiNola, Kaminsky, & Sternfield, 1968 (3rd ed.) Reporting Service for Children 563 Westview Avenue Ridgefield, New Jersey 07657	TMR	C	6 major domains subdivided into 4 areas each (e.g., social behavior, self-care, communication, basic knowledge)
Vineland Adaptive Behavior Scales Sparrow, Balla & Cicchetti, 1984 American Guidance Service Publishers Building Circle Pines, Minnesota 55014	0 to 30	N	5 major areas (e.g., communication, sociali-zation)
Y.E.M.R. Performance Profile for the Young Moderately and Mildly Retarded DiNela, Kaminsky, & Sternfield, 1967 Reporting Service for Children 563 Westview Avenue Ridgefield, New Jersey 07567	Pre-school EMR	C	10 domains with 10 subdivided areas in each (e.g., social behavior, self-help, safety, motor, manipulative skills)

*N = Normative, C = Criterion.

Adapted from W.A. Coulter & H.W. Morrow, *Adaptive Behavior: Concepts & Measurement.* New York: Grune & Stratton, 1978. Reprinted by permission.

AAMD ADAPTIVE BEHAVIOR SCALE

In 1965, the American Association on Mental Deficiency developed a project to study the broad dimensions of adaptive behavior. The project produced two adaptive behavior scales (Nihira et al., 1969), one designed for children aged 3 through 12, and the other for people 13 years of age and older. The scales have since been revised in a combined form

FIGURE 5.1

ABS-SE Domains and Subdomains

Part One Domains and Subdomains

DOMAIN 1   Independent Functioning
  Eating Subdomain
  Toilet Use Subdomain
  Cleanliness Subdomain
  Appearance Subdomain
  Care of Clothing Subdomain
  Dressing & Undressing Subdomain
  Travel Subdomain
  Other Independent Functioning
    Subdomain
DOMAIN 2   Physical Development
  Sensory Development Subdomain
  Motor Development Subdomain
DOMAIN 3   Economic Activity
  Money Handling & Budgeting
    Subdomain
  Shopping Skills Subdomain
DOMAIN 4   Language Development
  Expression Subdomain
  Comprehension Subdomain
  Social Language Development
    Subdomain
DOMAIN 5   Numbers & Time
DOMAIN 6   Prevocational Activity
DOMAIN 7   Self-Direction
  Initiative Subdomain
  Perseverance Subdomain
  Leisure Time Subdomain
DOMAIN 8   Responsibility
DOMAIN 9   Socialization

Part Two Domains

DOMAIN 10   Aggressiveness
DOMAIN 11   Antisocial vs. Social
  Behavior
DOMAIN 12   Rebelliousness
DOMAIN 13   Trustworthiness
DOMAIN 14   Withdrawal vs. Involvement
DOMAIN 15   Mannerisms
DOMAIN 16   Interpersonal Manners
DOMAIN 17   Acceptability of Vocal
  Habits
DOMAIN 18   Acceptability of Habits
DOMAIN 19   Activity Level
DOMAIN 20   Symptomatic Behavior
DOMAIN 21   Use of Medications

called the *AAMD Adaptive Behavior Scale,* 1974 Revision (Nihira, Foster, Shellhaas, & Leland, 1974). The purpose of the 1974 scale is to provide objective descriptions and evaluations of an individual's effectiveness in coping with the natural and social demands of the environment. A public school version of this scale was also developed, reflecting the need for an instrument appropriate to the school setting (Lambert, Windmiller, & Cole, 1975).

The 1981 revised *AAMD Adaptive Behavior Scale,* School Edition (ABS-SE) is significantly different from the 1974 Public School Version. Its two major purposes are: (a) screening, instructional planning, and evaluation of student progress, and (b) diagnosis and placement decisions. Although the same instrument is administered for both purposes, the way in which the raw data is scored and interpreted differs.

Like the earlier version, the ABS-SE consists of two parts. Part one is organized along developmental lines and evaluates individual skills in nine behavioral domains related to personal and community self-sufficiency and personal-social responsibility. These nine domains are further subdivided into subcategories. Figure 5.1 lists these domains and subdomains. Part two of the scale measures maladaptive-type behaviors related to social and personal adjustment. There are 10 domains in this part of the scale. There is one more domain area which is somewhat autonomous—"Use of Medications" (Domain 21).

This scale may be administered by either first-person assessment or third-party assessment. First-person assessment involves having someone who knows the person being assessed fill out the scale. The limitation of having the evaluator use the first-person method should be obvious: (a) the responder may not have access to all the information necessary to adequately answer the questions; or (b) the responder may have a biased view of the person being assessed. For a third-party assessment, the evaluator asks an informed observer questions directly from the scale and records the responses.

It is important to become familiar with the different ways of recording responses when administering this scale. There are three kinds of items in part one, differentiated according to scoring procedure. An example of the first type is presented below.

Figure A Item that Requires Selecting One Statement

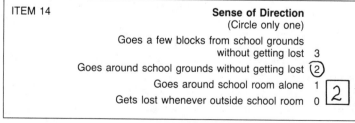

Four statements of possible behaviors are arranged in descending order of difficulty and are assigned corresponding numerical values. The examiner is instructed to circle the number of the statement which best describes the most advanced behavior of which the subject is usually capable. The second and third types require the evaluator to mark all statements that apply to the examinee. In one situation, all items are summed and recorded (see example below).

Figure B Item that Requires Selecting All Statements that Apply

ITEM 16	**Telephone**
	(Circle all that apply)
Uses telephone directory	1
Uses pay telephone	1
Makes telephone calls from private telephone	1
Answers telephone appropriately	(1)
Takes telephone messages	(1)
Does none of the above	0

Total: 2

In the other situation, all appropriate items are checked and then subtracted from a designated figure (see example below.)

Figure C Item that Requires Selecting All Statements that Apply and Subtracting from Total Possible

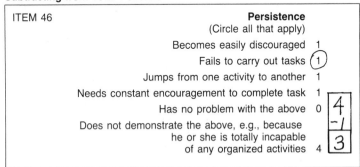

ITEM 46	**Persistence**
	(Circle all that apply)
Becomes easily discouraged	1
Fails to carry out tasks	(1)
Jumps from one activity to another	1
Needs constant encouragement to complete task	1
Has no problem with the above	0
Does not demonstrate the above, e.g., because he or she is totally incapable of any organized activities	4

$\frac{4}{-1}$ 3

There is only one type of item in part two. Here the evaluator is instructed to choose those statements which apply to the examinee and indicate the relative frequency with which each behavior occurs. Then each column is totaled and the sum is entered in the total box on the right, as shown in the following example.

Figure D A Part-Two Item

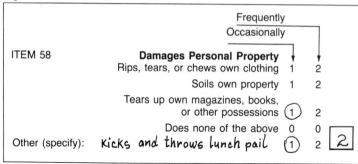

The results of the evaluation are used in two different ways depending upon the purpose of the assessment. Both techniques produce various derived scores and graphic profiles. If the purpose of the assessment was to gain information for instruction, the total raw scores for each domain are converted to percentiles, using either regular, EMR, or TMR referent groups. After this is accomplished, these percentiles can be graphically displayed on the profile (see Figure 5.2).

If the purpose of the evaluation was to obtain information to make an eligibility or placement decision, then a different procedure is followed. Here, the various domains of both parts of the instrument are organized into five factors: personal self-sufficiency, community self-sufficiency, personal-social responsibility, social adjustment, and personal adjustment. A factor score is determined (total of raw scores from each domain). The next step is to take the scores from factors 2, 1, and 3 and by the use of tables obtain a comparison score. This score is compared to norms for the same reference groups mentioned above and a measure of overall comparison (i.e., a percentile) is obtained. In addition to this comparison score, the total raw scores for each factor can be converted to scaled scores (again related to a given reference group); these scaled scores are then used to graphically display performance levels in a profile.

Interpretation of the scores requires practice and a good working knowledge of this instrument and test construction. General rules for selecting cutoff points are provided. These cutoffs can be used to determine critical ranges that indicate significant problems in adaptive behavior.

As stated previously, this recent revision is distinctly different from its earlier version. The standardization sample was increased but is still problematic because it only includes individuals from California and Florida. Another major change is the development of two different ways of using the obtained information: for instructional purposes and for placement decisions. Of particular note is the use of the comparison

FIGURE 5.2

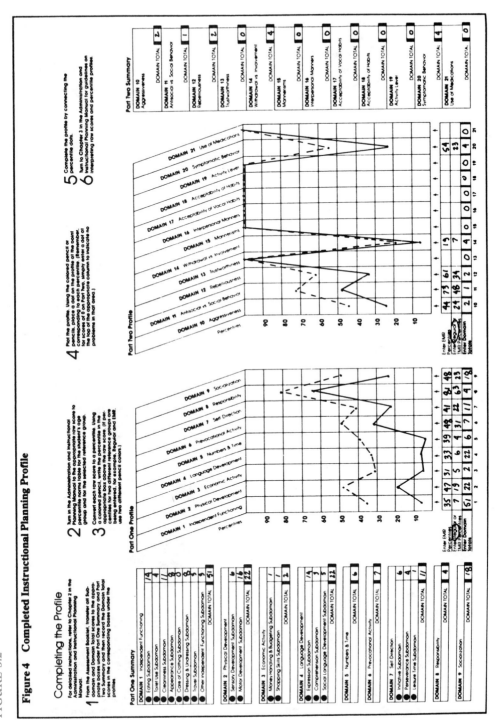

Figure 4   Completed Instructional Planning Profile

score, which is an attempt to help practitioners and decision-makers determine how a person's overall functioning compares to other members of various groups. This new edition straightens out the confusion between the instructional profiles for parts one and two that existed in the earlier version. This new edition also includes a guide designed for parents that helps explain this instrument and the obtained results.

THE VINELAND SOCIAL MATURITY SCALE

The *Vineland Social Maturity Scale* was developed in 1935 by Dr. Edgar A. Doll at the Training School at Vineland, New Jersey. Since then, it has undergone three revisions, the most recent in 1964 (Doll, 1965). It has been translated into Italian, Spanish, Swedish, German, and Japanese, and adapted for application with such diverse cultures as Hawaiian and Australian. The most comprehensive presentation of the Vineland scale can be found in the complete manual entitled *Measurement of Social Competence* (Doll, 1953).

The author's original purpose in constructing the scale was to provide a means of measuring social competence or "social maturity," which would help diagnose mental deficiency. Recognizing the need for an adaptive behavior component in the classification of persons as mentally subnormal, Doll sought to devise a measure "distinguishing between mental retardation with social incompetence (feeblemindedness) and mental retardation without social incompetence (which is often confused with feeblemindedness)" (Doll, 1965, p. 2). He defined conditions

Dr. Edgar A. Doll constructed the *Vineland Social Maturity Scale,* one of the first attempts to measure what we now call "adaptive behavior."

DECISIONS CONCERNING THE CLASSIFICATION OF STUDENTS AS MENTALLY RETARDED: THE IMPORTANCE OF ADAPTIVE BEHAVIOR

As previously mentioned in this chapter, levels of adaptive behavior functioning must be considered by those who decide if a person is mentally retarded. The recent AAMD manual *Classification in Mental Retardation* (Grossman, 1983) presents a number of case studies. Here are two of those in which adaptive behavior functioning is an important consideration. Read each one carefully and then decide if the specified individual should be classified as retarded. The decisions offered by AAMD can be found at the bottom of this page.

CASE STUDY #1: BILL

Bill, age 5, was evaluated after selection during kindergarten screening. Family is "poverty level" and has 6 children. Mother reported that Bill feeds self and dresses self except for shoe tying, that he tries to help around the house and with younger children (e.g., makes bologna sandwich for little sister); she says he watches TV a lot, but not Sesame Street; she has little time for reading to children or taking them to museums, etc. and says the home is busy and noisy. Psychologist reported Binet IQ of 68, with range of 4 testing levels, and Vineland of 78. He conversed with the psychologist freely, asked many questions about objects in room. He can count to 5 and recognizes words that are the names of commercial items, saying he learned them from TV.

CASE STUDY #2: CAMILLA

Camilla, age 8, youngest of 3 children. Parents have been concerned about her de-velopment since Camilla was 4 years old, primarily because of slow language development and slowness in development of self-help skills. Mother works parttime, but has spent a lot of time with Camilla from infancy, reading to child, playing with her, and attempting to stimulate language. Camilla now feeds herself with spoon and sometimes uses fork. Gross motor skills appear to be good, but fine motor skills are delayed. Camilla has good articulation, uses short sentences with correct grammar, but vocabulary is limited for age (e.g., failed vocabulary task on Binet for 6-year level) and is below developmental norms in language development. Has short attention span for age and requires many trials to master new material. Binet IQ was 70. Criterion-referenced test indicates recognition of about 25% of basic sight words; she recognizes functional words in context (LADIES, STOP, etc.) for very common words, but not such terms as ENTER HERE. Counts to 20 and understands concept of 4 objects. Repeated kindergarten and standardized achievement tests at school have consistently been 1½ to 2 grades below expected for age. In class and in everyday life, she appears to perform at a lower level than indicated by latest standardized test scores.

AAMD Decisions:
  Case Study #1—Bill: NOT RETARDED
  Case Study #2—Camilla: RETARDED

of mental deficiency as demonstration of intellectual inadequacy, of arrested mental development, and of social inadequacy.

The Vineland scales were recently revised substantially and renamed the *Vineland Adaptive Behavior Scales* (Sparrow, Balla, & Cicchetti, 1984). Now there are three versions of the scale: *Interview Edition, Survey Form; Interview Edition, Expanded Form;* and *Classroom Edition.* Of these three, the Survey Form is most similar to the earlier Vineland scales. The overall purpose of each of these versions is indicated in their titles. The first two scales are administered to individuals who know the person who is being assessed, usually parents or caregivers. The Classroom scale is typically filled in by the teacher. There are five major domains, one of which is optional, of adaptive behavior assessed by these scales: communication, daily living skills, socialization, motor skills, and maladaptive behavior (optional).

Administration and scoring of these scales are also different from earlier versions. Unlike before, where the different skill domains were intermixed, these new scales follow a domain structure where only items related to one domain (e.g., communication) are together. Raw scores are converted to standard scores, percentiles (both national and supplementary, which include norms of different disabled groups), stanines, age equivalents, and an indication of adaptive level. A sum of all domain standard scores can be converted to an adaptive behavior composite score (mean = 100, standard deviation = 15). By using the standard scores for each of the domain areas, a graphic representation of performance can be produced in profile form.

The Vineland has always been a popular measure of social competency (Coulter & Morrow, 1978); these new versions improve the earlier scales. For instance, problems with the limited standardization population of the earlier scales have been corrected. Because the 1984 versions are so new, little evaluative data is available on the usefulness of these measures in assisting decision-makers and teachers.

BALTHAZAR SCALES OF ADAPTIVE BEHAVIOR

The *Balthazar Scales of Adaptive Behavior* (BSAB) were developed in 1971 by Dr. Earl E. Balthazar at the Central Wisconsin Colony and Training School in Madison, Wisconsin, for use with severely and profoundly retarded individuals. This instrument has two sections, which together are designed to "measure the effects of treatment and training, and other types of programs for individuals in residential institutions, day care centers and clinics" (Balthazar, 1971, p. 3). Section I of this instrument focuses on the assessment of self-care skills, while Section II deals with social behavior. The subscales of this instrument include

Section I (Scales of Functional Independence)
1. Eating—drinking scales
2. Dressing—undressing scales
3. Toileting scales
Section II (Scales of Social Adaptation)
(Social Scale Categories)
Unadaptive Self-Directed Behaviors
   Scale 1: Failure to respond
   Scale 2: Stereotype (stereopathy), posturing, including objects
   Scale 3: Non-directed, repetitious verbalizations: smiling, laughing behaviors
   Scale 4: Inappropriate self-directed behaviors
   Scale 5: Disorderly, non-social behavior
Unadaptive Interpersonal Behaviors
   Scale 6: Inappropriate contact with others
   Scale 7: Aggression, withdrawal
Adaptive Self-Directed Behaviors
   Scale 8: Generalized, exploratory, recreational activity
Adaptive Interpersonal Behaviors
   Scale 9: Fundamental social behaviors: Non-communication
   Scale 10: Fundamental social behaviors: Social vocalization and gestures
   Scale 11: Appropriate response to negative peer contact
Verbal Communication
   Scale 12: Non-functional, repetitious, or inarticulate verbalizations
   Scale 13: Verbalization
Play Activities
   Scale 14: Object relations
   Scale 15: Playful contact
   Scale 16: Play activities
Response to Instructions
   Scale 17: Response to instructions
   Scale 18: Response to firmly given instructions
   Scale 19: Cooperative contact
Checklist Items
(Personal Care, Assisted or Unassisted, and Other Behaviors)

    The developers of the BSAB believe that it should be administered by direct observation in the subject's natural environment. They emphasize the importance of assessing the person while he or she is engaging in typical daily activities in familiar conditions. Section II can be scored by recording either the frequency of a given behavior or the occurrence of the behavior in a specified period of time (1-minute intervals).

The strength of the BSAB rests in the fact that it is minutely task-analyzed—each behavior required of the retarded subject is broken down into its smallest components. Figure 5.3 illustrates the fastidiously detailed definition of terms which precedes each subscale of the BSAB, Sections I and II.

Such precise detail is vital to the successful implementation of training strategies for severely/profoundly handicapped populations. When this instrument is administered properly, it is easy to proceed from testing to teaching—the trainer knows exactly at what point to begin programming for acquisition of a skill. The authors of the Balthazar Scale emphasize the intervention/programming function of the instrument over its identification/placement function. As do the AAMD scale developers, they recognize that the data derived from a measure such as this provide only part of the necessary information on the subject's total adaptive functioning. For this reason, "the scales are best utilized in an interdisciplinary setting offering a number of available services and disciplines" (Balthazar, 1973, p. 6).

ADAPTIVE BEHAVIOR INVENTORY FOR CHILDREN

The *Adaptive Behavior Inventory for Children* (ABIC) is one component of the *System of Multicultural Pluralistic Assessment* (SOMPA) developed by Mercer and colleagues (Mercer, 1977; Mercer & Lewis, 1977a, b). Several assumptions implicit in the development of the SOMPA can be seen in its name. First, assessment is conceived as a "system" rather than isolated, disjoint measurements. Second, the developers of this system acknowledge that American society is multicultural and pluralistic, regardless of the Anglo influence or status quo. In other words, there are

FIGURE 5.3 Balthazar Adaptive Behavior Scales: Definition of Items for the Eating Scales

Class I: Dependent Feeding
1. Mouth is open. Subject is fed orally. (The exception would be intravenous feeding).
2. Opens mouth voluntarily. Subject opens his mouth, but might have to be reminded or encouraged.
3. Opens mouth without physical stimulation. Subject opens his mouth voluntarily at the sight of food coming toward his mouth.
4. Removes food with mouth. Subject removes food from the spoon with his mouth.
5. Removes food with lips. Subject removes food from spoon with his lips.
6. Allows spoon to be removed from mouth. Subject does not bite or retain spoon, but allows it to be withdrawn.
7. Retains food. Subject retains all food from a spoonful without spitting or drooling (regardless of position).
8. Retains food in upright position. Subject eats in sitting position and does not spit or drool.
9. Manipulates food in mouth. Subject in some manner moves food in his mouth (chewing, biting, etc.).

From E.E. Balthazar, *Balthazar Scales of Adaptive Behavior, Part One: Handbook for the Professional Supervisor.* Palo Alto, Calif.: Consulting Psychologists Press, 1971, p. 10. Reprinted by special permission of Consulting Psychologists Press Inc., Palo Alto, CA 94306.

other non-Anglo cultures that need to be recognized. SOMPA attempts to consider the major implications of such a multicultural, pluralistic society, as reflected by Mercer (1977).

> The SOMPA presumes that all languages and cultures are of equivalent value and that linguistic and cultural differences must be taken into account when interpreting individual performance. The SOMPA assumes that the dominant Anglo core culture will continue to be perpetuated through the public schools as a matter of public policy and will continue to dominate the major economic and political institutions of American society. (pp. 187–188)

The *Adaptive Behavior Inventory for Children* is the section of the SOMPA designed to assess adaptive functioning of children 5 to 11 years old. The ABIC attempts to screen out of the school-aged population those children whose adaptive behavior skills lag behind the skills of their larger peer group. As a part of the SOMPA, the ABIC looks at the child's role performance in a variety of social contexts. Because it is normed on a typical school-age sample, the meaning of "adaptive behavior" for the purposes of this scale varies somewhat from the definition used by institution-based measures such as the Balthazar. Instruments of the latter type view adaptive behavior in terms of skills for which institutionalized children and adults need to be programmed. In contrast, the ABIC treats adaptation as "an important component for an assessment of populations that exist in the mainstream community" (Coulter & Morrow, 1978, p. 116).

The ABIC measures a child's adaptive functioning through a questionnaire completed by the child's mother (or other primary caretaker). The 242 items are grouped within six subscales.

1. Family role performance
2. Community role performance
3. Peer group role performance
4. Nonacademic school role performance
5. Earner/consumer role performance
6. Self-maintenance role performance

The questionnaires are then rated, and the raw scores are converted to scaled scores and plotted on the comprehensive SOMPA profile, along with scores from the other SOMPA subscales, without reference to the child's cultural background.

Clearly, the value of the ABIC lies in the fact that, as part of SOMPA, it relates performance to ethnicity and culture. It attempts to minimize cultural bias, not by posing as a "culture-free" device, but by analyzing children's adaptive behavior in the appropriate social-cultural

Jane Mercer and other advocates believe that a child's adaptive behavior must be evaluated in the context of his or her social and ethnic background.

context. In sum, the ABIC truly "operationalizes the two-dimensional definition of mental retardation advanced by the American Association on Mental Deficiency" (Mercer, 1978, p. 204). As a final note, be aware that the ABIC has received some criticism from practitioners. (See Reschly, 1982, for a discussion of this criticism.)

CURRENT ISSUES RELATED TO ADAPTIVE BEHAVIOR

Read page 134 for two experts' differing views on adaptive behavior.

As we have mentioned, some controversy still surrounds the concept and measurement of adaptive behavior. While much of the "hands-on" information concerning the assessment of adaptive behavior has already been presented in this chapter, there are a number of yet-unanswered questions related to both conceptual and practical issues. Coulter and Morrow (1978), in a most interesting discussion, have categorized some of the issues related to adaptive behavior measurement according to the two dimensions of psychological assessment. Most of the questions that these authors raise are not readily answerable, and they point out the need for further clarification through research. We fell that the points raised are worth citing as final thoughts for this chapter.

Adaptive Behavior and Identification/Placement:

1. Does the use of adaptive behavior measures reduce the bias toward minority groups?
2. What happens to those excluded from special services due to the inclusion of adaptive behavior measures?

3. Can the measurement of adaptive behavior become the more important factor in identifying mental retardation?
4. Should adaptive behavior be a determinant in the identification of other exceptionalities?
5. Is there any difference between intelligence and adaptive behavior between the ages of 0 to 5?
6. Does the concept of adaptive behavior have different meaning for the severely and profoundly handicapped?
7. Some practical issues:
   a. Should specific norms for various minority groups be used?
   b. How should adaptive behavior be measured for those 13 to 21 years of age?
   c. Who is the most appropriate source of information?
   d. Who should collect the data?
8. How should the validity of adaptive measures be examined?
9. Should a single, global score be adequate for the purposes of identification?

Adaptive Behavior and Intervention/Programming:

1. Is the measurement of adaptive behavior realistic, i.e., is it too vague a concept to measure?
2. How should adaptive behavior be envisioned? (e.g., how many domains?)
3. How extensively do we need to measure adaptive behavior?
4. Can those adaptive behavior skills that are lacking be acquired through training?
5. Can we define adaptive behavior in adulthood?
6. What behaviors from a social and prevocational perspective are important at the adolescent or upper functioning levels? (Coulter & Morrow, 1978, pp. 216–223)

As these and other issues are addressed, we will gain a better understanding of an often confusing concept. However, we are not at this point just yet. Huberty, Koller, and Ten Brink (1980), in a study that surveyed states' guidelines for determining classification of mental retardation, remarked that "there are some serious inconsistencies between states in their definitions of mental retardation, and some important omissions concerning the role and assessment of adaptive behavior" (p. 259). Patrick and Reschly (1982) found similar results. Table 5.3 lists a summary of these findings. What becomes readily apparent from these data is that there is indeed no uniformity from state to state about the type of definition used for determining eligibility for special services. Few states even specify what criteria they use

TABLE 5.3 Summary of State Educational Criteria for Mental Retardation and Primary Handicapping Conditions

State	Termin-ology[a]	Definition		Classification criteria			Max IQ[d]
		Intelli-gence	Adaptive behavior	Intel. test required	AB defined[c]	AB asses. required	
AL	MR	Yes	Yes	Yes	No	Yes	75
AK	MR	Yes	Yes	Yes	UK	No	75
AZ	MH	No	No	Yes	UK	No	NS
AR	MR	Yes	Yes	Yes	Yes	Yes	NS
CA	MR	Yes	Yes	No/Yes[b]	Yes	Yes	NS
CO	Other	Yes	Yes	Yes	No	No	73
CT	MR	No	No	No	Yes	No	75
DE	MH	Yes	Yes	Yes	Yes	UK	75
DC	MH	Yes	Yes	Yes	Yes	Yes	69
FL	MR	Yes	Yes	Yes	Yes	No	70
GA	MR	Yes	Yes	Yes	No	No	70
HI	MR	Yes	Yes	Yes	Yes	Yes	69
ID	MR	Yes	Yes	Yes	UK	Yes	79
IL	MI	Yes	Yes	Yes	UK	Yes	NS
IN	MH	Yes	Yes	Yes	Yes	Yes	70
IA	MD	Yes	Yes	Yes	Yes	No	85
KS	MR	Yes	Yes	Yes	No	No	NS
KY	MH	Yes	No	Yes	No	No	75
LA	MR	Yes	Yes	Yes	Yes	No	70
ME	Other	No	No	No	No	No	NS
MD	MR	Yes	Yes	Yes	No	No	NS
MA	NC	No	No	No	No	No	NS
MI	MI	Yes	Yes	Yes	UK	No	70
MN	MR	Yes	Yes	Yes	No	No	80
MS	MR	Yes	Yes	Yes	UK	No	75
MO	MR	Yes	Yes	Yes	UK	No	75
MT	MR	Yes	Yes	Yes	No	No	75
NE	EMH/MR	Yes	Yes	Yes	No	No	NS
NV	MH	Yes	Yes	Yes	No	No	70
NH	MR	Yes	Yes	Yes	UK	UK	79
NJ	MR	Yes	Yes	Yes	No	Yes	77
NM	MH	Yes	Yes	Yes	No	Yes	75
NY	MR	Yes	No	Yes	No	No	77
NC	MH	Yes	Yes	Yes	Yes	Yes	69
ND	MH	Yes	No	Yes	No	No	75
OH	MR	Yes	Yes	Yes	UK	Yes	80
OK	EMH/TMR	Yes	Yes	Yes	No	Yes	75
OR	MR	Yes	Yes	Yes	No	Yes	70
PA	MR	Yes	Yes	Yes	No	Yes	80
RI	MR	Yes	Yes	Yes	No	Yes	69
SC	MH	Yes	Yes	Yes	No	Yes	70

TABLE 5.3 (continued)

State	Termin-ology[a]	Definition		Classification criteria			Max IQ[d]
		Intelli-gence	Adaptive behavior	Intel. test required	AB defined[c]	AB asses. required	
SD	NC	No	No	No	No	No	NS
TN	MR	Yes	Yes	Yes	UK	Yes	75
TX	MR	Yes	Yes	Yes	Yes	Yes	70
UT	MR	Yes	Yes	No	Yes	Yes	75
VT	MR/NC	Yes	Yes	Yes	No	Yes	75
VA	MR	Yes	Yes	Yes	No	Yes	NS
WA	MR	Yes	Yes	Yes	UK	No	75
WV	MR	Yes	Yes	Yes	UK	Yes	70
WI	MR	Yes	Yes	No	Yes	Yes	70
WY	MR	Yes	Yes	Yes	Yes	No	NS
National summary							

[a] MR = mentally retarded, MH = mentally handicapped, MI = mentally impaired, MD = mentally disabled, NC = noncategorical, EMH = educable mentally handicapped, TMR = trainable mentally retarded.

[b] Intelligence test results required for TMR classification, but not used in mild mental retardation classification due to court order.

[c] AB = adaptive behavior, UK = unknown.

[d] Based on applying whatever criteria were stated to an IQ scale with a mean of 100 and an SD of 15. NS = not stated. Several states allowed classification of children with IQs above the criterion under certain conditions.

[e] LD = learning disabled, ED = emotionally disturbed.

(Frankenberger, 1984). It seems strange that most professionals in the field of special education accept the AAMD definition of mental retardation, yet in 1980 only 8 of the 41 states did so (Huberty et al., 1980). The data from the Huberty et al. (1980) study also suggest that the importance of adaptive behavior as a criterion for classification is not as widely recognized as some professionals would suggest.

SUMMARY

Although mandated by professional guidelines and by law, the use of adaptive behavior as a criterion for determining mental retardation is clouded by confusion. The available scales for assessing adaptive behavior are all based on different theories, and all evaluate different skills. We are confident that much of the confusion surrounding the conceptual and practical problems of adaptive behavior can be alleviated. As this decade progresses, it will be necessary to establish more uniformity of definition and to give more attention to adaptive behavior considerations on a statewide and national basis. Professionals in the field must attempt to answer those questions and issues raised by Coulter and Morrow (1978); it will be incumbent upon the states to address those questions raised by Huberty and colleagues (1980). Consideration of adaptive behavior is too important a concept to languish in continuing confusion.

PART TWO
Causes of Mental
Retardation

CHAPTER
SIX

Biological Causes of Mental Retardation

*T*he task of sorting out the causes of mental retardation is a formidable one. From the relatively primitive beginnings of the study of retardation in previous centuries to the advanced efforts of today, the search for causation has been a complex and continuing challenge for professionals from many disciplines. The goal of this chapter is to lay a firm foundation for an understanding of the many complexities of biological causes, known as **etiologies,** of retardation. In chapter 4, attention will be given to psychological and sociological factors.

Biological causes have been most often associated with relatively severe retardation. While we have identified hundreds of specific factors as causative agents, the number of unknown or at least unspecifiable (Maloney & Ward, 1978) causes of retardation still dwarfs the known and specifiable. In fact, causes are known for only 10 to 20% of the cases of retardation. A basic problem in discussing etiology is that cause has rarely been established for the largest and most representative group of mentally retarded persons, those who are mildly handicapped.

We can simply show the interaction between level of retardation and number of causes by dividing the levels into mild versus severe and

This chapter was contributed by Edward A. Polloway and James R. Patton

the causes into single (and specific) versus multiple (and unclassifiable). The combinations resulting in the greatest number of cases of retardation are (*a*) single causes and severe handicaps, and (*b*) multiple causes and mild handicaps. This two-group categorization generally follows the distinction suggested by Zigler and Seitz (1982). The single, powerful pathological influences will be highlighted in this chapter. The many factors that combine to cause mild retardation represent the overwhelming majority of causes of retardation and are discussed in chapter 4. The number of cases of retardation represented by single causes of mild retardation and multiple causes of severe retardation is relatively low. We can therefore conclude that *most* cases of mild retardation result from multiple environmental variables, perhaps interacting with multiple genetic factors, while cases of more severe retardation can be attributed to specific, and more frequently known, causes. Known and specifiable biological causes are referred to as *pathological, organic,* or *clinical*. Although these causes may certainly result in cases of all levels of retardation, we will pay particular attention to their etiological role in the more severe cases. In fact, pathological factors can be identified most often as causing the cases of retardation where the individual exhibits an IQ below 50.

Given the complexity of etiology, a logical question might be why educators, psychologists and other behavioral scientists should be concerned with the study of causation. As general knowledge, Kolstoe (1972) noted that familiarity with etiological factors facilitates multidisciplinary communication, is an essential element in professionalism in the field of mental retardation, and reflects the importance of being able to make accurate information available to parents. In certain situations, etiological information can contribute to more accurate diagnosis. Such information can assist in identifying high- and low-risk individuals, facilitating prescriptions for treatment through biomedical and, in some instances, educational intervention, and conveying to family members data on the possible hereditary and nonhereditary transmission of specific disorders (Chaney & Eyman, 1982). The role of teachers could include monitoring the effects of ongoing or progressive disorders that may hinder daily performance, preventing future occurrences through parent counseling, or effecting immediate change, as with child abuse.

While a general awareness of etiological influences is necessary for all professionals, the mechanisms of the specific causes discussed in this chapter may often prove too complex for someone without training in medicine and/or biology. Therefore it is important that intervention include input from various disciplines in determining if a cause can be specified or is even relevant to treatment. The fact that many etiologies cannot be identified should serve as both encouragement for future research as well as acknowledgment of current limitations in state of the art research.

The remainder of this chapter is divided into five major sections. Initially a discussion of biomedical terminology is presented, followed by a brief interpretation of the role genetics plays in development. The third section discusses some examples of specific causes, while the fourth looks at preventive and treatment measures. The final section explores some ethical issues.

TERMINOLOGY

To the student of biological causes of mental retardation, the translation of specific names for known causes into meaningful information can be most difficult. This section will provide ways to understand the labels ascribed to the various **syndromes** most often associated with mental retardation.

> A *syndrome* is a group of characteristics associated with a specific clinical disorder.

The terminology used to identify various syndromes comes primarily from three sources: (*a*) the conventional wisdom or practices often related to a specific historical era, (*b*) the names of the people who initially identified or described the syndrome, and/or (*c*) the descriptive biomedical terms related to features of the cause and/or the resultant effects.

Several examples illustrate the historical names for syndromes. Perhaps best known is the term *mongolism*, coined by J. Langdon Down in 1966 after its initial discovery by Seguin two decades earlier (Menolascino & Egger, 1978). For 100 years, this term prevailed simply because of Down's observations that one frequent characteristic of the syndrome is facial similarity to Asians. Jordan (1976) has suggested that the term's popularity can be traced to Rudyard Kipling's 19th century idea of the "white man's burden," associating mental inferiority with the alleged inferiority of non-Caucasian races. As Kolstoe (1972) noted, wide realization that the syndrome is found in all racial groups, including even Mongolians, aided in the retirement of the term by most professionals, although its use persists in lay publications.

Another example of a term established historically is *cretinism*. The term itself has an interesting history. Its source has been variously attributed to a Teutonic word for *chalky*, the French word *chretien*, stemming from the church's care for those affected, and the island of Crete (Jordan, 1976).

A second, more direct way to identify a clinical syndrome is to attach the name(s) of the researcher(s) who contributed to an understanding of the specific disorder. For instance, professionals now identify as *Down syndrome* the condition formerly called *mongolism*. Other relatively well known syndromes so named include *Tay-Sachs disease*, after the British and American physicians who described the characteristics in the 1880s, and *Lesch-Nyhan syndrome*, named for the researchers who identified the nature of this severe disorder in 1964.

Finally, the third source of syndrome labels is biomedical terminology. Although some of these terms are frequently used by lay persons, the meanings are often obscured by the forbidding sound of the labels. Actually, many of the specific labels should facilitate an understanding of the primary features of the disorder's causes and/or characteristics.

Table 6.1 lists some of the more common terms used to identify clinical disorders. For each entry, the specific derivatives are noted, along with their usual meaning, and one or two examples of specific uses.

Although labels are only an attempt to simply describe complex medical, biological, or behavioral phenomena, being familiar with the derivatives can be of great assistance in understanding the nature of various disorders and related terms. Several specific terms illustrate the system. For example *toxoplasmosis* would indicate a condition of (*-osis*) poisonous (*toxo-*) blood (*-plasm*). In fact, the clinical definition of *toxoplasmosis* is much more specific, but this analysis of the word provides a fair suggestion of its meaning. Another example would be *hydrocephalus*. Although the term refers to a disorder resulting from a blockage of cerebrospinal fluid, the translation of water (*hydro-*) on the head or brain (*cephalo-*) again illustrates the condition. Finally, a third clear example is the disorder called *myelomeningocele* (or *meningomyelocele*). As the term suggests, this condition is characterized by a saclike mass (*-cele*) on the spinal cord (*myelo-*), containing membrane tissue of the central nervous system (*-meningo-*).

TABLE 6.1 *Biomedical Terminology*

Stems and Affixes	Meaning	Example(s)
ab, abs-	from, away	abnormal, abscess
acro-	an extremity	acrocephaly
amauro	loss of sight	amaurotic idiocy
amnio	pertaining to embryonic sac	amniocentesis
anomalo	irregular	chromosomal anomaly
auto-	self, same	autism, autosomes
brachy-	short	brachycephalic
-cele, -coele	sac, cavity	meningocele
-cephalo-	head, brain	hydrocephalus
cranio-	skull	cranial anomalies

TABLE 6.1 (continued)

Stems and Affixes	Meaning	Example(s)
crypto-	hidden	cryptogenic
dys-	painful, disordered	dyslexia, dysplasia
-encephalo-	head, brain	encephalitis
endo-	inner, inside	endogenous
etio-	cause	etiology
ex-, extra-	outside, away from	exogenous
febr-	fever	febrile convulsions
fibro-	connective tissues	neurofibromatosis
fructo-	fruit	fructosemia
galacto-	milk	galactosemia
-gen-	born with, hereditary	genetics
glyco-, gluco-	sweet, sugar	glycogen, hyperglycemia
hemi-	half	hemiplegia
hydro-	water	hydrocephalus
hyper-	over, more than usual	hyperkinetic
hypo-	under, less than usual, lowered	hypothroidism
intra-	within	intracranial
-itis	inflammation of	appendicitis
-lepsy	seizure	epilepsy, narcolepsy
lipo-	fat	lipids
macro-, mega-	large	macrocephaly, acromegaly
meningo-	central nervous system membranes	meningitis
micro-	small	microcephaly
myelo-	marrow, spinal cord	myelomeningocele
-natal	birth	prenatal, postnatal
neuro-	nerve	neurofibromatosis
-osis	condition of	toxoplasmosis
-phagia	eat, swallow	coprophagia
-plasia	cellular growth	skeletal dysplasia
-plasma	blood	toxoplasmosis
-plegia	paralysis	monoplegia, paraplegia
poly-	many, much	polygenic
pseudo-	false, deceptive resemblance	pseudofeeblemindedness
-semia	sign, symptom	galactosemia
-somy, -some, soma-	body	chromosome, trisomy
thrombo-	clot	cerebral thrombosis
toxo-	poisonous	toxemia
-trophy	nutrition, nourishment	atrophy, dystrophy

From *Introduction to Military Medicine and Surgery*. Study Guide 6. Fort Sam Houston, Tex.: Academy of Health Sciences, U.S. Army, 1975. Reprinted by permission

Another stumbling block to a clear understanding of etiological processes is the science of genetics. The next section gives a primer of genetic principles and deviations.

AN INTRODUCTION TO GENETICS

Genetics can be defined as the study of hereditary and variation. As such, its scope is enormous, and its complexities significant. Advances in genetics in the past 150 years have been as impressive as in any area of science. Specifically, the contributions of geneticists to an understanding of the causes of mental retardation are particularly noteworthy.

The study of heredity begins with the study of **genes.** Genes are the basic biological unit carrying inherited physical, mental, or personality traits. Perhaps millions of genes are present in every complex, living organism, with thousands found within each cell. Genes occupy specific positions on **chromosomes,** the threadlike or rodlike bodies that contain genetic information and material.

Chromosomes vary widely in size and shape; but for human cells, the normal pattern is consistent. Each cell contains 23 pairs of chromosomes. The embryo initially receives one member of each pair from each parent. There are two types of chromosomes—**autosomes** and **sex chromosomes.** Autosomes are matching pairs and constitute 44 of the 46 chromosomes within the usual human complement (that is, 22 of the 23 pairs). Sex chromosomes make up the other pair. The letter X is used to represent the female sex chromosome, and Y to represent the male sex chromosome. At conception, an X chromosome is contributed by the mother, while either an X or Y is contributed by the father. The XX combination thus creates a female, and XY creates a male.

The precise and rather fragile sense of the roles of genes and chromosomes as building blocks of development is dramatically represented in mental retardation research. The two most prevalent general groups of biological causes of retardation are genetic transmission of traits and chromosomal abnormalities. However, even in these clearcut cases of genetic disorders, development is still shaped significantly by environmental influence.

GENETIC TRANSMISSION

In the simplest sense, traits can be transmitted from one generation to the next according to the make-up of a specific gene pair on a given chromosomal pair. Many specific characteristics can be traced to the presence or absence of a single gene. Transmission can occur basically through dominant or recessive inheritance. **Dominant inheritance** means that an individual gene can assume "control" over, or mask, its partner; and therefore will operate whether an individual gene pair is similar or dissimilar. **Recessive inheritance** indicates genes which, in a sense, "recede" when paired with a dissimilar mate, and therefore only are influential when matched with another recessive gene (homozygous).

Pairs of genes carrying the same trait are called *homozygous;* pairs carrying different traits are *heterozygous.*

The mechanics of dominant and recessive inheritance are illustrated in Figure 6.1. Capital letters indicate dominant traits; lowercase letters, recessive traits. In the common illustration of dominant inheritance shown in Example A, only one parent would have the specific dominant trait in question. Therefore it would theoretically be transmitted to two of four children of these parents. In the common illustration of recessive inheritance shown in Example B, probability suggests that at *each* conception, chances are one in four that the child will manifest the recessive trait (hh), two in four that he or she will be a carrier for the succeeding generation (Hh, hH), and one in four that he or she will be totally unaffected (HH).

Dominant inheritance obviously operates in a variety of common traits, including brown eyes and premature white patches of hair. However, its prevalence as a cause of genetic transmission of retardation is extremely small. Some specific examples include tuberous sclerosis and neurofibromatosis. Due to the nature of dominant inheritance, we could significantly reduce the prevalence of these and other dominantly inherited disorders if those affected would undergo voluntary sterilization.

These syndromes are discussed later in this chapter.

Recessive inheritance is commonly associated with blue eyes and with a variety of other innocuous traits. However, recessive traits also include a multitude of very rare disorders capable of producing severe handicapping conditions. Examples include phenylketonuria, Tay-Sach's disease, and galactosemia. Since transmission of recessive traits is primarily a function of the union of two carriers (see Figure 6.1), controlling these disorders would entail using genetic screening measures to identify unaffected carriers of the disorders.

A third type of genetic transmission is through sex-linked (or X-linked) inheritance. The name derives from a variety of recessive traits carried on the X chromosome. The problem is particularly significant for males. The female has two X chromosomes and, hence, a specific gene can be dominated by its mate. But the male (XY) will be affected by a single recessive gene carried on the X chromosomes, because there is no additional X whose genes might dominate the pathology-producing recessive trait. Instead, he has a Y chromosome which essentially determines sex rather than carrying genes which will counterbalance the X-linked gene. X-linked traits include colorblindness, hemophilia, Lesch-Nyhan syndrome, and a variety of other conditions which are found as often as 10 times more frequently in males than females. X-linkage has also been theorized as a basis for the inheritability of major intellectual traits and hence for the high percentage of retarded persons who are

Example A

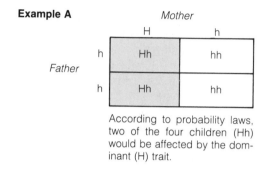

According to probability laws, two of the four children (Hh) would be affected by the dominant (H) trait.

Example B

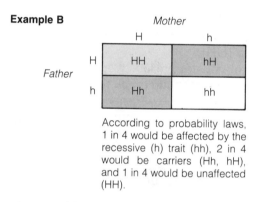

According to probability laws, 1 in 4 would be affected by the recessive (h) trait (hh), 2 in 4 would be carriers (Hh, hH), and 1 in 4 would be unaffected (HH).

FIGURE 6.1 Dominant and Recessive Inheritance

male (Lehrke, 1972a, b), but the validity of this theory has been widely disputed (Anastasi, 1972; Nance & Engel, 1972).

To complete our discussion of genetic transmission of traits, we must mention four concepts which can greatly influence the process: penetrance, expressivity, age of onset, and polygenic inheritance. **Penetrance** refers to the proportion of persons within a particular population who exhibit a given genetic trait. Many genes show incomplete or reduced penetrance. That is, for genes with low penetrance, relatively few of the people who have the gene will manifest the outward trait or symptom it causes. **Expressivity** is the severity of the trait. That is, the symptoms produced by a gene may vary in severity in different people. Because genes have varying penetrance and expressivity, syndrome variations are more the rule than the exception. This further accentuates the complexity of determining etiology, since individuals with similar genes can have widely varying physical and mental characteristics (e.g., Hashem, Ebrahim, & Nour, 1970).

Scarr and Carter-Saltzman (1982) referred to penetrance and expressivity as "fudge" factors because they are "concepts invoked to explain why the same gene, for the same disorder, fails to produce the same [outcome]" (p. 814). In addition, age of onset may differ significantly between and among disorders. In the case of Huntington's chorea, for example, onset may be as late as age 40 to 45, thus increasing the chances that the disorder may already have been transmitted to the next generation.

Note that this discussion relates to single gene anomalies and thus reflects the concept of one gene/one trait. In fact, most traits do not fit these simple Mendelian laws, and are transmitted via **polygenic inheritance.** That is, more than one gene pair affects the appearance of a particular genetic trait. In this case, "genetic predictions . . . have to be based on empirical data from population statistics. Simple genetic models just do not apply . . . " (Scarr, Carter-Saltzman, 1982, p. 804). Polygenic or multigenic inheritance will be discussed at greater length in Chapter 7.

This process has particular importance in the discussion of cultural familial retardation in chapter 7.

CHROMOSOMAL DEVIATIONS

A second major source of biological causes of retardation is chromosomal anomalies. Although the prevalence of these disorders is very small relative to the general population, they are significant contributors to the 10 to 20% of cause-specified cases of retardation.

Engel (1977) notes that at least 10% of all pregnancies begin with some chromosomal imbalance, but that most of these result in spontaneous abortion during the first three months of pregnancy. However, a small number of these children do survive to term and thus illustrate the potential effects of irregularities in the arrangement or alignment of the autosomes or sex chromosomes. Chromosomal errors can be identified in approximately 1 in 200 live births (Engel, 1977).

While genetic disorders are classified as hereditary, chromosomal problems are more accurately termed *innate,* since an abnormal chromosome arrangement is present from the moment of conception but need not be the product of hereditary exchange. Disorders of this type usually result from abnormalities in the process of **meiosis.** During meiosis, individual reproductive cells divide and then pair up to form the genetic foundation for the embryo. The normal process thus includes the contribution of 23 chromosomes from each parent to be paired again to form the new organism's complement of 46 chromosomes. Figure 6.2 illustrates the **karyotypes,** or graphic chromosomal pictures, for a male and female with normal patterns.

Several specific abnormalities can occur during the process of chromosomal arrangement and alignment resulting in either too much or too little chromosomal material being present. In **nondisjunction,** a given parental pair of chromosomes fails to "unjoin" or split at conception, thus resulting in the formation of a group of three chromosomes, called

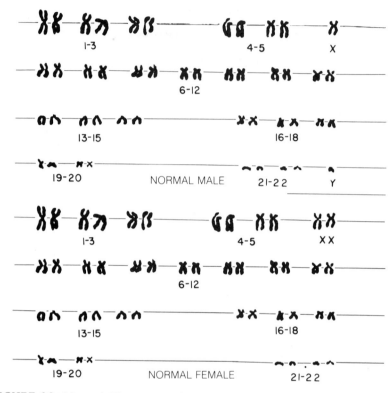

FIGURE 6.2 Normal Chromosomal Karyotypes

Figure 6.3 shows the karotypes for Trisomy 21, for a translocation, and for cri-du-chat, a syndrome caused by deletion.

Examples of the consequences of each of these four irregularities will be discussed later in this chapter.

a *trisomy*, in lieu of the normal pair. Trisomy 21, a trisomy on chromosome 21, produces Down syndrome, and is the most common cause of this problem. In **translocation,** a fragment of chromosomal material is located across from, or exchanged with, another chromosomal pair. For example, the translocation that results in Down syndrome occurs when a fragment broken off from the 21st chromosome pair attaches to a chromosome from group 15. **Deletion** indicates that a portion of the original genetic material is absent from a specific chromosome or pair. Finally, **mosaicism** indicates an uneven division in mitosis, creating a situation of unidentical cells of 46 or 47 chromosomes that cause a mosaic pattern.

ETIOLOGICAL CLASSIFICATION

The recent Manuals on Terminology and Classification of the American Association on Mental Deficiency (Grossman, 1973, 1977) provide a functional model for etiological classification. The Grossman system divides the many specific causes of retardation into 10 broad categories. This system has been tied to the generic International Classification of

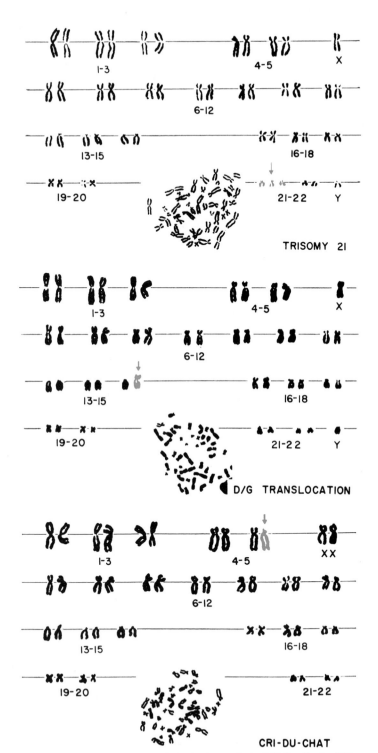

FIGURE 6.3

Karyotypes of
Autosomal Anomalies

From C.H. Carter, *Handbook of Mental Retardation Syndromes*. Springfield Ill.: Charles C Thomas, 1975, pp. 47, 49, 58. Reprinted by permission of Charles C Thomas. Publisher.

Diseases system developed by the World Health Organization and to the American Psychiatric Association's Diagnostic and Statistical Manual (DSM-III).

In the discussion below of particular etiological classifications as outlined in the Grossman manual (1983), the specific examples illustrating the categories are only representative samples and by no means an all-inclusive listing. There are imperfections in the AAMD system, due to the complexity of causes, the individual variations, and the difficulty in distinguishing retardation from other conditions. However, these problems are inherent in any classification system; they do not negate the system's value. Table 6.2 presents an overview of this classification system.

INFECTIONS AND INTOXICANTS

The first category underscores the variety of harmful substances, or **teratogens,** that can significantly affect pre- and postnatal development. The first widespread public exposure to the awesome power of teratogenic agents came from the thalidomide tragedy of the 1960s. Intended

---

TABLE 6.2   Etiological Classification System

.0 Infections and intoxications
   .01 Prenatal infections
      Congenital rubella
      Congenital syphilis
   .02 Postnatal cerebral infection
      Viral, bacterial
   .03 Intoxication
      Exposure to drugs, poisons
      Blood group incompatibility
      Lead poisoning
.1 Trauma or Physical Agent
      Prenatal, perinatal, postnatal injury
      Anoxia
.2 Metabolism or Nutrition
   .21 Lipid (fat) storage disorders
      Tay-Sachs
   .22 Carbohydrate disorders
      Galactosemia
   .23 Amino acid disorders
      Phenylketonuria (PKU)
   .26 Endocrine disorders
      Hypothyroidism (cretinism)
   .27 Nutritional disorders

      Malnutrition
      Dietary irregularities
.3 Gross Brain Disease (Postnatal)
      Neurofibromatosis
      Tuberous sclerosis
      Huntington's chorea
.4 Unknown Prenatal Influence
      Microcephalus
      Hydrocephalus
.5 Chromosomal Anomalies
      Cri-du-chat syndrome
      Down syndrome
      Sex chromosome disorders
         Klinefelter syndrome
         Turner syndrome
         XXX syndrome
.6 Other Conditions Originating
   in the Perinatal Period
      Prematurity
      Low Birth Weight
.7 Following Psychiatric Disorder
.8 Environmental Influences
.9 Other Conditions

Drawn from H.J. Grossman, *Classification in Mental Retardation* Washington, D.C.: American Association of Mental Deficiency, 1983, pp. 130–134 Reprinted by permission.

as a relaxant during pregnancy, this chemical caused severe physical deformities in many unborn children. The discussion below focuses on some of the specific infections and intoxicants that have a proven teratogenic effect.

The brain is especially susceptible to malformation through infection or intoxication during the first three months of pregnancy. Infection of the mother by rubella (German measles) early in pregnancy has been found to result in fetal defects in up to 50% of all cases. This is particularly significant because rubella is a disease of epidemic nature. Recently developed immunization procedures are helping to limit its incidence. In addition to retardation, congenital rubella can result in heart disease, skull deformities, blindness, and deafness and, as such, is one of the primary causes of severe multiple handicaps among children.

Congenital syphilis (and other venereal diseases) is another maternal disease which has been associated with damage to the central nervous system and severe retardation in the offspring. Perhaps the most alarming feature of this disorder has been its increasing prevalence in recent years after it had nearly been eradicated.

A substantial amount of research has investigated the effects of a variety of drugs and industrial chemicals on the fetus. Particular attention has been given to smoking, caffeine, lysergic acid (LSD), and other related drugs. Although the results are not yet clear, it would seem important to assume that any powerful chemical substance should be avoided as much as possible by pregnant women.

The most significant breakthrough within this domain has been with alcohol consumption. The problems associated with alcohol have been generally acknowledged for years. For example, Haggard & Jellinek (1942) noted that "infants born to alcoholic mothers sometimes had a starved, shriveled and imperfect look" (p. 165). However, despite this general suspicion of teratogenic effects, only recently has the nature of the fetal alcohol syndrome (FAS) been documented (Delaney & Hayden, 1977). Now identified by some as the third most common known cause of retardation (Smith, Jones, & Hanson, 1976; Umbreit & Ostrow, 1980). FAS is based on the direct toxic effects on the fetus caused by heavy alcohol consumption. The exact levels of consumption which cause FAS are not known, but those mothers who are alcoholic, who consume several drinks per day, or who engage in binge drinking, run a significant risk of damaging their children. Effects can include severe retardation, cranial and skeletal anomalies, and heart defects. Research continues on the risks of moderate drinking.

Lead poisoning (plumbism), leading to lead encephalitis, has been found to be permanently and progressively toxic to the central nervous system. It can cause seizures, cerebral palsy, and retardation. Although paints no longer contain lead, poisoning is still a factor in places where an infant has access to old, peeling paint. Conscious urban renewal is eliminating this problem through repainting with unleaded paints. However, increased blood levels of lead also can be caused by old lead water pipes, by prolonged breathing of lead-polluted air, as in towns with lead smelters and heavy traffic congestion, and by the young child mouthing and eating other objects containing lead. The President's Committee on Mental Retardation (PCMR, 1976b) has estimated that, in high-risk areas, up to 50% of all children show elevated lead levels in their blood. Analysis of their metal concentrations of lead and other elements has indicated higher levels for mildly handicapped than non-handicapped children (Marlowe, Errera, & Jacobs, 1983).

One other significant cause of retardation through infection or in-toxication is blood group incompatibility between mother and fetus. Most commonly, the condition occurs as a result of the Rh factor, a special protein on the surface of red blood cells. Rh-positive blood cells contain this protein; Rh-negative cells do not. When an Rh-positive man and an Rh-negative woman conceive an Rh-positive child, neither the mother nor the fetus is adversely affected. However, at birth, the mother's immune system will react to the fetus' Rh-positive blood by forming antibodies to the Rh factor. These antibodies remain in the mother's system and will enter the bloodstream of the *next* Rh-positive baby conceived, attacking its central nervous system. Rh incompatibility causes some 10,000 stillbirths yearly, while another 20,000 babies so affected are born deaf, epileptic, with cerebral palsy, and/or mentally retarded (Menolascino & Egger, 1978). Treatment of this immune response must prevent the creation of the destructive antibodies. One technique that has been developed is to vaccinate the mother with Rh immunoglobulin within 72 hours after termination of the first pregnancy (whether by birth, miscarriage, or abortion) and of each subsequent Rh-positive

Children who live in substandard housing may be tempted to eat peeling lead-based paints.

pregnancy. This immunoglobulin serum destroys the Rh-positive cells that pass from the infant's to the mother's bloodstream, thus inhibiting the development of antibodies that would otherwise attack the next fetus carried. This procedure does not alter the mother's immune response mechanism, but can remove the stimuli that engage it.

TRAUMA OR PHYSICAL AGENT

Insult to the brain during the prenatal, perinatal, and postnatal periods falls within this category. Particular examples include oxygen deprivation, accidents, and child abuse.

Perinatal refers to the period immediately following birth.

Oxygen deprivation, referred to most often as *hypoxia* or *anoxia*, can result from birth difficulties such as a knotted umbilical cord, extremely short or long labor, or breech birth. **Anoxia** has been associated with pronounced deficiencies in the affected infant, including lower IQ scores (Graham, Ernhart, Thurston, & Craft, 1962). However, these deficiencies may vary greatly and are often unstable; therefore, it is difficult to make safe judgments regarding the prognosis for an anoxic child (Robinson & Robinson, 1976). Other problems at birth which can produce trauma involve the mechanical act of delivery and the specific anesthetic procedures used.

A variety of postnatal traumatic events can occur throughout the development period and can cause disabilities. Head injuries account for the largest percentage of these events. As MacMillan (1977) notes, the two most frequent causes of injuries are car accidents and child abuse. Child abuse is of special concern, particularly because of the relationship between handicapped children and abuse. As Soeffing (1975) suggested in her review of the research in this area, child abuse can aggravate primary handicapping conditions. In addition to the direct striking of a child, other "disciplinary" techniques such as vigorous shaking, or whip-lashing the child have also been associated with brain hemorrhage and resultant retardation.

See chapter 7 also.

METABOLIC AND NUTRITIONAL FACTORS

This category includes the greatest number of specified causes of retardation. It includes those disorders that can be traced to dysfunction in the body's mechanisms responsible for the processing of food—so-called "inborn errors" of metabolism. In particular, imbalances related to fats, carbohydrates, and amino acids have been well-established as causative agents. Endocrine disorders and nutritional deficiencies are also properly classified in this category.

Metabolic disorders resulting from an increase in lipids, or fats, in the body's tissues are frequently progressive, degenerative diseases. The developmental profile is typically a normal progression until onset of the disorder, from which point the condition rapidly worsens. Tay-

Sachs disease, or infantile amaurotic idiocy, is inherited as an autosomal recessive trait and is disproportionately prevalent among persons of Ashkenazic Jewish backgrounds. Although still disproportionate among persons of Ashkenazic Jewish origin, recent findings have shown Tay-Sachs disease to occur more frequently among persons of gentile backgrounds than originally thought. Infants with Tay-Sachs disease appear normal at birth. From a point typically late in the child's first year, the disease follows a course of severe retardation, convulsions, blindness (or "amaurosis"), paralysis, and finally death by the age of 4. No cure has yet been found for Tay-Sachs disease. Other related disorders such as Spielmeyer-Vogt syndrome have later ages of onset but a somewhat similar profile.

An example of a carbohydrate disorder is galactosemia. This disorder is carried as a recessive gene and is characterized by the inability to metabolize galactose, a form of sugar found in milk. The manifestations of the syndrome can include retardation, liver and kidney dysfunction, and cataracts, although these effects vary significantly. Following identification of the disorder, the removal of dairy products from the child's diet has been found successful in interrupting the process of deterioration, although documentation of whether treatment results in normal intellectual functioning is lacking (Schultz, 1983).

Diet control can also overcome the effects of genetic transmission of amino acid disorders. Phenylketonuria (PKU), a disorder caused by an autosomal recessive gene resulting in mental retardation and frequently associated with aggressiveness, hyperactivity, destructiveness, and other disruptive behaviors. Davis (1981) is an example of the effectiveness of diet control. The successful story of PKU control is illustrated in Figure 6.4. Since originally described by Fölling in 1934, PKU has been virtually eliminated as an etiological factor in severe retardation, despite its incidence of 1 in every 12,000 to 15,000 births. Menolascino and Egger (1978) noted that, in spite of its low incidence, PKU has played a significant role in the field of mental retardation because it was the first inborn metabolic anomaly proven to cause the condition. It led to both increased research into etiology as well as to a pronounced change in the aura of hopelessness that once surrounded retardation.

Since 1964, most states have required examinations of the neonate through blood and/or urine screening tests within the first 4 days after birth. This test for PKU is simple and inexpensive. If the infant is found to have PKU, the elimination of protein-type foods such as fish, meat, and eggs from the child's diet can prevent the build-up of the harmful products of incomplete metabolism. Basic foods stressed are fruits and vegetables, while protein is provided by a special formula.

The results of this treatment have been most encouraging, Johnson and his colleagues (Johnson, Koch, Peterson, & Friedman, 1978) report

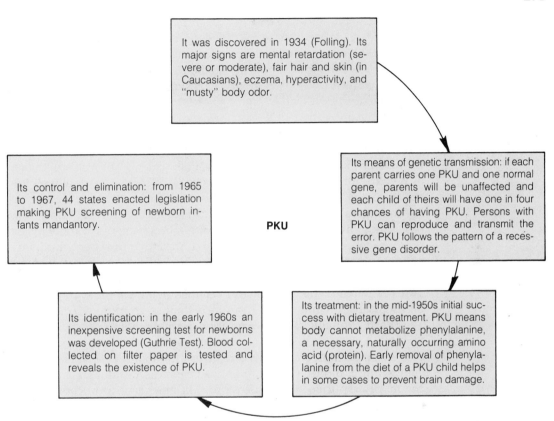

It was discovered in 1934 (Folling). Its major signs are mental retardation (severe or moderate), fair hair and skin (in Caucasians), eczema, hyperactivity, and "musty" body odor.

Its control and elimination: from 1965 to 1967, 44 states enacted legislation making PKU screening of newborn infants mandantory.

PKU

Its means of genetic transmission: if each parent carries one PKU and one normal gene, parents will be unaffected and each child of theirs will have one in four chances of having PKU. Persons with PKU can reproduce and transmit the error. PKU follows the pattern of a recessive gene disorder.

Its identification: in the early 1960s an inexpensive screening test for newborns was developed (Guthrie Test). Blood collected on filter paper is tested and reveals the existence of PKU.

Its treatment: in the mid-1950s initial success with dietary treatment. PKU means body cannot metabolize phenylalanine, a necessary, naturally occurring amino acid (protein). Early removal of phenylalanine from the diet of a PKU child helps in some cases to prevent brain damage.

From President's Committee on Mental Retardation, *Mental Retardation: The Known and the Unknown.* Washington, D.C.: U.S. Government Printing Office, 1976, p. 25. Reprinted by permission.

FIGURE 6.4

that a group of 148 treated PKU children did not significantly differ from the general population in the prevalence of congenital anomalies or major neurological defects. Intellectual level near or within the normal range is achievable.

However, there are still some problems. The diet itself can be unappealing, difficult to follow, and it may be difficult to balance protein control against the protein needs of developing children. Although the special diet is generally discontinued by approximately school age, some concerns are now also being raised about this practice. PKU also poses a threat to the offspring of an affected mother. Although cured themselves by dietary measures, these women can inadvertently harm their unborn children with their own metabolic imbalances during pregnancy. Consequences can include retardation, heart disease, and microcephalus (Schultz, 1983).

Lesch-Nyhan syndrome is a disorder identified in 1964 (Lesch & Nyhan, 1964) that is inherited as an X-linked recessive and thus is much more common among males. According to Nyhan (1976), this syndrome is the second most common metabolic disorder after PKU. The most striking manifestation of Lesch-Nyhan syndrome is an apparently uncontrollable urge to cause injury to oneself and, to a lesser extent, to others.

Typically, L-N children will begin extreme self-injurious behavior (SIB) after initially acquiring teeth. They may bite ferociously and, in their frenzy, rip and tear tissue (Libby, Polloway, & Smith, 1983). In fact, as Nyhan, Johnson, Kaufman and Jones (1980) stated, virtually all L-N children may be recognized by a "distinctive loss of tissue around the lips or fingers" (p. 26). Aside from SIB, L-N children may hit, pinch, and bite others, use obscene language, spit, and engage in a variety of disruptive actions due to their inability to control their own behavior (Hoefnagel, Andrew, Mirecult, & Berndt, 1965). As Fernald (1976) noted, the children are driven to such behaviors and unable to inhibit them. When unrestrained they may scream as if terrified of the pain they might inflict on themselves, while when restrained they seem more tractable.

Both biomedical and educational interventions have been attempted with L-N children. Drug treatment to alter the metabolism has proven efficacious on a short-term basis, although its effectiveness in eliminating SIB once the treatment has been discontinued has not been commonly reported. Continued work on biochemical processes in the brain offer great promise.

Educational interventions have included a variety of attempts at behavioral change with varying levels of success reported in the literature (e.g., Anderson, Dancis & Alpert, 1978; Bull & LaVecchio, 1978; Duker, 1975). Endocrine dysfunctions can also significantly affect mental and physical development. Hypothyroidism, the most common endocrine disorder, is the consequence of abnormally low levels of thyroid secretions. It has an estimated incidence of 1 in 5000 births and can be detrimental congenitally or postnatally. The congenital condition, caused by damage to the gland or by maternal dietary deficiencies, is also known as *cretinism*. It is characterized by small stature, dry grayish-white skin, large head, poor muscle tone, sluggishness, and severe retardation. However, if the syndrome has not been present *in utero* to a great extent or if it is acquired (an autosomal recessive trait), thyroid treatment can prevent or reduce the development of the physical stigmata and the onset of retardation. Inexpensive screening procedures based on the same blood sample used for PKU tests can detect this disorder at birth.

Another endocrine disorder which has received attention in recent years is Prader-Willi syndrome. The most significant characteristics of this disorder are retardation in motor and mental development, hypogenital development, insatiable appetite and hence obesity, and otherwise small features and stature (Wannarachue, Ruvalcaba, & Kelley, 1975). The biological mechanism underlying the syndrome seems to bring about a preoccupation with eating that has prompted observers to suggest that for a Prader-Willi child "life is one endless meal." This organic drive to consume may lead them to eating nonfood items as well as to stealing, gorging and foraging (Otto, Sulzbacher, & Worthington-Roberts, 1982). Current research points to the likelihood of an aberration in chromosome pair 15 as the source of the disorder (Nardella, Sulzbacher, & Worthington-Roberts, 1983). Additional information on the mechanics of the disorder and the effectiveness of various treatment options should be forthcoming in the next several years.

Nutritional disorders are associated with developmental deficiencies when they are reflected in diet inadequacies of mother as well as child. Gross malnutrition during the last 6 months of pregnancy or the first 6 months of life hinders the development of brain cells, potentially resulting in as much as a 40% deficit in the number of brain cells. Since later brain growth is in weight rather than in number of cells, the effects of malnutrition during this early critical period are irreversible (Cravioto, DeLicardie, & Birch, 1966; Winick, 1969). As Cravioto et al. (1966) pointed out, however, it is difficult to assess the true detrimental effect of poor nutrition because it tends to be associated with other conditions such as inadequate housing, substandard living conditions, poor hygiene, and poor prenatal care. It is problematic to assess the effects of malnutrition because it is always closely intertwined with environmental alternatives (Crnic, 1984). In addition, consideration must be given to the results of diets high in calories but lacking in important nutrients, and the potential effects of drug therapy on the nutrition of disabled persons (Springer & Fricke, 1975).

GROSS POSTNATAL BRAIN DISEASE

Included under this designation are several rare disorders carried as dominant traits. An individual affected by what might be termed "full-blown" postnatal brain disease is not likely to have children. Thus the incidence of this type of disease is affected by the reduced penetrance, variable expressivity, and late age of onset of the dominant trait. It can also be the result of genetic mutation.

Neurofibromatosis is also known as Von Recklinghausen's disease, for the man who first discovered the disorder in 1882. It is identified by light brown patches (called *café au lait*) and multiple nerve tumors which appear on the body. There are significant variations in expressivity and penetrance among cases. The location of the growth determines its effect on mental development, which will be severe if there is injury to the brain from the tumors. Otherwise, the subject may have normal intelligence.

Tuberous sclerosis is another skin disease carried by a dominant gene. The two words are derived from the Latin for "potatolike" and "destruction" and provide a graphic picture of the syndrome—that is, the tumors are similar to potatoes in their density and destroy the cells in the organs where they are found (Menolascino & Egger, 1978). The expressivity of the gene can result in great variation in characteristics of the people who have the disease. In the mild form, there is no resultant retardation or serious health problem; in the classical severe variety, tumors may result in dysfunction of any number of organs (e.g., brain, lungs, kidneys) followed by mental deterioration, epilepsy, and early death.

Another progressive disease is Huntington's chorea, a degenerative disease that attacks brain nerves and fibers. The classical symptoms are involuntary, jerky (*choreic*) movements, which give the disease its name, accompanied by mental deterioration, and, eventually, death. In fact, chorea is rarely a true cause of retardation as currently defined, simply because its onset is usually beyond the developmental period (Grossman, 1983). This disease presents a unique case since the offspring may inherit the dominant gene for chorea before the onset of the symptoms in the parent. Analysis of a family medical history is critical in the prevention of this disorder.

UNKNOWN PRENATAL INFLUENCE

This category was established to include all conditions that have an uncertain etiology and are present at birth. In actuality, medical science has now identified potential causes for many of these disorders. The category includes several cranial and cerebral malformations which are among the most common clinical types of retardation.

Children who have microcephalus are characterized by a small, conical skull, a curved spine that leads to a stooping posture, and severe retardation. The condition can be transmitted genetically, probably as an autosomal recessive trait, or it can be a secondary consequence of other causes such as congenital rubella. Individuals affected by microcephalus have been characterized as imitative, good-natured, and lively.

Hydrocephalus consists of at least six types of problems associated with interference in the flow of cerebrospinal fluid within the skull. The most common blockage type often results in the progressive enlargement of the cranium and subsequent brain damage. There is great variation in the physical manifestations of this condition; an enlarged skull is not present in all cases. Hydrocephalus may be caused by polygenic inheritance or as a secondary result of maternal infections or intoxications. Although the condition has been somewhat common, only relatively recently have its effects been greatly reduced in many infants by draining off the fluid via shunts, thus decreasing the cranial pressure. The shunts are valves or tubes surgically inserted under the child's skin to pump the fluid away from the brain and maintain proper flow. The results of early shunt treatment have been very encouraging in preventing head enlargement, which is then often associated with a decrease in the probability of retardation. Wolraich (1983) indicated that proper treatment can ensure the survival of affected children, although significant handicaps remain a possibility. Milder cases may escape detection, with no ill effects noted. For example, Einstein may have been affected by a nonprogressive, mild case of hydrocephalus (Beck, 1972).

CHROMOSOMAL ANOMALIES

Before the 1950s, causes of the disorders included in this category were unknown. However, research published by Lejeune and his colleagues (Lejeune, Gautier, & Turpin, 1959) and other cytogeneticists led to a much clearer understanding of the nature of chromosomal abnormalities. As mentioned earlier, aberrations in the number or arrangement of chromosomes are likely to have a damaging effect on the developing organism. Down syndrome and cri-du-chat syndrome are representative examples of autosomal disorders, while Klinefelter and Turner syndromes are the result of sex chromosome abnormalities.

Down Syndrome   This condition is by far the best known, most prevalent, and most frequently researched type of biologically caused retardation. For many lay persons, the concept of mental retardation itself is synonymous with a Down syndrome child. A reasonable estimate of the prevalence of Down syndrome is 5 to 6% of all retarded persons.

Study of the disorder has revealed three separate chromosomal causes. The first and by far the most common, Trisomy 21, is due to the failure of one pair of parental chromosomes to separate at conception, resulting in 47 chromosomes in the child. Since this particular abnormality has historically been found to be more common in children born to older mothers, researchers have suggested a variety of possible causes.

See Figure 6.3 and the earlier discussion of these chromosomal abnormalities.

Specific deleterious factors that have been suspected include medication and drugs, exposure to radiation, chemicals or hepatitis viruses, and the possible absence of a mechanism in the mother to spontaneously abort the child. It is important to realize that, although risk is related to age and increases to approximately 1 in 30 at 45 years old, advanced age is not the cause per se. Recent analyses have linked paternal age with Down syndrome and estimates have been made that in 20 to 25% of all cases of Trisomy 21, the extra chromosome is contributed by the father (Abroms & Bennett, 1980). Given the increased public awareness of the correlation between age and risk of occurrence and, subsequently, the more common decision to consider abortion (see p. 190), it is not surprising that a higher percentage of Down syndrome children are being born to younger parents (Zarfas & Wolf, 1979).

See Figure 6.3.

The second form of Down syndrome is caused by a translocation usually affecting chromosomal pairs 13 to 15 and transmitted hereditarily by carriers. Mosaicism, the uneven division that creates cells of varying chromosome number, has been identified as the third and least prevalent cause.

Down syndrome is generally associated with classical physical stigmata. The most common characteristics include a small stature, decreased muscle tone, large protruding tongue, short hands and neck, broad nose, shortened fifth finger, and upward slanting eyes. However, these features may vary greatly from one individual to another and, contrary to popular opinion, the number of characteristics present does *not* predict the level of intelligence (Belmont, 1971; Shipe, Neisman, Chung, Darnell, & Kelley, 1968). In addition, Down syndrome is also often associated with cardiac and respiratory defects.

Many of the behavioral characteristics traditionally associated with Down syndrome have generally not been documented in research. In particular, the stereotype of the young Down syndrome child who is cheerful, affectionate, rhythmic, and has unusual dexterity has not been empirically established (Belmont, 1971).

Most significant have been the data collected on the intellectual functioning of Down syndrome children. Typically, the syndrome has been assumed to most often result in moderate retardation, with a ceiling IQ of 70. Occasional anecdotal reports of talents (see Buck, 1955; Hunt, 1961) were considered more interesting or unique than typical.

Perhaps representative of the sentiments of many towards Down children is this statement: "You show me one mongoloid that has an educable IQ. . . . I've never seen one in my experience with over 800 mongols" (Restak, 1975, p. 92). Responding to this statement, Rynders, Spiker, and Horrobin (1978) provided a wealth of information on the question. Table 6.3 presents their review of 15 studies providing data on the intelligence of Down syndrome children. In addition to observing the violation of the alleged ceiling IQ levels, you should also note the three karyotypes. Generally, mosaicism has been associated with higher levels of functioning than Trisomy 21 or translocation (e.g., Hopkins, 1982).

See chapter 4 for more information on early intervention.

Optimistic data on the abilities of Down syndrome children continue to accumulate (e.g., Connolly, 1978). The successful efforts of early intervention seem to hold the key to the future. In a most positive statement, Rynders et al. (1978) conclude by suggesting that there may be a 30 to 55% chance of Down syndrome children functioning in the educable range.

TABLE 6.3 Down Syndrome Children's IQ Scores

Subjects by karotype	N	Mean	SD	Range
Trisomy 21	39	45	15	18–75
Translocation	41	53	17	28–85
Mosaicism	50	57	22	14–100

From J.E. Rynders, D. Spiker, and J.M. Horrobin, "Underestimating the Educability of Down's Syndrome Children: Examination of Methodological Problems in Recent Literature." *American Journal of Mental Deficiency*, 1978, *82*, p. 442. Reprinted by permission.

In addition to the encouraging data on intellectual development, recent efforts in the area of plastic surgery also hold promise for the future. Efforts, most notably in Israel and Germany as well as in this country, have demonstrated that the physical stigmata associated with Down syndrome can be significantly reduced. Such cosmetic intervention is further discussed at the end of this chapter.

OTHER CHROMOSOMAL ANOMALIES

A second form of chromosomal anomaly that has recently been documented is referred to as the fragile X or Martin-Bell syndrome (Richards, Sylvester, & Brooker, 1981). It has been postulated to represent, after Down syndrome, the most common clinical type of retardation. The disorder is caused by a deficiency in the formation of X chromosome. Fragile X has been associated with severe levels of retardation, although reports of its occurrence in individuals with various levels of retardation (and also with normal intelligence) suggest the need for caution (Daker, Chidiac, Fear, & Berry, 1981; Pueschel, Hays & Mendoza, 1983). The discovery of the syndrome provides an exciting direction for further research because it appears quite likely that many individuals for whom no cause was previously specifiable may have been victims of this disorder. A third type of autosomal abnormality is known as cri-du-chat (cat cry) syndrome, due to the high-pitched crying of the child caused by a related larynx dysfunction. This disorder is the consequence of the deletion of chromosomal material from pair 5. It generally results in severe retardation.

Abnormalities in the sex chromosomes have also been found to adversely affect development. Klinefelter syndrome is a condition in which males receive an extra X sex chromosome and thus have an XXY arrangement. The clinical pattern associated with Klinefelter syndrome includes frequent social retardation, sterility and underdevelopment of the male sex organs, and the acquisition of female secondary sex characteristics such as breasts. The syndrome is often associated with borderline or mild levels of intellectual retardation, with increasing deficits noted with an increase in X chromosomes (e.g., XXXY, XXXXY). The

FRAGILE X SYNDROME

Since its discovery, much attention has been directed toward a condition known as the *fragile X syndrome*. Scientists in various parts of the world are conducting research on this condition. Here are portions of an article by Jerry Bishop from *The Wall Street Journal* of January 29, 1982.

Gene Defect Linked To Retarded Males May Solve Mysteries

Does 'Fragile X Chromosome' Account for Many Cases Of Hereditary Condition?

By Jerry E. Bishop
Staff Reporter of The Wall Sreet Journal

A recently discovered genetic defect called the "fragile X chromosome" has been linked to many cases of mental retardation, and the finding is arousing great interest among researchers for the light it may cast on brain development.

Park S. Gerald, the chief of clinical genetics at Children's Hospital Medical Center in Boston, says that retardation linked to the defective chromosome is thought to be "about one-third as common as Down's syndrome." The latter occurs in about one of every 1,000 births. That means, Dr. Gerald quickly calculates, "there are about 500 male babies born (in the U.S.) every year with the fragile X problem."

The unfolding fragile X story may have even broader implications. For example, persons afflicted with fragile X retardation appear to be otherwise normal. That is,

incidence is relatively high: 1 in 400 male births. Although no specific cure exists, the condition can be alleviated through surgery and hormonal treatment. XXY boys have been found to have problems with auditory perception and receptive and expressive language and a general deficit in the processing of linguistic information (Bender et al., 1983).

A sex chromosomal disorder in females, Turner syndrome, results from an absence of one of the X chromosomes (XO). It represents the only syndrome with fewer than 46 chromosomes and this rarity is underscored by the fact that over 95% of all fetuses conceived with the XO pattern will be spontaneously aborted. Although Turner syndrome is not usually a cause of mental retardation, it is worthy of mention because it is often associated with learning problems, especially spatial and organizational difficulties. As with Klinefelter syndrome, Turner syndrome produces deviations from normal development, with lack of sec-

they don't suffer the facial deformities, uncoordinated movements and other physical problems seen in certain types of retardation. That suggests—and at this point it is only a conjecture—that the defective genes in the fragile X chromosome affect nothing other than brain development.

Furthermore, the fragile X has been linked recently to mild retardation in some females and to at least a few cases of autism. A new prenatal test to diagnose the fragile X makes possible abortions performed because prospective parents fear that children won't be completely normal.

Geneticists now are busy surveying institutions to determine how common the fragile X is in retarded males. About one-third of institutionalized patients suffer retardation of unknown cause. Presumably the fragile X will be linked to the conditions of some of these patients. In an Australian institution, Dr. Sutherland found that five of 205 retarded men possessed the fragile X, indicating that it might be related to 2.4% of the retardation in males.

Whether all male infants born with the fragile X chromosome will be retarded is an unresolved question. There are recent reports of normal males possessing what seems to be the same defect. So genetic counseling for women carrying the fragile X chromosome is problematic. Geneticists are reluctant to tell a pregnant woman that her baby is likely to be retarded. But the defect already has been made grounds for abortion.

Recently, researchers in New York announced that they had devised a test that detected the fragile X chromosome in a male fetus carried by a 31-year-old woman who had sought genetic counseling because she has a retarded brother. She elected to have the pregnancy terminated.

The advent of a test to diagnose the fragile X chromosome prenatally is sure to engender controversy, for it gives prospective parents an opportunity to impose a dubious intelligence test on an unborn child. Yet geneticists are quick to say that it is premature to make conclusions about the fragile X chromosome.

ondary sex characteristics, sterility, and short stature as common features.

One other abnormality of sex chromosomes that has attracted substantial attention is Jacobs or XYY syndrome. Although not often a direct cause of retardation, this disorder has been popularly indicted for causing behavior deviations. As Engel (1977) stated

> The discovery of the XYY deserves special mention, having been marred by the much overstated notion that bearers of two Ys were tall, dull, antisocial, aggressive beings compelled to perpetrate murder and larceny. As if to prove the point, a drunken murderer—made notorious by the senseless killing of eight women nurses—was reported by the press all over the world as the bearer of such an anomaly, a statement untenable in light of actual chromosome test results. (p. 113)

FIGURE 6.5
Sex Chromosomal
Abnormalities

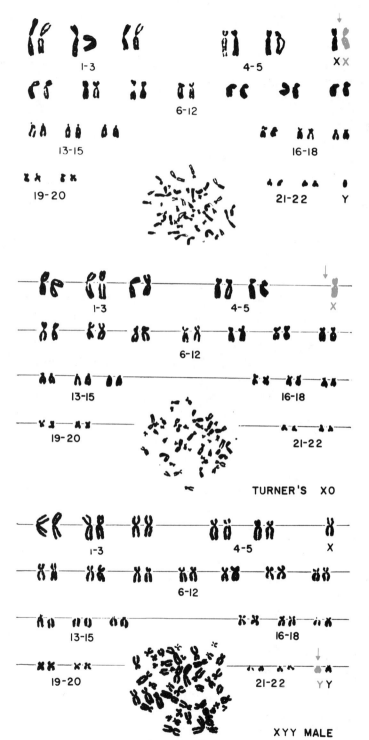

From C.H. Carter, *Handbook of Mental Retardation Syndromes.* Springfield, Ill.: Charles C Thomas, 1975, pp. 39, 43, 45. Reprinted by permission of Charles C Thomas, Publisher.

Although XYYs have been thought to be overrepresented in prison populations, there is no clear support for this belief and research indicates that their crimes have been more often against property than people, as was commonly assumed (Kauffman, 1977). XYY boys may show difficulties in some language skills (e.g., auditory discrimination or word retrieval), but may not differ significantly from nonhandicapped individuals (Bender et al., 1983).

GESTATIONAL DISORDERS

Deviations from the normal prenatal developmental period have been associated with delays in general intellectual functioning and/or specific learning difficulties. In particular, prematurity, low birth weight, and postmaturity are relevant, with the first two having received the most attention. Potential correlates of prematurity and low birth weight are illustrated in Figure 6.6 although no simple, certain cause-effect relationship exists for any of these factors.

Determining the effects of prematurity has been a difficult task. Extremely short pregnancies (less than 28 weeks) or very low birth weights (below 1500 grams, or 3½ pounds) indicate frequent problems;

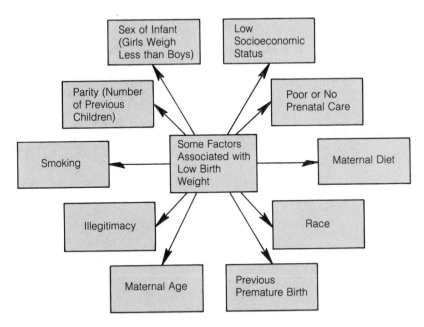

Prematurity: Gestation time of less than 37 weeks.
Low Birth Weight: Weight at birth equal to or less than 2,500 grams

From President's Committee on Mental Retardation. *Mental Retardation: The Known and the Unknown.* Washington, D.C.: U.S. Government Printing Office, 1976, p. 31. Reprinted by permission.

FIGURE 6.6 Low Birth Weight and Prematurity

but for less substantial deviations, the results are not as clear. Table 6-4 illustrates the relationship of prematurity, low birth weight, and handicaps.

The central question is whether prematurity directly leads to retardation. Menolascino and Egger (1978) indicated that while it did not, a combination of conditions could produce retardation. They stated

> A complex, but not unusual, example would be an infant born at 32 weeks gestation, weighing 4 pounds (1,800 grams), and displaying cyanosis and respiratory distress at birth, whose mother is a short, unmarried 17-year-old female from a low socioeconomic class. So many variables are present, and many of them are so difficult to quantify, that it is no wonder that consistent answers regarding prematurity and mental retardation are difficult to derive. (p. 230)

In addition to low IQ, prematurity has also been associated with an increased occurrence of cerebral palsy as well as attentional deficits.

Some of the deficiencies which these children develop can be attributed to life in the incubator. Exposing the children to sounds, fondling, and rocking while in the incubator may help overcome this sensory deprivation by resulting in improved sucking ability, attention skills, and test scores. However, the efficacy of these techniques has been questioned. It is possible that the beneficial effects dissipate over

TABLE 6.4 Prematurity, Low Birth Weight, and Moderate to Severe Handicaps

| Gestational Age (Weeks) | Handicap in Relation to Gestational Age | | |
	N Examined	N with Handicap	%
28	33	21	64
29–31	35	29	54
32–34	23	7	30
Total	91		

| Birth Weight (GM.) | Handicap in Relation to Birth Weight | | |
	N Examined	N with Handicap	%
950	13	11	85
950–1,150	20	14	70
1,150–1,350	32	13	41
1,350–1,500	26	9	35
Total	91		

From President's Committee on Mental Retardation, *Mental Retardation: The Known and the Unknown.* Washington, D.C.: U.S. Government Printing Office, 1976 (p. 31). Adapted from L.O. Lubchernno, M. Delivoria-Papadapolous, and D. Searls, "Long-Term Follow-up of Premature Infants, II." *The Journal of Pediatrics,* 1972, *80,* pp. 509–512. Reprinted by permission.

time, and thus they may not afford the benefits first ascribed to them (Robinson & Robinson, 1976).

RETARDATION FOLLOWING PSYCHIATRIC DISORDER

The relationship between retardation and psychiatric disorder is hazy when the disorder occurs during the developmental period. Benton (1964) lists the four interpretations of their association as follows: (a) the two may occur coincidentally; (b) a single, basic process may result in both the intellectual subnormality and the neurotic or psychotic behavior (e.g., severe organic brain dysfunction); (c) the retardation may be primary, with the subsequent stressful environment causing the psychiatric disorder; and (d) the psychological disturbance may be primary and result in intellectual deficiency. The fourth interpretation, retardation caused by disturbance, is the one which applies specifically to this etiological category.

The problem of differential diagnosis between retardation and emotional disorders is often a monumental one, and in many situations decided more by the bias of the professional making the diagnosis than by clinical agreement. Some observations about the interaction between these two handicapping conditions, however, are necessary. Maloney and Ward (1978) note, in reviewing their own research, that severity of mental illness in adults does not appear to relate to level of intelligence when group results are evaluated. The relationship for children, though, is much more substantial. Although debate will continue on the potential abilities of severely emotionally disturbed children, in reality they are most often at least functionally retarded (Baker, 1979). As Maloney & Ward (1978) stated

> One thing is . . . clear: the earlier the disturbance occurs (providing it is of significant duration), the higher the probability that it will interfere with intellectual development (p. 250).

Similarly, Russell and Tanguay (1981) reported that, while episodic psychotic illness may result in transient functioning in the mild or moderate ranges of intelligence, prolonged problems may permanently depress intelligence.

Regardless of the exact relation between the two disorders, behavioral and emotional disturbances do occur more often among retarded persons than in the general population (Beier, 1964; Polloway, Epstein, & Cullinan, 1984; Szymanski, 1980). Of special importance is the realization that behavioral disturbance is very often a concomitant problem leading either to institutionalization or to public school referrals for special class services. This fact increases the likelihood that the population of persons with retardation will frequently include many who might more appropriately be called *multiply* handicapped.

ENVIRONMENTAL INFLUENCES

Although the categories discussed so far represent hundreds of specific causes of mental retardation, the vast majority of cases are classified as having environmental causes, and thus fall into the familial, not the organic group. This category includes a variety of negative experiences (or the absence of positive interactions) that the child has encountered throughout the developmental period. The two terms used most frequently to describe this group are *cultural-familial retardation* and *psychosocial disadvantage*. Although these two terms carry somewhat different implications, the assumptions underlying both are that cause is not specified and that the condition is the result of the interaction of a myriad of variables. The great changes in the importance given environmental versus biological causes is well-illustrated by the following comparison, presented by the PCMR in *Mental Retardation: Past and Present* (1977, p. 137).

See the next chapter for more on the distinction between these two.

1912

Feeblemindedness in 85% of cases is inherited as a unitary characteristic, probably as a Mendelian recessive, and is not affected by environmental influences.

1975

General intelligence is "polygenic." The genetic component of mild retardation is inseparable from the debilitating effects of the poverty in which it most frequently occurs. Abnormal genes or chromosomes which generate more severe disorders account for 5% or less of the incidence of retardation.

The next chapter will delve more deeply into the causal factors that relate to the interaction of heredity and environment.

PREVENTION AND TREATMENT

Our emphasis on biomedical causes of retardation and the severe handicapping conditions that result may seem to present a bleak picture. The purpose of this section is to document the variety of tools, techniques, and procedures that have been developed to prevent, ameliorate, and/or treat biomedical retardation.

The progress in this domain has been particularly significant during the last 30 years. Inspired by a government commitment to prevent the occurrence of 50% of all cases of retardation by the end of the century (PCMR, 1976b), researches have tackled virtually all of the known causes of retardation. *In every case* a specific preventive measure has been found. Despite the pessimism that has been expressed in regard to the goal of preventing retardation, within the biomedical domain there have been substantial increases in knowledge.

BIOMEDICAL INTERVENTION

Preconception Preventive measures taken during this period can avert hereditary, innate, congenital, and other constitutional disorders.

Genetic counseling is an attempt to determine risks of occurrence or recurrence of specific genetic or chromosomal disorders. The tools of the genetic counselor include the family history and personal screening techniques. Study of the genetic and general medical history is particularly concerned with any evidence of spontaneous abortions or still-births, age and causes of deaths of relatives, and the existence of any intrafamily marriages that might bear on the presence of specific genetic disorders. Screening is primarily for carriers of recessive trait disorders. Blood samples can be analyzed rather easily and inexpensively. For example, Tay-Sachs screening costs about $20 (at the University of Virginia Hospital in 1980). Based on an understanding of the mathematical probabilities associated with recessive, dominant, or sex-linked inheritance, parents can then make an informed decision as to the risks of having a retarded child.

Other specific means of prevention are also available during this period. Immunization for maternal rubella can prevent women from contracting this disease during pregnancy. Blood tests for marriage licenses can identify the presence of venereal diseases. Adequate maternal nutrition can lay a sound metabolic foundation for later childbearing. Family planning in terms of size, appropriate spacing, and age of parents can also affect a variety of specific causal agents.

During Gestation Two general approaches to prevention are associated with this period: prenatal care and analysis for possible genetic disorders. A host of prenatal precautions can be followed to avert congenital problems. Adequate nutrition, fetal monitoring, and protection from disease are certainly the foundation of prenatal care. Avoidance of teratogenic substances resulting both from exposure (e.g., radiation) and from heavy personal consumption (e.g., alcohol and drugs) would also relate specifically to this period.

The analysis of the fetus for the possible presence of genetic or chromosomal disorders includes the techniques of **amniocentesis, fetoscopy, fetal biopsy, and ultra-sound.** Amniocentesis, which has become an almost routine medical procedure in the past decade, involves drawing out amniotic (embryonic sac) fluid for biochemical analysis of fetal cells. It is usually performed during the 14th to 16th week of pregnancy. This procedure is depicted in Figure 6.7. In the large majority of the

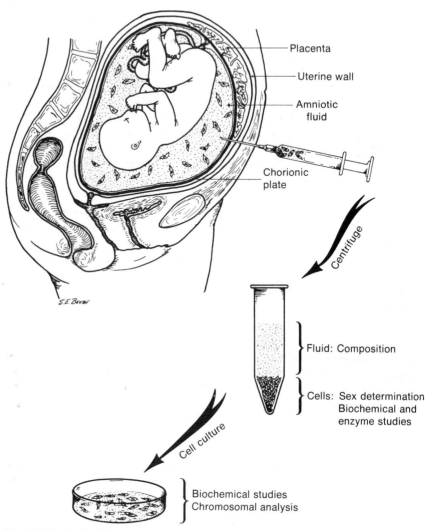

Placenta

Uterine wall

Amniotic fluid

Chorionic plate

Centrifuge

Fluid: Composition

Cells: Sex determination
Biochemical and
enzyme studies

Cell culture

Biochemical studies
Chromosomal analysis

From S.M. Tucker. *Fetal Monitoring and Fetal Assessment in High-risk Pregnancy.* St. Louis: C.V. Mosby, 1978. Reprinted by permission.

FIGURE 6.7 Amniocentesis

At the time of amniocentesis, interested parents can also find out the sex of the fetus.

cases where amniocentesis is used, the primary purpose is the detection of chromosomal errors such as Down syndrome.

Generally, the technique has been found safe. However, Tucker (1978) contends that there are certain specifiable risks to amniocentesis, of which the patient should be informed. They are

1. The risk factor to the mother and fetus is approximately 1%.
2. The culture of fetal cells may not be successful.

3. Repeated amniocentisis may be required.
4. Chromosome analysis, biochemical analysis, or both may not be successful.
5. Normal chromosome results, normal biochemical results, or both do not eliminate the possibility that the child may have birth defects or mental retardation because of other disorders.
6. In the case of undiagnosed twins, the results pertain only to one of the twin pair. (p. 38)

Those risks are the ones consistently specified. The chance of complications for either the mother or the fetus is approximately 1%.

Three purposes can be noted for these analysis techniques. Most encouraging, of course, would be that negative tests assuage parental fears or anxieties. Second, the results can confirm suspicions of disorders and then allow the parents the chance to find out what to expect. They also alert the physician to the need for careful monitoring prenatally, perinatally, and postnatally. Finally, the information can be used as a basis for undergoing a therapeutic abortion. This third option has generated quite a bit of controversy. Although the use of these techniques along with elective abortion has significantly reduced the occurrence of specific disorders such as Tay-Sachs disease (Scheiderman, Lowden, & Rae-Grant, 1978) and Down syndrome (Hansen, 1978), pressure from right-to-life groups has jeopardized the continuing funding and refinement of the procedures (PCMR Newsclipping Service, 1978). The issue of selective abortion is further discussed at the end of the chapter.

At Delivery Prevention at delivery is based on anticipating possible problems that may occur. MacMillan (1977) suggests that a pregnancy be considered high-risk and deserving of special attention whenever

1. The mother is under 20 or over 40 years of age;
2. There is the combination of low economic status and closely spaced pregnancies;
3. The expectant mother has a history of miscarriages, stillbirths, premature infants, and previous children with significant birth defects;
4. The expectant mother has chronic conditions such as diabetes, hypertension, and alcoholism;
5. The mother has Rh negative blood or her blood is otherwise incompatible with that of the fetus. (p. 145)

Several specific measures can be used to avert significant problems during the perinatal period. The most common is the Apgar test of vital signs (Apgar, 1953), an evaluation routinely given in American hospitals at 1 and 5 minutes after the birth of a child. On a scale of 0 to 2, the

GENETIC SERVICES AND COUNSELING

Genetic counseling is actually one part of what more properly may be called *genetic services* available throughout the nation. Genetic counseling refers specifically to communication, which is a most important part of the process of dealing with genetic disorders in a family. Genetic services offered by different agencies typically focus on a wide range of objectives, presenting a number of options to families and/or individuals. For example, this list reflects the genetic services available through the Department of Medical Genetics at the University of Virginia.

☐ Evaluation of children with suspected mental and/or growth retardation

☐ Diagnosis, coordination of care, and genetic counseling for children with congenital anomalies

☐ Cytogenetic confirmation of a suspected chromosome abnormality

☐ Genetic counseling for couples with a family history of a possible genetic disorder

☐ Tay-Sachs carrier screening for Jewish couples

☐ Genetic counseling and arrangements for prenatal diagnosis for chromosome abnormalities, neutral tube defects, inborn errors of metabolism

☐ Diagnosis and management of problems with short stature and skeletal dysplasias

☐ Evaluation and counseling of adults with medical disorders seeking assistance in family planning

☐ Counseling of black families concerned about sickle cell disease

☐ A source of assistance and/or information for any questions related to human genetics.

As is apparent from this list, nearly all of the services involve counseling. This process requires knowledgeable, skilled people who are qualified to deal effectively with different situations, with various types of people, and with a myriad of emotional crises. Counselors in general and genetic counselors in particular must be careful and sensitive to the needs of their clients. This process may involve

1. Discussion of the problem (i.e., the genetic disease);
2. Fundamental lessons in genetics;
3. Explanation of the mathematical probability of the risk or occurrence or recurrence;
4. Presentation of the options that are available;
5. Decision making (i.e., acting on a given decision);
6. Follow-up support.

Without question, there are a number of moral (e.g., abortion) and ethical (e.g., who should use this service) issues connected with genetic counseling; however, we must face these issues realistically and attempt to find solutions. We encourage you to find out more about genetic services available in your community. Additional information about where genetic services may be located can be obtained from the National Foundation/March of Dimes.

physician rates each of the following factors: heart rate, respiratory effort, muscle tone, skin color, and reflex response. An Apgar score of 8 to 10 means the newborn is healthy and responsive; scores of 5 to 7 and 0 to 4 indicate moderate depression and severe depression, respectively. Initial screening using the Apgar test or a similar scale can determine children "at risk" for specific disorders. Low 5-minute Apgar scores correlate with later neurological problems. Intensive intervention can begin for premature and other infants identified as having a particular difficulty.

The advent of computer-assisted obstetric measures has been particularly significant at this time. They assist in the close monitoring of both mother and child. One additional measure during the first 3 days after birth is injection of gamma globulin, which can prevent Rh-negative mothers from developing antibodies that might otherwise affect subsequent children. In the event a child is born to a mother who did not have the necessary injection at the time of an earlier birth (or abortion), a complete transfusion of the newborn's blood can prevent the destruction of its blood cells by the mother's antibodies.

Childhood Although prevention in the postnatal period is primarily achieved through environmental intervention, several biomedical considerations continue to be significant. Proper nutrition is of importance throughout the developmental period, and particularly during the 6 months after birth. Dietary restrictions for specific metabolic disorders should be maintained until no longer needed. Finally, avoidance of hazards in the child's environment can avert brain injury from causes such as from lead poisoning, ingestion of chemicals, or accidents.

COSMETIC INTERVENTION

While we have just looked at some of the avenues open for biomedical prevention or amelioration of specific causes of retardation, the fact remains that disorders with biological causes currently exist and will continue to be a problem in future generations. This section highlights measures that can be taken to reduce the additional detrimental effects on development and socialization attributed to physical characteristics common to many pathological conditions.

An article by Neisworth, Jones, and Smith (1978) discussed the problems of somatopsychology from a behavioral orientation. The authors suggested that atypical physical attributes such as facial disfigurements can serve as specific cues that influence the behavior of others and thus, indirectly, the handicapped person's behavior. This body-behavior conceptualization is illustrated in Figure 6.8.

Somatopsychology is the study of body variations related to psychological status.

In pursuing this argument, Neisworth et al. suggested that body-behavior cues can set the stage for a host of environmental interactions.

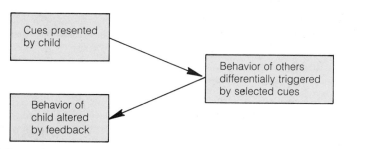

From J.T. Neisworth, R.T. Jones, and R.M. Smith, "Body-Behavior Problems: A Conceptualization." *Education and Training of the Mentally Retarded,* 1978, 13, p. 266. Reprinted by permission.

FIGURE 6.8 A Conceptual Model for Body-Behavior Cues

In particular, those that are most common would include ignoring—a very common "nonconsequence"—punishment through ridicule or assault, or reinforcement of inappropriate behaviors related to the specific handicaps. These reactions would be somewhat consistent with the radical behaviorist concept that retardation of any type is primarily the result of environmental variables, specifically a lack of stimulation and experiences and inappropriate or noncontingent reinforcement.

The implications of a body-behavior model for treatment are clear. They are direct extensions of Leland's (1972) concept of "invisibility," that is, the goal of having retarded persons blend into their environment so they are treated as nonretarded. The principle has validity for a variety of changes—from simple elimination of tongue protrusion (Leland, 1972) to complex language interchanges (Schiefelbusch, 1972).

Figure 6.9 illustrates the concept of invisibility for retarded persons, as related to age and level of severity. For those with severe handicaps, visibility is often a fact of life. For those moderately impaired,

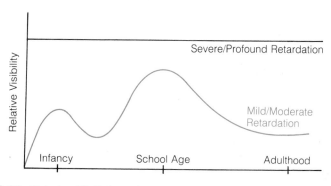

FIGURE 6.9 Relative Visibility of Retardation

visibility may vary, with increases soon after birth as the parents' awareness of a problem develops, followed perhaps by a small decrease reflecting acceptance and adjustment by others, to a later substantial increase in school with its learning and social challenges, and then a decrease during adulthood. The goal of professionals, therefore, must be to analyze these factors and hopefully intervene to keep the child as "invisible" as possible.

Cosmetic Prostheses Prosthetic devices are most often associated with functional purposes of reducing or eliminating a specific handicap. Examples include glasses, hearing aids, or artificial limbs. However, **prostheses** can also serve cosmetic goals, acting primarily to alter other people's perceptions of an individual. In one of the more interesting studies done on this idea, Shushan (1974) designed a before-and-after experiment using naive observers to evaluate photographs of retarded and nonretarded persons. He found that, by adding to the retarded people a variety of cosmetic aids such as sunglasses and fashionable hairstyles, he could influence the observers to perceive them as more normal.

Similar successes have been achieved in the area of plastic surgery. Of particular note has been the work of Milton Edgerton and his colleagues at the University of Virginia. Dramatic changes in appearance can be brought about through plastic surgery.

To illustrate the point further, many well-known celebrities have sought and undergone a variety of cosmetic changes. A strong case can therefore be made for the availability of these procedures to handicapped persons as part of their legal rights.

Cosmetic Learning A related concept is that of cosmetic learning, which Neisworth et al., (1978) describe as

> Teaching children ways of behaving that reduce the amount of
> attention they may call to themselves. Here, concern is not with
> physical features, but the focus is on behavioral characteristics
> that could contribute to a stereotype or cue too much attention
> and eventually devaluation. (p. 269)

Again, the principle of invisibility is relevant. Specific techniques that might be effective would include teaching the children to close their mouths, avoid drooling, walk without a shuffle, smile, and speak in a "normal" tone of voice.

ETHICAL CONCERNS

The incredible advancements in medical technology of the past several decades have enabled doctors and other professionals to sustain the lives of many handicapped individuals who in an earlier time would have perished. As a byproduct of these medical advances, however, both the medical profession and society in general have been confronted with the need to evaluate both the proactive and passive measures now available. It is critical to carefully consider the actions that can be taken before and after birth, once a specific handicapping condition has been identified.

Prior discussion concerning amniocentesis focused on its use to detect specific genetic disorders, most notably Down syndrome. Gradually, this practice has come under increased scrutiny. Public encouragement to screen for the disorder has led to more abortions. As Smith (1981) noted,

> The ease with which the abortion of Down syndrome fetuses is accepted as the best alternative, even by people who otherwise oppose abortion, may be related to the conventional wisdom or popular misunderstanding of the level of mental retardation or other disabilities associated with this condition. (pg. 9)

Smith questioned whether Down syndrome children had become defined as an out-group, something less than human, through the process of *pseudo-speciation*, i.e., the placing of human beings in a separate species on the basis of group characteristics such as race or handicap.

The question of selective abortion of handicapped individuals concerns more than just the case of Down syndrome. Lehr and Brown (1984) summarized the arguments in favor of the practice as including the possible need for intensive medical surgery, the potentially negative effects on the family (e.g., financial ability to care for the child and sibling resentment), and the drain of valuable resources from society. Included in the sentiments against the practice are the basic refutation of abortion for all, the consequential devaluing of humanness of handicapped persons, and the possible spillover effects into services for young children (i.e., if the fetus does not have the right to life, why should the child be entitled to support?). Ultimately, as Lehr and Brown (1984) have noted, the resolution of the issue has come down to the legal right of parents to make the decision about whether or not to give birth to the child.

The second major ethical concern is the question of the right to life of handicapped children after birth. Newspaper accounts of the cases of Baby Doe in Indiana, Baby Jane Doe in New York, and Phillip Becker, a Down syndrome teenager in California, have sensitized the American public to an issue that for years has been quietly debated within the private sanctum of professional circles. In most cases, the argument is whether a child's handicapping condition should be a primary factor in the decision to provide maximum medical care. In addition to the important legal questions involved (see Turnbull, 1983), philosophical issues are also significant in this arena.

Polloway and Smith (1984) identified the two diametrically opposed positions as the "quality of life" and the "sanctity of life" perspectives. From the former perspective, individuals with severe handicapping conditions are viewed as leading lives of meaningless existence full of suffering. Fletcher (1975), for example, posited that personal integrity should be placed above absolute biological survival. The quality of life concept was most dramatically revealed by the case at Johns Hopkins University Hospital involving a child with correctible duodenal blockage. Medical intervention was withheld because of the presence of Down syndrome. The child's anticipated quality of life was deemed insufficient to justify lifesaving medical intervention.

The alternative position challenges the ethics of euthanasia with handicapped persons, in either active or passive forms, and defends the unconditional right to life for all persons. This position is reflected in the basic policy statement developed by the American Association on Mental Deficiency (1975) which stated that " . . . the existence of mental retardation is no justification for the terminating of the life of any human being or for permitting such a life to be terminated either directly or through the withholding of life sustaining procedures" (p. 8). Consistent with this position, Walmsley (1978) questioned the notion that severely handicapped persons could be evaluated for their "essential lack of humanness":

> It is necessary that our society cease deluding itself by believing it can make a measure for humanness . . . A creature is a human being who is the product of the union of a man and a woman, is conceived by woman and born of woman. (p. 388)

In addition to the specific cases noted above, there are data to suggest that euthanasia is not rare. Duff and Campbell (1973) reported that, of 299 deaths of infants recorded in a New Haven hospital from 1970-1972, 43 (or 14%) could be attributed to withdrawal or withholding of treatment.

The increased attention to this issue demands professional scrutiny and advocacy (Cohen, 1981; Powell, Aiken, & Smylie, 1982). Smith (in press, 1984) noted special educators may be better informed than doctors concerning the possibilities and potentialities for the lives of individual handicapped children and thus are in a unique position to act as advocates. The Association for Individuals with Severe Handicapping Conditions (TASH) reflects the need for advocacy (see Figure 6.10). Although it is not the purpose of this brief discussion to conclude with a specific recommendation, professionals must carefully evaluate their position on this issue and be prepared to express and defend it.

BOARD TAKES STAND ON LIFE/DEATH ISSUE

In response to recent national events and to a request made at the Open Forum during the '82 conference in Denver, the Critical Issues Committee prepared the following policy statement, which was endorsed by the Executive Board:

"WHEREAS the right to life and liberty is guaranteed by our Constitution and Bill of Rights and,

WHEREAS the life and liberty of persons with disabilities are threatened by the prejudice which results from the ignorance generated by segregation and separation, and

WHEREAS this prejudice can only be overcome when the next generation of children born without disabilities grow up, play with, go to school with, live and work with their peers with disabilities,

WHEREAS The Association for the Severely Handicapped is extremely concerned with the increasing practice of withholding medical treatment and/or sustenance from infants based upon the diagnosis of, or prognosis for disability

THEREFORE BE IT RESOLVED THAT The Association for the Severely Handicapped opposes the withholding of medical treatment and/or sustenance from infants when the decision is based upon the diagnosis of, or prognosis for, mental retardation or related handicapping conditions,

AND FURTHERMORE this association reaffirms the right to equal medical treatment for all infants in accordance with the dignity and worth of these individuals, as protected by the Constitution and Bill of Rights of the United States of America,

AND FURTHERMORE this association acknowledges the responsibility of society and the government to share with parents and other family members the support of handicapped infants,

AND FURTHERMORE The Association for the Severely Handicapped acknowledges the obligation of society to provide for life-long medical, financial, educational support to handicapped persons to extend to them opportunities to achieve potential, equal and equivalent, to those opportunities, offered other/all members of our society.

Source: The Association for the Severely Handicapped *Newsletter*, June 1983, p. 1.

FIGURE 6.10

SUMMARY

Hundreds of specific factors have been identified as causes of mental retardation. Nevertheless, in the vast majority of individual cases, a specific cause can not be identified. We can tentatively generalize that specific biological causes are most often associated with moderate to profound retardation, while unknown cases are more frequently found within the mild range.

To understand etiology, we must appreciate principles of genetics, since a large percentage of biological causes stem from recessive, dominant, and sex-linked inheritance and from chromosomal abnormalities. In addition, other possible causes include prenatal infections and intoxications, brain injury, malnutrition, cranial malformations, disorders related to pregnancy, and psychiatric disturbances.

Prevention of retardation due to various pathological causes requires an intensive program that begins before the time of conception and continues throughout the developmental period. For every specifiable cause of retardation, a preventive measure of one type or another can be identified. Some of the most optimistic advances in recent years include genetic counseling and the screening of carriers for various disorders, amniocentesis, and careful perinatal monitoring. However, some of these procedures are—in spite of their clear use in preventing retardation—opposed by various groups within our society. In addition, cosmetic measures can also be used to attentuate some of the physical characteristics associated with retardation. Advances in medical terminology created difficult ethical problems that society must face.

CHAPTER SEVEN

Psychosocial Causes of Mental Retardation

See Table 6.2. According to the classification system used in the Grossman manual (1983) this category is designated as *environmental influences*.

Chapter 6 discussed the biological causes of retardation, that is, those specific, known causes of retardation that most often result in relatively severe impairment. In this chapter, attention shifts to the possible effects of multiple genes and/or a host of detrimental environmental factors. This separation is consistent with the distinction suggested by Penrose (1963) and Zigler (1966; Zigler & Balla, 1981) dividing the mentally retarded population into two groups: the organically impaired subgroup having an approximate mean IQ of 35 and a range of 0 to 70; and the familial subgroup representing those individuals at the lower end of the normal distribution of intelligence. This latter population, constituting the highest percentage of mildly retarded persons, is discussed here.

The initial and most basic problem raised is how to sort out the relevant etiological variables in a category that, by definition, includes unknown or at least unspecifiable factors. Though our central concern would be with children from poor families, other "environmental" causes have been associated with retardation in years past. In 1848, Samuel Gridley Howe discussed some of his thoughts on the causes of "idiocy."

This chapter was contributed by Edward A. Polloway and James R. Patton.

The moral to be drawn from the prevalent existence of idiocy in society is, that a very large class of persons ignore the conditions upon which health and reason are given to men, and consequently, they sin in various ways; they disregard the conditions which should be observed in intermarriage—they overlook the hereditary transmission of certain morbid tendencies, or they pervert the natural appetites of the body into lusts of divers kinds . . . and thus bring down the awful consequences of their own ignorance and sin upon the heads of their unoffending children. (pp. 2–3)

The dilemma of causation is reflected in the terms most commonly used today to refer to this category: *psychosocial disadvantage* and **cultural-familial retardation**. The former has grown in popularity since its introduction by Grossman in 1973.

Criteria for inclusion under this category requires that there be evidence of subnormal intellectual functioning in at least one of the parents and in one or more siblings where there are such. These cases are usually from impoverished environments involving poor housing, inadequate diets, and inadequate medical care. There may be prematurity, low birth weight, or history of infectious diseases but no single entity appears to have contributed to the slow or retarded development (1977, pp. 67–68)

The term *psychosocial disadvantage* has, to some degree, supplanted the term *cultural-familial* retardation. However, while the 1973 Grossman manual called the term *cultural-familial* retardation obsolete, this reference was revised in the 1983 manual. The importance of this term cannot be overlooked. As indicated by Heber (1959, 1961), *cultural-familial retardation* generally refers to a mild level of handicap with no organic defects. Heber indicated three basic considerations.

1. Evidence of retardation in at least one of the parents and in one or more siblings where there are such.
2. There is usually some degree of cultural deprivation present.
3. No intent in this category to specify either the independent action of, or relationship between, genetic and cultural factors in the etiology of cultural-familial mental retardation. The exact role of genetic factors cannot be specified since the nature and mode of transmission of genetic aspects of intelligence is not yet understood. Similarly, there is no clear understanding of the specific manner in which environmental factors operate to modify intellectual functioning. (pp. 39–40).

The third point is particularly cogent at this time. In the years that elapsed between the publication of these two manuals, research might have resulted in the clear analysis of these two key variables, genetics *(nature)* and the environment *(nurture)*. If this were the case, the adoption of *psychosocial disadvantage* (the definition of which makes no mention of genetics) and the rejection of *cultural-familial retardation* (which does not rule out genetics as a contributing factor) would have represented a logical shift in emphasis. This change in emphasis on genetics has been referred to as "the most potentially controversial change made by the Grossman manual" (Polloway & Payne, 1975, p. 14). However, in spite of the firm stand taken by the Grossman manual, the professional community had not then and has not now reached general consensus on the role of genetics in causing mild retardation. Robinson and Robinson's observation in 1970 is equally applicable today: "Nowhere is the nature-nurture controversy so alive as with respect to the etiology of this disorder" [mild retardation] (p. 627).

Given the complexity of the etiology of mild retardation, this chapter will investigate three theoretical perspectives related to causation: (a) the view that genetic factors are the primary determinants of development; (b) the view that environmental variables play the central role in influencing development; and (c) the interaction perspective, which stresses the importance of both of these determinants. In practice, the vast majority of theoreticians and researchers in the area subscribe to this third view, but we will look at all three perspectives to identify basic tenets of each position. Although the focus of the discussion here is on the dimension of measured intelligence, you should keep in mind that deficits in adaptive behavior also need to be present before an individual can be identified as mentally retarded. After a brief look at the population of mildly retarded persons, we will review these three basic positions, along with their implications for society in general and education in particular.

MILD RETARDATION: THE POPULATION

The characteristics of the mildly retarded individual are examined in more depth in the next chapter.

Before attempting to untangle the complexities of causation, we will answer the question, "Who are the mildly handicapped persons who have been associated with cultural-familial retardation or psychosocial disadvantage?"

This population represents the larger subgroup of those children and adolescents who have been labeled *mentally retarded*. Although prevalence estimates vary, we can assume that approximately 70 to 80% of all persons identified as retarded have mild handicaps and that the great majority of these individuals have been designated as within the cultural-familial group.

Dunn's (1973a) model provides a benchmark for analyzing the traditional mildly retarded population. He delineated five specific subgroups, three of which would be considered to be within the psychosocial domain. The designations, of course, do not represent true discrete groups; there is some overlap.

Neurologically handicapped children are those individuals whose retardation has a biological cause, but who show only mild impairment. This group might include, for example, those Down syndrome children who function at relatively high levels perhaps due to intensive early intervention efforts.

The second group would include multiply handicapped children. Probably the most frequent combination of handicaps would be retardation with emotional/behavioral disorders, due to the interaction of these impairments as well as to the biasing effects that behavioral disturbances can have on identification procedures. Other secondary handicaps that might be found in children within programs for the mildly retarded include motoric disabilities such as cerebral palsy, and speech and language disorders.

Dunn's other three subcategories are associated with psychosocial disadvantage and include Anglo (white), black, and bilingual children. In these cases, prevalence is much greater within either rural or inner-city communities where poverty is more common. For black children, dialectal variations from standard English could be a compounding factor, while for bilingual children (e.g., Puerto Rican, Chicano), the fact that English is often a second language may impede school achievement.

In the years since Dunn (1973) offered this model, significant changes have taken place in the EMR population. As Polloway and Smith (1983) indicated, the factors that have influenced this change included (a) definitional changes implicit in the Grossman (1973, 1983)

Children from poor communities are at high risk of showing mild mental retardation.

THE DILEMMA OF NATIVE AMERICANS

Recent court cases have documented and demonstrated the disportionate number of blacks *(Larry P. v. Riles)*, and Spanish-speaking *(Diana v. State Board of Education)*, students placed in classes for educable mentally retarded students. Without analyzing this litigation in detail, in all cases inaccuracies were found and changes were ordered. Another group of Americans who also are affected by procedural discrimination is Native Americans. The magnitude of the problem is highlighted in an excerpt from a report describing the situation of handicapped Navajos.

So many of his Native American problems are closely related to the problems confronting all reservation dwellers—poverty, ignorance, isolation, malnutrition, overcrowding, and disease. It is impossible to separate the basic needs of the handicapped Native American from those of his able-bodied brothers. Until overall living conditions improve on reservations, Native Americans will continue to develop handicapping conditions at a higher rate than the rest of the population, and those so afflicted will continue to live the lives of the lowest of the low, outcasts among outcasts in our society. (Haskins & Stifle, 1978)

A poignant example of the interaction of mental retardation and cultural values is depicted in the following vignette about Tom Whitefeather.

He's 18, and he has a choice to make. One of the social workers carefully explained that he could return to the reservation and live with his sister's family, or move to Mountain City and live in a small group residence. Both alternatives seemed fearful after living in Castle Rock State Home since he was 12. He was no longer sure of himself as a Lakota Sioux. On the other hand, he wasn't completely comfortable in the white man's world.

Tom had been committed to the institution by the court, after being found guilty of breaking into a hardware store, his third offense. A social worker's report pointed out that both parents were alcoholic. A court-appointed psychologist testified that Tom was "functioning in the mild mental retardation range."

The transcripts of the case show that representatives of the tribal council had petitioned the court to order that he be sent back to the reservation in their official custody. They testified that the staff at the institution were neither familiar with, nor understood the cultural values of their tribe. The petition was denied.

When Tom Whitefeather first came to the institution, it was recorded that he

manuals leading especially to increased concern for adaptive behavior; (b) the rippling effects of litigation (e.g., *Larry P. v. Riles*, 1972; *Diana v. State Board of Education*, 1970) challenging the use of the MR label and mandating special class placement for minority children; (c) the encouragement of a more restrictive concept of retardation as comprehensive rather than based solely on current status; (d) the successes of early intervention programs with disadvantaged children; and (e) the inclusion within EMR programs of individuals (e.g., Down syndrome) who previously would probably have been designated as trainable and served in TMR classes. As a consequence, the equation of EMR classes and cultural-familial retardation has been altered. No simple assump-

"walks slow . . . Will not take care of his clothes and possessions, and for the most part is uncommunicative. When he does talk, he mumbles. . . . He cannot be depended upon to carry out any working task."

Later notations in the records show that Tom's early negative attitude began to fade. He profited from educational classes and vocational training. Also, he developed acceptable work habits in the institution's laundry.

In a recent interview, a member of the tribe gave an explanation of his early failure at institutional life. "The white man's values are different from the Indian's. Members and families in the tribe may not show it outwardly, but they are a close-knit people. That's why most mentally retarded Indians should remain on the reservation. If they need help it will best be given by our own people."

The tribal member pointed out that once their highest values had to do with learning the world of nature. They had little need for competitive technocracy and the acquisition of many possessions like the white man, because the whole world was "always there and always available." It's not easy for the American Indian to solve the clash between his own and the white man's culture.

In an interview with the social worker responsible for placing Tom on the reservation or in Mountain City, it was learned that she had never been to the reservation, 120 miles away, and—to her best recollection—none of the staff had been there.

When the social worker carefully explained the choices he now can make, Tom sat silently, as if waiting for someone else to make the choice for him. This slow-moving, soft-talking young man with a record of personal development at Castle Rock State School is unable to verbalize the inner conflict—and maybe the wounds—he feels.

When he came, he was definitely a Lakota Sioux Indian. After six years away from the reservation, he wasn't sure. On the other hand, he heard that many persons in Mountain City were prejudiced against Indian Americans. Could he take that? Would he be able to get a job?

Tom is faced with the choice of entering one of two worlds that function differently and have little real understanding of each other. His inability to decide stems from his own confusion about himself, who he is and to whom he belongs.

Tom Whitefeather sits quietly while others are urging him to make a choice that may be impossible for him to make.

tions can be made that the only cause, or in some cases even the primary cause, for the intellectual deficits experienced by individuals within this population can be attributed to psycho-social variables. Because EMR classes are now more likely to be serving what MacMillan and Borthwick (1980) termed "a more patently disabled group" (p. 155), professionals must be aware of the increased presence of biological conditions as possible etiological factors.

The remainder of this chapter is concerned with those individuals who continue to be accurately identified as within the familial subgroup. The three perspectives on the etiology of psychosocial retardation are the hereditary, the environmental, and the interaction perspectives.

HEREDITARY POSITION

See chapter 1 for a discussion of the eugenics scare.

The study of the role of heredity in causing mental retardation has a long and somewhat vacillating history. The family pedigree studies associated with the eugenics scare at the turn of the century (e.g., Goddard, 1912) provided fuel to the fire by initially tying Gregor Mendel's theories of the simple genetic transmission of traits to the complex arena of human intelligence. Despite the quite apparent flaws inherent in these studies (Kanner, 1964; Kirk, 1964; Wallin, 1955), the study of mental retardation and that of genetics were nevertheless inexorably joined. The basic assumption of the early 20th century that intelligence was a fixed and stable trait merged comfortably with this perspective.

The hereditary position holds that intelligence, and familial retardation, is determined most significantly by genetic variables, not environmental variables. This genetic determinism stems from the mechanism of *polygenic inheritance*. Compared to the one gene/one trait association common in numerous disorders associated with retardation (e.g., PKU), polygenic refers to the interaction of many gene pairs and networks that, in combination, predispose an individual to a given level of intellectual functioning. The complexity of this phenomenon makes it extremely difficult to precisely evaluate the influence of genetics. Therefore, as noted in chapter 3, statistical data from population samples remain the basic measures available to researchers seeking to determine the merits of the hereditary position.

Several prominent researchers have advocated a strong genetic deterministic position; they include Arthur Jensen, William Shockley, Sir Cyril Burt, and Richard Herrnstein. In particular, Jensen's (1969) article "How Much Can We Boost IQ and Scholastic Achievement?" helped usher in a renewed debate during the 1970s. He was branded a racist, harassed and threatened, and his job and professional affiliations were challenged. However, an analysis of the genetic position requires a more detached, less sensational posture.

Much of the theoretical base for the genetic position relies on the interpretation of the *heritability* of intelligence. Heritability is defined as the proportion of total trait variance of a measurable characteristic that is directly due to genetic factors. For different traits, heritability could range from 0 to 1, according to what extent (from 0 to 100%) genetics determines intelligence. Since heritability for skin pigment, visual acuity, susceptibility to optical illusions, galvanic skin response, speed of visual information processing, reaction time, and related mental abilities has been established, Jensen (1973) suggests that environmentalists arbitrarily chose a point to begin denying genetic influences on intelligence.

Proponents of a strong genetic position have estimated a heritability of approximately .80 for intelligence, based primarily on IQ correlations from kinship studies within families and research with adopted children. The most often cited research includes studies of identical twins. Typically, the heritability figure is obtained by examining twins reared apart, because these pairs have all genetic factors in common. Their environments are different. A comparison of the IQs yields a measure of heritability for the population from which the samples are selected. The most widely cited research on twins (e.g., Burt, 1966; Shields, 1962) indicates that IQ correlations for twins reared apart is remarkably similar to IQ correlations for those reared together. Although these data appear to be extremely powerful when taken at face value, it should be noted that the studies have engendered controversy unto themselves; a discussion of the arguments about their validity will be provided later in the chapter. In addition, the use of heritability estimates is somewhat limited because (*a*) only group figures are available and (*b*) due to changes over time and among groups, the estimates are actually valid only for the groups from which they were obtained. It is important to note that heritability is specifically concerned with the *range* of individual differences in a trait. Thus a low genetic variance does not deny a genetic base, but rather indicates genetic similarity. Likewise, a low environmental variance does not refute the importance of environment but rather indicates that it is not substantially contributing to the individual differences. This point has led to Jensen's (1973) assertion that the environment acts primarily as a **threshold variable**—that is, some minimal requisite level of stimulation is required for normal development, but beyond this threshold, it has little importance as a basic determinant of intelligence.

SOCIAL CLASS AND RACIAL DIFFERENCES

Acceptance of a strong genetic position would lead to direct implications regarding any identified social class and social differences noted through intelligence testing. Social classes could be viewed as "breeding populations" that would produce an inevitable correlation between intelligence and the genetic base for the particular class (Jensen, 1969). Social mobility would theoretically increase this correlation, because the more able individuals would rise in class level (taking their superior genes with them), while the least able would drop to, or remain within, the lower class. The outcome of this mobility would be *gene pools* within social classes, which would then determine the genetic make-up of future generations born in that group.

In a highly mobile society, those stressing genetic determinism suggest that variance in intelligence *within* groups is thus constantly being transformed to variance *between* groups. Therefore, given equal opportunity, the differences between classes would tend to increasingly reflect real differences in biologically determined ability, as opposed to just arbitrary social discrimination. Thus, the removal of discriminatory barriers would ultimately lead to the establishment of biological barriers (Herrnstein, 1971). This system would differ from a closed, caste-type system where, by artificially hindering mobility, there would be greater within-class variance (Jensen, 1973). As support for this hypothesis, Waller (1971) reported that the greater the difference in IQ between father and son, the greater the son's upward (or downward) mobility.

Closely related to social class differences in intelligence is racial difference. In asserting the genetic viewpoint relative to group differences in IQ for black and white children, advocates have relied heavily on Shuey's (1966) review of research. Shuey concludes that there is a 15-point mean IQ gap between the races. In this review Shuey reports that the standard deviation of the IQ distribution for black children was found to be 12.4 (as compared to 16.4 for whites), thus resulting in a prediction that only approximately 15% of blacks would exceed the mean for whites. As an added rationale, Jensen (1973) cites isolated gene pools and assortative mating as contributing to the IQ disparity among races.

Assortative mating refers to the concept that "like marries like."

We can assume from this theoretical position that the high prevalence of mild retardation found among lower class and minority children would be seen as a direct function of polygenic inheritance within the social group. This conclusion would be compatible with the research of Reed and Reed (1965) who, in a modern-day genealogy study, conclude that approximately 1 to 2% of fertile retarded persons in one generation are responsible for 30 to 40% of the retarded persons within the next generation.

Clearly, the strong genetic stance is quite controversial. To provide a better perspective, we need to answer two questions. First, what are the ultimate social implications of adopting this position? Second, how valid are the data on which the theory is built? We will look at possible answers to these questions, borrowing specifically from the most vocal proponents of the viewpoint.

Social Implications Jensen (1973) suggests that there are two camps on the nature-nurture issue. He identifies them as (*a*) those holding what others have termed an *elitism/racism* conception, and (*b*) those holding what he calls the *egalitarian environmentalist* position, who deny genetic variability. He illustrates these camps with a 2 by 2 matrix design, shown in Figure 7.1. Jensen suggests that "True Environment," the situation in which the prevailing environmentalist position is the actual source of individual differences, is more acceptable within a democratic society than a True G position would be. But he also claims that an inaccurate False E situation would also be preferable, because it would be at least politically and socially harmless. Jensen speculates that this

Reality

Prevailing Hypotheses	Genetic	Environmental
Genetic	True G	False G
Environmental	False E	True E

From A.R. Jensen. EDUCABILITY AND GROUP DIFFERENCES. New York: Harper & Row, 1973, p. 20. Copyright © 1973 by Arthur R. Jensen. Reprinted by permission of Harper & Row, Publishers, Inc.

FIGURE 7.1 Hypothesis Regarding Source of Individual Differences

situation would then destroy the incentive to differentiate the False E position from the True E position through research. Acceptance of False E could result in needless frustration and hatred if discrimination is viewed as the sole reason for social inequality; when, in fact, genetic difference would be the actual reason for performance differences between races.

A related ethical issue is how to deal in practice with the theory of a genetic basis for racial difference in intelligence and thus in representation in special classes. Such a theory predicts the potential development of a national trend toward racial degeneration. This assumption leads to the prediction that higher reproductive rates of those who are at the "bottom" of society intellectually, educationally, and occupationally could handicap future generations by widening racial and social class gaps and thus promoting greater social inequality (Bajema, 1971). This premise is consistent with the opinion that the way to real equality may necessarily be a biological route.

Underlying any biological intervention to promote equality would be prevention through some form of birth control or through genetic engineering. While genetic engineering offers exciting and significant challenges for the near future, the idea of socially mandated birth control is only a new chapter in the continuing saga of the eugenics movement. The form of birth control advocated here is often voluntary sterilization (Shockley, 1974). Obviously sterilization is hardly a new idea; it has historically been the "treatment of choice" in thousands of cases throughout the country. Recent revelations in Virginia, for example, indicate that perhaps as many as 8,000 persons were unknowingly yet *legally* sterilized in state institutions between the height of the eugenics scare in the 1920s and the early 1970s. Although proponents of this policy today urge only programs of voluntary sterilization, in practice, both the relevant history of 20th-century America and the nebulous zone between informed consent and involuntary treatment cast doubt on whether the programs could be truly voluntary.

Although many of the laws enacted during the eugenics scare have since been revoked or at least the practices generally curtailed, the spectre of sterilization is bound to remain as long as the strong, highly deterministic genetic perspective continues to receive attention. Informed consent is now the watchword for such procedures, but, nevertheless, the question of parental approval will often supersede. It is critical that anyone discussing so-called eugenic measures distinguish between those disorders clearly associated with genetic transmission (e.g., PKU, Tay-Sachs disease) and those that are still speculative, such as familial retardation. At the same time, there is a need to divide those advocating a moderate genetic position from the radical self-styled genetic engineers.

Validity of the Data Base Many objections have been raised to the use of a figure of .80 for the heritability of intelligence. Any trait's heritability is not fixed, but rather is bound to a certain distinct population, period of time, and developmental situation (Cronbach, 1969; Scarr-Salapatek, 1971a,b). Thus the trait can change greatly over generations, due to environmental influences. Gage (1972) cites an analogy with the heritability of height, which may be extremely high for a given period, but clearly has increased tremendously over the long term of many generations. In addition, establishing heritability figures within groups does not permit assumptions to be made between groups (Gage, 1972). Since the heritability figures cited by genetic proponents were derived solely from Caucasian populations, whether they can be generalized to other groups would be very questionable.

A second consideration, closely related to the first but of greater significance, is the question of the validity of the use of several of the twin studies (i.e., Burt, 1966; Juel-Nielsen, 1965: Newman, Freeman, & Holzinger, 1937; Shields, 1962) as a data base for generating hypotheses on the importance of inheritance. In perhaps one of the most scathing attacks on the foundations of the genetic position, Kamin (1974) questions whether many of these identical twins had, in fact, been reared apart, as reported. For example, after reviewing the original case studies from the reports of Newman et al. (1937), Kamin offers the following analysis of these specific twin pairs allegedly reared apart.

> Ed and Fred's separation is at one point in the text described as "complete until their first meeting at 24 years of age." Further, "they lived without knowledge of each other's existence for twenty-five years." Their genes, during this period, appear to have impelled them to remarkably similar experiences. They each worked as electrical repair men for the telephone company, and each owned a fox terrier named Trixie. The case study, however, reports that "they even went to the same school for a time, but

never knew that they were twin brothers. They had even noticed the remarkable resemblance between them, but they were not close companions. When the twins were about eight years old, their families were permanently separated." This simply does not square with the earlier account of no knowledge of each other's existence for 25 years. . . .

The case study includes a photograph of the twins side-by-side "at the time of their first meeting. . . ." The twins are remarkably alike in appearance. They are wearing identical pin-striped suits, and identical striped ties. These, of course, might have been bought "at the time of their first meeting." Perhaps it is relevant to note that Fred was unemployed at the time of the study. (pp. 53–54)

Kamin (1974) further elaborates on the possible sources of bias within the selections of subjects for the Newman et al. (1937) study.

The twins were rewarded with considerable newspaper and magazine publicity; one threatened a legal suit because a magazine had described her as intellectually inferior to her twin. There was also a very tangible inducement offered to all twins by [Newman et al.]. They were treated to a visit at the Century of Progress Exposition then being held in Chicago. "Pair after pair, who had previously been unmoved by appeals to the effect that they owed it to science and society to permit us to study them, could not resist the offer of a free, all-expenses-paid trip to the Chicago Fair." To qualify for this reward,the twins had to attest to the fact that they had been separated, and that they were remarkably alike.

This raises a very serious issue. The facts about separation, in all the twin studies, depend heavily upon the verbal account of the twins themselves. When there are not tangible inducements, the twins are exhorted to make themselves available in the name of science. They receive free medical examinations, and enormous amounts of detailed individual attention from distinguished scientists. They could scarcely be blamed if, in a misguided effort to cooperate with science, or to bolster a sense of their unique worth, they were to stretch a fact or two. The report that "actual facts" concerning schooling were, "difficult to obtain" does little to allay anxiety on this score (p 54).

The other studies have also been criticized along similar lines. Kamin (1974) provides this analysis of several of the twins supposedly reared apart who participated in the Shields (1962) study.

Bertram and Christopher were separated at *birth*. "The paternal aunts decided to take one twin each and they have brought them up amicably, living next door to one another in the same Midlands colliery village. . . . They are constantly in and out of each other's houses." Odette and Fanny were separated from birth until the age of 12. The conditions of their separation seem to have been worked out by a specialist in experimental design. From the age of 3 until the age of 8 the twins were rotated every 6 months, one going to the maternal grandmother and the other to the mother. Joan and Dinah were separated at birth, but "reunited about 5." Their entire school careers were spent together in "a small country town." Joanna and Isobel were similarly "separated from birth to 5 years," and then "went to private schools together." When tested at age 50, their scores were virtually identical, and much higher than any other scores in the entire sample. Adeline and Gwendolen were not separated until their mother's death, when they were 9½. Gwendolen then moved to the maternal aunt's house, "at the other end of the village," and they continued their work "at the village school." (pp. 50–51)

Finally, questions have also been raised about the data from the studies by Burt (1966), who had been recognized as one of the foremost respected authorities within this field of study. The most damning evidence has been the suggestion that much of Burt's data was actually fictionalized. A recent biography by Hearnshaw (1979) suggests that many of the twin pairs reported in his study were simply created, along with Burt's two mysterious research collaborators, who may or may not have existed themselves. As Hawkes (1979) concludes, this biography confirms the suspicion that Burt "engaged in deliberate deception, fabricated research data and invented nonexistent 'colleagues' to support his theories about intelligence" (p. 673).

The above arguments notwithstanding, there continues to be considerable disagreement on the validity of these data bases and the implications that can be drawn from them. Fulker (1975), for example, in a review of Kamin (1974), contended that the book

lacks balanced judgment and presents a travesty of the empirical evidence in the field. By exaggerating the importance of what are, in reality, idiosyncratic details rather than typical features, (Kamin) totally avoids the necessity to consider the data as a whole. The cumulative picture is overwhelmingly in favor of a substantial (69–70%) heritability of IQ. (p. 519).

A recent very comprehensive review on the relationships between genetics and intelligence was provided by Scarr and Carter-Saltzman (1982). On this subject, they noted that, although removal of the flawed Burt research from collections of research on kinship groups reduced the overall magnitude assigned to the heritability for intelligence, both traditional and more contemporary studies nevertheless support at least a moderate genetic component. They concluded that the available data on both twin studies and adoption studies support the fact that heredity plays a major role in the determination of differences between individuals in intelligence. Henderson (1982), in a similar vein, noted that while the earlier kinship studies resulted in the hypothesis of a heritability of .80 for intelligence, recent data and interpretations yield a more conservative (though still substantial) estimate of between .30 and .60 (Henderson, 1982).

It is important to appreciate the problems of design associated with this type of research. Ideally, if a perfect design could be achieved, it would include the following characteristics: (*a*) identify *x* sets of twins (say, 20 sets); (*b*) separate them at birth; (*c*) place them into distinctly variant environmental settings; and (*d*) retest them periodically over an extended time. Unfortunately, in social science research, what usually is desired methodologically is achieved in practice only infrequently; this is especially true in the twin study research.

Despite recent research and criticism of earlier studies, the issue is unresolved. However, the moderate position that ascribes a key role, though clearly not the only significant role, to the genetic contribution seems to be an accurate interpretation of the data currently available.

ENVIRONMENTAL POSITION

Historically, the environmental view derives from John Locke's concept of the *tabula rasa*, which suggests that children are born with a blank slate on which the environment "writes" experiences and thus develops traits. Acceptance of this position would place a heavy responsibility on educators, because it implies that the mental development of a child can be immensely influenced by educational programs.

The strict environmental position holds that the primary determinant of a child's current level of intellectual functioning is his or her experiential background. Pasamanick (1959) has clearly stated this position.

> Except for a few hereditary clinical deficiencies . . . and for exogenous injury to neural integration, behavior variation does not seem to be the result of genetically determined structural origin. It is now possible to entertain a new *tabula rasa* theory hypothecating that at conception individuals are quite alike in intellectual endowment except for these quite rare hereditary neurologic defects. It appears to us that it is life experience and the sociocultural milieu influencing biological and psychological function which, in the absence of organic brain damage, makes human beings significantly different behaviorally from each other. (p. 318)

The radical behavioral position is also consistent with this extreme environmental perspective. Since from this view, all behavior (including

See Bijou's definition
of *mental retardation*
in chapter 2.

responses on an IQ test) is learned through interaction with the environment, retarded individuals are people who, because of inadequate or deficient experiences, have failed to learn appropriate behaviors or have learned inappropriate ones.

Bijou (1983) provided a particularly apt description of how "retarded development" can be conceptualized within behavior analysis theory. John B. Watson (1930), known as the "father of behaviorism," provided a controversial, yet eloquent, description of the environmental point of view.

> Our conclusion, then, is that we have no real evidence of the inheritance of traits. I would feel perfectly confident in the ultimate favorable outcome of careful upbringing of a healthy well-formed baby born of a long line of crooks, murderers and thieves, and prostitutes. Who has any evidence to the contrary?
>
> I should like to go one step further now and say, "Give me a dozen healthy infants, well-formed, and my own specific world to bring them up in and I'll guarantee to take anyone at random and train him to become any type of specialist I might select—doctor, lawyer, artist, merchant-chief and yes, even beggar-man and thief, regardless of his talents, penchants, tendencies, abilities, vocations and race of his ancestors." I am going beyond my facts and I admit it, but so have the advocates of the contrary and they have been doing it for many thousands of years. . . .
>
> The truth is society does not like to face facts. Pride of race has been strong, hence our Mayflower ancestry—our Daughters of the Revolution. We like to boast of our ancestry. It sets us apart. . . . Again, on the other hand, the belief in the inheritance of tendencies and traits saves us from blame in the training of our young. (p. 103)

The environmental position gained widespread support during the 1960s with the advent of Kennedy and Johnson's "War on Poverty," in particular with the Head Start program and with the widespread application of behavior modification techniques in public school and institutional programs for retarded children. In the next section, we will briefly outline environmental factors which may relate to retardation.

ENVIRONMENTAL CORRELATES OF RETARDATION

Psychosocial retardation has been closely linked to a number of specific variables within the poverty environment. Since a specific etiology is not likely to be pinpointed, however, our general focus must remain on the cluster of potentially debilitating characteristics of impoverished communities. Many theorists have concluded that lower class homes and communities function as deprived environments and are primarily responsible for children's educational handicaps. This thesis has, however, been challenged by others (e.g., Ginsburg, 1972), who deny the existence of the cultural deprivation phenomenon, and point to the vast majority of "economically handicapped" children who are not later identified in school as handicapped learners.

Before proceeding with a discussion of environmental variables linked with retardation, let us present two cautions. First Chan and Rueda (1979) stress the need to separate the effects of poverty from the essence of cultural differences. This distinction is quite useful, since it allows us to assess the negative effects of poverty without making judgments about cultural variance. Second, while a substantial amount of research has attempted to separate out specific environmental factors that relate to retardation, the various factors may often act in combination with each other. Although these variables are found more frequently within lower social class environments, we must nevertheless avoid assuming that these characteristics must, or even will, be present in a given home situation.

Within the poverty environment, parenting practices are as varied as they are within the general population, but authoritarianism and inconsistency are prevalent. Many parents emphasize external controls that may inadvertently stress, for example, the problems of getting caught for stealing over the avoidance of stealing for ethical reasons. Parents' reliance on punishment for control can lead children to imitate their aggressive models. Lack of structure and disorganization can also interfere with the child's need for stability. A lack of stimulation or excessive or inappropriate stimulation (e.g., bombardment of noise) may interfere with cognitive development.

The issue of language deprivation within the lower social classes is highly controversial. Bernstein (1961), in discussing class differences in

A nonstimulating environment can cause cognitive, intellectual, and physical deficits in children.

language in England, differentiates between the restricted code of the lower class and the elaborated code of the middle class. The former would be characterized by short sentences, simple structure, and a limited vocabulary; it could seriously limit thought processes. While Bernstein's theory has been applied to American ghetto children (e.g., Bereiter & Englemann, 1966), it has been challenged by many linguists, most notably LaBov (1970), who asserts that black dialect reflects a language difference rather than simply a class dialectal variation. The Bernstein hypothesis remains largely an unproven explanation of possible linguistic deficiencies and Bernstein (1970) himself has expressed concern over its interpretation.

Hess and Shipman (1965) expanded on aspects of Bernstein's thesis in their research with black mothers of various social classes. They contend that different types of parental control influence the child's later cognitive and social behavior. In general, the lower class family uses control which is less verbal, thus reducing the child's alternatives for action and thought. For example, the lower class mother is more likely to say, "Shut up!" than "Would you please quiet down? I am trying to talk to your brother." Over time, this kind of interaction could restrict the child's language and cognitive development. Hess and Shipman conclude that a deprived learning environment, such as is often associated with an impoverished home

> Produces a child who relates to authority rather than to rationale, who, although often compliant, is not reflective in his behavior, and for whom the consequences of an act are largely considered in terms of immediate punishment or reward rather than future effects and long-range goals. (p. 885)

Kagan (1970) has identified other psychological differences between lower class and more privileged children. He asserts that these differences emerge during the first 3 years of life and are stable over time. Kagan identifies seven such major variables: language, mental set, attachment, inhibition, sense of effectiveness, motivation, and expectancy of failure. All of these variables directly or indirectly influence school performance. Deficits in these areas could also limit the child in problem-solving skills.

In spite of this research, inappropriate patterns of parenting and child guidance are not necessarily inherent in the lower class home. As Chan and Rueda (1979) point out, these deficiencies are likely to reflect the parent's lack of access to data on techniques for enhancing psychosocial development. They base their argument on Hurwitz' (1975) finding that many poor persons live in a "communications environment devoid of meaningful information and knowledge" (p. 20). If this hypothesis is accurate, the implications for intervention are significant.

The family patterns within a lower class environment are more likely to include one absent parent, frequently the father. Thus the burden of child rearing falls heavily on mothers. Added to this problem are the large number of children in many families. The potential result is a decrease in each individual child's direct contact with adult models.

The practical problems involved in "making ends meet" within a culture of poverty are too often overlooked, and must also be considered. The time and effort spent within the middle class home to motivate and stimulate children may need to be devoted in a lower class home to a host of problems, including finding a job, finding suitable housing, and arranging for child care. In a culture where poverty is the overriding concern, parents do not have the luxury of planning for the future. Parents, as well as their children, may focus on the urgency of what can be obtained or accomplished at the moment rather than on setting goals for the future and planning accordingly (Hunt, 1969). The difficulties of daily living can make people feel fatalistic about the control they have over their environment and the value of even trying to improve their situation. A parent who is worried about finding money for daily meals will not see the problem of getting a child to a preschool program on time or of following through with a home-training program as a high priority. It is not surprising that educational concerns are often neglected.

Health problems can compound the detrimental effects of living in this environment. Particular concerns could include nutritional deficiencies, lack of resistance to disease, exposure to toxic substances, and inadequate medical care. Although these are quite obviously biological concerns, they tend to appear with a host of psychosocial factors and may jointly jeopardize mental development (Perkins, 1977).

Probably the clearest documentation of health problems with high-risk lower class children has been provided by Kugel (1967; Kugel & Parsons 1967). These researchers studied 35 children and found substantial evidence of short pregnancies and long labor, infectious **toxemia, anoxia**, prematurity, and neurological abnormalities. They indicate that their results negate the idea of inherited factors as the basis for mild retardation and rather indicate a combination of both psychosocial and pre- and postnatal biological factors as the specific causative agents. Kugel (1967) concludes his report by stating that

> By working diligently with this group of individuals when they are no older than 3 or 4 years of age, some of the pernicious factors can be ameliorated so that these persons need not be condemned to lifelong mental subnormality (p. 61).

Child abuse that may result in brain damage can also not be overlooked as a serious physical (as well as psychological) health hazard.

Although abuse is found across all social classes, evidence suggests that children with cognitive impairments may be subject to abuse up to 10 times more frequently than "normal" children (Sandgrund, Gaines & Green, 1974; Soeffing, 1975). The effects of child abuse thus may add to the other psychosocial causes of cognitive delay.

This discussion has only provided an overview of the types of problems that suggest a linkage between poverty and retardation. Since the overwhelming majority of individuals reared in lower class homes are *not* subsequently functioning retarded, however, the equation is far from perfect. A critical continuing need in research will be to attempt to determine if there are specific factors, or clusters of factors, most significant in negatively affecting a child's development. Trying to identify important correlates, Richardson (1981) reported that children identified as retarded were more likely to come from environments characterized by the following: five or more children in the family; living in the least desirable housing areas; crowded homes (a ratio of two or more people per room); and with the mother's occupation before marriage classified as semi-skilled or unskilled manual job. The next section discusses some specific aspects of early experience, as documented in classic deprivation and enrichment studies.

DEPRIVATION AND ENRICHMENT

Psychological research is replete with evidence concerning the effects of deprived environments on animals. Classic animal studies by Thompson and Heron (1954) and Krech, Rosenzweig, and Bennett (1956) point out that reductions in stimulation can produce learning deficiencies, inability to handle stress, and decreased cortical (brain) weight. There is little doubt that these studies prove the profound influence that environmental conditions have on mental processes in animals (Thompson & Grusec, 1970).

Of greater concern, however, are the studies done with young children. Studies done in orphanages in the middle part of this century provide vivid pictures. Due to lack of stimulation and thus sensory deprivation within these sterile environments, children showed cognitive, intellectual, and physical deficits (Dennis, 1960; Dennis & Najaran, 1957; Pinneau, 1955; Ribble, 1944). Although the mechanics of this deprivation have been debated, there is little doubt that the effects of a nonstimulating environment can be severe.

On the other hand, studies of early experience also illustrate the positive effects of enrichment in early experience. Rheingold and Bayley (1959; Rheingold, 1956) report that, by decreasing the ratio of children to caregivers within the orphanage, substantial cognitive gains could be realized. Dennis (1960) also found that developmental differences in children in orphanages could be attributed to regular contact and handling by adults. Although these findings are not directly applicable to the poverty environment, they do relate to the restrictive conditions found within some poverty homes, which can result in reduced learning opportunities (Coleman & Provence, 1957). It remained for a longitudinal study of early experiences to clearly demonstrate the potential for a radically altered life.

Influential Research Projects Perhaps the foremost name in research on early experiences is that of Harold Skeels. His research, beginning in the 1930s, when IQ was thought to be stable and genetically determined, helped lay the foundation for the massive intervention efforts of the 1960s. Due to the significance and even the romance of this research, we will discuss it in some detail.

The initial research effort of Skeels and Dye (1939) was concerned with investigating the reversibility of the effects of the nonstimulating orphanage environment. The program, which was unusual in its inception and implementation, was based on the observation of two female infants. In describing the children, Skeels (1966) writes: "The youngsters were pitiful little creatures. They were tearful, had runny noses, and coarse, stringy, and colorless hair; they were emaciated, undersized, and lacked muscle tone or responsiveness. Sad and inactive, the two spent their days rocking and whining" (p. 5). Though their chronological ages were 13 and 16 months, their developmental levels were 6 and 7 months, respectively.

Recognizing that it was impractical to place these children either with foster parents or an adoption agency, Skeels and Dye transferred them to an institution for the mentally retarded, not as residents but rather as "house guests." Each of the girls was "adopted" by an older retarded woman, who, under the supervision of staff, acted as a surrogate mother. The babies received the necessary parental care and attention for normal development. The appropriate levels of perceptual enrichment and physical stimulation were also provided. Six months after the transfer, the children were described as "alert, smiling, running about, responding to the playful attention of adults, and generally behaving and looking like any other toddlers" (Skeels, 1966, p. 6).

Buoyed by this experience, Skeels and Dye (1939) increased their experimental group to 13, by selecting 11 additional children from the orphanage. The mean IQ of this group was 64, and all but two of the children were classified as within the retarded range and thus judged by the state law as unsuitable for adoption. A contrast group of 12 orphanage children under 3 years of age was later selected for comparison. This contrast group was composed of four girls and eight boys with an average IQ of 86. Only two of these children were classified as mentally retarded.

While the contrast group remained in the orphanage and received minimal adequate health and medical services, the experimental subjects each received care on a one-to-one basis from an adolescent retarded woman. Each adolescent "mother" was given instructions on how to care for "her" child. They were instructed and trained on how to hold, feed, change, talk to, and stimulate the young children. No other direct educational experiences were provided for the children.

Two years later (Skeels, 1942) the groups were retested and the 13 experimental children showed an average gain of 28 IQ points. Of the 13 experimental children, 11 had IQs high enough to be eligible for adoption and were placed into good homes.

In 1965, more than 25 years after the original study had begun, Skeels located the subjects. His follow-up study reports that 11 of the 13 had married, and apparently all but one of the marriages were still intact. These adults had a total of nine children, all of normal intelligence. The adult's mean level of education was twelfth grade, with four having completed one or more years of college. All subjects were either self-supporting or functioning as homemakers. Their occupations ranged from professional work and business to domestic service for those two who had not been adopted. Their income was consistent with the national and state average at that time.

Meanwhile, the contrast group showed an initial drop in mean IQ of 26 points and as a result were generally not eligible for adoption. When located in 1965, the 11 subjects (one had died) were found to have a mean educational level of approximately the third to fourth grade. Four of the subjects in the contrast group were institutionalized and unemployed and were costing the state approximately $200 per month each. Those who were employed, with one exception, were categorized as "hewers of wood and drawers of water."

Skeels (1966) concludes his follow-up report with the following statement, which has served as a philosophical basis for subsequent early intervention programs.

> It seems obvious that under present-day conditions there are still countless infants with sound biological constitutions and potentialities for development well within the normal range who will become retarded and noncontributing members of society unless appropriate intervention occurs. It is suggested by the findings of this study and others published in the past 20 years that sufficient knowledge is available to design programs of intervention to counteract the devastating effects of poverty, socio-cultural, and maternal deprivation. . . . The unanswered questions of this study could form the basis for many life-long research projects. If the tragic fate of the twelve contrast group children provokes

even a single crucial study that will help prevent such a fate for others, their lives will not have been in vain. (pp. 54-55)

In one of the high-water marks of the environmental position, Skeels was subsequently cited for his research contribution in the late 1960s with a Kennedy Scientific Award (Dunn, 1973a). The participation in the ceremony of the experimental subject who completed college was impressive testimony to the potential of modifications of experiences on adult outcomes.

A second major study which significantly influenced the growing sense of the value of early intervention was conducted by Kirk (1958), who was interested in measuring the effects of an enrichment program on the social and mental development of retarded preschoolers. Kirk identified 81 children between the ages of 3 and 6 with an IQ range of 45 to 80 points. The two experimental groups contained 28 children living at home and attending a special nursery school and 15 children residing in an institution for retarded persons who also attended a nursery school. In the two control nonnursery school groups were 26 children living at home and 12 children in an institution. Cognitive measures were periodically obtained, and significant differences were reported between the groups. Those in the enrichment nursery school program reported IQ gains ranging between 10 and 30 points, while those without benefit of this stimulating environment declined in performance. Over a period of years the differences for each group were sustained.

The discussion of specific environmental factors and the classic studies on deprivation and enrichment create a strong empirical and emotional base for the environmental position. In addition to being an attractive stance within a democratic society, it also points the way toward methodology designed to reduce the occurrence of retardation. However, given the need to consider the genetic contribution, the most defensible position is one that acknowledges the interaction between the roles played by both nature and nurture.

INTERACTION POSITION

The interaction position holds that intellectual development cannot be solely attributed to either genetic or environmental determinants. This position acknowledges the importance of both of these variables as contributors to intelligence and thus as possible causes of retardation. A child's level of functioning would therefore be assumed to be a function of the interaction of inherited abilities and biological characteristics, as modified by environmental experiences.

Cancro (1971) makes the basic case for the interaction position when he states

The gene can only express itself in an environment and an environment can only evoke the genotype [inherited characteristic] that is present. In this sense, it may be very misleading to speak of one or the other as more important, even in theoretical terms (p. 60).

The most commonly accepted model for examining the interaction of genetic and environmental components was originally developed by Dobzhansky (1955). He theorized that inherited characteristics and constitutional restrictions (**genotype**) create a *range* within which a human trait develops. The behavior pattern that a person develops within this genetically endowed range is a function of the environment. The resultant behavior which emerges from the heredity-environment interaction is referred to as **phenotype**, which for this discussion would specifically refer to level of intellectual functioning.

Gottesman (1963) molded the concepts of Dobzhansky's (1955) conceptualization into a schematic paradigm, which is presented in Figure 7.2. Gottesman's hypothesized range for phenotypic development greatly increases as a function of genotype. For example, individuals with poor genetic endowment (genotype A), such as victims of recessive trait disorders or chromosomal abnormalities, would have a smaller range for phenotypic development, regardless of environment. On the other hand, those blessed with a richer genetic endowment (genotype D) have an extensive range for potential development.

To illustrate how the interaction phenomenon would apply, let us look at some generalized examples of the range of reaction, as it relates

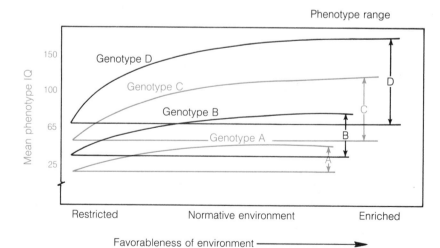

From N.R. Ellis, (Ed.). *Handbook of Mental Deficiency.* New York: McGraw-Hill, 1963, p. 255. Reprinted by permission.

FIGURE 7.2 Estimates of Reaction Range for Hypothetical Genotypes

to various situations. Consider first a Down syndrome child, whose range was restricted due to the results of chromosomal imbalance. Within an average environment, we will assume that the child will function at an IQ level of perhaps 45 to 55. However, given a restrictive environment (the orphanages of midcentury and some current institutions), this level might be depressed to 35. With an enriched environment through an early intervention program, an IQ in the 60s, or perhaps higher, is quite possible.

For a second example, consider the ghetto child with mildly retarded parents. Within the impoverished environment, the child's IQ might be expected to range between 65 and 80. Given a more restricted setting, some further depression might be anticipated. However, in an enriched situation, the range of reaction could be likely to include an average or near average level of functioning.

The actual magnitude of the potential range of reaction cannot be established, particularly for an individual case. However, recent estimates have placed it in the vicinity of 20 to 25 IQ points (Begab, 1981; Zigler & Balla, 1981). Accepting such a figure certainly encourages the development of effective intervention programs, but at the same time it falls short of the promise of total elimination of mild retardation. As Zigler and Seitz (1982) noted, such a middle ground between dogmatic genetic or environmental positions has "the advantage of generating energetic willingness to attempt interventions without unrealistic expectations about what they can accomplish" (p. 615).

In 1968, Smith offered a final note on the interaction model which still has merit for our discussion today. He states

> The hypothesized cause-and-effect relationship which exists between inheritance and the type of environment with which an individual is associated is subtle and not completely understood. Although genetic transmission is important, with research beginning to point to the possibility of eventually controlling heredity by manipulating DNA and RNA molecules, it is essentially irrelevant to the major concerns of education. Thus, the teacher's concern should be with manipulating the child's environment to maximize genotypic potential. (p. 20)

Acceptance of the importance of environmental factors should lead to a commitment to prevention that must include nonbiological intervention. The role of early intervention in prevention of mild retardation is discussed next.

PREVENTION

We have already looked at the implications of the genetic perspective for prevention—eugenic measures in general, and sterilization in particular. The focus here is on the impact of early intervention programs as a basis for preventing, in particular, mild retardation. Because mild retardation is usually diagnosed after the child begins school, the focus of these efforts is generally not on identified retarded children, but rather children from impoverished environments who are "high-risk" for later school-related difficulties.

The successes of the early enrichment studies we have already discussed paved the way for a variety of programs that sought to intervene with high-risk children before learning problems began. Bereiter and Englemann (1966) determined that the disadvantaged child typically shows strength in two areas on mental tests: immediate memory and rote learning. To capitalize on these assets, they designed a program with direct and repetitive instruction. In their program, the teacher constantly reinforced the children's appropriate responses. In addition, the program relied on a structural sequence of activities designed to enhance language development and later academic skills. Significant gains were reported both in IQ (mean increase of 16 points) and in achievement, where experimental subjects were as much as a year ahead academically at the time of their first grade placement. The DISTAR program (Direct Instructional System for Teaching Arithmetic and Reading) was a direct outgrowth of this project. The methodology used in this program has subsequently been applied to intervention efforts with students after their admission to school as part of Project Follow Through. The impressive benefits of direct instruction for averting academic and other school problems have been clearly documented by Becker (1977) and Becker & Carnine (1980).

Karnes, Hodgins, and Teska (1968) evaluated the effects of two preschool programs on 55 disadvantaged children. The experimental group of 28 children participated in a highly structured, cognitive and language development program. The control group of 27 children were enrolled in a traditional, nondirective type of preschool. After 7 months, the experimental group achieved significant gains in intellectual functioning and on other measures of language development and academic readiness. Karnes et al. conclude that their highly structured program was more effective than the traditional approach in developing intellectual functioning, language abilities, perceptual development, and school-related skills.

Gray and Klaus' (1965) early training program was "an attempt to offset the progressive retardation commonly observed in the schooling of culturally deprived children" (p. 887). The intervention began before each child started school and continued through the first years of school. By focusing on preschoolers, the program was intended to be preventive rather than remedial. The experimental groups received summer enrichment activities plus weekly home visits during the school year. The program was designed to improve the disadvantaged subjects' attitudes toward and aptitudes for achievement. The results showed intelligence score gains for the experimental group over a 39-month period (Gray & Klaus, 1968).

The publicized benefits attained through these types of early intervention efforts fueled the commitment of the government to begin a large-scale program aimed at disadvantaged children. During the Johnson administration's War on Poverty in the mid 1960s, therefore, Head Start was initiated to provide direct services to 4-, 5-, and 6-year-old children. To some extent, Head Start began with the assumption that lower class homes functioned as culturally deprived environments. The program was designed to compensate for this deprivation. However, in more recent years, Head Start has gradually developed an orientation that is more consistent with the cultural framework of the community.

The Head Start movement has gone through three somewhat distinct stages of growth (Payne & Mercer, 1974). The initial stage, the halcyon period (1965–1967), was characterized by an abundance of funds, euphoria, and basically anecdotal support of the efficiency of the program. During the next stage, the critical period (1967–1969), the publicized "fade out" of gains and the failure of some participating children by around third grade led to criticism of the program. For the most part, this skepticism was spearheaded by a report known as the *Westinghouse Report* (Cicirelli, 1969). During this period, concern for empirical justification of the program overshadowed the previous reliance on descriptive reports. Although serious methodological questions have been raised about this report, it nevertheless led to widespread pessimism and very nearly to the termination of the program (Zigler & Seitz, 1982). A relevant point made by McVicker Hunt (Pines, 1979), one of the foremost advocates of preschool programs, was that it had been naive to assume that one summer or year of nursery school would be enough to let poor children catch up with their middle class peers. The third stage, the consolidation and refinement period (1969–1973), evolved from these critical years. It reflected the needs of the programs to change their purposes and procedures and to document their gains in order to justify their existence.

Much of the criticism directed at these intervention programs was focused on the nature of the service delivery systems rather than on the validity of the concept of early intervention itself (Hawkridge, Chalupsky, & Roberts, 1968; Pines, 1966; Spicker, 1971). Therefore, rather than assuming simply that compensatory education is unworkable, as Jensen (1969) indicated, advocates have identified specific features that predict successful efforts to enhance young children's development. These considerations include

Although the Head Start program is a major part of overall efforts to reduce school-related difficulties, it is not per se a program of prevention of mental retardation. See LaVor and Harvey (1976), Zigler and Cascione (1977), and Ensher, Blatt, and Winschel (1977) for more on the Head Start movement relative to retardation.

1. Curricular models which emphasize cognitive or academic competencies and development produce the largest intellectual increases.

2. Most successful programs are highly structured and incorporate a specified plan of learning sequences which lead children to stated objectives.

3. Structured programs which are not cognitively or academically oriented produce intellectual gains only when they incorporate strong oral language development programs.

4. The concept of critical periods of learning has remained largely unproven, but programs focusing on younger children have a number of distinct advantages.

5. Home intervention appears most helpful when it supplements a short-term preschool program.

6. Time is critical. Each activity should be selected based on its maximum contribution to the child's learning.

7. Longitudinal intervention programs are justified because children continue to develop after the initial year of programming.

8. Follow-through efforts into the primary grades may be necessary to sustain the achievement gains. Curriculum and methodology must be modified to accommodate children who have had the benefit of compensatory education in the preschool years.

9. Favorable adult—student ratios are characteristic of virtually all successful early intervention programs.

10. Programs are best evaluated by achievement measures and related skills acquisition rather than IQ gains. Not only are the former amenable to intervention, they are the basis for subsequent school performance.

EMPHASIS ON YOUNGER CHILDREN

See chapter 10 for more on current early education programs.

As a function of some of the limitations that resulted from Head Start and similar programs, the more recent trend has been to focus on younger children. As Caldwell (1970) comments, "none of the known studies that began enrichment programs as late as age 6 produced gains as large as those of either Skeels and Dye (1939) or Kirk (1958)" (p. 722). Taking note of the success of infant programs, those in charge of program development have therefore shifted their emphasis toward the first years (or months) of life.

The Milwaukee Project (Garber & Heber, 1973; Heber & Garber, 1971; Strickland,1971) received attention in professional journals as well as in the popular media. It exemplified the spirit of the infant education movement. Garber and Heber (1973) refer to the project as an habilita-

CHILDREN AT RISK

Most of us are aware of the constant reminders telling us that we are "at-risk" for something that is not beneficial to us. Those who smoke are at-risk for lung cancer or respiratory problems; people who don't wear seatbelts/shoulder harnesses are at-risk for serious injury if they are involved in an accident. Some of us through no fault of our own are considered at-risk drivers because we are male and under a certain age. Recently we have been told that our nation is at-risk because of the current state of our educational system. While these are realities of an adult nature, there are other circumstances, just as serious, that affect a much younger group. Many children across the nation are at-risk for school failure and, possibly, classification as mildly retarded. Most of the young children who are likely to have problems later in school do not necessarily display overt signs at an early age.

One of the major dilemmas in implementing early intervention programs is knowing which children are at-risk. Unfortunately, there is some confusion about what professionals mean by "risk" (Keogh, 1983). One definition is: "A risk factor is any ascertainable characteristic or circumstance of a person or group of persons that is known to be associated with increased probability of having, developing, or being adversely affected by a process producing a handicapping condition (Garber & McInerney, 1982, p. 134). Common examples of risk factors which are frequently cited include socioeconomic status of the family, intellectual abilities of the parents (especially the mother), and number of children in the family.

Keogh (1983) concluded that there are three types of children who are at-risk. Her categorization further highlights the point that there are important differences in the way we should conceptualize at-risk children.

☐ Established risk: Children in this category have known medical conditions which affect their lives.

☐ Suspect risk: These children have developmental histories that suggest that there is some form of biological problem; however, it is not readily apparent.

☐ Environmental risk: Children who fit this group have no known medical or biological problem, but they do experience life situations (e.g., family, school) that are associated with possible problems.

When considering whether children are at-risk or not, it is important to evaluate not only the children about whom we are concerned but also to investigate other external factors, such as their homes and life events. If efforts to identify and provide services to at-risk children and families are well designed and systematically implemented, fewer children should fail at school and fewer will be placed in special education.

tive effort aimed at preventing intellectual deficiencies in children identified as "high-risk." The project used an intensive educational program for very young children, beginning during the first few months of life. After a survey of the inner-city living environment, Garber and Herber concluded that poverty conditions produce a high-risk potential for mental retardation by virtue of the mother's intelligence, socioeconomic status, and community of residence.

The project was a long-term study of the effects of intervention beginning 6 months after birth. The experimental design had two components: maternal rehabilitation and infant stimulation. Forty mothers with IQs of 70 or less and their infants were selected as subjects for the study. The maternal rehabilitation program reeducated the mothers for later vocational positions and trained them in child-rearing and homemaking skills.

The infant stimulation program began before the child reached age 6 months. The typical sequence of events gave the child a teacher in a one-to-one relationship until the infant reached 12 months of age; at that time, the pair was joined by a second teacher-infant pair. At 15 months, the two children began instruction with only one teacher. At 18 months, small groups were formed for teaching. Structured teaching groups were then continued throughout the rest of the program. The curriculum was designed to focus on the major language and cognitive needs identified for this group of children.

A carefully detailed program of measurement included comparisons on physical and developmental measures, intelligence scores, learning tasks, and language tests. Strickland (1971) reports that the experimental group began to acquire vocabulary rapidly between ages 19 and 25 months, while the control group (children who did not go through the program) had limited vocabulary until after age 28 months. At 32 months, the experimental children were using full sentences, while the control children were using unconnected words. Starting at age 36 months, a grammar test was given every 3 months, with the experimental group registering significantly higher gains at each interval. When the children were reaching age 42 months, the IQs of the experimental children were reported to average 33 points higher than the control children. In concluding their interim report, Garber and Heber (1973) noted

> Infant testing difficulties notwithstanding, the present standardized test data, when considered along with performance on learning tasks and language tests, indicate an unquestionably superior present level of cognitive development on the part of the experimental group. Also, the first wave of our children are now in public schools. None have been assigned to classes for the retarded. (p. 10)

Garber and Heber's data supported the hypothesis that declines in cognitive functioning typical of a low socioeconomic population could be reversed through early infant intervention.

Without question, the "Miracle in Milwaukee," as this project became known, was very influential in resurrecting the concept of compensatory education which had been so severely criticized by Jensen (1969) and others. However, a number of questions have arisen over the years about the miraculous nature of this program. Even in the afterglow of the initial publicity given the program, Page (1972) raised concerns about several significant aspects of the program. He questioned, in particular, the possible bias in sampling of the population under study, the testing procedures, and the inaccessibility of the project data to external review by professionals. More recently, Page and Grandon (1981) noted:

> The Milwaukee Project, even after 14 years, seems seldom to have appeared in refereed science journals, and details remain clouded. Yet its fame has been remarkable, particularly for its central claim: Working with available materials and intensive personal attention, we may raise children 30 IQ points; indeed, we may move them from dull normal to superior in intelligence.
>
> If this claim is true then the Milwaukee Project deserves its apparent image as the high-water mark of environmentalist accomplishment. And, repeatedly, writers advocating interventions have cited this project as such, even though it only had, as it in effect still has, the status of a series of press releases supported with occasional brief, undetailed addresses to uncritical professional audiences. An event of this kind, whether or not properly understood, can take on a mythic quality and become a pillar in one's ideology about the origins of human nature and the proper directions for social reform (p. 240).

These authors then provided a detailed analysis of the study and an evaluation of its scientific merits.

It is safest to conclude at this time that, while the Milwaukee Project stands as a symbolic representation of the value of early intervention, the research underlying it has become shrouded in a host of methodological and legal concerns. You may wish to consult Garber and Heber (1981), Page and Grandon (1981), and Hernstein (1982) for retrospectives on the project.

A second project that sought to improve the futures of disadvantaged children is the Carolina Abecedarian Project (Ramey & Haskins, 1981; Ramey and Campbell, 1984). The project was initiated in 1972 with infants and children believed to be high-risk for subsequent school failure. Children in the experimental group of the preschool intervention effort were placed in a child-centered, prevention-oriented day care program until the age of 5. The curriculum provided the students was cognitively and socially focused with an emphasis on language development (Ramey & Haskins, 1981). Data summarized a decade after the study had begun (Ramey & Campbell, 1984) indicated that, while children in the experimental group continued to score at or near the national average in critical skill areas, control subjects evidenced a significant achievement gap which began after 18 months of age and persisted throughout formal schooling.

A third project geared to young children was the Ypsilanti Carnegie infant education project (Lambie & Weikart, 1970). Two theoretical assumptions underlay this project: (*a*) preventive intervention must begin even before the preschool years, because that is the time the environment exerts its greatest influence, and (*b*) home teaching for the infant and parent can be the foundation of a successful program.

The basic strategy involved home teaching by public school instructors, who were each assigned to a family and who provided one-to-one instruction with the parents and the child. As the teacher developed a strong relationship with the family, he or she could become keenly aware of the child's development and could provide the parents with relevant information. The program was essentially concerned with promoting the effectiveness of the parents.

Weikart and Lambie (1970) found that home instructional programs have specific advantages which other programs do not provide. They note the following.

1. The convenience to the mother working in her own home aids the success of the program.
2. The information documented by the teacher and provided to the mother is directly related to the mother-child pair.
3. As the mother and teacher develop a trusting relationship, the teacher can give real and genuine information.
4. Based on the working relationship between the teacher and family, the ability to establish a link between family and school is greatly enhanced.

Although the target population for many early intervention programs has been poverty children who are high-risk for later problems, including mild retardation, the trend toward early intervention for the more severely handicapped has certainly also become stronger in the past decade. Although rarely concerned with the virtual prevention of retardation and related handicaps, Allen (1978) and others have noted that this type of intervention often has the following purposes.

1. Provide support to parents and family of the child;

2. Prevent the acquisition of maladaptive forms of behavior (e.g., self-stimulation) that may develop in the absence of appropriate interaction with adults;

3. Ameliorate the severity of the handicap;

4. Prevent the occurrence of secondary handicaps such as emotional disorders and muscular-skeletal disabilities;

5. Acclimate the child to a basic learning routine.

PREVENTION: PERSPECTIVE

Chapter 3 discussed various biomedical preventive procedures that have resulted from more sophisticated scientific knowledge. This chapter highlighted preventive programs related to psychosocial causes. To tie these areas together, Figure 7.3 is a summary of the causes of retardation in a framework based on curative emphasis. Primary prevention refers to the total prevention of a handicapping condition, such as with rubella vaccination, fetal surgery for hydrocephalus, or genetic counseling for

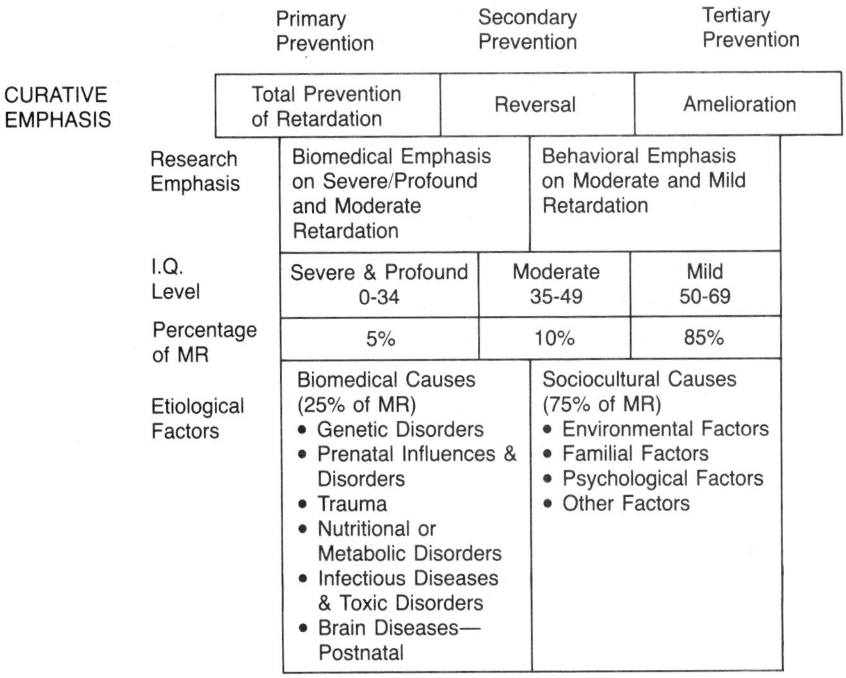

	Primary Prevention	Secondary Prevention	Tertiary Prevention
CURATIVE EMPHASIS	Total Prevention of Retardation	Reversal	Amelioration
Research Emphasis	Biomedical Emphasis on Severe/Profound and Moderate Retardation	Behavioral Emphasis on Moderate and Mild Retardation	
I.Q. Level	Severe & Profound 0-34	Moderate 35-49	Mild 50-69
Percentage of MR	5%	10%	85%
Etiological Factors	Biomedical Causes (25% of MR) • Genetic Disorders • Prenatal Influences & Disorders • Trauma • Nutritional or Metabolic Disorders • Infectious Diseases & Toxic Disorders • Brain Diseases— Postnatal	Sociocultural Causes (75% of MR) • Environmental Factors • Familial Factors • Psychological Factors • Other Factors	

From: Stark, J.A. (1983) The search for cures in mental retardation. In F.J. Menolascino, R. Neman, & J.A. Stark (Eds.), *Curative aspects of mental retardation: Biomedical and behavioral advances.* Baltimore: Paul H. Brooks Publishing Company, © 1983: (Figure 3, page 5, used with permission).

FIGURE 7.3 Prevention of Retardation

recessive trait disorders. Secondary prevention refers to early diagnosis, reversal of the condition, and a cure for a specific disorder. An example is the implementation of a restrictive diet for PKU children. Finally tertiary prevention, which has been the primary focus of this chapter, is ameliorating handicaps and maximizing future development. It includes early intervention programs geared to both parent training and support as well as child development and instruction (Stark, 1983).

Although we have reason to be optimistic about the strides made to combat psychosocial retardation, the successes that have been achieved are tempered by the obvious need for greater commitment in this area. The question remains whether our society is willing to devote the necessary resources to significantly alter the incidence of psychosocial or cultural-familial retardation and thus to significantly reduce the general prevalence of retardation.

Clarke and Clarke (1977) examined the status of preventive measures in the field as related to the PCMR's (1972) doubtlessly optimistic goal of reducing the incidence of retardation by 50% before the end of the 20th century. They conclude that, within the area of pathological causes, major advances have begun to affect the known causes and thus that we can anticipate a substantial decrease in numbers within this smaller group. However, within the much larger domain of mild retardation, Clarke and Clarke conclude that a 50% reduction is not very likely to be achieved, hence dooming any possibility of realizing the PCMR's goal.

One possible source of neglect may be the result of professionals' increased concern for the severely handicapped. As Haywood (1979) notes, the laudable focus in the research given to this previously unserved and virtually ignored population may have inadvertently drawn attention away from mildly retarded children. It is unlikely, however, that this reason could be offered as a source of our lack of general societal commitment. We therefore must look instead to governmental policy.

Certainly one problem is related to the funds earmarked for all handicapped children under P.L. 94–142. Although, in most states, services begin at birth or age 3, many mildly retarded children will not be identified until school age. Therefore, these children are not likely to be classified during early childhood, which would be a prerequisite for benefiting from early intervention services. We certainly do not advocate a wholesale effort to label young children. However, it is critical that we continue to acknowledge that programs for high-risk children make good sense on humanitarian, sociological, and finally financial grounds. As Robinson and Robinson (1976) note, "efforts to improve the life situations of the poor may be the single most important step toward prevent-

See also Sells & Bennett, 1977.

There have been significant decreases in the number of mildly retarded children served in many school districts. This reduction, however, more often reflects stricter diagnostic guidelines (e.g., the increased emphasis on adaptive behavior and the lowering of IQ limitations to 70) rather than the implementation of preventive programs. That is, the population identified as mildly retarded has now changed, and thus the decrease in prevalence. (see Polloway & Smith, 1983).

ing mental handicap" (p. 178). Only through programs and related research (Zigler, 1978) can this significant reduction be achieved.

In conclusion, let us restate the basic premises of this chapter. Although advocates of the genetic stance remain active in proffering ideas concerning the bases for individual differences (see Jensen, 1980), it is apparent that children reared in restricting conditions do not develop and mature as well as their more privileged peers. In a nation wealthy in resources and rich in energetic people, the negative consequences of an unstimulating environment must be diminished through the most promising intervention strategies. As Baroff (1974) notes, "equality of opportunity is a ghastly charade if individuals are so stunted by early experiences as to be unable to take advantage of the opportunities our society offers" (p. 116). By facilitating children's cognitive, academic, social, and emotional development, we increase the chances of having a future population of healthy, self-sufficient, mature adults. Basically, intervention strategies must center on identifying high-risk children and establishing intervention strategies designed to facilitate the development of each individual child.

SUMMARY

Despite the numerous specific biological factors that can be identified as causes of mental retardation, the vast majority of cases stem from unknown causes within the realm of environment and/or polygenic inheritance. The terms *cultural-familial retardation* and *psychosocial disadvantage* refer to the population whose retardation is associated with these factors.

The hereditary position draws from assumptions about the frequency of mild retardation found within specific families. Support for the genetic viewpoint has been drawn from the study of parents and their children, siblings, and, most significantly, from identical twins. This position carries clear implications for biologically oriented intervention measures such as sterilization; therefore, the rationales behind it must be carefully weighed.

The environment position is based on a number of specific factors that may negatively affect development. Specific correlates of retardation would include a host of variables related to poverty, including parenting practices, health problems, linguistic concerns, and daily living difficulties. Classic early intervention studies such as the longitudinal research of Harold Skeels have provided an empirical foundation for this position.

Acceptance of the environmental position or the concept of the interaction between heredity and environment would dictate a commitment to intensive intervention with young children in order to prevent learning problems from beginning. A variety of models such as Head Start and the Milwaukee Project have been developed to accomplish this purpose. Achieving a significant reduction in mild retardation presents a continuing challenge to our nation.

PART THREE
Major Concerns
and Issues

CHAPTER EIGHT

Family Issues

Even though families with a mentally retarded member have been among the leading advocates of the rights of the handicapped, there were very few references to parents in the early mental retardation literature. During the mid-1940s and early 1950s, a few papers dealing with the parents of mentally retarded children began to appear. Since the mid-1950s, the literature dealing with parents of the mentally retarded has vastly grown. Several factors have contributed to this increased concern, one of which was the formation of the President's Panel on Mental Retardation in 1961 by President Kennedy. This panel provided considerable impetus for research and development into the prevention of mental retardation, the care, education, and rehabilitation of affected individuals, and the development of more comprehensive community-centered clinical and social services. The emphasis that the President's Panel placed upon community-based services influenced the amount of attention given to parents and families of mentally retarded individuals. However, because of the Panel's broad scope of action, its effect upon parents may have been a bit diffuse.

A second major cause of increased professional attention to parents is research on the influence of the home environment on child

---

This chapter was contributed by Diane Browder, Eric D. Jones, and James R. Patton.

development. Early research revealed the detrimental effects of environ-mental deprivation (e.g., in institutions of that era) and the benefits of early stimulation (see Hess & Shipman, 1965; Skeels, 1966; Skeels & Dye, 1939; Spitz, 1945, 1946a, b). This research spurred development of early intervention programs and encouraged the prevailing view that the home is a more favorable environment than an institution. More recently, Nihira, Meyers, and Mink (1983) have demonstrated the influ-ence of the home environment on the mentally retarded child and vice versa. Literature also supports the benefits of parent involvement in the child's educational program (e.g., Adubato, Adams, & Budd, 1981; Cheseldine & McConkey, 1979; Miller & Sloane, 1976; Salzberg & Vil-lani, 1983; Schreibman, O'Neill, & Koegel, 1983).

A third, and probably the most important, factor in bringing par-ents to the attention of professionals has been the vastly increased politi-cal strength of the parents. During the past two and a half decades, individual parents and parent organizations, such as the Association for Retarded Citizens, fought in the courts and lobbied in state and federal legislatures to secure basic legal rights for their children. In the vast majority of the cases, they have been successful. In summary, it has taken a combination of enlightenment through research and demonstra-tions of political clout to bring the parents of mentally retarded individu-als to the attention of professionals. While it is regrettable that this atten-tion has been so long in coming, it has, happily, arrived.

PROBLEMS IN RESEARCH TECHNIQUES

Although the issues concerning families of mentally retarded persons are now receiving more attention, they frequently are presented with judgments and generalizations that cannot be made from the existing research. In the last few years authors have noted the shortcomings of previous research and have begun to take new approaches to defining and meeting family needs (e.g., Blacher, 1984; Beckmen-Brindley & Snell, 1984; Nihira, Meyers, & Mink, 1983).

One methodological problem in previous research is the tendency to make statements about "families" based on research with one family or a few parents (e.g., Emde & Brown, 1978). While the study of small samples can reveal useful insights for similar families, the generalizabil-ity of the findings probably does not extend to the widely heterogeneous group of people with mentally retarded family members.

A second methodological problem is in the conceptualizations of the family. Research assumed that the family consisted of the traditional members (father, mother, children). Further, one member, the mother, has been studied alone to make inferences about the family unit. Even when a traditional family structure exists and the mother provides most of the care for the mentally retarded member, the mother should not be viewed in isolation from the family unit (Beckman-Brindley & Snell, 1984). Within the family unit, relationships exist between the various family members. For example, the mother has a relationship with her spouse, her nonhandicapped children, and the mentally retarded child. Her relationship with her mentally retarded child is influenced by her other relationships. Besides the omission of family-centered research, studies have not kept pace with the changing demographic patterns of families in our society.

FAMILY PATTERNS

Single-Parent Families Most public policy is built around the image of the traditional family. The discrepancy between that image and the reality of many families seems to be increasing. Coates (1978) reported that the number of families headed by females has increased more than 250% since 1950. The number of children who live with a single mother increased by approximately 40% between 1970 and 1976. Coates predicts "approximately 45% of the children born in 1976 will have lived with a single parent for some time before reaching 18 years of age" (p. 35). The increasing number of single-parent families appears to be an important consideration for agencies which provide services to the mentally retarded—especially when family intervention is involved. As there is very little research on single-parent families with mentally retarded members, we have no adequate means for policy makers to analyze and program for the needs of these families.

Young Mothers Females under the age of 15 currently constitute the only group in the United States with a significant expansion in birth rate (Coates, 1978). Mothers who are in their early teenage years contribute 20% of the live births each year. And 80% of the high-risk infants born each year are born to mothers under 15 years of age. In addition to a variety of congenital defects which identify at-risk infants, there is a higher probability that these infants will not be cared for as well as if they had been born to an older and more experienced woman.

Fathers As women increasingly have sought employment outside the home, men have begun to take on more responsibilities in the home. When fathers have been included in parent-child interventions, their contributions have been beneficial (see Bronfenbrenner, 1974; Heber & Garber, 1967; Lindsley, 1966). Ironically, in most studies which report the positive effects of the fathers' participation, their participation was not sought. Research is needed to identify the nature of the relationship of fathers to their mentally retarded children and their most effective involvement in intervention programs.

The following examples, based on real people, illustrate this complexity of family patterns. In Family A, the unit consists of a recently divorced father and a three-year-old mentally retarded son. The father's mother (also single) provides respite care on weekends. During the day the father is employed as a laborer and takes his son to a day care center. The father is considering marriage with a woman who has two school-aged children. In Family B, the unit consists of a father, mother, an older son, and a mentally retarded daughter. The mother cares for the children and home full-time. Although the father works outside the home in a service profession, his hours and work place are flexible, so he can return home during the day if needed. In Family C, the unit consists of two parents with professional careers outside the home. They have two young children and have recently adopted a mentally retarded adult woman whose parents are dead. This woman is employed during the day. The children are in school and day care. In Family D, the mother has two mentally retarded children. She recently separated from her husband, who was physically abusive to her and the children. The mother receives little support from her parents, who live in another state. She has applied for welfare.

Obviously, many more family patterns could be described. However, these four examples illustrate how family issues concerning the mentally retarded member cannot be separated from the family structure. This family structure can influence attitudes and resources for providing an optimal family environment for the mentally retarded member.

As the concept of the family broadens, so does the concept of which member(s) in the family can participate in the education of the mentally retarded member. In the traditional family concept, the mother is viewed as the one who has the time and responsibility to provide home training. However, recent research has included both parents (Fox & Roseen, 1977; Holmes, 1982; Singh, 1980), fathers only (Cheseldine & McConkey, 1979), and siblings (Angney & Hanley, 1979; Sobsey & Bieniek, 1983; Colletti & Harris, 1977). If this trend is extended to other family members with the skills and resources to contribute to a child's education, research could emerge with grandparents, aunts or uncles, or long term, live-in family friends.

A third methodological problem in the research to date has been the type of dependent variable and measurement used. For example, a popular approach has been to use questionnaires to assess parents' attitudes. Parents may answer such questionnaires with what they perceive to be the preferred answer, rather than with their true feelings. Additionally, even the identification of "true" feelings does not reveal the short and long term events influencing these feelings. Crnic, Friedrich, and Greenberg (1983) have suggested the need to examine families in their environments. Direct observation of families' skills, preferences, and resources may provide the most useful information for families and professionals.

A fourth methodological problem has been the search for pathology in families with a mentally retarded member. While a mentally retarded member *may* require more resources and *may* create stress if family resources are limited, the *a priori* assumption that a mentally retarded member has a detrimental effect on a family can bias the focus and results of research. Few studies have explored the contribution the mentally retarded person has made to the family. Nor has the literature described families who are bonded together by the entry of a special child. One resource for such research is families like example C, who choose to adopt a mentally retarded person.

Begab (1969) commented on the variance noticed in different groups of parents:

> Most [parents of the mentally retarded] are normal average, well-adjusted people, some are maladjusted; others are neurotic, mentally incapacitated, or intellectually inadequate. They differ greatly in their usefulness to the community, in their personal adjustment, in their capacity for parenthood, and in their skill in handling life's many problems—including mental retardation. (p. 74)

Given that families differ greatly, families with a mentally retarded member share some challenges. Depending on family resources, these challenges may be greater for some than others. Although this chapter cannot describe every issue a family might face, it is intended to help parents and professionals identify and meet challenges in a family with a mentally retarded member.

FAMILY ADAPTATION

Adjustment to a mentally retarded child has been a topic of much of the literature on families. Blacher (1984) reviewed 24 such articles that suggested stages of adjustment. For example, Emde and Brown (1978) described attachment between the mother and special child as including the stages of: 1) denial, 2) mourning, and 3) development of acceptance. Rosen (1955) described five stages including: 1) awareness of the problem, 2) recognition of the problem, 3) seeking for the cause, 4) seeking for the solution, and 5) acceptance of the problem. While the presence of a mentally retarded person does require family adjustment, the process is an evolving one influenced by many factors besides the parent and child (e.g., financial resources, educational opportunities, social support). In reviewing the research on family adjustment, Blacher (1984) noted the numerous methodological flaws in this research and questioned the usefulness of describing stages of adjustment.

Similarly, Crnic, Friedrich, and Greenberg (1983) criticized the tendency of professionals to classify families' adjustment. Rather, Crnic et al. (1983) suggested that professionals look at adaptations to stress and the family's coping resources and ecological environments as systems to mediate the family's response to stress. A good approach to understanding family adaptation is to examine some potential phases and study how families may alleviate their stress during each.

INITIAL DIAGNOSIS

In a complex society like ours, which places such a high premium on the skills attributed to intelligence, the realization that a child is mentally retarded can be a disappointment to parents. Raech (1966) has said that one of the most trying emotional experiences a couple could ever face is the diagnosis of their child's mental retardation. Obviously, facing such a diagnosis as a single parent could be especially difficult.

Prior to a diagnosis, parents may suspect that something is wrong. In two studies (Carr, 1970; Drillien & Wilkinson, 1964), almost half the mothers of children with Down syndrome suspected something was wrong with their children before a formal diagnosis was provided. However, the exact nature of the disability may not concur with the parents' suspicion. Depending on which of the child's behaviors seem different or abnormal to the parents, the parents may suspect a medical problem, deafness, or behavior or learning problems.

The term *mental retardation* may not be understood by the parent. The parent of a mildly retarded child may associate the term with the physical characteristics of Down Syndrome or the skill deficits of the severely retarded child. To this parent, the term *mentally retarded* may seem inappropriate for a child who perhaps does not look different and

A UNIQUE PARENTAL PERSPECTIVE

We who work with retarded people are always inspired by parents who do those things which make their retarded child a significant part of the family. It is typical for proud new parents to send out birth announcements of their new family member. Usually, these announcements are full of excitement and satisfaction. But how do you tell people that your newborn is re-tarded? Most of the time, this information is carefully disguised or withheld. To be sure, this is not an easy task nor one that parents enjoy doing.

Sometimes interesting items come to our attention and we do not know from where they came or who gave them to us; the following material falls into this category. It is a real birth announcement, but its authors are unknown. It demonstrates one of the most positive parental attitudes we have seen. We have omitted information such as the child's name, date, and time of birth because it is not necessary; the important message is contained within the parents' words. This retarded child is lucky to be introduced into a family like this one.

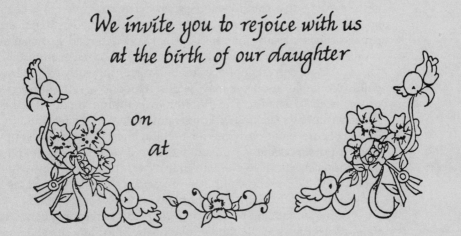

We invite you to rejoice with us
at the birth of our daughter

on

at

It is our belief as Latter-day Saints that we all lived a pre-earth life with our Heavenly Father. Certain valiant spirits were selected at that time for special missions during an earth life. One of these spirits has been chosen for our family. Our daughter is a child with Down's Syndrome. We feel privileged to be entrusted with the care of this special child, who will return to her Heavenly Father at the end of her earth life and resume, for all eternity, her valiant status with her body and intellect completely restored.

who has some academic skills. Even the parents of a severely retarded child may assume the term means an inability to learn, which does not apply to their child.

When professionals describe parental "acceptance" of the diagnosis, it may be unclear what parental behaviors are expected to reflect "acceptance." An adaptation that *is* required is for parents to seek or accept education and treatment for their child. These services are often associated with a classification system. For example, to receive most special education services the child must be classified as handicapped. If professionals classify the child as mentally retarded to make services available, the parents must agree for the child to receive these services. Or, parents of a preschool-age child may seek out early treatment for the child. Available resources may be designated as serving the *handicapped* or the *mentally retarded*. The parent may continue to question the use of the term *mentally retarded* while agreeing to the child's receipt of services. Or, to secure better services for a child, the parent may "shop" for a different diagnosis (e.g., autism, learning disabilities). Since our special education classification system is imprecise, the parent may obtain more than one label for the child. These various parental responses can be viewed as adaptive, since they obtain services for the child.

Professional actions that may help the parent are: 1) to refer the parent to services at the time of diagnosis; 2) to state the child's level of disability honestly, including acknowledgment of the imprecisions in classification and the variability of children's progress; 3) to emphasize the child's strengths and similarities to other children; and 4) to refer the parents to "experienced" parents and other professionals who can help them locate resources to cope with the challenges. Professional actions that may hinder the parents' adaptation are: 1) to withhold from the parents information on labels that will be used for the child with and by other professionals; 2) to criticize the parents if they do not use the same labels for their child that professionals prefer; 3) to provide a label without information about its characteristics or potential services; 4) to refer to the child by label rather than by name (e.g., "your mentally retarded child" versus "Jane"); or 5) to deny that the child has special life-long needs.

The process of adapting to receipt of special services after receiving the child's diagnosis probably will not be an immediate or easy one, even with professional support. Other ecological variables also impinge on this process. Dr. Philip Roos (1975), former executive director of the Association for Retarded Citizens (ARC) and father of a mentally retarded child, describes several parental feelings. Following Roos' (1975) descriptions are examples of ecological variables that could contribute to these feelings.

1. *Loss of self-esteem.* A defect in one's child may be interpreted as a defect in one's self, particularly when a parent identifies closely with his child. Life goals may be abruptly and radically altered, including loss of the fantasy of immortality through one's children.

2. *Shame.* Parents may anticipate social rejection, pity, or ridicule and related loss of prestige. Social withdrawal may be a common consequence.

3. *Ambivalence.* The simultaneous experience of love and hatred normally experienced by parents toward their children is likely to be greatly intensified toward a retarded child. The retarded child's relative lack of achievement and tendency toward irritating behavior are likely to be sources of continuing parental frustration. Frustration, in turn, generates anger and resentment which may lead to death wishes toward the child and feelings of rejection, typically accompanied by guilt. Inconsistent behavior, sometimes alternating between rejection and overprotection, can be expected.

4. *Depression.* Chronic feelings of sorrow are to be anticipated as a nonpathological reaction to having a mentally retarded child. Most parents are disappointed in their child and are concerned about his future. To some, mental retardation symbolizes the child's death, and hence precipitates a brief reaction similar to that associated with the loss of a loved one.

5. *Self-sacrifice.* Some parents adopt a "martyr" attitude and sacrifice all personal pleasures for the child. The retarded child may become the focus of such parents' total interests, often to the detriment of other family members. Family disruption, including marital conflicts, may accompany this pattern. The retarded child may become the focus of mutual blame and criticism by the parents.

6. *Defensiveness.* Parents may become acutely sensitive to implied criticism of their child and may react with resentment and belligerence. In extreme cases, parents may deny the existence of the retardation, rationalize the child's shortcomings, and seek professional opinions to substantiate their own contention that "there is really nothing wrong" with their child. (pp. 343–44)

FROM BEING A PROFESSIONAL TO BEING A PARENT

It is difficult indeed to convey adequately what it is like to have a son or daughter who is severely mentally retarded. Unless we actually are in such a situation, then we *really* can't experience the trials, frustrations, successes, and other feelings that are part of daily life with a severely handicapped child. The following comments of Ann Turnbull, excerpted from *Parents Speak Out*—a collection of writings by parents of handicapped children who are also professionals in the field—express her experiences of living with her severely handicapped stepson. Her words effectively relate some of her feelings concerning the "ups and downs" of being a parent of a handicapped child. What makes these selections especially poignant is that Ann is an eminent special educator who professionally works with parents of handicapped children. Her story illustrates the transition from being a professional to being a parent.

I can vividly recall when I spoke 3 years ago to an interagency committee in a nearby community on the topic of deinstitutionalization. At the time I was a strong advocate for the quick return home of substantial numbers of mentally retarded persons from state institutions. [At one point, Ann remarked that she couldn't understand how certain parents could oppose having their child return home.] Immediately a mother of a mentally retarded son flew to her feet and began berating me in front of the group. While shaking her finger in my face, she screamed, "Do you know what it is like to live with a mentally retarded child?" I felt both embarrassed and defensive. After trying to explain my comment, I responded (probably in somewhat of a self-righteous way), "No, I don't know what it is like, but in 2 weeks I will begin to find out. My husband and I will be bringing his mentally retarded son home from an institution." She smiled at me as if to say, "Are you ever in for it"; yet my confidence in approaching the new parental roles and responsibilities was unshaken. I had three degrees in special education with an emphasis in mental retardation, several years of teaching experience in public schools and a residential institution, and was on the university faculty. Being with mentally retarded children was a way of life for me. I thought to myself, "Just wait. I will show you that it really is not all that difficult to be a parent."

Rud [Ann's husband] and I took a leisurely trip through New England and picked Jay up on our return at his school in Massachusetts [Jay's first day of deinstitutionalization]. We were very happy to see him and filled with excitement and anticipation as we packed his things in the car. After a tearful good-bye to Sue and Dom D'Antuono, we started the trip back home to North Carolina. We stopped early on the first afternoon at a motel, so we could have a relaxing swim before dinner. As we approached the pool, Jay's temper tantrum started, and it did not end for a seeming eternity. He kicked and screamed and cried. Finally, when he calmed down, he got in the pool but would not budge from clenching the railing on the side. A girl much younger than Jay was swimming laps beside him. Her father, who was beaming with pride and clapping at her performance, turned to me and said, "Do you always have this much trouble with him?" I absolutely froze. I could not muster any kind of response. I wanted to shout, "Give me time. I've been his mother for less than a day." I choked my tears back and insisted that we go back to the room. Throughout the remainder of the trip home, the question kept echoing in my mind, "Do you always have this much trouble with him?"

For one who thought she knew, the last 3 years have, indeed, been a humbling experience. The 24-hour reality test has standards far higher than any examination I ever took while earning my three degrees. In fact, the three degrees may have been more a hindrance than a help in meeting my new parental responsibilities. I had always been taught to be objective and to consider the facts of a situation. All of a sudden, I had an ache in my heart, a knot in my stomach, and tears welling in my eyes. It did not take long for it to dawn on me that the mother from the interagency meeting was right—I was in for a startling experience.

In Jay's first months home, I faced many of the emotional reactions that parents typically encounter immediately after the birth of a handicapped child. Almost all of my friends were professionals whose work related to the developmental problems of children. Many of them reacted to Jay as a patient or client, rather than as a child. I became very angry at their offhand remarks, and as a result, some of my closest friendships were abruptly ended. One friend commented, "I've never seen a child with such a big head." Another said, "Doesn't Jay remind you of an autistic child, the way he stares off in space?" I was very confused . . . and felt alienated from many of my professional colleagues who were advising me to be objective and to remove myself from the emotion of the situation. In many encounters I was getting the message that they thought I was an obnoxious and hostile parent. I had been on the inside long enough to know what professionals think about parents who refuse their advice. I could remember having those feelings myself about parents. That's what really hurt. I felt both parental anger and sorrow over some of my own professional mistakes in previous interactions with parents.

What goes on in training programs in the name of education is sometimes shocking. It has become very prevalent in special education departments of colleges and universities to offer courses on working with parents. I cringe at the thought of some of the course syllabi I have reviewed. In many of these courses, very limited attention is directed toward helping parents solve the day-to-day problems which almost invariably are encountered, yet weeks are devoted to the "psychological insight approach to parental guilt." Many such courses are a fraud and tend to insure further conflict and unsatisfactory relationships between parents and professionals. *Extended practicum with families of handicapped children and the provision of respite care for families should be standard requirements* for courses which purport to prepare students for working with parents [emphasis added].

Moving from a professional to a parental role has been a sometimes painful and difficult task for me. It has caused me to engage in tremendous self-examination. Being Jay's mother has also resulted in an extended growth process for me. As much as anything, I have learned how much I do not know. Now, I am ready to learn.

TABLE 8.1 Examples of Ecological Variables

Variables	Potential Reactions
1. —Strangers stare or make negative comments about the child —Friends and other family members have children without handicaps who receive positive comments from family and strangers —Caring for the child requires forfeiting a career or other plans —Grandparents or neighbors aren't willing to babysit this child —Handicap was inherited from parent	Loss of Self-Esteem
2. —Parents recall an action during pregnancy or childbirth that they consider the cause —Family or strangers suggest that parents are somehow to blame	Shame or Guilt
3. —Child does not cuddle or smile until later in infancy —Child has disturbing behaviors: cries a lot as an infant, has intense tantrums —Child requires a great deal of caretaking time —Friends and family do not find the child appealing	Ambivalence
4. —Child has a degenerative disease —Child does not reach an expected developmental milestone —Parents' attempts to teach the child new skills are unsuccessful —Friends and family offer no support or support that doesn't relate to current stress —Loss of spouse or deterioration of marital intimacy.	Depression
5. —Religious institution, family, or others encourage large commitment of time and other resources —Relationships with family members or friends are strained	Self-Sacrifice
6. —Parents receive a lot of criticism from acquaintances, family, professionals —Parents' values differ from others (e.g., different lifestyle than professional) —Parents' skills or information are not credible to professional	Defensiveness

As these examples suggest, many events outside the parents may influence the parents' adaptations to their child. As parents gain strategies to cope with the ecological variables, their adaptation process can be enhanced.

SKILLS TO COPE

After the child has been diagnosed, the parents continue to face the challenges of the child's special needs. Recent studies have shown the increased stress experienced by these families (Beckman, 1983; Friedrich & Friedrich, 1981; Holroyd & McArthur, 1976). For example, Beckman (1983) looked at the influence of certain child characteristics on stress. The five characteristics included rate of child progress, responsiveness, temperament, repetitive behavior patterns, and the presence of additional or unusual caregiving demands. All characteristics except rate of progress were related to the stress reported by parents. The types of stress reported included parent problems such as poor health or mood, excess time demands, negative attitude toward the child, overprotection, lack of social support, overcommitment, and pessimism; and family problems such as lack of family integration, limits on family opportunities, and financial problems.

Although families respond differently to stress, little information exists on how families with mentally retarded members can buffer or mediate stress. One approach might be to acquire skills to teach the mentally retarded person new skills and to manage problem behaviors. Numerous studies have demonstrated that parents can be effective teachers to their mentally retarded child (e.g., Casey, 1978; Filler, 1976; Sobsey & Bieniek, 1983) and can change the child's socially inappropriate behaviors (Adubato, Adams, & Budd, 1981; Luiselli, 1978). Siblings also can be effective teachers (e.g., Angney & Hanley, 1979; Colletti & Harris, 1977). Helping a mentally retarded person acquire new skills may make family life more pleasurable (e.g., if tantrums are reduced) and may make the family member who teaches feel competent.

Unfortunately, most of the research with families of mentally retarded individuals has focused only on family training to help the special member improve. This training may not buffer other stress and, in contrast, may create more stress as family time is invested in this manner. What the family also needs are strategies to supplement skills as teachers and to help balance teaching with overall family functioning.

Folkman, Schaefer, and Lazarus (1979) have delineated five types of coping resources that they hypothesize can moderate the effects of stress. Crnic, Friedrich, and Greenberg (1983) further suggest that these resources may help families cope with the stress that may arise in adapting to a mentally retarded family member. First, the physical and mental health of a family member (e.g., parent) may help the individual cope with the stress of caretaking, behavior management, school conferences, and so on that are required with a mentally retarded member. Second, problem-solving skills, including the ability to search for and analyze information and generate various courses of action, can help the family member in either a crisis or a long-term problem situation (e.g., the child is approaching 21 and will finish school). Third, social networks of supportive relationships can help families maintain community involvement and cope with problems. Fourth, utilitarian resources, such as income and SES, have been linked to family adaptation by Nihira et al. (1983) and Farber (1970). The final resource Folkman et al. (1979) suggest as a coping resource is the individual's personal beliefs including feelings of self-efficacy and belief in some higher purpose (e.g., religious faith). It is important to remember that the influence of these resources is hypothetical. Future research with families should evaluate their impact.

While the coping resources mentioned can be changed by the family members, other ecological variables that may influence ongoing adaptation can be more difficult to alter. Bronfenbrenner (1977) has described four levels of influence on the individual including: 1) interactions within immediate settings like home, school, or work; 2) interrelations among major settings; 3) the formal and informal social structures like neighborhoods, governmental agencies, and school systems; and 4) the ideological institutional patterns of the culture and subcultures (e.g., "the American work ethic"). These various systems influence the individual's access to coping resources and can introduce variables that may not change in the family's lifetime. For example, resources for a community's needed adult programs may require public awareness and legislative action. In such a community, aging parents may find no acceptable solutions for their mentally retarded adult child's need for a long-term residence. Parents may become understandably frustrated and angry. Hentoff (1977) provides a graphic illustration of a father's reaction to the failure of a system to meet the needs of his child.

> At one of the first New York City Board of Education meetings I went to, a black father got up to speak. He had been a school dropout in the south, I learned later, came north, worked at a string of menial jobs, and eventually wound up in a dead-end factory slot which paid him some ninety dollars a week. His hope was his child, and he had watched her fall farther and farther behind each year of school.
>
> The black father was very angry. "You people," he said to the board, "operate a goddamn monopoly, like the telephone company. I got no choice where I send my child to school. I can

only send her where it's free. And she's not learning. Damn it, that's *your* responsibility, it's the principal's responsibility, it's the teacher's responsibility that she's not learning.''

The more or less distinguished members of the Board of Education looked on impassively.

"When you fail, when everybody fails my child"—the father's voice had gotten thick with rage and no little grief—"what happens? Nothing. Nobody gets fired. Nothing happens to nobody except my child." (p. 4)

PLANNING THE FUTURE

In a recent movie entitled *The Natural*, a baseball player must cope with life not turning out like he expected it to. When a family has a mentally retarded child, unless chosen through adoption, the child is not what the parents expected. A child is often viewed by a parent as an investment in the future or a claim to immortality. While the mentally retarded child may have many accomplishments, he or she is less likely to follow the career and family dreams of the parent than other children might. Olshansky (1962, 1966) describes the feeling parents of a mentally retarded child have as chronic sorrow. As mentioned in the previous section, these feelings are not "neurotic" but, rather, are a reaction to conditions of our society that are difficult or impossible to change. For example, the mentally retarded person probably will face personal prejudice and discrimination in services and employment.

Planning for the mentally retarded person's future and the future of the family can be difficult. When the child is very young, parents often cannot predict the child's eventual level of independence. Older parents worry about their own health and mortality. Providing parents with answers to the questions presented earlier in this chapter can help parents know what to expect. Referring parents to older parents may help them anticipate and plan for the future.

It seems to be as difficult for many professionals to accept the concept of chronic sorrow as it is for the parents of mentally retarded children to accept (on terms dictated by professionals) the fact that their child is mentally retarded. The concept of acceptance, as it is frequently viewed by professionals, is tied to the notion that parents of mentally handicapped children go through stages of increased acceptance, until they finally reach a point of mature acceptance. Many descriptions of different stages have been published, but, as mention previously, there is little solid evidence to suggest that parents actually progress through stages. Also, there is a tendency to make value judgments about a given parent's ability to cope with a child's retardation. In the absence of empirical support for a hierarchy of stages of acceptance, it would be invalid and potentially destructive to subscribe to that notion. A more acceptable idea would be periodic acceptance or adjustment, which is

For a detailed discussion of possible stages of acceptance, see Wolfensberger, 1975.

influenced by families' coping resources and the systems in which they function. Throughout their lives as parents of a mentally retarded child, the parents may have a wide range of reactions. It is important to remember that they probably do not pass through those reactions in any exact sequence. Rather, their behaviors and feelings are apt to be influenced by various problems confronting them. For example, obtaining certain services for their elementary school child may help them temporarily adjust to certain problems. Later, perhaps when the child displays signs of sexual activity, these same parents may react again with frustration, apparent guilt, or any of a number of other similar crisis reactions. It may helpful and (we believe) appropriate to consider parent acceptance of their child's mental retardation as cyclical, dependent upon the presenting problem. Thus the idea of recurring distress or chronic sor-

CONCERNS OF NONRETARDED SIBLINGS

The effects on parents of having a retarded member in the family have been documented in many different places; however, the effects of this member on the nonretarded siblings has received much less attention. Siblings also have concerns and questions about their handicapped brother or sister. Unfortunately, their confusion often remains because special education professionals have not tried to explain the situation to them or answer their questions.

Powell and Ogle (1985) have identified seven major areas about which nonhandicapped siblings may have concerns, voiced or not, and list examples of questions these nonhandicapped siblings might have. While Powell and Ogle were considering handicapped children in general, their examples are appropriate to situations where a family member is retarded.

Concern	Question
Cause of the handicap	Why is my sister handicapped?
	What caused the handicap?
	Will future brothers and sisters also be handicapped?
	Whose fault is it?
The child's feelings	Is my brother in pain?
	Does he have the same feelings I do?
	What does he think about?
	Does he know me?
	Does he love me and my parents?
	Why does he behave so strangely?

row becomes believable, and a more useful approach. A caring professional will try to be sensitive to the way the parent is reacting to any given problem, and provide the needed support or send the parents to someone else who can help them deal with their feelings as well as the current situation.

PARENT-PROFESSIONAL RELATIONSHIPS

The range of reactions expressed by parents of handicapped children reflects the difficulties they confront in attempting to meet their own needs and those of their children. Society has charged parents with the responsibility of raising handsome, healthy, intelligent, and socially adequate children. Not only are parents expected to raise those children, they are expected to maintain their own emotional stability while doing

Prognosis	Can my sister be cured?
	Will she improve?
	Can she grow out of this?
	Can treatment really help?
Needed services	What special help will he need?
	Who are these professionals who work with him?
	What do they do with him?
How to help	What am I supposed to do with my sister?
	What can I expect from her?
	Can I help teach her?
	How can I interact with her?
	Should I protect her?
Where the child lives	Why does my brother live at home?
	Wouldn't an institution be better for him?
	Why doesn't he live at home?
	Aren't institutions bad for handicapped persons?
The future	What will happen to my sister in the future?
	Will she always be with us?
	Will she go to school?
	Will she get married and have a family?
	Will she ever live on her own?

Source: Howell, T.H., & Ogle, P.A. (1985). *Brothers & sisters—A special part of exceptional families*. Baltimore: Paul H. Brookes Publishing, pp. 45–46.

it. When they encounter problems rearing their children, most parents seek advice and counsel from a variety of sources, including their own parents, friends, relatives, and the popular media. The advice they receive may be helpful, it may be irrelevant, or at times it may be out of fashion; but most parents cope fairly well with the task of raising their children and obtaining appropriate advice.

Parents of mentally retarded children feel the same social pressures as parents of normal children. However, meeting those demands is a much more difficult assignment. Much of the advice which is available to parents of normal children is often not as useful to parents of the handicapped children. Common sense is often not sufficient for coping with unusual problems. In many cases, the parents of mentally retarded children come to the conclusion that they cannot effectively meet their own needs and the needs of their child without professional help.

PARENT-PROFESSIONAL PARTNERSHIP

If relationships between professionals and parents can be designed with cooperation and coordination in mind, many family needs can be met. During the initial stage of the relationship, the parents and the professionals should identify and agree upon (a) the child's eligibility and needs for service, (b) the short- and long-term objectives of treatment, and (c) the priorities for treatment. Unless the parents and professionals can basically agree on the needs of the child and the objectives and priorities for treatment, the relationship will probably not be productive.

Agreement on the needs of the child and the nature of suggested programming is necessary, but not sufficient, for a good working relationship. The professional and the parents must work together to maximize the child's development. Effective coordination of efforts may be more readily obtained if the parents and the professionals can all identify and agree upon their respective roles. Heward, Dardig, and Rossett (1979) list seven roles commonly assumed by parents of handicapped children. Those roles are (a) teaching, (b) counseling, (c) managing behavior, (d) parenting nonhandicapped siblings, (e) maintaining the parent-to-parent relationship, (f) educating significant others (such as relatives and neighbors), and (g) relating to the school and community. Without even listing the roles of various professionals, it should be apparent that many roles are held in common by parents and professionals. Most mentally retarded children spend a greater portion of their time with their parents than with professionals. Since parents have access to a wide variety of potential reinforcers, the child can be provided with an effective program, if the professionals and the parents can coordinate their efforts. The child will make maximal progress if any instructional program is consistently administered in both school and home settings.

Interchange of information is extremely important to maintain a productive treatment program, as both parties need to be aware of the child's progress in each setting. When changes in the program are sought, both parties should be informed. A parent-professional relationship which meets the preceding criteria may not be easy to develop, may be difficult to maintain, and may not produce the desired results as quickly as might be wished. Despite these problems, the development of a good parent-professional relationship is advantageous for the welfare of the child. Neither professional nor parents alone can provide a comprehensive and consistent program; they must work as partners. Turnbull (1978), stepmother of a mentally retarded child and professional special educator, has offered suggestions for professionals who work with parents. They include

1. Professionals must acquire humility and the honesty to say "I don't know."
2. Courses on working with families of the retarded should include a practicum with families of the handicapped and should teach skills to help parents solve day-to-day problems of living with a retarded child.
3. Respect is an essential ingredient in the parent-professional relationship.
4. Parents and professionals must work together if handicapped children are to reach their full potential.
5. Handicapped children need to have personal relationships with individuals outside the family. These relationships are also important to assure the parents that others love their child and seek opportunities to be with him or her. (adapted from pp. 136–140)

Professional Mishandling of Parents Unfortunately, parents of retarded children have not always received the help they need from professionals. Roos (1975) contends that too often professionals deal with parents in an unproductive and pejorative manner.

Problems of Obtaining Diagnosis Parents frequently have difficulty with professionals when they seek a diagnosis of their child's condition. While parents may already suspect retardation, the actual diagnosis can be a very upsetting experience, as we have discussed. Diagnosticians are often keenly aware of the parents' anxieties, and they too may feel considerable anxiety when delivering the diagnosis. Unfortunately, the attempts of some professionals to reduce their own anxiety in addition to the anxieties of parents sometimes result in mishandling of the diagnostic process (MacMillan, 1977). Roos (1975) claims that the professionals, operating from the medical model, often consider mental retardation to be an uncurable condition.

They (professionals) generate self-fulfilling and self-limiting prophecies which threaten to mitigate [sic] against the development of mentally retarded persons. Parents are usually sensitive to such defeatist attitudes and either adopt similar expectations or resent those who hold negative expectations toward their child. (p. 341)

Recent research supports Roos's claim. Abramson, Gravink, Abramson, and Sommers (1977) surveyed 215 families whose preschool children were diagnosed as mentally retarded. Of the sample, 94% sought advice from medical doctors. Only 18% of the families in the sample indicated that they received sympathetic and informative advice. Regarding the nature of the advice, Abramson et al. report

For the most part advice consisted of an objective and clinical portrayal of the situation (27%), another referral (24%), or an attempt to minimize the symptoms (14%). A bleak prognosis, misinformation, and [advice to] love [and] treat the child as a normal child accounted for 9%, 5%, and 3% respectively. (p. 29)

It is not surprising that the responses of 51% of the families ranged from feelings of great dissatisfaction to uncertainty about the advice they had received. Considering that most physicians have not been given extensive training regarding the nonmedical care and treatment of mentally retarded persons, it is not surprising that they do not provide parents with adequate nonmedical service. Most of the problems involved in rearing a mentally retarded child are not primarily medical problems.

Abramson et al. (1977) did find that the parents were more satisfied with the medical services than with the nonmedical services provided by physicians; "77% of the sample was either satisfied or very satisfied with the medical treatment their child had received" (p. 29). Other writers (for example, Carr, 1974; MacMillan, 1977; Wolfensberger, 1967; Zwerling, 1954) report that callous and insensitive treatment frequently accompanies the negative and hopeless type of diagnosis. It is certainly possible that some professionals may present a stern or callous attitude as a defense against their own anxiety. In other cases, they may feel that they have to convey the diagnosis as a grim reality to the parents in order to force them into action.

In deference to medical personnel, we must acknowledge that there are many persons very knowledgeable of nonmedical matters; we hope that there will be more interchange between the two groups in the future. We must also remember that physicians are not responsible for most diagnoses of mental retardation. Educational agencies are responsible for most of the diagnoses. Physicians usually diagnose the more severe cases of mental retardation, or cases accompanied by physical features or disabilities, when the child is young. Educators and administrators who represent educational agencies have also mishandled a great many parents who were seeking services for their children. They have just managed to do it with a little less notoriety.

Jensen (1950) has reported another frequently occurring error in the diagnostic process. Too often professionals encourage parents to be overly optimistic. Eventually, the reality of the child's limitations becomes apparent and the result is disillusioned parents. False encouragement also tends to delay diagnosis. And without diagnosis, needed services may not be available for the affected child or other family members.

There is some justification for a delay in diagnosis if the diagnostician suspects, but is not certain, that the child is retarded. In those instances a re-examination or further referral is appropriate. Diagnosticians should be aware, however, that delays and additional referrals can cause parents to "shop around." Anderson (1971) defines "shopping" as

> The retarded child's parents making visits to the same professional or to a number of professionals in such a manner that one visit follows another without resolution of a resolvable problem. (p. 3)

While some professionals regard "shopping" as symptomatic of the parents' inability to accept the diagnosis, others (including Anderson, 1971; Keirn, 1971; Roos, 1975) claim that shopping may indicate a search for services. Keirn (1971) arbitrarily defines a shopping parent as one who pursues a third professional evaluation. He surveyed 218 families and found that only six—less than 3% of the families—could then be identified as "shoppers." Consultations with different professionals should take place if the intent is to provide a thorough diagnosis and comprehensive services. The number of parents who shop for magic cures may be so minimal that the negative connotation of the term probably does not fit the majority of the parents seeking additional professional services. Much assistance could be given to parents if one professional would consolidate previous evaluations and encourage them to return for services (Keirn, 1971).

Parents as Patients   Parents of retarded children operate under considerable emotional stress. Some professionals identify the parents' emotional stress as the primary problem, suggesting a role of parents as patients. Instead of receiving the services and information which could be used to meet their needs and those of their children, some parents have been subjected to psychotherapy and counseling. Psychological treatment regimes are unlikely to succeed, if they do not provide the parents with other benefits, including (*a*) an understanding of the nature of mental retardation and (*b*) information to help them identify and meet the needs of the children.

Professional Omniscience—Omnipotence An omniscient-omnipotent attitude (i.e., all knowing and authoritative) manifested by some professionals represents another kind of inappropriate treatment of parents. Professionals have too often made important decisions affecting the welfare of a child without consulting with the parents. It has also been a common practice of some professionals to withhold information from parents. Their rationale for denying parents access to information is usually based upon the assumption that such information would be too threatening or destructive (Roos, 1975). Furthermore, it is naive to assume that current legal provisions such as P.L. 94–142 have eliminated the willful withholding of information from parents. Legislative mandates apply only to documented information, but professionals frequently maintain private notes which are not available to parents. Although there is some justification for maintaining private notes before a decision is made, there is less justification for withholding information from parents if it is related to decisions which have been made or are being made regarding their child—especially in the areas of evaluation, placement, and service delivery.

Total responsibility for the success or failure of a working partnership between parents and professionals is the responsibility of both parties, demanding cooperation and coordination. While we have been stressing the professional responsibility for making the relationship work, at times parents are responsible for the failure of some relationships to become productive. Some parents indeed have denied that their child was retarded, have neglected important needs of the child, have declined to participate in goal setting, have rejected professional aid, have distrusted the motives of professionals, and have held unrealistic expectations for the relationship. The list of the sins of omission and commission could be expanded for each party. What is very important to note is that the development of the parent-professional partnership should be considered an ethical responsibility, a practical necessity, and for professionals, now a legal obligation.

PARENTS AND THE RIGHT TO EDUCATION

Chapter 9 discusses the legislation and litigation which has affected the welfare of all mentally retarded individuals. The Education For All Children Act, P.L. 94–142, has specific relevance to the parent-professional relationship. The discussion here highlights some important points of P.L. 94–142 as it relates to parents.

Two of the expressed purposes of P.L. 94–142 are

1. To insure that a free appropriate public education which includes special education and related services are available to all handicapped children.
2. To insure that the rights of handicapped children and their parents are protected. (Sec. 121 a.1)

The assurance of procedural due process for the parents and the child is essential to fulfillment of the handicapped child's educational and other needs. The education agency may not unilaterally decide the needs of the child, the child's eligibility for service, or what services shall be provided. This local education agency must attempt (and document its efforts) to obtain the written informed consent of the parents before any activity related to evaluation or the delivery of special education services may be carried out. The parents' consent must be obtained in all of the following situations: prior to evaluation for eligibility, before implementation of the IEP, at the completion of each annual review, and prior to any change in placement or re-evaluation. In addition parental consent may be revoked at any time.

The rights of parents are not limited to approving or disapproving proposed placements, services, and activities. Parents also have the right to attend and participate in the development of their child's IEP. They have the right to veto any decisions and to recommend activities and services for their child. They have the right to request a re-evaluation of their child or a review of the child's placement and IEP. The parents' role in the development of the IEP is extremely important, because the IEP determines what constitutes an appropriate education.

According to P.L. 94–142, parents of children suspected of or identified as being handicapped are entitled to other rights as well. These additional rights include

1. The right to inspect any educational records with respect to identification, evaluation, placement, and the provision of a free appropriate education. (Sec. 121a. 502)
2. The right to obtain an independent evaluation: If the independent evaluation is to be submitted at an IEP meeting or at a due process hearing, it must have been conducted by a qualified examiner who is not employed by the education agency responsible for the child's education. (Sec. 121a. 503)

    If an agreement cannot be reached between the parents and the educational agency, regarding the provision of a free appropriate education and related services, either party has the right to seek settlement in a due process hearing.
3. The right to receive parent counseling and training as a related service (Sec 121a. 13(6)): If it is determined that this service is necessary to meet the special needs of the child and if the par-

ents agree to participate, then the educational agency must provide this service. Providing parent counseling and training is not intended to allow educational agencies to train parents to shoulder the burden of educating their handicapped child themselves. The intent of that provision is: (*a*) to help parents understand their child's special needs; (*b*) to provide them with information about child development; and (*c*) to enable parents a method for supplementing the child's educational program whenever appropriate.

The protection guaranteed by these procedural safeguards for both handicapped children and their parents is an essential component of the delivery of an appropriate education. The potential adversarial relationship that often develops between parents and professionals when these safeguards are applied tends to strain many partnerships. Although this type of relationship can develop and is most undesirable, it is essential that these legal safeguards be available to parents. Since it is possible for an adversarial relationship between parents and professionals to develop, we might ask whether it should be avoided for the child's sake. When either party—the school or the parents—becomes more concerned with their own interests than with the interests of the child, it is indeed the child who suffers. Differences in opinion should be able to be worked out before it is necessary to invoke due process procedures. When in disagreement, parents and professionals might be able to ensure an appropriate education for a child by working together for the child's benefit.

ROLES OF PARENTS

PARENTS AS MEMBERS OF ORGANIZATIONS

Parents of handicapped children have gained important political power in recent years. Although some parents on their own have been able to obtain certain services for their handicapped children, it has been the collaborative efforts of parent organizations that have had a significant impact on securing services for mentally retarded people.

One of the largest organizations concerned with the education and care of mentally retarded persons is an organization founded by parents. Although the Association for Retarded Citizens (ARC) is now a large complex diversified organization, it had simpler beginnings. Roos (1975) has described the development of ARC from its grass roots beginning to its present status as one of the largest and most influential organizations representing mentally retarded citizens. In 1950 many local parent organizations came together to form the National Association for Retarded Children. In 1973 the name was changed to the National Association for Retarded Citizens, reflecting a change in perspective from just children to all people. NARC is known as the Association for Retarded Citizens. Roos pointed out that there has been a gradual trend for nonprofessionals to become involved as members and as leaders in ARC.

The rapid growth of ARC attests to its ability to help meet the needs of mentally retarded persons and their families. Roos (1975) reports that "from 125 member organizations with approximately 13,000 active members, it has grown to over 1600 state and local units and a membership of approximately 250,000 in 1974" (p. 348). As of 1980, there are approximately 1900 state and local units, with approximately 1,000,000 members.

While ARC has always attempted to meet parents' needs for support and information, it also has expanded beyond this important self-help role. On the national and local levels, ARC has entered into four important areas: (*a*) provision of programs and services for mentally retarded citizens, (*b*) political lobbying and litigation, (*c*) citizen advocacy, and (*d*) monitoring and evaluating programs. A current emphasis of ARC is to secure publicly supported services which mentally retarded persons are entitled to as citizens.

Reviewing the impact of parent organizations in general and ARC in particular, Roos (1975) states

> In summary, the day of the naive parent struggling impotently to find desperately needed services for his retarded child is now past. Parent organizations in the United States, primarily under the aegis of NARC, have matured into strong, sophisticated advocates for the retarded and their families. No longer alone and helpless, parents have demonstrated that they can be valuable assets in behalf of their own children as well as in behalf of all retarded, wherever they may be. (p. 353)

PARENTS AS BEHAVIOR MANAGERS

Parents of retarded children have often had to raise their own children, but they have not always been regarded as competent to do so, as Kurtz (1978) points out.

> Social forces and human service arrangements have diminished the status of parents and reduced their incentive to assume their role as powerful agents in the child's development. This is especially true for parents who feel inadequate and ill prepared. Human service agencies have communicated to parents that someone else can do the job better. By taking major responsibility for services, professionals in schools and health and social service agencies have undermined the position of parents. (p. 452)

Fortunately, parents have been receiving more recognition as key figures in their child's development. Research in the area of early childhood education with "at-risk" children (Bronfenbrenner, 1974) and early intervention for handicapped children (Boyd, 1979; Clunies-Ross, 1979; Shearer & Shearer, 1972) has highlighted the importance of parental involvement in early childhood development programs.

CONCLUSION AND SUGGESTIONS

Professionals have continued to develop an interest in the problems faced by families with handicapped members. The quality of research has continued to improve, and as a result many important issues have been identified. For this reason, research on this topic will be needed and should be encouraged for many years yet. It is particularly important to be mindful of certain indicators of future problems such as demographic changes. The relevance of certain demographic changes, such as the higher incidences of teenage mothers, single parents, and working mothers, is not a problem of the future but a reality of the present. It is important to study the family structure rather than focusing on one member in isolation from the family.

The importance of obtaining adequate samples and conducting sound research cannot be overemphasized. Whatever services are available to mentally retarded persons and their families are frequently made available by virtue of various policy-making agencies. It is most important that these policy makers base their decisions on information that reflects the facts, rather than on our best guesses.

SUMMARY

Professional interest in the families of retarded people is a relatively recent phenomenon. While we do not have much reliable research on the topic, we do know that the parents of a child diagnosed as mentally retarded are apt to have a range of emotional reactions. The caring professional must be realistic yet positive in presenting a diagnosis and helping parents face the future. The professional can greatly help the family by steering them toward various formal and informal sources of support. Educators who deal with parents of mentally retarded children have the additional moral and legal responsibilities of cooperating to plan and monitor the children's educational programs. Through various organizations, parents have come to be recognized as a major force in shaping public policy toward handicapped people.

CHAPTER NINE

Legal Rights

SECURING THE RIGHTS OF MENTALLY RETARDED CITIZENS

> The right to be human based upon the principles of equality, is applicable to all individuals. However, this democratic principle is too often violated in relation to the mentally retarded citizens. There is today a significant movement, initiated by parents and professionals, to establish the legal rights of the retarded. It is certainly ironical that these concerned individuals are advocating the "establishment" of basic human rights, when in reality the rights of the retarded under the constitution should be no different than those of the nonretarded citizens. Consequently, the issue confronting society is not the establishment of basic human rights, but the enforcement of the rights guaranteed every individual. (Drew, Hardman, & Bluhm, 1977, p. 101)

Drew and colleagues aptly describe the present situation; advocates of mentally retarded citizens still are attempting to establish that certain rights should be claimed by all citizens, rather than privileges earned by a few. No matter how apparent it may seem, we must first establish that mentally retarded persons are indeed entitled to those rights guaranteed

This chapter was written by James R. Patton and Thomas J. Zirpoli.

all citizens and only then can we enforce their application. In the past, scant acknowledgment has been given to the personal and civil rights of those who are mentally retarded.

Wald (1976) suggests that the rights to which mentally retarded individuals are entitled are those that define a man or woman as a human being. In addition, she suggests that these rights carry obligations for the individual as a member of society. The status of mentally retarded persons as contributing members of society is precisely what needs to be underscored if rights—supposedly granted to all citizens— are to be secured for those labeled retarded.

LEGAL TERMINOLOGY

Proponents of any social change movement, such as the push for handicapped rights, need to become familiar with the language of the law, because legal remedy is currently the tool with which they can legitimize change. Effectively advocating for the rights of disabled persons requires an understanding of the need for legal action, the significant legislation to date, the arguments upon which court action is based, and the juridical language in which it is couched. We will address the first three points further in this chapter; for the fourth we are providing a condensed glossary of legal terms. Consult the glossary for a clarification of such concepts as *equal protection, due process*, and *least restrictive alternative*.

ISSUES REGARDING MENTALLY RETARDED PEOPLE

Throughout history, mentally retarded people as a group have been misperceived in a number of ways ranging from Martin Luther's idea of retarded people as demonic to Justice Holmes' infamous perception of them as social parasites (*Buck v. Bell*, 1927). As we saw in chapter one, the treatment accorded the mentally retarded population has reflected the sociopolitical influences of a given time. It is demonstrated in many ways, including practices such as institutionalization for custodial and protective purposes, compulsory sterilization laws and, most recently, the preclusion of many mentally retarded people from acquiring education and/or training services.

Indiana has the dubious distinction of enacting the first compulsory sterilization law.

Although a more acceptable semantic substitute has not become popular, the term *mental retardation* itself conjures up many misconceptions. Kurtz (1977) believes that the general public conceptualizes *mental retardation* from a medical perspective as a sickness. Sociological categorization of mentally retarded persons may imply deviancy status (that is, at significant variance from the norm). Even today we tend to accentuate the disabilities rather than the abilities of these people. Attitudes and perceptions such as these can easily lead to decisions and patterns of treatment that are decidedly antithetical to both egalitarianism and normalization.

What may be more alarming is that the public will develop stereotypes negatively associated with mentally retarded persons. For instance, not too long ago, the Nebraska Supreme Court, in upholding the state's compulsory sterilization law, stated "that mental deficiency accelerates sexual impulses and any tendency toward crime to a harmful degree" (*In re Cavitt*, 1967). Just as possible is the likelihood that the mentally retarded person will be considered "an eternal child" who never really attains what we call *adulthood*. It is not uncommon to hear people, who should know better, referring to retarded adults as children. This interpretation can trigger what Perske (1972) refers to as *overprotection*, which limits people's individuality and personal growth.

All too often, mentally retarded people are regarded as a singular, homogeneous group. Perhaps this happens because stereotypes and generalizations are easy to use. This notion of homogeneity must be replaced in the minds of the general public by a more appropriate, individualistic notion of them. As is true of those with normal intelligence, there is much variance among mentally retarded persons. If people can understand that all of those who are mentally retarded are not at the lowest end of the intelligence continuum, can become aware of the concepts of adaptive/functional behavior, and can consider retarded people more like us than unlike us, then they will have more accurate notions of the individuality and heterogeneity of retarded persons.

Suspect Class   As a group, mentally retarded individuals have been vulnerable to purposeful unequal treatment and, as you might expect, have not enjoyed a position of political influence. As a result, they often need legal protections. As Gilhool (1976) says

> Past stigmatization, isolation, and irrational exclusion of the mentally retarded provide a strong basis for arguing that a legislative administrative classification which excludes or differentially burdens retarded citizens is suspect, subject to strict scrutiny, and justifiable only by a compelling interest of the state. (p. 183)

Litigation in a variety of areas has identified other characteristics by which people have been classified and discriminated against. These characteristics include sex, race, alienage, and illegitimacy. The rationales used in these court decisions for defining suspect classes of people with special rights (or without certain rights) have had some bearing on the litigation involving mentally retarded people.

Best Interests versus Legal Rights   From time to time the principles of best interest and legal rights of an individual have come into conflict. When the state acts under the best interest principle, it does so in one of two ways. If the state acts in the best interest of the individual, it does so based on the theory of *parens patriae* (that is, the state is the father of the country and of its citizens). If the state acts in the best interest of society, it does so based on the theory of police power (that is, the power to impose restrictions upon private rights that are related to general welfare of the public). This legal principle can impose upon the rights of an individual, as evidenced in many sterilization cases in which the state interceded on behalf of the general welfare of the public. The principle of *parens patriae* seems on face value to be harmless, but situations can arise in which use of this principle negates the individual's right to due process under the law.

LEGAL ARGUMENTS

CONSTITUTIONAL GROUNDS

The Fourteenth Amendment to the Constitution contains two frequently invoked clauses: (*a*) the *due process* clause ("nor shall any State deprive any person of life, liberty, or property, without due process of law") and (*b*) the *equal protection* clause ("nor deny to any person within its jurisdiction the equal protection of the laws"). Many of the rights secured and services established for mentally retarded people during the last few years have been achieved through litigation firmly based on constitutional grounds, particularly on these two principles. Table 9.1 presents constitutional arguments that have been used most frequently in cases involving mentally retarded persons. This table provides only a brief guide to the constitutional basis for much of the recent litigation; it is not an exhaustive list of all previous, present, or future bases for litigation.

Table 9.2 is a summary of court cases important to special education.

Since the equal protection clause of the Fourteenth Amendment has been the backbone of civil rights and rights for the handicapped, we will look at it in depth. There are two types of equal protection analyses (that is, the application of equal protection to a specific claim): (*a*) "traditional"/"rational basis" analysis and (*b*) "strict scrutiny"/"new equal protection" analysis. Turnbull (1975) provides a historical perspective and explains some factors that are responsible for the type of analysis employed in litigation.

> Until the era of the Warren Court, the application of equal-protection guarantees to claimed violations of individual rights usually resulted in a finding that the governmental action was above constitutional reproach. When the "traditional" equal-protection analysis failed to yield results that corrected obvious abuses of individual rights, the Warren Court fashioned "new equal protection" analysis. Which of the two equal-protection analyses it applied depended principally on the nature of the complaining party, the nature of the complainant's interest or the right being infringed upon by the government, and the ability of the government to justify its action. (p. 14)

TABLE 9.1 Constitutional Arguments Affecting Handicapped Persons

Constitutional Argument	Constitutional Basis (Amendment)	Explanation	Example of Application
Equal protection	14th	No state shall deny to any person within its jurisdiction the equal protection of the laws	Right to education
Due process (substantive)	5th (federal) 14th (state)	Legislation must be reasonably related for the furtherance of a legitimate governmental objective	Right to appropriate classification Right to treatment
Due process (procedural)	5th (federal) 14th (state)	Guarantees procedural fairness where the government would deprive one of his property or liberty	Placement Rights in the criminal justice system
Freedom from cruel and unusual punishment	8th	Protection from punishment that is found to be offensive to the ordinary person, that is unfair, or that is grossly excessive to the offense	Right to refuse treatment Right to treatment Rights in prison
Freedom from slavery and involuntary servitude	13th	No person shall be forced or coerced into working	Right to work (institutional)
Freedom of speech and the right to vote	1st	Free exercise of basic rights	Right to education

When the courts apply the rational basis analysis or traditional analysis, they invoke a two-pronged test. First, the courts ask whether the purposes sought by the state are legitimate state purposes. Second, they investigate whether there exists a "rational" correspondence between the purposes of the state action and the classification.

If the courts apply the new equal protection analysis, they set into motion a test that contains three major features. First, the situation must involve a suspect classification. Second, a fundamental interest must be at issue. Third, if the first two criteria are met, then the courts demand that the state demonstrate a "compelling interest," based on necessity, not on convenience (Turnbull, 1975).

FEDERAL STATUS AND REGULATIONS

Another mechanism for securing the rights of mentally retarded citizens that has had a significant effect is federal legislation. The 1975 passage of

The Education for All Handicapped Children Act (EHA, P.L. 94-142) was noteworthy because it established a federal statutory basis for providing free public education to *all* handicapped children. Although Congress passed this legislation in 1975 and President Ford signed it into law in that same year, its implementation did not actually commence until September of 1978.

As a result, more cases appealing to this legislation to combat any violation are being initiated. However, it was not until 1982 that a case using EHA arguments made it to the Supreme Court (*Board of Education v. Rowley*). This law will be examined later in this chapter.

Two other important laws, enacted in the 1970s, are the Vocational Rehabilitation Act of 1973 (P.L. 93-112) and the Developmental Disabilities Assistance and Bill of Rights Act of 1975 (P.L. 94-103), which was amended in 1978 (P.L. 95-602). Section 504 of the Rehabilitation Act has also been referred to as the "Bill of Rights" for handicapped people. It provides for a private right to action on the part of handicapped citizens who believe they have been discriminated against because of their handicapping condition. This legislation addresses a range of areas: education, employment, accessibility, health and social services, and affirmative action. The Developmental Disabilities Act ensures the rights and dignity of all developmentally disabled individuals and assists states in the development of comprehensive plans to provide services to these people. This legislation requires each state to set up a State Developmental Disabilities Planning Council, which oversees the plan for improving services to this group, and an independent agency, which provides protection of, and advocacy for, human, civil, and legal rights.

Other active federal statutes that have varying degrees of importance for mentally retarded people include the Elementary and Secondary Education Act of 1965 (P.L. 89-110), amended in 1974 (P.L. 93-380); the Vocational Education Amendments of 1968 (P.L. 90-576); the Adult Education Act (P.L. 19-230); and the Social Security Act.

For a complete listing of federal legislation for handicapped individuals prior to P.L. 94-142, see La Vor, 1976: for a brief elaboration on most of the legislation mentioned above, see Ballard, 1976.

STATE CONSTITUTIONS AND STATUTES

Since it is incumbent upon each state to provide education for its citizens by virtue of compulsory education laws, it would follow that this legislative mandate would be a strong basis for arguing that these same services be afforded to handicapped children. Although referring specifically to the right to education issue, Turnbull (1975) poignantly states the importance of state mandates.

> The case law on the right to an education is not based solely
> upon federal and constitutional arguments. And not surprisingly,
> the federal equal-protection and due-process arguments are not
> as likely to be a secure ground for establishing the right to edu-

cation as is the guarantee of education imposed on the state by
its constitution or statutes. (p. 6)

Turnbull goes on to say that nearly all states have constitutions which
contain provisions for educating their children, and that many states
have provisions for the education of all children, including handicapped
children.

State and federal statutes and regulations are most useful for litigation when they incorporate constitutional claims. Litigation of recent
years has demonstrated the success of this relationship.

EDUCATIONAL RIGHTS

INTRODUCTION

The importance of education is generally recognized and supported.
The Supreme Court in the landmark *Brown v. Board of Education* (1954)
decision clearly commented on the value that education can have on
one's life.

> Today, education is perhaps the most important function of state
> and local governments. Compulsory school attendance laws and
> the great expenditures for education both demonstrate our recog-
> nition of the importance of education to our democratic society. It
> is required in the performance of our most basic public responsi-
> bilities, even service in the armed forces. It is the very founda-
> tion of good citizenship. Today it is a principal instrument in
> awakening the child to cultural values, in preparing him for later
> professional training, and in helping him to adjust normally to
> his environment. In these days, it is doubtful that any child may
> reasonably be expected to succeed in life if he is denied the op-
> portunity of an education. Such an opportunity where the state
> has undertaken to provide it, is a right which must be made
> available to all on equal terms.

With the proliferation of legal cases in the last few years, there has
been a shift in focus from a systems-centered decision-making process to
one which is more child-centered. What this means is that individual
characteristics must be considered when educational decisions are
made. Overriding concepts such as appropriate education and least restrictive environment, while vague and wanting in definition, demand a
child-centered perspective.

RIGHT TO EDUCATION

Is Education a Fundamental Right? To many people, education is considered a fundamental right that the authors of the constitution definitely incorporated into their masterpiece. The Supreme Court, in

TABLE 9.2 Summary of Early Litigation Affecting Special Education

Right Addressed	Litigants	Year	Highest Level of Judicial Review
Right to education	*Brown v. Board of Education*	1954	U.S. Supreme Court
	Pennsylvania Association for Retarded Children v. Commonwealth of Pennsylvania	1972	U.S. District Court (Pa.)
	Mills v. Board of Education of District of Columbia	1972	U.S. District Court (D.C.)

Issues	Implications of Litigations	Arguments Used
Segregation of students by race Impact of racial segregation on the child's motivation to learn	Segregation by race unanimously declared unconstitutional Established importance of education for advancement Established policy in favor of equal educational opportunity Generalized the purposes of education not its fundamentality	Equal protection
Class action suit—challenging the exclusion of mentally retarded children from free public education Access to education for all retarded citizens Particular learning needs of the mentally retarded	Consent agreement of both parties Established a right to education for mentally retarded children Established that all mentally retarded children could gain from education and training Demanded appropriate education Demanded preschool services if normal children received such Provided tuition grant assistance Provided due process mechanisms Required the identification of mentally retarded children not already identified Provided for education in the least restrictive setting	Equal protection Due process State statutes
Class action suit—exclusion of all exceptionalities Access to education Use of waiting lists	Extended the logic of *PARC* to all handicapped regardless of the degree of the impairment Gained procedural safeguards Required a timetable of implementation Acknowledged alternatives of placement	Equal protection Due process District of Columbia Code

TABLE 9.2 (continued)

Right Addressed	Litigants	Year	Highest Level of Judicial Review
	San Antonio Independent School District v. Rodriquez	1973	U.S. Supreme Court
	Lebanks v. Spears	1973	U.S. District Court
	Maryland Association of Retarded Children v. Maryland	1974	Circuit Court of Baltimore County
	In the Interest of H.G., A Child	1974	Supreme Court of North Dakota
Right to appropriate classification and placement	*Hobson v. Hansen*	1967	D.C. District Court
	Smuck v. Hansen	1969	D.C. Circuit Court

Issues	Implications of Litigations	Arguments Used
Claim that a discrimination exists due to being in a poorer school district Challenge to state-financing scheme Assertion that education is a fundamental right	Rejected wealth discrimination claim Left open the fundamentality of some identifiable quantum of education Reaffirmed the importance of education Indicated that denial of education could be used in terms of denial of freedom of speech and right to vote	Discrimination Equal protection

Challenged Louisiana's failure to provide education/training to a large number of mentally retarded children	Consent agreement
	Two features not found in *PARC* or *Mills*
	  1) Education—oriented toward the goal of making every child self-sufficient or employable
	  2) Educational services to adults who were not given services as children
	Acknowledged additional factors for evaluation of mentally retarded besides intelligence
		Equal protection

Class action suit on behalf of mentally retarded and physically handicapped children being denied free public education	Began to address "appropriateness" issue Required the state to provide the necessary funding	State statutes
Equal educational opportunity	Involved the highest level of judicial review prior to 1975 and P.L. 94-142	State constitution Equal protection
School classification Challenging ability grouping Denial of educational opportunity to poor public school children	Stated that ability grouping is related to educational purposes Stated that schools cannot use IQ to place children in ability tracks Addressed the consequences of being labeled *mentally retarded* Suggested a close review of classification practices	Due process Equal protection

TABLE 9.2 (continued)

Right Addressed	Litigants	Year	Highest Level of Judicial Review
	Larry P. v. Riles	1972	California District Court
	Diana v. State Board of Education	1972	California District Court
	Doe v. San Francisco Unified School District, et al.	1973	California Superior Court
	Lou v. Nichols	1974	U.S. Supreme Court

San Antonio Independent School District v. Rodriguez (1973), stated that education is not a fundamental right, guaranteed either explicitly or implicitly by the constitution. While initially this is a shocking statement, nevertheless there are some encouraging implications from the *Rodriguez* decision. In Rodriguez, there is ostensible mention of the im-

Issues	Implications of Litigations	Arguments Used
Class action suit concerning the misplacement of Black Elementary school children in classes for the educable mentally retarded Serious injury resulting from such placement	IQ tests not rationally related to purposes of segregation based on ability to learn in the regular classroom Enjoined schools from placing Black children in EMR classes primarily on the basis of IQ measures Required procedural due process Established that the burden of proof is on the defendants Recognized that adaptive behavior assessment is important Wary of proposed ratio system asked for by plaintiffs	Due process
Class action suit concerning the misplacement of Spanish-speaking children in classes for the mentally retarded	Refrain from using IQ tests with Spanish-speaking children as presently exists Translation of tests into native language Retest children already in classes for the mentally retarded Required the development of norms appropriate to the specific population	Due process
Damages sought for diminished earning capacity Charges of negligence and misrepresentation	New area of claims on public entities Schools accountable even after a student graduates	State of California Statutes
Meaningful education being denied Chinese-speaking children Misplacement	Recognized that certain school practices effectively deny meaningful opportunity for education Required bilingual instruction	Civil Rights Act 1964

portance of acquiring basic minimal skills required for the exercising of the first amendment rights of free speech and involvement in the political mechanism of voting. Therefore, denial of educational services to any individual may impede the acquisition of the basic minimal skills and consequently a denial of constitutional rights. Although *Rodriguez* did not establish the right to education as fundamental, it did reaffirm the importance of education and implicitly denounced the denial of such action.

Basic Arguments Table 9.2 summarizes some of the early litigation affecting special education. As can be seen in the table, the arguments most frequently employed by plaintiffs in right to education cases include establishing the importance of education, using equal protection and due process claims and addressing statutory provisions in the federal and state constitutions. In addition to these important arguments, another factor of critical significance that was established in the *Pennsylvania Association for Retarded Children v. Commonwealth of Pennsylvania* (1972) and in *Mills v. Board of Education of the District of Columbia* (1972) cases is that all mentally retarded individuals can benefit from education and/or training. Without this established fact, substantial opposition could be lodged against providing educational services for many mentally retarded individuals who have been excluded from the schools. Recently this issue of educability has resurfaced (Kauffman & Krouse, 1981; Noonan, Brown, Mulligan, & Rettig, 1982) in a new context; it will be discussed in the next chapter.

Exclusionary practices that have kept many mentally retarded children out of school have existed for a long time. It was not until the early 1970s that legal challenges to exclusionary policies were successfully waged. This litigation was to pave the way for later federal legislation that would significantly alter the delivery of educational services to exceptional people.

PARC v. Commonwealth of Pennsylvania. Early in January, 1971, the Pennsylvania Association for Retarded Children and the parents of 13 mentally retarded children filed a class action suit in federal court on behalf of all mentally retarded persons between the ages of 6 and 21 who resided in the Commonwealth of Pennsylvania and who were excluded from receiving educational services. At issue was the prevailing policy that denied these school-age children access to public education. As referred to earlier, expert testimony that highlighted the benefits that all mentally retarded individuals could gain from education and training weighed heavily in this case. Although settled by means of a court-approved consent agreement in October, 1971, the PARC settlement had a profound impact on special education and mentally retarded children. It established a precedent guaranteeing access to a publicly supported education for all mentally retarded people. By reason of due process rights and equal protection claims, the plaintiffs were able to establish that certain Pennsylvania statutes were unconstitutional. Implications of this decision which would have long-lasting effects on the delivery of services are listed in Table 9.2.

Mills v. Board of Education. Not long after the consent agreement in
PARC was reached, a civil suit was filed in the District of Columbia. In
this case, the parents and guardians of seven children charged that the
Board of Education was denying these children a publicly supported
education. All of the plaintiffs in this case qualified as "exceptional." In
August, 1972, Judge Waddy ruled in favor of the plaintiffs and in effect
declared that a publicly supported education was the right of all exceptional children, regardless of the type and severity of the exceptionality.
Mills actually extended many of the achievements and legal guarantees
that *PARC* won for mentally retarded people to include all exceptional
individuals. Defendants claimed that there were insufficient funds for
carrying out the judge's decision and providing education to all exceptional children. Judge Waddy's reply reflected the attitude of many concerning the exclusionary practices so long in effect.

> The District of Columbia's interest in educating the excluded chil-
> dren clearly must outweigh its interest in preserving its financial
> resources. If sufficient funds are not available to finance all of the
> services and programs that are needed and desirable in the sys-
> tem, then the available funds must be expended equitably in
> such a manner that no child is entirely excluded from a publicly
> supported education consistent with his needs and ability to ben-
> efit therefrom. The inadequacies of the District of Columbia pub-
> lic school system whether occasioned by insufficient funding or
> administrative inefficiency, certainly cannot be permitted to bear
> more heavily on the "exceptional" or handicapped child than on
> the normal child. (*Mills v. Board of education*, 1972)

As is readily apparent, the argument of limited financial resources was
not accepted as sufficient reason to exclude children from receiving an
appropriate education. Clearly, this rationale will not be sufficient for
exclusionary purposes in the future. Nonetheless, financial resources
are limited and, even with P.L. 94-142 and its recent amendments
(P.L. 98-199) in effect, these financial issues demand our attention.

   After *PARC* and *Mills*, right to education litigation was filed in
many other states as well. As a result, mentally retarded students began
to acquire various educational rights that had been denied previously.
Moreover, many of the provisions formulated in the PARC consent
agreement were incorporated into the framework of EHA.

RIGHT TO AN APPROPRIATE CLASSIFICATION AND PLACEMENT

Basic Arguments The most frequent charges in the legal cases involving
placement decisions have involved violations of equal protection and
due process. MacMillan (1977) offers an explanation of the typical equal
protection claim that can be raised in relation to special class placement

for educable mentally retarded students. "The contention is made that a child placed in a special education class is denied equal educational opportunity because his options are reduced . . . and because the quality of the EMR program is poorer than that of the regular class" (1977, p. 290).

The due process arguments are based on the contention that the procedures used for classifying a child or for placing a child in a special class (such as administration of certain tests) may deny substantive due process. Correspondingly, the denial of proper procedural safeguards before and after evaluation also violates the procedural due process clause of the constitution. The thrust of the opposition to misclassification centers on the chronic effects of labeling a child. Many people vehemently object to the stigma associated with being placed in a class for mentally retarded students. It is interesting to note, however, that the available research does not provide strong evidence that these labels have negative effects (Gottlieb & Leyser, 1981; MacMillan, Jones, & Aloia, 1974). Others react just as violently to the segregation and isolation of special class placement.

The use of intelligence measures as the prime criterion for determining placement has long been under scrutiny. As shown in Table 9.2, the problems of intelligence testing have come under fire in a number of legal decisions. *Hobson v. Hansen* (1967), *Larry P. v. Riles* (1972), and *Diana v. State Board of Education* (1970) have specifically looked at the placements of children after being classified mainly on the basis of IQ tests.

In *Hobson v. Hansen* (1967), the denial to poor school children of educational services equal to those of the more affluent was determined to be unconstitutional. The court found that students were being "tracked" into ability groups on the basis of instruments that seemed to be biased against black students and those from lower socioeconomic groups. In *Larry P. v. Riles* (1972), the Federal District Court for Northern California decided that IQ tests could not be used as the sole determinant in the placement of black students in classes for educable mentally retarded children. In January of 1984, the 9th Circuit Court of Appeals affirmed by a 2-1 margin the lower court opinion, thus moving this case closer to review by the Supreme Court (Cordes, 1984).

Just as *Larry P.* specifically concerned the problems of black children being misclassified, other cases also litigated in California have focused on the problems that other ethnic groups encountered in placement decisions. In *Diana v. State Board of Education* (1970), the injured party, representing Spanish-speaking children, argued that many such students had been placed in EMR classes on the basis of individual intelligence tests with cultural bias. Specifically, the children involved in this lawsuit primarily spoke Spanish but were given intelligence tests in English. Although *Diana* was settled out of court, it resulted in clear changes in the methods and procedures used for identifying and placing students in EMR classes.

It would be misleading to suggest that these were the only lawsuits involving appropriate classification and placement, or that all litigation has been decided in the same way. In a class action suit filed in an Illinois federal district court (*Parents in Action on Special Education [PASE] v. Hannon*), the use of intelligence tests to place minority students in EMR classes was found to be a valid procedure. The findings in *PASE* are in direct opposition to those in *Larry P.* and have added even more confusion to an already controversial area.

Nevertheless, the misdiagnosis and misplacement of students remain areas of professional concern. There is also interest in the effects this litigation will have on special education. Cordes (1984) remarked that some experts feel there has been little change in the schools. On the other hand, Smith and Polloway (1983) suggested that such concern has resulted in a more conservative posture of classifying students as retarded, especially mildly retarded (EMR).

LEGISLATIVE BASIS OF EDUCATIONAL RIGHTS

While there is a rather impressive list of legislation addressing the needs of exceptional people, no federal or state statutes have held the significance, meaning, or potential that two pieces of federal legislation enacted in the 1970s have had on the establishment of certain educational rights for disabled individuals. The two laws that have been praised, cursed, and discussed at length are the Rehabilitation Amendments of the Vocational Rehabilitation Act of 1973 (P.L. 93-112) and the Education for All Handicapped Children Act (P.L. 94-142), amended in 1983 as P.L. 98-199.

See LaVor, 1976.

VOCATIONAL REHABILITATION ACT OF 1973
Although it took over four years for the regulations finally to emerge, the Vocational Rehabilitation Act, passed in 1973, has been acclaimed as a truly landmark piece of legislation. The intent of this law was to encourage equal opportunity for handicapped people and to determine discriminatory practices that affect this group. The spirit of the law can be recognized in the following excerpt.

> No otherwise qualified handicapped individual in the United
> States, as defined in Section 7(6), shall, solely by reason of his

handicap, be excluded from the participation in, be denied the benefits of, or be subjected to discrimination under any program or activity receiving Federal financial assistance.

Although most of our attention has been directed to the nondiscriminatory section of this law, this is only one part of the act. In addition, this legislation requires that each state education agency do the following.

1. Develop and implement comprehensive and continuing state plans for meeting the current and future needs for providing vocational rehabilitation services to handicapped individuals and to provide such services for the benefit of such individuals, serving first those with the most severe handicaps, so that they may prepare for and engage in gainful employment.

2. Evaluate the rehabilitation potential of handicapped individuals.

3. Conduct a study to develop methods of providing rehabilitation services to meet the current and future needs of handicapped individuals for whom a vocational goal is not possible or feasible so that they may improve their ability to live with greater independence and self-sufficiency.

4. Assist in the construction and improvement of rehabilitation facilities.

5. Develop new and innovative methods of applying the most advanced medical technology, scientific achievement, and psychological and social knowledge to solve rehabilitation problems and develop new and innovative methods of providing rehabilitation services to handicapped individuals through research, special projects, and demonstrations.

6. Initiate and expand services to groups of handicapped individuals (including those who are homebound or institutionalized) who have been underserved in the past.

7. Conduct various studies and experiments to focus on long neglected problem areas.

8. Promote and expand employment opportunities in the public and private sectors for handicapped individuals and to place such individuals in employment.

9. Establish client assistance pilot projects.

10. Provide assistance for the purpose of increasing the number of rehabilitation personnel and increasing their skills through training.

11. Evaluate existing approaches to architectural and transportation barriers confronting handicapped individuals, develop new such approaches, enforce statutory and regulatory standards and requirements regarding barrier-free construction of

public facilities and study and develop solutions to existing architectural and transportation barriers impeding handicapped individuals. (Ballard, 1976, p. 136)

THE EDUCATION FOR ALL HANDICAPPED CHILDREN ACT

What has been referred to as a revolutionary event in the history of special education and the educational rights movement is P.L. 94-142, enacted & signed into law in November, 1975. While the thrust of this law was not new—parents and professionals had been advocating for educational rights for a long time—this was the first time that a federal statute had been enacted to address these issues.

As this law encompasses a wide range of guarantees and assurances, it will be helpful to take another look at the more salient features of this act. The Virginia State Department of Education Division of Special Education (1977) has provided the following encapsulation.

1. Assurance that extensive child identification procedures are being used;
2. Assurance of a "full service" goal and a detailed timetable for achieving it;
3. A guarantee of complete due process procedures;
4. Assurance that regular consultations are held with parents or guardians;
5. Maintenance of programs and procedures for comprehensive personnel development including inservice training;
6. Assurance that special education services are provided to all handicapped children in the "least restrictive" environment;
7. Assurance that nondiscriminatory testing and evaluation procedures are being used;
8. Assurance that policies and procedures have been adopted to protect the confidentiality of data and information;
9. Assurance that individualized programs for all handicapped children are available;
10. Assurance that an effective policy has been initiated to guarantee the right of all handicapped children to a free, appropriate public education, *at no cost* to parents or guardians.
11. Assurance that a surrogate will be named to act for any child when parents or guardians are either unknown or unavailable, or when child is a legal ward of the state. (pp. 8-9)

To many teachers, the requirement to develop individual education programs of the law has been a true burden; to others, it symbolizes at last the progress that has been made in guaranteeing the educational rights of handicapped children. Regardless of personal perceptions of the IEP, it does represent a commitment to provide services that are appropriate to the needs of the student. This document can be considered a form of accountability that should reflect the guarantees of the Act suggesting educational appropriateness in the least restrictive setting.

Although the actual format of IEPs differs from one school system to another, every IEP should include the following components, as mandated by the law.

1. The student's present level of educational functioning;
2. Annual goals that the student is expected to achieve;
3. Short-term instructional objectives;
4. Listing of the specific services including special education and related (e.g., speech, physical therapy) services that have been determined essential to the student;
5. The amount of participation in the regular classrooms that is appropriate for the student;
6. Temporal data: dates for initiation of services and for expected termination of these services;
7. Evaluation procedures utilizing objective criteria to determine if the student is meeting the short-term instructional objectives;
8. Annual review: an approximate date must be set at which time the student's progress is reviewed. (Smith & Payne, 1980, p. 123)

In 1982, new regulations were proposed that suggested many changes on how EHA should be implemented. Much public outcry resulted and, after many public hearings and thousands of written responses, the broad changes were withdrawn. The following year, the EHA was amended as P.L. 98-199, retaining the original act's provisions. However, there were some changes: The revised act provides modest increases in the authorization levels for EHA programs, establishes several new or expanded programs, re-establishes a consumer advisory council on handicapped educational issues, promotes administrative flexibility, clarifies ambiguous terminology, and strengthens certain key features of the law, such as evaluation requirements.

Although P.L. 94-142 has been hailed as the culmination of the movement for securing rights for the handicapped, this law has also raised some questions, caused some concern, and even inspired some outright criticism. One of the most perplexing problems involves the concept of mainstreaming. The implementation of this concept preceded the establishment of a firm research base that supports it (Patton & Payne, 1985). Gottlieb (1981) noted that we may be more concerned with placing students in the least restrictive environment than with educating them there. Furthermore, if we follow the intent of this law and reintegrate many students back into regular classes without adequately preparing teachers and students, then perhaps we are doing more of a disservice than a service to those reintegrated exceptional students.

RELATED LEGAL ISSUES

RIGHT TO HABILITATIVE SERVICES

Closely related to the question of educational rights is the right to receive appropriate education and training or habilitative services in an institutional setting. Three landmark cases in this category, *Wyatt v. Stickney* (1972), *O'Connor v. Donaldson* (1975), and *Pennhurst v. Halderman* (1981), all of which address the issue of institutional care, are discussed in chapter 14. *Wyatt* was the first case to establish the constitutional right of residents of mental hospitals and mental retardation facilities to receive appropriate habilitative training. The right to *refuse* unnecessary treatment was the subject of *O'Connor v. Donaldson*, which established that a nondangerous person capable of functioning safely on his own or with the help of a willing, responsible advocate could not be confined in a residential institution.

The *Pennhurst v. Halderman* case has confounded the picture. In this case, plaintiffs argued that the residents at Pennhurst were being denied adequate treatment; their claims were based on constitutional grounds. The federal court agreed with their complaint. On appeal, the Third Circuit Court of Appeals affirmed the lower court decision but based its judgment on statutory grounds—the 1975 Developmental Disabilities Assistance and Bill of Rights Act. The appeals court stated that this legislation created substantive rights for retarded individuals to habilitative services. In 1981, the United States Supreme Court reversed the appeals court decision. The high court recognized the inadequate conditions at Pennhurst, but did not feel that the Congressional intent of the DD Act created rights and required adequate treatment. McCarthy (1983) summarized the high court's position:

> [T]he Supreme Court declared that the Act was not intended to create new substantive rights; it was designed to *encourage*, but not to *mandate*, better services for the developmentally disabled. (p. 519)

McCarthy goes on to suggest that the Supreme Court position seems to be that it will strictly interpret funding legislation and will not demand that states provide services that are not explicitly stated in the laws. A dilemma arises because it is unlikely that states, in times of fiscal austerity and on their own initiative, will improve conditions and provide more services to institutionalized persons.

Although judicial principles, theories, and decisions can be complex, two basic assumptions behind the decision-making process in cases such as these described above should be made. "First, human and constitutional rights are not divisible and may not legally be parcelled out according to the mental, emotional, or physical attributes of a person; and, second, the unequal person is entitled to equal treatment under the law" (Turnbull, 1975, p. 427). As this statement points out, society recognizes that people are categorized into groups, but human and constitutional rights are not.

RIGHT TO LIFE-SAVING INTERVENTION

Within the last few years, much media attention has been given to the issue of withholding treatment from certain disabled individuals. Two celebrated cases have been *Guardianship of Becker* (1981,1983) and *United States v. University Hospital, State of New York at Stony Brook* (1983), better known as the Baby Jane Doe case. Both of these cases involve major issues which are typically associated with all such cases: parental and family autonomy, appropriateness of governmental intervention, and the question of quality versus sanctity of life. What tends to be missing is concern for the best interest of the child.

The original *Becker* cases (*In re Phillip B.*, 1980) has received much publicity (see the vignette in this chapter for background information). This earlier litigation was not successful in obtaining the corrective sur-

THE LIFE AND TIMES OF PHILLIP BECKER

Over the course of the last few years, considerable attention has been given to the situation of Phillip Becker, his natural parents, and other significant people in Phillip's life. Early events in Phillip's story highlight a number of critical issues, which relate to other retarded individuals as well. Foremost among these issues is the elusive concept of "quality of life" and how it is interpreted by the courts.

Phillip Becker is now in his late teens. However, when this story first became publicized, he was 11 years old. Phillip suffered from a congenital heart impairment and needed corrective surgery. His cardiovascular system was overtaxed and was sure to continue to deteriorate, eventually leading to a sudden heart attack or most certainly early death (probably by age 30). The crux of the problem was that

Phillip's natural parents refused to allow the surgery to be performed.

Eventually, the Juvenile Probation Department (California) sought a court order to permit the surgery to take place. After testimony was given by both sides, the juvenile court judge affirmed the parents' position. His decision was based primarily on the lack of proof that Phillip would die immediately if surgery were withheld and on the principle of parental sovereignty (i.e., the parents acting in the best interest of the child—especially when making life/death decisions). This lower court ruling was upheld by the Court of Appeals, and subsequent requests by the attorney general's office to the California Supreme Court and to the U.S. Supreme Court were refused, thus letting the previous decision stand.

gery which Phillip needed to prolong his life. Parental sovereignty won out over governmental interest in such matters. Recent guardianship proceedings have allowed Phillip to have new surrogate parents and to receive the corrective surgery that he needed. What is interesting in the Becker case is the legal means used to obtain the desired results— guardianship proceedings. Herr (1984) has noted that "the jurisdiction of state courts to resolve *Becker*-type disputes does not depend on constitutional or section 504 violations . . . the remedy . . . was established under a traditional guardianship statute" (p. 33).

The other type of "withholding treatment" case is exemplified by the Baby Jane Doe case. In this type of case, unlike *Becker*, where the child is older and his abilities are known, the individual is newly born and typically severely or profoundly handicapped. In this particular case, the hospital, with the parents' consent, chose not to perform certain surgical procedures which were needed to correct various physical problems. The government attempted to obtain the infant's medical records to determine whether the child's rights were being violated. The govern-

---

The courts have favored parental autonomy over the state's interest in intervening in family matters. The "quality of life" issues that are raised in this litigation stem from attitudes of the parents and several doctors in this case. Their stance was based on the following beliefs which surfaced during the testimony.

1. Phillip's life is not a "life worth living" (since he is mentally retarded).

2. If the surgery is performed, then Phillip would most probably outlive his parents and thus be devoid of their supervision and attention. As a result, he would not receive quality care.

3. The risk of surgery is too great. Testimony by doctors indicated that the risk of death was at most 10%.

The first two positions implied that Phillip was better off dead than alive, an opinion

open to criticism. The last position was best addressed by Baines (1980): "The operation carries a 10% maximum risk of death, as compared with the 100% certainty of greatly premature death" (p. 132).

Upon reflection, two salient questions remain. They poignantly summarize the plight of Phillip and others in situations like his.

☐ Who among us is in a position to determine what is a "quality" life?

☐ Has Phillip's life received less protection because he is mentally retarded? (Baines, 1980, p. 132)

UPDATE:
There have been some significant changes in Phillip's life since these earlier proceedings occurred. First, custody of Phillip has been given to his foster parents (the Heaths). Second, corrective surgery was performed on Phillip.

ment's position was that the treatment program selected (or the lack of one) might be a violation of Section 504. In this case, the federal district judge denied the government access to the child's medical records.

The Baby Jane Doe case and other situations like it have caused much professional reaction. Organizations such as the American Association on Mental Deficiency, the Association for Retarded Citizens, and The Association for Persons with Severe Handicaps (TASH) have taken positions against withholding of treatment. TASH (1984) has published a monograph on this topic entitled, *Legal, Economic, Psychological, and Moral Considerations on the Practice of Withholding Medical Treatment from Infants with Congenital Defects.*

Another effect of the Baby Jane Doe case is Congressional action to include "Baby Doe" provisions in amendments to the Child Abuse Prevention and Treatment Act, originally enacted in 1974. The purpose of these provisions is to protect infants with disabilities. This legislation has been supported by a large number of professional organizations with one notable exception—the American Medical Society. Instances where treatment is withheld or withdrawn are referred to in this legislation as medical neglect.

RIGHT TO EXTENDED SCHOOL YEAR

Another issue associated with the education of retarded students is whether they and other handicapped students under EHA are entitled to an extended school year if such services are deemed necessary to provide an appropriate education. Originally litigated as *Armstrong v. Kline* (1979), and consolidated upon appeal with other cases as *Battle v. Commonwealth of Pennsylvania* (1980), these cases considered whether significant gaps (i.e., summer break) in the educational programs of certain children cause losses in skill development (regression) and, if so, whether these students should have their school year extended. Both decisions found the defendant's policy of limiting educational services to a maximum of 180 days inflexible, and that it prevented students from receiving an appropriate education.

RIGHT TO LIVE IN COMMUNITY SETTINGS

Additional Congressional action (S.2053), the "Community and Family Living Amendments of 1983," is attempting to facilitate efforts to provide more community-based services by redirecting federal Medicaid matching dollars from institutional to community settings. If these amendments become law, the reduction in monies available to institutions and the increased availability of Medicaid monies for family home and community-based settings should encourage states to maximize the number of individuals who are in community settings. Another provision of these amendments is for states to develop comprehensive long-range plans for effectively establishing community-based services.

CONCLUSION: PERSISTING PROBLEMS

It is safe to say that much progress has been achieved in recent years with regard to guaranteeing the educational rights of mentally retarded learners. However, we believe that there are some areas that will remain confusing and problematic in terms of what is legally substantiated. These problem areas include

1. Exclusionary practices—Will many mentally retarded people still be excluded from receiving services?

2. Assessment procedures—Until special classes are racially and ethnically proportional, will there continue to be concern as to the methodology used in placement decisions?

3. Summer programming—Should students identified as mentally retarded be granted educational services during the summer?

4. IEPs—Will there continue to be problems associated with determining the goals and providing services necessitated by individual programming?

5. Economic considerations—Is the general public going to be willing to finance the costs of educating handicapped students—especially during times of economic stress?

6. Involvement of parents—Will the trend to include parents as integral members of the parent-professional partnership continue? Should they be forced to participate if they don't show interest?

7. Appropriateness and least restrictive alternative—Are we really sure we know how to define these concepts?

It is obvious that these questions need to be addressed. Some tentative answers may be offered; however, the passage of time alone will provide the complete answers. We must be cautious, and guard against potentially damaging results, described by Rosen, Clark, and Kivitz (1977) as "backlash to normalization and deinstitutionalization policies far worse than the conditions that generated progress" (p. 353).

UNWELCOMED IMMIGRANTS

Not long ago, there was an article in *Sports Illustrated* ("From Russia With Love") about a Soviet immigrant named Max Blank. While the *SI* article was about this 6' 8-½" high school basketball star, we were more interested in his younger brother. In describing the travels of the Blank family to the United States, *SI* reported:

> But the Blanks continued on to Italy; they spent eight months in
> the village of Ladispoli, west of Rome, waiting for a special

waiver that would enable Max's younger brother, Yakov, a Down's syndrome child, to enter the U.S. A 1952 immigration statute prohibits the admission of aliens who are mentally retarded without such a waiver.

We located Section 212 of the Immigration and Naturalization Act entitled "General Classes of Aliens Ineligible to Receive Visas And Excluded From Admission." The first part of Section 212 is presented below.

GENERAL CLASSES OF ALIENS INELIGIBLE TO RECEIVE VISAS AND EXCLUDED FROM ADMISSION

Sec. 212 (a) Except as otherwise provided in this Act, the following classes of aliens shall be ineligible to receive visas and shall be excluded from admission into the United States:

(1) Aliens who are feeble-minded;

(2) Aliens who are insane;

(3) Aliens who have had one or more attacks of insanity;

(4) Aliens afflicted with psychopathic personality, epilepsy, or a mental defect;

(5) Aliens who are narcotic drug addicts or chronic alcoholics;

(6) Aliens who are afflicted with tuberculosis in any form, or with leprosy, or any dangerous contagious disease;

(7) Aliens not comprehended within any of the foregoing classes who are certified by the examining surgeon as having a physical defect, disease, or disability, when determined by the consular or immigration officer to be of such a nature that it may affect the ability of the alien to earn a living, unless the alien affirmatively establishes that he will not have to earn a living;

(8) Aliens who are paupers, professional beggars, or vagrants;

The waiver about which the Blanks were waiting to hear is Form I-601 which is entitled "Application of Waiver of Grounds of Excludability." This form and $35.00 are submitted to the office of Immigration and Naturalization Service when applying for permanent residency. Although there seem to be supportable arguments for excluding certain individuals from becoming citizens of this country, we will let you decide whether retarded individuals should be one group of such individuals.

GLOSSARY OF LEGAL TERMS

Act A law passed by a legislature. Synonym for *statute*.

Amicus curiae (pl. *amici*) "Friend of the court." This term refers to a third party—a person or organization—who, while having no direct legal interest in the outcome of a lawsuit, submits briefs and, on occasion, evidence to a court in support of a position. In a number of landmark cases, organizations such as the Association for Retarded Citizens, the American Association on Mental Deficiency, and the United States Department of Justice have filed *amicus* briefs in support of the developmentally disabled plaintiffs.

Appeal   An application to a higher court to reverse, modify, or change the ruling of a lower court. An appeal is usually based on the lower court's interpretation of the law or on the manner in which it conducted a case. The United States Supreme Court is the highest court of appeals in the country.

Bill   A proposed statute, not yet law.

Brief   A lawyer's written summary of the law and/or facts involved in a particular case.

Cause of action   The legal damage or injury on which a lawsuit is based. There must be a cause of action, or legal "wrong," for a court to consider a case; (in *Wyatt v. Stickney*, denial of treatment and maintenance of harmful conditions in institutions gave rise to causes of action for violation of constitutional rights).

Class action   Most lawsuits are individual actions. A class action is a lawsuit brought by one or more named persons on their own behalf *and* on behalf of all persons in similar circumstances ("similarly situated"). A court's ruling in a class action suit applies to all members of the "class." For example, the court's ruling in the Willowbrook case applied to all 5,000 people who were residents of Willowbrook State School when the suit was filed, not just the few in whose names the suit was filed.

Common law   The body of law derived from historical usage, as opposed to statutory (written) law.

Complaint   A formal legal document submitted to a court by one or more persons (the plaintiffs), alleging that their rights have been violated. A complaint specifies one or more causes of action, names those who have allegedly violated the plaintiff's rights (the defendants) and demands that the defendants take certain corrective action (relief).

Adapted from S.J. Taylor & D. Biklen, *Understanding the Law: An Advocate's Guide to the Law and Developmental Disabilities*. Syracuse, N.Y.: Syracuse University and the Mental Health Law Project, 1979. Pp. 3-11. Reprinted by permission. The authors would like to thank Michael Lottman, Lee Carty, Harold Madorsky, and Lesley Lannan for their assistance in the preparation of this paper.

Consent (informed consent) An intelligent, knowing, and voluntary agreement by someone to a given activity or procedure, such as a medical operation, a scientific experiment, or a commercial contract. An informal consent requirement is a particularly important tool for safeguarding the rights of retarded people—a group who often have difficulty understanding the implications of proposed activities or procedures—especially if activities or procedures are proposed which involve risk, may be irreversible or have an irreversible effect, or will be physically, psychologically, and socially intrusive. Three conditions must exist before informed consent can be given: (*a*) The person must be capable of understanding the circumstances and factors surrounding a particular consent decision; (*b*) information relevant to the decision must be forthrightly and intelligibly provided to the person; (*c*) the person must be free to give or withhold consent voluntarily.

Consent agreement (consent judgment or consent decree) A court-ratified and enforced agreement between the opposing parties to suit, resolving the contested issues. Reached after the initiation of a lawsuit, a consent agreement, because it is ratified by a court, carries the same weight as any other court order. The Willowbrook case, *NYSARC v. Carey*, resulted in a consent agreement. For a plaintiff, a consent agreement minimizes the cost and time of continued litigation and avoids the risk of receiving an unfavorable ruling from a court.

Constitutional right A right guaranteed by the United States constitution or the constitution of the state in which a person resides. For example, the rights of *due process* and *equal protection* are specified in the 14th Amendment to the United States constitution. Constitutional rights are rarely self-explanatory. They are interpreted by courts in specific cases. A federal constitutional right supersedes federal or state law. The landmark right-to-treatment and right-to-education lawsuits (like *Wyatt v. Stickney* and *PARC v. Pennsylvania*) have been based on constitutional arguments.

Cruel and unusual punishment The prohibition contained in the 8th Amendment to the United States constitution. This constitutional argument has been made in lawsuits regarding institutions for the mentally retarded and mentally ill as well as prison cases and cases challenging the death penalty. In *NYSARC v. Carey*, for instance, the court ruled that conditions at Willowbrook represented a violation of residents' right to be free from cruel and unusual punishment, because the residents were subjected to intellectual, emotional, social, and physical harm while in the custody of the state.

DD Act (Developmentally Disabled Assistance and Bill of Rights Act) A federal law (P.L. 94-103 as amended by P.L. 95-602) designed to assist states in assuring that persons with developmental disabilities receive the services necessary to maximize their potential through a system which coordinates, monitors, plans, and evaluates those services and which ensures the protection of the rights of persons with developmental disabilities. The DD Act requires states receiving federal DD money to have in effect a protection and advocacy system for people with developmental disabilities. (Also see *Protection and advocacy system*.)

Declaratory relief   A formal finding by a court of the plaintiff's rights in a lawsuit. In effect, a court affirms the constitutional or statutory rights claimed by the plaintiffs. Declaratory relief is usually coupled with a court order granting injunctive relief.

Defendant   The party against whom a lawsuit is filed.

Development disabilities   A general, noncategorical term which subsumes terms for specific "severe, chronic" disabilities like mental retardation and cerebral palsy. The meaning of terms such as "developmental disabilities" varies from state to state, depending on particular statutes or regulations. The DD Act amendments (P.L. 95-602), passed in 1978, define developmental disability as follows:

> The term "developmental disability" means a severe, chronic disability of a person which—
> (A) Is attributable to a mental or physical impairment or combination of mental and physical impairments;
> (B) Is manifested before the person attains age twenty-two;
> (C) Is likely to continue indefinitely;
> (D) Results in substantial functional limitations in three or more of the following areas of major life activity: (i) self-care, (ii) receptive and expressive language, (iii) learning, (iv) mobility, (v) self-direction, (vi) capacity for independent living, and (vii) economic self-sufficiency: and
> (E) Reflects the person's need for a combination and sequence of special, interdisciplinary or generic care, treatment, or other services which are of lifelong, or extended duration and are individually planned and coordinated.

Due process   A right guaranteed under the 5th and 14th Amendments to the U.S. Constitution. The concept of *substantive due process* refers to all citizens' fundamental rights to life, liberty, and property. For example, in the *Donaldson* case, the Supreme Court ruled that the state of Florida had deprived Kenneth Donaldson of his rights under the 5th and 14th Amendments by involuntarily confining him in a custodial institution. *Procedural due process* refers to the fairness of procedures involved in any action which deprives people of their rights. Recent court rulings and legislation apply due process requirements to educational and treatment decisions. For instance, in *Mills* the court ruled that parents or guardians are entitled to due process regarding the school classification and placement of their children. Courts have interpreted the right of due process to require at a minimum that a person receive *reasonable notice* and the opportunity for a *fair hearing* prior to being deprived of legal rights.

Equal protection A right guaranteed by the 14th Amendment. This clause of the U.S. Constitution states that all citizens are entitled to equal protection under the law—that is, to be free from discrimination in the exercise of rights except where the state demonstrates a rational basis or compelling interest for apparently unequal treatment. In *Brown v. Board of Education of Topeka, Kansas*, the U.S. Supreme Court prohibited racial segregation in schools on the basis of the equal protection clause. The concept of equal protection has served as the foundation for landmark right to education and right-to-treatment suits on behalf of persons with disabilities.

Finding of fact A determination of the facts in the case, made by a judge or jury. A finding of fact is distinct from a conclusion of law, which only a judge can make.

Guardian An individual who has the legal authority to make decisions on behalf of another. There are many types of guardians (sometimes also called *conservators* or *committees*), and guardianship rules vary by state.

Guardian ad litem A person appointed by the court in a lawsuit to represent the interests of a person lacking capacity. A *guardian ad litem* is sometimes referred to as *next friend* or *law guardian*.

Habeas corpus An order (*writ of habeas corpus*) issued by a court to release a person from unlawful confinement.

Injunctive relief An order from a court which requires or prohibits the performance of specific acts, in order to remedy the violation of legally protected rights. In *Halderman v. Pennhurst State School*, the court-ordered injunctive relief consisted of the replacement of Pennhurst, a state institution for the developmentally disabled, with community services for all of Pennhurst's residents. Injunctive relief is often accompanied by *declaratory relief*.

Jurisdiction The authority of a court to hear and decide a suit.

Least restrictive alternative The legal concept that the government must accomplish its purposes in a manner which least infringes upon the rights of its citizens. The concept of least restrictive alternative means that services for disabled persons must be provided under the least confining and most normalized and integrated circumstances consistent with their needs. In education, this concept implies a preference for "mainstreaming," or integrated education, over segregated education in a special school or class.

Money damages Court-awarded financial payment for injuries suffered by one party due to the action or inaction of another. Damages are usually paid to the plaintiff by the defendant and may be either compensatory (to reimburse the plaintiff for loss or expenses) or punitive (to punish the defendant and deter future misconduct).

Motion A request to the court in the context of a specific case to take some action relating to the case.

Opinion A judge's statement of the reasons for a decision.

Order A judge's ruling.

Ordinance A local law, that is, a city, town, or county law.

P.L. (Public Law) The designation of a federal law. The numbers following "P.L." refer respectively to the session of Congress during which the law was passed and the order in which the law was passed in that session. For example, P.L. 94-142 was the 142nd law passed during the 94th Congress.

Party The plaintiff or the defendant in a lawsuit.

Petitioner The party appealing a court's decision to a higher court. Synonym for *appellant*. Also sometimes used to identify the plaintiff in certain courts or types of cases.

Plaintiff The party who brings a lawsuit, alleging a violation of rights. The plaintiff is always named before the defendant in a case title; for example, Donaldson is the plaintiff in *Donaldson v. O'Connor*. Upon appeal, the order of names is reversed.

Pleadings The documents submitted to a court in the pretrial stage of litigation. The term is used broadly to refer to the plaintiff's initial complaint, the defendant's answer and the plaintiff's reply to the answer, and is sometimes used more narrowly to refer to the plaintiff's complaint.

Precedent A prior court decision in a relevant case, cited in the interpretation of law or constitutional provision. A court may or may not accept a precedent as authoritative in interpreting the law in a specific case, depending on the factual similarities between the cases and the jurisdiction in which the precedent arose.

Preliminary injunction A form of injunctive relief. A preliminary injunction is a temporary order to prevent a party from taking certain actions pending the court's final decision.

Private cause of action An individual's ability to seek relief from a court for violation of a statutory or constitutional right (see *standing*). A statute is said not to create a private right of action when it provides for remedies other than individual court proceedings and when there is no apparent legislative intent to allow individuals to sue when their rights under the statute are violated.

Protection and advocacy system (P&A) A state system of protect and advocate for the rights of people with developmental disabilities, as provided by the DD Act. The DD Act requires states receiving federal DD money to establish a P&A system and provides for federal allotments to fund this system. Under the DD Act, the P&A system must be independent of any agency which provides services to persons with developmental disabilities and must have the authority to pursue legal, administrative and other apparent remedies. (Also see *DD Act*).

Relief The remedy to some legal wrong or violation of one's rights. Plaintiffs seek from the court certain types of relief against the defendants, such as declaratory relief, injunctive relief, writs of *habeas corpus* (release), or money damages.

Remand An order by a higher court returning a case to a lower court for further action consistent with the higher court's decision.

Respondent The winning party at the trial level in a case that has been appealed. Synonym for *appellee*. Also used to mean the defendant in certain courts or cases.

Review A re-examination of a court's decision by that same court or by an appeals court.

Section 504 Section 504 of the Rehabilitation Act of 1973, as amended. Section 504 outlaws discrimination against any handicapped individual by any organization receiving federal funds. Section 504 is often discussed in conjunction with Section 503 of the Act, which obliges every employer receiving more than $2,500 in federal money to take affirmative action to hire and promote handicapped persons.

Shall/may The term "shall" in a law, regulation, or court order is mandatory, while the term "may" is discretionary. The term "may" allows flexibility in a party's actions, including the flexibility not to act at all.

Sovereign immunity The legal doctrine which protects the state and federal governments from certain kinds of suits in certain courts, on the general theory that the government ("sovereign") should be free to exercise its authority within reasonable limits. This immunity may be lost when the government exceeds its authority or acts in an unconstitutional manner. Recent laws and court decisions have greatly narrowed the concept of governmental immunity from suit.

Statute A law passed by a state or federal legislature. Synonym for *Act*.

Statute of limitations A statute which specifies the period of time within which a lawsuit must be brought after an alleged violation of rights. A person loses his or her right to sue after the time period has elapsed.

Stay A court order postponing the enforcement of a court ruling pending future legal action, such as an appeal to a higher court.

Summary judgment A judge's ruling on the law in a case where the judge holds that the facts are not in dispute.

Temporary restraining order A form of emergency injunctive relief, issued (often without a hearing) to preserve the status quo for a brief period pending a full hearing before the court. A party must show that immediate and irreparable harm will result if the order is not issued. For longer-term relief before the court's final decision, a preliminary injunction is necessary.

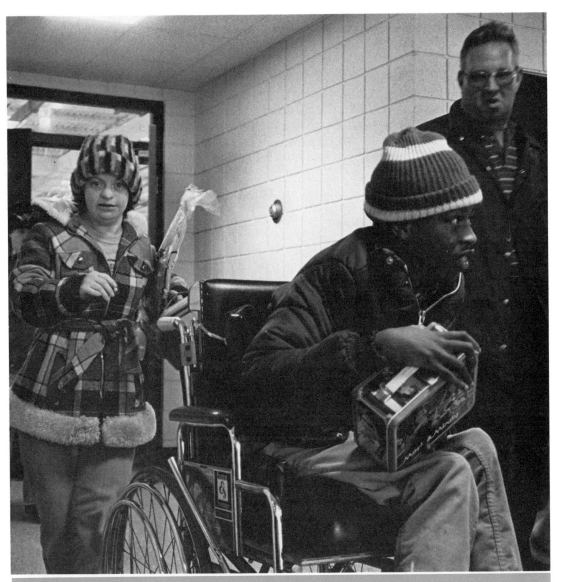

PART FOUR
Programming
Options

CHAPTER TEN

The Educational Assessment Process

S o far we have looked at the history of services to mentally retarded people, the evolving definition of mental retardation, certain causes of the condition, and characteristic features of many retarded individuals. It is now time to turn to information on dealing with retarded students. This chapter describes in some detail how individuals are identified and subsequently classified as mentally retarded. In particular, in this chapter on the assessment process, we will focus on the administrative context of assessment, legislative reform and the overall assessment process, from identification through placement. Two related chapters that deal in depth with the assessment of two characteristics that combine to define mental retardation are the ones concerning intelligence (chapter 4) and adaptive behavior (chapter 5).

To begin, educational assessment of exceptional students is a multifaceted process. It may be performed for one of two different reasons: for classification or for educational programming. Wallace and Larsen (1978) capture the essence of this distinction when they state that educational assessment techniques are administered

This chapter was contributed by Robert Marshall Davis and James S. Payne.

1. To identify and sometimes label for administrative purposes those children experiencing learning problems who will probably require special educational help, and

2. To gather additional information that might be helpful in establishing instructional objectives and remedial strategies for those children identified as handicapped learners. (p. 5)

We will address both of these dimensions throughout this chapter.

THE ADMINISTRATIVE CONTEXT

Since 1970, the educational literature has been saturated with articles, books, and speeches on accountability—and the public seems to concur. Public pressure at school board meetings, in the press, in defeating levies at the polls, has, at the least, supported the professional movement to develop standards for accountability. As a result, new legislation, known as *Standards of Quality*, has been adopted by many State Boards of Education to mandate performance, professional, and system accountability. In addition, P.L. 94-142 (The Education for All Handicapped Children Act of 1975) has created a national legislative mandate for school systems to provide each handicapped child in need of special education and related services a written **Individualized Educational Program (IEP)**. The IEP must include statements of the child's present levels of performance, annual (long-term) goals, and instructional (short-term) objectives. Furthermore, the child's progress and the IEP must be reviewed at least annually. The passing of P.L. 94-142, according to Van Etten and Van Etten (1976), "requires teaching accountability. . . . Any arguments about the need for accountability are now moot. It appears to be the law of the land" (p. 4). According to Thorndike and Hagen (1969), "sound decisions arise out of relevant knowledge of the individual. . . . The more we know about a person that relates to our present decision, and the more accurately we know it, the more likely we are to arrive at a sound decision about him or a wise plan of action for him" (p. 8). It is against this backdrop of public pressure, legislative mandate, and the professional educator's need for accurate information and accountability that the assessment process unfolds.

To fully appreciate the complexities involved in educational assessment, you must look at the process of decision making which precedes the actual assessment of any given student.

One of the primary functions of any school administration is to make decisions (Griffiths, 1959). Administratively, most school systems include a department often referred to as *Special Services* and/or *Pupil Personnel Services*. This administrative unit is responsible for tasks such as referring students suspected of having disabilities, identifying those students who do have disabilities, classifying those students according to legal guidelines, and conducting a multifactored assessment to develop specific recommendations for implementing instructional prescriptions. For this reason, it is imperative that decisions made by this office be accurate, be based on information thorough enough to reflect the student's needs, and provide the kind of implementation that assures sustained educational accountability. In addition, decisions made in regard to children suspected of having or identified as having a handicapping condition must now conform to certain legal requirements, as set forth in P.L. 94-142.

LEGISLATIVE REFORM

The Education for All Handicapped Children Act is probably the most significant federal school legislation since the enactment of Title I of the Elementary and Secondary Education Act of 1965. According to Goodman (1976), P.L. 94-142 can be envisioned as

> Promising an end to the inglorious custom of treating persons with disabilities as second class citizens. It appears that P.L. 94-142 will bring schools closer to the principles of democracy on which the Nation was founded by opening classrooms to a new student clientele. (p. 6)

This legislation is the fulfillment of the goal of many professional special educators—to assure each exceptional child the opportunity for an appropriate education unfettered by inappropriate administrative constraints and inadequate public resources.

The purpose of P.L. 94-142 is to make certain that needed services reach all handicapped children. The federal government has authorized the spending of up to three billion dollars by 1982 in aid to the states, which is much more money than had previously been provided. In order to receive this aid, the states are required to provide evidence that they are doing all within their power to help all handicapped children receive needed services. "In two decades the federal government has moved from a position of little concern or involvement to become a major partner with the local and state public education programs for the handicapped" (Kirk & Gallagher, 1979, p. 475).

In essence, the public schools now have the responsibility for providing quality educational programs for all children, including mentally retarded children, regardless of the severity of the handicap. These programs must be instructionally appropriate and individually designed to the greatest extent possible. In addition, each handicapped child is by law entitled to reassessment at least once a year.

All school districts are required to begin an intensified effort to

Public Law 94-142
94th Congress, S. 6
November 29, 1975

An Act

To amend the Education of the Handicapped Act to provide educational assistance to all handicapped children, and for other purposes.

Be it enacted by the Senate and House of Representatives of the United States of America in Congress assembled, That this Act may be cited as the "Education for All Handicapped Children Act of 1975".

Education for All Handicapped Children Act of 1975, 20 USC 1401 note.

EXTENSION OF EXISTING LAW

SEC. 2. (a)(1)(A) Section 611(b)(2) of the Education of the Handicapped Act (20 U.S.C. 1411(b)(2)) (hereinafter in this Act referred to as the "Act"), as in effect during the fiscal years 1976 and 1977, is amended by striking out "the Commonwealth of Puerto Rico.".

(B) Section 611(c)(1) of the Act (20 U.S.C. 1411(c)(1)), as in effect during the fiscal years 1976 and 1977, is amended by striking out "the Commonwealth of Puerto Rico,".

(2) Section 611(c)(2) of the Act (20 U.S.C. 1411(c)(2)), as in effect during the fiscal years 1976 and 1977, is amended by striking out "year ending June 30, 1975" and inserting in lieu thereof the following: "years ending June 30, 1975, and 1976, and for the fiscal year ending September 30, 1977", and by striking out "2 per centum" each place it appears therein and inserting in lieu thereof "1 per centum".

(3) Section 611(d) of the Act (20 U.S.C. 1411(d)), as in effect dur-

P.L. 94-142 has laid out specific procedures for identifying, assessing, and providing educational services for all handicapped children.

locate and appropriately identify and serve all retarded children, regardless of their level of disability. Smith, Neisworth, and Greer (1978) address the issue as it relates to the moderately retarded, and they conclude that

> The upshot of this legislation (P.L. 94-142) is that children who are adjudged to be moderately retarded, whether they reside in a residential institution or at home, will be provided an appropriate educational program on a continuous and longitudinal basis. Congress and the Courts will no longer sanction the "warehousing" of children in institutions, and no longer will school districts be given the "option" of deciding whether they can afford to provide for moderately retarded children. . . . Parents can look forward to the time when their moderately retarded youngsters will be given opportunities to develop the range of basic skills necessary for them to function in the community within reasonable, but legal, limitations. (p. 193)

In particular, the law specifies that first priority be given to those children not currently receiving an education at all, and that second priority be given to the most severely handicapped children whose current education is not considered adequate. Public school education of the severely and profoundly retarded (and multiply handicapped) remains controversial. Some advocate groups, such as The Association for the Severely Handicapped, and professionals urge the integration of severely handicapped students into the public schools wherever conceivable. As Brown, Branston, Hamre-Nietupski, Johnson, Wilcox, and Gruenewald (1979) conclude,

> Severely handicapped students will be increasingly more competent because of better educational services and longitudinal exposure to nonhandicapped models [in the public schools]. If severely handicapped students and nonhandicapped students are taught to interact in a variety of ways starting from early age, there is little doubt but that the attitude and performance discrepancies currently observed can be substantially reduced. (p. 13)

On the other hand, a statement opposing the wholesale integration of severely handicapped students into the public schools has been made by Burton and Hirshoren (1979).

> To place the severely and profoundly retarded student into self-contained classes in the public schools . . . is inappropriate and inconsistent with the intentions of P.L. 94-142 and reflects a simplistic answer to a very complex problem. . . . Nowhere, in any of the litigation and legislation since the PARC decision of 1971, is there a clear mandate or requirement for the physical placement of all severely and profoundly retarded children in the public schools. What the law does mandate is that a free appropriate education, in the least restrictive environment, be provided. . . . The public school, in terms of physical plant, staffing, and tradition, is generally not the most appropriate nor is it the least restrictive delivery system for services to the severely and profoundly retarded. (pp. 601–602)

This refers to the case *Pennsylvania Association for Retarded Children, v. Commonwealth of Pennsylvania*, in which the court first established the right of all students to education in the least restrictive environment.

Although this point of view has not met with many favorable reactions from champions of the integration of severely handicapped students into regular schools, it nonetheless raises some very important questions regarding the concepts of "appropriate education" and "least restrictive environment." Recent litigation focuses on some aspects of these issues. For example, in *Matthews v. Campbell* (1979), parents of a 13-year-old severely/profoundly retarded boy sued their public school district to provide a residential care facility with 24-hour care for their son, who had been placed in a public school program and was living at home. They felt that the public school could not provide adequately for their son. The initial ruling gave the school district 6 months in which to demonstrate that it could provide an appropriate educational program.

At the end of that time, the case was reviewed; the judge found that the boy should be placed in a residential program for 6 months and his progress compared with that during the public school program. Because there was no suitable residential program near enough to the child's home community, the court decided on a plan proposed by the school district involving a combination of public schooling and residence in a specially staffed apartment. At the time of this writing, the boy is in that program and no final decision has been handed down. In any case, the school district is, in effect, paying for a local residential facility. What seems to be clear from this case and others is that appropriate placement must be decided on an individual basis—in the courts, if necessary.

ASSESSMENT

Administratively, **assessment** implies collecting information on an individual for the purpose of making decisions about that person. The assessment process refers to the comprehensive gathering of data, as suggested by Salvia and Ysseldyke (1981).

> Assessment in educational settings is a multifaceted process that involves far more than the administration of a test. When we assess students, we consider the way they perform a variety of tasks in a variety of settings or contexts, the meaning of their performances in terms of the total functioning of the individual, and likely explanations for those performances. Good assessment procedures take into consideration the fact that anyone's performance on any task is influenced not only by the demands of the task itself but also by the history and characteristics the individual brings to the task and by factors inherent in the setting in which the assessment is carried out. (pp. 3–4)

While labels per se may not be important, they are a necessary tool in complying with the law and thus in determining eligibility for special services. Handicapped students must be so classified if their school districts are to receive federal funding under P.L. 94-142.

The first goal of assessment may be to identify a child as handicapped, for instance, to find that his intellectual performance and adaptive behavior fit the definition of "mental retardation." Mentally retarded students may be assessed in order to classify them or to determine an individual's current strengths and weaknesses. Regardless of the intent, the ultimate goal of educational assessment is to provide an appropriate program and/or treatment plan for the students.

This assessment process may involve the use of formal and/or informal tests. It is important to make a sharp distinction between *assessment* and *testing*. Assessment is *not* synonymous with testing. Ysseldyke (1978) states that "tests are tools which may be used in the assessment process" (p. 269). Highlighting the relationship of testing to the assessment process, Gunzburg (1958) has suggested that the purpose of assessment is to "put test scores in their proper context and to relate them to the person tested rather than to the test used" (p. 258). It is imperative that the assessment process obtain the kind of information about a handicapped child that allows educators to choose appropriate teaching strategies as well as to produce guidelines for instructional objectives, methods, and materials that can be incorporated into the IEP. A combination of formal tests, informal tests, observation, and a case history may provide a useful and thorough methodology for assessing retarded children.

The assessment process is an ongoing function which does not end with the writing of a report. Sattler (1974) has noted that assessment also "involves communicating the findings to interested parties, interpreting the results to parents . . . and participating in decision-making activities" (p. 3).

P.L. 94-142 ensures the quality of assessment procedures and services by specifying legal safeguards. Some of the basic rights dealing with assessment ensured by P.L. 94-142 include

1. The right to due process, which protects the student from being labeled erroneously or denied an equal education. Specifically, all records must be kept confidential. The parents must be an active part of the team which evaluates the child, places the child in special education, and develops the IEP. In addition, if the parents disagree with the school's placement, they have the right to an independent evaluation and a hearing in front of an impartial third party.

2. Protection against discriminatory testing in diagnosis. In the past, standardized tests have been used to identify handicapped children. These tests were often (if not always) biased against ethnic minority children. A child can no longer be identified as handicapped on the basis of a single test. Furthermore, the testing must be done in the child's native language.

3. Team assessment. Handicapped children must be assessed by a multidisciplinary team, and placement must be decided by a team which includes at least the child's parents, teachers, and a school administrator. All tests must be administered by trained personnel.

4. Multifactored assessment. All areas of suspected disability must be assessed. This might include vision, hearing, communication, and health, among others.

5. Ongoing review. The IEP must include a date for the beginning and end of all special services, and must be reviewed at least annually. A child can no longer be labeled "mentally retarded," stuck in a special class, and remain there, regardless of the progress made.

FUNCTIONS OF ASSESSMENT DATA

Special education assessment involves examination of intelligence, achievement, personality, perceptual-motor development, aptitude, interests, social maturity, and specific subject areas. Medical, social, psychological, educational, speech, language, and hearing data are all used, with varying importance depending on the individual, to make educational decisions. Ysseldyke (1978) suggests five functions of educational assessment: screening and identification, classification and placement, intervention planning, program evaluation, and evaluation of progress.

IDENTIFICATION AND SCREENING

The essence of identification and, more specifically, early identification, is prevention through intervention. It is possible that, if problems are identified early, intervention can remediate the problems of some children, limit the effects of handicaps in other children, and in many cases prevent the development of secondary handicaps. P.L. 94-142 requires the identification, location, and evaluation of all handicapped children who are between the ages of 3 and 21 as of September 1, 1980 (provided state laws do not limit education for children aged 3 to 5). This translates into large-scale preschool screening and identification programs.

Child-Find   The first step involved in identification is **child-find.** As Lillie (1975) suggests, "Before children can be screened, they must be found; i.e., someone must bring them to a screening location or provide their names and a way to get in touch with them" (p. 248).

As we saw in chapter 2, most child-find projects have relied on public awareness campaigns. Unfortunately, there is no convincing documentation indicating the most productive approach to early identification. The choices between referral and screening modes, between community-based efforts and outside agencies, between mass campaigns and personal contact, and between screening all children and screening only handicapped children are difficult to make. These questions must be fully examined before a valid and reliable approach to early identification of mildly retarded children can be implemented. Compounding the problem are community differences. As we have seen, children with relatively severe retardation are easier to identify at an early age—even at birth in many cases. But in certain communities—both rural and sparsely populated and certain urban, lower socioeconomic communities—retarded children may still be taken home and ignored, if not hidden away. Finding these individual children is a difficult task.

No matter how thorough a preschool child-find program is, the majority of children with mild retardation usually will not be identified until after they begin school. Therefore, the responsibility for "finding" most mildly retarded children rests with the classroom teacher, who should report students who are "high risk" of showing learning handicaps.

A last, but not least, concern is the impact of early identification on parents. To discover that your child is "mentally retarded" is painful. Parents must be assured that the child will receive a thorough and accurate diagnosis. In dealing with parents whose young child has been identified as mildly mentally retarded, professionals should not dwell on the "problem," but should quickly move to those interventions that will enhance the child's functioning and solve problems the parents have with the child.

See chapter 8 for a comprehensive discussion of this topic.

Screening **Screening** is intended to identify those children who might need special services, so that they can be assessed in more depth. Basically, a screening test divides individuals into two groups: those who are possibly handicapped or delayed and those who are not handicapped or delayed. Once the screening procedure identifies a student potentially in need of special services, then further assessment is in order. A screening procedure may falsely identify some children as "high risk" when they are *not* handicapped or, conversely, may not identify certain children who are actually handicapped or delayed.

Frankenburg (1972) suggests considering the following factors before screening begins: (*a*) the frequency of the particular condition being screened for; (*b*) the severity of the condition; (*c*) the availability of a particular treatment or remediation which would be effective; (*d*) the time the screening takes place; (*e*) the detectability of the condition; (*f*) the value of early detection; (*g*) the cost-effectiveness of the procedure.

The primary purpose of screening is to *recognize* those students who need a more complete diagnostic study. A child who is identified on a screening test does not necessarily need a full battery of standardized tests. Frequently, formal or informal observations as well as frequency counts of observed behavior can determine the need for further assessment.

An example of a new screening test, which can be used with preschool, kindergarten, and first grade students, is REFER: Rapid Exam for Early Referral (Kunzelmann & Koenig, 1980). While REFER is individually administered, it takes only 4 to 5 minutes to give to each child. After a 15-second practice, the child performs each of four simple, preacademic tasks. The teacher merely counts correct responses. If the child gets statistically low scores on all four items, he or she is referred for further diagnosis. If he or she gets three out of four low scores, rescreening in 3 months is recommended. According to the authors, the test successfully predicts which students will need special education services, before the teacher and child waste time with inappropriate educational programming. Screenings like this promise to ease the problem of identifying mildly retarded children when they first enter school.

In summary, the major function of screening is to quickly examine a large number of individuals to identify the ones who are so clearly "at risk" of being handicapped that more intensive assessment and diagnosis are warranted.

CLASSIFICATION AND PLACEMENT

Historically, tests have been used for the purpose of making classification and placement decisions. For instance, criteria are specified for establishing the nature and degree of retardation of individual students. Many state education agencies recommend that children receive individual psycho-educational evaluations and be classified before they are placed in special education. In addition, most states prescribe the nature of the evaluation for different categorical placements. For example, as we have seen, one criterion for "mental retardation" is an IQ of 70 or below on standardized measures of intelligence, such as the Wechsler Intelligence Scale for Children-Revised (WISC-R) or the Standford-Binet, along with impairments in adaptive behavior as clinically determined.

A Look at Assessment Instruments To perform an in-depth educational assessment, the team should use a variety of types of assessment instruments. Table 10-1 lists many of these.

Standardized tests are formal instruments widely used for measuring and evaluating an individual's strengths and weaknesses. The procedures for administering and scoring these tests are strictly prescribed and must be followed exactly. Many standardized tests are norm-referenced; that is, they have been given to large numbers of subjects, and the results of those tests can be used for comparing an individual's performance to that of the norm group. Most intelligence and achievement tests are both standardized and norm-referenced. Although they are useful, let us not forget that a formal standardized test is simply a collection of behavior samples reflecting how a person performed at one given moment. Thus, a student's deficits must be analyzed and interpreted within the context of the testing situation.

Another type of test useful in educational assessment is the criterion-referenced test. These tests are often made up by classroom teachers, although there are published versions. Criterion-referenced tests compare a student's performance on a task to a mastery level rather than to the performances of other students (McLoughlin & Lewis, 1981).

Informal assessment may involve giving questionnaires or inventories of certain skills; observing the child with or without a checklist of target behaviors; interviewing the child, the parents, or other concerned people; and a variety of other assessment techniques.

Specific assessment tools used for evaluating intelligence and adaptive behavior are discussed in chapters 4 and 5.

TABLE 10.1   Methods Used in Assessment

A. Objective tests and standardized measures
   1. Standardized tests and measures
      a. Achievement tests
      b. Mental and intelligence tests
      c. Tests of motor skills and abilities
      d. Aptitude and readiness tests
      e. Physiological measures and medical examinations
      f. Personality and adjustment tests
      g. Interest inventories and attitude scales
   2. Unstandardized short-answer objective tests
      a. Simple recall or free response tests
      b. Completion tests
      c. Alternate response tests
      d. Multiple-choice tests
      e. Matching tests
   3. Improved essay types of tests consisting of questions so formulated that they can be scored on a fairly objective basis
   4. Scales for analyzing and rating a performance or a product.
   5. Tests involving evaluation of responses using projective methods
B. Evaluation of behavior by less formal procedures
   1. Problem-situation tests
      a. Direct experience
         (1) Experiment to be performed
         (2) Actual life situation to be met
      b. Indirect approach
         (1) Improved essay-type examinations
         (2) Expressing judgments about described situations
         (3) "What would you do?"
   2. Behavior records concerning in- and out-of-school activities
      a. Controlled situations
         (1) Use of checklists, rating scales, score cards, codes for evaluating personality traits, behavior, attitudes, opinions, interests, and so on
         (2) Self-rating devices, "Guess-Who?"
         (3) Time studies of attention, activities
         (4) Photographs and motion pictures
         (5) Stenographic reports
         (6) Dictaphone and tape recordings
      b. Uncontrolled situations
         (1) Log or diary; autobiographical reports
         (2) Anecdotal records, behavior journals
         (3) Records of libraries, police, welfare agencies, and so on
         (4) Still or motion pictures
         (5) Tape recordings
   3. Inventories and questionnaires of work habits, interests, activities, associates, and the like
   4. Interviews, conferences, personal reports
      a. With the individual learner
      b. With others, such as parents or associates
   5. Analysis and evaluation of a creative act or product, such as a poem, music, and constructions
   6. Sociometric procedures for studying group relationships
   7. Evaluation of reactions using projective and expressive techniques
      a. Psychodrama and play techniques
      b. Free-association tests
      c. Interpretation of reactions to selected pictures and drawings
      d. Interpretation of free oral and written expression
      e. Interpretation of artistic and constructive products

From Leo J. Brueckner and Guy L. Bond, *The Diagnosis and Treatment of Learning Difficulties*, Englewood Cliffs, N.J.: Prentice-Hall, 1955, pp. 8–10. Reprinted by permission of Prentice-Hall, Inc., Englewood Cliffs, New Jersey.

TESTING THE LIMITS OF STUDENTS

The assessment of handicapped students often involves the use of formal, standardized, norm-referenced instruments. In an effort to obtain the most useful information about a student, there are times when alternative testing procedures may be indicated. One recommended procedure is referred to as *adaptive assessment* or *testing the limits*. This technique has been discussed thoroughly by Sattler (1982) and is highlighted below.

Testing of limits. The standard administrative procedures should be followed, if possible, in all cases. The only exceptions are those discussed in the test manuals (e.g., changing order of tests if necessary, eliminating spoiled tests, etc.) or those necessary to test handicapped children. However, there are times at which examiners desire to go beyond the standard test procedures (testing of limits) in order to gain additional information about the child's abilities. These occasions may be infrequent, but when they occur, the information gained from testing-of-limits procedures can be helpful, especially in clinical settings. Any successes obtained during testing of limits, of course, cannot be credited to the child's scores. *All testing-of-limits techniques should be used only after* *the scale has been administered using standard procedures.*

A number of different testing-of-limits procedures are now considered.

1. *Additional cues.* How much help is necessary for the child to answer a question correctly? To answer this question, you may provide a series of cues to the child. You can show the first step in solving the problem, after which you can provide a series of additional steps if needed. Or you might begin by asking the child how he or she went about trying to solve the problem. This question can be followed by asking the child to try to answer the problem again, or by providing the first step in reaching the correct solution, or by informing him or her where the method was wrong and then asking him or her to try again. The more cues that are needed before success is achieved, the greater the degree of possible learning disability or cognitive deficit.

2. *Establishing methods used by the examinee.* There are many different ways of solving the test questions.

All assessment data may be used for **interindividual** or **intraindividual** comparisons. Interindividual assessment compares one person with a norm (that is, with other people). An example of an instrument of this type is the WISC-R (Wechsler, 1974). Intraindividual tests identify a person's relative strengths and weaknesses. An example is the Peabody Individual Achievement Test (Dunn & Markwardt, 1970). Certain norm-referenced tests may be used for both interindividual and intraindividual comparisons.

To learn how the child went about solving the problem, you may simply ask what method was used. Some children will be able to verbalize their method, while others will not, even though they have answered correctly. On digit span tests, for example, the task can be solved by grouping the digits in pairs of two, three, or more digit sequences, by recalling them as a number (4—1—3 as four hundred and thirteen), or by recalling them as distinct digits in sequence. The method used may be related to learning efficiency or to personality features, or it may have no particular import. Asking how the child solved the problem may give you additional insight about how well the task was understood.

3. *Additional time limits.* When the child fails a test because of time limits, you can readminister the test without time limits (after the examination has been completed), in order to determine whether the child can solve the problem.

4. *Alternate scoring.* As a result of the help provided during the testing-of-limits phase, the child may pass tests. During the test proper, too, the child may solve a problem after the time limit has been reached. In such cases, an alternate IQ can be calculated, and both the standard and alternate scores reported. However, the alternate IQ must be interpreted cautiously because it has no normative basis. Little is known about the meaning of alternate scores, but it is possible that they are related to learning potential.

One of the problems associated with helping procedures introduced during the testing-of-limits phase is that these procedures may invalidate the results of retesting occurring at a later date. You must therefore carefully consider the benefits and costs of testing limits. If retesting may be needed in the near future with the same test, then the testing-of-limits procedure in all probability should not be used. However, if the goal is to evaluate the limits of the child's abilities on the test, and there is no reason to plan on a retest in the near future (say within the next twelve to twenty-four months), testing of limits may be quite useful.

SOURCE: Sattler, J.M. (1982). *Assessment of children's intelligence and special abilities* (2nd ed.). Boston: Allyn and Bacon.

Inter-individual differences are used for classification and for grouping children in special classes or ability groups. . . . Intra-individual differences are used to organize an instructional program for a particular child in conformity with abilities and disabilities, without regard to how he or she compares with other children. (Kirk & Gallagher, 1979, p. 30)

Clearly, many different kinds of tests are available for gathering data for making educational decisions. Too often, decision makers rely entirely upon test scores instead of evaluating the kinds of behaviors sampled by the test as well as the way in which the person earned the score. It is the responsibility of the assessment team to interpret all interrelationships among pieces of assessment data, not merely to report test scores (McLoughlin & Lewis, 1981). The significance of this process has been noted by Smith (1969).

> Specialists in the measurement and evaluation of human behaviors are asked to estimate children's behavioral capabilities and achievement in a variety of dimensions and for a number of purposes. It is alarmingly clear that the accuracy of these estimates is critical since these data are used to make significant decisions. The results of behavioral assessments are being used to do things to people. . . . Those using this information must know the meaning, limitations, and appropriateness of every evaluative procedure employed with youngsters. (p. 11)

Pupil Placement in Special Education P.L. 94-142, as well as state laws, mandates that each school division operating a special education program must develop and adopt local policies that establish a systematic plan for pupil screening and referral; diagnosis, educational planning, and reporting; implementation; and follow-up. As part of these responsibilities, the local educational agency must ensure that a Special Education Eligibility Committee exists at each school. This committee is charged with determining whether an individual child is eligible for special education services.

Legally, the identification of a child as handicapped and subsequently eligible for special education services requires interdisciplinary action. In practice, in most school districts a child must go through the following assessments before being placed in special services for the mentally retarded.

1. An educational evaluation by the teacher to determine what the student has learned and whether this person is presently having problems.

2. A speech, language, and hearing evaluation by a speech clinician to determine whether or not the child has difficulties in these areas *which may be interfering with learning*.

3. A psychological evaluation by a psychologist to determine how the student learns and what is the best way to maximize learning.

4. A sociological evaluation by a visiting teacher to obtain information about the student's behavior at home and how the home situation may affect learning.

5. A medical evaluation by a physician to determine whether medical factors may be interfering with learning.

Along with this multifactored evaluation, every mentally retarded student has certain rights to confidentiality and due process. These rights are guaranteed by law and provide personal safeguards that are essential if an appropriate educational opportunity is to be achieved.

These rights are summarized in Table 10.2.

TABLE 10.2 Rights of Each Handicapped Student

Confidentiality

1. *Notice.* The state educational agency must notify the parents concerning the type of data sought, the sources from which data will be collected, and the uses to be made of the data; the policies and procedures to be followed regarding the storage, disclosure to third parties, retention, and destruction of the data; and the rights of children and parents regarding the data.
2. *Access Rights.* Parents have the right to examine data relating to their children.
3. *Hearing Rights.* Parents have the right to request a hearing to question the accuracy and appropriateness of the data.
4. *Consent.* Parental consent must be given before a child is formally evaluated and before data are disclosed to anyone other than officials of participating agencies or used for purposes other than those specified to the parents (see Notice above).
5. *Safeguards.* Participating agencies must protect the confidentiality of data at all times; at each participating agency one official must assume responsibility for assuring the confidentiality of data; all personnel collecting or using data must be trained in the state's policies and procedures regarding confidentiality; and each participating agency must keep a current list of employees who are permitted access to the data.
6. *Destruction of the Data.* Within 5 years after the personally identifiable data are no longer needed for providing educational services to the child, they must be destroyed. The child's name, address, and phone number and information on grades achieved, attendance record, grade level, and year completed may be maintained indefinitely.
7. *Children's Rights.* Upon reaching majority, children have the same rights of privacy as those accorded to parents.

Due Process

1. *Notice.* Parents must receive notification regarding proposed changes in the identification, evaluation, or educational placement of the child or regarding refusals to make such changes. Parents must also be informed in their native language, if feasible, of their rights and the procedures available to them.
2. *Access Rights.* Parents have the right to examine all relevant data regarding their child's identification, evaluation, and educational placement.
3. *Consent.* Parental consent must be obtained before the child can be formally evaluated or a change made in his or her educational placement.
4. *Hearing Rights.* If parents disagree with the agency's identification, evaluation, or educational placement of the child, they have an opportunity for an impartial due-process hearing conducted by the state or local educational agency. At the hearing parents can be represented by anyone of their choice and can submit an independent evaluation of their child.
5. *Appeal Rights.* Any party aggrieved by the findings and decision of the hearing may appeal to the state educational agency, which must conduct an impartial review and make an independent decision. Any party which is not satisfied with this decision may bring civil action in a court of law.

From K.W. Laub & P.D. Kurtz, "Early Identification," in J. Neisworth & R.M. Smith (Eds.). *Retardation: Issues, Assessment and Intervention.* New York: McGraw Hill, 1978, pp. 262–266. Reprinted by permission.

ASSESSMENT OF SEVERELY HANDICAPPED STUDENTS

Assessing severely and profoundly retarded students or those with multiple handicaps presents some special difficulties. Most standardized instruments are not appropriate because (*a*) severely handicapped children were not included in the norm groups, (*b*) scoring procedures are not designed to accommodate extremely low scores, (*c*) many of these children have sensory deficits, and (*d*) results cannot be translated into educational prescriptions (Simeonsson, Huntington, & Parse, 1980). As an alternative, many school systems are using criterion-referenced assessment or developing their own "curriculum-referenced checklist" (White & Haring, 1978), which breaks down the school's curriculum into specific assessment targets, details procedures for uniform assessment of each child, and gives specific criteria for determining mastery of each skill. Thus the curriculum-referenced assessment results can be immedi-

CONSIDERATION OF THE CONDITIONS OF ASSESSMENT

There is much talk about the many factors which can influence how well a person performs under formal testing conditions. However, the test results seldom indicate any of these conditions. Some publishers and authors of tests are beginning to acknowledge this important aspect of the assessment process. Concern for the administrative, student-related, and environmental conditions that might affect test performance are exemplified below. This type of information is being promoted in tests published by PRO-ED. We support the inclusion of this information and feel that it should be collected every time a formal test is given.

ADMINISTRATION CONDITIONS

A. Subtests administered in one session_____
   two sessions_____ three or more_____
B. Tested completely individually_____ Tested partially in group_____ Size of group_____
C. Administered by:
   Experienced Examiner_____
   By other. Specify (Classroom Teacher, Trainer, etc.)_____
   _____

ately translated into instructional objectives for each child. As Smith and Smith (1978) comment, "Because learning for these students is often a tedious venture, major skills and the minute splinter skills of which they are comprised frequently become goals and objectives covering a substantial part of the school year" (p. 57).

Most assessments of severely and profoundly handicapped students cover communication skills, self-help skills, social skills, motor skills, and preacademic or cognitive skills. It is critical that assessment tools used with severely handicapped students precisely analyze each child's performance level in each of these domains. Several such systems are now available. One system, the Uniform Performance Assessment System (UPAS) (White, Edgar, & Haring, 1978), produces an overall score as well as communication, gross motor, social/self-help, and preacademic scores. Its scales are built on the hierarchical development

STUDENT-RELATED CONDITIONS

	Poor				Good
A. Energy level	1	2	3	4	5
B. Attitude toward test	1	2	3	4	5
C. Rapport with examiner	1	2	3	4	5
D. Perseverance	1	2	3	4	5
E. Visual acuity	1	2	3	4	5
F. Hearing acuity	1	2	3	4	5
G. State of health:					
General	1	2	3	4	5
During testing	1	2	3	4	5

H. Notes and other considerations _____
_____
_____

ENVIRONMENTAL CONDITIONS

A. Place(s) tested _____
_____

	Interfering				Not Interfering
B. Noise level	1	2	3	4	5
C. Interruptions	1	2	3	4	5
D. Distractions	1	2	3	4	5
E. Light	1	2	3	4	5
F. Temperature	1	2	3	4	5

G. Notes and other considerations _____

of certain critical skills in each domain. UPAS is designed to be used four times each school year, in order to give precise information on child progress that can be used in planning further instruction.

INTERVENTION PLANNING

Diagnosis without remediation through educational prescription would make the assessment process useless. Therefore, once we know what the problem is, we attempt to remediate it by applying the appropriate treatment. Assessment data must specify where the child is in instructional terms ("John can do two-digit addition problems without carrying") to let the teacher know the next step in instruction (McLoughlin & Lewis, 1981).

The ultimate goal of assessment is to provide the student with an appropriate instructional program. It therefore is necessary to diagnose specifically what must be provided. The process of tying specific diagnosis to explicit educational programming has been called *prescriptive teaching, clinical teaching* (Lerner, 1981) and *diagnostic-prescriptive teaching.*

> Clinical teaching differs from regular teaching because it is planned for an individual child rather than for an entire class; for an atypical child rather than for the mythical "average" child. . . . Clinical teaching implies that the teacher is fully aware of the individual student's learning style, interests, short-comings and areas of strengths, levels of development and tolerance in many areas, feelings, and adjustments to the world. With such knowledge, a clinical teaching plan that meets the needs of a par-

Educational assessment should be tied to instructional decision-making

ticular child can be designed and implemented. An important aspect of clinical teaching is the skills of interpreting feedback information and the need for continuous decision making. (Lerner, 1981, p. 125).

The complete prescriptive teaching process can be viewed as a cycle, with each stage of the process a point along a circle, as shown in Figure 10.1. Prescriptive teaching is especially critical in the education of severely and profoundly retarded students, because individual variations in beginning skills levels are so marked.

The Individualized Educational Program represents the transformation of the assessment of the handicapped child into a documented plan of action. Addressing the need of each student for a specifically designed program, the IEP also functions as a guide for instruction, as a basis for evaluation, and as a means of communication. Without question, the IEP is an integral part of the diagnostic-prescriptive process.

PROGRAM EVALUATION

To judge the effectiveness of different intervention strategies, program evaluation after the fact is necessary. Tests and other assessment proce-

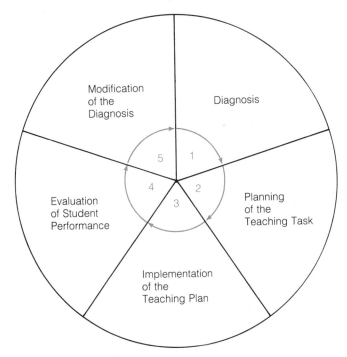

FIGURE 10.1 Diagram of the Clinical Teaching Cycle

From J.W. Lerner, *Learning Disabilities: Theories, Diagnosis and Teaching Strategies* (3rd ed.). Boston: Houghton Mifflin, 1981, p. 125. Reprinted with permission.

dures are used to evaluate program effectiveness as well as alternative interventions. Evaluations of medical treatments, the appropriateness of alternative placements, and/or different curricular interventions can be made.

EVALUATION OF PROGRESS

Data are needed to make decisions regarding the extent to which an individual student is making progress on social, educational, medical, and/or psychological programs. Emphasis here is on comparing actual and expected progress. A good example of this is in the annual review of the IEP, where the team evaluates whether the short-term instructional objectives and long-term goals have been achieved.

THE WHOLE PROCESS—ONE EXAMPLE

To realistically tie together all the components of the assessment process, let us now look at an example of an actual placement process. This example, which concerns a mildly retarded child, typifies the usual procedures involved in the assessment process. It is diagrammed in Figure 10.2.

1. The student, David, is referred by his Classroom Teacher (using an appropriate referral form), or by other appropriate persons and/or agencies, for further assessment. (The Elementary Supervisor may be contacted prior to referral by the Classroom Teacher.) It is important to note that a referral may be initiated by the parent.

2. David is observed by the Resource Teacher to obtain additional screening information regarding his educational strengths and weaknesses, and behavioral and/or emotional problems. She also gathers the results of *existing* routine vision, speech, language, and hearing exams, preschool medical exams, and all group readiness, achievement, and intelligence tests. A conference is held with David's parents to discuss his learning problems prior to a meeting of the Child Study Team.

3. Referral to the Child Study Team is made because David's screening records reveal:
   a. Significant differences in academic performance (low) when compared with classmates; and
   b. Significant discrepancy between ability and achievement.
   The Child Study Team consists of at least four of the following persons, who are appointed by the School Principal:
   a. Principal or designee
   b. Referring teacher
   c. Resource teacher

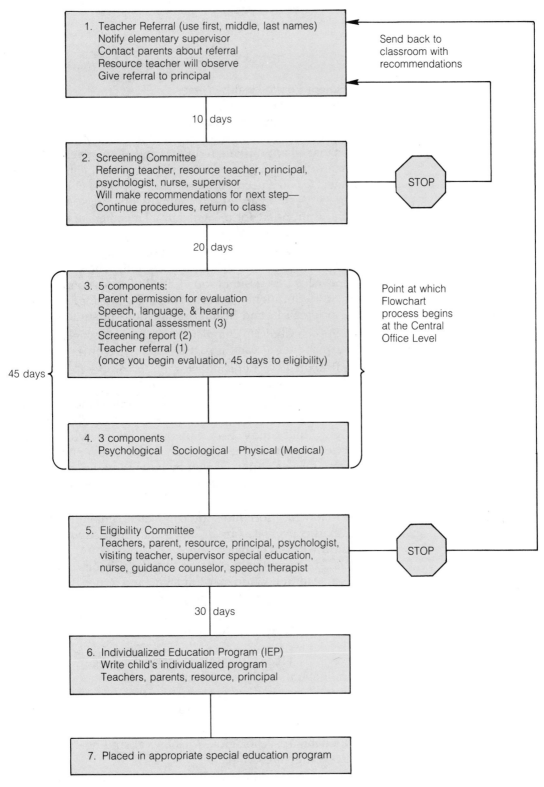

FIGURE 10.2 Procedures for the Identification, Evaluation, Confirmation, and Placement of Special Education Students

    d. School Public Health Nurse

    e. Other teachers as appropriate

    f. Other building or county personnel as appropriate

    The process moves to step 4 when the Child Study Team decides that all appropriate resources and alternatives within the regular school program have been exhausted in efforts to better meet David's needs and that he is suspected of being handicapped. A summary of the committee findings is completed on the appropriate form, signed by all members of the committee, and forwarded to the Resource Teacher.

4. The Resource Teacher asks the School Principal to obtain David's parents' permission to evaluate him. The Principal uses an inclusive permission form entitled "Permission for Evaluation" for educational, speech, language, hearing, psychological, sociological, and health examinations of students.

5. The Speech Clinician completes a speech, language, and hearing report (not already a part of David's record).

6. The Resource Teacher completes (on the proper form) an Educational Assessment of David.

7. The Resource Teacher sends to the Central Office (in care of Psychological Services) a copy of the Classroom Teacher referral, the Child Study Team Summary, the speech, language, and hearing report, the Educational Assessment, and the Permission for Evaluation (signed by parent), and retains a copy. Completion of this step denotes an official special education referral.

8. The following procedures are completed simultaneously:

    a. David is evaluated by or under the direct supervision of a Certified Psychologist.

    b. David's parents are contacted by the School Public Health Nurse for follow-up on completion and return (to school) of health examination (on proper form).

    c. An educational evaluation is completed including direct observation and appropriate testing, both formal and informal.

    d. David is given a complete speech/language and hearing evaluation.

    e. David's parents are contacted by the Visiting Teacher for completion of the sociological evaluation.

9. The Resource Teacher is sent a copy of each of the evaluation components (psychological, sociological, and health examinations) as they are completed.

10. The Resource Teacher completes and send to the Supervisor of

Special Education a form entitled "Scheduling Eligibility Committee Agendas." A copy of this form is forwarded to the School Principal.

11. The Supervisor of Special Education checks the completed form of Scheduling Eligibility Committee Agendas against the Flow-Chart in the Special Services Office. The form and chart agree with each other, so the Supervisor of Special Education schedules a date for the Eligibility Committee Meeting. The agenda of the scheduled meeting is sent to the School Principal one week prior to the date of the meeting.

12. A memo of the results of the Special Education Eligibility Committee meeting is sent to the School Principal on day following the meeting.

13. The Special Education Eligibility Committee Report of Recommendations is sent to the School Principal one week following the committee meeting.

14. The School Principal contacts David's parents to inform them of the recommendations of Special Education Eligibility Committee and to invite them to participate in the development of David's Individualized Education Program (IEP).

15. The School Principal arranges a meeting of the School Building IEP Committee, appointed by School Principal, which shall include, but is not limited to the following:
    a. School Principal or designee (chairperson)
    b. Teacher(s) (general and/or special)
    c. The parents and David (because David is old enough to understand what is taking place)
    d. Other specialists as appropriate and designated by School Principal

    These specialists could include the psychologist, speech/language clinician, physical therapist, or anyone else with pertinent information.

    If David's program were to be implemented in another school, the participants of IEP Committee would be cooperatively selected by the referring and receiving School Principals. It is recommended that the IEP Committee meet in the school the student will be attending. David would not be placed in the special education program until the IEP is completed.

16. The IEP Committee develops an IEP for David, which is signed by all members, including David's parents.

17. The School Principal places David in the special education program, as determined by the IEP. A copy of the IEP is sent to the Central Office.

18. Transportation arrangements are made by the referring School Principal and Transportation Office because David will attend a different school as a result of the new class placement.

19. All of these evaluation components and related correspondence and information are filed in David's Pupil's Confidential Record and placed in the office of the School Principal or Guidance Counselor. A card is placed in David's Pupil Cumulative Record to indicate the existence of the confidential record. A duplicate copy of this information is maintained in the Special Services Office.

The Eligibility Committee includes at least three members knowledgeable about the characteristics and educational needs of handicapped children. This committee is composed of such persons as the supervisor of special education, a school psychologist, a physician or nurse, a visiting teacher or school social worker, a school principal, a guidance counselor, a special class teacher, parents, a regular class teacher, and a speech clinician. A summary of the deliberations, findings, and recommendations of the Eligibility Committee is maintained. It includes the names, positions, and signatures of the persons participating in each meeting. A report is made and is included in each pupil's eligibility folder. All special education assignments must be reappraised at least every 3 years if the student's assignment to special education services continues beyond that time.

In addition, as we have seen, an IEP for each handicapped child must be developed and annually reviewed. Along with the statements of present educational performance and short-term objectives and long-term goals, the IEP includes statements of the specific educational services to be provided the child, the projected dates for initiation of the services and anticipated duration of the services, and specific criteria to measure progress.

SUMMARY

The assessment process affects the retarded student during every stage of service delivery from identification to intervention. P.L. 94-142 has helped to standardize the process; the law provides both regulations for and the spirit which should underlie assessment procedures.

The initial step in the process is identification. Included here are child-find efforts both in the school and the community and screening of those who are referred. The actual educational assessment involves both the analysis of the student's educational needs, with appropriate prescriptions for instruction, and the evaluation of the program's effectiveness. The assessment process requires multidisciplinary input from medical, psychological, speech and language, sociological, and educational specialists. In addition, the student and his or her parents are involved throughout the assessment.

CHAPTER ELEVEN

Educational Programming

W e have already dealt with the causes, characteristics, and assessment of various levels and types of mental retardation. Now it is time to go a step further by focusing on the critical task of developing and implementing educational programs which give each mentally retarded individual, regardless of his or her unique limitations, the opportunity to participate in the activities of the daily environment to the greatest extent possible.

We will discuss a number of key aspects of the educational programming process. First, we will look at the complementary roles of the teacher and learner in the process of special education. Second is a discussion of the critical task of selecting appropriate learning objectives for mentally retarded students, followed by a look at a sampling of curricular objectives geared to meet the needs of students who are classified at three general levels of mental retardation—mild, moderate, and severe and profound. Third, we will describe the components of the educational programming process in detail. And finally, we will focus on some specific instructional methods which are often useful for working with handicapped learners.

This chapter was contributed by Ruth A. Payne, James S. Payne, and Jill C. Dardig.

THE ROLE OF THE TEACHER AND LEARNER

The educator's goal in teaching is to identify adaptive behaviors for each individual and carefully structure the educational environment so that learning is likely to occur. Meeting this goal involves going through the steps in the educational programming process detailed later in this chapter so that the retarded student (*a*) acquires a wide variety of adaptive skills; (*b*) learns when and where to use those skills; (*c*) generalizes specific skills to other settings; and (*d*) maintains the skills over time. The educator must keep these four objectives for the learner in mind. In this way, the tasks of the teacher and learner will be complementary. Let us now look at these four tasks in more detail.

In this chapter, the terms behavior, skill, and objective will be used interchangeably.

ACQUIRING A WIDE VARIETY OF ADAPTIVE BEHAVIORS

Mentally retarded persons need to function successfully in school, home, job, and community settings. To do so, they need skills in many areas, including self-care, mobility training, communication, social interaction, academics, health and safety, leisure time, and vocational pursuits. Therefore, teachers must be concerned with targeting useful learning objectives in all of these areas, rather than focusing solely on the traditional academic subjects such as reading, writing, and math. In fact, when teaching students who are severely and profoundly developmentally delayed, teachers often find that academic skills are neither relevant nor adaptive learning objectives and may concentrate entirely on skill areas such as self-care, motor, and nonverbal communication.

LEARNING WHEN AND WHERE TO USE THE SKILLS

Retarded students must learn to observe and respond to environmental cues which signal that a particular behavior is, in fact, adaptive and appropriate in that setting. Along with being able to perform a skill to a certain level of mastery, students must recognize the conditions under which a behavior should be performed. For example, when is it appropriate to approach, shake hands, and introduce oneself to another person? At a party when a new person arrives, on the street to a complete stranger, or in a work setting while in the midst of completing a task? Or when is it appropriate to use the operation of adding numbers? When making a withdrawal from a checking account, when estimating the total cost of groceries to be purchased, or when asked to find the product of two numbers? Or when should you reach and grasp an object? When handed a soft toy, a bowl of hot cereal, or when you are within reach of another person's hair or eyeglasses? Discrimination tasks like these require mentally retarded learners to observe each setting to determine relevant cues and then quickly and reliably decide which behavior from their repertoire is appropriate. The teacher must structure the educational program so that students learn to attend to relevant cues, make adaptive responses, and receive positive consequences for their efforts.

GENERALIZING ADAPTIVE BEHAVIORS TO OTHER APPROPRIATE SETTINGS

This factor is a corollary to the one just discussed; that is, the retarded person must be able to identify similar settings in which a behavior is appropriate and respond correctly in those settings as well. For example, the situations of obtaining lunch in a variety of "fast food" restaurants, repotting several types of plants and flowers, and filling out employment applications for different clerical jobs all (within each situation) have similar but not exactly the same elements which a person should recognize as cues for a particular set of adaptive behaviors. Also, the person must be able to generalize his or her responses from the training situation to the actual real-life environment in which the behaviors should occur. It appears that many practitioners and researchers are currently paying more attention to this instructional challenge, as shown by the increasing number of articles in the *Journal of Applied Behavior Analysis* and other journals. These articles focus on the use of generalization training techniques as integral parts of their programs.

MAINTAINING THE PERFORMANCE OF NEW BEHAVIORS OVER TIME

Behaviors must continue in the person's repertoire past formal training into future environments and situations that he or she will encounter throughout life. Here again, instructional programs can be structured to facilitate both generalization and maintenance of new behaviors through systematic manipulation of program variables such as training materials, instructors, and reinforcement schedules.

SELECTING FUNCTIONAL BEHAVIORS

One key to successful educational programming is the selection of functional behaviors (Guess, Horner, Utley, Holvoet, Maxon, Tucker, & Warren, 1978). A functional skill or behavior is one which is useful to students and will give them some appropriate control over their environment in terms of obtaining positive and consistent consequences. A behavior which is not functional for a student will probably not be maintained in his repertoire over time. For example, the teacher may need to decide whether or not it is functional for a mildly retarded high school student to be able to identify Roman numerals (M, C, L, etc.) or to be able to name the parts of speech in a sentence (simple subject, indirect object, etc.). Is it functional for junior high level moderately retarded students who already have good fine motor skills to spend time randomly stringing beads? Teachers must ask if their particular students would benefit in the long run from this type of specialized training.

Would the skill be useful in the students' real-life environments? Is the skill age-appropriate? Would they retain the skills over time? If not, they must choose more useful behaviors upon which to focus their time and attention.

Regardless of the student's level of functioning, the educator should ask the following questions when selecting each target skill for an individual educational program.

1. Is it a functional skill? Is the skill one which will be useful and adaptive for that individual?

2. Will the learner be able to use the skill in the immediate environment(s)? Will use of the skill produce positive environmental consequences for the learner in daily interactions?

3. Will the learner be able to use the skill often? Behaviors which are used often are likely to be better maintained over time.

4. Has the student demonstrated an interest in learning the skill? If a student can demonstrate, verbally or nonverbally, a preference for learning a particular skill, this already existing motivation can be valuable in carrying out a successful instructional program.

See chapter 3 for more on the need of retarded students for success experiences.

5. Is success likely in teaching this skill? The successful acquisition of a new skill is rewarding to teacher and learner alike, and can make future success more likely.

6. Is the skill a prerequisite for learning more complex skills? For example, the fine motor skills of reaching, grasping, and releasing are prerequisites to various self-help skills like self-feeding and hair washing as well as the skill of writing; the skill of identifying different denominations of coins is a prerequisite of paying for purchases in a store and verifying that the correct change has been given.

7. Will the student become more independent as a result of learning this skill? Mentally retarded people have traditionally been regarded as being primarily dependent upon the care of others in order to meet their needs. However, most individuals with mild retardation can learn to lead totally independent lives; individuals who are moderately retarded can become productive and semi-independent in their daily living skills; and even individuals in the severe and profound categories can often learn some basic skills which make them less dependent upon others— for instance, using the bathroom independently, manipulating toys and other objects, moving around a room, or using a six-picture communication board (Gruber, Reeser, & Reid, 1979). Teaching independence skills means helping the individual

exert the greatest degree of control possible over his environment and hence his own life.

8. Will the skill allow the student to qualify for improved or additional services, or services in a less restrictive setting? Frequently, specific criteria have been established for admission to a particular educational program. For example, young children may have to be toilet trained for admission to a day care program, adults may need to demonstrate good self-care and homemaking skills to be admitted to a group home in the community, and adolescents may need to demonstrate mastery of basic functional academic skills in order to be considered for enrollment in a vocational training program.

9. Is it important to modify this behavior because it is harmful or dangerous to self or others? Some mentally retarded individuals (usually individuals in the lower functioning levels) have learned maladaptive behaviors such as rocking, hand-wringing, head-banging, and hitting, which may not only interfere with learning other adaptive skills, but also may be physically harmful to themselves or others. In structuring an educational program, teachers must use procedures to reduce these undesirable behaviors when they occur, along with teaching appropriate substitutes which will get the student social attention, stimulation, or another positive consequence in a more normal, productive way.

CURRICULUM AREAS

As we have seen, the label "mental retardation" is used to encompass children and adults with a very wide range of skills and needs. Therefore, curricula designed for mentally retarded individuals will cover a wide range of content areas and levels of difficulty, even within each of the three major subgroupings: severely and profoundly mentally retarded, moderately or trainable mentally retarded, and mildly or educably mentally retarded. Curricula designed for moderately, severely, and profoundly retarded individuals are often structured to encourage implementation virtually from birth to death, rather than just during the typical school-age period of 5 to 18 years.

CURRICULUM FOR THE SEVERELY AND PROFOUNDLY MENTALLY RETARDED

In the past, many people assumed that severely and profoundly mentally retarded people could not learn, and that their only needs were for physical protection and custodial care. Now it is recognized that, given an appropriate instructional program, these individuals can learn to take an interest in and respond to their environment and master basic skills in a variety of areas.

One basic behavior which is a prerequisite to learning almost all other skills is attending. Attending is actually a category of behaviors which can include skills such as focusing the eyes, turning the head, and orienting the body towards a stimulus for a particular amount of time. Since much learning takes place through imitation of others, it is obvious that focusing attention is a critical first step in the learning process. Along with attending, typical curricular objectives for profoundly retarded students may include responding to stimulation, familiar people, and objects by cooing, smiling, relaxing, or moving body parts; social skills such as making eye contact or touching another person; motor and verbal imitation; gross and fine motor movements like head control, reaching, grasping, sitting, and protective behaviors; and following simple directions. Teachers are concerned with increasing and improving the variety, rate, and quality of the adaptive responses the child or adult can make.

Since many profoundly retarded individuals also have severe physical handicaps which limit their voluntary movement, a comprehensive curriculum usually involves putting them in proper positions for work, play, and rest, passive exercising to encourage and permit functional use of their bodies and prevent further deformities from developing, and providing a variety of auditory, tactile, and visual stimulation which the person would not normally have access to because of impaired mobility or sensory deficits. This group of learners provides a particular challenge to teachers to select appropriate objectives, devise and select adaptive equipment (easy-to-grip eating utensils, communication boards, mobility aids), use appropriate rewards, and find ways to record each learner's progress towards objectives that reflect and make evident even very small improvements in behavior.

Curriculum for severely mentally retarded learners can include the elements described above, along with more advanced skills in the areas of physical development, self-care, and communication and socialization. Often gestures, signs, or symbols are the preferred communication mode, rather than oral speech and language.

Since most severely and profoundly mentally retarded persons are identified at birth or soon after, educational programming can begin early, in either a residential (institutional) placement, day program, or home setting. School-age and adult programs are also important in teaching daily living skills and in ensuring that the learner continues to use adaptive behaviors previously learned.

Because of their special needs and medical problems, services are often provided not only by teachers and home trainers but also by occupational therapists, physical therapists, language specialists, and prosthetic equipment experts. All of the people who provide services need to work as a team to create a coordinated, useful educational program for these students.

CURRICULUM FOR THE MODERATELY MENTALLY RETARDED

Learners in this category can benefit from training in many areas which will eventually prepare them for semi-independent or supervised living and working situations. Self-care skills such as toileting, dressing, self-feeding, and good grooming are often worked on first, along with physical development and oral or signed communication. As students progress through a school-age educational program, areas such as interpersonal interaction and social behaviors (in school, home, work, and community settings), functional academics like writing one's own name, address, and telephone number, recognizing "survival words" like "exit," "ladies' room," and "poison," basic money use, counting, telling time, and constructive leisure-time activities (sports, crafts, gardening, puzzles) are included. For older students, the emphasis shifts towards acquiring good work habits (e.g., being on time, completing tasks), social skills required on the job which are critical for vocational success (Rusch, 1979), as well as specific job skills, housekeeping chores (preparing simple meals or making beds), community-access behaviors (using public transportation and eating in restaurants), and human sexuality.

One important skill is getting to and from work. See page 330 for a lesson plan used to teach retarded adults to ride the bus.

Postschool placement opportunities for moderately retarded learners often involve work activity centers or sheltered workshops; and, as more facilities become available in the community, placement at a group home (Janicki, Mayeda, & Epple, 1983). Educational programming continues in these settings to help individuals cope with the changing demands of their environment (Schulman, 1980).

CURRICULUM FOR MILDLY MENTALLY RETARDED LEARNERS

This category represents the largest group of retarded learners and probably the widest range of skills and needs. As we have seen, most mildly retarded learners are identified at school and not before; they do not usually have additional significant physical or sensory impairments. The majority will go on to live independent lives in the community involving home, marriage, job, and family. Few will attend college, but some will obtain postsecondary vocational training. However, the home environments and causes of developmental delay vary widely, and must be considered by the teacher when structuring an educational program.

See chapter 4.

Curricular objectives in a program for mildly handicapped children are often somewhat similar to those found in a "regular" classroom. Academics such as reading, writing, and math are normally taught, with a focus placed on teaching functional academic skills which will enable the student to succeed in the community and at home. Reading is taught primarily for protective and informational purposes (reading food labels

LESSON PLAN FOR RIDING THE BUS

Riding the city bus
COURSE

A. Campbell
TEACHER

October 18
DATE

I. *Instructional Objectives*
  a. Students will board a parked city bus properly (wait until door is open, climb steps, deposit money, and sit down).
  b. Students will disembark from city bus at specified point/sign in school lot (will ring buzzer, stand, and depart from back door when stopped).
  c. Students will role-play what to do when lost or when they have missed their correct stop, using the parked bus as setting.

II. *Lesson Presentation*
  a. Introduction: Discuss what we are doing today: present as practice to facilitate next week's field trip.
  b. Perceived Purpose: Next week we are going to the Barracks Road Shopping Center by bus. We have to know how to get on and off the bus to do this.
  c. Review of Previous Tasks: Students will identify city bus stop signs—selecting bus stop signs from a group of photographs of community signs (road signs, street signs, etc.). Will review that it costs 75¢ to ride the bus, each time you get on.

III. *Task Sequence*
  a. Task: Students will board a parked city bus.
    1. Learning Activity: The instructor will model the sequence, stating what she is doing at each step.
    2. Concrete Practice: Students will board the bus three times as practice, receiving verbal prompts as needed. Will remain on bus on last trial.
  b. Task: Students will disembark from the city bus.
    1. Learning Activity: While riding around the parking lot in the bus, the instructor will state the sequence for disembarking.
    2. Concrete Practice: Each student will identify the "bus stop" at which to get off, and, following verbal directions for each step, will ring buzzer, stand up, and walk out opened back door when bus has stopped.
  c. Task: Students will role-play obtaining help when lost.
    1. Learning Activity: Bus driver will state three steps to take while on bus: walk up to driver and state you are lost, state destination, ask for help—may show ID card here.
    2. Concrete Practice: Following the instructor's model, each student will role-play asking the bus driver for assistance in accordance with the three steps.

IV. *Special Student Considerations—Individualized*
  Due to J's speech impediment, he will be provided with a "destination card" to show driver in Task c-2, so that he will not have to rely on his speech.

V. *Special Student Considerations—Group*
  Remind students to get on and off the bus one at a time.

and recipes, newspaper ads, and signs) and secondarily for enjoyment as a constructive leisure-time activity. Writing skills involve useful everyday tasks such as filling out employment applications and writing business and social letters. Math skills emphasize all aspects of money handling, including budgeting. Other subjects taught include science, social studies, effective oral communication, health, and human sexuality. Older students learn about apartment living, marriage and family responsibilities, and community resources, in addition to a heavy emphasis on job preparation, including skills like locating job openings in newspapers and displaying correct behavior during a job interview (Kelly, Wildman, & Berler, 1980). Many mildly retarded high school students have the opportunity to learn a trade through specialized school-sponsored vocational training or on-the-job training in the context of a full or half-day work study program.

One additional skill area which should be targeted for mildly retarded students is skill in being assertive. Most mildly retarded adults will live unsupervised in the community. Because they may interact at times with people who attempt to take advantage of them financially, socially, or sexually, they need to be able to refuse to do things that are against their wishes or judgment and follow through on their refusal. Instructional programs can give students the opportunity to learn and practice assertive behaviors for many occasions through role-playing and other techniques (Bregman, 1984).

The instructional materials commonly used in mildly handicapped programs are, especially at the younger levels, often similar to or even the same as materials used in regular classrooms. For example, learning centers can be used effectively with these students to individualize instructional tasks and promote active learning and independent functioning. Materials for older handicapped students, especially print materials, are generally "high interest, low readability." These written materials are geared towards the more sophisticated interests of older students, yet are written at a lower grade level so the students can understand them more easily.

In all three of these curricular categories, it is important to remember that there often will be overlapping objectives and materials across categories. Therefore, although many of the excellent curriculum guides currently available for retarded learners state that they are geared for one particular category of student, they may, in fact, also be very useful for one or both of the other two classifications.

EDUCATIONAL PROGRAMMING

Educational programming for mentally retarded students involves many interrelated components. Educational programs must be designed, implemented, and evaluated systematically so that decisions will be made that have an optimal effect on the development of each individual learner.

The programming process described below can be applied to all educational programs, regardless of the learner's age, placement, or level of retardation. It is a process which, based on an assessment of an individual's current skills and needs, first determines what specific skills need to be learned to help the individual function more successfully in his environment, and then determines the arrangement of the teaching-learning environment in the best possible way to facilitate acquisition and maintenance of adaptive behaviors.

ASSESSMENT

The first step of the process is determining exactly what skills the student already can do in each important area of functioning. As was emphasized in chapter 6, educational assessment techniques should be concerned with obtaining information about the learner which will lead directly to developing an appropriate educational program.

A comprehensive educational assessment should lead to several outcomes. The first is an overall picture of the student's functioning level. Second, the assessment should pinpoint specific strengths and weaknesses in the student's behavioral repertoire. Third, the assessment should lead to the logical next steps in the student's development. These steps are often the next steps on an assessment scale. Rather than providing one single score or label, the assessment should yield many individual items of information and point to many different areas where instruction would be beneficial in moving the person towards more independent functioning.

An educational assessment which is a criterion-referenced or curriculum-referenced measurement of a student's mastery of specific, observable behaviors is usually more program-oriented than a norm-referenced measure of behavior. Criterion-referenced assessments provide specific information which leads to the formulation of instructional objectives, while norm-referenced assessments are more useful for providing information upon which placement decisions may be based. Many standardized achievement and intelligence tests fall into this second category.

Various formal and informal assessment methods are listed in Table 10.1.

There are hundreds of behavioral criterion-referenced assessment tools available which either include a range of skill areas or focus on one or two discrete areas (e.g., sight word vocabulary, math facts, and dressing behaviors). These tools vary as to their usefulness and objectivity, and must be examined carefully and individually (Walls, Warner, Bacon, & Zane, 1977). Special care must be taken when selecting an assessment instrument for use with profoundly retarded, multihandicapped individuals. Attention should be focused on use of instruments which credit lower-functioning individuals with rudimentary behaviors and slight improvements in skill levels. Many teachers choose to develop their own assessment tools as well. Several disciplines (for example, language therapy and physical therapy) have highly specialized but useful tools which are currently in use. In selecting one or more assessment tools, care must be taken to match their complexity and difficulty with the functioning level of the student, so that the data that are collected are meaningful.

GOALS AND OBJECTIVES

Teachers can draw on a number of sources to determine appropriate educational goals and objectives. Of course, as we discussed earlier, a goal's relevancy is the degree to which it is functional for each particular individual. Goals and objectives can be drawn from curriculum guides geared for a particular population or from assessment tools which measure important adaptive behaviors, or may be developed through the careful observation of a learner's needs in a variety of everyday settings.

Goals usually refer to overall, long-term purposes of educational programs. Examples of long-term goals might include improving self-care skills like clothing selection, learning a trade like furniture refinishing, or learning to make a weekly home budget. Instructional or behavioral *objectives* usually refer to logically arranged sequences of specific, short-term steps towards meeting the program's overall goals. These objectives are important so that educational programs can be not only planned but also evaluated on the basis of learner progress towards meeting specific criteria. Behavioral objectives are statements which specify an observable behavior, the conditions under which the behavior will occur, and the acceptable standard for accuracy against which the performance will be measured. Sample behavioral objectives for students at four different functioning levels might be:

- ☐ (Mild) Given a help-wanted newspaper ad, the student will say the meanings of four abbreviations with 100% accuracy.
- ☐ (Moderate) Given five coins of five different denominations, the student will arrange them in order from most valuable to least valuable at least four out of five times.
- ☐ (Severe) Given a toothbrush, paste, and cup of water, the student will brush teeth, moving brush along all surfaces and using a circular brushing pattern for at least 2 minutes.
- ☐ (Profound) When his name is called, the student will maintain eye contact with the teacher for at least 2 seconds within 5 seconds of the cue.

METHODS

Instructional methods involve actively structuring the learning environment to promote learning of targeted objectives. Specifically, the teacher is concerned with choosing appropriate antecedents and consequences of behavior so that learning can take place efficiently and effectively. These variables and corresponding instructional strategies and techniques will be discussed at length later on in this chapter.

MATERIALS

Instructional materials which help promote active learning of targeted skills should be selected. Materials can run the gamut from texts and other print materials, workbooks, dittoes, audio and videotapes, records, films, models, realia, games and toys, to teaching machines, computers, programmed learning materials, and prosthetic equipment. Teachers should use materials which closely match the student's ability level and lead directly to skill acquisition. Materials geared for regular classrooms can often be used or adapted, particularly for use with mildly handicapped students. Many teachers and other specialists develop their own instructional materials, which are usually less expensive than commercially produced materials and often more motivating for their students to use, as they can be personalized.

ACTIVITIES

Teachers also plan individual and small and large group activities which lead to the acquisition of target behaviors. Activities can involve performing motor behaviors, talking, gesturing, writing, role-playing, sorting, counting, and so on. Activities should be varied to add interest to the curriculum and should provide many opportunities for learners to make active responses. Whenever possible, activities should take place in the real-life environment (such as a store or laundromat), so that the difficult transition from the simulated to the real-life environment is made easier.

EVALUATION

The progress of learners towards meeting targeted objectives needs to be measured on a regular basis. Progress, or lack of progress, will signal to teachers when to move on to more complex objectives and when to change instructional methods, materials, and activities so that failure situations are avoided and success facilitated. Progress data to guide educators in the decision-making process may be obtained in many different ways and can be collected on a daily or weekly basis.

This six-step educational programming process helps achieve an integrated educational program based on individual student needs. It is closely related to the process and requirements mandated by P.L. 94-142 in relation to the Individualized Educational Plan (IEP).

THE IEP

Every handicapped child has an Individualized Educational Plan which outlines and integrates the educational programming process discussed above. Programs which serve mentally retarded adults or preschoolers sometimes call their plans by a different name such as Individual Habilitation Plans (IHPs), but these plans usually contain the same components as IEPs.

IEPs contain seven major elements, each of which will be discussed briefly in relation to the educational programming process.

1. Statement of present levels of functioning. These levels are determined by the assessment process.

2. Prioritized annual goals. These goals may be selected and arranged in order of importance, using the criteria for selecting functional behaviors discussed earlier in this chapter.

3. Short-term instructional objectives. These statements should be written as behavioral objectives, so that a clear direction is provided for instruction and ongoing evaluation of student progress is possible. Educators can use the many references available which identify and discuss suitable learning objectives for a wide range of mentally retarded learners (Haring, 1977; Kolstoe, 1976; Snell, 1978; Stephens, Hartman, & Lucas, 1978; Van Etten, Arkell, & Van Etten, 1980).

4. Special education and related services. Especially with more severely handicapped students, services are often required in addition to those provided by a classroom teacher in order to provide a program which meets all of the child's educational needs. These may be services provided directly to a child, such as speech or physical therapy or special transportation, or family services delivered by a psychologist or parent trainer.

5. A statement describing the extent of the child's participation in regular educational programs. The extent of participation (which can legitimately vary from no participation to almost full-time involvement) varies according to the child's special needs and limitations and is determined by the expected benefits to the individual handicapped student on a case-by-case basis.

   See chapter 12 for discussion of "mainstreaming" and the least restrictive environment.

6. Timeline of the initiation and duration of services. These services must be provided in the amount and sequence scheduled by the interdisciplinary team.

7. Objective criteria and evaluation procedures. By writing salient behavioral objectives, gearing instruction directly towards their acquisition, and using reliable and valid devices to regularly record behavior, this requirement can easily be met.

THE INTERDISCIPLINARY TEAM

This group of individuals has the task of providing a comprehensive, appropriate educational program. P.L. 94-142 mandates the role of the interdisciplinary team to include making placement decisions and formulating and implementing IEPs. The rationale behind the use of an interdisciplinary team is that mentally retarded students (as well as students with any type of handicapping condition) have a wide variety of needs which can best be met through input from people with a broad range of training, experience, skills, insights, and perspectives. Team members can include, for example, teachers, psychologists, school administrators, parents, student advocates, nurses, social workers, physical, occupational, and language therapists, and even the student himself. Each discipline has a unique and important contribution to make to this team effort (Copeland, 1976; Finnie, 1975; Pearson, 1972; Robinault, 1973; Vanderheiden & Grilley, 1976). The exact composition of each team is determined by the needs of the individual student. Often the size of the team grows as the severity of the students' handicaps increases. This group of individuals must put forth a coordinated effort to make decisions about such critical areas as assessment tools and methods, instructional objectives, educational placement, instructional strategies, and evaluation. To maximize their effect and to avoid duplication of efforts, teams should meet regularly to plan and review programs and carefully delineate each person's responsibilities. Unfortunately, teams do not always function as smoothly in practice as they do in theory, due in part to the realities of the very heavy case loads that many professionals are obliged to have. One recent development which has potential as a time-saving device for interdisciplinary teams is the use of microcomputers. Microcomputers enable team members to efficiently collect and store student data, rapidly and accurately analyze these data, and easily produce multiple, legible copies of reports for use in educational planning (Smith & Wells, 1983; Nolley & Nolley, 1984). Microcomputers have the additional advantage of freeing team members from routine, time-consuming paperwork, allowing more time for direct delivery of services to handicapped individuals.

CHARACTERISTICS OF THE MENTALLY RETARDED STUDENT AND IMPLICATIONS FOR EDUCATIONAL PROGRAMMING

Chapter 3 discussed several characteristics which are typical of many mentally retarded learners and should be considered when structuring educational programs. The first characteristic concerns a tendency to have an external "locus of control"; that is, mentally retarded individuals may perceive that they have little control of the environment or the consequences of their actions. The teacher can use several strategies to help students become more "internally oriented." First, skills must be chosen which are adaptive and functional for individual students, so that they may actually achieve a measure of control over their environment. Second, instruction should teach the students to associate their actions with their consequences, and then to anticipate in advance what a consequence would probably be so that an appropriate behavior may be chosen. A very effective strategy for teaching this type of skill is role-playing, which allows the student to repeatedly practice, in a non-threatening situation, choosing and using suitable adaptive behaviors (Stephens, 1978). Another strategy involves the use of a social learning contract, which spells out, in writing or in pictures, the environmental factors which link various situation-specific behaviors and their possible positive, negative, and neutral results.

A second characteristic concerns the high "expectancy for failure" shown by many mentally retarded learners. This rather negative orientation is readily understandable, as many mentally retarded people have long histories of failing to learn new skills, usually as a result of poor (or nonexistent) educational programming. Not only may they anticipate failure when trying to learn new tasks, they may even refuse to attempt them at all.

Teachers can counteract this nonproductive trait in several ways. First, they should look closely at the results of their assessments and set reasonable, achievable goals and objectives based on the student's demonstrated level of functioning in each skill area. Second, they should structure the instructional program for success by breaking down objectives into small learning steps (via task analysis) and using a rich schedule of positive reinforcement. Third, they can reward effort and improvement as well as perfect performance. These and other similar strategies can help to make students more willing to try new tasks and lead to positive comments such as "I *can* do it," which indicate that the student expects to succeed rather than fail.

A third characteristic of mentally retarded learners is "outer-directedness," or a tendency to rely on external cues or instructions for behavior. For example, if a student needs help with her work, she may always wait for the teacher to notice her problem and tell her how to proceed. In this case, teachers can reward more "innerdirected" behaviors such as actively asking the teacher for help or independently identifying several possible solutions to the problem and then trying each one until a solution is reached.

Of course, teachers must look beyond general characteristics which may or may not apply to the individual learner and plan programs based on each individual's unique characteristics.

INSTRUCTIONAL METHODS .

In this section of the chapter, we will describe a variety of methods which may be used to help students learn new, adaptive behaviors and eliminate inappropriate ones from their repertoires. After we look at the key environmental variables which affect learning, we will briefly review several educational techniques. However, before teachers decide to try one or more of these techniques, especially those designed to reduce behavior, they should read and study further to ensure that each technique is correctly used.

Many of the topics to be covered in this section are characteristic of good educational programming in general and are not by any means the sole property of special education. However, some of the strategies that will be presented are quite effective with mentally retarded students. The special effectiveness of these techniques stems from the fact that they were developed to address many of the learning problems displayed by this group of students.

LEARNING

The past decade of research in special education has brought about the discovery of some important relationships between teaching and **learning.** These findings are shifting attention from speculation about the internal circumstances of learning to systematic studies of the effect of environmental conditions on learning. Learning is an extremely complex process; yet the teacher can exercise much control over the environmental variables that affect learning to make it a more efficient and successful experience for mentally retarded students.

The conditions or events that precede behavior are often referred to as **antecedents** and include such things as scheduling, environmental arrangement, and presentation of materials, verbal directions, or other stimuli. All of these events and conditions, when skillfully arranged, can increase learning. **Consequent events,** such as rewards or punishments, can, if made contingent upon the occurrence of appropriate or maladaptive behavior, greatly facilitate learning as well. Figure 11.1 illustrates the interrelationship between antecedents, consequences, and behavior. The effective teacher learns and uses strategies and methods that ensure that positive behavior change, or learning, takes place. This

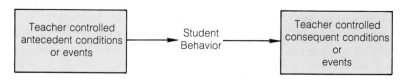

FIGURE 11.1 Paradigm of Teaching and Behavior Change

type of learning system is produced by manipulating both antecedent events and contingent consequences appropriate to each child.

Although there are many skills involved in teaching, the true and only test of the effectiveness of instruction lies in determining if a new skill is learned. Obviously, if the student learned, the instruction was effective; if the student did not learn, then the instruction was ineffective. This remainder of this section deals with the important interaction and relationship of antecedent and consequent events in the learning process.

Before continuing this discussion, however, one important question must be resolved. What is learning? Learning has been defined in a variety of ways, such as the acquisition of knowledge, skills, and attitudes and the development of awareness and insight. In any case, learning is demonstrated when a change in behavior occurs. This change in behavior may indicate the acquisition of various bits of knowledge, skills, and attitudes; without these important changes in a student's observable actions, we have no way to determine that learning has occurred. Therefore, the focus of instruction must be on teaching observable, measurable behaviors to mentally retarded individuals. This orientation is commonly called a "behavioral approach" to teaching and learning. An abundance of further information on behavioral techniques and documentation of its numerous applications to teaching skills to mentally retarded learners may be found in many texts (Mercer & Snell, 1977; Neisworth & Smith, 1978; Thompson & Grabowski, 1972; Walker & Shea, 1980) and professional journals (*Journal of Applied Behavior Analysis, Behavior Modification, Journal of the Association for the Severely Handicapped, Mental Retardation*).

ACQUISITION AND MAINTENANCE

We must differentiate two specific stages of learning which were mentioned at the start of this chapter: **acquisition** and **maintenance.** Acquisition learning refers to the initial attempts at development of a skill or chunk of knowledge. Maintenance learning refers to the ability to retain this skill or knowledge over a period of time. Maintenance learning can not be equated with memory, because maintenance implies more than remembering. It takes the learner from the initial grasp of a fact, concept, or skill during acquisition to its solid establishment in his response repertoire over time. Perhaps it can best be viewed as a combination of remembering and continued use of the learned material.

The differences between acquisition and maintenance learning result in several important teaching considerations. These include the determination of each stage's needs relative to the antecedents and consequences of the targeted behavior.

The first consideration deals with the consequences of behavior. For the acquisition stage, the production or shaping of responses requires a **continuous** schedule of **reinforcement.** Continuous reinforcement is a one-to-one correspondence between behavior and consequence; that is, every time the student performs the skill to be acquired, he or she receives a tangible or intangible reward from the teacher. Examples might include the teacher praising the student each time he buttons a button correctly, praising every word or sentence read aloud correctly, or giving a token every time a child raises her hand when she wants to speak. Whether word recognition, hand-raising, self-toileting, or using sign language is the particular skill targeted for acquisition, the sooner the reinforcement is given after the response is observed, the greater the efficiency of the learning experience.

However, while new skills are acquired most efficiently through continuous reinforcement, they can be maintained most efficiently with **intermittent reinforcement.** Research indicates that a one-to-one correspondence between behavior and consequence is not as important during maintenance as it is during the acquisition stage. In fact, behavior which has been reinforced intermittently after the acquisition phase tends to become very firmly established in the student's repertoire over time. During maintenance, reinforcement should be varied over time and frequency of occurrences; a teacher might reward the child at the end of every two or three pages or stories read, when he has completely dressed himself, or occasionally at the end of the day for appropriate hand raising.

We will cover specific types of consequences to use in greater detail later in this chapter.

The second consideration resulting from the differences between these two learning stages deals with the relative necessity of antecedents for learning. During the initial stage, frequent and varied stimuli will need to be presented to students to ensure that the skill will be acquired. For example, for a mentally retarded student to learn a vocabulary list, the same words may have to be presented often in a variety of ways. The same words may be presented through flash cards or teaching machines, written as spelling words, or cut out of magazines. The words may be presented several different times throughout the day every day for a while. Once the student has learned the words to a certain level of proficiency, they will not have to be presented as often in formal training sessions. They can be maintained through periodic review of the words which have been incorporated into the student's reading assignments.

Third, based on the importance of continuous reinforcement and frequent, varied presentation of antecedents to learning, it follows that, for new behaviors to be acquired, they must be taught directly and intentionally. There are always exceptions to this rule, but educators, especially teachers working with mentally retarded students, must assume the responsibility to actively teach whatever it is that should be learned and not rely on incidental or chance learning. Only through direct teacher-student instruction can the requirements for consequences and antecedents be fulfilled. However, during the maintenance stage, techniques ranging from worksheets to student tutors can play a valuable role when used properly.

Using our example involving the vocabulary list, the student could be given one-to-one or small group instruction involving modeling during the acquisition stage of learning new words. Peer tutoring would be another way to help the student acquire and practice this skill (Cooke, Heron, Heward, & Test, 1982). These approaches would ensure that each individual student had frequent opportunities to respond to the presented stimuli (flash cards, and so on) and to receive correction or reinforcement immediately. After the child has progressed to a predetermined percentage of correct responses, then self-directed seatwork or large group practice periods would probably be sufficient.

Whether the skill is naming colors, writing one's own name, collating papers, or doing long division, this change in teaching conditions is necessary to reflect progress from the acquisition to the maintenance stage of learning.

These considerations of the differences between acquisition and maintenance learning dictate how teachers approach the task of meeting students' educational needs and their subsequent class and lesson plans. There are two apparent problems that can result from the misuse and confusion of the teaching techniques for these two stages.

The first problem has been clearly and succinctly discussed by Lindsley (1964). It concerns the continued use of acquisition-type techniques for maintenance stage learning. For example, after a child has learned all the primary colors, the teacher may continue to directly teach the differences between red and yellow, when the child could easily handle an assignment on his own with a worksheet or educational game. This type of teaching can be counterproductive for three reasons: (*a*) it wastes teacher and student time that could be spent on acquisition of other learning tasks; (*b*) it restricts the student from getting over what Lindsley calls the "acquisition hump," to go on to further skill development; and (*c*) the time could be better spent on maintenance stage learning of the task. He notes that "it is almost as unkind to crutch-trap a handicapped person as it is to deny him a crutch in the first place" (1964, p. 65). It is not uncommon to discover that some teachers of mentally retarded students are guilty of this offense. This is due in part to the misperception that these students *need* to spend extra time and effort on acquisition-type activities, even after they have mastered the skill.

The concept of denying the crutch to the student illustrates the second problem, which can result from the use of teaching techniques

COMPONENTS OF EFFECTIVE INSTRUCTION

Much time is spent discussing the effectiveness of programs, materials, and people. Most programs implemented today, educational or other, include mechanisms for evaluating effectiveness. However, what does "effective" instruction mean? On a general level, responding to this query is relatively easy. An answer to the question would probably imply that some type of progress or learning takes place. Reflection obscures the meaning of this question, making it difficult to answer.

Other related but more specific questions—To what specific skills are we referring: academic, social, or what? Does time come into play here; is rate of learning important?—are critical to any analysis of effective instruction. Moreover, effective instruction implies the most facile acquisition of a wide range of knowledge or skills in a psychologically healthy, appropriately structured learning environment. Furthermore, effective teachers do certain "things," called *components of effective instruction.*

The figure presented below highlights a number of significant facets of effective instruction (from a teacher orientation) that help learning occur. As can be seen from the diagram, the essential components are divided into three phases, although some overlapping exists. For a more extensive discussion of this model, see Polloway and colleagues (1985).

Antecedents to teaching	Teaching behaviors	Follow-ups to teaching
☐ *Physical dimensions* ☐ classroom arrangement ☐ seating ☐ classroom furnishings ☐ environmental factors ☐ *Social dimensions* ☐ teacher variables ☐ student variables ☐ school variables ☐ parent variables ☐ *Organizational dimensions* ☐ acquisition of materials ☐ scheduling ☐ grouping ☐ record keeping ☐ *Instructional dimensions*	☐ Clear communication ☐ Matching of instructional techniques to corresponding stages of learning ☐ Active engagement of students ☐ Appropriate use of specialized and/or adaptive strategies ☐ task analysis ☐ prompting ☐ adapting materials and activities ☐ Consistent monitoring of progress (data collection)	☐ Useful feedback to students ☐ motivational ☐ corrective ☐ Practical methods of record keeping ☐ Careful evaluative and planning activities

SOURCE: Polloway, E.A., Payne, J.S., Patton, J.R., & Payne, R.A. (1985). *Strategies for teaching retarded and special needs learners* (3rd ed.). Columbus, OH: Charles E. Merrill.

geared for maintenance learning during the acquisition stage. This involves attempting to teach mentally retarded students new skills through methods that solely provide them opportunities to learn and work on their own, such as completing worksheets, sorting items, or viewing films. Rather than carefully programming new skills, this misuse leaves the students to their own devices to try to cope for themselves, without the continuous feedback and reinforcement they usually need for acquisition learning.

Resolving these problems involves careful assessment of the student's skill development during instruction. As the student shows evidence of learning and improvement (i.e., reaches a pre-established level of correct performance), a gradual phasing out of the components of the acquisition-type teaching should be instituted towards the goal of reliance on maintenance activities. If the student has significant trouble with the transition, the teacher can again use more frequent reinforcement and directive techniques before attempting to move the child away from the acquisition stage (Lindsley, 1964).

ANTECEDENT EVENTS

A teacher must understand and consider a number of strategies and techniques which are antecedents to learning if programming is to be effective. These include those events or activities which prepare for, facilitate, and guide learning. The teacher who develops and perfects an array of antecedent instructional skills is on the way to building a solid foundation for becoming effective. The antecedents to learning that we will discuss include task analysis, the formulation of class rules, prompting, consideration of classroom environment, and planning/scheduling.

Task Analysis **Task analysis** is one of the major skills all teachers of students with learning problems must master, particularly teachers of students with all degrees of mental retardation. Through task analysis, a terminal learning objective is set and a sequence of objectives is established, which, if mastered, will lead to the attainment of the terminal objective. Simply stated, *task analysis* is the breaking down of a large skill into its component behavioral parts. For example, the skill of using the telephone involves recognizing numbers, matching numbers on paper to those on the dial, dialing the phone, speaking appropriately into the phone, and using the phone book. Or, the skill of making a bed involves assembling two sheets, a blanket, a pillow, and case and putting each one on the mattress in a particular order. In both examples, each of these subobjectives can also be further broken down into smaller steps, and each component can be separately and directly taught. The degree to which each task must be broken down depends upon the learning needs of the individual student; in general, the more severely handicapped the student, the more finely the task must be analyzed.

Many everyday skills can be taught through task analysis.

In some cases, a sequence of subgoals for a particular task is available to the teacher in the form of diagnostic tests, teacher manuals, actual commercial teaching programs, or curriculum guides. For instance, if a person wanted to know something about the series of steps required in self-feeding, this information could be obtained from a tool like the *Balthazar Adaptive Behavior Scales* (Balthazar, 1971, 1973). This test breaks down self-feeding into small sequential steps which, when followed, will greatly help the teacher plan and execute a program to teach self-feeding. In the area of language, a teacher can obtain a sequence of steps for teaching language from a number of commercial language programs. One such resource that is widely used with mentally retarded students is *DISTAR* (Science Research Associates), which begins with something as simple as teaching singular statements such as "This is a cup" and moves to teaching complex statements such as, "Hand me all the cups that are blue and are not broken." Several similar programs are available in the areas of math and reading, and many programs focusing on self-help skills for more severely handicapped students are on the market as well. Unfortunately, not all of what needs to be taught is readily available in commercial form; therefore, various tasks must be analyzed and the subgoals determined by the individual teacher.

Rules Another antecedent to behavior involves classroom **rules.** Many children, and most mentally retarded children, seem to function best in situations in which they know what is expected of them. Students need to be aware of what will and what will not be tolerated. An explanation, demonstration, and posting of classroom rules prior to any violations is often a sound practice in antecedent instruction. Mentally retarded students need not be placed in a situation of having to test limits to determine classroom rules, since the teacher can clearly explain acceptable and unacceptable behavior. Classroom rules should be few in number, clearly defined, written or illustrated by pictures, and posted for quick referral. Consequences, both positive and negative, should be used consistently when rules are followed or broken.

The learning of the rules is facilitated by reviewing them regularly, immediately notifying violators after each and every infraction, and frequently praising students for obeying the rules.

Prompting **Prompts** are antecedent stimuli that are presented to the learner along with the task being taught in order to increase the chances that the correct response will be given. Prompting can consist of a variety of techniques, including physical prompts, verbal cues, highlighting or accenting, and imitation.

Becker, Engelmann, and Thomas (1971) have suggested several guidelines for increasing the effectiveness of prompting. All prompts should be gradually withdrawn, or faded until they are no longer required. The prompt used should be the least possible one, in order to facilitate **fading.** The instructional task stimuli should precede the prompt to make sure the learner attends to the task rather than the prompt.

Physical Prompts. This technique consists of physically assisting the child in performing motor movements. For example, a teacher can teach a child to raise the arm towards a toy by firmly holding the child's wrist and raising the arm until contact is made with the toy. In this example, the prompt can be faded as the child begins to exert some control, by the teacher physically just starting the arm movement and reducing the pressure of the grip to barely holding or touching the wrist. This fading process is repeated until the teacher is not touching the child's wrist at all.

A similar prompting technique has been used to help mentally retarded children learn to use a pencil or crayon. At first, the child's writing hand is grasped so that the teacher is actually doing the marking, then gradually the pressure is reduced to the point of a light touch, and finally the child marks with the writing utensil, completely unassisted.

Verbal Cues. Verbal cues can accompany the task and assist in producing the correct response. Voice inflections and verbalization (modeling) of the correct response with the child are two common ways to use this technique. For example, learning the names of colors can present difficulties for young mentally retarded children. For a child who can respond correctly to all primary colors and all secondary colors except orange, the following procedure could be implemented. The teacher could show the child an orange block, hold it up, and ask "What color is this?'' Before the child can answer incorrectly, the response "orange" is given by the teacher. Within a very few trials, the child should respond simultaneously with the teacher. Gradually the teacher can fade the cue by reducing her vocal prompt until it is inaudible, while continuing to imitate the mouth movements of the response "orange." Gradually these cueing lip movements can be eliminated also.

Highlighting. Building cues into instructional materials can involve the highlighting or accenting of some critical features or dimensions of a correct response which must be selected from several possible choices. Some of the most common ways are to make the correct response bigger, present it louder, or highlight it in a contrasting color or sound from the other possible choices. These somewhat artificial cues should gradually be faded as the student consistently selects the right answer, so that he does not become totally dependent upon them over time.

Another example of the use of accenting in the educational setting is placing lines on the floor to designate quiet study areas and play areas where talking is permitted. A similar technique can be used to remind students of safety areas. For example, to teach a child to stay out of the way of a swing, a teacher could draw a line around the swing set and instruct the students not to cross the line while another child is seated in the swing. This same technique is used at the high school level in many shop classes. Circles are drawn on the floor around the power equipment, and only one person can be in the circle at a time. In both cases, circles or lines are antecedent stimuli used to prompt students not to get in the way of others. Eventually, when students learn the safety rules through a combination of praise and negative verbal feedback, the lines are no longer needed and can be faded out.

Imitation. Mentally retarded students learn a great deal through imitating the behavior of others. It is imperative that teachers be aware of the power of this type of learning and keep in mind the fact that mentally retarded individuals imitate both inappropriate as well as appropriate behavior. Therefore, the use of good models—both adults and peers—is of paramount importance. **Modeling** is a process that involves the use of both antecedent events (the model actually demonstrating the behavior) and consequences (positive reinforcement for correctly imitating the modeled behavior). For the teacher wishing to improve imitative learning in the student, three components need to be kept in mind: simplify, demonstrate, and repeat.

To simplify imitative movements, a teacher may need to exaggerate, to restrict actions to short time spans, or to model in some sequence moving from simple to complex. For example, in teaching a child to greet other people, a teacher initially could model the handshake and verbal hello, and later, perhaps through modeling or other means, work on the qualitative and more complex skills such as eye contact, tone of voice, and duration of interaction.

Although many children may try to imitate, some may find it difficult, no matter how well the behavior is demonstrated. For a mentally retarded student who has difficulty imitating, it is important to actually teach the skill of motor or verbal imitation. Imitation usually is taught by a combination of instruction, demonstration, and prompting techniques.

Classroom Environment   Lindsley (1964) coined the phrase *prosthetic environment* when referring to environments that are intentionally designed to facilitate learning. It is without question that classroom environments should be considered an important part of the process of learning, particularly with respect to providing appropriate antecedents to learning.

Prosthetic environmental strategies can include seating (or prone position) arrangements that stimulate responding and discourage distractions, AV equipment that assists in highlighting and emphasizing important points, charts that consistently remind students of certain rules, furniture and areas that encourage interaction and sharing, manipulative games that promote the development of fine motor skills, and mobiles and other stimulating items which vary in color, texture, and size to attract the attention of more severely handicapped students.

It was not too long ago that the majority of special education classes were small, underequipped, and located in undesirable areas of the school building. Even today, many classrooms continue to fit this description.

Most certainly there are physical limitations in all schools, but regardless of the physical barriers and restrictions, the teacher must provide an environment that will allow for small group instruction, individual work, and a nonseated area for children to become involved in interesting activities. For multiply handicapped students whose mobility is impaired, the environment must be flexible enough to allow them to be positioned in a variety of ways and locations. Whether the classroom is small and self-contained or a part of a new, open-classroom pod, flexible arrangements are essential for developing a prosthetic environment.

Planning and Scheduling   The school day schedule is seldom put together so as to increase the opportunities for learning. The importance of a well-planned schedule, however, cannot be overemphasized. The tempo and pace of instruction are dramatically affected by the schedule of events that take place daily. By weaving interesting, creative, and exciting activities throughout the day and by alternating the nature of

Student: Joan Boaks

Objectives: Long-range: Student will name all primary and secondary

colors on command; e.g., "What color is this?" "Red."

Specific lesson: The student will be able to point to the correct colored

object (red and yellow) upon verbal command (e.g., point to the red cup)

at least 90% of the time.

Materials: Red cup, yellow cup, shield (blotter), raisins

Method of Presentation: Place the red and yellow cup upside down in

front of the student. Shield the cup from the student's view of the

blotter. While shielded, place a raisin under one of the cups (e.g.,

yellow), take the shield away and say, "Pick up the yellow cup."

When the child picks up the yellow cup, let the child have the raisin.

If an incorrect choice is made, say, "no, this is yellow" and take the

raisin and repeat the process. Be sure to alter the placement of the

cups so the student does not learn position placement rather than color.

Evaluation of lesson: Date _____:

	Trials Correct	Trials Incorrect
Red		
Yellow		

Total percent correct = _____

Projected needs:

Child's reaction to lesson:

FIGURE 11.2 Lesson Plan Format

the activities (e.g., seatwork, individual instruction, or group instruction, and verbal, motor, and writing activities), teachers can plan a program that will be interesting and enjoyable as well as educationally profitable.

Scheduling involves the development of a daily plan made up of a series of specific lesson plans. The daily schedule ensures that there will be enough activities for the day and, conversely, that there will be enough time for each activity.

Lesson Plans. A well-planned daily schedule helps the teacher in effective instruction. After the teacher determines students' specific needs, a plan for meeting individual needs emerges through the use of lesson plans. A lesson plan focuses directly on the learning objectives which are written on the child's IEP. In it, the teacher states exactly what will be taught to each student and how it will be taught. The important aspect for teachers is not the specific plan format to be used but the inclusion of information regarding what they plan to teach. Figure 11.2 illustrates a typical lesson plan.

CONSEQUENT EVENTS

No matter how well the antecedent events have been presented, learning cannot take place without providing consequences which signal to the students that their responses are correct or incorrect.

Consequences may be items, activities, or events. These positive or negative consequences must come immediately after the response as well as be contingent upon it. To be contingent means that the consequence occurs if, and only if, the behavior precedes it. It serves to increase or decrease the behavior it follows.

The Functions of Consequences Consequences are feedback mechanisms that predominately serve two functions: (*a*) to motivate children and (*b*) to control children who act inappropriately. Motivation implies the need to increase some behaviors, while control implies the need to decrease certain responses. Furthermore, the behaviors (in both motivational and control situations) to be addressed can be either academic or social.

However, we must emphasize that the effect of a particular consequence on behavior is entirely an individual matter; what is reinforcing to one person may be neutral or even punishing to another. Therefore, consequences must be selected on an individual basis and used only as long as they have the intended effect of strengthening or weakening behavior. This critical information may only be obtained when detailed records are kept on each student's daily progress. Keep this key concept in mind when reading the rest of this section.

A TOKEN ECONOMY

The following is a description of a token economy by a teacher who has implemented nine different token economies: one with preschoolers, two in homes with parents or retarded children, four at the elementary level, and two at the secondary level (one a work study program).

In a typical token economy, the teacher gives children points, poker chips, check marks, or other tangible objects as rewards or reinforcers for desirable behavior. The points or objects are later used as a medium of exchange with which the child can "buy" a variety of goods (e.g., candy or toys) and services (e.g., recess, tutoring help, or privileges). For example, a teacher may give a child tokens for correctly completing a specified number of arithmetic problems or for staying in his or her seat for a specified period of time. Later, the child may exchange the tokens for a desired object or activity. Tokens may be issued to individual children, to small groups, or to entire classes for designated achievements or social behaviors.

Recent research has shown that, essentially, token economies are miniature economies with characteristics of supply, demand, inflation, recession, and socioeconomic levels that are predictable in terms of economic theory.

Token economies are *not* recommended for all teachers. I would suggest if a teacher has one or more of the following characteristics, he or she should consider *not* using a token system:

1. Doesn't like the idea or philosophy of using money as a basis for transactions in the classroom.
2. Detests keeping records of any kind.
3. Is personally disorganized.
4. Lacks a sense of humor and/or has a chip on the shoulder.
5. Sees nothing wrong with how the children are presently learning.
6. Lacks energy and ambition and is unwilling to take the time to plan and prepare adequately.

If the teacher does not have any of these characteristics, a token economy may be his or her "cup of tea."

Motivation Motivational-type consequences can be used to accelerate either academic or social behaviors. Typical types of positive consequences or reinforcers used to motivate mentally retarded children are praise, food, toys, and games. For example, a student may be praised for completing a math assignment, assembling a circuit board, making sure his work is correct, keeping his head erect for 10 seconds, or following directions. Academic or social performance may also be strengthened through the use of tokens, activities, or other positive consequences. General experience and an abundance of research suggest that children perform both quantitatively and qualitatively better when properly motivated through the systematic application of positive consequences.

Many types of positive reinforcers are available to the teacher, including social reinforcers, tangible items, activities, and tokens. Social reinforcers include such things as praise and physical contact like hugging or shaking hands (Hall & Hall, 1980a). Common tangible reinforcers are food, toys, books, records, and notebooks. Recreational, sports, and even educational activities can also be used as positive consequences by giving students an opportunity to participate in something they find pleasurable. Tokens in the form of poker chips or points, which can be exchanged for desirable tangible items and activities, can also be very effective in producing positive behavior change. Involvement of the student in self-charting of behavior and planning of contracts (Salend & Ehrlich, 1983) can increase the chances of success in any reinforcement program.

Several factors should be considered when using positive reinforcers. First, the positive consequences should be presented immediately following the appropriate behavior. If there is a lapse in time, an intervening behavior, perhaps even an inappropriate one, may accidentally be reinforced. Second, in a sense, there is a continuum of types of reinforcers ranging from tangibles to activities to tokens to social. This continuum begins with reinforcers that are more artificial, in that they are not always available immediately contingent upon behaviors in the natural environment (how often will a child or adult obtain a tangible reward after doing a home or work task?). This continuum ends with more natural reinforcers like tokens (money is a token reinforcer with which most of us are familiar), praise, and attention. Therefore, it is helpful to use reinforcers at the higher end of the continuum if they are effective for a particular mentally retarded student, in order to prepare him for the outside world. If the person responds only to lower level reinforcers, they may be used in combination with higher level ones so that these more natural consequences gradually become reinforcing. However, food reinforcers should be used with great care to avoid problems such as allergies, weight gain, etc. (Shevin, 1982).

For a discussion of teacher characteristics and use of the token economy, see page 350.

One last factor concerning choice of reinforcers must be mentioned. The teacher will need to be very creative in this area, especially when working with profoundly retarded, multiply handicapped individuals who may not be motivated by praise, tangible items, tokens, or even food (they may have eating and digestive problems). In this type of case, the teacher can try various types of auditory, visual, and tactile stimulation like music, colored lights, rubbing with lotion, and water play to see if they are effective reinforcers (Wolery, 1978).

Control   Control-type consequences are commonly used to decrease or decelerate disruptive, disturbing, or other inappropriate behaviors. These consequences present an unpleasant event contingent upon and immediately following an undesirable behavior. This contingency causes the behavior to decrease in frequency. As is true in the case of positive motivational consequences, negative control-type consequences must be chosen on an individual basis, and mildly unpleasant consequences (for example, ignoring, verbal reprimands, loss of points or privileges) should be tried before more restrictive consequences (such as timeout) should be used. Whenever negative consequences are used to decelerate inappropriate behavior, the teacher must *always* select an appropriate substitute behavior to teach to the student and use positive consequences to make this learning possible. For example, a student who is frequently out of her seat may earn points exchangeable for recreational activities when she is in seat and on task, while losing points for out-of-seat behavior. Or a student may receive a loud "No" when engaging in self-stimulation like hand flapping, and receive praise and attention for using his hands in appropriate ways like playing with toys or feeding himself.

The vast majority of teaching interactions with mentally retarded individuals should and do involve positive interventions, and a relatively small proportion involve negative contingencies. However, negative consequences are sometimes necessary, and we will cover several typically used ones in this section.

Typical negative consequences employed in classrooms for the mentally retarded involve loss of points or checkmarks, loss of a special privilege, or loss of free time. These contingencies may be effective for reducing certain undesirable behaviors of some children.

Timeout is a procedure used to decrease behavior. It involves withdrawal of positive reinforcement (Hall & Hall, 1980b). The technique of timeout involves the temporary removal of an individual from the setting in which an inappropriate behavior has occurred, thus preventing him from receiving positive reinforcement. The student may be placed in a safe but nonstimulating area or room for a brief time period. When he returns to the original setting, the student is directed to engage in appropriate behaviors and reinforced for his successful efforts. This combination of timeout and positive reinforcement is often effective in bringing about positive behavior change. One consideration as to the use of timeout is that its effectiveness as a decelerating consequence will be due in large part to the high rate of positive reinforcement in the classroom and its absence in the timeout area. Without these two elements, the procedure will be of limited usefulness.

More aversive consequences are occasionally used with mentally retarded individuals who have seriously self-destructive behaviors like head-banging, biting their own hands and other body parts, and rumination. Consequences such as unpleasant tastes, smells, sounds, or sensations have been used effectively to reduce these life-threatening behaviors in some individuals. Staff using these procedures must be expertly trained prior to and well-supervised during the actual implementation, and must prepare and carry out simultaneous positive programs to teach these individuals functional skills. Along with this discussion of using aversive consequences, we want to point out that many educators are successfully employing only positive techniques to reduce inappropriate behaviors. Such techniques involve reinforcing behaviors other than or incompatible with the inappropriate behavior, and reinforcing successively lower and lower rates of the target behavior until it is eliminated (Denny, 1980; Repp & Deitz, 1979; Tarpley & Schroeder, 1979).

Again, further reading and study must be completed before a teacher attempts any of the procedures mentioned in this section, particularly those involving negative consequences (Foxx, 1982).

SUMMARY

Effective teaching of retarded students requires careful assessment, detailed instructional planning, and individualized behavior and learning management—the same ingredients all good teachers use with their pupils. But in addition, teachers of retarded students need to choose curricula and specific educational targets that will be functional for their students and help them succeed in their everyday environments. Educational programs for retarded students will often focus on practical daily living skills that increase students' independence, rather than on academic skills. Teachers must be thoroughly familiar with the common learning characteristics of retarded students, and match their instructional strategies and materials to each student's needs. It is particularly important that the teacher create a learning environment that increases the students' chances for success, by carefully analyzing the tasks, drawing up lesson plans and daily schedules, making students aware of classroom rules, and prompting desired responses. The consequences that students receive for making responses must be thoughtfully chosen if they are to be effective in motivating students to learn or in controlling their behavior. The teacher must also know whether the student is acquiring or maintaining the skill. In sum, teaching retarded students requires not only standard teaching skills but specialized knowledge and careful management.

CHAPTER
TWELVE

Placement Alternatives

The trend today toward providing appropriate, beneficial, humanistic services to retarded persons in our society has led to changes within the existing structure of American schools as well as to the development of entirely new educational alternatives. The goal is no longer to hide the handicapped from view, but to habilitate them. A guiding principle is "normalization"—the idea that mentally retarded people should lead lives as much like yours and mine as possible. For children this principle has been reflected, in part, in the mandate for education in the least restrictive environment in which the child can succeed. This principle often leads to "mainstreaming"—placing the child in the regular classroom or school for some portion (or all) of the school day. Kneedler, Hallahan, and Kauffman (1984) note that the related movements of mainstreaming and deinstitutionalization have had their greatest impact in the area of mental retardation.

This chapter deals with various program alternatives available to mentally retarded individuals. We will look at placement alternatives for infants and young children, for school-aged children and youth, and for adolescents and adults. We will also look at the position statements of

This chapter was contributed by Allen K. Miller, Cecil D. Mercer, and James S. Payne.

the National Association for Retarded Citizens (1978) on mainstreaming mentally retarded students into the public schools.

PROGRAMS FOR INFANTS AND PRESCHOOL-AGED CHILDREN

As we have seen, the more severe the handicap, the earlier the child is likely to be identified as mentally retarded. Consequently, most educational programs for infants and preschool-aged children are designed for the moderately to profoundly handicapped, those with multiple handicaps, or those who can be identified as being at high risk of having significant delays by the time they reach school age. There are three major models used for working with young retarded children: the home-based model, the center-based model, and a combination of home- and center-based services (Heward & Orlansky, 1980). All rely heavily on the involvement and participation of the child's parents, with parents providing actual instruction in most cases.

HOME-BASED MODEL

In the home-based model, the child receives services at home from a parent, usually the mother. In most programs, a professional or paraprofessional trainer comes to the home to identify areas of need, develop an instructional program, teach the mother how to teach the child, and monitor progress. Techniques of behavior modification, task analysis, and developing systems to chart progress are typically taught (Cegelka & Prehm, 1982). The visiting teacher may also provide some direct instruction to the child. According to Karnes and Zehrbach (1977, p. 22), "home-based programs seem to lend themselves well to sparsely populated areas, to clusters of small towns, and to rural areas" as well as to parents who feel more comfortable keeping their child at home for emotional or cultural reasons. The home-based program has the additional advantage of providing instruction in the natural environment, but it has the disadvantage of isolation. That is, the child does not have contact with other children, both retarded and nonretarded. And while the parents receive help regularly, they do not have the chance to meet other parents and professionals to share experiences and (often) frustrations.

See chapter 8 for more on the effect on parents of having a retarded child.

One well-known home-based program is the Portage (Wisconsin) Project. This program serves handicapped children up to age 6 who show at least a 1-year developmental lag. Approximately half the children served are mentally retarded (Karnes & Zehrbach, 1977). The program uses both professional and paraprofessional home teachers, who usually visit the homes once a week. The emphasis is on teaching the parents to use behavior modification techniques with their children. The project uses the *Portage Guide to Early Education*, a curriculum which includes 450 skills organized by normal developmental sequence. In addition, the staff works with other community agencies to provide services to the child and family.

A slightly different approach is taken by the RIP (Regional Intervention Program) in central Tennessee (Eller, Jordan, Parish, & Elder, 1979). In this program, parents come to the Nashville center for an initial individualized training program that meets 5 days a week for as long as necessary. This training program is run by other parents who have been through the program with their own children. Parents are taught to record data, choose instructional goals, reinforce desirable responses, and teach their children. Instruction of the child also begins at the center, and staff members watch the parents work with the children and help the parents improve their teaching skills. At the end of the parent training program, parents return home and provide all services for their child. In order to enter the program, the parents must agree to work in the center for 6 months after the intensive intervention with their own child has ended. Once this intensive work is completed, the center serves as a liaison to follow up on the child's educational placement and progress. RIP focuses on children under age 5, and over half the children begin the program at age 3 or younger. It has the extra advantage of being an informal parent support group.

CENTER-BASED PROGRAMS

In center-based program, most instruction and services are provided at the center itself. Parents bring their children to the center, where instruction is often provided by both staff members and parents. According to Karnes and Zehrbach

> These programs tend to be for the older preschool child and/or the more severely handicapped child who can benefit from special equipment such as sound amplifiers or orthopedic equipment and from highly trained personnel such as physical and occupational therapists, psychiatrists, and special medical personnel. (1977, p. 23)

In these programs, the preschool children have the opportunity to interact with other children and with teachers, learning social skills that they will need for success in school. Many centers provide a combination of individualized, small-group, and large-group instruction.

One center-based program is the Model Preschool Center for Handicapped Children at the University of Washington in Seattle. The Center offers a variety of programs, including (*a*) an infant learning program for Down syndrome infants; (*b*) an infant program for other "at risk" infants; (*c*) programs for Down syndrome preschoolers—an early preschool for children from age 19 months to 3 years, an intermediate preschool for children aged 3 to 4, an advanced preschool for children aged 4 to 5, and a kindergarten for 5- to 6-year-olds; (*d*) preschool programs for severely handicapped children (Karnes & Zehrbach, 1977). These developmental programs all work towards helping the children function as normally as possible, with the eventual goal of placement in programs in their home communities.

COMBINATION HOME- AND CENTER-BASED PROGRAMS

In these programs, children receive instruction both at home and in a center. These programs combine the advantages of the other models. Again, parents are trained, often at the center, to teach their children. The staff may also visit the home to observe the child and parent, as well as to discuss the child's progress. For example, the Teaching Research Infant and Child Center in Eugene, Oregon, serves moderately to profoundly handicapped children ages 1 to 18 (Fredericks, Baldwin, Moore, Templeman, & Anderson, 1980). It includes a classroom for children aged 1 to 3 and one for children aged 3 to 6, as well as classes for older children. The curriculum is based on the *Teaching Research Curriculum for the Moderately and Severely Handicapped* (Fredericks et al., 1976), using developmentally sequenced materials and task analyses of skills. Daily center teaching involves both individualized and group instruction. In addition, the teachers train the parents to work on jointly chosen instructional programs which are coordinated with the school programs and designed to extend the school day. The home teaching periods last from 10 to 30 minutes each day.

In some home and center programs, the parents work at home with children up to around age 3, at which time the child begins to go to the center. The Saginaw D.O.E.S. Care Program in Saginaw, Michigan, is one such program. It serves handicapped children, including the mildly and moderately retarded, from birth to age 8. In the D.O.E.S. program, home trainers, working under the direction of professional staff, visit the home until the child reaches age 3. From age 3 to 8, the children attend classroom programs focusing on individual learning needs.

PROGRAMS FOR CHILDREN AND YOUTH

The free public school system was established in the United States shortly after the War of 1812 (Pulliam, 1968). Before that time, most children had been educated in church-sponsored programs in which the provision of equal education for all children was not a concern. During the early part of the 19th century, state laws were enacted that required communities to provide educational opportunities but did not require mandatory attendance. These efforts at mass education emphasized the

"MAINSTREAMING" REVISITED

Since the implementation of the Education for All Handicapped Children Act of 1975, there has been much mention of the concept of mainstreaming. Often associated with the notion of placing students in the least restrictive environment, mainstreaming implies the integration of handicapped students into regular education. Some authorities, however, point out that some regular education settings may be more restrictive, rather than less restrictive. Regardless of the restrictiveness debate, there are other important issues relevant to the practice of mainstreaming retarded students. The following list includes some of the major concerns facing educators and researchers dealing with this topic.

☐ In light of the presumed benefits of having handicapped students educated as much as possible with their nonhandicapped peers, we still lack a solid research base that supports this idea.

☐ There may be more interest in mainstreaming students than in what happens to them afterwards.

☐ What are the practical and financial implications of mainstreaming preschool-aged children?

☐ If the mildly retarded population has changed over the last few years, then two notes of caution arise: (1) earlier research on mainstreaming mildly retarded students is probably not applicable to the present population; and (2) this new lower functioning EMR group is probably not as capable of being mainstreamed as former EMR students.

☐ No definite conclusions about the success or failure of mainstreaming efforts can be drawn from the existing corpus of research.

☐ If suitable retarded students are to be successfully integrated into regular education settings, they will have to
　　—acquire those classroom-related survival skills and behaviors which are required in these settings
　　—develop appropriate social skills (i.e., social competence)
　　—participate in cooperative ventures with nonretarded peers so that the retarded students can be perceived as performing reasonably well.

☐ There is a great need to (1) identify programs that seem to successfully mainstream students; (2) examine the components of these programs; and (3) disseminate this information.

importance of curricular content and not the individual needs of children. For the most part, children with mental and physical limitations were kept out of school. This situation changed with the advent of compulsory attendance requirements, which began in Rhode Island in 1840. The entry of retarded youngsters into the public schools meant that the public schools needed to offer an array of programs. We can group the current program alternatives used for educating school-aged retarded youngsters into 16 types. As illustrated in Figure 12.1, the programs may be divided into four major categories: those based in regular classrooms, in special classrooms, in special schools, and in other settings.

During the last few years, the trend has been to provide services to exceptional children without segregating them from students who do not have learning problems. This trend—mainstreaming—requires that all exceptional children (including the mentally retarded) be taught in

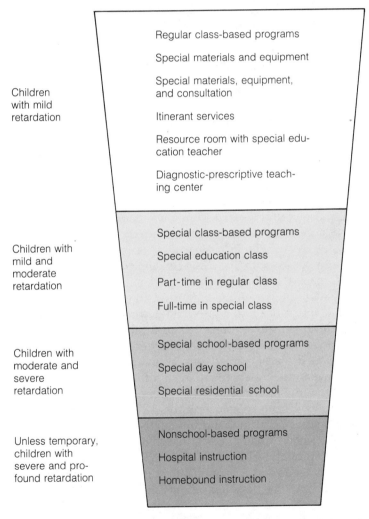

Children with mild retardation

Regular class-based programs

Special materials and equipment

Special materials, equipment, and consultation

Itinerant services

Resource room with special education teacher

Diagnostic-prescriptive teaching center

Children with mild and moderate retardation

Special class-based programs

Special education class

Part-time in regular class

Full-time in special class

Children with moderate and severe retardation

Special school-based programs

Special day school

Special residential school

Unless temporary, children with severe and profound retardation

Nonschool-based programs

Hospital instruction

Homebound instruction

FIGURE 12.1 Models for Educating Retarded Pupils According to Level of Program Segregation and Degree of Retardation

Some programs work with very young retarded children.

See chapter 14.

Chapter 9 presents a thorough discussion of the most significant recent litigation over rights of the developmentally disabled.

the regular classroom whenever possible. Within school systems, the expansion of regular classroom-based programs reflects recent efforts to educate children within the mainstream of the educational process. Mainstreaming has influenced institutional programs by suggesting that institutions be reduced in size and located as close as possible to the area from which their residents are referred. Mainstreamed regular class programs are more readily geared to mildly retarded children, where the special class and special school programs are designed primarily to serve children whose retardation is more severe, or who have other handicapping conditions. As with its close cousin, the **deinstitutionalization** movement, mainstreaming has gained momentum from a recent profusion of litigation and resulting significant legislation. Most of the legal action in this arena has highlighted the detrimental effects of segregating school children by exceptionality and of labeling students as *retarded*, *disturbed*, and so forth. Today mildly retarded children seem to be readily mainstreamed, desegregated, and nonlabeled, but more severely retarded and even moderately retarded children are still not easily accommodated within the public schools or community living. As the program alternatives move from regular classroom to special school-based programs, segregation, labeling, and the degree of retardation of the child increase. MacMillan (1982) notes that the retarded child should be placed in the program alternative closest to the regular class that the student's own needs and characteristics will allow, and the instructional arrangement should be flexible to allow as much meaningful integration of the retarded student into mainstream education as possible. In addition, when establishing objectives for any retarded child, it is important to make only a tentative commitment to a program level and not consider placement in any program as permanent or terminal. Educators should provide handicapped students with programs that will maximize their potential and allow them to function in society. Opportunities for moving retarded children from more segregated programs to more integrated programs should constantly be considered, and changes made whenever feasible.

P.L. 94-142

The 1975 Education for All Handicapped Children Act (P.L. 94-142) has been, to date, the most significant piece of legislation to affect the education of handicapped children and youth. In the area of educational placement for handicapped children and youth, two specific legal guarantees are relevant:

Chapter 9 discusses at length the stipulations of 94-142.

1. Assurance of the availability of an appropriate *public* education for all handicapped children at no cost to parents.
2. Assurance that special education will be provided to all handicapped children in the "least restrictive" environment.

Basically, these assurances impel educators to ensure that no child shall be rejected from services on the basis of handicap and that every child shall be integrated with his or her normal peers to the maximum extent possible. Let us now turn to the specific alternatives available for placement of retarded students.

REGULAR CLASS PROGRAMS

The ultimate goal guiding educational placement is to provide the most beneficial services to retarded children with minimal segregation from their peers. This goal can be accomplished in the **regular class** programs for some students, with a variety of instructional arrangements. The

Individualized education is crucial for handicapped students in all settings.

child's needs and those of the other children in the class dictate which arrangement should be used. Again, constant reevaluation is needed to determine the appropriateness of the placement, based on the changing needs of the child.

Special Materials and Equipment Occasionally regular classroom teachers are able to teach mildly retarded pupils in their classrooms with the help of some special education materials. The material may be a high interest, low vocabulary reading series, a programmed reader, a job-related math book, or any material or hardware that allows the teacher to individualize instruction. This level of special education support requires a regular classroom teacher who is highly skilled with a sensitivity for the individual needs of retarded learners.

Special Materials, Equipment, and Consultation In this plan, the regular classroom teacher is provided with special materials and limited consultation from a special education teacher. The consultation may consist of demonstrating the use of certain materials or equipment, assessing the child's needs, developing teaching strategies, or providing an inservice training program. This level of support also requires that the regular classroom teacher be highly skilled and sensitive to the needs of retarded children. In essence, to use either of these plans, the regular classroom teacher should be working with a moderate to small pupil-to-teacher ratio (approximately 5 to 12 students per teacher).

Itinerant Services An itinerant program supplies regular class teachers with regular consultative and instructional services for their retarded pupils. An **itinerant teacher** usually operates from a central office and visits the school periodically, usually working in individualized or small-group instruction with students who have special needs that hamper their scholastic progress. This alternative is often used with students who have vision or language disorders. Since these services are limited in scope and only provided weekly or biweekly, the basic responsibility for the education of the retarded children remains with the regular class teacher. Occasionally the itinerant services are bolstered through school-based tutors who are either volunteers or teacher aides. Also, student tutoring helps teachers to individualize instruction; it is gaining popularity as a technique for assisting regular class teachers with retarded learners (Christoplos, 1973). Moreover, peer tutoring has been successfully used to (*a*) improve academic skills; (*b*) foster self-esteem; (*c*) help the shy youngster; (*d*) help students who have difficulty with authority figures; (*e*) improve race relations; and (*f*) promote positive relationships and cooperation among peers (Mercer & Mercer, 1985).

Resource Room with Special Education Teacher In the **resource room** plan, the special education pupil remains in a regular class and receives special education through the coordinated efforts of the regular class teacher and the resource room teacher assigned to only that school. Models for resource instruction vary substantially among schools. For example, Reger and Koppman (1971) note that

> Resource room programs for children with problems are not new, but there seems to be a large degree of variation among programs and there is not universal understanding of this kind of approach. (p. 460)

The child may be placed in the resource room for all academic instruction, returning to the regular class only for lunch, art, and physical education, for instance; or may have resource room instruction only for particular problem areas such as reading and language arts. The flexibility of the resource room plan allows it to accommodate the different needs of both teachers and children.

See Figure 12.2.

    The resource room has been primarily used as a placement alternative for children with learning disabilities. However, several investigators (Barksdale & Atkinson, 1971; Hammill, Iano, McGettigan, & Weiderholt, 1972) have recognized the resource room plan as an alternative for educating mildly retarded children. Bradfield, Brown, Kaplan, Rickert, and Stannard (1973) have demonstrated the feasibility of educating mildly retarded children in the regular classroom. In their study, the regular class teachers who received the retarded children were assisted in developing "precision teaching" skills. Their findings indicate

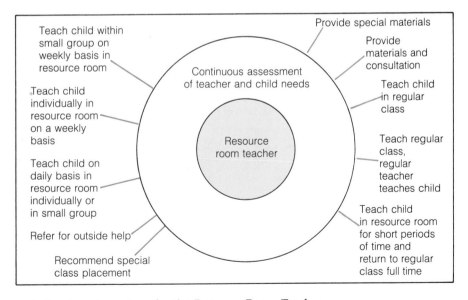

FIGURE 12.2 Service Alternatives for the Resource Room Teacher

HELEMANO PLANTATION AGRICULTURAL TRAINING CENTER

Designing productive programs for retarded adults can be a challenge to tax the limits of one's creativity. One progressive and innovative example is the Helemano Plantation in Hawaii. This program was described not long ago in an article entitled "Opportunity For The Retarded, Inc. Says 'Nuts' to Counting Bolts" written by Patricia Rowe. Selected portions of this article, which appeared in the Summer 1984 issue of *Human Development News*, are presented below.

On the Hawaiian island of Oahu, the hazy tropical climate has been kind to the local fruit industry. The lush Dole pineapple plantations employ thousands of workers, giving rise to a lively local economy, nourished by sunshine, and the growing population.

Nearby, on the Helemano Plantation, farm laborers harvest a variety of tropical fruits and vegetables; a baker pulls a cake out of the oven; a clerk rings up a sale at the country store. All the workers on this plantation contribute their vital share to the local economy. What is extraordinary is that most of them are victims of developmental disabilities.

The Helemano Plantation is owned by Opportunities for the Retarded, Inc., (ORI) a private organization dedicated to the philosophy that developmentally disabled persons are perfectly capable of being productive members of society. Founded in 1980 by Susanna Cheung and a group of parents and professionals from the Honolulu area, the project currently serves 62 people with moderate to severe disabilities and utilizes 18 acres of land valued at 1.8 million dollars.

In planning the community, Cheung and her collaborators were guided by their conviction that subjecting the developmentally disabled to institutionalization or jobs performing the most menial of chores is a senseless and insensitive waste of human life. The community features a work center with a diverse group of enterprises, a residential living program, and supportive services such as counseling, job placement assistance, an educational institute and a recreational facility.

ORI's environment—a combination of workplace and residence—enables retarded persons to have stability and training opportunities, to harness hidden talents, to revitalize mind and body, and to earn a good wage. However, ORI's services are not limited to the retarded client population, but are also offered to the local residents, making the ORI enterprise truly unique.

Many of the local residents are Asian immigrants who have no knowledge of

that the academic skills, attitudes, and social behavior of retarded children in the regular classroom improved as much as or more than that of retarded children in special classes. Walker (1974) has compared the effectiveness of resource rooms and special classes with mildly retarded children; he concludes that "the academic and social-emotional needs of

English or western culture. Other local residents need to learn a trade or to have a communications link to the outside world. In an isolated rural setting such as this, the ORI complex offers the entire community a chance at normalcy and a hope for a better life.

The delivery of services to the entire community not only promotes understanding and goodwill between the developmentally disabled client population and the local residents, but encourages the formation of the most basic of support networks—friendship. "Some people think the developmentally disabled take but do not give," observes Executive Director Cheung. "This is a myth. The developmentally disabled *can* contribute to the community, which is why the thrust of our whole program is community involvement and service."

ORI was initially funded with a $400,000 grant from the Department of Housing and Urban Development and $1.5 million from Community Development Block Grant funds and the Hawaii State Legislature. It also received development funds from the Hawaii Department of Health, the United Way and other private sources. While 20 percent of the farm is now self-sufficient, within the next five years all segments of the work center are expected to be completely self-supporting.

The work center's bakery, cafeteria, giftshop and country store are guaranteed success, Cheung explains, because of their location next door to the Dole Pineapple Center, which attracts 700 visitors daily. These enterprises, together with the farm and a nursery, make a total of six areas, from which clients may choose one in which to receive training, with the eventual goal of job placement.

On the job, senior citizens assist the client population in area of food preparation, nursery operation and retail sales. The current median client salary exceeds a dollar per hour. Ceramics and Hawaiian craft programs are provided for those requiring more therapeutic activities.

The farm employs the greatest number of residents on the plantation. Cheung's management is certainly not lacking in good business sense. "If we are farmers, we must be good farmers and plant good crops," she says.

The residential program, which enables clients to balance work skills with independent living skills, consists of several boarding homes located near the training facility and offers residents supervisory assistance from home counselors. There is a 10 to 20 percent turnover rate among the resident client population. Short-term housing (on a fee-for-service basis) is available for emergency or vacation needs and for parents who visit their children on the facility premises. Parents, however, are encouraged to take their children home for periodic weekend visits to foster a greater sense of normalcy.

the mentally retarded child can be met as well, if not better, in the resource program as in the special class" (p. 289).

The current trend is to have resource teachers provide their services within the regular classroom as opposed to a separate resource room. By providing services in a regular classroom, greater transfer of learning and greater maintenance of learned concepts should occur than if resource help is given in a special setting (Gearheart, 1980).

Although the resource room is gaining popularity as an instructional plan for educating exceptional children, its efficacy has not been extensively examined. Using learning disabled children, Sabatino (1971) found evidence which indicates that daily contact (40-minute sessions) with the resource room teacher was more effective than semiweekly 30-minute sessions. Until research suggests otherwise, it appears that the resource room will remain as a model for educating exceptional children within the mainstream.

Diagnostic-Prescriptive Teaching Center In this relatively new plan, children are taken for short periods of time to in-school centers staffed by a team of special educators and diagnosticians. The center staff members assess the child's performance and develop an individual educational strategy. The child returns to his regular class, but his instruction is based on the program recommended by the center's staff.

SPECIAL CLASS PROGRAMS

Special class programs provide a self-contained instructional environment for the child who is unable to fully profit from education in the regular classroom. Classes of this kind are usually restricted to approximately 10 to 15 students, often with an aide available to provide instructional assistance to the teacher.

Special Education Class **Self-contained special classes** are designed for children who cannot keep up with the instructional pace in a regular classroom. Generally, the special class consists of a group of children who have been identified as exceptional and thus in need of extraordinary treatment, for instance, mentally retarded, emotionally disturbed, or learning disabled students. As with the resource room, the children may receive their total academic instruction within the self-contained class or they may have their academic day divided between part-time self-contained class instruction in certain subjects and regular class instruction in other areas. Although the special class students usually participate in regular physical education, art, and music classes, they are segregated from the mainstream of education. For years, studies and reviews (Cassidy & Stanton, 1959; Dunn, 1968; Johnson, 1962; Rubin, Krus, & Balow, 1973) have been questioning the efficacy of special class programs for mildly retarded children. In commenting on the special class, Dunn (1973b) has stated

> The self-contained special-class plan has been most severely criticized when used with slow-learning and disruptive children. Too often the plan has been used to put out of sight pupils the regular teachers do not want. It is to be hoped, however, that this

practice will not disguise the appropriateness of the plan, especially for children with severe learning disabilities and for
younger children. Certain of these children may need an intensive, specialized curriculum to learn specific skills so as to take a
greater part in the regular school program later in their school
careers. (p. 28)

Smith and Arkans (1974) caution professionals not to become en-
gulfed in the mainstreaming effort to the point of abolishing the self-
contained classroom. They note that it is not feasible for a classroom
teacher who is responsible for the education of 20 to 40 students to
simultaneously meet the educational demands of children with severe
learning problems. They further note that the effectiveness of resource
rooms has not been demonstrated with moderately retarded children. In
essence, it appears that the self-contained program represents a viable
model when used to educate those students who require it. Mercer
(1983) notes that when the special class is deemed appropriate, the following criteria are essential:

1. The special class teacher should be trained to teach the types of
   students in the class.
2. The students should be selected on the basis of learning or social-emotional problems, *not* on the basis of socio-economic status or race.
3. Each child should receive intensive and systematic instruction
   tailored to his unique needs.
4. A wide variety of teaching materials and resources should be
   available to the teacher.
5. The class size should be considerably smaller than a regular
   class.
6. A variety of teaching styles is needed to accommodate the different needs of the pupils.
7. Each pupil's progress should be constantly monitored. Reintegration into the mainstream should be considered when it appears feasible.
8. The class should have administrative support. (p. 153)

Gearheart (1980) suggests that self-contained special classes should
be used with more seriously involved or multiply handicapped individuals. In recent years there has been a strong movement to keep students
out of special classes, since these classes do segregate the special student
from the regular students. On the other hand, the special class may be
the only public school setting that is educationally appropriate for many
moderately and severely retarded students. And, in fact, a self-contained class in a regular school does allow more integration—on buses,

on the playground, in the lunchroom—than a separate school for handicapped students.

SPECIAL SCHOOL PROGRAMS

In the past, school districts placed the majority of their mentally retarded students in special schools. Under this arrangement, students were bussed to a day school which was developed solely to serve exceptional students. The chief advantage of the special school is in providing complete control over the child's curriculum and daily life. This allows for manipulation of all variables within the learning environment—scheduling, physical facilities, instructional climate, and so forth—to best benefit the individual student. On the other hand, the absence of any contact with normal peers presents an unrealistic picture of the world and eliminates any benefits that could be gained through modeling and socialization with other children. As a result, few school districts continue to use special schools for mildly or moderately handicapped students (although some districts still have special classes for severely and multiply handicapped students).

Special Day School A child whose handicap is so severe as to prevent him from functioning in a regular school may attend a **special day school** on either a part-time or full-time basis. In systems combining regular and special day schools, the most severely disabled children are bussed to a central school for part of the day for essential educational services that are not provided in their home schools. In systems where services for the retarded are not available in the regular school, they may receive their entire educational program within a special day school. For sparsely populated regions, it may be economically difficult to provide special classes in each local school; hence the district may feel that it is "necessary" to use a special school instead.

Special Residential School In cases where a retarded child's educational and social disabilities are so pronounced as to warrant round-the-clock attention, he or she might attend a **special residential school**. Facilities of this kind have very low pupil-staff ratios, which benefit the students by allowing for intensive instruction. However, segregated schools deny retarded pupils the opportunity to interact with nonhandicapped peers, and as such, contradict the normalization principle and the "least restrictive environment" provision of P.L. 94-142. Nonetheless, there are, and will continue to be, certain severely handicapped persons who require the highly specialized treatment offered in residential facilities. Many of these children have physical disabilities that require close attention. The environment of a residential school may, then, for many severely retarded and multiply handicapped children, be the least restrictive in which they may function effectively. However, ac-

Some educators would claim that all students—no matter how severe the handicap—should be placed in regular schools (see Brown et al., 1979).

cording to P.L. 94-142, educators must monitor each child's progress so that he or she can be moved to a less restrictive environment as quickly as possible.

OTHER PROGRAMS
Hospital tutelage and homebound instruction are the two most common alternatives for school-age children who are physically unable to be transported to school.

Hospital Instruction Hospital instruction is usually furnished to students who are recovering from an illness or accident, in which case it is understood to be a temporary plan. However, for children confined to a hospital or convalescent home for serious, chronic afflictions, hospital instruction is a continuing process, usually carried out by itinerant or regular class teachers.

Homebound Instruction Homebound instruction is similar to hospital instruction in that it is designed for students who are either temporarily or permanently confined to their homes. Itinerant or regular class teachers usually furnish the instruction. Since it is costly and segregates the child, the use of this plan should be minimized.

As noted by Dunn (1973b), the assignment of a child to an educational program is influenced by the characteristics of the child, his school, his parents, and the community. Child-related variables include the nature of the disability, motivation, academic skills, and behavioral characteristics. School variables include the nature of the regular class program, availability of appropriate special education facilities, and competence of special educators. The parental and community factors include parental support, home environment, and community services.

Although these factors influence placement decisions, the strongest determinant, in keeping with the prevailing trend toward mainstreaming, should be the attempt to educate handicapped children in as normal a setting as is feasible. The child should be integrated as much as possible within his school, home, and local community. In essence, programs which segregate disabled children from the normal environment should be implemented only as a last resort.

NARC POSITION STATEMENTS
With the advent of P.L. 94-142 and the normalization and mainstreaming movements, the National Association for Retarded Citizens (1978) has offered several position statements to guide classification and placement procedures as they related to the mentally retarded student in our public school systems.

Position #1 The principle of mainstreaming in education is best embodied in those programs that offer a variety of instructional alternatives appropriate to students who need specialized services. To the greatest possible extent, handicapped and nonhandicapped students should be allowed to interact socially and academically during the course of the school day. For maximum efficiency, every school system should have a stated policy and guidelines for implementing the mainstreaming principle, and both regular and special teachers should be involved in planning and carrying out the policy. Careful consideration also should be given to establishing a flexible system which will allow appropriate transition and movement within the system as dictated by the individual learning needs of each child.

Position #2 Mainstreaming procedures must be conducted in carefully planned stages, including the development of school policies covering (*a*) procedural guidelines and clear delineation of responsibilities; (*b*) in-service education for both regular and special class teachers; (*c*) careful orientation of students to avoid unnecessary sensitization to individual differences; and (*d*) involvement of parents in formulating education objectives, student evaluation and development of individual educational plans, and the employment of special support personnel.

Position #3 As a general rule, all mentally retarded students should be integrated into the mainstream of public education to the maximum extent possible in accordance with the least restrictive placement provisions specified in Public Law 94-142. However, integration per se should not be considered an educational goal. Rather, it should be viewed as a viable means of facilitating the acquisition of social, academic, and life skills needed by mentally retarded persons to live in a world populated

Programs like the Special Olympics help retarded students learn skills they can use in interacting with nonhandicapped children.

by handicapped as well as nonhandicapped persons. As stated previously, the specific type of educational placement for a given child must be based on an Individualized Educational Plan. Thus, a variety of placement options will be necessary, including resource teaching programs in conjunction with regular class placement, special classes with integration in one or more academic subjects, and self-contained programs within the public school building for some children with highly specific or unusual learning needs, such as the profoundly retarded and multiply handicapped student. In all cases, placement in any component of the service continuum should be based on continuing evaluation of student progress, and feedback from this evaluation should be used to modify both student placement and the educational delivery system.

Position #4 Mainstreaming must be viewed as affecting all students and teachers in the public schools, and traditional patterns of educational services delivery must be modified in the direction of individualized programming for all students. Individualization is a concept that must take on many and varied forms and must not be restricted to written Individualized Education Programs. Simply stated, every individual must be educationally treated as an individual. Individualization should help to alleviate the problem of designing curricular objectives primarily for average ability students and help provide a wide range of educational experiences which will benefit all students, regardless of their learning needs.

Position #5 Future classroom teachers must be prepared to develop educational programs for students with a wide range of functional abilities and to interact positively with children from diverse cultural backgrounds. Their daily efforts must be supported by special teachers who have been trained to provide the necessary diagnostic, prescriptive, and instructional assistance to deal with the unusual learning needs of exceptional students. Teacher-training institutions should also help provide in-service education programs for their former graduates who are being called upon to function within mainstreaming programs.

Position #6 A national public information campaign is needed to educate our citizens about the mainstreaming movement and its implications. The campaign should focus upon the promotion of positive attitudes toward mentally retarded persons and upon the need for creating an educational environment in which all students may learn that vast differences among persons are a real part of the human experience. Thus, it is no longer acceptable for children to be separated from one another on the basis of categorical differences, nor for education to be structured solely according to traditional ability or age groupings. The ultimate success of mainstreaming will largely hinge upon public acceptance of the fact that individualized education planning and instruction are desirable for all students, handicapped and nonhandicapped alike.

Position #7 NARC supports the establishment of a national evaluation effort to assess the efficacy of mainstreaming within the public schools. They recommend a systems approach involving evaluation, feedback, revision, and monitoring. Suggested areas for evaluation emphasis might include: (*a*) the acceptance or rejection of mentally and physically handicapped students by their peers in regular education classes; (*b*) the efficacy of regular class placement for mentally retarded students with differing degrees of handicaps, ages, and backgrounds; (*c*) the cost-effectiveness and cost-benefit associated with mainstreaming; and (*d*) the relationship of mainstreaming to the short-term educational and life skills performance of mentally retarded persons.

PROGRAMS FOR ADOLESCENTS AND ADULTS

We will look at today's programs for retarded adolescents and adults in terms of orientation of change. A program can attempt to change the behavior of the individual to meet the environment, or modify the environment to meet the specific needs of the individual. From this perspective, programs for retarded adolescents and adults can be classified according to their treatment orientation: changing the environment, changing the individual, changing both the environment *and* the individual, or removing the individual from society. Programs for retarded adolescents and adults tend to be oriented toward teaching specific useful skills and behaviors rather than basic skills which can be generalized across settings, which are emphasized in programs for school-aged children. Programs for retarded school children can have any of these change orientations, although the normalization concept would seem to suggest training the individual to function in the "normal" environment.

CHANGING THE ENVIRONMENT

Reflecting the traditional thinking of a medical model, which situates a problem within an individual and attempts to "cure" it, most programs have focused on changing the individual. The emphasis of these traditional programs is on molding or training the individual to function within the society. However, in several select programs, the emphasis is reversed; the environment is altered to accommodate the individual. Although the prevailing philosophy in mental retardation services stresses placing disabled persons in living conditions that are as normal as possible, these recently conceived residential alternatives take a different tack. Most of these programs create discrete societies where retarded persons may live, sheltered from the rejection and failures too often experienced in society. The founders of such enterprises as Camphill Village, Innisfree Village, and Dan Torisky's program believe that, in this kind of protective environment, retarded persons can achieve a feeling of belonging, develop their own social connections, and enjoy useful, productive lives. Because they are self-contained and (ideally) self-sufficient communities, one could argue that these programs are normal in the same way that an ethnic community could be a normal, though different, segment of the larger community.

A new farm community in Hawaii for retarded adults is described on pages 376–77.

Camphill Village   The Camphill movement, the foremost program which adapts the environment to the individual, has inspired the establishment of similar communities throughout the world. In all respects, Camphill is more than just a program—it is a philosophy. Camphill villages are based on the thinking of Rudolf Steiner, who provided the basic tenets of the Camphill movement. Today Karl Konig and Carlo Pietzner are the most prominent proponents of Steiner's thinking.

For information and literature write to Camphill Village U.S.A., Inc., Copake, NY 12516.

Born in Austria, Steiner was deeply influenced by the philosophical writings of Goethe, who believed in a spiritual realm beyond man's sensory experiences. Steiner believed that these psychic forces must be used to restore a sense of humanistic values to a materialistic world and that latent in every person is an enhanced consciousness that can be developed through proper training. During a resident tutorship, Steiner became interested in the application of his theory to mentally retarded people. One of the individuals he tutored was a sickly, retarded youth whom others thought incapable of normal cognitive development. With his typical enthusiasm, Steiner took on the responsibility of educating the boy. After a 2-year period of intensive training, the boy was functioning on the same level as his peers. This experience laid the groundwork for Steiner's development of a new approach for educating the mentally retarded (Scientific Seer, 1969).

Konig, a Viennese pediatrician and an avid student of Steiner, encouraged and guided the practical application of Steiner's teachings (Pietzner, 1966). The ensuing approach to the education of the mentally retarded became known as *curative education*. The basic beliefs are

1. Every child has a right to be educated; there is no justification for speaking of ineducable children, with the exception of a very small minority (Konig, 1966).

2. Instead of embracing a high-pressured approach to treatment, curative education favors a humanistic approach which believes that the individual develops from stage to stage toward a sound maturity (Scientific Seer, 1969).

3. The retarded need a stable, supportive environment in which they know they are accepted as equal and treated accordingly (Konig, 1966).

4. Retarded children need group instruction and intensive, individualized instruction which focuses on each child's area of disability in order that they do not feel segregated from the society.

In 1939, Konig began the Camphill movement in Aberdeen, Scotland, in the form of a school for physically, emotionally, and mentally handicapped children. The initial success of this school led to the establishment of similar schools throughout England and Europe. Concern for the students after they surpassed school age led to the establishment of the first Camphill Village (Botton) in Yorkshire, England, in 1954. Pietzner (1966) has said that the most striking aspect of the movement is its concern for the retarded adult. The first such village was founded in the United States in 1961 by Pietzner. Steiner, Konig, and Pietzner have implied that the purpose of Camphill is to cure the retarded, but in actuality the "cure" is basically achieved by providing the retarded with a tolerant, sympathetic and compromising minisociety.

Each member of these villages produces according to his ability and receives according to his needs. There is no staff-client dichotomy, and the emphasis is on establishing healthy interpersonal relationships. All members of the community share the ownership and profits of labor as equal partners. Staff members are referred to as *coworkers* and are fully committed members of the community. The staff consists primarily of adults, who usually receive assistance from local volunteers functioning as temporary workers. Each coworker is a houseparent to a group of villagers, who together represent a family unit. Every "family" has a separate house of its own.

The entrance criteria for adult villagers require that each member be able to care for his own physical needs and require no medical or custodial care. In addition, those who can meet the social standards of the normal community are not permitted to be villagers. This attitude is derived from the belief that the best place for the retarded adult is in the security of his or her own home. Konig realized that a Camphill village "family" is only a substitute for the natural security of an individual's own family; he has recommended that the retarded adult be kept at home, if at all possible (Konig, 1966).

The goal of each village is economic self-sufficiency; to this end, each community has its own livestock and vegetable garden. Surplus food and the products manufactured in the village are sold to neighboring communities. Although the objective is to be self-sufficient, tuition is charged to the villagers' parents, and outside donations are accepted to reduce the operating costs.

Villages of this type are becoming increasingly popular throughout the world. At present, there are 25 such communities in Europe, South Africa, and the United States. Nevertheless, this type of program has not been extensively publicized in this country. Perhaps this can be attributed to Camphill's contradiction of our traditional methods of dealing with the mentally handicapped, that is, assisting in the development of salable, vocational skills.

Innisfree Village Innisfree Village, located in the Blue Ridge Mountains near Charlottesville, Virginia, is modeled after Camphill Village, U.S.A. Heinz and Alice Kramp founded Innisfree, which means "inner freedom," in 1971. The village was developed as an alternative to what the Kramps (among others) perceived as the largely inadequate care provided by public and private institutions in this country (Howard, 1971).

For information and literature write to Innisfree Village, Route 2, Box 506, Crozet, VA 22932.

Innisfree was built on the concept that a natural environment and a community of peers will allow the handicapped individual to function as a productive, self-respecting member of a society. Under these conditions, a member will have every opportunity to maximize his potential. The founders describe Innisfree as

> A place where a person can say, "I am retarded, this is my way of life, this is where I can function. I live in a community where I need not be told that I am a member—I know I am a member, doing interesting things, good work and having something that is mine." (Innisfree Village, p. 10)

Innisfree Village molds the lives of villagers and staff into one family. The staff members and their children share homes with the retarded adults. Each member is given vocational instruction commensurate with his skills and interests. The social life and recreational facilities at Innisfree promote camaraderie and help develop a feeling of communal living. Economically, Innisfree, like the Camphill communities, has self-sufficiency as its goal, although currently it is dependent on tuition and outside resources.

Marbridge Ranch Marbridge Ranch is another community adapted to the needs of the mentally retarded and handicapped. The ranch reflects Western style living, and the surroundings project an atmosphere of collective living. It provides the opportunity for retarded individuals to develop fraternal roots in a setting which offers employment, family living, and social exchange. Emphasis is on developing personal relations, and little distinction is made between the staff and the residents. The retarded are taught ranch skills suitable to their abilities. Each member of the ranch is expected to produce to the fullest of his potential and to share with the other members of the community.

Dan Torisky's Program Dan Torisky's program, as advertised in national media (*Time*, 1970), represents a large commercial venture. Torisky had the idea that national or state parks, with their recreational and lodge facilities, would provide an excellent environment in which

BEGINNING A COMMUNITY

Designing a worthwhile program for retarded adults can be a challenge to tax the limits of one's creativity. In each different location, a program must teach clients the particular work skills their community finds useful. Applying this principle to the culture of the Hawaiian Islands, long-time vocational expert Susanna Cheung of Honolulu created "Opportunities for the Retarded, Inc.," a nonprofit vocational preparation project for the retarded adults.

One of Cheung's goals for her new agency is to develop a 5-acre tract of land just outside Honolulu into a self-sufficient farm community where retarded adults can live and work together. In the dialogue that follows, Cheung describes the Pua Melia plantation and the program she hopes to develop there.

There are 5 acres, 3 of which are already developed. There are a million beautiful trees already planted, and millions of ti leaves, which are used here to decorate flowers, to make baskets, to wrap around chicken, and all that. We have already been offered 7¢ a piece for the ti leaves we harvest. So with this we can do a lot of vocational training. We can train our clients to cut the ti leaves and wash the leaves and stack the leaves, and we can sell them.

When we develop the other 2 acres, we will grow vegetable crops, especially Chinese vegetables, which are controlling the market in San Francisco and Canada. Our people are capable of doing the harvesting; they can prepare the soil, and pack and pick the produce. So when we produce melons and vegetables, we can export. We are not just looking into a local market; and we will not be competing with local labor.

With 2 acres we want to do this. With another we want to keep chickens, of course, and a couple of pigs. The pig is important here you know—for the luau and for making "Kalua pig". . . .

So, when you think about this piece of land it will not just provide us with vocational training, it also provides us and lays the groundwork for self-sufficiency.

How many clients will the farm facility accommodate?

Right now we want to have quality control; in other words, we don't want to have 200 to 300 workers so our Board of Directors decided that to keep the quality we want to grow slowly—not more than 100 people.

What inspired you with the idea of creating a farm community where retarded persons can live and work?

It's funny, I grew up in the city, and I've never even lived on a farm. But I know the idea is not new on the mainland. I had read some books, and I knew of similar projects in New York, and in Virginia. But it's strange, and I don't understand why this kind of thing has not been done in Hawaii where we have warm weather all year 'round. When I read the book, *The Good Earth*, I felt as they did—that you've *got* to have *land*. I believe that when you have land, you can survive.

I read these things on the mainland and was inspired, but more so, it really confirmed what I believe and I'm determined to get it done, to show in Hawaii, we've got to have something like that in order for the handicapped to survive and to demonstrate that they can be self-sufficient. With retarded people, they must compete with the labor market, and how many employers can really hire the handicapped? Not too many. And also, not very many retarded people really can handle a full-time job. So, therefore, when you have this piece of farmland, you can create so many jobs and you can provide shelter, supervision, and employment. We do not want to force employers to hire our people and then call it "mainstreaming" or "normalization." You cannot make the majority accept the minority. You cannot force them. But we can *show* that things can be done—we can be self-sufficient.

So you hope the project will create a community where retarded people can generate their own livelihood without having to compete?

That's right. You know, retarded people do grow up to be adults. Most people just think of them as children—it never dawns on them they will be adults. They will be old. Unfortunately they don't have a college to go to; they don't have a full-time job to do. But I think that in Hawaii agriculture could be one answer.

What has been the overall public response to Pua Melia idea thus far?

Well, there are many dimensions. All the professionals are overwhelmed. They say what a exceedingly good idea it is and they're all very supportive. But when you come to apply for money and grants, they all give you the red tape this and that. Strange, there are farmer's home loans, but they are all for normal people. When you have a group of retarded adults, it's "who are you?"

Getting money to start this project has been very difficult. As we are a new organization, we don't have much credit. Yet here we are asking to borrow $350,000 and

we've been operating just one month! You can imagine the difficulty. But the Board members and parents are willing and determined, and I know it will come through.

How do you respond to opponents who accuse you of building an institution at Pua Melia?

Oh, people will always say that. Once you talk about establishing a live-in agricultural community, they immediately ask what about it is so different from Waimano [the state-supported residential facility]? Such a large group of people living together. My response is natural: I live in an institution—and I wouldn't mind living in such a beautiful institution as Pua Melia. The definition is the key. What *is* an institution? Think for example of people who live in a townhouse development or some type of community that is so confined into one area. They form a community association and a neighborhood board and limit this to only these certain people living together. And that's an institution. When you talk about a university, that's an institution. The university has its dorms, its restaurants, its bookstore, and classrooms all in one complex, and that's normal. If it's good for a university, why is it so different and so bad for the retarded? I can't understand that. I don't argue with the word "institution." Yes, we have an institution. But what's wrong with that? I think people make the institution. How you make it normal and prepare people is what is important. It's the lifestyle in question, not the word "institution."

What are your long-range goals for the farm project?

I would like to see an extensive boarding facility, training area, a restaurant, and a country store.

retarded and handicapped individuals could live and develop. To staff the parks, he advocates employing the mentally retarded and physically handicapped, who, under supervision, could maintain and service all aspects of the facilities. Supervisors could check work standards and maintain an acceptable level of work.

Torisky envisions the community as a viable alternative to the system of institutional care. He has argued that many retarded and handicapped individuals living in institutions do not belong there and that each member of society should be allowed to lead a productive life. To finance his idea, Torisky traveled throughout the state of Pennsylvania securing potential support. Today his dream has become a reality, as Otocsin State Park in central Pennsylvania is staffed by retarded and handicapped individuals who are former inhabitants of the state institutions.

CHANGING THE INDIVIDUAL

Chapter 15 details career education alternatives for retarded adults.

In this approach, the individual is viewed as the subject for change; hence, the majority of the programs described here prepare retarded persons for gainful employment in society.

Special Education/Work Study Special education/**work study programs** were developed to blend academic course work with vocational experience. These programs are located in community-based residential facilities and public school systems. The student population consists of youths who have problems functioning in the regular classroom and have been identified as potential dropouts.

Work study programs are described in depth in chapter 13.

The guiding principle for the work study movement dictates that educators should provide a program which they believe is appropriate to the student's abilities instead of forcing the pupil to adapt to the traditional high school program. The aim of the program is to develop the student's potential for future employment through on-the-job experience and classroom instruction.

Throughout the program, the classroom experiences for vocationally oriented students are geared to the development of job-related skills. They receive instruction in telling time, making change, reading want ads, and similar competencies requisite for employment. Mandell and Gold (1984) noted that one advantage of work study programs is that students are able to learn a vocational skill through on-the-job training in the community while continuing to receive remedial classroom instruction that emphasizes basic academic skill development.

Vocational Education In this country within the past century, a multitude of facilities have been constructed and programs inaugurated for the express purpose of rehabilitating handicapped workers (Brolin, 1982; Oberman, 1965). In 1918, Massachusetts became the first state to enact legislation allocating funds to agencies that train disabled persons for employment (Roberts, 1965). Other states quickly followed the lead and provided similar benefits for such agencies. In 1920, Congress passed the Smith-Fess Bill (Industrial Rehabilitation Act), the first national ordinance advocating vocational rehabilitation. This bill appropriated monies to state governments interested in developing and maintaining occupational training programs for disabled workers. During the years following the Smith-Fess Bill, numerous pieces of legislation (including the Barden-LaFollete Act, 1943, the Vocational Rehabilitation Amendment, 1954, and the Vocational Act Amendments, 1968) advanced the development of services in vocational centers. The resultant fiscal endowments have allowed these schools to evolve to the extent that, today, they can furnish a full spectrum of education and rehabilitation services.

Vocational education is a part of the total educational program in that the school's program prepares students for future gainful employment. Training of this kind is typically offered to all students in the school system, including mentally handicapped individuals who can benefit from standard instruction offered in an occupational setting. Unlike the special education-work study program described above, which begins in junior high school and continues until graduation, a vocational education program of this type usually does not accept students until the sophomore or junior year of high school. Also, the training program of vocational education usually focuses on specific work abilities. There is less concern for the tangential job-related skills than in special education-work study; emphasis is on developing competencies for a particular trade.

Vocational Rehabilitation Education and rehabilitation services are provided by various specialists: physicians, nurses, psychologists, occupational therapists, teachers, employers, social workers, and rehabilitation counselors. The success of a program rests on the ability of these professionals to work together as a team.

In programs in which a vocational rehabilitation counselor is available, the counselor coordinates the services of the other team members into a unified effort. As team coordinator, he is visible throughout the entire corrective process. For example, in the early stages of diagnostic evaluation, the counselor, with the interdisciplinary team, analyzes all vocationally significant data regarding a student and relates them to occupational requirements. Also, within the framework of the team structure, the counselor develops the rehabilitation plan and discusses it with each individual student. The counselor is responsible for ensuring that the job on which the student is placed is suitable for the individual. Finally, the counselor follows up on the client in the job situation and evaluates adjustment. The counselor must possess vast knowledge about specific jobs as well as know a great deal about the needs of employers, how to establish rapport with them, and how to carry out a detailed placement plan from acquisition to development to maintenance (Payne, Miller, Hazlett, & Mercer, 1984).

The rehabilitation counselor represents a link between the school program of the mentally retarded and the world of work. As a counselor, he can help the students to confront their disabilities, understand their abilities and limitations, and engage in a program leading to a more productive life.

Program Perspective We have implied that the rehabilitation process is a smooth operation. Unfortunately, there are many major obstacles hampering projects that attempt to assist retarded clients. Although they have received vocational/rehabilitation services, individuals may present problems which hinder the program. For example, the retarded person may fail to appear for an evaluation, may be habitually tardy to training classes, or may arrive at a placement interview in unkempt, shabby dress. The family also may undermine the best efforts of the rehabilitation counselor, deliberately or otherwise. For example, a young retarded adult may have no transportation to his appointments. The family may move frequently or may feel antagonistic to any community workers. Other problems which might bar an individual's progress are unrealistic aspirations, lack of emotional stability, inadequate communication skills, and poor work motivation (Younie & Rusalem, 1971). One factor which has received little attention in the past is employers' attitudes toward handicapped workers. Recent writings suggest that employers be involved throughout the vocational education process, in order to preserve their understanding of handicapped workers and to ensure their commitment to the program (Petzy, 1979; Steinmiller & Retish, 1980).

In addition to these impediments, internal conflicts have reduced the effectiveness of vocational rehabilitation programs, vocational schools, and work study programs. The scope of training services, as we have said, often involves the interweaving of various professional disciplines. Unfortunately, the necessary cooperation between professionals has not always been forthcoming, and many vocational programs have stagnated. Brolin and Kokaska (1979) suggest that, in the future, there must be more cooperative efforts between agencies, businesses, organizations, and parents of handicapped individuals. Agencies need to work together and stop becoming entangled in territorial rights, professional jealousies, and theoretical differences.

Wells (1973) reports that vocational education has struggled to maintain its niche in schools and has historically faced not only an unfavorable image but also apathy, which originates from both the school and community. The negative image of vocational education has an impact on the retarded population. Dunn (1973b) states, "Vocational and technical schools have tended to bar low IQ pupils because of their alleged tarnishing effects on the status of these facilities" (p. 175). The 1968 amendments to the Vocational Education Act of 1963 stipulate that 10% of the federal funds allocated to vocational education programs must be used to provide comparable services to the handicapped. Brolin and Kokaska (1979) state that this 10% allotment of funds to be set aside for the handicapped as per the 1969 amendment was continued with the enactment of the Educational Amendments of 1976, P.L. 94-482. One stipulation that was added is that state and local funds must match 50% of the federal monies allocated to vocational education programs, thus increasing the total fiscal support available for the future.

The number of cooperative vocational rehabilitation and special education-work study programs has diminished during the last few years. According to Garrett, the percentage of federal vocational rehabilitation financing spent annually on research and demonstration projects for the retarded has dropped from a high of over three million dollars in 1965 to under one million dollars in 1970 (Dunn, 1973b). Perhaps the lack of coordination among these programs and the resultant inefficiency could be ameliorated if the programs were organized under one central administration. If these problems can be overcome and internal conflicts resolved, the full potential of vocational programs to help retarded persons achieve more independence and mobility through gainful employment may be realized. In turn, this would enable retarded adults to have a broader base for self-determination in their future growth and development.

CHANGING BOTH THE ENVIRONMENT AND THE INDIVIDUAL

The philosophy that programs for habilitating the retarded should concentrate on changing both the environment *and* the individual has led to the creation of **sheltered workshops** for moderately to severely retarded adolescents and adults. The National Association of Sheltered Workshops and Home-Bound Programs (1961) established this definition of sheltered workshops.

> A nonprofit organization or institution conducted for the purpose of carrying out a recognized program of rehabilitation for physically, mentally, and socially handicapped individuals by providing such individuals with remunerative employment, and one or more other rehabilitating activities of an educational, psychosocial, therapeutic, vocational, or spiritual nature. (p. 17)

Basically, a sheltered workshop is a structured environment in which retarded people can learn necessary work habits, receive training in particular skills, and eventually gain salaried employment either within the workshop itself or through placement in the community. Of course, each sheltered workshop is unique to the characteristics of the people served, the local community, and the administrators and workers.

Sheltered workshops may be classified according to the eventual employment of the retarded adult as either **transitional, extended,** or **comprehensive** (Gold, 1973). A transitional workshop concentrates on the development of vocational skills so that the disabled worker will eventually gain employment in the larger community. This type of operation serves mainly the mildly retarded population. An extended workshop provides long-term employment to disabled individuals (usually moderately, severely, and profoundly retarded) who cannot secure employment in competitive industry and will remain dependent on the workshop for future employment. The comprehensive workshop, which is the most common, includes both transitional and extended services.

Nonvocational services are also frequently provided to assist retarded adults in personal and social adjustment. Cohen (1971) has listed such areas as "travel, communication, the ability to handle money, self-care, appearance, and recreation" (p. 416) as essential points of focus for preparing the retarded adult for a place in the community.

The work found in sheltered workshops varies according to the abilities of the workers, the surrounding community, and the local industry. For the most part, each workshop conforms to the needs of the local industries and trains workers for employment in those areas. Cohen (1971) categorizes the specific work production into three groups: manufacture of new goods, subcontracts to local businesses, and repair of products.

The sheltered workshop is a valuable tool in the provision of rehabilitative services for retarded adults, particularly the moderately and severely retarded. Its chronically inadequate fiscal situation notwithstanding, the workshop model has great potential as a vocational alternative for retarded workers.

REMOVING THE INDIVIDUAL FROM SOCIETY

Since the advent of the normalization movement, which is built upon the philosophy that all handicapped persons are entitled to life in an environment as culturally normal as can be managed, the practice of banishing disabled persons from the public eye is no longer acceptable. Large public institutions for the mentally retarded and mentally ill, once condoned as warehouses for deviants thought unworthy of an ordinary existence as human beings, have been upturned by an outgrowth of normalization known as the *deinstitutionalization* movement. Spurred by increasing exposure of inhuman conditions within many large, remote institutions, by volumes of recent litigation over "handicapped rights," and by widespread acceptance of normalization as a principle, deinstitutionalization in the 1970s included three basic processes.

1. Preventing admission into institutions of persons who could be served in alternative facilities.
2. Returning to the community all residents who, through proper training, could function in local settings.
3. Reorienting existing institutions to make habilitation, if at all possible, the goal.

Suran and Rizzo (1983) note that current attitudes toward institutionalization in the field of mental retardation are that it should be prevented whenever possible, and, when necessary, it should occur in small, community-based residences. See chapter 14 for a detailed treatment of deinstitutionalization and institutional reform.

SUMMARY

Placement alternatives for mentally retarded individuals vary with the age of the individual, the level of severity of the handicap, and the individual's home and community. Infants and young children are served in home-based programs, in center-based programs, and in combination programs. While the home-based programs offer advantages, especially in sparsely populated areas, center-based programs more nearly approximate the school setting which is the ultimate goal of the mainstreaming movement. Once the child reaches school age, alternatives include a continuum of services ranging from regular class placement with special help to the special residential school. When the child reaches adolescence and then adulthood, the focus changes from educational to vocational. Many retarded adults are trained in work study programs or vocational education to work in competitive employment, while other, more severely retarded, adults work in sheltered workshops. Still others move into special communities of retarded and nonretarded workers, where each person contributes to the best of his or her ability. Choice of the most appropriate, most effective placement is not always clear; it must be based on consideration of the needs of the individual, the family, and the available community resources.

CHAPTER THIRTEEN

Career and Vocational Programming

O ur society places a great emphasis on each person's ability to support himself or herself and on that person's ability to contribute to the society-at-large. Even people with conditions like mental retardation are not exempted from this social requirement. Yet, statistics (Bowe, 1978; Levitan & Taggart, 1977; Martin, 1972) have shown that many mentally retarded persons in our society are either unemployed or underemployed. Many explanations for this vexing problem have been advanced. For example, vocational training programs for the retarded have often been narrowly focused; that is, these programs are often predicated upon the development of only one of two specific skill areas. Some programs have prepared their clients for a job market that no longer exists. In some extreme cases, there is no career and/or vocational preparation program at all.

While this information is factually correct, it represents a negative or pessimistic view of career preparation for the mentally retarded. For instance, from the time of Edward Seguin in the 1850s to Richard Hungerford in the 1940s to the present concern over career education, work-

---

This chapter was contributed by Mary Beirne-Smith, Laurence J. Coleman, and James S. Payne.

ers in the field of mental retardation have recognized the need to prepare each mentally retarded person to be a contributing member of society. In fact, in the 1850s, Edward Seguin firmly stated that occupational preparation should have a place in educational programs. A century later, Richard Hungerford outlined a comprehensive program of vocational education. His program, entitled "Occupational Education," was designed to build vocational and social competence skills. The program included occupational education, vocational training, and vocational placements (Hungerford, DeProspo, & Rosensweig, 1948). Today practitioners in the field are seeking to provide more realistic vocational training for mentally retarded students, as well as to integrate them into regular vocational training programs.

Whether you are optimistic or pessimistic about career programming for the mentally retarded, professionals in this area need to move forward in the development of stronger career preparation programs that prepare the mentally retarded individual to be gainfully employed and to fit naturally in the society.

In this chapter, we will discuss past and present career and vocational programming practices relating to mentally retarded students. The chapter is divided into two major sections. The first section takes a close look at the development of the concept of career education, elements of a career preparation program, and a number of issues that have been raised by the evolution of the concept of career education. The second section of the chapter discusses the specifics of the later stages of career education; that is, topics relating directly to vocational preparation. Such topics as vocational assessment, vocational placement and follow-up, and issues related to vocational education are explored.

EVOLUTION OF THE CONCEPT OF CAREER EDUCATION

Career education for all children became a national priority in 1971, when U.S. Commissioner of Education Sidney P. Marland called attention to the insufficient preparation of our nation's youth for careers beyond high school. Marland (1971) described career education as embodying three basic points: (*a*) career education is needed by all students, regardless of whether they will eventually work in a sheltered workshop or local plant or go to college, (*b*) career education should occur throughout the educational career of the individual, starting in kindergarten and continuing into adulthood, and (*c*) career education is meant to give the individual a start in making a living. Marland's postulations about career education seem to have the following implications for mentally retarded students.

TRANSITION FROM SCHOOL TO WORK

The need to better prepare retarded students for life after high school has been recognized by local educational agency personnel, documented in the literature, and targeted nationally as a top priority. There are three major phases of this process: (1) secondary level curricula, IEP management, and career development; (2) transitional management; and (3) availability/appropriateness of postsecondary options.

The prospect of retarded adolescents adjusting to the world of work and community living depends greatly on how well various groups function. The cooperative efforts of local education personnel, vocational rehabilitation counselors, postsecondary education staff, adult service providers, and various community agencies that assist retarded young adults are vital to this transition process. There has been too little cooperation among these important groups and there have been too few attempts to study this entire transition process.

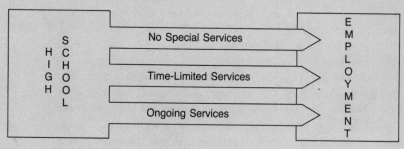

Major Components of the Transition Process

1. Since a person assumes varying roles throughout life, and these roles are a function of both the social system and the person's experiences, it is imperative that mentally retarded students have educational opportunities that allow them to learn to assume different roles in the society.

2. It is essential to view the person as a whole. Only by considering the varied aspects of a person's present circumstances and his or her probable future circumstances can effective education be implemented. Thus, career education for mentally retarded students will require a knowledge of each individual's career strengths, as well as weaknesses.

3. A wealth of knowledge and experience is necessary to reach specific career education goals. Moreover, these goals are often

The transition process can be visualized in the opposite figure. The middle phase, transitional management, includes three alternative pathways:

☐ No Special Services: Some students simply find their own way to the world of work, relying on their own resources. Some students have no other choice!

☐ Transition with Time-Limited Services: This option refers to short-term services (e.g., vocational rehabilitation, postsecondary vocational training), which lead to employment.

☐ Ongoing Services: This linkage refers to some type of employment with ongoing support provided to the worker and to the employer. This concept of "supportive employment" is relatively new.

Overall, transition efforts should (1) maximize students' performance and movement through programs; (2) increase awareness of their interests, aspirations, and educational needs; and (3) increase the availability of appropriate programming options.

The Office of Special Education and Rehabilitative Services (OSERS) has this topic as a national priority. This federal office has funded several major transition projects. The general types of projects and the number funded within each category are

☐ service demonstration model projects (6)

☐ youth employment projects (5)

☐ postsecondary demonstration projects (8)

☐ cooperative model projects (2)

☐ personnel preparation projects (7)

For information regarding the funded projects, contact OSERS.

complex and can be realized only through the cumulative effect of an educational program which proceeds from kindergarten through grade 12 and beyond.

4. Placement in real vocational situations is a vital part of education for each student. This situation is no less necessary for mentally retarded students.

5. All persons, including the mentally retarded, have a right to an education suited to their needs and capabilities.

HISTORY OF CAREER EDUCATION

Various writers trace the history of career education from several different time periods that preceded the rapid growth of career education in the early 1970s (cf., Cegelka, 1979; Herr, 1977; Hoyt, 1982; Kolstoe, 1981;

Smith & Payne, 1980) to contemporary concern over how to implement this concept most effectively. While these authors do not always agree as to exactly where or when this movement began, it is generally agreed that vocational education and related legislation have provided much of the framework upon which career education has been built. For example, Cegelka (1979) states that monies which were made available through the Smith-Hughes Act in the early 1900s secured the place of vocational education in the United States. She also states that later legislation, such as the Vocational Education Act of 1963, extended vocational services to many groups of individuals who previously had not received such services, including handicapped students.

Smith and Payne (1980) report that both events such as the passage of the 1962 Manpower Development Training Act, the Vocational Rehabilitation Act (P.L. 93-112) and the accompanying Section 504 (1973) (which is essentially a civil rights act for the handicapped), and the concern of major professional organizations such as the Council for Exceptional Children (CEC) and the American Association on Mental Deficiency (AAMD) with this evolving concept have intensified its impact. Smith and Payne also point out that special education has played a major role in the evolution of the career education movement. For example, from the early 1940s onward, special educators such as Richard Hungerford and his associates have emphasized the need for mentally retarded students to develop occupational skills. This emphasis on providing direct work experiences led to the development of the cooperative work study programs in the 1960s (Kokaska, 1968). These work study programs for mentally retarded students were based upon the premise that the school could only provide limited in-house work experiences. At the same time, educators felt that industry in the community could provide much better and more realistic work experiences for mentally retarded students. Therefore, school personnel sought to establish cooperative arrangements with community industries. The school's goal was to produce a student with good vocational skills; the businesses gained a person who had at least minimal job skills; and the student received an education that met his or her specific needs. Commenting on the merits of work study programs, Dunn (1973b) states that these programs have been one of the most innovative features of secondary curricula over the last decade.

While all of these movements were taking place, many people, including Marland (1972), noted with alarm that many of the nation's youth were not involved in vocational preparation programs, that the dropout rate from the public school system was very high, and that most of the functional career preparation and training given to school aged youngsters was offered during the last year or two of high school. Disturbed by the lateness and brevity of programs which sought to adequately prepare students for different careers, Marland called for the formulation of a comprehensive, educationally based career program. Thus, the concept of career education was born.

DEFINING CAREER EDUCATION

Career education and **vocational education** are not synonymous; career education has a broader meaning. According to the Division on Career Development of The Council for Exceptional Children, "career development is a process which facilitates responsible and satisfying life roles— that is, student, worker, family member, and citizen—through the utilization of teaching, counseling, and community interventions." Thus, career education and vocational education both accept the idea that schools are supposed to prepare students for participation in the larger society; however, career education and vocational education differ in their interpretation of this idea. Vocational educators attempt to prepare students to enter the job market as competent, employable wage earners. To this end, vocational education focuses on the high school student who will soon be seeking full-time employment. Vocational educators perform such functions as assessing students' work potential, helping the workers-to-be explore different work possibilities in their community, and availing them a number of trial work experiences through which they can identify their own preferences. Career educators, on the other hand, see as their mission preparing students for participation in adult life. Thus, career education's emphasis extends from the elementary grades through secondary school and beyond. Because of this difference in orientation, vocational education is actually a subcategory of career education. Extending this distinction, we can see that other aspects of the school curriculum—reading, writing, science, math, family life education, consumer education, sex education—might also be subsumed under the broad heading of career education because they are components of an educational program that purports to prepare students for future life.

Yet, career education is even larger than the combination of these elements, because it is the unifying vehicle that ensures that an individual has more than an even chance to become a contributing member of the society. For example, in the past, most elementary pupils at some point would discuss different kinds of jobs and workers associated with those jobs. Yet, these discussions were often a matter of happenstance; that is, they often happened by chance. However, through the adoption of career education, these discussions—at whatever school level—will become a required part of the curriculum. Thus, students will be continually exposed to different careers as they move up to higher grades. Career education will also help youngsters to see how such basic subjects as reading and math will enable them to succeed on certain jobs.

MODELS OF CAREER EDUCATION

One of the most comprehensive career education models that has been developed to date has been described by Brolin and Kokaska (1979). Their model is three-dimensional and consists of competencies, experiences, and stages. They describe 102 subcompetencies which comprise 22 major competencies. These 22 major competencies are clustered into three curriculum areas: daily living skills (a sample competency is buying and preparing foods), personal-social skills (e.g., acquiring self-confidence), and occupational guidance and preparation (e.g., exhibiting sufficient physical-manual skills.) The student can develop each competency during the four career education stages: career awareness, career exploration, career preparation, and placement and follow-up. In the career awareness stage, which extends through elementary school, the child learns of the value of working toward a goal and developing academic and social skills, and is introduced to 15 different career clusters. According to Herr (1976), these 15 clusters include the 20,000 job titles listed in the *Dictionary of Occupational Titles*. The fifteen clusters are

1. Construction Occupations
2. Manufacturing Occupations
3. Transportation Occupations
4. Agri-Business and Natural Resources Occupations
5. Marine Science Occupations
6. Environmental Occupations
7. Business and Office Occupations
8. Marketing and Distribution Occupations
9. Communications and Medial Occupations
10. Hospitality and Recreation Occupations
11. Personal Service Occupations
12. Public Services Occupations
13. Health Occupations
14. Consumer and Homemaking Occupations
15. Fine Arts and Humanities Occupations

The career exploration period is devoted to studying examples of jobs within these clusters and measuring the child's interests and skills against the demands of specific careers. One of the goals during this stage is to demonstrate to each pupil the fact that there is a range of possibilities within any job title. For instance, a file clerk, a secretary, and an administrative assistant would all be office workers. Brolin and Kokaska see this stage as occurring during late elementary school. However, Kolstoe (1975) argues, on the basis of his experience, that exploration should be implemented in the secondary school, probably in late junior high.

In the career preparation stage, students learn the actual competencies required in their chosen line of work. For mentally retarded pupils, the development of performance skills and attitudes for an actual job are stressed. The placement/follow-up stage involves placing students on a job and providing the necessary assistance to ensure that they are successful. These final phases require much coordination between the school and the community. As students pass through these stages, they should become increasingly able to assume the many roles that will be required of them at school, within the family, and in the community.

Clark's (1979) School-Based Career Education model consists of four elements: (*a*) values, attitudes, and habits; (*b*) human relationships; (*c*) occupational information; and (*d*) acquisition of job and daily living skills. Career awareness begins in kindergarten and continues throughout elementary school. Curricula for grades K-9 delineate specific goals for each of the four elements during this stage. Career exploration occurs during junior high school. Career preparation begins in high school and continues to post-secondary settings. Figure 13.1 illustrates Clark's career education model.

CAREER EDUCATION AND THE MENTALLY RETARDED

Since the goals of career education are appropriate for all students, career goals for mentally retarded individuals are similar to those for the nonretarded. How these goals become realized is the difference between mentally retarded and nonretarded students. These differences are a function of the individual's general and specific characteristics.

To discuss this process for mentally retarded students, we need to distinguish between career education for mildly retarded students and career education for moderately to profoundly retarded students. The behavior of mildly retarded children and adults only minimally reduces their career options. The vast majority of them will be capable of independent living as adults, and many will no longer be labeled or recognized as mentally retarded after they leave school. Mildly retarded individuals make up approximately 80% of those labeled "mentally deficient." On the other hand, moderately to severely retarded persons exhibit patterns of behavior that disrupt their learning and interaction with others so much that their career options are sharply limited. As adults, they will frequently be dependent upon support from others in order to function within the community. Throughout their lives, they are likely to be perceived as mentally retarded or, at best, as different from their neighbors. This group constitutes approximately 20% of the population of mentally retarded people.

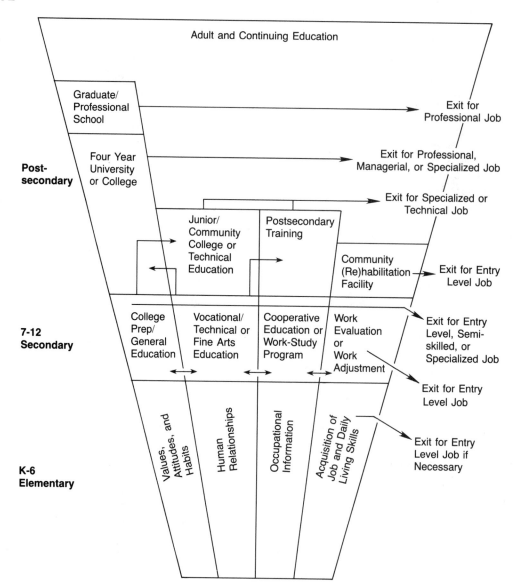

FIGURE 13.1 Clark's School-based Career Education Model

From G. M. Clark, *Career education for the handicapped child in the elementary classroom*. Denver: Love Publishing, 1979. Reprinted by permission.

Given these distinctions between the two groups, it is apparent that the knowledge and skills mastered by each group will greatly differ; thus, their particular career capabilities and needs will differ.

The need for career education for mentally retarded students is strongly supported by research on their community and postschool adjustment. The data for postschool adjustment of mentally retarded individuals comes from studies employing different sampling techniques, different definitions of *adjustment*, and different statistical techniques. Consequently, there are often inconsistencies among interpretations of these studies. As might be expected, the results of these studies show that mentally retarded persons have varying degrees of success in adjusting to life following school. Generally, though, most studies indicate that mentally retarded adults, even those recently released from institutions, are capable of adjusting to community living if given proper training. The following i. a synopsis of information derived from reviews and studies of mildly retarded workers by Heber and Dever (1970), Kokaska (1968), and Brolin, Durand, Kromer, and Muller (1975).

1. Job success is a function of attitudes and personality, rather than IQ. Intelligence is not a significant reason for job success.

2. Retarded adults seem to be particularly susceptible to changes in the economy; that is, the rate of employment is closely tied to economic conditions. When the economy is in a downward cycle, retarded workers seem to get and hold fewer jobs. The converse is also true.

3. Since mentally retarded employees are often the last to be hired and the first to be let go, they often must live in substandard dwellings.

4. Mentally retarded workers tend to hold unskilled or semiskilled jobs. Brolin et al. (1975) report that 50% of their sample held jobs in service occupations (dishwashers, waitress, maid, janitorial work); 12% were in clerical and sales work; 9%, in structured occupations, such as shop work, carpentry, and maintenance. The remaining workers held jobs in such areas as farming and fishing, machine trades, and benchwork occupations. While these are low-level jobs, these findings illustrate the wide variety of positions mentally retarded adults can assume.

5. Mentally retarded persons generally tend to hold unrealistic career goals. Most see themselves in skilled and professional occupations. This finding is in marked contradiction to their actual job status.

6. Mentally retarded individuals are often underemployed; that is, they are not attaining their occupational potential and are employed in jobs below their ability level. This may be due to employer attitudes, supervisors' concerns for high production rates (Payne & Chaffin, 1968), or to poor vocational training programs.

7. A great many mentally retarded people get married and raise

ASSESSMENT OF CAREER APTITUDES AND INTERESTS

Various instruments are available for assessing aptitudes, interests, and competencies related to career development; some of these are discussed in this chapter. One recently developed instrument, the *Occupational Aptitude Survey and Interest Schedule* (OASIS) (Parker, 1983), is particularly relevant.

The OASIS Aptitude Survey is a standardized measure designed to assess strengths and weaknesses in several aptitude areas related to the work world for students in grades eight through 12. The subtests of the Survey are based upon the major domains of verbal, numerical, spatial, perceptual, manual dexterity, and general ability factors derived from extensive analyses of existing aptitude tests. The content, item format, and administration procedures for each subtest are described below.

1. *Vocabulary.* Measures verbal ability. Every item presents a list of four words, two of which are either antonyms or synonyms. Examinees read and select the appropriate pair for each of 40 items.

2. *Computation.* Assesses numerical ability. Thirty arithmetic and algebra problems posed in a multiple-choice format offer five alternative answers.

3. *Spatial Relations.* Measures spatial aptitude. Inspection of a two-dimensional figure, and the subsequent choice of the three-dimensional figure that can be constructed from the initial drawing, is required.

4. *Word Comparison.* Determines a general perceptual level. Each item demands that subjects judge whether its two sets of words, numbers, or nonsense syllables are the same or different. One of

families. Their marital success seems comparable to that of the nonhandicapped population.

8. Mentally retarded individuals who have participated in work/ study programs tend to respond better to occupational demands and are more employable than those who have not been in such programs.

These findings clearly indicate that mildly mentally retarded adults are capable of being successful workers and making successful community adjustments. These results also suggest that being a successful worker and adapting in the community is a consequence of learned behaviors. Therefore, these learned behaviors can be analyzed in terms of

two speed subtests in the OASIS-AS, it features 95 items for attempted completion within a five-minute limit.

5. *Making Marks.* Assesses manual dexterity. Speed is also involved in this subtest, which requires subjects to draw three lines in the form of an asterisk in individual boxes as rapidly as possible.

The OASIS-Interest Schedule is a standardized tool to assist junior and senior high school students in exploring their vocational interests in a comprehensive, understandable, nonsexist, and concise format. The Interest Schedule was designed to accompany administration and results of the OASIS-Aptitude Survey so that career investigation and planning might be undertaken in as informed a manner possible. The 12 scales of the Interest Schedule are based upon the major occupational categories derived from analyzing all major occupational research to date, as described in the manual. Each scale consists of 20 items, half of which are job or career titles and half of which are job activities, to which subjects respond "like," "neutral," or "dislike." The 12 areas are:

☐ artistic
☐ scientific
☐ nature (e.g., outdoor work)
☐ protective (e.g., law enforcement)
☐ mechanical
☐ industrial
☐ business detail
☐ selling
☐ accommodating (e.g., hair care)
☐ humanitarian
☐ leading/influencing
☐ physical performing

Source: Polloway, E. A., Payne, J. S., Patton, J. R., & Payne, R. A. (1985). *Strategies for teaching retarded and special needs learners.* (3rd ed.). Columbus: Charles E. Merrill. Reprinted by permission.

the requisite skills and knowledge needed for successful functioning and can be taught as part of a comprehensive career education program.

Information from studies conducted by Saenger (1957) and Stanfield (1973) indicate that more severely retarded individuals can likewise make successful adjustments to family life and be productive members of their communities. While the data from such studies clearly illustrate the reduced career options for moderately to severely retarded adults, these data also show that such persons can engage in productive work at sheltered workshops and community centers. More recently, moderately and severely retarded workers have been placed successfully in competitive employment, performing such jobs as kitchen utility worker, porter, elevator operator, dishwasher, groundskeeper, janitor, and assembly line worker (Rusch, 1983; Schutz, Jostes, Rusch, & Lamson, 1980; Wehman, Hill, & Koehler, 1979). According to Rusch, a *survey-train-place-train* model facilitates nonsheltered employment for severely handicapped individuals. Using this model the job counselor would: "(*a*) survey potential employers to determine important skills that need to be trained; (*b*) train students to perform these skills; (*c*) place trained clients into nonsheltered settings; and (*d*) provide long-term follow-up training" (p. 503).

CAREER EDUCATION ISSUES

We have now looked at our conceptions of the nature of career education, its current status, and its value for mentally retarded people. While many other educators share these views, you should not infer that these views are universal or that all debate regarding these matters has ceased. In fact, Brolin and D'Alonzo (1979) state that many of the points already discussed in this chapter are issues that must be resolved if handicapped students are to receive the major benefits of the career education movement. The six critical issues they delineate are: (*a*) Should career education be primarily job-centered or life-centered? (*b*) Should career education be infused into all levels of the curriculum, or should it be a separate program? (*c*) Who should be responsible for ensuring that handicapped students are included in career education? (*d*) Can the goals of mainstreaming and career education be accomplished at the same time? (*e*) What is to happen to former ways of teaching that do not emphasize career education, and to courses and materials associated with these teaching approaches? (*f*) How will teacher preparation programs foster the development of career education skills in new teachers?

Obviously, we do not have the ultimate answer to any of these issues, but we do have some reasoned opinions about each one of them which we will share with you.

Issue One Career education, in our opinion, should be life-centered as well as job-centered. Past and present evidence indicates that too heavy a reliance on a job-centered perspective to the exclusion of such aspects as attitude training has caused many of the problems, such as underemployment and unemployment, presently faced by mentally retarded and other handicapped adults.

Issue Two One of the problems with current school curricula is that there is no overall mechanism which prepares each student for life. Most children in our schools learn to read, write, and compute. A few even learn some vocational skills. It is our belief that career education can provide the comprehensive framework to bring all of these educational elements together, so that the individual can more easily move through different life experiences. To do so means infusing career education throughout the curriculum, so that students see the functional uses of the skills they learn, so that they get an integrated, realistic view of their skills.

Issue Three Special educators, now and for some time in the future, must be responsible for ensuring that mentally retarded students are included in career education programs. Since special educators are moving away from providing direct teaching of all handicapped students, career education will provide special educators with another avenue to ensure that the handicapped receive an appropriate education.

Issue Four As Brolin and D'Alonzo (1979) have pointed out, mainstreaming and career education can greatly enhance the chances of success for all handicapped students by providing them with more lifelike experiences, and by relating the instruction which they receive to real-life existence.

Issue Five Obviously, many courses, materials, and teaching approaches will be supplanted in favor of more career-oriented substitutes. However, these formerly useful mechanisms also superseded other courses, materials, and teaching approaches. Our concern should be how to get the most out of the things which will be changed as a consequence of career education.

Issue Six Ensuring that career education concepts are systematically included in teacher preparation programs is a difficult goal, compounded by the fact that many teacher preparation programs are still struggling with the task of teaching general educators to deal with handicapped students. Recently, MacArthur, Hagerty, & Taymans (1982) proposed a program that includes integrating program changes with service delivery systems, coordinating efforts of educational specialists with those of other disciplines, involving the business community and the public sector in developing community-based programs, analyzing and demonstrating cost-effectiveness, and disseminating information about effective programs. As this approach is refined and others are developed, career education will become an integral component in teacher education programs.

CRUCIAL ELEMENTS OF A CAREER PREPARATION PROGRAM

Whether you rely upon the tenets of career education (for example, see Brolin and Kokaska, 1979) or some other vocational preparation model to develop a systematic view of how to ultimately prepare mentally retarded students for the world of work, several crucial elements must be present for any career preparation program to succeed. Among the elements which are crucial to any preparation program's chances for success are adequate program objectives, provision of counseling services, and a distinct stage where specific vocational skills are developed. However, these three elements are not the only ones that can cause a career preparation program to succeed or fail. But if one or any combination of the three elements is missing, then the program is less than optimal. It will not have clear direction if program objectives are not clearly delineated; without counseling services, program participants will probably not always select wise alternatives when they are confronted with career decisions; and unless some specific vocational skills are developed at some point during the career preparation program, many participants will leave the program without useful vocational skills.

DEVELOPING PROGRAM OBJECTIVES

A first priority in the development of a comprehensive career preparation program is the development of a set of program objectives (Smith & Payne, 1980). While not all career preparation programs will have all of the same objectives, due to differences among student characteristics, jobs available in the community, and so on, certain objectives should be included in most programs. A first objective that should lead off any career preparation program is to develop a continuing career profile of the student's skills and interest. Since all students enter any program with different skill and interest levels, these skills and interests must be assessed to determine an appropriate beginning training level for each student. For example, if a young man is interested in auto mechanics and has been working in this area already, he would probably be placed ahead of others just beginning an auto mechanics training program. As the student moves through the program, the instructor should gather and record additional information that reflects the trainee's changing or developing skills and interest. This information can then be used to motivate the student, as well as to convince employers that he is a desirable candidate.

A second program objective should be to engage each student in actual or direct job experiences and activities. This objective is important because, as the National Association for Retarded Citizens has stated, many programs that attempt to train retarded persons for different kinds of work have been too academically oriented; that is, the programs have tended to stress reading, writing, and other "school" skills over "life" skills (Payne, Polloway, Smith, & Payne, 1981). This oversight can be corrected by allowing the student on-the-job training opportunities in any reasonably safe environment, be it a typical school, a factory, or a sheltered workshop. A third related objective for all career preparation is to develop entry level job skills for every student. By this, we mean that students work on actual job sites to learn how to adjust to the demands of the job and fellow workers, as well as to begin building a repertoire of the specific skills requisite for employment in this area of work. For instance, the best way for an aspiring cement mason to learn the latest mortaring techniques is to apprentice with a skilled craftsman, under whose direction he can handle genuine masonry tools and do the actual cementing. Concrete experiences of this kind are particularly crucial for mentally retarded students, for whom modeling and imitation are recognized as among the most effective teaching techniques (Payne et al., 1981).

The fourth important objective that should be included in all programs is to provide job placement and follow-up services for students who have completed, or will complete, the preparation program. Since many of the mentally retarded persons we are concerned with will qualify for services from vocational rehabilitation or other agencies, these personnel can often provide placement and follow-up services. In other instances, the public schools may have their own vocational placement facilities, regardless of who conducts them. The important point here is that placement and follow-up services are included as one of the goals of the career preparation program.

PROVIDING COUNSELING SERVICES

Another essential ingredient in a career preparation program is the availability of counseling services. Before discussing the two primary kinds of counseling (personal and career counseling) that are to be used with mentally retarded students, let us first define the term **counseling** and describe the counseling process. According to Hansen, Stevic, and Warner (1972), counseling may be defined as

> A process that assists an individual in learning about himself, his environment, and methods for handling his roles and relationships. Although individuals experience problems, counseling is not necessarily remedial. The counselor may assist an individual with the decision-making process in educational and vocational matters, as well as resolving interpersonal concerns (p. vii).

The elements of this definition indicate a number of counseling goals and roles that the counselor plays during the process. A major goal of the counseling process is to help the client become more self-sufficient and independent. The counselor helps his clients to achieve this goal by showing them that they can shape many of the circumstances that affect their lives. A specific role of the counselor is to help the individual to develop and explore alternative ways and means for dealing with problems or conflicts; a second role of the counselor is helping the client to overcome obstacles to progress in any area. As a result of information derived from the counseling process, the client is better able to make decisions which will lead to a resolution of any uncertainties and conflicts that may remain. The vocational counseling process follows this general format.

Counseling is usually divided into a number of different subareas, such as personal counseling and career counseling. But as Hansen et al. (1972) point out, the process is essentially the same in both instances. However, a crucial difference between career counseling and personal counseling is that career counseling calls for a substantial knowledge of occupational materials, options, and other concerns. For example, a career counselor must be knowledgeable about career/vocational assessment and the local job market and the characteristics and needs of local employers, as well as the characteristics of the population with which he or she will be working.

DEVELOPING VOCATIONAL SKILLS

The culminating phase in the career education process involves the development of some specific vocational skills. While we will explore this topic more extensively in the next section, we want to give you an overall view of what events should take place at this time. Initially, as we have already seen, the skills of all students should be assessed. Next, present and projected jobs should be analyzed to determine what skills are necessary to perform these jobs. Once this is done, students should be trained on the basis of their present skill level, interests, and projected job availability. Following training, students should be placed on permanent job sites. Follow-up services to the worker and employer should be provided to minimize the effects of any problems that may develop. Finally, the program should be evaluated to assess how well the student has been prepared for employment.

VOCATIONAL PREPARATION

Our focus now turns to the events which take place during the period when the mentally retarded student is actually being prepared for gainful employment, competitive or otherwise. In this section, we will discuss topics ranging from traditional vocational options for the mentally retarded to program evaluation to issues related to vocational education.

TRADITIONAL VOCATIONAL OPTIONS FOR THE RETARDED WORKER

High School Work Study Programs The high school work study program is the type used most frequently for teaching vocational and occupational skills to mildly mentally retarded youth. According to Kolstoe (1975), the high school work study program usually runs over a 3-year period which encompasses the 10th, 11th, and 12th grades. In the first year of the program, lessons such as transportation, budgeting, peer relationships, personal hygiene, and measurement are emphasized. These units are usually part of the academic portion of the program, which covers half of the school day. While the student spends approximately half the day in the formal classroom setting, the other half is spent in more practical instruction. In this part of the program, job analysis, job explorations, as well as specific assessment of the student's vocational skills and interests, begin. During the second year of the program, the students further refine their skills by learning how to complete job applications and how to behave in a job interview. At this time, the students should develop some rudimentary skills in a number of work areas, such as clerical work, food service, carpentry, or automobile repair. During the third year of the program, students begin to concentrate on work skill refinement in one or two specific areas. At this time, part of the day is spent on an actual job, and the remaining time is spent in school. As the third year draws to a close, students are spending more time on the job and less time in the school.

There are five phases in the special education/work study program: vocational exploration, vocational evaluation, vocational training, vocational placement, and follow-up. These phases are incorporated into a work-oriented special education curriculum of actual skill training experiences and job-related classroom instruction. In the first phase, vocational exploration, the student is familiarized with the nature of various occupations and their skill requirements. During this prevocational stage, two separate sets of assessment take place. The students are evaluated to determine what their vocational capabilities are and what types of jobs they may be interested in. Simultaneously, a job analysis is performed within the community. Lawry (1972) defines job analysis as "a systematic way of observing jobs; determining the significant worker requirements, physical demand, and environmental conditions; and reporting this information in a concise format (p. 27)." In addition, Brolin (1982) stated that a job analysis is concerned with "what, why,

See Figure 13.2.

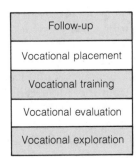

FIGURE 13.2 Phases in the Special Education-Work Study Program

and how" a worker fulfills the requirements of the job. Vocational evaluation, the second step, involves experiences with different job skills prescribed in order to determine the vocational abilities and preferences of the student. The vocational training stage is designed to develop job skills in the pupil's general area of preference. To help prepare the student for a variety of occupations, his training covers a wide range of job skills, usually at the semiskilled level. The choice of specific job skills such as typing or bricklaying is based upon the previous assessments. As a person advances in the program, he is exposed to a variety of actual on-the-job experiences under the supervision of the special education faculty. Once he has tried several jobs for brief periods, he will begin to seek permanent employment. Vocational placement consists of locating a job for the individual upon his graduation from high school. Follow-up entails counseling to help the newly employed student deal with any difficulties encountered on the job. This phase may also involve further training or replacement, should the student be unable to adjust to the first assignment.

Sheltered Workshops The vocational education option that is most often used with the moderately to severely retarded has been called the *sheltered workshop, rehabilitation workshop* (Brolin, 1982) or *community work center*. Regardless of which name is used, these facilities have several common characteristics.

1. Clients/employees usually work on contractual jobs.
2. These contract jobs are usually of short duration; therefore, a staff person is needed to bring in new jobs.
3. Most tasks are broken into small steps.
4. Jobs usually proceed in an assembly line fashion; one part is added at each step of the process until a final product is completed.
5. The facility may or may not provide vocational assessment and training for persons outside of the center.

In order to attain the goal of employment for the retarded, a workshop essentially delivers four services: work evaluation, work adjustment, work experience, and placement and follow-up. Each individual is given an evaluation of his basic abilities; he is assessed in various work settings to determine work limitations and capabilities. A work adjustment program is used to train the adolescent or adult in general work skills, such as "punctuality, dependability, personal habits, cooperation with supervisors, cooperation with fellow employees, proper use of materials and equipment, and the ability to work under pressure" (Cohen, 1971, p. 423). The work experience phase is the progressive development of specific work skills needed for successful employment.

This phase usually follows a step-by-step procedure from simple to complex tasks. At each skills level, the individual's work is observed to determine his level of functioning. The purpose is to match the worker's aptitudes as closely as possible to an appropriate occupation. To this end, work experience training covers a wide spectrum of work skills ranging from unskilled assembly line tasks to highly complex assignments. The placement and follow-up services offered in a sheltered workshop parallel those furnished by special education work study and vocational education programs. Cohen (1971) described the placement and follow-up stage as follows.

> During this crucial period, the individual should be provided opportunities for selective job placements, either within the workshop or within the community. Appropriate on-going services should be available to ensure his successful adjustment to the community working situation. (p. 423)

The considerable variety of services and facilities needed in a sheltered workshop requires a large budget. While it is theoretically possible for an industry of this nature to be economically self-sufficient, it is impossible in practical terms. Due to the extensive time required to train individuals for job success, workshops rarely become self-sufficient. Massie (1962) has said that, in order for such businesses to be self-supporting, they must accept only the higher IQ applicants. Since the sheltered workshop is an effective means of training workers of almost all intellectual levels, that admission criterion would severely limit the potential of the program to serve the entire retarded population (Doll, 1958). For this reason, workshops rely on various sources of assistance: federal, state, and local grants; community resources; foundation grants; and individual financial contributions.

The two major obstacles to the success of the sheltered workshop are its economic dependence on outside sources (Kolstoe & Frey, 1965)

A sheltered workshop can provide a severely handicapped student with the opportunity to be productive and earn wages.

and a general inability to provide a wide scope of occupational tasks for the varied skills of the retarded workers. Gold (1973) points out that most contracts received from the participating local industries engage the workers in only menial, monotonous tasks for notoriously paltry wages. This limits the possibility for maximizing the potential of all the clients in the workshop. Gold (1973) offers suggestions for future workshop policy which might reverse this trend. He recommends that industrial contracts be required to have the following characteristics.

1. Tasks should challenge workers to learn new skills.
2. Adequate time must be allowed for production and training of workers for the tasks.
3. Full-time human labor, rather than automation, should be emphasized.
4. A variety of skills should be required to fulfill the contract.
5. Both the workshop and the worker should profit from the contract.

Finding suitable contracts and training the workers requires thought and planning. Brown, Wright, and Hitchings (1978) suggested a variety of sources, from the state directory of manufacturers to community service clubs such as the Kiwanis, as sources of potential contracts. They further suggested that workshop staff visit the potential contractor, task analyze the jobs to be done, train their workers to do the specific job, and continually evaluate ongoing job performance.

VOCATIONAL ASSESSMENT

An individual's occupational aptitudes may be assessed either by using written tests or by observing work samples. Written vocational assessment devices can be grouped into at least two categories: **aptitude tests** and **interest inventories.** Aptitude tests measure the abilities and traits of an individual in a certain area. For example, an aptitude test which measures typing abilities should indicate whether or not a person can type or can learn how to type. Results of these tests are most often used to predict an individual's chances for success in a certain field. Examples of aptitude tests that measure career related skills are the General Aptitude Test Battery (U.S. Department of Labor, 1970) and the Nonreading Aptitude Test Battery (U.S. Department of Labor, 1970). On the other hand, interest inventories assess the student's feelings and preferences about certain types of occupations rather than measuring potential proficiency. The Gordon Occupational Checklist (Gordon, 1967) and the Minnesota Vocational Interest Inventory (Clark & Campbell, 1966) are two such devices. Another currently popular interest inventory is the AAMD-Becker Reading Free Vocational Interest Inventory (R-FVII)

(Becker, 1975). This test is composed of sets of three pictures from which the individual must choose one picture that shows an activity he or she would most like to do. The sets provide scores relating to 19 different interest areas such as food service, clerical, and laundry service, 11 of which typically appeal to males and 8 of which are usually chosen by females. The test takes less than 1 hour to administer, and is especially appropriate for use with individuals who have low verbal and reading skills.

Another way to assess work skills is through a work sample or job simulation. This procedure evaluates each individual's rate of production and general job-related behaviors. Brolin (1982) offered the following suggestions for making the most of this procedure. The job sample or work sample should be written up and organized in such a way that the tasks required are arranged sequentially from the least demanding to the most difficult. The students should be allowed to practice each task and master it completely before proceeding to the next task; in this way, they can master each task necessary for the production of a particular good or service.

One example of a job simulation device is the Jewish Employment and Vocational Service Work Samples (JEVS) package. Brolin (1982) described these work samples as being composed of 28 tasks that measure worker skills in 14 general industrial categories. During the evaluation, which covers a 2-week period, the person being evaluated is required to perform work-related tasks that vary from the simple (lettering signs) to the complex (disassembling and rebuilding equipment).

While these instruments and procedures do yield valuable information about students' vocational capabilities, they have frequently been criticized for several reasons. First, the reading level for many of the paper-and-pencil tests is too high for many retarded students (reading levels for these instruments are usually at or around a sixth grade level). Second, there are few, if any, items relating directly to females. Third, socioeconomic differences are ignored (a preponderance of items reflect a middle-class orientation). Finally, the racial and cultural diversity of the population of this country is not reflected in the items which make up the tests. Work sample evaluations are criticized because they are expensive and time-consuming, often requiring extensive travel to and from the work site.

VOCATIONAL PLACEMENT

Once a student has acquired some vocational skills, either the school or some other agency such as vocational rehabilitation seeks to place the student on a permanent job site. Smith and Payne (1980) suggest a number of procedures to aid the placement specialist in this process. Their suggestions can be summarized as follows.

1. Make as many personal contacts with local employers as possible.
2. Use local clubs to advertise your program, as well as to secure information concerning placement sites.
3. Become more selective in the use of job sites as the program grows.
4. Consider employers as an integral part of the program. Use them at different levels of the program; for example, the prevocational as well as the vocational level.

Additionally, technological advances such as computerized occupational information systems (Kruger, 1980) can provide job placement specialists easy access to information about job possibilities and job requirements.

FOLLOW-UP AND EVALUATION

Once a student is placed on a permanent job site, the placement specialist is charged with the responsibility of following the student's progress to ensure that he is successful on the job. Brolin (1982), as well as Phelps and Lutz (1977), noted that, initially, follow-up services should occur frequently and then become less frequent. For a short period, the follow-up services to the student and the employer may occur daily, then once a week, and finally on a monthly to yearly basis. Much of the information gained during this period can also be used to assess the effectiveness of the program in preparing the student for the present job. This relationship between follow-up and evaluation procedures makes it possible for future as well as present program participants to benefit from the information gathered.

The provision of follow-up and evaluation services continues to be one of the weakest links in the vocational preparation program for the mentally retarded. The provisions of P.L. 94-142 calling for annual review and an increase in communication between school personnel and state vocational rehabilitation personnel (Capobianco & Jacoby, 1966) have proven to be insufficient mechanisms for ameliorating the problem. However, we can reasonably assume that, as school programs continue to improve and as job counselors improve their own job placement skills and the job-seeking skills of mentally retarded individuals, follow-up services will be increased or greatly strengthened.

PROGRAMMING ISSUES

Vocational preparation of retarded students has come a long way, but we do not have all the answers yet. At least two problem areas remain.

The first problem concerns the difficulty of the written material that is used in vocational programs for mentally retarded students. The reading level of much of this material is too high even for mildly retarded pupils. Vocational and special educators have struggled with this problem for some time without being able to bring it to a reasonable conclusion. In a recent publication, Coleman (1977) outlined a possible solution. Preliminary research which he has conducted indicates that a modification of *Basic English*, which was developed by Ogden (1934) and his associates, enables retarded readers to understand vocationally related materials. Coleman translated materials from a standard form to a Basic English format, using the 850 words of that system. He thus reduced the readability level of the material to third or fourth grade level and below. While the results of this research should be interpreted with caution, this approach holds promise for the future.

Problem number two relates to what to do when a mentally retarded person resigns or is fired from a job. While a similar event would not cause as much concern with a nonretarded person, it does seem to cause a good deal of consternation on the part of family, friends, and professionals who work with handicapped people. The crucial issue here is whether a job termination should be more frowned upon for retarded workers than for the rest of the labor force. We feel that a mentally retarded employee has as much right as the next person to like or dislike a job and his or her coworkers and to leave an unpleasant or unproductive situation if necessary. To deny this fact, we believe, is to deny equal rights (and responsibilities) to the mentally retarded adult, and is contrary to the thrust of normalization.

SUMMARY

In this chapter, we have taken a broad look at career and vocational programming for mentally retarded students. Career education is aimed at helping all students prepare for life as well as for a job, and should extend through the entire period of schooling and beyond. However, career education programs for the mildly retarded need to be different from those for moderately to severely handicapped people, largely because mildly retarded students often disappear into the general population once they leave school. Consequently, the vocational/career prognosis for the mildly retarded student is generally good, while the prognosis for the moderately to severely retarded worker is somewhat more restricted. For any student, a career education program should include specific program objectives, counseling services, and development of specific vocational skills. Vocational preparation programs for the mildly retarded are often high school work/study programs, while the more severely retarded attend sheltered workshop or rehabilitation workshop programs.

CHAPTER FOURTEEN

Institutions, Institutional Reform, and Deinstitutionalization

To most people, mention of the word *institution* conjures an array of unpleasant thoughts and scenarios. Many people's perceptions of institutional life have been shaped largely through exposure to the media or from third party sources; most people have never actually visited a state or private institution. Motion pictures such as *One Flew Over the Cuckoo's Nest* and *Titicut Follies* have dramatically depicted some of the injustices associated with institutional settings. While there have been and still are injustices committed toward the institutionalized person, what we read in the newspaper and watch on the television emphasizes the sensationally negative aspects of institutions. We are not defending the institutional concept from bad press; we simply recognize that today there are positive efforts being made as well. In this chapter, we will attempt to be unbiased in our descriptions of the major components, issues, and trends relevant to institutions for mentally retarded children and adults.

See chapter 1. Historically, much has happened between the time when Guggenbühl first founded the Abendberg in the mid-1800s and current thinking about institutions. Facilities for mentally retarded people, for

This chapter was contributed by Frances E. Patton, James R. Patton, and Jayne Anne Maresca.

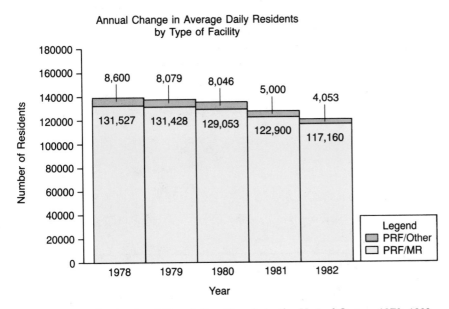

Annual Change in Average Daily Residents
by Type of Facility

FIGURE 14.1 Institutional Population Trends in the United States, 1978–1982.

From L. L. Rotegard, R. H. Bruininks, & G. C. Krantz, "State Operated Residential Facilities for People with Mental Retardation, July 1, 1978–June 30, 1982," *Mental Retardation*. 1984, *22*, 69–74.

the most part, have operated on the premise that these individuals should be removed from society. It has only been recently that institutional programming has been criticized for its custodial nature and reevaluated from either of two major but distinct directions: (*a*) for its inhibiting and debilitating effects on the institutionalized resident, and (*b*) for its potential for education and rehabilitation. In this chapter we will explore each of these positions.

To appreciate the scope of the issue, it may be helpful to look at some statistics. Not all studies report the same statistics; however, the figures are close enough to convey the magnitude of the situation. Rotegard, Bruininks and Krantz (1984) report that the number of mentally retarded persons in institutions between 1960 and 1977 had not changed drastically. Figure 14.1 shows the population of institutions for the mentally retarded and for the mentally ill between 1978–1982.

In a series of studies published from 1976 to 1982, Scheerenberger (1976a, 1976b, 1977, 1982) systematically examines certain demographic variables of more than 200 public residential facilities (PRFs). A more detailed representation of the decline in institutional populations between the years of 1970 and 1981 is presented in Figure 14.2. Data from this study, which further elaborates on the scope of the institutional population of PRFs in this country, have been summarized by Scheerenberger (1982).

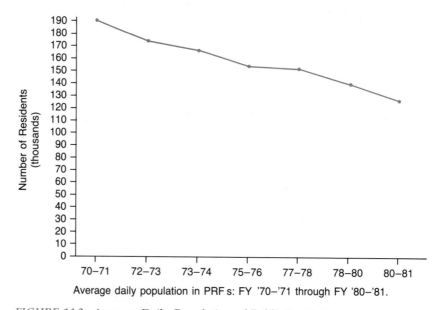

Average daily population in PRF s: FY '70–'71 through FY '80–'81.

FIGURE 14.2 Average Daily Population of Public Institutions

From R. C. Scheerenberger, "Public Residential Services, 1981: Status and Trends," *Mental Retardation*, 1982, *20*, 210–215. Reprinted by permission.

1. The total related bed capacity of the 282 PRFs (100%) for Fiscal Year 80–81 was 133,528—32,182 less than in Fiscal Year 75–76.

2. The average daily resident population reported by 282 PRFs (100%) for Fiscal Year 80–81 was 125,799—27,785 less than Fiscal Year 75–76. The range was 9 to 2,232 with a median of 309, down 171 from 480 reported for Fiscal Year 75–76.

3. The decrease in resident population between Fiscal Year 75–76 and Fiscal Year 80–81 was reported as 18.09%.

4. 57% of the residents were male and 43% were female.

5. The average overall chronological age was 31.91 years.

6. Approximately 80% of the residents were severely or profoundly retarded.

7. There were 5,133 new admissions reported by 261 PRFs (93%). The total estimated new admissions for all operational PRFs was 5,547, a 33% decrease from the 8,308 admissions for Fiscal Year 75–76.

8. The total operational budgets for the 282 PRFs was $3,580,956,203, excluding construction costs. Of this amount, 82% was spent on salaries. Per diem costs ranged from $25.61 to $213.00 with a mean of $77.99. This represented a 117% increase since Fiscal Year 75–76.

In order to describe the many complexities of the institutional setting, we will use the remainder of this chapter to explain the processes and intricacies of institutional life. In addition, we will discuss many of the issues arising from this type of placement and comment on some recent reforms and current trends.

THE CERTIFICATION/COMMITMENT PROCESS

Commitment of an individual to an institution for the mentally retarded or the mentally ill requires legal proceedings conducted according to the guidelines established by each state. For example, in the Commonwealth of Virginia, certification for voluntary commitment is initiated when the parent or guardian of the disabled person contacts the facility to seek approval for admission. Within 30 days after the request, officials of the facility must observe the candidate for *no more than 48 hours* to determine whether or not there is "sufficient cause to believe the person is mentally retarded or mentally ill." If the evaluators find no such "sufficient cause," the applicant is denied admission. Otherwise, the facility endorses his or her candidacy, and the individual's eligibility for admission becomes a judicial matter. The parent or guardian next must petition in local district court for eligibility proceedings, and a judge determines if the candidate is "willing and capable of" requesting voluntary commitment. The judge then offers the candidate admission and prescribes a minimum period of treatment once he or she accepts.

As described, voluntary commitment can be accomplished with relative ease, since all parties apparently agree upon the desired outcome. Thus legal action is a mere formality. Involuntary commitment is also legal, but is far more problematic—both practically and morally. Again, the Virginia Code provides an example that is representative of most jurisdictions. It is possible that in a case of parent/guardian-initiated contact, the individual under consideration does not wish to be certified for admission to an institution. He may still be observed by the facility, found eligible by the local district court judge, and offered the opportunity to apply for voluntary admission. If, however, he does not accept voluntary commitment, the judge advises the individual of the right to a commitment hearing and to counsel, which the court provides. The following process ensues.

1. A commitment hearing is held as soon as possible, allowing for preparation of defenses and witnesses.
2. The judge summons a physician licensed in Virginia and skilled in the diagnosis of mental retardation and/or mental illness.
3. The physician is given the opportunity to personally examine the individual and certifies that he or she has cause to believe:

    a. The person is/is not mentally ill or mentally retarded.

    b. The person does/does not present an imminent danger to self or others.

    c. The individual does/does not require involuntary hospitalization.

4. The judge hears the evidence and observes the individual in question.

    a. The following factors are considered in the judge's decision:

        1. The person does/does not present an imminent danger to self or others as a result of mental retardation or illness.

        2. The person has/has not otherwise been proven to be so seriously mentally ill or retarded to be substantially unable to care for self.

        3. There is/is not any less restrictive alternative to institutional confinement and treatment, other alternatives having been investigated.

5. If the judge finds #1 and #2 above to be positive while finding #3 to be negative, the individual shall be subject to court-ordered outpatient treatment, day treatment in a hospital, referral to community mental health clinic, or other appropriate treatments necessary to meet the needs of the individual.

6. If the judge finds all three considerations above to be positive, the individual will be certified for admission, and removed to a facility for a designated period of hospitalization not to exceed 180 days.

7. The individual may appeal the involuntary commitment to the circuit court within 30 days of commitment order, and is entitled to trial by jury.

8. At the expiration of 180 days:

    a. The individual may be released.

    b. The individual may be readmitted involuntarily by further petition and order of the court.

    c. The individual may be recommitted for treatment on a voluntary basis if he or she so wishes to change his or her status.

Several obvious practical problems arise from this process. For one, the handicapped person's right to counsel, though acknowledged on paper, is in practice abridged simply because very few lawyers to date have been trained in the field of developmental disabilities or are well-grounded in legal rights of the handicapped. Moreover, this procedure presupposes that the local district court judge is qualified to determine if a disabled person is "willing and capable of" seeking or refusing voluntary commitment. It further assumes that this judge has the expertise to ascertain, in the limited time spent in hearings, which type of facility best suits the individual's needs.

The moral question arises when one considers the handicapped person's right to treatment, first established in *Wyatt v. Stickney* (1972). Does right to treatment imply its corollary—the right to refuse treatment? If so, involuntary commitment may be a violation of human rights. If not, should this not be established as a separate right? With the current trend toward deinstitutionalization, civil rights advocates have become increasingly concerned with this aspect of "handicapped law."

The actual legal steps toward certification for admission comprise but one facet of the entire commitment process. You may wonder what would prompt the parents or guardian of a mentally retarded person to seek institutionalization for their disabled child or ward. MacMillan (1977) suggests that there are many factors beyond deficient mental functioning that impel the decision to institutionalize. He believes there must be an additional negative component that renders the individual "superfluous or threatening" in the eyes of his or her caretakers. A study of institutional admissions policies (Eyman, O'Connor, Tarjan, & Justice, 1972) found that the candidates for institutionalization most likely to be admitted were young relative to the group studied, had compounding physical disorders, and/or exhibited serious deficits in adaptive behavior. Certain family factors may color the placement decision. One factor that may affect the decision to institutionalize is family disorganization. A large percentage of institutionalized children come from single parent homes, although it is unclear whether the presence of a severely retarded child in the home disrupts marriages or whether divorce generates circumstances where the task of raising such a child becomes overwhelming. Another factor may be low socioeconomic status (SES). The actual incidence of severe mental retardation does not favor any particular social class; however, the decision to institutionalize may be skewed by SES. One study of institutional populations (Eyman, Dingman, & Sabagh, 1966) observed that residents of institutions are more likely to come from lower class backgrounds. The researchers suggest that more lower class parents perceive the institution as an environment preferable to what may be a deprived home. Eyman and colleagues (1966) also note that higher SES parents tend to place their retarded children sooner and that the willingness of higher SES parents to institutionalize a child is directly related to the number of normal children in the home; that is, the more normal children in the family, the more likely parents are to institutionalize a retarded child.

Community attitudes add another dimension to the question of whether or not to institutionalize a retarded family member. If the prevailing viewpoint of the community into which a severely retarded child is born reflects a fear of "deviant" human beings, the parent(s) of this

FOSTER GRANDPARENT PROGRAM

If you have not visited a residential facility for retarded individuals recently, you may be surprised to see senior citizens on the grounds of the facility. These senior citizens are foster grandparents (FGPs).

The Foster Grandparent Program, a federally supported program that began in 1965, provides an opportunity for senior citizens who are 60 years or older and who have low income to serve individuals with special needs who are no older than 21. The foster grandparents serve on a regular basis, usually four hours daily, five days a week, in such places as institutions, public schools, day care centers, and other nonprofit agencies. They bring their skills and experiences, as well as their kindness, patience, and understanding.

This program is beneficial to all parties involved. Institutions receive free assistance with their programs, and the retarded children benefit greatly from the additional attention. The foster grandparents receive the following benefits:

nontaxable hourly stipend, which is not considered wages or compensation; transportation or transportation allowances; one meal per day; annual physical examinations; accident and liability insurance while on the job; uniforms (you will see them wearing smocks); vacation and sick leave; regular training; annual recognition.

In institutional settings, it is amazing to see profoundly retarded youngsters who are unable to communicate in any traditional fashion respond positively to their FGP. Little language is used because the physical proximity of the FGP is usually enough. FGPs are generally assigned to two children each day and may provide companionship, attend to the personal needs of the individual (dressing, feeding, or toileting), and provide social contact. If you desire more information about this program, you can either contact the regional office of ACTION or call toll-free (800) 424-8580.

child will likely be under considerable social pressure—subtle or otherwise—to separate the "deviant" from those who find him offensive; that is, to hide the child in an institution. Not all parents respond to these community attitudes and not all public sentiment is so rejecting; but when these two variables interact, institutionalization becomes more probable.

THE INSTITUTIONAL SETTING

ORGANIZATION OF A LARGE RESIDENTIAL INSTITUTION

As is true in any large organization, the operation of a residential institution is carried out on two levels: administration and personnel. The administrative level deals with management aspects such as budget, admissions, and coordination of services. The remaining personnel are those staff members who implement the programs which the administration directs.

Administration   Not surprisingly, the traditional large public residential institution presents a myriad of managerial problems, and the consequent reduction in the quality of care provided to residents has long been an issue. Since the 1960s, many institutions have adopted an organizational system called **unitization** in an effort to improve their efficiency. Unitization takes a number of different forms but has three basic elements (Raynes, Bumstead, & Pratt, 1974).

☐ Individual buildings are grouped into units according to certain broad attributes, such as age and severity of handicap.

☐ Unit directors assume responsibility for admission, treatment, and release of residents on their respective units.

☐ Staff members are assigned permanently by unit.

Figure 14.3 illustrates the unitization in the organizational structure of a large residential facility in Virginia. Each discrete center (Child Development, Community Adjustment, and so on) represents a unit as described.

Institutions that have adopted the unit plan have generally been attempting to improve the quality of care for residents. Increasing the consistency of staff-client interactions and allocating staff time more equitably are typical objectives. However, research findings have turned up a substantial discrepancy between the hoped-for improvement and actual upgrading of care. Raynes et al. (1974) examined the effects of reorganization by units in a public facility of some 1200 residents. Though the purpose of the reorganization was to devote more resources to the fulfillment of resident needs, the researchers found little evidence of the desired change 4 years later. Apparently, administrative changes such as the unitization attempted in this institution are not sufficient to redirect the attitudes that determine resident care practices on the building level. For this, policies should focus not on administration, but on the institutional staff.

Personnel   Three types of staff are essential to the operation of a residential institution. Psychologists, teachers, counselors, and social workers comprise the professional staff, whose job it is to habilitate the resident toward more adaptive functioning and eventual return to the community. The direct care staff are the ward attendants, nurses, and other employees who work in direct, continuous contact with the residents, attending to their more basic and custodial needs—feeding, dressing, toileting, medicating, and so forth. The third type are maintenance personnel—janitors, groundskeepers, and others who concern themselves with upkeep of the physical plant, though they may have

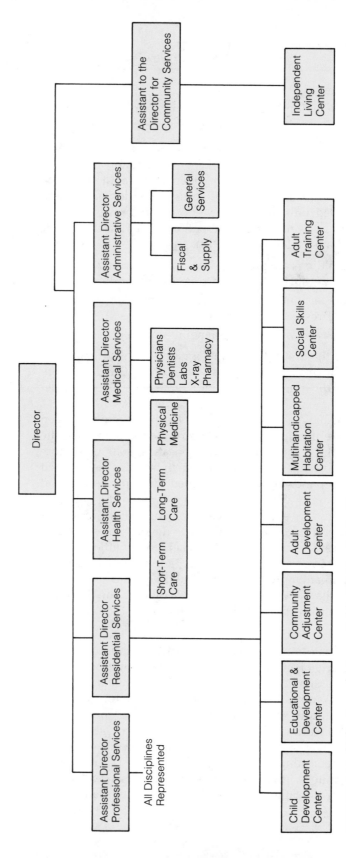

FIGURE 14.3 Utilization of a Large Public Residential Facility

numerous contacts with residents throughout the day. It is these three groups of employees, particularly the direct care staff, who set the tone, the psychological climate, in which daily events transpire. Their attitudes and interactions are far more powerful than upper level policy decisions in determining whether the disabled persons in their care will be abused, ignored, or genuinely served.

Conflict between the goals of the professionals and those of the direct care staff often creates tension in the ranks to the detriment of joint efforts. The differing responsibilities of professionals and direct care personnel lead them to see residents in dissimilar settings, either in the office or on the ward, which in turn biases each group's perceptions of the resident. Whereas professionals look toward eventual rehabilitation for the retarded client, smooth operation of the ward takes priority for the attendants. Consequently, a high-functioning resident, from whom attendants might enlist help in cleaning bedpans or monitoring other residents, can become a bone of contention between the professionals who wish to remove him from the institution and the direct care attendants who want him to stay. Furthermore, attendants generally frown upon professional staff activities which tend to disrupt routine or agitate the residents. These forces, often combined with officiousness from the better educated professionals, generate the tension that often contributes to what is usually a high staff turnover rate.

Personnel shortages, as reflected in the high turnover rate, present a persistent problem in institutional operation. Latkin, Bruininks, Hill, and Hauber (1982) surveyed 75 public and 161 nonpublic facilities for mentally retarded persons in order to examine staff turnover rates. They reported annual turnover rates ranging from 2 to 157% for public institutions (mean—32.8%) and from 0 to 400% for private community settings (mean—54.2%). MacMillan (1982) notes that economic opportunity in the outlying community influences the rate of staff change. Obviously, employees will be more likely to leave the institution if they believe there are other jobs available elsewhere. In addition, attendant turnover tends to vary directly with the ratio of professionals to custodial workers; that is, the greater the proportion of professionals relative to attendants, the higher will be the attendant turnover. It would seem that most direct care workers find their jobs more palatable when supervision by professionals is kept to a minimum.

In recent years there has been concern among professionals about the potentially detrimental effect high staff turnover may have on the mentally retarded. One study, conducted by Munro, Duncan, and Seymour (1983), investigated the effect of front-line staff turnover on the behavior of 140 residents living in a unit of an institution. The investigators found, to their surprise, that staff-turnover had little impact on resident behavior. They interpreted the results as suggesting that

retarded persons may learn to cope well with the seemingly unstable situation. Also, the most important factor affecting resident
behavior may not be turnover rates, but the nature of staff residents' relationships (whether new or established), the quality of
residential living environments, and the consistency by which
programs are carried out. . . .

Turnover can eliminate staff who are considered incorrigi-
ble, "burned-out," or abusive toward residents (pg. 331).

Underfinancing is another chronic affliction of both public and private institutions, and one that exacerbates personnel shortages and low
staff morale. In an economic system which maintains the notion that net
price equals net worth, meager salaries mean low prestige and failure to
attract the most qualified personnel. As a rule, professionals who seek
work in public institutions are not leaders in their respective fields, although there are exceptions. In more than a few cases, the medical personnel are those unable to obtain a state license. Likewise, the inveterate
custodial staff are less likely to be the truly dedicated public servants
than those who simply could not find jobs elsewhere. **Institutional
peonage,** which results when the more capable residents are forced to
work without pay, is a frequent by-product of deficiencies in the number
and quality of personnel. Clearly, the unfortunate outcome of relying on
an underpaid, underqualified, overworked staff to conduct the daily
business of a complex organization can only be to prevent the institution
from fulfilling its stated purpose—service to the disabled.

POLITICS OF THE INSTITUTION

As we have mentioned, to many people who have never seen the inner
workings of a large residential facility for the retarded, the word *institution* is a distasteful one that provokes images of horror and human suffering. Unfortunately, for many of those who have "experienced" an
institution in one way or another, the reaction is the same. The following is a description of the scene that confronts an uninitiated visitor to a
ward for 82 low-functioning residents (mean IQ of 15.4) in a 3000-bed
state facility for the mentally retarded in Southern California. The authors, MacAndrews and Edgerton (1964), recount their impressions of a
group that today forms the majority of the institutional population—
severely and profoundly retarded individuals.

Words, however well-chosen, cannot begin adequately to convey
the combined sights, sounds, and smells which initially confront
and affront the outsider on his first visit. What follows is at best
an approximation.

Despite the size of Ward Y, the simultaneous presence of
its 82 patients evokes an immediate impression of overcrowding.

Additionally, most of the patients are marked by such obvious malformations that their abnormal status appears evident at a glance. One sees heads that are too large or too small, asymmetrical faces, distorted eyes, noses, and mouths, ears that are torn or cauliflowered, and bodies that present every conceivable sign of malproportion and malfunction. Most patients are barefooted, many are without shirts, and an occasional patient is—at least momentarily—naked. What clothing is worn is often grossly ill-fitting. In a word, the first impression is that of a mass—a mass of undifferentiated, disabled, frequently grotesque caricatures of human beings.

Within moments, however, the mass begins to differentiate itself and individuals take form. A blond teen-ager flits about rapidly flapping his arms in a birdlike manner, emitting birdlike peeping sounds all the while. A large Buddhalike man sits motionless in a corner, staring straight ahead. A middle-aged man limps slowly in a circle, grunting, mumbling, and occasionally shaking his head violently. A shirtless patient lies quietly on a bench while a small patient circles about him, furiously twirling a cloth with his left hand. A blind youngster sits quietly digging his index fingers into his eyes, twitching massively and finally resolving himself into motionless rigidity. A red-haired patient kneels and peers intently down a water drain. A portly patient sits off in a corner rocking. Another patient rocks from a position on all fours. Still another patient, lying supine, rolls first to one side then to the other. Several patients walk slowly and aimlessly around, as if in a trance, showing no recognition of anyone or anything. A microcephalic darts quickly about, grinning, drooling, and making unintelligible noises. An early twentyish mongol wearing an oversized cowboy hat strikes about with his hands firmly grasping the toy guns in his waistband holsters. Others smile emptily, many lie quietly, still others from time to time erupt into brief frenzies of motion or sound.

A few patients approach the newcomer to say "Daddy," or "Wanna go home," or to give their name or to offer some paradoxical phrase such as "tapioca, too, ooga, ooga." One or another patient may attempt to touch, pull, or grasp the stranger, but such attempts at interaction are usually of the most fleeting duration. Others may approach and observe from a distance before moving away. Most pay no attention to a new face.

In the background, strange and wondrous sounds originate from all sides. Few words can be distinguished (although many utterances, in their inflection, resemble English speech); rather, screams, howls, grunts, and cries predominate and reverberate in a cacophony of only sometimes human noises. At the same time, loud and rhythmic music is coming out of the loudspeaker system.

There are, finally, the odors. Although many patients are

Institutions have made great progress since this bulletin board was assembled in the early 20th century. The small metal tags identified the eight groups of "pupils"; from left to right, top to bottom, as: "cretins, gelatinoids, hydrocephalic, isolated congenital cases, microcephalic, congenital (one of two or more cases occurring in a family), excitable, paralytic."

not toilet-trained, there is no strong fecal odor. Neither is there a distinct smell of sweat. Yet there is a peculiar smell of something indefinable. Perhaps it is a combination of institutional food and kitchen smells, soap, disinfectant, feces, urine, and the close confinement of many human bodies.

In sum, Ward Y and its inhabitants constitute a staggering visual, auditory, and olfactory assault on the presupposedly invariant character of the natural normal world of everyday life. Here, to a monumental degree, things are different. (p. 313–14)

Even today, this type of reaction by first time visitors to institutions for the developmentally handicapped is not uncommon. The authors relate an honest account of their thoughts and feelings as they walk through the institution. In this account, there is no mention of abusive or cruel practice toward residents, contrary to treatment of some residents in years past. However, there is a disservice, possibly as unjust as abuse or overcrowding occurring in institutions today. This disservice is the adherence to strict routine. Below is a description by Cullari (1984) relating the day-by-day events of severely and profoundly retarded persons in an institution.

It is 6:30 A.M. in section D of Blossom Hall. Bobby, along with 19 other profoundly mentally retarded clients who live there, is awakened. Today three aides are working on the section. Many of the clients are nonambulatory and have a number of other physical problems.

By 7:30 A.M., all of the clients are changed, toileted, shaved, and dressed. Bobby and the rest of the section are brought down to the dining room for breakfast. Each staff person moves from one client to another feeding everyone except the handful that can help themselves. A respirator is nearby for those who are prone to choking on food. At 8:15 A.M. everyone is back on the section, and oral hygiene begins. One aide remains in the central day room with most of the clients, while the other two aides are in the bathroom brushing teeth.

By 9:00 A.M. everyone is finished, and the aides take turns for their breaks. Until these are over, only two aides remain on the section. One of them supervises the 20 clients, while the other starts the housekeeping chores, such as bedmaking, that they also must do. Bobby is quietly rocking in his chair. Many of the other clients are rolling on mats placed on the floor.

Just before lunch, one of the aides marks the "progress" that the clients made on the assigned program plan, even though she didn't have time to actually carry it out. Her supervisor is usually in the main office completing paper work and rarely does he check whether programs are carried out.

That afternoon, Bobby and the other clients are seated in the day room in front of the T.V. He doesn't seem to be too interested in the soap opera that's on. The three aides sit together and gossip about the latest rumors going around the Center. Interaction with the clients is limited to keeping everyone seated and fairly quiet. Some of the clients are leafing through Sears catalogues.

At three o'clock, the afternoon shift begins. One aide called in sick, so there will only be two assigned to the section. After everyone is changed or toileted, the ambulatory clients are prepared for outdoor activities. These consist of a 20-minute walk around the Center. The nonambulatory clients are again placed on mats on the floor.

Shortly after dinner is over, the clients are prepared for bathing. Some of them were supposed to see a movie that night, but it had to be cancelled because of the shortage of staff. At eight o'clock, the supervisor comes down to help with the bathing.

One person undresses the clients, while the other two bathe, dry, and put pajamas on everyone. Bobby is the last one to finish. At 9:30 P.M., he is put to bed. (p. 28)

RESIDENTIAL CONFINEMENT CHALLENGED: HALDERMAN V. PENNHURST STATE SCHOOL AND HOSPITAL

On December 13, 1979, the United States Court of Appeals for the Third Circuit affirmed in a 6–3 opinion the right of every mentally retarded person to receive habilitative care in the least restrictive setting possible. The appeal which led to this recent acknowledgment of handicapped rights arose from a March, 1978, decree ordering the close of Pennhurst State School and Hospital, a large, state-run residential institution in southeastern Pennsylvania.

In the original action, begun on May 30, 1974, Terri Lee Halderman, a 20-year-old retarded resident of Pennhurst, filed suit on behalf of herself and all present and future residents of the facility, alleging that subhuman conditions and the lack of habilitative programming at Pennhurst violated their statutory and constitutional rights.

In the first phase of the nonjury trial, begun in April, 1977, the court spent 32 days hearing testimony to establish the truth of Halderman's allegations. By the end of this exposition, any illusions of Pennhurst State School and Hospital as a facility for the "care and training" of mentally retarded persons were erased. These excerpts from the opinion of presiding Judge Raymond Broderick suggest the quality of "care and training" afforded to residents there.

> Pennhurst is almost totally impersonal. Its residents have no privacy—they sleep in large, overcrowded wards, spend their waking hours together in large day rooms and eat in a large group setting. . . .
>
> All residents on Unit 7[20] go to bed between 8:00 and 8:30 P.M., are awakened and taken to the toilet at 12:00–12:30 A.M., and return to sleep until 5:30 A.M. when they are awakened for the day, which begins with being toileted and then having to wait for a 7:00 A.M. breakfast.
>
> The physical environment at Pennhurst is hazardous to the residents, both physically and psychologically. There is often excrement and urine on ward floors, and the living areas do not meet minimal professional standards for cleanliness. Outbreaks of pinworms and infectious disease are common.

A routine that is remarkably similar to this one is adhered to in most mental wards nationwide. While there is nothing deliberately cruel about the practices, MacAndrew and Edgerton (1964) and Cullari (1984) relate, neither is there any attempt to transcend the utterly custodial nature of what institutions call "treatment." "In many institutions, programming is virtually nonexistent, staff interaction with clients is minimal, and activities are limited to watching T.V., looking at pictures in books and magazines, short periods of "workshops," and long periods of rocking" (Cullain p. 28).

Obnoxious odors and excessive noise permeate the atmosphere. Such conditions are not conducive to habilitation. Moreover, the noise level in the day rooms is often so high that many residents simply stop speaking.

Residents' records commonly contain a notation that they would benefit from specific types of programming. However, such programming has, for the most part, been unavailable. The average resident receives only 1½ hours of programming per weekday and no programming on weekends. No one, except those in school, gets more than 3½ to 4 hours per day. If one factors out those programs which are not considered beneficial, the average drops to about 15 minutes per day.

On the whole, the staff at Pennhurst appears to be dedicated and trying hard to cope with the inadequacies of the institution. Nearly every witness who testified concerning Pennhurst stated that it was grossly understaffed to adequately habilitate the residents.

The Broderick court held that confinement at Pennhurst clearly deprived residents of their right to nondiscriminatory habilitation, to minimally adequate care, to due process, equal protection, and freedom from harm, and to treatment by least restrictive means. Broderick ordered the eventual close of Pennhurst and arrangement of suitable community settings to which residents could transfer. Moreover, he ordered that Individual Program Plans be developed for each remaining resident and monitoring procedures be established for the duration of the facility's operation.

Pennhurst officials and their various codefendants appealed this decision in 1979, only to have the new court reaffirm the right to the least restrictive mode of habilitation and the private right of action to enforce that right. Although the appeals court did not mandate Pennhurst's termination, it upheld 38 of the 41 paragraphs of Broderick's order, along with his belief that retarded persons will benefit most from community placement.

Since the 1979 U.S. Court of Appeals decision, the U.S. Supreme Court twice declined to uphold the lower court decisions. However, after the Supreme Court remanded the case back to the lower courts in January 1984, out-of-court negotiations began between the parties involved in this case. By fall 1984, a settlement had been achieved in which the state agreed to close Pennhurst by July 1, 1986, thus ending 10 years of litigation. Although this famous case will soon be resolved, *Pennhurst* will remain a catchword in the movement to depopulate institutions.

Structure is essential in the care of persons who are mentally impaired, and routine is an effective management tactic for those charged with their care. However, routine easily becomes rigidity, and the purpose is twisted from one of assistance to one of control, in settings where employees regard residents as subhuman creatures who require little more than to be kept alive. That such a destructive attitude has historically shaped the "treatment" of institutionalized populations is one of the major criticisms of the system.

MEANS OF CONTROL

Routinization is but one means of control regularly exercised in the institutional setting. Isolation, mechanical restraints, and aversive treatment techniques such as drug therapy and electric shock are used as well, at times to an extent that is unjustified by any real need.

Aversive treatment techniques comprise an extreme form of behavior modification designed to eliminate maladaptive behaviors characteristic of severely retarded children and adults. In the past decade, scores of studies have demonstrated the effectiveness of various aversive conditioning techniques in suppressing such behaviors as body rocking (Baumeister & Foreharnd, 1972), persistent vomiting (Kohlenberg, 1970), and self-induced seizures (Wright, 1973) that impede the retarded person's learning of adaptive skills or cause him or her physical harm. Wallace, Burger, Neal, Van Breno, and Davis (1976) surveyed 207 public residential institutions for the mentally retarded on their use of aversive treatment, defined as the "application of any of the following noxious stimuli in contingent relationship with a behavior . . . electric shock, physical punishment, chemical irritants, and auditory irritants" (p. 17). Of the 115 (56%) of the institutions that replied, 53 (54%) allowed aversive treatment to be practiced with particular residents. Each of these 53 users, and 74% of the responding nonusers, condoned the use of aversive conditioning as a legitimate mode of treatment. Of all respondents, 87% felt that a multidisciplinary team rather than a single individual should approve or disallow the use of aversive techniques with each individual. However, only 17% of aversive treatment users were found to be in compliance with the regulation by the Joint Committee on Accreditation of Hospitals Standard requiring parental approval for use of aversive treatment with legally incompetent clients.

Drugs are also widely used to pacify chronically disruptive residents. Dispensing of drugs for this purpose is legally restricted to prescription by the in-house physician. Yet institutional practices vary from administration of lawfully required dosages (for instance, for epileptics) to extreme overuse. In the latter case, drugs such as thorazine or stelazine become a conventional control over a wide range of undesirable behaviors, and "hyperactivity" acquires a definition that is spuriously loose. Planning programs to alleviate boredom and help vent "hyperactive" energy would minimize the need for chemical control (Biklen, 1977).

Mechanical restraints provide another effective imposition of control on "hyperactive" behavior. Devices such as straitjackets (*camisoles*), restraining sheets on beds, and restraining chairs are widely used to calm recalcitrant residents or inhibit self-destructive behavior. Biklen (1977) has documented countless incidents of overzealous restraining practices.

> We saw a teenage girl wearing a camisole being led into an isolation room where there was only a mat on the floor. The room was barren. One attendant spoke to another. "We took her over to the hospital this morning to give her an enema. We had to put the camisole on her in order to do it." The girl remained expressionless. I asked why she needed an enema. The attendant told me, "Well, she's on such heavy doses of tranquilizers, it's necessary" (p. 45).

Forced seclusion is a type of restraint also justified as a deterrent to self-abuse. This involves removal of the offending resident to a solitary, locked ward or room for what may become an indeterminate length of time.

There are guidelines for control of aberrant behavior on the books. But, in practice, another type of seclusion—isolation of the physical plant from contact with outlying communities—typically ensures that such dicta will be roundly ignored. Most large, public residential facilities are reluctant to entertain inquisitiveness from the outside for much the same reason that many businesses fear IRS audits. Authorized inspection can prove disastrous for those who insist on dodging regulations. The traditional mental institution avoids this by affirming its status as a separate entity by erecting high walls and fences around prison-like buildings remote from population centers. When the institution reinforces its public image of deviance, myths born of ignorance and fed by separation compel its continued isolation.

Isolation can be psychological and emotional as well as physical. Censorship of mail, monitoring of visits, restrictions on outside travel, and rationing of telephone privileges all cut off institutionalized persons from what Biklen calls "potential allies." Segregation by sex controls the mating of "undesirables" and prevents potentially volatile alliances between residents. The psychological isolation created by these abnormal circumstances flourishes within the impervious, obdurate, cage-like facilities which historically house institutionally retarded people. The language of architecture in such "Siberias of human service" (Turnbull, 1980) is clearly that of control.

Although aversive techniques are widely used as a means of control, institutions have begun to use positive measures more frequently. Marks and Wade (1981), for example, found that providing praise and edibles to residents for contact with material which they did not destroy significantly reduced the frequency of destruction of leisure materials. In another study, Smith, Piersel, Filbeck, and Gross (1983), eliminated food stealing by a severely retarded female through response cost and positive reinforcement. These instances clearly support the idea that positive techniques, rather than sole reliance on aversive techniques, may be and should be used more often in institutional settings.

SOCIALIZATION

Critics of institutions have long attested to the debilitating effects of institutional life on the cognitive and social functioning of the residents. The eternal monotony of routinized feeding, toileting, dressing, and so on, the mass movements at scheduled times, the rationing of clothing and possessions, the monumentally drab environment provide little of the intellectual challenge needed for cognitive growth. Segregation, overcrowding, and understaffing encourage routinization and preclude opportunities for positive social contact. Vitello (1976) summarizes the research on child development as follows.

1. The earlier a child is institutionalized, and the longer he remains, the greater will be his cognitive and behavioral deficits.

2. Institutionalized children from enriched backgrounds show greater loss of cognitive and behavioral functions than do those from impoverished environments. The latter may actually demonstrate gains if the prior setting was less nurturant than the institution.

3. It is possible to increase environmental stimulation and positive social contact within institutions to promote cognitive and behavioral growth; however community alternatives are, in the aggregate, more effective.

MacMillan (1982) notes that, in tests done on institutionalized children, impairment is more pronounced for verbal IQ than performance IQ. He suggests remediation through more frequent meaningful verbal interactions between children and staff. Personality, as well as cognitive, disorders are more common in institutionalized than noninstitutionalized retarded populations. Zigler (1966) found a common trait of young retarded residents to be an unusually strong desire for contact with an approving adult. Yet the impersonality of institutional settings, where overworked employees have little time (or inclination) to individualize, denies warm contact to those who need it most. A debilitating cycle is then activated, in which, according to Zigler, a resident who cannot get sufficient adult attention becomes more childishly dependent and makes no progress toward acquiring independent living skills. In this case, disability is both a cause and a result of institutionalization.

Learned Helplessness A similar phenomenon repeatedly observed in institutional settings is known as **learned helplessness.** Are the passivity and resistance to learning that are characteristic of retarded persons in institutions a cause for commitment? Or are they the product of an environment inimical to learning? Or do retarded people in large residential facilities actively learn not to learn? Researchers have identified learned helplessness in animals (Overmier & Seligman, 1967) and in humans (Seligman, 1975) as a pattern of submissiveness which develops when the victims repeatedly discover that their actions are of no consequence, that outcomes are beyond their control.

Learned helplessness is especially common in large institutions, where residents continually see aversive stimuli meted out for no apparent reason. Attendants often punish residents indiscriminately out of their own frustration or ignorance about the needs of retarded persons. Residents often victimize each other in random fits of pent-up energy, for example, striking an unsolicited blow to the nearest shin. Similarly, persons suffering from seizures find themselves totally helpless in the face of recurring inexplicable and traumatic events. DeVellis (1977) observes that learned helplessness is brought on by a person's inability to predict or deter such aversive events and is abetted by frequent recurrence of outcomes over which the person is powerless. A person who has learned not to learn will be (*a*) more submissive, (*b*) less responsive to stimuli, and (*c*) less able to connect his or her actions with consequences. The syndrome can be cured by forcibly leading the afflicted individual through actions that halt particular aversive stimuli. For instance, a victim might need to be dragged several times through the motion of removing herself from the path of a hair-pulling wardmate before she realizes she can avoid that particular irritation. But she will eventually catch on. Learned helplessness is best prevented by teaching individuals at an early age that outcomes *do* follow logically from their actions, and by repeatedly exposing them to situations they can control. For institution personnel, this involves allowing the resident opportunities to initiate and end simple activities, to express a preference when choices are available, and to handle objects that can be easily manipulated. Direct care staff should be alerted to the importance of letting the residents exert some influence over their environment.

Other Behavior Disorders Critics have identified several other maladaptive behavioral syndromes that seem to be institution-induced. Levy and McLeod (1977) describe a condition called **functional retardation,** in which institution residents react to their stressful living conditions by self-stimulating (rocking, hand weaving, and so on). They liken these stereotyped behaviors to those shown by normal individuals who have been deprived of sensory stimulation for extended periods.

Biklen, from his observation of six state schools and five mental hospitals in 1977, concludes that the rigid, condemning living environment characteristic of most mental institutions induces the very behavior it is designed to control. In the few facilities he examined with relaxed, accepting climates and no locked wards, Biklen found none of the violent acting-out that calls for seclusion or restraints. In contrast, he found that in the traditional cold, regimented institutions where locked wards were part of the aversive treatment repertoire, residents up-ended furniture, banged heads, bit, kicked, and screamed—quite likely in *response* to their being caged and isolated for hours with nothing to do. Logically, frustration and its manifestations which warrant restraints can be abated if residents are given meaningful ways to spend their time and a pleasant, accepting atmosphere in which to do it. Otherwise, the natural response is rebellion.

CURRENT OPINION ON INSTITUTIONALIZATION

The history of institutional service has progressed along waves of widely fluctuating public sentiment, and residential treatment of retarded people remains to this day an emotional issue. The prevailing opinion on institutionalization in its present form is that the large public residential facility is an abnormal, unhealthy environment in which efficiency of operation dominates the needs of residents as a group and of individuals in particular. For all the lip service paid to rehabilitation, the goal of "treatment" in most existing public facilities is permanent residence. Care is, at best, custodial. Beyond this general agreement, opinions on how best to correct an error of such magnitude vary. Wolfensberger (1975) sides with the most severe critics, charging that present-day institutions are unsalvageable and should be dismantled.

In addition, Menolascino and McGee (1981), believe that "the new institution . . . is still a system that generally dehumanizes and depersonalizes its residents" (p. 219). Others, such as Ellis et al. (1981), believe that, with a deep structural overhaul, many institutions can be made more humane and more rehabilitative and that, once revamped, they should be included as a part of a continuum of services available to the mentally retarded and their families. The bottom line is in either case a massive effort toward institutional reform.

INSTITUTIONAL REFORM

Three major developments within the past decade have greased the wheels of the institutional reform movement.

1. Judicial backing of the handicapped individual's right to the least restrictive conditions necessary.
2. Exposure of abominable conditions in large public residential institutions.
3. Widespread-approval of *normalization* as a goal for those labeled *deviant*.

THE LEGAL IMPETUS

A number of court decisions and legal actions involving the interpretation of the constitutional guarantee of certain rights have catalyzed the process of institutional change. Many arguments used to obtain services and privileges have been based on Section One of the Fourteenth Amendment, which lends itself well to any attempt to establish rights for mentally retarded people.

> All persons born or naturalized in the United States and subject to the jurisdiction thereof, are citizens of the United States and of the State wherein they reside. No State shall make or enforce any law which shall abridge the privileges or immunities of citizens of the United States, *nor shall any State deprive any person of life, liberty, or property without due process of law,* nor deny to any person within its jurisdiction to equal protection of the laws. (emphasis added)

Legal channels for creating and inspiring change have been used very effectively in the past two decades. Yet, it was not until 1972 that the federal courts significantly became open to the crusade for institutional reform. The first court decision to have a major impact on altering the conditions in institutions was concerned with the right to treatment.

Right to Treatment   The legal impetus for reform was dramatized in the litigation of a landmark case, *Wyatt v. Stickney,* on April 13, 1972. This case had a direct impact on the adequacy of services in residential facilities for mentally retarded individuals. The plaintiffs in this class action suit built their case on the grounds that the residents of the Partlow State School (Alabama) were being denied their right to treatment. While this was a class action suit, it was originally filed by the legal guardian of Ricky Wyatt against the Alabama Department of Mental Hygiene in 1970. Specifically, in the *Wyatt* case Ricky Wyatt (named plaintiff) represented all residents in the state of Alabama who were involuntarily confined in the state's hospitals.

In a class action suit, a designated plaintiff brings an action on behalf of himself and all persons in a similar situation.

The decision of Judge Johnson of the District Court of the United States for the Middle District of Alabama, North Division, declared that the constitutional rights of the retarded under the Fourteenth Amendment were being violated. The failure of this state to provide proper treatment in its residential facilities moved the court to draw up a precedent-setting 22 page appendix which defined minimum treatment standards for the state school to adopt. The order and decree of the *Wyatt* decision was comprehensive in its coverage of residents' right to treatment and habilitation, records and review, physical environment, medication, and admissions policies. A summation of the minimum treatment standards includes:

1. Borderline or mildly retarded individuals shall not be placed in residential institutions.

2. Admission to a residential institution shall be granted following the determination that the client-environment match is the least restrictive habilitative setting.

3. Institutions must attempt to move residents in the following manner.
   a. To a less structured living environment;
   b. From larger to smaller facilities;
   c. From larger to smaller living units;
   d. From group to individual residence;
   e. From segregated to integrated community living; and
   f. From dependent to independent living.

To summarize the importance of *Wyatt*, let us look at what was achieved. First, the case applied specifically to mentally retarded people in institutions. Second, the court issued a set of minimum standards and monitoring procedures in residential facilities that would serve as a model to other states. Third, the case recognized the constitutional rights of the mentally retarded resident.

It is not surprising that many judicial proceedings deal with essentially the same or identical issues. What is intriguing is that judicial proceedings under similar situations may reach decisions which are diametrically opposed (Scheerenberger, 1976b). This was exactly the situation in the class action suit of *Burnham v. Department of Public Health* in Georgia (1972), in which a completely different decision from the *Wyatt* decision was reached. Judge Smith, presiding in the United States District Court for the Northern District of Georgia, recognized that individuals in mental institutions have a moral right to treatment. However, he did not rule that there was a legal obligation for such treatment (Scheerenberger, 1976a). As a result, there was a legal discrepancy between *Wyatt* and *Burnham*. Resolution would come on appeal of *Wyatt* to the United States Court of Appeals, Fifth Circuit. During the course of the appeal, the case of *Wyatt v. Stickney* changed to *Wyatt v. Aderholt*, due to a change of defendants. The Court of Appeals essentially upheld the earlier decision of *Wyatt v. Stickney*, reemphasizing that the mentally retarded resident has a constitutional right to treatment. Furthermore, the decision allowed the federal courts to enter into other cases of this nature, as well as to set standards and monitor their implementation.

Another suit that had an impact on institutionalized people, also decided by the Fifth Circuit Court of Appeals, was *O'Connor v. Donaldson* (1975). A number of issues were addressed in this case in which Donaldson (the plaintiff) was committed to an institution in 1957 by his father. It was determined that the defendants were aware at the time of

Donaldson's placement that he was neither reckless nor dangerous to himself or others. In addition, once he was institutionalized, Donaldson received neither adequate treatment nor therapy. The decision by the court awarded the plaintiff $38,000 in compensatory and punitive damages, which were to be paid personally by the defendants. In this particular case, the defendants were held personally liable. Subsequently, the case was sent to the Court of Appeals, where the original decision was upheld. *O'Connor v. Donaldson* is significant in that it established the illegality of involuntarily institutionalizing a person who is not dangerous and who is able to function without institutional care.

Since 1980, there have been two major suits brought to the United States Supreme Court regarding the rights of institutionalized persons. *Pennhurst State School and Hospital v. Halderman* (1981) and *Youngberg v. Romeo* (1982) established the rights of habilitation and protection from harm for the mentally retarded residing in institutions. It has taken many years to establish these legal rights. Professionals and advocates must work to ensure that future cases continue to define and support the rights of all residents of institutions.

> See the discussion of the Pennhurst case for more on the latest litigation on rights of institution residents.

DIMENSIONS OF DEINSTITUTIONALIZATION

Securing the legal right-of-way for institutional reform is, as with all social change movements, only the first step in a long journey. The crucial factor—public attitudes—cannot be changed by legislation. At the heart of the movement for change must be acceptance by all parties of the legitimacy of the deinstitutionalization principle, and cooperative effort toward its realization.

Successful institutional reform requires support on four dimensions.

1. Community and residential personnel must provide every opportunity for retarded clients to be served in the least restrictive local setting.
2. A person whose condition requires residential placement should be so placed no longer than is absolutely necessary.
3. Institutionalized retarded persons who can function in the community should be transferred there as soon as possible.
4. All phases of residential programming should emphasize independence and personal growth consonant with the deinstitutionalization principle.

The linchpin of the institutional reform movement is the belief in the principle of normalization, or most recently referred to as social role valorization by Wolfensberger (1983). He defines the goals of socially valued roles as 1) reducing or preventing the differentness or stigmata which may devalue a person in the eyes of observers; and 2) changing societal perceptions of a devalued person or group so that a given characteristic or person is no longer seen as devalued.

Deinstitutionalization is one crucial goal of institutional reform and a natural corollary to the normative principle. According to the National Association of Superintendents of Public Residential Facilities for the Mentally Retarded (1974), deinstitutionalization encompasses the following processes.

1. Prevention of admission by finding and developing alternative community methods of care and training,
2. Return to the community of all residents who have been prepared through programs of habilitation and training to function adequately in appropriate local settings, and
3. Establishment and maintenance of a responsive residential environment which protects human and civil rights and which contributes to the expeditious return of the individual to normal community living whenever possible.

In the language of human service, this principle translates to a developmental model of continuous services ranging in desirability from the natural home to the residential institution. Any point along the continuum depicted in Figure 14.4 may be the "least restrictive environment," depending on the needs and capabilities of the retarded individual, but in general movement along the continuum should be toward the home as far as possible and away from the home only in the case of clearly demonstrated need.

CURRENT TRENDS

Smaller Community-Based Facilities   The important dimensions that distinguish alternatives to placement in the traditional public mental institution are size and geographic location. Large centralized structures are giving way to more numerous smaller facilities built to ensure more accessibility to population centers. Scheerenberger (1976a) reports a 74% increase in the number of public residential facilities (PRFs) operating in the United States—from 135 in 1964 to 235 in 1974.

Since 1974, Scheerenberger (1982) reports an additional 47 PRFs (total 282), which represent a 16% increase. This wave of new construction is offset by the declining population of existing facilities and the

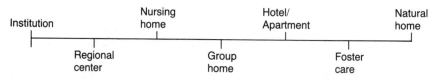

FIGURE 14.4   Continuum of Placement Alternatives

consistently smaller bed capacity of new ones. Scheerenberger's analysis of census statistics for 176 PRFs revealed an 8.9% total decrease in population over the 1969 to 1974 period, and a decrease of 15.9% for the older PRFs between 1964 and 1974. Between 1975 and 1981, based on 282 PRFs, Scheerenberger (1982) reports a 18.09% decrease in total population. The older facilities in his study, those built prior to 1964, ranged in bed capacity from 169 to 3,178, with a median of 1,014. Those constructed since 1964 varied from 10 to 1,508 beds, with 318 the median. The trend toward reduced size is clear.

Figure 14.5 graphs the increased number of institutions and their decreased size.

The countermovement to the traditional isolation of large public institutions is evidenced by an increasing number of alternative services arising in and around communities—from regional centers of 200 beds and less (for example, in California and Connecticut) to small group arrangements such as nursing homes, group homes and apartments, and foster homes.

See chapter 15 for more detailed discussion of community services.

More Severe Handicaps Change is also apparent within existing large institutions, most notably in the characteristics of the residents. One

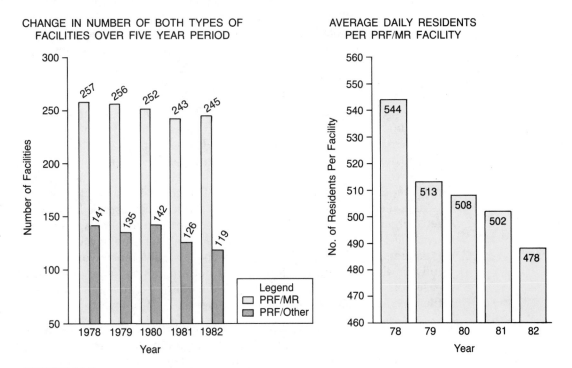

CHANGE IN NUMBER OF BOTH TYPES OF FACILITIES OVER FIVE YEAR PERIOD

AVERAGE DAILY RESIDENTS PER PRF/MR FACILITY

FIGURE 14.5

From L. L. Rotegard, R. H. Bruininks, & G. C. Krantz, "State Operated Residential Facilities for People with Mental Retardation: July 1, 1978–June 30, 1982," *Mental Retardation*, 1984, 22, 69–74. Reprinted by permission.

TABLE 14.1 First Admissions to Public Residential Facilities

Year	Mild %	Moderate %	Severe and Profound %
1922–23	40.4	35.2	14.3
1931–35	45.7	30.2	15.6
1941–45	43.3	29.4	14.9
1951–55	32.1	35.6	22.4
1963–64	28.2	21.5	50.3
1973–74	17.6	19.3	63.1

From R. C. Scheerenberger, *Deinstitutionalization and Institutional Reform.* Springfield, Ill.: Charles C Thomas, 1976. Reprinted by permission.

consequence of the push toward normalization has been a dramatic reduction in the number of mildly-to-moderately retarded persons admitted. Table 14.1 shows the distribution of first admissions to public residential facilities since 1922, as reported by Scheerenberger (1976b). Clearly, the normalizing trend has accelerated since the mid-1950s to the point where, in 1975, 63.1% of all first admissions and 71.2% of the total institutional population were severely retarded and finally, in 1981, Scheerenberger reports that approximately 80% of the population was severely or profoundly retarded.

One outcome of housing an increasingly disabled group of people is the need for more technical centralization in the large institutions. Severe mental retardation is most often accompanied by serious physical disorders, often as part of a syndrome such as cretinism, a metabolic or genetic disorder, or a physical trauma. Consequently, a facility undertaking the care of a large concentration of severely handicapped residents will require a trained medical staff as well as a substantial arsenal of therapeutic equipment and supplies. This could easily lead to a return to the medical model of institutional service, as described by Wolfensberger (1975), in which medical personnel dominate the administrative staff, hospital routines are followed, and terminology is medical ("patients," "nursing units," and so on). The difference would hopefully be that modern institutions will not attempt to "cure" the "disease" of retardation but rather will use medical technology to mitigate the physical problems of retarded residents.

Legal Protection The legal problems of institutionalized retarded individuals comprise a neglected area that is beginning to receive increasing attention as institutional reform progresses. Three relatively recent innovations, advocacy, Human Rights Committees, and ombudsman services, are currently used to safeguard the rights of those who are developmentally disabled.

The primary function of a handicapped rights advocate is to help retarded persons exercise their rights. Retarded people as a *class* are represented by many local, state, and national organizations that lobby for such global concerns as federal aid and right to appropriate education. The President's Committee on Mental Retardation, the Council for Exceptional Children, and the Association for Retarded Citizens are such organizations. Advocacy for retarded *individuals*, both for those living in the community and those remaining in institutions, poses a different challenge. Most retarded persons in the community find the business of merely surviving sufficiently complex, much less dealing with legal rights. Three types of advocacy programs are used in different jurisdictions to protect retarded citizens against denial of rights: state agencies, citizen advocates, and legally trained advocates. Scheerenberger (1976b) emphasizes the role of natural parents as advocates. Though not all parents are suitable for the task, conscientious parents are encouraged to have themselves appointed guardians should their retarded son or daughter need such supervision beyond the legal age of adulthood.

Most of the Human Rights Committees (HRCs) began in the 1970s as a result of the lawsuits and rights movement. The HRCs work within an institution and are designed to protect the rights of institutionalized mentally retarded persons. Kemp (1983) reports that, of 74 state resident facilities surveyed, the HRC was responsible for a wide range of functions. Some of these include review of behavior management programs, investigation of grievances, complaints and alleged rights violations, review of research programs, investigation of abuse and neglect, advocation or protection of resident rights and review of client care including a humane environment and adequate services. The most commonly reported cases brought before the committees were behavior modification programs and the use of psychotropic medication to control behavior.

The **ombudsman** in public institutions is a new concept, not yet a force in residential care. Still, reform advocates look to the future possibilities of ombudsmen as major change agents. Mallory (1977) defines an ombudsman as "one whose role is to protect the rights of individuals seeking services from government agencies and educational systems." Ombudsmen in an institution for mentally retarded residents are charged with protecting persons hurt by rules and procedures which support institutional structure and ignore divergent resident needs. Specifically, (*a*) they address grievances a resident might have with the management and negotiate for a solution, and (*b*) through their own investigation, they identify bugs in the system and recommend to administrators tactics for correcting problem areas. Where an advocate would be an outsider and thus limited in influence over internal operations, the ombudsman works within the institution in a position independent of administrators and other staff. For maximum effectiveness, an ombudsman should be

1. Thoroughly versed in the inner workings of the institution—fiscal policy, regulations, communication patterns, and so on;
2. Secure in his or her position, so that criticisms need not be tempered by fear of reprisal;
3. Afforded full investigative power within the institutional system;
4. Trained in legal issues, characteristics of developmentally disabled persons (especially severe and profound retardation), and organization and management of residential facilities.

Ombudsman services as described have tremendous potential for effecting institutional reform from within. Should the concept take hold, ombudsmen will be valuable agents for increasing accountability of institutions to taxpayers, lawmakers, and human rights advocates, and for availing due process to institutionalized residents.

Economics: Community vs. Institution   Existing large institutions cannot be depopulated until enough alternative sites have been constructed to absorb the new releases. People cannot merely be released from institutions and sent home. Like all worthwhile social endeavors, this takes money. Whether or not a community has sufficient revenues to build new facilities for retarded citizens depends on a number of variables—the local tax base, state and federal aid contributions, the priority given to mental retardation services, and so forth. In a sense, new construction also generates money, in that employment rises and the community gains a new investment asset, but this is a separate issue. Construction costs are finite, while operational costs may continue indefinitely. Despite arguments to the contrary, operating costs for small, community-based facilities are substantially lower than the cost of residential services. Edgerton, in 1975, charged that claims of lower expense for smaller facilities were simply unsubstantiated. However, a 1979 study by Intagliata, Wilder, and Cooley, comparing costs of institutional and community alternatives, upholds the original claim that community facilities are less expensive to operate.

Table 14.2 lists comparative data which represent the expenditure for a single resident in a variety of settings, from an institution to the natural family. According to the data reported by Intagliata et al. (1979), it is more economical to place retarded individuals in a community setting.

TABLE 14.2 Cost for Residential Services

Setting	Cost (Resident/Year)	*Cost (Resident/Day)
Institution	$14,630	$40.10
Group Home	$9,255–$11,000**	$25.35–$30.15
Family Care	$3,310	$ 8.60
Natural Family	$2,108	$ 5.80

*Daily figures added.
**Variation depends upon residents' level of disability.
Data from J. C. Intagliata, B. S. Wilder, and F. B. Cooley, "Cost Comparisons of Institutional and Community Based Alternatives for the Mentally Retarded Persons," *Mental Retardation*, 1979, 14(6), 155. Reprinted by permission.

REFLECTIONS ON DEINSTITUTIONALIZATION

The final goal of the normalization process and of its adjunct, deinstitutionalization, is to allow every retarded individual the opportunity for a happy, meaningful life. To this end, retarded persons will be removed from institutions if at all possible and placed in physical settings that mirror home life. Estimates of the number of institutionalized persons who qualify for transfer run as high as 50% of the total residential population (Scheerenberger, 1976b). Thus, in order to achieve the goal of deinstitutionalization, great numbers of people will be uprooted from familiar settings and transplanted into surroundings to which they must quickly adapt. Many normal individuals do not adjust easily to new surroundings; what, then, is the prognosis for retarded people, who are actually identified by their deficits in adaptive behavior? Logically, there will be a substantial number of retarded persons for whom a hasty exit from the institution will *not* mean a happy life. In other words, it is possible for deinstitutionalization to obscure the goal of normalization.

To read about some positive aspects of institutions, see page 439.

"The relocation syndrome" has long been a problem in homes for the aged, especially since Medicare legislation in the early 1970s began to exact improved care standards in nursing homes and to reduce residency where possible. Reports on the yearly number of elderly persons who die soon after moving to or between nursing homes vary from 3% (Cochran, Sran, & Varano, 1977) to 34% (Bourestrom, 1973).

The "least restrictive environment" movement has created a similar set of circumstances and has sparked a similar surge in the death rate and incidence of serious depression among the mentally retarded population. Cochran and colleagues (1977) observed the "relocation syndrome" in a study of 250 former residents of a large centralized facility in Maryland who were transferred en masse to Great Oaks, one of six smaller regional centers newly erected to serve retarded adults near their family homes. The following account is typical of the five residents who suffered the symptoms.

> Joan, a 52-year-old white, profoundly mentally retarded female, was considered normal at birth and had no serious illnesses or injuries, although her developmental landmarks were all extremely delayed. She remained at home, attended no school programs, and was somewhat overindulged until the time of her parents' death. She was admitted first to a psychiatric facility and, shortly thereafter, to Rosewood Center, where she resided for 18 years. No depression occurred at Rosewood and she was in good health. At the time of transfer to Great Oaks Center, she was rather quiet and fearful, but not particularly depressed. A few days following transfer, however, she ceased eating, became increasingly depressed, and spent a great deal of her time weeping. Her depression lasted 3 to 4 weeks, during which time she lost approximately 15% of her body weight. There was poor response to high caloric dietary supplements and antidepressant medications. She improved gradually and has done well subsequently (p. 10).

Though only five out of the 250 relocated residents reacted in this way, they suffered severely and perhaps unnecessarily. One of the five eventually died of pneumonia. Coffman and Harris (1980) have documented a parallel set of symptoms which they call *transition shock*. This condition is analogous to the adjustment problems of recent divorcees, ex-prisoners, and returning veterans, and the "culture-shock" experienced by cross-cultural travelers such as exchange students and VISTA volunteers. Certain common characteristics other than symptoms exist.

1. Cue problems—Responding inappropriately to cues that were relevant in the old environment but not in the new (e.g., bells signaling mealtime in institutions), as well as failing to respond to cues peculiar to new environment.
2. Value discrepancies—for example, personal traits developed by rigid institutional routine—sluggishness, dependence, inability to make decisions—will normally not be valued in the community.
3. Emergence over time—as with "relocation syndrome," problems associated with transition shock do not occur immediately, but incubate for 1 or 2 weeks. Perhaps it is at this time that the special treatment afforded to newcomers gives way to routine.

The symptoms manifested by a "shocked" former resident attempting to adjust to a new environment—depression, withdrawal, shyness, wistfulness, irritability, sleep disturbances, incontinence—often mis-

The call for a more realistic appraisal of residential care typifies what has been called "deinstitutionalization backlash." Many people now recovering from years of rampant anti-institutionalism inspired by various court cases have begun to realize that residential services indeed may be appropriate for those severely and profoundly handicapped persons for whom community placement is far from "least restrictive." Institutions have potential value in that they offer

- ☐ A concentration of mental retardation specialists and medical personnel;
- ☐ A setting where the necessary medical and technological support systems can be housed most economically;
- ☐ A structured and systematic lifestyle, which severely and profoundly retarded persons usually require;
- ☐ A "home" among peers characterized by individual attention and care, in contrast to the mainstream community where retarded people generally bring up the rear;
- ☐ A location where qualitatively sound and ethically sanctioned research—both pure and applied—can take place; accomplished by encouraging in-house staff who demonstrate the requisite research skills/interest and by cooperating on joint ventures with universities and other research groups;
- ☐ A vector for developing community awareness, understanding, participation, and acceptance of persons who are mentally retarded;
- ☐ A bona fide training site for (a) residents—acknowledging a resident's potential as well as his or her limitations; (b) staff; and (c) community service personnel.

These positive aspects of residential facilities have been achieved by some institutions and are the goal of others. However, the value of any institution is maximized when it is located in a community setting and when certain prerequisites are met; some of these include

- ☐ Providing salaries that are competitive with other human service occupations and establishing incentives that attract and keep qualified, dedicated staff;
- ☐ Instilling morale that fosters interest and pride in the daily duties of the staff;
- ☐ Providing training that is relevant, motivating, and enriching;
- ☐ Demonstrating results so that the staff can see that their efforts are making a difference;
- ☐ Developing a cooperative relationship with related agencies, with universities, with parent groups, and with the community;
- ☐ Ensuring humane and ethical standards that are openly and equitably advocated by the administration on behalf of all residents;
- ☐ Creating an overall climate of hope, understanding, and determination.

lead observers to ill-informed conclusions that the individual has permanent behavior disorders. Persons unfamiliar with developmental disabilities tend to forget that mentally retarded people experience the full range of human emotions; they fail to recognize that transition shock is an emotional reaction, and that despondence, loneliness, anxiety, hostility, and so on are feelings no less salient for retarded than for normal persons.

For the newly deinstitutionalized, the road to social integration is full of obstacles. That these can become overwhelming is evidenced by the soaring rate of readmissions which presently follows on the heels of mass exodus from institutions. It is often difficult to discern which problems are the fault of ineffective (or nonexistent) preparation by the institution, which are inseparable from the transition process as described, and which stem from deficiencies in the ability of the new setting or receiving staff to accommodate new community members. Where the institution is to blame, difficulty can be sidestepped with an extensive preparation program that involves

1. Contact with staff members from both the present and receiving facilities as proof to the client of continued interest in his welfare,
2. Visits to the new residence prior to the move,
3. Family participation in the moving and adjustment processes,
4. Assignment of a personal advocate (chosen by the individual if possible) well in advance of the move to advise and support the retarded person.

Where problems arise from the individual's particular emotional response to change, patience on the part of the receiving staff and sympathetic counseling from both ends are the best weapons. The person should be reassured that the depression is probably only temporary.

Expectations of success or of failure heavily influence the new community member's ease of transition. The person given thorough preparation and ample support in the new role will naturally have better expectations for his or her own adjustment. Equally important is a general public belief that mentally retarded individuals can lead meaningful lives if given the necessary training and support. This encompasses teacher expectations in school and employer expectations on the job. Public sentiment can be affected in subtle ways. If the name of a new community facility implies deviance, if residents are called "patients" or "inmates," or adults are referred to as "children," the community at large will have understandably low expectations, and will behave accordingly. In that kind of climate, normalization is not possible.

READMISSIONS

The number of yearly releases from public institutions rose almost 150% between 1963 and 1974. While this is impressive, a far more dramatic figure for the same period is the 500% increase in readmissions. As the statistics in Figure 14.6 indicate, deinstitutionalization has been largely a process of reinstitutionalization, shuffling retarded residents through a devastating experience in independent living, then reeling them back in. The primary reason for unsuccessful placement, as reported by 136 public facilities (Scheerenberger, 1977), was a lack of supportive services in the community. Table 14.3 itemizes these neglected services.

QUALITY OF LIFE

Too often, a retarded person's failure to adjust in the new setting is the fault of ill-conceived alternative placement by overzealous reformers. Community facilities are not inherently normalizing; in fact, they can be as restrictive as the worst institution if the setting is inappropriate and the residents are unsupported by the services they require. Up to this point, we have implied that smaller size means superior service. A fair inquiry into institutional reform compels that we question these blind assumptions. Balla (1976) examined the impact of institutional size on aspects of care provided to residents. He attempted to determine

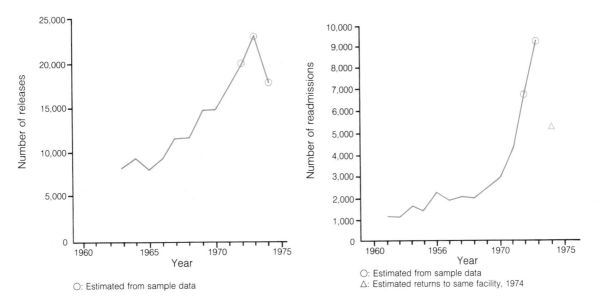

O: Estimated from sample data

O: Estimated from sample data
△: Estimated returns to same facility, 1974

FIGURE 14.6 Institutional Releases and Readmission of Mentally Retarded Individuals, 1960–1975

From J. W. Conroy, "Trends in the Deinstitutionalization of the Mentally Retarded," *Mental Retardation*, 1977, *15*(4), 44–46. Reprinted by permission.

TABLE 14.3 Primary Reasons for Readmissions as Reported by 135 Public Residential Facilities. 1973–1974

Reason	n	%
Community rejection	31	22
Lack of community services:	70	50
Activity centers & sheltered workshops	(12)	(9)
Advocacy services	(1)	(1)
Behavior management programs	(16)	(12)
Comprehensive services	(23)	(17)
Counseling	(5)	(4)
Day care	(11)	(8)
Education/Training	(13)	(9)
Employment	(9)	(6)
Family support	(2)	(1)
Follow-along services	(39)	(28)
Living accommodations	(27)	(19)
Medical services	(21)	(15)
Parent training	(4)	(3)
Failure to adjust	64	46
Family:	24	17
Could not adjust	(21)	(15)
Moved	(3)	(2)

From R. C. Scheerenberger, *Deinstitutionalization and Institutional Reform.* Springfield, Ill.: Charles C Thomas, 1976. Reprinted by permission.

whether certain structural elements common to large institutions foster practices that downgrade the quality of care, but found too little empirical data from which to draw strong conclusions. Balla's findings can be summarized as follows.

1. No data could be found supporting the supposition that smaller facilities return more residents to the community.
2. There is little significant correlation between the size of a facility and the adaptive behavior of residents.
3. There is no significant correlation between proximity of a residential facility to the home and frequency of visits by family members.
4. The *type* rather than *size* of an institution seems to determine the quality of care, with smaller, community-based facilities being generally more resident-oriented than large, isolated institutions.

Balla found that, of four types of residential facilities, group homes (7 to 57 beds) were the most resident-oriented, followed by small regional centers (10 to 116 beds), then average-sized regional centers (150 to 300 beds). Large, centralized institutions were the least resident-oriented. Orientation of care practices varied predictably across institutional types; however, *within* each group, the size of the facility had no bearing on orientation. Clearly, it is incorrect to presume a retarded person will be better served in a smaller facility simply because it is smaller. Regional centers can easily become surrogate institutions, and nursing homes have tremendous warehousing potential. It is equally wrong to expect that locating within a community will automatically make a facility more normalizing. Nor should we translate removal from the institution "as soon as possible" to mean "immediately if not sooner." As mentioned previously, preparation for community life cannot be rushed; neglecting that crucial readiness period all but assures that the client will become one more casualty of institutional reform.

FINAL THOUGHTS

As is true for any reform movement, the claims of those who seek to abolish public residential institutions are best regarded with a degree of healthy skepticism. Several points need to be stressed.

First, it is possible to abolish the residential institution. However, that portion of the retarded population who reside in institutions is entitled to quality care. There will probably always be some severely handicapped persons who are unable to function in the community, for whom the institution provides the least restrictive environment. To impose unrealistic standards of a "culturally normative environment" on such individuals is to deny their constitutional rights. Equal opportunity may at times mean unequal treatment. To quote MacMillan (1977),

> We should not get carried away with treating retarded individuals as though they were normal; because they are retarded, they have a right to special services, which may not be altogether normal. (p. 509)

Second, because residential institutions for the mentally disabled are as much a social phenomenon as any "institution" in the generic sense (marriage, baseball, whatever), to abolish such settings is to treat only the symptoms of a larger "social disease." The history of residential treatment has proven that institutions basically mirror prevailing social attitudes about the retarded. However, it is much easier to charge institutions with wrong-doing than to indict a nebulous public conscience. As Biklen (1977) says,

> It would be easy to recommend that a dirty ward be cleaned or that shabby clothes be replaced by new and stylish clothing, but

> such changes would not expunge those forces which create dirty wards and ill-clothed inmates. (p. 35)

Ultimately, the fault is not with the sadistic attendant who feeds residents lighted cigarettes but with the social attitudes that allow such actions to go unpunished.

Realistically, institutions will be around for a long time. As demonstrated by the exorbitant readmissions rate, it would be disastrous to eradicate institutions at a time when the track records of community service models are so poor. Vitello (1976) describes the ideal residential institution as one (not beset with staffing, crowding, and fiscal problems) in which

    ☐ Life support facilities are the best available, and include comprehensive, medical, and therapeutic care;

    ☐ Living arrangements emulate the family unit;

    ☐ Large-group activities are subordinate to small-group and individual activities;

    ☐ Service is decentralized.

Clearly, upgraded residential institutions are needed to fill the present void of decent community services. We should work on changing the attitudes and approaches that cast institutions as dungeons, so that institutions can actually be part of the deinstitutionalization process—one phase in the transition to least restrictive environments.

CHAPTER
FIFTEEN

Adulthood and Community Issues

*I*n recent years, we have witnessed a dramatic change in the lives of mentally retarded adults. Many retarded people are now living in community settings and are dealing with the same problems and complexities of adulthood that all of us face. For some mentally retarded adults, community living is not too difficult; for others, everyday life poses major challenges. This chapter will highlight some issues related to community living.

One of the purposes of the institutions established in the mid-1800s was to give disabled people skills necessary for successful reintegration into community life. As pointed out in chapter 1, the reasons why people were institutionalized changed over time, partly because few individuals successfully adjusted to community living. At the same time, powerful efforts to keep retarded persons away from society emerged. This condition lasted for many years and only recently has the community integration movement blossomed again.

Many factors are responsible for this renewed interest in creating community settings for retarded individuals: emphasis on individual rights; evidence of successful community experiences of some retarded adults; and attempts to provide living situations that are as close to

This chapter was contributed by James R. Patton and Janis L. Spiers.

normal as possible. This principle of normalization, championed by Nirje and Wolfensberger, can be applied to all facets of life; however, it is particularly relevant to community living.

Although most professionals advocate the development of programs designed to initiate or maintain mentally retarded adults in the community, most would also agree it is shortsighted to deny that the issue is complex. Kleinberg and Galligan (1983) remarked that "the view that community-living arrangements are necessarily more 'normalizing' than are traditional institutions is too simplistic" (p. 21). They emphasized that programmatic intervention is critical to successful adjustment, implying that without it community placement may not be much better than institutional placement. Professionals should also consider what successful community adjustment means to retarded individuals themselves, in addition to applying their own criteria.

COMMUNITY ADJUSTMENT

When we speak of community adjustment, we are referring to three major factors: (a) characteristics and behaviors of the individual; (b) demands placed upon the mentally retarded adult to live and function adequately in the community setting; (c) interaction effects. A fair amount of research has been devoted to studying the individual prior to and after the move into a community setting. Moreover, researchers (Hull & Thompson, 1980; Willer & Intagliata, 1981) have emphasized the importance of environmental factors. Nevertheless, there has not been much examination of community settings. Even less research has been directed at inspecting what Rappaport (1977) referred to as the "person-environment fit." Heal, Sigelman, and Switzky (1978) highlighted the situation.

> What has not yet been systematically considered is the possibility that one residential environment might be optimal for a client with one set of characteristics, while another is optimal for a client with a different set of characteristics. Suggestive evidence from related fields pinpoints the interaction of person and environment as a significant determinant of behavior. (p. 240)

Most students classified as educably mentally retarded (mildly retarded) in school environments are likely to adjust to life in the community. However, this adjustment may be more difficult for other retarded adults. Researchers have established two general approaches to studying community adjustment. One technique is the use of follow-up studies of previously institutionalized people or of noninstitutionalized persons. This type of research dates back to the early part of this century.

The second type of study involves the attempt to predict successful community adjustment. These studies are sometimes called *prognostic* studies (Rosen, Clark, & Kivitz, 1977).

FOLLOW-UP STUDIES

Over the years many follow-up studies have been performed. In general, through the years these studies suggest that individuals who were either deinstitutionalized or "graduated" from school settings were able to adapt successfully to community living. When retarded adults did not succeed in community settings, it was usually because of maladaptive behavior (Intagliata & Willer, 1982). Keep in mind that community adjustment is complex and that simple descriptions of it may be inadequate. It is also worth noting, as McCarver and Craig did in 1974, that much of the follow-up research has methodological flaws (Heal et al., 1978).

For a comprehensive review of both follow-up and prognostic studies see McCarver & Craig, 1974.

Criteria for successful community adjustment   One of the methodological problems in the follow-up studies conducted to date has been inconsistency in selecting and defining criteria for successful adjustment to community life. Although much of the research has used similar criteria, there has been no effort to standardize criteria, making comparisons between studies difficult. On the other hand, it *may* be necessary to vary some specific criteria to understand the idea of "person-environment fit."

Successful community adjustment has been defined in different ways. Willer and Intagliata (1981) presented five areas of functioning which are related to adjustment: self-care, community-living skills, behavior control, use of community resources, and social support. McCarver and Craig (1974) identified eight major criteria by which to gauge a community adjustment. Within each of these major categories, more specific variables may be considered. Rosen, Clark, and Kivitz (1977) summarize the adjustment variables identified by McCarver and Craig as follows:

1. Living environment (type of residence, amount of rent or mortgage payments, residential stability, satisfaction with living quarters);

2. Type of employment (place of work, skill level, job requirements);

3. Job changes (general stability, mobility up or down);

4. Savings and money management (debts, bank accounts, budgeting, installment buying);

5. Sexual problems (venereal disease, promiscuity, prostitution, homosexuality, illegitimacies, marital adjustment, exploitation);

6. Antisocial behavior (legal problems, arrests, delinquency, acts of violence);

7. Marriage and children (sexual adjustment, contraception, parental responsibility, health of children);

8. Use of leisure time (social contacts, recreational activities, hobbies, reading, travel). (Rosen, Clark, & Kivitz, 1977, pp. 142–143)

Although this list provides us a basic reference from which to organize our thinking about how to define successful community adjustment, previously performed follow-up studies have not always used these criteria. An example of the follow-up study is a classic study performed during the early 1960s of 53 mentally retarded persons who were released from Pacific State Hospital between 1949 and 1958 (Edgerton, 1967). Actually, 110 individuals successfully completed a vocational training program at Pacific State Hospital, but for practical purposes 53 people were selected to be contacted personally. This study was designed to gain a greater appreciation of the everyday lives of mentally retarded persons who had been released from an institution. In this study, Edgerton and his colleagues decided to focus on the following areas, which these researchers believed to be factors in community adjustment.

1. Where and how the ex-patients lived,
2. Making a living,
3. Relations with others in the community,
4. Sex, marriage, and children,
5. "Spare time" activities,
6. Their perception and presentation of self, and
7. Their practical problems in maintaining themselves in the community. (Edgerton, 1967, pp. 16–17)

Subjects in this study ranged in age from 20 to 75, with an average age of 35. There was an even distribution of men and women. The mean IQ of all subjects was 64.

Through interviews with the subjects and other people associated with the subjects (neighbors, relatives, friends, and employers), Edgerton and colleagues gained much information on the everyday lives of the subjects. Approximately 17 hours of investigation were devoted to each of the 53 people involved in the study. Overall, Edgerton's subjects were coping with life in the community; however, there were some areas that were troublesome. The authors point out that many of the subjects had a difficult time dealing with the stigma related to the label of *mental retardation*. They spent a great deal of energy and time "denying" their retardation and attempting to "pass" as normal. Major areas in the everyday lives that were problematic for the subjects centered on (*a*) making a living; (*b*) managing sex, marriage, and reproduction; (*c*) using leisure-time activities. To cope with these problems and to help pass as normal, many of the subjects developed relationships with "benefactors." Similar in many ways to the role of advocates today, the benefactor would assist the mentally retarded person in coping with problems of everyday living.

In 1972 and 1973, 12 years after the original study, Edgerton and Bercovici (1976) were able to locate 30 of the original 53 subjects. Again using interviews and participant-observation, the researchers focused on factors of community adjustment similar to those in the 1960–61 study. This time subjects were also asked to compare their present lives with their situations 10 years earlier. Researchers rated each subject's present adjustment with that of 1960–1961 and found that 8 subjects had improved, 12 had not changed, and 10 seemed to have regressed. While the researchers note that they were not able to predict very well from their original data how a person was to be doing at a later date, some general statements could be made. As length of time in the community increased for the subjects, there seemed to be fewer feelings of stigmatization, less concern with trying to deny their retardation, and less need for benefactors.

In this follow-up study, a number of points raised by the researchers are worth reiterating. First, adjustment is a multidimensional and complex concept. Second, as Edgerton and Bercovici point out, "social adjustment . . . may fluctuate markedly, not only from year to year, but from month to month or even from week to week" (1976, p. 495). Third, perhaps what constitutes good social acceptance from the mentally retarded person's viewpoint may differ significantly from the criteria used by professionals. This situation is reflected in the following statement.

> After many years of community living, persons once institutionalized as mentally retarded could . . . develop their own collective and individual views of what constitutes good social adjustment. If, as we suspect, our criteria of adjustment will continue to emphasize competence and independence while retarded persons themselves emphasize personal satisfaction, then our dilemma is even worse than we had all previously recognized. (Edgerton & Bercovici, 1976, p. 495)

In 1982, 20 years after the original study was conducted, Edgerton and his associates again set out to locate and examine the lives of people who were previously studied (Edgerton, Bollinger, & Herr, 1984). Of the original 48 subjects from whom information was gathered in 1960–61, only 15 were identified as being able to provide adequate data in 1982.

This group was a much older one, with an average age of 56 years. We know little about older mentally retarded people, especially those who live in community settings, and these data, while limited, provide some information. Using data gathering techniques similar to earlier efforts, the researchers ranked the subjects in the following areas: life satisfaction, social competence, life stress, relative dependence on benefactors, quality of life, and degree of improvement in life circumstances over the last 10 years. In the last category, five were stable, four had gotten worse, three had improved, and the others were undetermined because no agreement could be reached. Overall, the subjects conveyed a sense of hope, as reflected in Edgerton and colleagues' comments: "They [the subjects] believed that the future could be better and that their efforts could make a difference; they would pursue a better life by a variety of means" (1984, p. 350).

PREDICTING SUCCESSFUL COMMUNITY ADJUSTMENT

It would be wonderful to be able to predict successful and unsuccessful adjustment outcomes for mentally retarded individuals leaving either an institutional or school setting. As Rosen, Clark, and Kivitz (1977) state

> The fact that some retarded persons can succeed in the community while others fail suggests the need to determine, before their discharge from institutional or special school programs, which persons have the greatest potential for successful adjustment to independent living. (p. 171)

A number of researchers have had precisely this goal in mind. Unfortunately, the results of the research on the prediction of community adjustment have not supported any one combination of predictor variables. It would seem that IQ might be useful as a predictor variable; however, studies have not confirmed this hypothesis (Willer & Intagliata, 1981).

Typically, prognostic studies have concentrated on characteristics of the individual, which can include variables such as IQ and age, institutional-related factors (age at admission, training received, length of institutionalization), personality, emotional status, physical status, academic ability, vocational skills, and physical appearance. Up to now, most research has placed a greater premium on cognitive variables than on some of the others. To be able to better predict the outcome of community adjustment, we need to consider some alternative approaches to this type of research. Future researchers may do well to study social skill and personality variables in more detail for their prognostic value. It also seems prudent to consider those factors that are community-related. That is, it may prove to be very helpful in predicting community adjustment to know something about the community which an individual is entering.

Heal and colleagues (1978) have identified five aspects that should be carefully considered in preparing mentally retarded individuals for adaptation to the community environment. They are

- ☐ community attitudes and behaviors toward residential facilities and their residents;
- ☐ zoning controversies and regulatory obstacles;
- ☐ availability, adequacy, and access to community resources/support services;
- ☐ role of benefactors, friends, or advocates;
- ☐ characteristics of the residential service system itself. (p. 229)

CHARACTERISTICS OF LIFE IN THE COMMUNITY

Where do they work and sleep? What do they do? How do they spend their day? Some mentally retarded persons are fully integrated and actively involved in their community: working and receiving pay checks, establishing a home, entertaining friends, and participating in local events. Others spend much of their time alone or involved in activities that serve only to occupy time.

The complexity of each mentally retarded person's life, the variety of experiences, and the opportunities to develop and assume responsibilities all depend on the availability of appropriate community resources, public and private attitudes, and the strengths and weaknesses of the individual.

Work, home, and play comprise the major endeavors of adult life. With the thrust of normalization and deinstitutionalization, community options in each of these areas that facilitate the participation of mentally retarded persons in these normal rhythms and routines are growing. The following sections describe some options for retarded individuals in employment, housing, and leisure. We will not give specific standards or criteria by which to evaluate each model. However, you should consider the expectations and constraints of each program and how these affect the community life of the mentally retarded adult.

EMPLOYMENT

The routine and rhythm of work, the work tasks, the socializing associated with work, all these become part of the pattern of normalization. Leaving the house each morning, boarding the bus, punching in, coffee breaks, arguing with friends or foe, lunch, back to work, and then returning home, another day passed and another dollar earned. (Wolfensberger, 1972)

Work is no less significant for the retarded person than for anyone. Social changes, as well as changes in public policy, have allowed more retarded people to enter the work force and share in the benefits of gainful employment. During the past few years, advances in the technologies of task analysis and vocational prosthetics have greatly revised the employment forecasts for retarded persons. Once thought to possess little potential for gainful employment, even the most severely retarded individuals are now demonstrating the ability to perform complex vocational tasks when provided with appropriate and systematic training (Bellamy, Horner, & Inman, 1979; Bellamy, Sowers, & Bourbeau, 1983; Karan, Wehman, Renzaglia, & Schutz, 1976). In addition, federal legislation—specifically, the Rehabilitation Act of 1973—has mandated that existing vocational programs and resources include handicapped persons. These developments have greatly expanded vocational possibilities for mentally retarded adults. Positions and employment alternatives have been created within the community for purposes of vocational habilitation, and opportunities have opened within the regular job market.

Habilitation implies that most retarded persons are entering the work force, rather than reentering, as *rehabilitation* would suggest.

Vocational habilitation programs are built upon three values and procedures which differ from the processes of regular employment, as they seek to

☐ Produce workers, not goods;

☐ Accept those individuals who lack job skills, rather than take those with the most skills; and

☐ Train their best workers to leave, retaining their least productive persons.

It is interesting to note that this third objective sometimes creates conflicting feelings among the staff. It can be difficult for a supervisor to see her best workers move on, leaving her with a less able group. Nevertheless, the goal is to move these workers on to regular employment if at all possible. These programs serve to provide mentally retarded individuals with a meaningful daytime activity, training in job skills, and payment for productivity. They usually offer a progression of tasks varying in their requirements of independence of performance, accuracy, and speed. Most of these programs receive some form of economic subsidizing to offset costs of operation.

Vocational habilitation programs may be transitional in nature, emphasizing training and eventual placement in a more independent position, or serve as long-term sites for persons who cannot work in more demanding and less structured situations. Where the ultimate goal for habilitation is placement in a regular job site, retarded persons do not always meet this goal, nor do all need to progress through the habilitation system in order to secure competitive employment.

Today many communities offer a continuum of employment possibilities for mentally retarded adults. Economic conditions, the extent and adequacy of systematic training procedures, the flexibility of the worksites to facilitate adjustment, and the individual's abilities and deficits interact to determine where along the continuum a specific person may be found at a given time.

Activity centers   In many areas, local associations for retarded citizens, church groups, and other private organizations have developed programs to provide daytime activities for a more severely retarded population who require continuous supervision. These activity centers serve severely retarded persons who are older than school age and considered to be too handicapped to meet production criteria within workshop settings, though some may move on to these settings. Many of these individuals lack appropriate behavioral and motor skills required in sheltered workshops. Activity centers provide training in prevocational and vocational skills such as simple assembling tasks. However, they stress increased self-sufficiency over employability and place a greater emphasis on teaching daily living skills such as travel, safety, grooming, and communication. They also typically include recreational and socialization programs, as well as the opportunity for work and pay.

Sheltered workshops   Usually located in one large facility, sheltered workshops offer an assortment of job experiences to train vocational skills and behaviors within simulated work situations. Generally comprehensive in nature, providing both long-term and transitional placements, they may serve mild, moderate, and severely retarded persons, and often individuals with other handicapping conditions. Although activity centers are sometimes considered to be a form of workshop, sheltered workshops are usually of two types: transitional and long-term. Transitional workshops train clients for eventual competitive employment and often place a strong emphasis on production; clients in these settings may have to meet established production quotas. Long-term or extended workshops (Heward & Orlansky, 1984) provide training to clients who are likely to continue in this setting for a long time, resulting in less emphasis on rate of production. It is also possible to find some workshops that offer both types of training.

Most sheltered workshops provide basic rehabilitation services including screening, evaluation, training, placement, and follow-up. Programs focus on developing individual competency in a variety of tasks and the personal behaviors and attitudes associated with good working performance: promptness, attention to task, sociability, grooming, safety, and so on. Assignments within a workshop may include refinishing and restoring used goods, crafts, or contracted work such as cleaning headphones for airlines. As workshops strive to expand an individual's abilities and potentials and develop a repertoire of marketable job skills, the quality of the services offered depends on the number and variety of outside contracts the workshop can procure. This need requires that one or more of the staff members devote much time to securing contracts. These staff members must be knowledgeable about local businesses and aware of the workshop's production capabilities. Their job is to "sell" the services of the workshop to business and industry (Brolin, 1982). Long-term contracts are desirable because they provide a steady, reliable source of work and income to the workshop. Workers within sheltered workshops are usually paid on a piece work basis at rates comparable to local production rates.

An example of a successful attempt to train and employ severely handicapped workers in a long-term workshop setting is the Specialized Training Program (STP). This model was originally developed at the University of Oregon and replicated in six western states (Bellamy, Sowers, & Bourbeau, 1983). Although workers in these settings do possess acceptable behavior and motor skills, they are severely handicapped and are considered to be inappropriate recipients of vocational services. Yet, the clients in the STP programs are capable of productive work.

Transitional employment   There are also intermediate employment steps between sheltered workshops and competitive employment for many handicapped persons. These positions are usually created through vocational (re-)habilitation programs to provide an opportunity to generalize skills learned within a sheltered facility to a real work site. They allow for decreasing supervision and segregation and increasing autonomy and integration through preparation and control of the work environment and use of a visiting vocational counselor. Retarded persons may work in small groups within a regular industry and receive continuous or close supervision, or they may be individually mainstreamed into the work force with just minimal and periodic special support. Another approach, which is being implemented in Hawaii, involves the use of job coaches (COMTEP, n.d.). After a suitable place of employment has been secured for a client, job coaches go with the client to the job site and provide any assistance the worker may need in adapting to the new situation. These coaches are gradually withdrawn so the worker is able to function independently. This model increases individual workers' chances to adjust to their jobs. Because the coaches provide the necessary assistance, the employer does not have to. In either instance, supervision shifts from actual skill training to monitoring of performance and satisfaction. Some school systems are also using this model in work study programs with retarded high school students, placing them within garages, hospitals, or good service programs, for example. These intermediate positions are significant in helping retarded individuals advance to independent employment, as they lessen the

INDEPENDENT LIVING

Timmy and Carol Savage presently live in an apartment, on their own and as independent as any couple could possibly be. Tim spent 37 years of his life in the state's institution for the mentally retarded, after which he lived in a group home. Tim now works full time sanding picture frames for ACME Industries, while Carol performs routine maid services for the Best Western Inn. According to Tim, and incidentally confirmed by the landlord, "We pay on time, every time. We don't get behind."

Tom Houston, housing developer for the handicapped with Mental Retardation Services, explains it has been a long process of educating landlords and neighbors alike that the mentally retarded are more similar to, than different from, those pegged as normal. "Many landlords have very legitimate concerns about disabled individuals, because if a tenant is impeded in his performance of his duties as a tenant, it could result in a loss to the landlord."

The Savages have access to a Citizens Advocacy program which matches a non-handicapped volunteer from the community with a "special-friend," which will hopefully develop into a lasting friendship. The lay person acts as an advocate for the human and legal rights of the mentally retarded person. It is simply one more way that his differences can be diminished, and a volunteer grows in his understanding of the handicapped.

Houston feels compelled to assure a prospective landlord that where a handicapped tenant has inadequacies, there will be a professional, or a lay person like a Citizen Advocate, to compensate. Some people like the Savages need little supervision. They have demonstrated a consistency of behavior that assures a landlord they are able to handle most of their duties as tenants with little guidance from others.

When a client is deemed ready for independent living, Houston helps him work out an agreement for monthly rent payments, including utilities, which are not to exceed ¼ of the individual's gross income.

Once an apartment is found to suit everyone's purposes, a 1-year lease is signed. In so doing, the client is guaranteed his rent subsidy will be renewed annually for the next 5 years.

"Some landlords are very responsive," said Houston, calling him up when they have a vacancy because they like the program and go out of their way to help the tenant. For our landlords, "it's just a cut-and-dried agreement, strictly business. He wants to know, 'Am I going to get my checks on time? Is my lease going to be violated?'"

Houston says over and over again that these tenants are turning out to be reliable. They like structure and adhere rather consistently to a routine once good habits are taught them. But Houston is quick to point out that "it's not a humanitarian thing. It's a good business deal."

"I wouldn't be on the phone to you," he tells a landlord, "if I didn't feel it was good business."

differences between sheltered work and competitive job sites and facilitate the transfer of skills.

Competitive employment Many retarded persons are employed in regular jobs and receive minimum wage. These jobs are usually unskilled or semiskilled labor such as janitorial or dishwashing (Crain, 1980). Some are self-employed and hire themselves out as yardworkers or housekeepers. These individuals obtain positions through their vocational programs or locate jobs independently through friends, word of mouth, or their own ability. Most retarded persons who find jobs in competitive employment are mildly retarded, though there are examples of severely handicapped persons working as cafeteria and fountain attendants, baker's helpers, racket stringers, duplicating machine operators, and more (Cook, Dahl, & Gale, 1977). Competitive employment that retarded workers assume varies greatly, depending on the person's abilities and training, the employers' attitudes, and the flexibility of the work environment.

Characteristics of employability Many studies have been conducted to identify those characteristics which are associated with successful employment of the mentally retarded. The results of this research indicate that personal and social skills are more directly related to employability and job stability than measured intelligence or physical dexterity. Those characteristics which tended to predict job success include (Kolstoe, 1961; Sali & Amir, 1970)

- [ ] Positive attitude towards the work sites;
- [ ] Motivated behaviors—promptness, pride;
- [ ] Ability to get along with supervisors and coworkers;
- [ ] Ability to communicate with more than one-word response;
- [ ] Physical attractiveness—grooming, good health, appropriate height-weight ratio;
- [ ] Fair motor coordination.

The ability to adjust socially to the work environment is seen as the most crucial factor in acquiring and maintaining a position. Occupational failure may be caused by the inability to get along with employers, poor attendance and punctuality, poor personal appearance and manners, and irregularity of moods and behaviors. Environmental constraints such as problems obtaining reliable transportation, family difficulties, and lack of appropriate referrals and support also hinder successful employment for some individuals.

Successful competitive employment appears to be directly related to motivation and the ability to adjust and respond to the vocational and social demands of the job situation. In 1969, Kantner again confirmed that IQ was not a significant predictor of success and that, of 82 subjects studied, only 6% lost their jobs due to an inability to perform certain skills necessary for the job task. These studies strongly imply that vocational programs must emphasize the development of good personal adjustment and general job skills if they are to be effective. Employability must be stressed over productivity, with centers providing training in areas such as interviewing skills, social and conversation skills, using transportation services, reporting in when sick or late, in addition to developing actual task-oriented manipulative skills. This shift in emphasis has begun in many workshops and job training centers.

School systems are also incorporating career development exercises into their curriculum for special classes to help build realistic job aspirations and awareness of responsibilities (See Brolin & Kokaska, 1979). Training programs are attempting to seek better "fits" between the social demands of a particular work setting and the personal and communication skills of the individual. These improvements in early and well-focused programs should improve the possibility of competitive employment for most retarded persons.

LIVING ARRANGEMENTS

Where people live determines to a great extent how they live. This seems obvious when applied to persons within institutions, and it is also true of those residing in the community. For a mentally retarded person, having a home in the community may mean having a local address, yet spending hours alone in a room not knowing anyone or how to do anything. Or it may involve walking over to greet the neighbors, catching a bus to the store, planning meals, and maintaining an apartment. Clearly, community living requires more than physical location. It demands involvement and interaction with the neighborhood and surrounding environment, and training in the necessary skills. Often, interaction with the community has been negative. Zoning laws that regulate the establishment of group homes unfairly discriminate against retarded people. Community opposition to the establishment of group homes has also been documented (Kastner, Reppucci, & Pezzoli, 1979; Lubin, Schwartz, Zigman, & Janicki, 1982; Seltzer, 1984).

Many forces and perspectives have influenced the development of community residential facilities (CRF) for mentally retarded adults (Baker, Seltzer, & Seltzer, 1977). Wolfensberger (1969) has strongly advocated the establishment of small residences within neighborhood settings, having live-in house parents and a family orientation, and using generic community services. He also suggests using foster care and adoption as means to individually mainstream retarded persons. Other individuals still believe that the retarded need to be protected and benevolently guided on a day-to-day basis, often limiting their exposure to

Future developments in community living for many retarded adults may be significantly influenced by the outcome of the Supreme Court case, *Cleburne Living Center v. City of Cleburne*, which focuses on the effect zoning ordinances have on the rights of retarded citizens to reside in the community.

the community due to fear of the risks involved. Still another view focuses on establishing a "psychological sense of community" (Sarason, 1974) by organizing handicapped residents into a cohesive and independent group—in settings apart from the general public. An emphasis on acquiring daily living skills through planned activities defines still other settings as having a training orientation and function.

The dominant orientation that a CRF has is a function of the characteristics and needs of the residents who live in it. CRFs vary by size, location, number of residents, staffing patterns, and degree of handicapping conditions residents have. The orientation of the CRF also determines the facility's responses to the following issues associated with services for its residents:

☐ Degree of autonomy allowed or developed within the residents;
☐ Restrictions placed on residents: required activities, curfews, etc.;
☐ Residents' role in determining house/facility policies;
☐ Residents' responsibilities within the facility;
☐ Degree of privacy allowed;
☐ Sexuality of residents;
☐ Resident's length of stay: long-term or transitional;
☐ Emphasis on community involvement;
☐ Atmosphere created through decorations and furnishings;
☐ Actualizing the normalization principle.

Some mentally retarded persons remain in their families' homes rather than move to an alternative community arrangement. Yet many of these same issues and perspectives—specifically those affecting autonomy and responsibility—are pertinent to the home setting also. Whether in a private home or community facility, it is the match between an individual's needs and the setting's emphasis which ultimately defines the quality of the housing arrangement.

A number of community living arrangements have been developed, although their availability may be limited. Moreover, the quality of any given option may vary greatly from one setting to another. The following are general descriptions of community living arrangements found in many parts of the country.

ICF-MR programs Intermediate Care Facilities for the Mentally Retarded (ICF-MR) provide 24-hour care, including nursing, medical support, training, and therapeutic support to its residents. Theoretically, these facilities provide necessary services to a more involved clientele in a less restricted environment—the community. However, some observers (Taylor, McCord, & Stanford, 1981) have suggested that certain states have used the federal Medicaid monies which accompany these facilities to create "mini-institutions."

Group homes   The group home is the most common community living arrangement established by social services or private organizations for mentally retarded adults. In these homes, a group of retarded residents lives within a residential neighborhood, receiving support and supervision from live-in counselors. Some are transitional in focus, preparing residents to move to more independent situations. Others serve as long-term residences. Sometimes several homes may be located near each other and staffed by a single resident manager. These settings, known as congregate homes, provide a living environment suited for more capable residents because supervision, counseling, and assistance is minimal. Many evoke images of comfortable family settings—using large old houses where possible, decorated with the memorabilia and belongings of the residents and encouraging a sense of responsibility and contribution by household members. They provide a sharp contrast to sterile institutional settings.

Most of these homes attempt to provide training in daily living skills and community awareness through direct experiences. Areas emphasized include self-help skills, household management, basic academics, socialization, leisure activities, and travel and safety skills.

Daily programs are usually divided into client participation in a day activity such as work, school, or center and an evening activity involving household chores such as cooking and clean-up and receiving instruction in a skill area or enjoying a social or leisure activity. Figure 15.1 outlines the weekly schedule at one group home.

Group homes can be categorized according to size and population. The number and characteristics of the residents may also affect the degree of personalization, socialization, training, and integration offered to the retarded individuals. These models include

1. Small group homes have 10 or fewer residents, 2 staff persons, and a relief staff. Residents are usually 20 to 30 years old, involved in a day activity or employed, and mildly or moderately retarded. Most homes fit into this category.

2. Larger group homes offer a more specialized professional staff and usually serve older and more handicapped persons. Due to increased numbers of residents and lower staff-to-client ratios, they tend to be more restrictive and provide fewer opportunities for resident autonomy or involvement in decision making. This category can be divided into medium-sized homes serving 11 to 20 residents, larger homes with 20 to 40 people, and mini-institutions having 41 to 80 residents.

	MONDAY	TUESDAY	WEDNESDAY	THURSDAY	FRIDAY	SATURDAY	SUNDAY	SATURDAY	SUNDAY
	All clients are at work or school during the day. 4–5 p.m. Clients arrive home. Work on personal hygiene, socialization, and daily living skills.							Residents sleep in.	Church (optional)
	5–6 p.m. Dinner Preparation and Table Setting			5–7 NIGHT COLLEGE	5–6 p.m. Dinner Preparation and Table Setting			Residents prepare and clean-up breakfast and lunch (with staff help as needed)	
	6–7 p.m. Dinner and Clean-up				6–7 p.m. Dinner and Clean-up			Shopping or Group Activities or Individual Activities	3–5 p.m. *Required Activities* / Meal Selection
	7–9 Coffeehouse (every other week)	7–9 p.m. Free Time	6:30–9:30 p.m. TUTORS	7–8 p.m. Dinner and Clean-up	7–9:30 p.m. Recreational Activity		7–9 p.m. Free Time	*Residents usually plan and implement their own weekend schedule as much as possible.	Housework
	Individualized Tutoring by House Staff		(with clients from 7–9 p.m.)	8–9 p.m. Free Time			Individualized Tutoring by House Staff		Food Shopping
	9–10 p.m. Personal Hygiene, Daily Living Skills, Socialization	Throughout Evening Personal Hygiene, Daily Living Skills, Socialization	9–10 p.m. Personal Hygiene, Daily Living Skills, Socialization		9:30–10 p.m. Personal Hygiene, Daily Living Skills, Socialization		9–10 p.m. Personal Hygiene, Daily Living Skills, Socialization		

FIGURE 15.1 Weekly Resident and Staff Schedule at One Group Home

3. Mixed group homes function as halfway houses. They are transitional in nature, serve individuals other than the retarded, and often provide a place for convalescing rather than training.

4. Homes for older adults typically serve individuals over age 50. These residences may be shared with nonretarded elderly persons. They are often secluded, with residents not likely to be involved in outside activities.

Group homes for retarded persons, as well as for other handicapped people, are controversial. Community opposition, usually from neighbors, has often been a major barrier to providing less restricted living options. Although neighbors fear that their property values will decrease if a group home is established in their neighborhood, real estate values of homes in the same communities as group homes do not seem to decrease (Wiener, Anderson, & Nietupski, 1982). Seltzer (1984) found that efforts to educate the public about retardation and group homes were positively correlated with community opposition. She also observed that "opposition is less likely when the community becomes aware either after the residence begins operations or more than 6 months before it opens" (p. 7). The implication of these findings is that it might be better to adopt a "low-profile" entry strategy rather than a "high-profile" (i.e., intensive community education programs) one when establishing a community residence.

Protected settings   Certain community living arrangements afford retarded people protected settings with more support than group homes. These include foster home settings and sheltered communities.

Foster home settings are designed to integrate retarded individuals into the most normalized setting of all—a family. Three different types of foster settings are available in Hawaii:

☐ Care homes: licensed family or residential homes that provide room, board, and personal care

☐ Boarding homes: licensed homes that provide room and board to ambulatory individuals needing minimal care and supervision

☐ Companion homes: licensed private family homes that provide a homelike environment and an active program of training for adults; a similar setting is available for children and is called a "teaching home"

Sheltered communities, which were discussed in chapter 9, are typically located outside the community proper. Some of these settings attempt to insulate the retarded individuals from a public that is viewed as unable or unlikely to accept handicapped adults. Other settings encourage participation in the mainstream of community life, only sheltering the retarded adults from dealing with the complexities of community living (see the insert on Helemano Plantation).

Community training programs Workshop dormitories have been developed in some areas as boarding school-type models for individuals working in sheltered workshops. These dormitories are programmatically or administratively attached to the vocational training efforts of the workshop. Although they stress community living skills, vocational learning is usually given a greater emphasis. These training programs and dormitories are generally transitional in nature.

Similar training models also exist on the grounds of some institutions. These are frequently called *community preparation programs* and are designed to give residents some controlled, structured experiences with the increased independence, risks, and responsibilities they will encounter if and when they are deinstitutionalized. Typically using a cottage or building located somewhat apart from other institutional facilities, these programs provide training in telling time, managing money, using public transportation, doing household chores, social skills, and legal rights. Participants may also commute daily to an employment site within the community. The quality of these settings as preparation for community living depends on their ability to replicate or progressively involve residents in the actual circumstances they will encounter when they move beyond the institutional grounds and shelter.

Apartment programs Apartment programs represent the least restrictive alternatives within community residential programming. The degree of supervision, support, and training provided to the residents depends on the individuals' needs. Some residents will require support in the areas of money management, cooking, and/or household skills. Others may demand services only at times of crisis. Residents within these programs are usually less severely handicapped than those in other models and have better personal and social adjustment skills. Most are employed competitively or at workshops. Variations of this model include

1. Apartment clusters—Several apartments in close proximity to each other, sharing the supervision of a central staff person.
2. Single or resident apartments—A live-in arrangement in which a nonretarded person shares a home or apartment with one or more retarded individuals.
3. Independent apartment living—One or more retarded individuals living within an apartment, receiving support and assistance on a periodic basis from a nonresident staff person.

RECREATION AND LEISURE TIME

Mentally retarded persons can advance in health and physical fitness, mobility, language, social skills, and self-esteem through participation in recreational activities (AAHPER, 1966; Wilson, 1974). Like all persons, the retarded need recreational activities to provide a change in daily schedule and to forestall boredom. Unfortunately, most retarded individuals remain outside the mainstream of community life with regard to recreational activities and the use of leisure time.

Though many mentally retarded persons express interest in a wide range of activities, the recreational repertoire of most retarded individuals consists of passive events such as watching TV or movies, listening to records, walking, and looking at magazines. If handicapped bus passes are available, some will ride buses for hours on end. Few retarded adults go to parties, plays, or initiate social get-togethers. Sometimes this is due to the overprotection of families or benefactors. Their activities are restricted to those they can do alone or with family members, and to those that avoid contact with strangers or new places (Katz & Yekutiel, 1974). This limited use of leisure time results from factors associated with both the individual and the community. Although recreational difficulties are not inherent to the condition of mental retardation, many mentally retarded adults do not have recreational skills because of limited experiences or instruction, slow or uneven physical development, or the lack of friends with whom to learn or play. A lack of community funds, trained personnel, and until recently awareness of the mentally retarded adult's need for recreation has also contributed to this problem. This situation may be compounded by transportation difficulties. Ironically, these difficulties may be more pronounced for persons living in more independent settings such as apartments, as they may have less accessibility to peer groups or transportation than persons living in group or family homes.

Recreation programs   Recreation programs for retarded people have existed for many years within institutions, though these programs have been more concerned with keeping residents occupied and providing relief for staff than developing leisure skills. However, advocates for the retarded have demanded that community recreational opportunities available to normal individuals be extended to handicapped persons also. Communities have begun responding publicly and privately by developing special programs and modifying regular services. Examples include

☐ Special overnight or day camps for retarded people
☐ Special Olympic programs
☐ Therapeutic recreation classes and programs
☐ Mainstreaming into regular recreation facilities and classes

Other innovative projects have sprung up over the past few years. Retarded individuals in Milwaukee have formed a group to publish a local newspaper—the *Milwaukee Citizens*. The Mohawks and Squaws, a social organization in Massachusetts, was developed to provide retarded persons with a club atmosphere—a place to belong. Recently, these retarded persons have begun to successfully hire themselves out as consultants, specializing in mental retardation. Drama groups, craft guilds, jogging clubs, cooking groups, and other activities for retarded persons have increased over the past few years. Parents, teachers, and service providers have realized the importance of developing home-centered hobbies, and have included instruction of card games, checkers, plant growing, stamp collecting, and other leisure projects into their curricula or service plans. Manufacturers have begun to produce games that do not rely on reading skills, but use color codes and shapes to facilitate play. The development of special equipment such as modified bowling balls and walkers for ice-skating has broadened opportunities to participate in sports. Specialized curricula such as *Ho'onanea Program: A Leisure Curriculum Component for Severely Handicapped Children and Youth* (Wuerch & Voeltz, 1981) have been developed specifically to address this area. The removal of physical and attitudinal barriers has also expanded the options available to retarded adults.

Until recently, a mentally retarded individual's use of leisure time was characterized more by a lack of choice and knowledge than an expression of true interest. As with other skill areas, retarded persons need intentional and systematic instruction in the use of leisure-time skills in order to develop hobbies and to participate in activities with confidence. Communities are beginning to respond with preparation and opportunities enabling retarded individuals to make choices and to gain personal and social enrichment through recreational activities.

MOBILITY

The ability to travel about one's environment develops an awareness of other people and places and facilitates a sense of personal control over the environment. In our society, the ability to move from one place to another is essential. Remaining in one fixed location is viewed as odd and limiting.

Mobility is complex for mentally retarded persons. Most do not have driver's licenses or cars. They must depend on others for rides, walk, or use public transportation systems. Independent travel skills also require certain intellectual and physical abilities.

Each of these options presents its own unique limitations and requirements for retarded individuals. Riding with friends or caretakers forces the retarded person to be dependent on other people. Walking limits destinations to a reasonable radius. An individual must also know how to cross streets, as well as knowing where and how to go. Public transportation systems present the most complex array of limitations and requirements. They limit destinations to routes covered and travel must be within the system's hours of operation. This system may thrust individuals into a world that relies on reading, telling time, determining correct change (if passes are unavailable), and discriminating locations with a fast and impersonal pace. Mentally retarded individuals generally have difficulty under these circumstances.

Safety is another concern relating to independent travel. What if a retarded person gets lost? Being in public places such as bus stops or walking on streets may expose retarded individuals to perplexing situations, and they may become disoriented and confused. Traveling in groups may offer more safety and security for the individual. Proponents of normalization, however, discourage having small "packs" of retarded individuals walking or riding together, as this tends to isolate and mark them as a generalized set rather than as individuals (Wolfensberger, 1972).

These limitations, difficulties, and dangers are real issues which can restrict retarded individuals' ability to travel and ultimately confine them to staying home. However, many of these problems can be overcome simply through sequential systematic training. Other concerns will take community awareness and willingness to change existing formats.

Many educational, vocational, or residential programs for retarded persons are now including instruction in street safety and mobility skills. Individuals are learning general rules such as crossing only on green lights and at crosswalks and looking both ways; they are also developing a repertoire of known paths to points of interest. Mildly and moderately retarded persons are being taught how to ride buses. They initially receive close supervision and guidance, which is phased out so that the skill comes under control of independent use. Retarded persons are being taught how to recognize buildings and environmental cues as destination points and how to determine when lost. Practice in asking strangers for help, in locating the police, in using identification cards and the telephone, and in responding to harassment is also included in the developing curricula for travel. Money skills are also being taught in conjunction with riding the bus. The social skills and etiquette of being a passenger, such as appropriate conversation or responses to strangers, are being taught. Special transit services have also been developed in some communities to aid the physically and severely handicapped. They offer special wheelchair lifts and supervision.

Great advances have been made in many areas of training and modifications to encourage and enable retarded individuals to enjoy more people and places through travel. These advances need to be extended to all cities, and other areas need to be explored and developed. The hours that buses run to certain areas and facilities need to be increased so that the social and community activities and participation of retarded persons are not limited to (typically) 7:00 A.M. to 7:00 P.M. Color coding the names on buses so that reading deficits would not cause unnecessary handicaps would also facilitate this skill. Some form of public transportation needs to be extended to retarded and nonhandicapped persons living in more rural areas.

Out-of-town travel may present even more complex challenges for retarded people. Making reservations, changing connections or terminals, managing schedules, taxis, hotels, tips, luggage, and many other intricate components of long distance travel by bus or plane can overwhelm mentally handicapped travelers. Some airlines do provide special services for retarded passengers, but this again places them in the position of being singled out as different and dependent on others. Costs often also keep these individuals from enjoying this form of adventure. Out-of-town travel still holds many limitations for the mentally retarded, yet it presents an interesting and exciting challenge for educators and professionals to analyze and break into manageable parts.

ISSUES RELATED TO COMMUNITY LIVING

Frustrated, puzzled, jubilant, overwhelmed, bored, or busy, mentally retarded people react to their environments like everyone else. Their work experiences, use of leisure time, relationships, decisions, competencies, and self-images are determined not only by the opportunities available to them, but also by their individual aspirations, needs, and interpretations of these interactions. Thus, any descriptions of their lifestyles must include personal as well as environmental variables. Several areas have been identified in which the variety, nature, and quality of an individual's development as a community member is significantly affected by the mix of these two dimensions.

PUBLIC ACCEPTANCE

Public acceptance and understanding are interrelated processes which are crucial for the successful and active integration of retarded adults into our communities. The public in general and communities in particular support the deinstitutionalization of retarded persons. The degradation and pathos of institutions, as reported by Blatt and Kaplan (1966) and Rivera (1972), has angered many. People also support the need for mentally retarded persons to live in communities as an extension of social equality, equal opportunity, and humanitarian rights (Gallup, 1976). However, these attitudes are abstractions; when the time comes to hire a retarded person or watch a house down the street become a group home, attitudes may change.

A RESOLUTION FOR COMMUNITY ACTION

The Association for Persons with Severe Handicaps (TASH, formerly The Association for the Severely Handicapped) has formulated the following policy statement concerning the integration of developmentally disabled persons into community environments. It contains a plan for action and describes how community living should be examined.

DEINSTITUTIONALIZATION POLICY

To realize the goals and objectives of The Association for the Severely Handicapped, the following resolution is adopted: In order to develop, learn, grow and live as fully as possible, persons with handicapping conditions require access to services which allow for longitudinal, comprehensive, systematic and chronological age appropriate interactions with persons without identified handicaps. Such interactions must occur in domestic living, educational, vocational and recreational/leisure environments. Specifically, handicapped individuals should: 1) participate in family-like and/or normalized community based domestic living environments; 2) receive educational services in chronological age appropriate regular educational environments; 3) receive training in and access to a wide variety of vocational environments and opportunities, regardless of functioning level; and 4) participate in a wide range of normalized recreational/leisure environments and activities that involve persons without identified handicaps. The Association for the Severely Handicapped believes that the above conditions must be met in order to provide quality service and that these conditions can only be met by community-based services. Therefore, The Association for the Severely Handicapped resolves that it will work toward the rapid termination of living environments and educational/vocational/recreational services that segregate, regiment and isolate persons from the individualized attention and sustained normalized community interactions necessary for maximal growth, development and the enjoyment of life.

Once in the communities, many mentally retarded persons encounter resistance and discrimination in employment, housing, education, and public service. Reports have circulated of neighbors verbally and physically opposing the construction of group homes for the retarded on their blocks. As mentioned earlier, zoning ordinances have been quickly enacted or dusted off to prevent such moves in many communities.

Public attitudes towards the mentally retarded vary in their intensity and conclusions. Yet several questions seem to arise with most persons who are considering having retarded persons within their own communities. People are often concerned about increases in taxes to support group homes or workshops, declines in property value due to having retarded individuals within the neighborhood, the safety of their children, and how they should react to a retarded person if they meet on the street or in local stores. Wolpert (1978) has shown that these concerns are generally unfounded in his studies of the effects of group homes in New York City's neighborhoods. However, such questions, if ignored, can prevent the acceptance and active social integration of the retarded persons; anger and fear can be self-perpetuating. These concerns and feelings can develop into legal battles holding up the opening of group homes, or cold stares and avoidance of retarded persons in the neighborhood.

Fortunately, initial fears and reactions can be prevented or changed. Most stem from a lack of public understanding of what mental retardation is and is not. A Gallup poll taken in 1974 revealed that most people viewed the mentally retarded in general terms, believing that mentally retarded persons are unable to live independently and require close and constant supervision. As most retarded persons are only mildly handicapped, this view is drastically incorrect and limiting. These low expectations of the retarded and the fears associated with them often dissolve when "normal" individuals meet retarded persons and see their abilities and potential. Several studies have shown that public attitudes and acceptance of the mentally retarded improved after expected undesirable consequences of integration did not occur (Ebron & Ebron, 1967; Hamilton & Bishop, 1976; Hollinger & Jones, 1970; Jaffe, 1966; Semmel & Dickson, 1966). This research indicates that positive experiences in living with retarded people promotes more positive attitudes towards them (Kastner, Reppucci, & Pezzoli, 1979).

To facilitate acceptance of mentally retarded persons, community services must acknowledge and address the need for public education keeping in mind the admonitions of Seltzer (1984) presented earlier in this chapter. Efforts must be made to inform the public about the nature and causes of retardation and how to respond and react to retarded individuals. As all mentally retarded persons do not make positive adjustments to the community, service providers must assure the public of their support and ability to respond in times of crisis or concern.

The deinstitutionalization project of New York state serves as a model of comprehensive community education and involvement. Public media displays providing information on the needs and nature of mental retardation, task forces comprised of community members to locate appropriate group home sites, and speakers bureaus to address community concerns form the basis of this campaign to educate and obtain support. Similar efforts are also concentrated in the schools to foster acceptance of the mentally retarded in the up-and-coming generation.

Nothing is more essential to the eventual success of the community mental retardation services movement than the good will,
acceptance, and support of the general public. Whether directly
as neighbors or employers of retarded persons, or indirectly as
voters guiding public officials with regard to zoning issues, program proposals, and agency budgets, the general public's knowledge and attitudes are largely responsible for the nature of the
community in which retarded people live. That community can
accept or reject, help or impair. While the effects of mental retardation on instrumental and expressive functions is real, the extent to which mental retardation constitutes a daily problem for
an individual depends heavily on the extent to which other people are tolerant, helpful, and adjustive to the differences of mentally retarded persons. (Kastner et al., 1979)

There are also efforts to foster acceptance of mentally retarded students in the schools. Programs that provide structured interactions of
nonhandicapped children with severely retarded children have increased the social acceptance of these retarded students (Voeltz, 1982).
Nonhandicapped students are likely to understand retarded persons
better if they are provided structured opportunities to interact. Although we do not know what long-term effects these interactions may
have, we hypothesize that positive attitudes established during the
school period may extend into adulthood.

QUALITY OF LIFE

It seems funny and ironic to me, that most people spend an exorbitant amount of time trying to distinguish themselves as
unique and different while all that a handicapped person wants
is to be just like everyone else. (A Citizen Advocate, 1978)

In 1967, Edgerton used the term "cloak of competence" to describe
the lives of 48 newly deinstitutionalized persons. He was referring to
their efforts to pass as normal through the assumption of the roles,
behaviors, expressions, and mementoes of their nonretarded neighbors,
and by denying to themselves the appropriateness of their label and
previous years in isolation. As we saw earlier in this chapter, these individuals were aware of the negative connotations society has attached to
the label *mentally retarded*. They considered public disclosure of their
condition to be devastating, because it would result in their segregation
and exclusion. They would not even admit that they were, or had been,
"retarded." They devised excuses and pretenses, or "cloaks," for covering up their deficits in an attempt to acquire and maintain acceptance.

The terms our society uses to define adulthood—*independence* and
productivity—and the roles we expect adults to assume—worker, partner, parent, and household manager—contrast sharply with the public

images and expectations the label *mental retardation* evokes. In fact, the expression *mentally retarded adult* seems contradictory to many misguided people who think that retarded people are childlike, dependent, and unable to make decisions. Retarded adults are not children. They are adults, attempting to establish themselves in the community and to form their own self-images.

For these individuals, the only criteria on which to judge personal value and competence are their achievement and material attainment relative to nonretarded persons in the community. Having a job, a sweetheart or spouse, a room or home of their own, and personal possessions has become the hallmark of normalcy for many retarded persons and their major goal. Yet, even when these have been acquired, individuals may still feel that they risk exposure through daily blunders or failures, and remain caught in a whirlwind of stress—coping with the frustrations of what they are, struggling to be what they are not.

Mentally retarded adults want to be part of a system which is still hesitant to welcome anyone who is different. They are forced to strive for sameness, yet must deal practically with their uniqueness. The imminence of disclosure and its disastrous consequences may lessen as the retarded individual does meet with some acceptance (Edgerton & Bercovici, 1976); yet we can imagine that the label is never a comfortable one. As for all individuals, the development of a positive sense of self, so critical for daily living, is a life-long endeavor for mentally retarded adults. The stakes are a bit higher for them, and the cards are slightly stacked against them.

FRIENDSHIP

A sense of belonging, of feeling accepted, and of having personal worth are qualities brought to life through friendship. Friendship creates an alliance and a sense of security. It is a vital human connection.

Mentally retarded people want and need friendship like everyone else. Yet they are often denied opportunities to form relationships or to develop the skills necessary to interact socially with others. Their exposure to peers may be limited because they live and work in sheltered or isolated environments. They typically lack a history of socializing events such as school clubs, parties, or sleepovers that help to develop or refine personal skills. They may not know how to give of themselves to other people and may be stuck in an egocentric perspective. Retarded persons may also respond inappropriately in social situations unless instructed otherwise. Many people shun retarded individuals who freely hug or kiss strangers when greeting them. Some retarded persons have speech problems, making communication difficult. Other factors may further hinder their ability to attract and keep friends. Mildly retarded individuals often avoid associating with other retarded persons for fear of emphasizing their own stigma. The normal community, however, may be reluctant to incorporate these retarded individuals within their smaller social circles, given what are often real differences in interests.

With few contacts and opportunities, retarded persons may attempt to befriend strangers or unwitting individuals. Many attempt to become social acquaintances with their professional contacts. In their effort to maintain those contacts and relationships they have developed, some retarded individuals will overcompensate: calling their friend too many times, talking too long on the phone, demanding attention, and not being able to let up. Unfortunately, these behaviors tend to make people uncomfortable and hesitant to interact with retarded persons for fear that they will have to "hurt their feelings" at some later date. Some mentally retarded persons have also been victimized or exploited by some "friends"—a situation which unfortunately may be a normal risk.

A friend can play a vital role in the adjustment of a retarded individual to community living, by providing emotional support and guidance through the exigencies of daily life. Certain organizations have begun to address the mentally retarded adult's need for friends by constructing social opportunities with realistic peer groups. Examples of these include the Mohawks and Squaws, a social club for retarded adults in which members plan their own parties and projects, and Citizen Advocacy programs which sponsor one-to-one relationships between a community volunteer and a retarded individual for the purpose of aiding adjustment. Researchers in behavior training have also begun to devise strategies for teaching retarded individuals appropriate social skills, such as how to address strangers, initiate conversations, and respond in various social situations.

SEXUALITY

Sexuality, marriage, and parenthood are probably the most controversial areas of normalization for the mentally retarded. The sexual development of mentally handicapped persons is greatly affected and determined by the myths, concerns, and ignorance of parents, professionals, and the general public. Some of these myths include

- ☐ Mentally retarded people are not interested in sex.
- ☐ They are oversexed.
- ☐ They lack the ability to comprehend information regarding their sexuality.
- ☐ They lack the ability to responsibly control their sexual desires.
- ☐ They have enough difficulties without becoming involved with the risks of a sexual relationship.

☐ They will reproduce their kind.

☐ They cannot adequately care for a child.

Because of these fears on the part of their caretakers, many mentally retarded people have been "sheltered" from sex information, references to love or dating, and opportunities to interact with members of the opposite sex. More dramatically, thousands of retarded individuals have been sterilized in order to avoid the consequences of their sexuality, if not the issue itself.

With the movement toward less restrictive living conditions, mentally retarded persons are returning to or remaining in the community. Many professionals would argue that sexual development and interaction be part of the retarded adult's life and that the right to sexual expression not be prohibited. The increased independence and patterns of social interaction now available to the retarded in the community necessitate, in practical terms, that this issue no longer be ignored. Parents, public school systems, group homes, and training programs are beginning to provide the mentally retarded with sex education.

SEXUAL KNOWLEDGE AND ATTITUDES OF THE MENTALLY RETARDED

It is impossible to characterize the degree of sexual interest and capabilities of mentally retarded individuals by virtue of their label. The nature of the retardation may, however, have both direct and indirect effects on sexual development, awareness, and knowledge.

1. Mentally retarded persons appear to be delayed in development of secondary sex characteristics, as compared with the normal population. The greater the degree of retardation, the more significant the delay in sexual development (Mosier, Grossman, & Dingman, 1962).

2. Mentally retarded persons usually are not involved with a variety of interpersonal activities such as clubs, parties, and dating in which to develop appropriate social skills with persons of the opposite sex and to make contacts.

3. Their sexual activities are more likely to be considered inappropriate due to their visibility. This is generally because retarded adults live under close supervision, in "goldfish-in-a-bowl" circumstances, rather than because of innate perverseness (Johnson, 1971).

4. Difficulty with language comprehension may impede their understanding of the vocabulary or medical terminology most commonly used when teaching about sex. They will generally rely on using more descriptive expressions (Johnson, 1971).

5. They generally lack the sources of information which supplement direct instruction about sex because they do not have an informed peer group (there is little "locker-room talk"), and they may not be able to read printed materials or have access to them.

6. They tend to be more affected by their inhibition or imposed prohibitions of sexuality than their own need for expression and often have extremely moralistic views about sex (Rosen et al., 1977).

7. Sex roles within marriage are defined in terms of providing shelter and support to children, rather than the sexual relationships between husband and wife (Rosen et al., 1977).

8. Sex role development may be impaired for persons who have lived in institutions and were only exposed to persons of the same sex.

Sex education   More parents and educators are recognizing that sex education is needed for mentally retarded adolescents and adults. Yet sex education programs, adequate materials and curricula, and qualified instructors are still limited. Existing programs often emphasize hygiene, morality, and prohibitions (Rosen, 1970, 1972) rather than focusing on sexual awareness and behaviors and larger social and emotional development. However, many innovative approaches and programs have begun within community services, institutions, schools, and homes to help mentally retarded adolescents and adults explore and enjoy this aspect of their humanity appropriately and responsibly. Systematic instruction—using discussions, role playing, and programmed experience—is being provided in the following areas:

1. Issues related to anatomy—Health care, body processes and changes, conception, pregnancy;

2. Means of sexual expression—Masturbation, heterosexuality, homosexuality;

3. Sexual responsibility—Birth control, venereal disease, parenthood;

4. Interpersonal relationships—Appropriate behaviors with strangers, friends, boyfriends and girlfriends;

5. Values, morals, and laws;

6. Decision-making skills and practices.

Obviously much information on human sexuality is available. The detail and scope of what should be presented to retarded persons needs to be individually determined, according to the person's intellectual abilities and physical and social needs. Contrary to earlier beliefs, most severely, moderately, and mildly retarded persons are able to learn socially appropriate sexual behaviors and to demonstrate responsibility and self-control (Johnson, 1971). Birth control is a difficult area for some retarded persons to master, due to the complexities of some methods or the requirement of daily awareness and responsibilities. No perfect method for retarded individuals has been determined, although many individuals are able to use the IUD, pill, or diaphragm with much success. Sterilization does not need to be viewed as a necessary consequence of being mentally retarded.

MARRIAGE AND PARENTHOOD

The issues of marriage and parenthood are closely allied with sexuality, and elicit similar concerns from the community regarding the rights of retarded adults. The laws within many states still restrict and prohibit marriage between "feebleminded" persons, and allow the courts to remove a child from a retarded mother on the grounds that her condition renders her unfit. As with the area of sex, most retarded persons do not receive instruction regarding the responsibilities of marriage and child rearing, or how to initiate or maintain these roles. However, some advocates are beginning to accept marriage for individuals with IQs over 50 (Rosen et al., 1977).

It has been estimated that the marriage rate among mildly retarded persons is only slightly below the national average (Ingalls, 1978). They appear to marry persons of higher intellect, to complement the skills of their partners, and to depend on each other for companionship and support. Mentally retarded women marry more frequently than retarded men. Previously institutionalized persons have a lower incidence of marriage than individuals who remained in the community and progressed through special programs or classes (Rosen et al., 1977). Some of the problems encountered by mentally retarded couples include low income, difficulties managing money, erratic employment or low job status, limited social skills or outlets, and difficulties in planning for the future. Though little research has been conducted on the long-term status of married mentally retarded persons, with "appropriate preparation, training and continued understanding help . . . mildly retarded adults . . . make as good a marital adjustment as nonretarded persons in the same socioeconomic circumstances" (Katz, 1972).

Many retarded individuals view marriage as an important role in life—a symbol of acceptance and normalcy and a needed means of belonging and sharing. In addition to desiring marriage, a few retarded individuals also wish to have children. Of all the issues regarding the retarded, this one still stirs the hottest taboos, fears, and debates. Two major concerns arise regarding parenthood and the mentally retarded: (*a*) will they pass on their condition? and (*b*) can they be suitable parents?

In response to the first concern, only 15% of the causes of mental retardation are due to genetically-known factors and thus directly transmittable. The majority of cases of retardation are due to psychosocial factors. Parents—retarded or not—who have few economic resources often produce children who are at high risk of becoming retarded. These infants require lots of stimulation as well as adequate diets to insure normal development. The mental retardation of the parents, as well as their economic capabilities, may interfere with their ability to provide this kind of care, unless outside support and training in child care and nutrition is given.

Can mentally retarded people be suitable parents? There are no ready answers to this question. Little research has been conducted on the ability of the mentally retarded to be adequate parents. Individuals have speculated that retarded parents may be prone to abuse their children because they are frustrated. Others have wondered how grown nonretarded children will view their retarded parents. Attempts to find answers to these questions will have to take into account the economic constraints faced by most retarded adults. The criteria used to evaluate effective parenting will need to reflect the values of their low socioeconomic group rather than the middle class. The availability of support and training in infant stimulation and mothering techniques will also affect the competence of retarded adults to function as parents.

The rights of mentally retarded individuals to express themselves sexually, to marry, or to reproduce will remain controversial for some time. However, our past means of coping with these issues—through isolation of the retarded, mass sterilization, and legal and physical prohibitions—have proven to be largely ineffective, dehumanizing, contradictory to our belief of normalization, and damaging to the individual and possibly to society in general. Mentally retarded people are sexual beings. Given their intellectual limitations, they need support and guidance in this area. Appropriate training, information, and an awareness of alternatives are necessary if mentally retarded adults are to be able to direct their sexual needs and energy into personally and socially constructive channels.

LIFELONG LEARNING

Continuing education has received growing emphasis in our country as a means towards professional advancement, a recreational outlet, and an opportunity to enrich life. It is becoming more necessary as society becomes more complex. Community colleges and universities have begun offering many credit and noncredit courses at low fees to encourage the participation of the general public. For the most part, such opportunities have been limited to the intellectually "normal."

Recently, however, it has been recognized that mentally retarded adults not only have a right to continue their education beyond the public school years, but they also have a great need to do so. As retarded people learn slowly, they must continue their training in community living skills beyond age 22 if they are to adapt to the changes in our society and reach the maximum level of independence. Lifelong learning is simply a logical endeavor for retarded adults. At some community colleges, special programs, which recruit and provide educational services to retarded adults, have been established.

In answer to those needs, adult education programs for the mentally retarded have begun. Based on the Metro College for Living in Denver, Colorado, and Night College in Austin, Texas, over 25 programs have been developed across the country since 1970. These programs emphasize and enact the concept of normalization—over 75% are held on college or university campuses and operate during normal hours. The students select their classes, register and pay fees, arrange their own transportation as independently as possible, and have a responsibility to attend. Although most of these programs are still coordinated and funded by special (not generic) services, an impetus for their adoption by regular continuing education facilities is growing.

These colleges serve as a meaningful activity for retarded persons during their leisure hours. They emphasize daily living skills and functional academics, such as those outlined in Table 15.1. They also provide an opportunity for retarded adults to socialize and develop a group of college friends. Teachers are usually volunteers from the local university programs or the community in general, and are trained in the basics of classroom management and the learning characteristics of retarded students.

The College for Living and Night College programs have broadened the opportunities for retarded adults to expand their behavioral repertoires and to participate in activities that foster dignity, responsibility, and contribution. They are a source of pride for the participants, and provide first-hand experiences for persons interested in pursuing careers in the human service field. Because they use regular college campuses and community resources, they also help educate the nonretarded about the potential of the handicapped. In the words of a Night College teacher from Charlottesville, Virginia,

> When I took my legal rights class on the bus to go register to vote for the coming election, we got the usual stares from the other passengers as two of my students had Down syndrome and elicited the "Ah, yes, that one's retarded" looks. Yet the

TABLE 15.1 Course Offerings—Night College, Charlottesville, Virginia

I. Communication	**III. Sex Education, Hygiene, and Personal Adjustment**
Talk and Say A Lot	Looking Good
Keep on Talking	You and Others I
Community Checklist	You and Others II
For Your Own Writing	Understanding Yourself
Using the Telephone	**IV. Community Education**
The Communication Workshop	Riding the City Bus
II. Money and Money Management	How to Find and Keep a Job
Money Skills Assessment	Know Your Community I
Simple Money	Know Your Community II
Money I	Living on Your Own
Money II	First Aid and Home Safety
Using Your Money	Driver's Education
Community Checklist	What's Cooking: The Basics in Good Eating
Budgeting	**V. Leisure Time**
Opening a Checking Account	Fun in your Free Time
	Bicycle Safety
	Swimming and Water Safety
	Art and Nature
	Photography

> stares really increased as my students' discussion on pari-mutuel
> betting and the zoning ordinance was overheard. Intelligent
> words from faces thought to hold blank minds—that was a real
> education for those people on the bus!

Some higher functioning mentally retarded individuals enter into military service as a means of pursuing postsecondary training. How well they do in their military occupations is not well documented; however, they may encounter problems, as highlighted by Patton and Polloway (1982):

> For those not familiar with military service, some of the more
> recognizable military demands placed on the person involve orga-
> nization, discipline, socialization, and following directions and
> orders. In addition, various academic skills may be necessary,
> depending on the soldier's duties or military occupational spe-
> cialty [MOS]. (p. 81)

ADVOCACY

Advocacy has been defined as the representation of the rights and interests of oneself or others in an effort to bring about change which will eliminate barriers to meeting identified needs. During the past two decades, advocacy has become a popular and potent consumer movement.

Social services have been criticized for resisting changes, being bogged down in red tape, being inaccessible, slow to move, and impersonal (Wolfensberger, 1972). Communities are still imposing legal and social bulwarks against the retarded. Parents of retarded children, retarded adults themselves, and interested friends have begun to actively and collectively remove these barriers by investigating the services needed by retarded individuals, evaluating the appropriateness of those services delivered, and serving as catalysts for changes. Operating on a one-to-one basis or as a group, through long-term relationships or in times of crisis, within the courts or at the supermarkets, advocates identify, protect, and assert the rights and interests of mentally retarded people within our society. In addition to helping handicapped citizens receive needed services and opportunities, advocates also serve as models of acceptance and thus help change public attitudes towards persons with disabilities. Several types of advocacy now exist.

Systems and legal advocacy have been highly instrumental in affecting legislation such as P.L. 94-142 and in altering the nature of many institutions and improving the quality of those remaining. Citizen advocates have played a major role in the lives of many retarded persons, helping them to get jobs, stay in school, learn to ride the bus or use the bank, and providing a sense of caring and companionship to individuals

TABLE 15.2 Types of Advocacy

Systems (Corporate) Advocacy

Advocacy by:	An independent collective of citizens
In order to:	Represent the rights and interests of groups of people with similar needs
	Pursue human service system quality and progressive change

Legal Advocacy

Advocacy by:	Attorneys-at-law
In order to:	Represent individuals or groups of individuals in the litigation or legal negotiation process

Self-Advocacy

Advocacy by:	Individuals whose rights are at risk of being violated or diminished
In order to:	Represent one's own rights and interests; speak on one's own behalf

Citizen Advocacy

Advocacy by:	A mature, competent, volunteer citizen
In order to:	Represent, as if they were his own, the rights and interests of another citizen

who often have few friends. Self-advocacy is a much newer concept and is growing through efforts such as People First, which is a movement of retarded individuals who have organized themselves on local, state, and national levels, to identify common needs and develop lobbying power.

Though a relatively new social movement, advocacy has been heralded as the major force which can and will assure success for the mentally retarded individual within our communities.

SPECIFIC SERVICES IN THE COMMUNITY

It seems quite logical to say that any given community differs on many dimensions from any other community. However, certain services may be universally needed for enhancing the life of mentally retarded adults. Everyone needs certain services in order to maintain a certain standard of successful living. Gilhool (1976) has presented a system for categorizing services into four types.

1. Type I services—Available to all citizens; retarded would use, as would general population (e.g., garbage collection, police protection, education, employment services);
2. Type II services—Available to all citizens; retarded would use in special ways (e.g., access to buildings);
3. Type III services—Available only to some citizens; retarded would use if they qualify in "some" category (e.g., public assistance, Medicare, Medicaid);
4. Type IV services—Available only to mentally retarded citizens (e.g., supervised residential services).

Gilhool suggests that type I and type III services are most often the services from which mentally retarded individuals have been excluded in the past. Education would fall under type I.

Regardless of the classification system used, certain basic services should be afforded the mentally retarded citizen who lives in the community and retarded adults should be taught to use them. Table 15.3 briefly explains the major areas that need to be considered. While most of the services presented in Table 15.3 relate to Gilhool's type IV, access to other, more common services generally available to the total citizenry is also needed. Many communities have established a system of service delivery whereby those services listed in the table are being provided. Other communities, often located in less urbanized areas, suffer from inadequate and insufficient mechanisms for providing these essential services. It is of paramount importance that communities make every effort to meet the needs of those special citizens who may need special services.

TABLE 15.3 Essential Services for Retarded and Other Handicapped Persons

Category	Description

1. Developmental programs
  a. Day activity
  b. Education
  c. Training
	Includes a variety of educational and care programs appropriate for a person's age and severity of handicapping conditions.

2. Residential services
  a. Domiciliary
  b. Special living
    arrangements
	Includes out-of-home living quarters: 24-hour lodging and supervision, and less supervised living arrangements for less severely handicapped persons (e.g., supervised apartment).

3. Employment services
  a. Preparation
  b. Sheltered (including work
    activity)
  c. Competitive
	Includes a continuum of vocational evaluation, training, and work opportunity in supervised and independent settings.

4. Identification services
  a. Diagnosis
  b. Evaluation
	Includes efforts to identify presence of disabilities and their probable cause(s), and to assess and plan service needs of the disabled person.

5. Facilitating services
  a. Information and referral
  b. Counseling
  c. Protective and socio-legal
  d. Follow-along
  e. Case management
	Includes a variety of actions needed to insure that disabled persons are informed of available services, assisted in getting services, provided protection of rights and guardianship if needed, and given continued review of plans to insure that services are appropriately delivered.

6. Treatment services
  a. Medical
  b. Dental
	Includes appropriate medical care, prosthetic devices needed for maximum adjustment, and dental care.

7. Transportation	Transportation to training, work, and other activities.
8. Leisure and recreation	Structured and unstructured leisure opportunities as needed.

From E. I. Meyen, *Exceptional Children and Youth: An Introduction*, Denver: Love Publishing, 1978. Reprinted by permission.

EMERGING AREAS OF CONCERN

Many variables affecting the adjustment of the mentally retarded adult within the community have arisen during the recent renewal of emphasis on normalization. It would be impossible to discuss all the persons who have fallen between the cracks, the areas neglected or lagging behind, or the new trends and resources which have recently developed. However, we will highlight some of these issues as areas of future concern.

THE MENTALLY RETARDED OFFENDER

One area worthy of study that has drawn the attention of only few professionals is the problems arising when mentally retarded persons encounter the criminal justice and correctional systems. While retarded criminals are not necessarily a new phenomenon, there have been relatively few efforts to address this issue. In general, studies indicate that the majority of those people incarcerated in state prisons are "undereducated, underskilled, and come from culturally and financially impoverished backgrounds" (March, Friel, & Eissler, 1975, p. 21).

Some studies have estimated that close to 10% of the total prison population could be classified "legitimately" as mentally retarded (Brown & Courtless, 1967). If we extend this consideration to those individuals who are in the borderline range of retardation, then estimates of "exceptional offenders" in the penal system increase to 40%. A special article appearing recently in *The Washington Post*, while suggesting a conservative estimate of 5% of the prison population as mentally retarded, highlights the extent of the problem.

> There are at least 25,000 retarded people in the nation's prisons, and some studies suggest that the number may be double that, or triple. This means that possibly one out of every 20 of the 500,000 prisoners in the United States is mentally retarded. Their crimes include murder and armed robbery, but many are more innocuous offenses, such as "cheating" cab drivers because they didn't understand about paying. (DeSilva, 1980)

Although there definitely seems to be a disproportionate number of mentally retarded people in the penal system, the implication that mental retardation causes criminality should be avoided. Biklen (1977), in reference to the high estimates of the number of mentally retarded individuals in prison, suggests that "the figure may not reflect any greater propensity of the mentally retarded than other segments of the general population toward crime" (p. 52). Then what explanation might there be for this disproportionality? The hypotheses offered to account for this overrepresentation revolve around two major domains: (*a*) certain characteristics of mentally retarded people and (*b*) the functions of the legal-correctional system. The problems encountered by the exceptional offender are not solely limited to the criminal justice system, but extend into the correctional system as well.

The criminal justice system   Just how an individual enters the criminal justice system varies from case to case. Biklen (1977) presents three plausible explanations for why a disproportionate number of mentally retarded people wind up in prison.

1. Retarded persons may be at risk of being easily influenced by delinquent peers;
2. The retarded may have far fewer occupational roles available to them and so may choose crime as an available activity;

3. The retarded may experience greater frustration than the average person in a highly competitive society and thus may choose delinquency as an act of rebellion. (p. 52)

Another hypothesis suggests that the mentally retarded criminal lacks many of those skills that are necessary for avoiding being caught. In addition, some professionals suggest that being a criminal may give some individuals certain status that they would not achieve from normal community living. Finally, many mentally retarded individuals may not comprehend that they are breaking the law and that their actions may carry certain unpleasant consequences. Another relevant consideration may be the low socioeconomic status of many retarded adults.

After a person allegedly has committed a criminal act, some type of intake procedure ensues. At this point, some potential problems can develop. First, many law enforcement officials are not able to recognize that a person is mentally retarded, sometimes resulting in the unfair handling of such a suspect. Second, often confessions are obtained quite readily from the mentally retarded offender who wants to please authority figures or who is intimidated by threatening language used in interrogation. Third, even though there are programs that have been designed to inform mentally retarded adults of their legal rights, few individuals who are arrested are aware of their constitutional rights.

As we progress through the criminal justice process, we note that more problems emerge at the adjudication stage. The following list summarizes these obstacles to justice.

1. Competency to stand trial—A mentally retarded person found incompetent to stand trial may be receiving the equivalent of a life sentence without parole, as the trial is merely delayed until competency is achieved. For all practical purposes, mentally retarded offenders probably will not become competent. In the case of *Jackson v. Indiana* (1972), the Supreme Court ruled that an individual could only be held for a "reasonable" length of time, at which time either civil commitment procedures must be initiated or the person must be released.

2. Insanity plea—This plea actually pertains to the issue of culpability for one's actions. At the present time, much confusion still remains over the suitability of the insanity defense with mentally retarded offenders. Even if a person is relieved of criminal culpability by virtue of insanity, commitment proceedings would most likely be initiated.

3. Plea bargaining—It is not uncommon for the sake of expediency to "plea bargain" many cases (that is, the offender agrees to plead guilty to a lesser charge). In effect, rather than going to

trial with a plea of "not guilty" or attempting to establish an insanity defense (which are both time consuming and expensive), a plea bargain is obtained, most likely resulting in imprisonment.

4. Court appointed counsel—Marsh and colleagues capture the essence of this problem: "Court appointed attorneys often do not have the time to expend as much effort on an indigent as a regular client" (1975, p. 24).

5. Probation—In order to be placed on probation rather than be incarcerated in many areas, it is necessary for an individual to have or gain steady employment. For many mentally retarded individuals this may not be likely (Marsh et al., 1975).

With these and other obstacles facing the mentally retarded offender, it is no wonder that an inordinate number of them enter the penal system.

The mentally retarded offender in the correctional system For most, if not all, of those individuals imprisoned, the experience is one of brutality, degradation, frustration, helplessness, and loneliness. Mentally retarded individuals who are placed in harsh prison environments can be quite susceptible and vulnerable to this institutional lifestyle.

To this day, there are very few prison programs designed for the exceptional offender. Marsh and associates recognized this problem and offered a reason for it.

> Since prisons are not designed to treat the mentally retarded, it is no surprise that little programming exists that attends to this group's special needs. Furthermore, the low funding priority of most correctional systems insures that programs must be geared to the average rather than the retarded inmate. (1975, pp. 24–25)

To maximize treatment and habilitation of handicapped offenders in the correctional system, Menolascino (1974) stated that it is necessary to consider three major areas: (*a*) classification and diagnosis; (*b*) treatment; and (*c*) pre-release planning and parole. He went on to explain the implications.

> With early identification of the degree of retardation and emotional problems (if any), a more realistic approach may be made to an individual's rehabilitation needs. The treatment of a retarded offender must include special education and vocational training so that the offender acquires the skills to get along in the outside world. Lastly, halfway houses (Keller & Alper, 1970) should be utilized for the transition from a correctional institution to the community, buttressed by a strengthened system of parole officers who are trained to manage retarded offenders with a more humanistic approach that stresses acceptance and hope. (p. 9)

Some correctional centers have developed distinct units for mentally retarded offenders; often these units are referred to as units for the developmentally disabled. Regardless of the name, the intent of these units is to provide specialized services for these handicapped offenders. Although there are some problems inherent in this type of program (for instance, lack of trained staff), this is definitely a step in the right direction.

We have attempted to highlight some of the more important issues connected with mentally retarded offenders. We hope that as more attention is given to their needs and problems, more pervasive, systematic, and effective services will be observed in an effort to assure the right to treatment.

ELDERLY MENTALLY RETARDED ADULTS

Elderly retarded adults have been called an "invisible" population. Community programs typically focus on serving the retarded child or young adult, and do not seek or identify the aged. Little research has been conducted on the characteristics of the elderly retarded—where and how they live, how they age physiologically and sociologically. Yet given our knowledge of the community adjustment patterns of the retarded in general, and the experiences of the nondisabled aged in our society, we can make certain assumptions about lifestyles of elderly mentally retarded people in our communities.

1. They are likely to be unemployed, given the general attitudes towards the retarded and old age.

2. They are likely to have severely reduced incomes and savings, as the retarded generally have short employment records and usually earn minimum wages.

3. Their interaction with the community will be minimal. Most elderly persons in our society live in protected or isolated settings such as nursing homes or boarding houses for the aged.

4. Their intellectual abilities will decrease. This is true for the normal population, though it has been hypothesized that mentally retarded people's IQs may decrease faster than those of their nonretarded age mates (Dickerson et al., 1974).

5. The changes and functional losses experienced by all aging persons may be experienced by the retarded at an earlier age (45 or 50), due to an actual speeded-up aging process or the community's reaction to their physical and functional gray hairs (Dickerson, Hamilton, Huber, & Segal, 1974).

Despite the apparent marginal existence of elderly retarded people, this group and their daily health, economic, social, and housing needs have been largely ignored or neglected. There are many possible reasons why services to the elderly retarded are few and far between (Hamilton & Segal, 1975).

1. There are not very many professionals familiar with the gerontological aspects of mental retardation.
2. The elderly are often dependent on others for transportation, and service locations are often not accessible.
3. Funding is scarce.
4. There is no agency to coordinate existing services.
5. Generic service programs are reluctant to view the elderly retarded as clients.
6. Community attitudes towards the retarded tend to be negative.
7. Most people are unaware of problems of elderly retarded people.

Because elderly retarded adults remain an unidentified group without a strong cohesive consumer voice, their problems have not been addressed in most communities by generic or special services. However, within the past five years, several service agencies and private organizations across the country have begun to recognize the special needs of this group. Many innovative programs have developed, including specialized employment opportunities, self-awareness and assertiveness groups, social-recreational programs, special dental care, and appropriate housing options.

Mentally retarded persons are now living longer due to advances in medicine and social practices; yet we are just beginning to address their right to grow old with dignity. Much still needs to be done with regard to professional knowledge, community awareness, and personal preparation if we are to expand the principles and philosophy of normalization to this population, and recognize our responsibilities to retarded persons of all ages.

SERVICES TO RURAL COMMUNITIES

Community services for retarded citizens have developed rapidly in urban areas during the past 15 years or so. The development of these comprehensive services and resources, however, has not been as rapid or as extensive in less populated rural areas. Rural communities, for the most part, still remain less receptive to and unprepared for the integration of retarded individuals and are often unable to maintain handicapped persons within community residential facilities.

A dispersed population, distance from professional services, small base with which to fund programs, transportation difficulties, and the rural tendency toward preference for independence and resistance to outside influence have been cited as reasons for this lag in the development of services, despite recent legal and social changes (Talkington, 1971). The number of handicapped persons identified greatly exceeds the services available for them in most rural areas. This disparity between services needed and provided has forced many rural families to institutionalize their retarded member. Where most communities are now only institutionalizing their more severely and profoundly retarded and multiply handicapped children, the admissions from rural areas still include larger numbers of higher functioning individuals who need special education and vocational services (Talkington, 1971).

It is critical that services be extended from the regional centers of more populated areas to these rural districts, and more preferably, that local rural resources be developed to serve those in need. Several projects along these lines have begun. Some institutions and social service agencies are establishing diagnostic, evaluative counseling centers in counties, and in a few instances, shifting control of these centers to local agencies. Workshops and activity centers have also been developed in some rural areas, although transportation and the need for extensive outreach services remain as blocks to effective and far-reaching support services within rural areas.

SUMMARY

More attention, in our opinion, needs to be directed toward the issues of mentally retarded adults living in the community. This chapter has attempted to sensitize you to many of these issues. With the continuing trend toward keeping handicapped adults in community settings, we will need to provide these individuals with a full range of appropriate services. To accomplish this task, it is important to understand the major problems, to recognize the complex nature of these problems, and to formulate ways of addressing them. In this chapter, we have reviewed the issues of community adjustment, what it is like to live in the community for the mentally retarded adult, some of the major problems encountered in community settings, specific services that should be available to all handicapped people, and some areas that need to receive more professional attention and effort.

PART FIVE
Future

Future Horizons

As futurists . . . we are like Pointillist painters of the Neo-Impressionist period. We paint large and small dots which do not provide a holistic image or "feel" for a future. The reason is clear: Unless we confine ourselves to strictly technological systems, it is exceedingly difficult to consider the tremendous number of elements and interactions between them which are characterisic of complex human and societal systems. It is not yet possible to deal simultaneously with a very large number of variables (some quantitative and some qualitative) so as to minimize disharmony or discordance in the total system. Thus our scenarios for the future are more like a series of dots on the the canvas than a cohesive image. (Linstone, 1977, p. 3)

The purpose of this chapter is to suggest a few of the "dots" that may eventually contribute to a holistic image of the field of mental retardation in the future. This task will include a mixture of forecasting of new issues and projection of present needs into the future.

This chapter was contributed by James R. Patton.

PREDICTING THE FUTURE

As Linstone suggests, the challenge of predicting the future is a monumental one. Basically, predictions of what will transpire at some later date are based on what we already know. Some error must always be acknowledged in any prediction, because we cannot foresee certain unknown, intervening variables which will affect the future. Nevertheless, we must persevere in our efforts and at very least try "to anticipate the consequences of alternative courses of action" (President's Committee on Mental Retardation, 1976b, p. 38).

The business of certain agencies, institutions, and professions is largely that of prediction. Insurance companies, for instance, rest their profit margins on their ability to predict certain statistics (life expectancies, number of auto accidents, injuries, and deaths; thefts and fires, etc.). Institutions of higher learning use certain variables such as high school grade point average and SAT scores to predict success in college. Meteorologists live and die by making predictions. Since they are constantly being evaluated by the public, they are highly accountable for their forecasts. Prognosis is also used in medicine. In all of these examples, we can see that certain events are projected from existing facts.

Those of us interested in the field of mental retardation are very much concerned about where we have been, where we are today, and where we will be in the future. As mentioned previously, the best we can do without the gift of clairvoyance is to base our hunches on the trends and changes that the field of special education is presently experiencing. Social forecaster John Naisbitt based his popular, insightful *Megatrends* on this premise: "The most reliable way to anticipate the future is by understanding the present" (p. xxiii). Unfortunately, that persistent element of the unknown lurks before us; therefore, to adopt a simplistic view of the future denies the possibility of major turning points or what Kuhn (1970) calls revolutionary change in scientific thinking. On this note, Naisbitt points out that, while certain broad tendencies can be noted (e.g., the shift from a national to a world economy), no one can predict what specific form our future society will take. Attempts to describe it in detail, he feels, "are the stuff of science fiction and futuristic guessing games" (p. xxiii). A simplistic view of the future ignores the impact of sociopolitical factors that can significantly alter the course of events.

JOURNEY INTO THE FUTURE

Mindful of these cautions, let us begin our venture into the future. We make no pretense to be able to predict the future of special education à la Huxley, Orwell, Wells, Asimov, or Rodenberry, although much of what will be suggested may seem as fantastic as their works. Nonetheless, as the validation of many notions presented in *Brave New World* proves, the line between fiction and reality is a tenuous one, and even the most extravagant predictions can become credible.

The major topics addressed in this chapter are general in nature and by no means exhaustive of the possibilities. They were chosen because they exemplify certain ongoing trends and suggest likely future directions. We merely ask that you be aware of the complexities of prediction, the many facets of the area of mental retardation, and the interaction of both of these. Most importantly, we suggest that you be imaginative and creative, extending your thinking even beyond what we will present.

CHANGES IN SOCIETY

Before we can approach topical issues, it is essential that we understand the changes and influences which our society will probably experience. The social and economic structure of mankind has progressed through three major stages (hunting and gathering, agricultural, and industrial) and is currently in a fourth stage (postindustrial).

The pressures placed on an individual vary significantly with the unique demands of a given social system. The ability to succeed in school was not very important in the agricultural society of the 18th century where manual labor was esteemed. The industrial revolution introduced new social demands characterized by the need for semi-skilled and skilled workers; training for these jobs and certain requisite abilities became mandatory for success in this era. As we advance from an industrial to a postindustrial society, the types of skills demanded by social institutions, and particularly by the workplace, have begun to change dramatically. Naisbitt (1984) presented the following information.

> MIT's David Birch has demonstrated that of the 19 million new jobs created in the United States during the 1970s—more than ever before in our history—only 5% were in manufacturing and only 11% in the goods-producing sector as a whole. Almost 90%, then—17 million new jobs—were not in the goods-producing sector. (p. 8)

Linstone (1977) posits that the years ahead will be characterized by the themes of *communication* and *information*. He states that "The change from an energy to an information society is of such depth and magnitude that it boggles the mind" (p. 5). To Naisbitt (1984), the "restructuring of America from an industrial to an information society will easily be as profound as the shift from an agricultural society to an industrial society" (p. 9). While the transition from agriculture to industry took 100 years, the shift from an industrial to information-based society has taken only 20. Naisbitt believes the change has happened so quickly that many people are only just now realizing it.

The implications for mentally retarded persons in this new era of social and economic structure are profound. On the one hand, there will be more of a demand for knowledge and intelligence, as Sagan (1977) envisions. These emerging demands could portend more problems for those who are mentally retarded. On the other hand, however, the application of new technological and scientific advances resulting from the demands for the acquisition of more knowledge could forecast optimism for mentally retarded individuals, particularly in the areas of prevention and programming.

EMERGING CONCERNS

Commensurate with the technological advances characteristic of this hypothesized postindustrial social structure, noticeable changes will also emerge in terms of social attitudes and perhaps the concept of retardation itself. At this point, let us speculate on what we may be able to expect in the future. Note that in the sections that follow, there may at times be a fine distinction between what we predict will happen and what we would like to see happen.

ATTITUDES

Attitudes are eminently important because they are usually indices to behavior. Harth (1977) remarks that attitudes "represent a verbal statement about how one feels toward a particular construct" and later goes on to say that "people hold rather strong and divergent attitudes about mental retardation" (p. 4). This becomes quite noteworthy in regard to the mentally retarded population, when we consider that attitudes are highly correlated with the availability of services and programs, the interactions of people with the mentally retarded, and the self-esteem of the retarded individual (Guskin, 1977).

Historically, social attitudes toward deviant populations or individuals have placed the blame for the deviancy upon those who, for various reasons, are different. Ryan's (1976) powerful book, *Blaming the Victim*, describes this phenomenon as it relates to placing the blame for poverty on its victims. As a result of this type of thinking, most intervention programs are designed to change the individual but not the system. Rappaport (1977) proposes that what is required is a paradigm which involves a "person-environment fit," emphasizing the relationship between individuals and their social and physical environment. A perspective that includes this notion of person-environment fit would benefit the mentally retarded by encouraging society to look more broadly at the full range of potentialities, needs, and problems of mentally retarded citizens. Society must move away from blaming the person to a more transactional model. There are signs that this is beginning to happen.

One alternative perspective has been suggested by Bogdan (1980). He is skeptical of the concept of mental retardation and considers it to be socially constructed. His approach is to look at mental retardation through the eyes of those who are retarded—a view seldom solicited. Bogdan remarks that "this approach involves suspending, as much as possible, one's own assumptions about people one talks to and attempting to see the world from their perspective" (p. 75). Adopting this perspective, we are likely to get a very different view of what retardation is.

Prevalence figures owe their existence to definitions and to other variables that may influence them (e.g., age, sex, geography). Most professionals now support prevalence figures of 1% or lower over the often-cited figure of 3%. These lower figures are reflected in the recent data on the number of students classified as mentally retarded and served in the schools (refer to figure 2.4). Whether the decreases witnessed over the last few years will continue remains to be seen. Nevertheless, these changes may have a significant effect on how we conceptualize and provide services to this population, as Smith and Polloway (1983) have clearly suggested. It seems likely that we may need to pay more attention to those students whom we call *slow learners* for two reasons: (a) they have typically been in need of special assistance; and (b) this group is becoming more populated by students who were formerly served in special education.

There are strong pressures in the field of special education to reexamine the process and the effects of labeling individuals as *mentally retarded*. To date, there still is no strong evidence that negative effects result from labeling students mentally retarded (Gottlieb & Leyser, 1981; MacMillan, Jones, & Aloia, 1974). However, many professionals are concerned about labeling and efforts to evaluate its effects are warranted.

Seeking to update conventional views on the nature of mental deficiency, Mercer (1973a; 1977) conceptualized retardation from a sociological perspective in terms of "an achieved social status in a social system" (p. 3) and of role expectations. In this model, appropriate behavior varies from role to role; as a result, mental retardation is suspected when certain role expectations are not fulfilled.

As time progresses, let us hope that classification models stress more often the notions of adaptive behavior, cultural factors, various social roles, and person-system interaction, as Hobbs (1975) described.

> The development of a classification system that takes into account (for individual children in particular settings) assets and liabilities, strengths and weaknesses, linked to specified services required to increase the former and decrease the latter. (Hobbs, 1975, p. 281)

Definitions should recognize that individuals vary considerably and consequently have different needs. Hallahan and Kauffman (1976)

EMERGING DEVELOPMENTS IN PRENATAL ASSESSMENT

The following article describes a new technique, *chorion biopsy*, that can detect various prenatal abnormalities. It seems to have some distinct advantages over other current techniques like amniocentesis.

Prenatal Testing 'Revolution' Reported

BAR HARBOR, Maine (AP)—A new method for detecting birth defects and determining sex as early as the seventh week of pregnancy will "revolutionize" prenatal testing, says the first American doctor to use the technique.

The procedure, called chorion biopsy, will someday be as routine as amniocentesis, the current prenatal testing method, said Dr. Eugene Pergament of Michael Reese Hospital and Medical Center in Chicago.

Like amniocentesis, chorion biopsy can be used to detect such disorders as Down's syndrome and sickle-cell anemia and to determine the sex of the fetus. However, while the results of amniocentesis are not available until about the 20th week of pregnancy, chorion biopsy yields results by the seventh to 10th week.

If defects are found, the mother can elect to have an abortion, which is much simpler and safer during the first three months of pregnancy than it is later.

Pergament told The Associated Press that he has used the new technique on six women. One elected to have an abortion when the test showed that her child had one too many copies of chromosome 16. Pergament said the child would not have survived.

IN ANOTHER, the procedure was unsuccessful, but it did not affect her pregnancy, Pergament said. The other four women are having normal pregnancies and should give birth in four to five months, he said.

The new technique was described recently during a seminar on genetics at Jackson Laboratory in Bar Harbor.

propose the use of a broad definition of mild handicaps, with the concomitant use of as many behaviorally specific descriptors as necessary.

> Many children could then acquire multiple labels, but with such a degree of behavioral specificity the labels would perhaps be less pejorative and facilitate communication among professionals and lay persons alike. (p. 29)

This approach meshes neatly with Hobbs' (1975) suggestions and remains attractive to this day.

Regardless of changes in the professionally accepted concept of mental retardation, this term will probably remain in our vocabularies. Public interpretation of the term will continue to be a significant variable

Chorion biopsy is done by inserting a tube through the mouth of the womb and snipping a tiny sample of tissue from the chorion, the precursor of the placenta. Because the chorion has the same genes as the fetus, it can be examined for genetic information.

Amniocentesis—sampling of the fluid around the fetus—cannot be done until at least the 16th week, because there is not enough fluid present before then.

Also, amniocentesis captures so few cells that it takes four weeks to grow the cells and test them for defects.

Chorion biopsy allows the testing to be completed in a day or less.

Two other research groups, at Thomas Jefferson University in Philadelphia and at Yale University, are also experimenting with the technique, but they have not yet used it to make a diagnosis.

DR. LAIRD Jackson, leader of the group at Thomas Jefferson, said it is of "overwhelming" importance to diagnose birth defects in the seventh to 10th week rather than the 20th week.

"This is a distinctly different time than a five-month pregnancy, where you've seen something that looks like a baby when you've done the ultrasound," he said. A seven-week fetus is just 4 inches long.

The procedure may also eventually allow certain birth defects to be corrected, said Dr. John Hobbins, head of the Yale group.

"It may herald a whole new era of fetal treatment," he said. "In some cases we're going to be able to do something by being aware of it (a birth defect) early."

Chorion biopsy has already been tried on a small number of patients in the Soviet Union, China, England and Italy, Pergament said.

In Milan, Dr. Bruno Brombati used it with at least 72 women, Pergament said. The procedure caused miscarriages in two of Brombati's patients, according to Hobbins.

The researchers all agreed that the procedure seems to be safe, but more testing is needed to prove it.

Honolulu Star-Bulletin Friday, August 26, 1983

---

in society's treatment of its mentally retarded citizens. For this reason, our efforts should be directed toward fostering favorable attitudes toward the retarded and removing the stigma associated with the label.

Professional interest over the last few years has shifted away from mildly retarded people toward the more severely retarded (Patton & Payne, 1985; Strichart & Gottlieb, 1983). Haywood (1979) remarked that, while there has been a demonstrable redirection of resources away from moderately and mildly retarded persons, there has been "an increase in the volume of research and services directed toward severe and profound retardation" (p. 429). All of these groups require professional inquiry, yet one should not be sacrificed for the sake of the other.

Granted that there are many vital areas associated with the field of mental retardation which could be addressed, we have selected five broad categories as worthy of attention. Within these topical areas, numerous other issues are revealed. Much of what is presented represents either an update of current research and technology, reflections on what needs to be, or thoughts about what might be.

PREVENTION

In March of 1976, the President's Committee on Mental Retardation published its report to the president entitled *Mental Retardation: Century of Decision*. In this publication, the committee listed a number of goals, objectives, and recommendations which were to be achieved before the year 2000. Two of these goals are directly associated with prevention.

> Goal: At least 50% reduction in the incidence of mental retardation from biomedical causes by the year 2000.
>
> Goal: Reduction of the incidence and prevalence of mental retardation associated with social disadvantages to the lowest level possible by the end of this century. (pp. 135, 137)

Prevention is a critical factor in controlling the incidence of mental retardation. However, it is interesting that few programs exist which are directed toward primary prevention (Begab, 1981). In this section, we will review some of the breakthroughs already achieved and consider the future.

A statistical feature common to both biomedical and psychosocial prevention that bears mentioning is birth rate. This is a critical dimension in that it directly influences the incidence of mental retardation—as birth rate increases, so does the number of children who will be diagnosed as *retarded*. Furthermore, as society becomes technologically more sophisticated, a conflict arises between our ability to prevent some mental retardation by technical means and the fact that infants who would not have survived in the past can now be kept alive and will survive due to technical advances. This conflict raises critical ethical, moral, and legal questions.

Biomedical issues Biomedical intervention will undoubtedly have a great impact on the prevention of retardation in the future. Biomedical intervention programs can be introduced at the preconceptive, prenatal, birth/perinatal, and postnatal stages of development.

Preconceptive prevention is a type of "quality control" (Fletcher, 1974). Smith and Smith (1978) stated that techniques safeguarding quality control and preventing mental retardation before conception include proper immunization against certain diseases, proper nutritional standards, diagnostic genetic intervention, and proper family planning. We can easily see that these strategies require some type of education or dissemination of information to prospective parents. Since the purpose of these techniques is to prevent mental retardation prior to conception, they rely heavily on early identification of high-risk situations. Genetic counseling can provide critical information for family planning after certain diagnostic tests have been executed. Panati (1980) reported that, in 1980, over 200 genetic counseling centers were operating in the United States. Most of these provide fetal analysis and immediate postnatal testing in addition to screening prospective parents. Often, genetic analysis will identify carriers of defective genes whose future offspring have a chance of being affected. Therefore, the ability to detect this situation early—before conception—can have a dramatic effect on prevention.

As a result of genetic counseling, some parents are now faced with the decision of whether or not to have children. On the horizon, however, there is hope that some, if not all, of these genetic problems can be resolved eventually before conception. Scientists from many fields (genetics, cytology, biomedicine, biochemistry, and molecular biology, among others) are combining their talents, expertise, and research in the promising scientific area called *cytogenetics*, the branch of biology that deals with the study of heredity and variations (Fletcher, 1974). For example, earlier in this decade, medical researchers from Harvard, Yale, and Boston's Children's Hospital Medical Center developed a technique in which a *single gene* can be isolated and examined for flaws. In this process, chemical agents called restriction enzymes are used to slice a

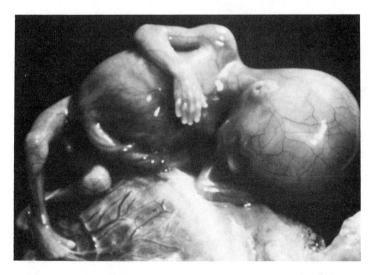

Not too long ago, photographs of a fetus *in utero* were the stuff of science fiction. Perhaps surgery *in utero* to correct deformities will be possible—if not commonplace—in the near future.

IS THERE A CURE FOR MENTAL RETARDATION?

The following article, which appeared in *The ARC News*, examines whether mental retardation can be "cured." As discussed in this chapter, it is foolish to consider whether we can cure all forms of mental retardation. What the following information compiled by ARC does do, however, is elaborate on some emerging technology in which research is attempting to ameliorate many forms of mental retardation having biological/organic etiologies.

What are the prenatal, perinatal, and postnatal origins of mental retardation? When should we have treatment intervention? If we could focus on how cells move out into the brain's network, could we find a cure? When is the circulatory system of the brain developed? What is known about effects of peptides in the brain? How can we tell if we cure mentally retarded people?

Treatment and cure are dependent on knowing the causes. The scientists agreed that locating and understanding a cause, and then interrupting it before it affects the nervous system is the first step to be achieved in the search for cures. And the causes are many. They may occur during fetal development or after birth. They may be inherited. Mental retardation can also result from childhood diseases, such as measles, or from accidents which result in brain damage. At least 250 factors, either alone or in combinations, have been identified or suspected as causes in the occurrence of mental retardation.

Relating the cell biology of the brain to specific behavioral operations represents one of the most challenging issues facing neurobiologists. Part of the difficulty can be traced to the extreme complexity, first of behavior, and then of the brain itself. Researchers find the difficulties in establishing causal relationships of this type intimidating, if not downright overwhelming.

Scientists know that the first brain cells form a core and remain stationary while newer cells bypass this core and migrate to their proper stations. This developmental process is extremely vulnerable to disease and to the destructive forces of drugs and alcohol. When the fetus' development is hampered by the levels of alcohol consumed by the mother, brain cells sometimes form normally but position themselves abnormally. Although this mispositioning also can be due to genetic factors, most cases are associated with diseases, infection, and potentially harmful substances such as drugs and alcohol. If we could find a treatment for diseases that gain access to the developing unit, per-

DNA chain into thousands of its component genes and radioactively tag each gene *in vitro*, just as marine biologists might tag fish they wish to study. Thus isolated, a gene can be analyzed for inherent defects or missing material (Parati, 1980). Continued research such as this will lead to great advances in the emerging field of gene therapy. Unhealthy genes can be "overhauled" and defective parts replaced with healthy genetic information. The curative potential of gene therapy is stagger-

haps we could cure the mental retardation brought about by this dilemma.

Some neuroscientists have concluded that dendrites within the brain's cerebral cortex hold the key to solving the mystery of mental retardation. Dendrites are the parts of the brain's nerve cells which conduct impulses. These impulses cross a gap, or synapse, and stimulate the contact points on nearby brain cells. Research has shown that a major period of dendritic growth occurs during the last 3 months of fetal development. In the newborn brain much of this synaptic material is in place. The density of this synaptic material increases until age 12 or 14, and production of synapse points then begins to drop off. Still, some disorders can cause the branches to simply disappear, to malform, or to crumble.

Scientists also believe that neuropeptides may represent a new approach in the treatment and possible cure of mental retardation. Neuropeptides are strings of amino acids found throughout the brain. One peptide in particular which has been tested several times is melanocyte-stimulating hormone (MSH). Several studies showed that the active core of MSH improved attention. Three studies with mentally retarded individuals indicated that certain deficits, traditionally assumed to be irreversible, may be influenced by peptides. Certain enzymes which break down the peptides' amino acids and may affect the brain are also being studied. When the enzymes do not function correctly (either through insufficient or overabundant amount), the peptides cannot function properly either.

Many arguments surround the area of genetics. Some argue that "just an extra chromosome" cannot be the cause of mental retardation. Others point out that the increasing age of fathers and mothers is associated with several chromosomal disorders leading to mental retardation. It has been suggested that Down syndrome might be attributable to a particular part of a gene and not part of an extra chromosome.

There still is much more we need to know before cures will be found. We need to know more about the brain's structure. We need to know more about synaptic connections. We need new ideas about what to look for in analyzing some postnatal cases of mental retardation. We need to know more about physiology and placenta support systems. We need information on how mentally retarded people process and use data. And we need more research. The ARC (Association for Retarded Citizens) has demonstrated its leadership by undertaking the search for cures and is committed to finding answers to these questions.

ing; diabetes, hemophilia, Tay-Sachs, PKU, and even cancer could conceivably be controlled, if not eradicated, by perfecting gene transplants. The promise of this form of preconceptive medicine is great and should be encouraged. Yet it must also be monitored because it offers the opportunity for ethical abuses.

Prenatal prevention takes many forms. Adequate nutritional intake is a must for pregnant women if the birth of infants with physical and mental defects is to be prevented. Malnutrition has been shown to be associated with premature births, low birth weight, and reduced mental functioning (Begab, 1974). This problem can be controlled. Through more efficient educational programs directed toward providing proper nutritional information and through technological advances like dietary supplements or nutritional meal systems delivered by mail (Beevy, 1978), the improper nutritional health of prospective mothers could be reduced drastically or (theoretically) eliminated completely.

Prenatal techniques such as sonography, ultrasound, and amniocentesis can effectively diagnose defects in the fetus. Through amniocentesis, the most common of these procedures, it is possible to detect approximately 80 of over 2000 known genetic disorders. The ability to collect fetal information will make this technique increasingly valuable as preventative gene analysis becomes more commonplace.

If we have the instruments to detect prenatal problems today, then what options or techniques might we possibly have in the future? Currently, the typical options after detection are few—terminate the pregnancy or carry the fetus to term and deal with the defective infant. In the not-too-distant future is the possibility of embryonic medicine, where fetal surgery can be requested to redress certain deformities *in utero*. Pines (1973) describes another future possibility—the prenatal programming of the developing brain.

Although the most highly developed of early creatures, *Homo sapiens* has the unenviable distinction of being the species with the longest period of vulnerability after birth. A neonate is quite helpless, and the probability of an infant's survival without assistance and protection is scant. As we know, various birth traumas (such as anoxia and breech birth) can account for a number of conditions associated with mental retardation. Although traumatic birth episodes will always be with us, the frequency of these unfortunate events will decrease as medical techniques continue to be refined and developed.

Commensurate with the continued sophistication of medical knowledge and service delivery, the science of screening newborns for metabolic deficiencies will continue to be perfected. Defects such as PKU, hypoglycemia, galactosemia, and hypothyroidism, among others, can all be detected and subsequently treated early in an infant's life. What must be forestalled is the unacceptable paradox of researchers developing the technology but not applying it, for whatever (usually economic) reason.

As discussed in chapter 15, the issue of withholding treatment from severely handicapped infants has received, and will continue to receive, much attention. So far, the courts have supported parental sovereignty in cases of this type; however, federal legislation may change this dramatically. The Critical Issues Subcommittee on Infant Concerns of The Association for Persons with Severe Handicaps (TASH, 1984) has issued recommendations:

1. Increase public and professional awareness of the issues pertaining to infanticide/euthanasia.
2. Support of legislation that prohibits the discrimination of medical treatment to infants who are also mentally retarded.
3. Support of federal, state, and local legislation and policies that increase services to families of infants who are severely handicapped.

As far as the prevention of mental retardation in the early childhood years is concerned, Smith and Smith (1978) emphasize the need to minimize environmental hazards, implement early stimulation projects, and reduce the incidence of child abuse. Correspondingly, systematic efforts to educate the public should be encouraged. The effectiveness of these programs must be evaluated, because the mere existence of educational programs does not by any means guarantee the acquisition of needed information.

If technology and, more importantly, its application to the problems associated with mental retardation continue to blossom, then there is a real chance that the incidence of mental retardation due to biomedical causes *can* be reduced by 50% by the year 2000. But this goal will not be achieved without public support and encouragement.

Psychosocial issues   The future of the issues surrounding the psychosocial causes of retardation remains difficult to predict. The psychosocial variables of socioeconomic status, poverty, race, environment, and culture have been related to the causes of retardation; but unfortunately, the questions they raise do not lend themselves to clear solutions. It would be marvelous to eliminate poverty and to attenuate the problems faced by people of the lower socioeconomic classes, but we must be realistic. Even though the PCMR's goal of reducing the incidence and prevalence of mental retardation to the lowest level possible in the next 20 years is most admirable and even conceptually believable, we nonetheless face many entrenched institutional obstacles. Let us consider a few of them.

First, regardless of our seemingly uncontestable intentions to eliminate poverty, in actuality this goal may be impossible. The perception of poverty being eliminated may indeed be achieved, but the reality of poverty will no doubt persist. In the 1976 Report to the President (PCMR, 1976), the President's Committee cautioned that poverty should be viewed as a dual concept.

> The question of poverty is two-sided. Absolute poverty is officially measured in the United States as a fixed standard of real

> income based upon the prevailing cost of a minimum human diet. The percent of the population below this level has declined from 22.4 in 1959 to 11.9 in 1972. However, the proportionate distribution of incomes in American society has changed very little in that time, with the lowest fifth of the population receiving a steady 4.5 to 5.5 percent of the aggregate income in each year in the United States from 1947 to 1972. This creates, the futurists suggest, a persistent condition of relative poverty. Projection of the continued decline of absolute poverty to near-zero could still leave the level of relative poverty unchanged. (pp. 42–43)

Both dimensions of poverty pose continuing obstacles to the reduction of psychosocial causes of retardation in the future. Clearly, it is the institutional dimension of relative poverty which poses a continuing obstacle to the reduction of psychosocial causes of retardation in the future.

Second, our well-established notions and attitudes toward the concept of cultural deprivation may need to be redressed. Frequently, little acknowledgment is given to the strengths of children who arrive daily at school from what is believed to be a "deprived" environment. Barring the financial distinction between middle class and low socioeconomic status (SES), and the differences in educational opportunity that distinguish classes separated by income, there are few things intrinsically enriching about middle class culture that would, by contrast, render lower class environments "deprived." A child's use of nonstandard English, for example, need not spark the conclusion that the child's home life is substandard; rather, the language is a product of cultural factors not found in higher SES homes. The fact that most schools adhere to middle class mores and standards ensures that problems will arise if we insist that the student from a nonmiddle class background conform without question to this system. Ginsburg (1972) believes that children who are poor and who live in what we often refer to as "culturally deprived" environments actually have skills and strengths that are sufficient for adequate cognitive development, but that these skills and strengths are different from those of middle class children. The real tragedy may rest in the fact that "the language and intellectual skills that poor children do have are frequently ignored by the schools they attend" (Rappaport, 1977, p. 251).

As standards of living improve, as more programs directed toward upgrading impoverished areas increase, as more efforts to provide early intervention to children "at risk" for school failure are established, and as our conception of cultural deprivation matures, the opportunity to prevent cases of mental retardation due to psychosocial causes will undoubtedly increase. Generalized amelioration will only occur if there are *drastic* changes in our social structure. Such drastic changes are not likely.

TECHNOLOGY

Nowhere can we find more reason for optimism than in the application of technological advances to the area of mental retardation. Those of us in the field of special education may owe the Soviets more than we can imagine for launching Sputnik in the late 1950s; this event sparked a technological renaissance which has been felt in every aspect of our lives. Many professional disciplines have joined together to influence divergent areas of special education; this multidisciplinary flavor is embodied in the interest in human exceptionalities shared by a great many physical and social scientists, engineers, and medical personnel. The engineering field, for instance, has contributed a tremendous list of achievements that includes prosthetic limbs, speech synthesizers, recording instruments, and computerized wheelchairs. Moreover, the near future promises an updated list onto which will be added biofeedback techniques, cosmetological devices, meals delivered through the mail, and a staggering array of computer-related possibilities.

This developing technology appeals to us as a salve for many of the pressing problems of the day; yet it also creates some ethical problems.

> In science-based affairs, especially those of a biological kind like medicine, the hypothetical quickly becomes the actual. Future questions foreseen are suddenly present and pressing. The time lag is negligible between the theoretically possible and the clinically feasible. It is said that prophecy foreshortens time, that it treats what is to come as if it were a present fact. In this sense prophecy is a major part of biomedical ethics in these days. (Fletcher, 1974, p. xiv)

Obviously, one of the significant correlates to advancing technology is the ethical overlay with which we must also concern ourselves. As Linstone (1977) states, "It has become increasingly apparent in the last several years that science and technology can no longer be considered 'neutral'" (p. 18). Issues such as abortion, brain research, the withholding of treatment, the administration of controversial treatments (such as psychosurgery, chemotherapy, and electroshock), euthanasia, and aborted fetal experimentation can all be classified as "indeterminable issues" (Begelman, 1978). Their actual ethical value is not readily apparent; there is no general consensus as to what is right or wrong. As Begelman notes, "their resolution depends upon complex legal or philosophical arguments not yet established as valid" (p. 44).

Whether or not these ethical issues are amenable to philosophical solution, they must be addressed and taken seriously, especially in relation to the mentally retarded population. We know all too well that the most vulnerable are invariably the least powerful and the mentally retarded fit this "rule." Consequently, it is incumbent upon us to ensure that some form of protection is provided to this vulnerable population by legal safeguards and standards of ethical practice. Lacking such protections, technology and science, no matter how beneficial, could supersede their bounds.

SERVICES

Over the last ten years, services to people with mental retardation have been guided by the general principle that *all* retarded individuals are entitled to the same rights and privileges as nonretarded persons. Related to this is the notion that all retarded individuals can learn and benefit from the services provided. Whether most retarded individuals are receiving appropriate services is difficult to determine. Many are and many others, especially those who have been moved out of special settings, are not. With this in mind, there appear to be three major questions: (*a*) Are retarded individuals receiving necessary services? (*b*) For those who are receiving them, how are they delivered? and (*c*) What is the quality of the services? We will now examine the services available to retarded people at three levels: infant and early childhood, school age, and transition/adulthood.

Infant and early childhood For many severely handicapped infants, there will continue to be increasing numbers of infant stimulation centers. In many areas of the country, such services are available to parents of severely retarded infants. In a similar vein, many parent support groups have been established. These groups afford parents of severely retarded children a chance to talk openly with other parents about common problems they face. As these children get older, special classes will be available at no expense to the parents. Also, more teachers are being specifically prepared to work with preschool handicapped youngsters.

Most mildly retarded children are not identified until they reach school age. Therefore, many students identified as "at risk" for being classified mentally retarded are served in early intervention programs. There are strong indications that these early efforts have positive outcomes on later performance (Lazar & Darlington, 1982; Rogers-Warren & Poulson, 1984). Although these programs seem to be effective, we do not know exactly what specific variables within these programs are responsible for the gains.

School age Over the last few years, great strides have been made in developing methodologies and curricula for teaching severely and profoundly retarded individuals. Concern for chronological age-appropriate programming and the development of functional skills is great. However, there has also been some controversy regarding the *educability* of these individuals. Professionals have discussed whether some severely handicapped individuals have the right to an education, or can benefit from it (Kauffman & Krouse, 1981; Noonan, Brown, Mulligan, &

Rettig, 1982). This issue is likely to persist, especially in times of limited financial resources.

In the mild/moderate area, the pressing issue is the nature of this new mildly retarded population. If MacMillan and Borthwick's (1980) contention that this mildly retarded group is becoming more lower functioning is correct, then we may need to reexamine how we serve this group. Questions about whether this new mildly retarded population can be mainstreamed are also relevant (Polloway, 1984).

School subject areas that should be emphasized to strengthen the curriculum of mildly retarded students include social studies, science, art, and music. These subjects are usually relegated to second-class status, resulting in either inappropriate or poor instruction (Patton & Payne, 1985). Two other skill areas that should be strengthened are social skills and thinking skills. Gresham (1982) has argued pervasively for the inclusion of social skills training if we want mildly retarded students to be successfully integrated into regular education. With the increasing availability of microcomputers in schools, the opportunities to develop thinking skills should be enhanced.

Because we still do not have any definite conclusions regarding the success of mainstreaming, we must continue to evaluate this policy. Of particular interest will be information about what makes certain mainstreaming efforts successful and whether mainstreamed settings are appropriate for meeting students' needs. Our zeal to *place* students in the mainstream of regular education should not supersede our concern to *educate* them once they are there (Gottlieb, 1981).

Transition/adulthood Although it has always been important, transition from school to community is finally receiving the national attention it deserves. Many programs intended to facilitate this transition have been started. Schools are developing curricula that better prepare students for life after school. School systems and those agencies that assist disabled adults (e.g., Division of Vocational Rehabilitation) are working together in new ways. Community colleges are setting up innovative programs for mildly retarded young adults.

Quality of services Providing services, whether to teachers or to students, does not in itself ensure effective or high quality results. To guarantee the best return on our efforts we must strive for improvement in a number of areas. Although they are ten years old, Hobbs' (1975) comments remain accurate.

> Services for all kinds of children remain a tangled thicket of conceptual confusions, competing authorities, contrary purposes, and professional rivalries, leading to the fragmentation of services and the lack of sustained attention to the needs of individual children and their families. (p. 282)

TECHNOLOGY AND MENTAL RETARDATION

The effects of technology on the lives of mentally retarded persons are amazing. Recently, the Association for Retarded Citizens was awarded monies to support a number of bioengineering projects. Descriptions of these projects appeared in a recent issue of *The ARC* and are reprinted below.

Grants Boost Program

More than a quarter of a million dollars awarded the ARC Bioengineering Program means that several exciting designs can move quickly into development and into the lives of people needing greater independence and mobility in their battle over handicaps.

Dr. Al Cavalier, Bioengineering program director, announced five projects that will be funded through the generosity and wisdom of two organizations and several federal and Texas state agencies.

The projects will consist of the development of:

1. Computer systems for the remediation of problems in logical thinking and memory.
2. A computer-based device to improve physical conditioning and verbal skills.
3. A tray for self-feeding.
4. A crib to provide an interactive environment for infants.
5. A major technology conference and establishment of an electronic information system.

Memory remediation

"Technology to Enhance Special Education: Remediation of Problems in Logical Thinking and Memory" is the title of an 18-month project to develop computer-based instructional systems using two popular personal computers.

The goal is to remediate deficiencies of children who are mentally retarded or learning-disabled to improve their memory processes and logical reasoning.

"Memory problems are believed to exist in the large majority of people with mental retardation," Cavalier explained. "If deficiencies of these underlying processes remain uncorrected, they compound higher-level areas of functioning and frustrate remediation efforts."

The instructional systems will combine techniques for teaching efficient cognitive strategies with the unique strengths of computers in logical analysis, memory and motivation, Cavalier said. The systems would also maintain a record of each student's performance for review by parents and teachers.

Among several project objectives are the assessment of the need for such systems, transformation of descriptions into practical, affordable tools, systematic evaluations of their effectiveness and to recommend to the federal government a marketing plan to distribute the technological aids.

The systems will be field tested in the Dallas Independent School District.

Funding for the 18-month project will be $152,307 from the U.S. Department of

Education, Office of Special Education Programs, Division of Educational Services.

Information on project results and the availability of educational software will be widely shared among ARC members.

Improvement of skills

Development of a prototype of a computer-based device to improve simultaneously the physical health and cognitive skills of persons with mental retardation is planned as a two-year project.

"The device will incorporate vivid audio and video features to motivate and maintain participation in jogging, rowing and bicycling activities while providing interactive instruction in language and other skills," Cavalier said.

Field evaluations using state and local ARC units will provide valuable information on necessary refinements of the device and suggest guidelines for its use for parents and professionals, Cavalier noted.

For this 24-month project, The Meadows Foundation has provided $30,000 for initial development of the prototype and The Zeta Tau Alpha Fraternity $12,500 for the field evaluations.

Zeta Tau Alpha is a national service organization which helped the Bioengineering Program progress through its first stages. The Meadows Foundation in Dallas was created in 1948 by independent oilman Algur H. Meadows to enrich the quality of life for the people of Texas.

Tray for self-feeding

Two years is proposed for construction and field testing of a unique technological aid that will provide more independence in feeding for individuals with mental re-

tardation and severe physical handicaps. The device also will allow persons to choose foods and to pace their own rate of consumption. Field evaluations of the device as well will also involve state and local ARC units.

"The self-feeding tray is designed to be a low-cost alternative to robotic arms to permit people who are severely physically-involved and mentally retarded to feed themselves," Cavalier said. "The self-feeding aid is a three-sectioned tray which pushes food onto spoon-shaped projections attached to each section whenever a client desires a particular food. The person then moves his head forward, selects a food and removes it with his mouth."

Funding for the tray is $30,000 from The Meadows Foundation for initial development of the prototype and $12,500 from Zeta Tau Alpha for its field testing.

Interactive Crib

Another exciting project serving very young individuals—babies—will be the design and construction of a prototype of an interactive crib.

Using computerized devices, the crib's design will stimulate a handicapped infant's natural curiosity, provide captivating information through a variety of sights and sounds in response to the infant's behaviors, and encourage developmentally-progressive actions. Miniature video screens, recordings of voices and sound effects, colored knobs and buttons and a gentle vibration pad are among possible features of the crib.

Following development of the prototype, the crib will be tested for further refinement prior to completion of the design and subsequent marketing.

The Meadows Foundation is providing $15,000 in start-up funds. More funds are being sought for completion of the project.

Information pool

A national conference titled "Technology and the Developmentally Disabled" and the establishment of a computerized knowledge base and information referral system will be the focus of a project funded by the Texas Planning Council for Developmental Disabilities.

The conference is planned for February 1985 and will explore ways technology can serve people with developmental disabilities. The conference as well as a "state of the art" survey in Texas are expected to yield information on experts, products, hardware and software vendors, organizations, documents and other resources involving the use of technology with disabled people.

The project also will include development of a major pool of knowledge and information on computer applications for people with developmental disabilities, maintained by the Bioengineering Program at ARC National Headquarters.

ARC is involved in these activities as a subcontractor to the University of Texas at Arlington, Graduate School of Social Work. ARC will be advising UTA on the survey, conference and database. Additionally a computer system will be established to set up the database at ARC National Headquarters for telephone access by parents and professionals across the country.

Official publication of the Association for Retarded Citizens of the United States Volume 33, Number 4, Fall 1984

What seems to be needed is better coordination of services, answers to certain curricular questions (such as what should be taught and how it should be taught), evaluation on many fronts (teaching per se, materials, and methods), and improvements in the training of personnel. National authorities have examined the quality of education in general. If the quality of services is to be improved, then all of those professionals who interact with mentally retarded individuals must be prepared properly. For teachers, this means that teacher-training programs must be sensitive to the ever-changing demands placed upon both the teacher and the student. It also means that the typical in-service model must be drastically revised so as to provide the necessary information in the most efficacious manner. Competence must be demonstrated not only by teachers but also by community mental health workers, social workers, law enforcement personnel, juvenile officers, lawyers, judges, physicians, and anyone who can have a significant impact on the mentally retarded individual.

PARENTS AND FAMILIES

The child is an integral part of a small social system, composed of the child and people and settings important in his development. The child cannot be effectively treated apart from this system; yet in practice episodic treatment of the isolated child is the rule. (Hobbs, 1975, p. 279)

As Hobbs points out, if we wish to help a mentally retarded individual of any age, then we must understand that this person is always a part of an existing system. Typically, this system is the family. A look at early intervention projects indicates that there definitely has been attention given to the inclusion of at least one parent in most projects. If we are to improve services to families in the future, then most assuredly we will have to involve the whole family and have to provide a number of various services. Among the services which are warranted are counseling, respite care, informational resources, and active involvement of parents and families in the programming of their retarded child. Hobbs (1975) refers to this active involvement aspect as "a new partnership among public agencies, professional people, and parents to achieve an optimal balance of shared, long-term responsibility for exceptional children" (p. 279).

Keniston and the Carnegie Council on Children (1977) have interpreted this need for services into family policy statements. Keniston and the Council use the term *public advocates* to mean those individuals whose efforts are directed toward improving conditions for children. The policy statement they offer provides suitable goals which we should strive to achieve. The components of this family policy include

1. Public advocates should support jobs for parents and a decent living for all families.
2. Public advocates should support more flexible working conditions.
3. Public advocates should support an integrated network of family services.
4. Public advocates should support proper health care for children.
5. Public advocates should support improved legal protection for children outside their families. (pp. 216–220)

RIGHTS OF THE MR

In chapter 15, we presented the rights to which the mentally retarded are entitled as championed by various groups. At this time, we feel that it is worthwhile to present a list of legal rights for mentally retarded persons that we think should be acknowledged; we should all support, protect, and defend these rights.

Some of these rights require further investigation.

Right to life
Right to bodily integrity
Right to have a guardian

Right to live in the community
Right to a family life (with parents/family)
Right to privacy
Right to employment, income, and economic security
Right to be a parent
Right to education
Right to appropriate placement and classification
Right to treatment (medical, training, psychiatric)
Right to refuse treatment
Right to be free from harm
Right to be free from cruel and unusual punishment
Right to be free from involuntary servitude
Right to the least restrictive alternative (education, placement, etc.).

In addition, two other rights need to be mentioned. One of these rights stems from the concept of "dignity of risk" (Perske, 1972), and the other right was proposed by the International League of Societies for the Mentally Handicapped (1969). In our work with the retarded, it has become increasingly apparent that above all, mentally retarded individuals should also be afforded

The right to take risks
The right to be respected.

Until mentally retarded people are in a position to enjoy these rights, then indeed they will continue to be second-class citizens, denied the rights to which all citizens are entitled.

FINAL THOUGHTS

We hope that the future will be characterized by improved conditions for all of those who are handicapped. There is much reason to believe that influences such as advocacy groups, interest groups, and most importantly, social attitudes, will continue to shape the quantity and quality of programs and services for those who are mentally handicapped. Table 16.1 summarizes many of the topics discussed in this chapter and suggests trends and implications of various sociopolitical forces.

Presaging future change as we are attempting here can be an intriguing business. There is, however, a caution to be heeded. Those of us in the field must refrain from promising more than we can deliver; we must avoid such grandiose claims as were made by many of the early pioneers in this field in the first half of the 19th century—claims which later proved to work to the detriment of mentally retarded people.

TABLE 16.1   Relationship of Trends and Implications

Trends If these trends occur . . .	Implications* We would expect . . .

VALUES**

1. Individuals no longer judged on the basis of economic productivity	Reinforcement of national policy of educating every handicapped person to maximum potential (2,3)
2. Greater emphasis on self-actualization	
3. Continued focus on the equality of all groups	Less emphasis on vocational training in educational programs for the handicapped; and greater emphasis on subjects such as art and music (2,7)
4. Decentralization	
5. Stronger community ties	
6. More manageable government and social institutions	Increased acceptance of handicapped persons who cannot work (1,2)
	Reinforcement of handicapped persons' full participation in society's mainstream (2,3,4)
7. Expansion of knowledge system to include spiritual, subjective, and creative knowledge	More handicapped persons living in the community rather than in institutions (3,4,5,6)
8. Increased feeling of wholeness and connectedness of all persons	More normal social relationships for handicapped persons; less alienation (4,5,8)
9. Public participation in scientific and technological issues	Increased attention to the whole individual, including attitudes and spirit, in service delivery (2,7,8)
	Increased resistance to labeling and categorical funding systems (8)
	Increased interactive approach in service delivery (8)
	Increased involvement of handicapped persons and their families in planning, implementing, and monitoring programs and treatments (9)

ECONOMICS

10. Continued shift to an information/service economy	Decreased government program funding (16)
11. More information/service jobs, including more jobs involving computer operations	Forced competition for dollars between programs for handicapped and other programs at all levels of government (16)
12. Physical demands on factory workers reduced by increasing use of computers	Increased litigation and political pressure on behalf of the handicapped (16)
13. Fewer persons overall entering work force in the 1980s; however, increasing numbers of women entering work force	Increased pressure for federal ''block funding'' (16)
	Reduction in the power of federal laws that are enforced by funding incentives and sanctions (16)
14. Decreased unemployment	

TABLE 16.1 (continued)

Trends If these trends occur . . .	Implications* We would expect . . .
15. Growing underemployment resulting from increasingly higher educational levels required for jobs 16. Slowed economic growth 17. Application of management techniques and new technologies increasing productivity and reducing costs in the service industries	Need for an increase in efficiency and coordination among services agencies (16) Increased employment opportunities for the handicapped (10,11,12,13,14) Increased number of routine jobs potentially available for the mentally handicapped (17) Curricular changes in educational programs to increase emphasis on information skills (10,11) Unavailability of some jobs to handicapped persons because of spiraling educational requirements (15)

SOCIAL INSTITUTIONS

18. Greater variety of family types 19. Smaller families 20. More single-parent and two-career families 21. Changes in traditional husband/wife roles 22. Changes in service delivery patterns and demands for new services 23. More flexible work schedules 24. Lifelong learning 25. Return to smaller communities 26. Increased costs for social services/ decline in volunteers 27. Continued decline in birth rate and school enrollment	Greater demand for extended day school programs (18,20,21) Growing demand for paid child advocates (18,19,20,21) Easier accommodation of work schedules to meet special needs of handicapped persons (23) Increasing need to develop and extend educational opportunities for handicapped adults (24) Need to develop curricula and to train personnel for the instruction of handicapped adults (24) Use of surplus educational facilities for adult instruction (24,27) Need for better coordination and communication among service agencies, particularly in rural areas (25,26) Need to fund, recruit, and train a wide variety of auxiliary personnel to supplement a diminishing corps of volunteers (26) Possible opportunity for increased individualization of educational programs, allowing more handicapped students to receive more of their education in regular classes, or decline in support for regular teachers and increased resistance to integration of handicapped students because of school budget cuts (27)

TABLE 16.1 (continued)

Trends If these trends occur . . .	Implications* We would expect . . .
TECHNOLOGY	
28. Continued expansion of human physical abilities through the use of technology 29. Better communications through use of technology 30. Continued problems in disseminating information 31. Continued economic problems in supporting the research and development of new products 32. Continued problems with standards and certification of new products	Greater opportunity for handicapped persons to participate in mainstream of society, including school and work force (28,29) Increased sharing of information vital to the development and dissemination of new assistive devices (29) Continued need for government to disseminate information, coordinate and support research and development, establish standards and quality control (30,31,32) Continued increase in politicization of the handicapped (29,30,31,32) Greater opportunity for handicapped persons to obtain information and resources and to communicate with others having similar problems (29)
MEDICINE	
33. Continued dissemination of new diagnostic techniques and medical technology 34. Improved neonatal care 35. Increased control of disease through immunization, screening, and better record keeping 36. Continued problems in reaching all citizens with health care service	Decrease in the incidence of cerebral palsy (33,34) Fewer handicaps ascribed to premature birth (33,34) Reduction in genetic disorders through amniocentesis and abortion; continued need to develop treatment for genetic disorders (33) Reduction in acquired handicapping conditions (35) Continued need to develop better methods of reaching citizenry for immunization and screening (36)

*Numbers in parentheses following each implication designate the trend(s) from which that implication was inferred.

**Some panel members believed that these trends would not occur, that instead an even greater emphasis would be placed on economic productivity, competitiveness, and individual material success.

From N. Safer, J. Burnette, & B. Hobbs, "Exploration 1993; The Effects of Future Trends on Services to the Handicapped," *Focus on Exceptional Children*, 1977, *11*(3), 21–23. Reprinted by permission.

Simply stated, there is and will continue to be a distinct need for continued research with, about, and for the mentally retarded in many areas, among them training and education, community living, and prevention. More importantly, we need new knowledge, developed by creative thinkers using both existing theories and new paradigms. Although it is essential that research, both basic and applied, be encouraged, systematic evaluation of the effectiveness and value of this research is also warranted. As Hobbs (1975) has pointed out, major policy decisions in the field of special education have historically been made without verification of validity or effectiveness. However, this caution should not inhibit creative thinkers; if anything, it should embolden them.

Ultimately, the field of special education must grow, improve, and prosper—because if it does not there may indeed be a backlash, initiated by both those whom we wish to serve and those to whom we appeal for financial support. Rosen, Clark, and Kivitz (1977) offer a sobering thought which may temper any unrestrained optimism with a touch of reality.

> As professionals who have accepted the responsibility for training the mentally retarded, we now bear a moral responsibility to go beyond the obvious, the commonplace, and the relatively simple educational problems in habilitation in order to find ways of teaching essential life-enriching behaviors and skills. If we do not accept this aspect of our role, we may be faced with a backlash to normalization and deinstitutionalization policies far worse than the conditions that originally generated progress. Such backlash would be difficult to deal with because it would come from the mentally retarded themselves and from their families if we fail to fulfill our promises to them for better lives. It will also come from the general public when it no longer wishes to provide the financial support to take the risks for persons who fail to become integrated into the mainstream as "ordinary citizens." (pp. 353–54)

The future in many ways can be influenced by what we do or, at the very least, try to do today. The times are such that we can no longer remain passive observers, but must become active participants in the problems and needs of the mentally retarded population. Our attention should be focused not only on retarded persons but also on the public, because the key to the future rests there. Without positive public sentiment toward those who are mentally retarded, nurtured by what happens today and reflected in financial support for our efforts, the future outlook for the handicapped is not favorable. It then becomes evident that our foremost goals should incorporate the elements of social acceptance of mentally retarded people, active participation on the behalf of all advocates, and the continued search for new knowledge.

GLOSSARY

Acquisition The initial development of a skill or chunk of knowledge.

Adaptive behavior "Degree and efficiency with which the individual meets the standards of personal independence and social responsibility expected of his age and cultural group" (Grossman, 1983).

Amniocentesis Analysis of amniotic fluid during second trimester of pregnancy to allow for biochemical analysis of fetal cells; can indicate presence of genetic and chromosomal disorders and tell sex of fetus.

Anoxia Lack of oxygen severe enough to cause tissue damage; can cause permanent brain damage and retardation.

Antecedents Conditions or events that precede learning.

Aptitude test Test, often standardized and norm-referenced, of an individual's relative abilities in a variety of fields.

Autosomes 22 matched pairs of chromosomes (44 out of normally present 46). *See Sex chromosomes.*

Career education Education that prepares the individual for all the roles he or she will assume as an adult, including the roles of worker, citizen, and family member.

Cerebral palsy Any neuromuscular disability resulting from damage to the brain at birth or during early developmental years.

Child find Often the first step in the process of identifying children in need of services; generally involves a public awareness campaign.

Chromosomes   Threadlike bodies which contain genes that occupy specific loci.

Clinical judgment   Judgment based on experience rather than measurement; its use in determination of retardation puts thrust of diagnosis on the individual examiner.

Cognitive-developmental theory   As proposed by Piaget, suggests that each individual progresses through stages of development where specific cognitive skills are acquired via interaction with and adaptation to the environment and perception of that environment. Includes four orderly stages of development.

Comprehensive workshop   A sheltered workshop which includes transitional and extended workshop services.

Concrete operational stage   Third stage in Piaget's cognitive-developmental theory, during which the child learns to classify and to solve concrete problems; lasts approximately from age 7 to age 11 in nonretarded children.

Consequences   Subsequent events which, if made contingent, can facilitate learning.

Construct validity   The extent to which a test measures the factors which comprise the ability or skill the test purports to measure.

Continuous reinforcement   One-to-one correspondence between response and reinforcing consequence; best used to teach new responses.

Cultural-familial retardation   General category for causes of cases of mental retardation with no organic defects present.

Deinstitutionalization   Movement to decentralize large public institutions and move residents into smaller local centers and family settings, so as to provide the most natural and least restrictive environment in which handicapped persons can live and maximize their potential.

Deletion   In genetics, process where a portion of original genetic material is absent from a specific chromosomal pair.

Developmental model   Model which suggests that cognitive development of retarded individuals generally follows same sequence as nonretarded, at a slower rate.

Developmental period   Time between conception and the 18th birthday (Grossman, 1983).

Deviation intelligence quotient   In contrast to ratio IQ concept, assumes IQ is normally distributed; distributes IQ on normal curve with 100 as average and standard deviation which is same for every age level.

Difference/defect model   Model which suggests that cognitive development of retarded individuals is qualitatively different from nonretarded individuals and therefore requires different teaching strategies.

Dizygotic   Twins who developed from two separate fertilized eggs.

Dominant inheritance   Inheritance in which individual gene has control or can mask the other gene in the pair.

Down syndrome   A chromosomal anomaly which accounts for largest percentage of cases of moderate and severe retardation. Generally accompanied by clinical manifestations such as epicanthic folds, large tongue, broad flat bridge of nose, and poor muscle tone.

Educationally subnormal   Intellectually inadequate children needing special academically oriented education.

Etiology   The cause or causes of a given condition.

Expectancy   The way in which an individual approaches a task or situation based on experiences in previous similar situations.

Expectancy for failure   Individuals who have accumulated failure experiences set lower aspirations and goals in an effort to avoid additional failure.

Expressivity   The severity of a given genetic trait.

Extended workshop   A sheltered workshop which provides long-term employment for workers who cannot secure competitive employment in the community due to their handicap.

Fading   An antecedent approach used in teaching where the student responds to a cue or prompt which is gradually faded away.

Feedback   Information given to learner (or system) following a specific response.

Formal operational stage   Fourth stage in Piaget's cognitive-developmental theory, during which the child learns to think abstractly and reason by logic; begins around age 11 in nonretarded children.

Functional retardation   Retardation of institutional residents maintained or worsened by their stressful living conditions; often includes engaging in self-stimulation.

Gene   The basic biological unit influencing the inheritance of traits.

Genetics   The study of heredity and variation.

Genotype   An inherited characteristic which delineates a range within which a human trait develops.

Grand mal   The most severe type of epileptic seizure, in which the individual has violent convulsions, loses consciousness, and becomes rigid.

Grouping of material   Clustering information prior to presentation to facilitate memory and recall.

Grouping of students   The arrangement of the environment in such a way as to make it possible to work with students in the most effective, efficient manner.

Heritability   The proportion of total trait variance that is directly due to genetic, measurable factors.

Imitation   Process of acquiring behavior through observation of another person; can be intentional or unintentional.

Incidence   The number of new cases of a condition identified within a population over a specific period of time.

Incidental learning   Learning which takes place outside a formal structured learning environment.

Individualized Education Program (IEP)   A written document required by federal law to detail the year's plan for every handicapped child.

Input organization   Organization and storage of information so it can be recalled when needed.

Institutional peonage   System in which institutional residents are induced to work without pay in order to maintain the institution.

Intelligence   The ability to adapt, achieve, solve problems, interpret incoming stimuli to modify behavior, accumulate knowledge, or respond to items on an intelligence test; cannot be measured directly.

Intelligence quotient (IQ)   Mental age divided by chronological age and multiplied by 100; gives an index of intellectual performance relative to others in the same age group.

Interest inventory   Test, usually not standardized or norm-referenced, of an individual's expressed interest in a variety of fields; may be in checklist or other informal format.

Interindividual   Comparison of one individual to other individuals.

Intermittent reinforcement   Reinforcement that is delivered after some, but not all, occasions of a behavior; best used to teach a student to maintain an acquired response.

Intraindividual   Comparison of strengths and weaknesses of one individual.

Itinerant teacher   Provides regular education teacher with consultation and some instructional services on a limited basis; provides support for the regular teacher, who still has the major responsibility for the child's educational program.

Karyotypes   Graphic chromosomal pictures.

Learned helplessness   A pattern of submissiveness which develops in institutional residents when they discover that their actions are of no consequence and outcomes are beyond their control.

Learning   The process whereby practice or experience results in a change in behavior which is not due to maturation, growth, or aging; cannot be directly measured or observed.

Locus of control   How one perceives consequences of his or her own behavior. Can be either *internal* (events resulting from one's own behavior) or *external* (events resulting from outside forces).

Long-term memory   Ability to retrieve information from storage after a few days to months.

Maintenance   The ability needed to retain skills or knowledge over time.

Mastery learning   Presenting material to a student at whatever rate that student can learn it satisfactorily.

Mediation   A verbal learning process whereby an individual "connects" a stimulus and a response.

Meiosis   Process where gametes divide and pair up to form genetic foundation for an embryo.

Memory   Ability to retrieve information that has been stored.

Mental age   A measure of intellectual level (as performance on a mental measurement test) recorded independently of chronological age.

Mental retardation   "Significantly subaverage intellectual functioning existing concurrently with deficits in adaptive behavior, and manifested during the developmental period" (Grossman, 1973).

Mildly retarded   Individuals who deviate mildly below the normal range of intelligence and adaptive behavior. Can usually benefit from academic instruction and are often referred to as "educable" mentally retarded.

Modeling   An approach to teaching where the teacher demonstrates part or all of the behavior to be learned and the student repeats the action immediately.

Moderately retarded   Individuals functioning below mildly retarded; usually identified at birth or shortly thereafter. Educationally referred to as "trainable" mentally retarded, with program emphasis on self-help and basic survival skills, along with appropriate academic and vocational training.

Monozygotic   Twins who developed from the split of a single fertilized egg.

Mosaicism   Uneven division of cells in mitosis, resulting in unequal or extra chromosomes.

Nondisjunction   Failure of one parental pair of chromosomes to split correctly resulting in a trisomy such as Down syndrome (Trisomy 21).

Observational learning   Learning that results from watching demonstrations by others.

Ombudsman   One whose role is to protect the rights of individuals seeking services from government agencies.

Operant conditioning Systematic arrangement of environmental events and consequences so as to result in changes in behavior.

Outerdirectedness Looking to others for guidance or cues in developing appropriate responses in demand situations.

Penetrance Proportion of individuals within a particular population who possess a given gene and exhibit its genetic trait.

Performance Observable behavior; can be basis for determining whether learning has occurred.

Petit mal A type of epileptic seizure in which the individual loses consciousness, usually for less than half a minute; may occur very frequently in some children.

Phenotype An actual human trait that develops as a result of the interaction between the inherited trait (genotype) and the environment.

Phenylketonuria (PKU) An inherited metabolic disease which can cause severe retardation; can now be detected at birth and the detrimental effects prevented with a special diet.

Polygenetic inheritance Inheritance in which more than one gene pair affects the appearance of a particular trait.

Predictive validity The extent to which test performance predicts some other behavior.

Preoperational stage Second stage in Piaget's cognitive-developmental theory, during which the child begins to use symbols and to imitate actions of others; lasts from approximately age 2 to age 7 in nonretarded children.

Prevalence The total number of cases of a disorder existing within a population at a particular place or at a particular time.

Profoundly retarded Individuals who function at the lowest level of retardation demonstrate retarded development in all areas, along with little communication or interaction with the environment. Heavy dependence upon others to meet their basic physical needs.

Prompts Stimuli presented along with task being presented, in order to increase probability that the correct response will be elicited.

Prosthetic devices Artificial parts designed to replace absent ones, such as arms or legs.

Psychometric Test which purports to measure intelligence or mental ability.

Ratio IQ The ratio gives an index of a child's test performance relative to others in his age group; however, the absolute difference between MA and CA has a diminishing influence on IQ as the child gets older.

Recessive inheritance   Inherited traits which recede when paired with dominant genes and are therefore only influential when matched with another identical recessive gene.

Regular class program   In special education, system where the student is in the regular education program but receives support through modification of regular materials and special education materials.

Reliability   The extent to which a test consistently yields the same or similar results upon repeated administrations.

Resource room   Provides extra help for areas of greatest need for children in regular classrooms.

Screening   Processes used routinely with all children to help find strengths and weaknesses and to identify individuals in need of more complete diagnostic study.

Selective attention   Focusing attention on the relevant dimensions of a learning task.

Self-contained special class   Special separate class for handicapped children; generally used when it is felt that the individual will not benefit from any regular class instruction or activities.

Sensorimotor stage   First stage in Piaget's cognitive-developmental theory, during which the child makes purely physical responses to the environment; lasts from birth to approximately age 2 in nonretarded children.

Severely retarded   Individuals who function at a level between "moderately" retarded and "profoundly" retarded; includes a high incidence of other handicaps, though they can generally communicate and interact with the environment to some extent. Severely retarded people generally do not benefit from academic training, but can learn self-help and communication skills.

Sex chromosomes   One pair of chromosomes, which determine sex of individual (out of normal 23 pairs). *See Autosomes.*

Sheltered workshop   A structured environment where individuals can learn work habits, receive training, and find salaried employment either within the workshop or in the community.

Short-term memory   Ability to retrieve information from storage after a few seconds to a few hours.

Significantly subaverage intellectual functioning   "Performance of two standard deviations below the mean on an intelligence test" (Grossman, 1973).

Social learning theory   Theory which suggests that individuals interacting with the environment will either exhibit approach or avoidance behavior, depending on the expectancy of and value attached to the reinforcement or goals.

Special day school   Special school for more severely disabled students who cannot function in the regular school environment.

Special residential school   Generally considered the most restrictive educational placement; usually considered with only the most severely handicapped students, who require 24-hour care.

Standard deviation   Unit used to measure the amount by which a particular score varies from the mean with respect to all the scores in a norm sample.

Standard error of measurement   A reliability measure; indicates the amount by which a subject's actual score is likely to differ from his true score (i.e., the score he or she would get if the test had no margin of error).

Standardized test   Any test, usually norm-referenced, which has been given to a large number of subjects and for which standard procedures for administration, scoring, and interpretation are published; standard procedures must be followed for results to be valid.

Subaverage intellectual functioning   "An IQ of 70 or below on standardized measures of intelligence. This upper limit is intended as a guideline; it could be extended through 75 or more, depending on the reliability of the test used" (Grossman, 1983).

Syndrome   A group of characteristics associated with a specific clinical disorder.

Task analysis   Breaking down of a large skill into its behavioral components.

Teratogens   Substances that can negatively affect pre- and postnatal development.

Threshold variable   Description of environment as a minimum requisite level of stimulation required for normal development; as of yet not defined adequately (see Jensen, 1973).

Toxemia   Condition resulting from toxic substances in the blood; in pregnant women, can result in problems in the fetus.

Transfer   Ability to apply previously acquired knowledge to new tasks or problems.

Transitional workshop   A sheltered workshop which concentrates on development of vocational skills so that the workers will eventually gain employment in the community.

Translocation   Process where a fragment of chromosomal material is exchanged with incorrect chromosomal group; can result in Down syndrome.

Unitization   Attempt to improve large institutions by breaking them into "units" which are generally self-sufficient and have specific goals and responsibilities, along with permanent staffing.

Validity   The extent to which a test measures what it purports to measure.

Vocational education   Education that prepares the individual for a specific trade or job or group of trades or jobs.

Work study programs.   Programs developed to maximize a student's potential future employment through a combination of on-the-job experience and classroom instruction.

REFERENCES

Abramson, P., Gravink, M., Abramson, L., & Sommers, D. (1977). Early diagnosis and intervention of retardation: A survey of parental reactions concerning the quality of services rendered. *Mental Retardation, 15*(3), 28–31.

Abroms, K. K., & Bennett, J. W. (1980). Current genetic and demographic findings in Down's Syndrome: How are they presented in college textbooks on exceptionality? *Mental Retardation, 18*, 101–107.

Adubato, A., Adams, M. K., & Budd, S. (1981). Teaching a patient to train a spouse in child management techniques. *Journal of Applied Behavior Analysis, 14*, 193–205.

Allen, K. A. (1978). Early intervention for young severely and profoundly handicapped children: The preschool imperative. *AAESPH Review, 3*, 30–41.

Altman, R., & Talkington, L. W. (1971). Modeling: An alternative behavior modification approach for retardates. *Mental Retardation, 9*(3), 20–23.

Amante, D., Van Houten, V. W., Grieve, J. H., Bader, C. A., & Margules, J. H. (1977). Neuropsychological deficit, ethnicity, and socioeconomic status. *Journal of Consulting & Clinical Psychology, 45*(45), 524–35.

American Association for Health, Physical Education, and Recreation. (1966). *Recreation and physical activity for the mentally retarded*. Washington, DC: Author.

American Association on Mental Deficiency. (1975). *Position papers of the AAMD*. Washington, DC: AAMD.

American Psychiatric Association. (1980). *Diagnostic and statistical manual of mental disorders.* (3rd ed.). Washington, DC: Author.

Anastasi, A. (1972). Four hypotheses with a dearth of data: Response to Lehrke's "A theory of X-linkage of major intellectual traits." *American Journal of Mental Deficiency, 76,* 620–22.

Anastasi, A. (1982). *Psychological testing.* (5th ed.). New York: Macmillan.

Anderson, K. A. (1971). The "shopping" behavior of parents of mentally retarded children: The professional person's role. *Mental Retardation, 9*(4), 3–5.

Anderson, L., Dancis, J., & Alpert, M. (1978). Behavioral contingencies and self-mutilation in Lesch-Nyhan disease. *Journal of Consulting and Clinical Psychology, 46,* 529–536.

Angney, A., & Hanley, E. M. (1979). A parent-implemented shaping procedure to develop independent walking of a Down's syndrome child: A case study. *Education and Treatment of Children, 2,* 311–315.

Apffel, J. A., Kelleher, J., Lilly, M. S., & Richardson, R. (1975). Developmental reading for moderately retarded children. *Education and Training of the Mentally Retarded, 10,* 229–35.

Apgar, V. (1953). A proposal for a new method of evaluation of the newborn infant. *Current Researches in Anesthesia and Analgesia, 32,* 260–64.

Arthur, G. (1950). The Arthur Adaptation of the Leiter International Performance Scale. Chicago: C. H. Stoelting.

Azrin, N. H., & Foxx, R. M. (1971). A rapid method of toilet training the institutionalized retarded. *Journal of Applied Behavior Analysis, 4,* 89–99.

Baines, R. A. (1979). Unequal protection for the retarded? *Amicus, 4,* 128–32.

Bajema, C. J. (1971). The genetic implications of population control. *Bio-Science, 21,* 71–75.

Baker, A. M. (1979). Cognitive functioning of psychotic children: A reappraisal. *Exceptional Children, 45,* 344–48.

Baker, B. L., Seltzer, G. B., & Seltzer, M. M. (1977). *As close as possible: Community residences for retarded adults.* Boston: Little, Brown.

Balla, D. A. (1976). Relationship of institution size to quality of care: A review of the literature. *American Journal of Mental Deficiency, 81,* 117–24.

Ballard, J. (1976). Active federal education laws for exceptional persons. In F. J. Weintraub, A. Abeson, J. Ballard, & M. LaVor (Eds.), *Public policy and the education of exceptional children.* Reston, VA: The Council for Exceptional Children.

Balthazar, E. E. (1971). Balthazar Scales of Adaptive Behavior, I: Handbook for the Professional Supervisor. Champaign, IL: Research Press.

Balthazar, E. E. (1973). Balthazar Scales of Adaptive Behavior, II: Scales of Social Adaptation. Palo Alto, CA: Consulting Psychologists Press.

Bandura, A. (1969). *Principles of behavior modification.* New York: Holt, Rinehart, & Winston.

Barksdale, M., & Atkinson, A. A. (1971). Resource room approach to instruction for the educable mentally retarded. *Focus on Exceptional Children, 3*(4), 12–15.

Barlow, C. F. (1978). *Mental retardation and related disorders.* Philadelphia: F. A. Davis.

Baroff, G. S. (1974). *Mental retardation: Nature, cause, and management.* New York: John Wiley.

Baroff, G. S., & Tate, B. G. (1967). Training the mentally retarded in the production of complex production: A demonstration of work potential. *Exceptional Children, 33,* 405–8.

Barton, E. S., Guess, D., Garcia, G., & Baer, D. (1970). Improvement on retardates' mealtime behaviors by time out procedures using multiple baseline techniques. *Journal of Applied Behavior Analysis, 3,* 77–84.

Baumeister, A. A., & Forehand, R. (1972). Effects of contingent shock and verbal command on body rocking of retardates. *Journal of Clinical Psychology, 28,* 586–87.

Baumeister, A. A., & Muma, J. (1975). On defining mental retardation. *Journal of Special Education, 9,* 293–306.

Bayley, N. (1969). *Manual for the Bayley Scales of Infant Development.* New York: Psychological Corporation.

Beasley, C. R. (1982). Effects of a jogging program on cardiovascular fitness and work performance of mentally retarded adults. *American Journal of Mental Deficiency, 86*(6), 609–613.

Beck, E. (1979, September). Brave new world of intelligence testing. *Psychology Today,* 27–41.

Beck, J. (1972). Spina bifida and hydrocephalus. In V. Apgar & J. Beck, *Is my baby all right?* New York: Simon & Schuster.

Becker, R. L. (1975). Reading Free Vocational Interest Inventory. Washington, DC: American Association on Mental Deficiency.

Becker, W. C. (1971). Teaching reading and language to the disadvantaged— What have we learned from field research? *Harvard Educational Review, 47,* 518–543.

Becker, W. C. (1977). Teaching reading and language to the disadvantaged— What have we learned from field research? *Harvard Educational Review, 47,* 518–543.

Becker, W. C., & Carnine, D. W. (1980). Direct instruction: An effective approach to educational intervention with the disadvantaged and low performers. In B. B. Lahey & A. E. Kazdin (Eds.), *Advances in Clinical Child Psychology* (Vol. 3, pp. 429–469). New York: Plenum Press.

Becker, W. C., Englemann, S., & Thomas, D. R. (1971). *Teaching: A course in applied psychology.* Chicago: Science Research Associates.

Beckman, P. (1983). Influence of selected child characteristics on stress in families of handicapped infants. *American Journal on Mental Deficiency, 88,* 150–156.

Beckman-Brindley, S., & Snell, M. E. (1984). Family perspectives on parent participation in educational and behavioral programs. Unpublished manuscript, University of Virginia.

Beevy, J. (1978). *Applications of biomedical and related technologies to instructional issues in the education of the severely and profoundly handicapped student.* Paper presented at the Fifth Annual Conference of the American Association for the Education of the Severely/Profoundly Handicapped, Baltimore, October.

Begab, M. J. (1981). Issues in the prevention of psychosocial retardation. In M. J. Begab, H. C. Haywood, & H. L. Garber (Eds.), *Psychosocial Influences in Retarded Performance: Issues and Theories in Development* (pp. 3–28). Baltimore: University Park Press.

Begab, M. J. (1969). Casework for the mentally retarded—Casework with parents. In W. Wolfensberger & R. A. Kurtz (Eds.), *Management of the family of the mentally retarded.* New York: Follett.

Begab, M. J. (1974). The major dilemma of mental retardation: Shall we prevent it? Some social implications of research in mental retardation. *American Journal of Mental Deficiency, 78,* 519–29.

Begelman, D. A. (1978). Ethical issues for the developmentally disabled. In M. S. Berkler, G. H. Bible, S. M. Boles, D. E. Deitz, & A. C. Repp (Eds.), *Current trends for the developmentally disabled.* Baltimore: University Park Press.

Beier, D. C. (1964). Behavioral disturbances in the mentally retarded. In H. A. Stevens & R. Heber (Eds.), *Mental retardation: A review of research.* Chicago: University of Chicago Press.

Bellamy, G. T., Horner, R. H., & Inman, D. P. (1979). *Vocational habilitation of severely retarded adults—A direct service technology.* Baltimore: University Park Press.

Bellamy, G. T., Sowers, J., & Bourbeau, P. E. (1983). Work and work-related services: Postschool options. In M. E. Snell (Ed.), *Systematic instruction of the moderately and severely handicapped* (2nd ed.). Columbus, OH: Charles E. Merrill.

Belmont, J. M. (1966). Long-term memory in mental retardation. In N. R. Ellis (Ed.), *International review of research in mental retardation* (Vol. 1). New York: Academic Press.

Belmont, J. M. (1971). Medical-behavioral research in mental retardation. In N. R. Ellis (Ed.), *International review of research in mental retardation* (Vol. 5). New York: Academic Press.

Belmont, J. M., & Butterfield, E. C. (1977). The instructional approach to developmental cognitive research. In R. V. Kail & J. W. Hagen (Eds.), *Perspectives on the development of memory and cognition.* Hillsdale, NJ: Lawrence Erlbaum.

Belmont, J. M., & Butterfield, E. C. (1971). Learning strategies as determinants of memory deficiencies. *Cognitive Psychology, 2,* 411–20.

Bender, B., Fry, E., Pennington, B., Puck, M., Salonblatt, J., & Robinson, S. (1983). Speech and language development in 41 children with sex chromosome anomalies. *Pediatrics, 71,* 262–266.

Benton, A. L. (1964). Psychological evaluation and differential diagnosis in H. A. Stevens & R. Heber (Eds.), *Mental retardation: A review of research*. Chicago: University of Chicago Press.

Bereiter, C., & Englemann, S. (1966). *Teaching disadvantaged children in the preschool*. Englewood Cliffs, NJ: Prentice-Hall.

Bernstein, B. A. (1970). Sociolinguistic approach to socialization: With some reference to educability. In F. Williams (Ed.), *Language and Poverty* (pp. 25–61). Chicago: Markham Publishing.

Bernstein, B. (1961). Social class and linguistic development: A theory of social learning. In H. A. Halsey, J. Floud, & C. A. Anderson (Eds.), *Education, economy, and society*. New York: Free Press.

Bienenstok, T., & Coxe, W. (1956). *Census of severely retarded children in New York State*. Albany, NY: Interdepartmental Health Resources Board.

Bijou, S. W. (1966). A functional analysis of retarded development. In N. R. Ellis (Ed.), *International review of research in mental retardation* (Vol. 1, pp. 1–19). New York: Academic Press.

Bijou, S. W. (1983). The prevention of mild and moderate retarded development. In F. J. Menolascino, R. Neman, & J. A. Start (Eds.), *Curative Aspects of Mental Retardation: Biomedical and Behavioral Advances* (p. 223–241). Baltimore: Paul H. Brookes.

Biklen, D. (1977). Myths, mistreatment, and pitfalls: Mental retardation and criminal justice. *Mental Retardation, 15*(4), 51–57. (a)

Biklen, D. (1977). The politics of the institution. In B. Blatt, D. Biklen, & R. Bogdan (Eds.), *An alternative textbook in special education*. Denver: Love Publishing. (b)

Binet, A., & Simon, T. (1961). The development of intelligence in children. Training School Bulletin, No. 11, 1961. Reprinted in J. J. Jenkins & D. G. Paterson (Eds.), *Studies in individual differences*. New York: Appleton-Century-Crofts, Prentice-Hall.

Bishop, J. E. (1982, January 29). Gene defect linked to retarded males: May solve mysteries. *Wall Street Journal*.

Blacher, J. (1984). Sequential stages of parental adjustment to the birth of a child with handicaps: Facts or artifact? *American Journal on Mental Deficiency, 2*, 55–68.

Blatt, B., & Kaplan, F. (1966). *Christmas in purgatory*. Boston: Allyn & Bacon.

Bogdan, R. (1980). What does it mean when a person says, "I am not retarded"? *Education and Training of the Mentally Retarded, 15*(1), 74–79.

Bourestrom, N. C. (1973). *Relocation report no. 3: Preparation for relocation*. Ann Arbor: Institute of Gerontology, University of Michigan and Wayne State University.

Bowe, F. (1978). *Handicapping America, barriers to disabled people*. New York: Harper and Row.

Bower, A. C. (1978). Learning. In J. P. Das & D. Baine (Eds.), *Mental retardation for special educators*. Springfield, IL: Charles C. Thomas.

Boyd, R. D. (1979). Systematic parent training through a home based model. *Exceptional Children, 45,* 647–48.

Bradfield, R. H., Brown, J., Kaplan, P., Rickert, E., & Stannard, R. (1973). The special child in the regular classroom. *Exceptional Children, 39,* 384–90.

Bregman, S. (1984). Assertiveness training for mentally retarded adults. *Mental Retardation, 22,* 12–16.

Bricker, D. D., & Dow, M. G. (1980). Early intervention with the young severely handicapped child. *JASH, 5,* 130–42.

Brolin, D. E. (1982). *Vocational preparation of persons with handicaps.* (2nd ed.). Columbus, OH: Charles E. Merrill.

Brolin, D. E. (1978). *Life-centered career education: A competency-based approach.* Reston, VA: The Council for Exceptional Children.

Brolin, D. (1982). *Vocational preparation of retarded citizens* (2nd ed.). Columbus: Charles E. Merrill.

Brolin, D. E., & D'Alonzo, B. J. (1979). Critical issues in career education for the handicapped student. *Exceptional Children, 45,* 246–53.

Brolin, D. E., Durand, R., Kromer, K., & Muller, P. (1975). Postschool adjustment of educable retarded students. *Education and Training of the Mentally Retarded, 10,* 144–49.

Brolin, D. E., & Kokaska, C. J. (1979). *Career education for handicapped children and youth.* Columbus, OH: Charles E. Merrill.

Bronfenbrenner, U. (1974). *A report on longitudinal evaluations of preschool programs. Volume II. Is early intervention effective?* Washington, DC: Department of Health, Education and Welfare Publication No. (OHD) 76–30025.

Bronfenbrenner, U. (1977). Toward an experimental ecology of human development. *American Psychologist, 32,* 513–531.

Brown v. Board of Education (1954). 347 U.S. 483.

Brown, A. L., Campione, J. C., & Murphy, M. D. (1974). Keeping track of changing variables: Long-term retention of a trained rehearsal strategy by retarded adolescents. *American Journal of Mental Deficiency, 78,* 453–66.

Brown, B. S., & Courtless, T. F. (1967). *The mentally retarded offender.* Washington, D.C.: The President's Commission on Law Enforcement and Administration of Justice.

Brown, L, Branston, M. B., Hamre-Nietupski, S., Johnson, F., Wilcox, B., & Gruenewald, L. (1979). A rationale for comprehensive longitudinal interactions between severely handicapped students and nonhandicapped students and other citizens. *AAESPH Review, 4,* 3–14.

Brown, L. F., Wright, E., & Hitchings, W. (1978). Guidelines for procuring work contracts for sheltered workshop clients. *Career Development for Exceptional Individuals, 1*(2), 88–96.

Brueckner, L. J., & Bond, G. L. (1955). *The diagnosis and treatment of learning difficulties.* Englewood Cliffs, NJ: Prentice-Hall.

Buck v. Bell (1927). 274 U.S. 200.

Buck, J. N. (1955). The sage: An unusual mongoloid. A. Burton & R. E. Harris (Eds.), *Clinical studies in personality* (Vol. II) (p. 455–481). New York: Harper.

Bull, M., & LaVecchio, F. (1978). Behavior therapy for a child with Lesch-Nyhan syndrome. *Developmental Medicine and Child Neurology, 20,* 368–375.

Bunker, M. C.,Lambdin, M. A., Lynch, H. T., Mickey, G. H,. Roderick, T. H., Van Pelt, J. C., & Fosnot, H. (1972, April 30). Will my baby be normal? *Patient Care.*

Burnham v. Dept. of Public Health, 349 F. Supp. 1335 (N.D. Ga. 1972), rev'd, 503 f.2d 1319 (5th Cir. 1974).

Burt, C. (1966). The genetic determination of differences in intelligence. *British Journal of Psychology, 57,* 137–53.

Burton, T. A., & Hirshoren, A. (1979). The education of severely and profoundly retarded children: Are we sacrificing the child to the concept? *Exceptional Children, 45,* 601–2.

Bush, W. J., & Waugh, K. W. (1982). *Diagnosing Learning Problems* (3rd ed.). Columbus: Charles E. Merrill.

Cain, L. F., Levine, S., & Elzey, F. F. (1963). *Manual for the Cain-Levine Social Competency Scale.* Palo Alto, CA: Consulting Psychologists Press.

Caldwell, B. (1970). The rationale for early intervention. *Exceptional Children, 36,* 717–27.

Cancro, R. (Ed.). (1971). *Intelligence: Genetic and environmental influences.* New York: Grune & Stratton.

Capobianco, R. J., & Jacoby, H. B. (1966). The Fairfax plan: A high school program for mildly retarded youth. *Mental Retardation, 4*(3), 15–20.

Carr, J. (1970). Mongolism: Telling the parents. *Developmental Medicine and Child Neurology, 12,* 213–21.

Carr, J. (1974). The effect of the severely subnormal on their families. In A. M. Clarke & A. D. B. Clarke (Eds.), *Mental deficiency: The changing outlook* (3rd ed.). New York: Free Press.

Casey, L. O. (1978). Development of communicative behavior in autistic children: A parent program using manual signs. *Journal of Autism and Childhood Schizophrenia, 8,* 45–59.

Cassel, T. Z. (1976). A social-ecological model of adaptive functioning: A contextual developmental perspective. In N. A. Carlson (Ed.), *Final report: The contexts of life: A social-ecological model of adaptive behavior and functioning.* East Lansing, MI: Institute for Family and Child Study, Michigan State University.

Cassidy, V. M., & Stanton, J. E. (1959). *An investigation of factors involved in the educational placement of mentally retarded children: A study of differences between children in special and regular classes in Ohio.* Cooperative Research Project No. 043. Columbus: The Ohio State University.

Cattell, R. B. (1947). *The measurement of intelligence of infants and young children.* New York: Psychological Corporation.

Cattell, R. B. (1950). Culture Fair Intelligence Test: Scale 1. Champaign, IL: Institute for Personality and Ability Testing.

Cegelka, P. T., & Prehm, H. J. (1982). *Mental retardation: From categories to people.* Columbus, OH: Charles E. Merrill.

Cegelka, P. T. (1979). Career education. In D. Cullinan & M. H. Epstein (Eds)., *Special education for adolescents: Issues and perspectives.* Columbus, OH: Charles E. Merrill.

Chan, K. S., & Rueda, R. (1979). Poverty and culture in education: Separate but equal. *Exceptional Children, 45,* 422–28.

Chaney, R. H., & Eyman, R. K. (1982). Etiology of mental retardation: Clinical vs. neuroanatomic diagnosis. *Mental Retardation, 20,* 123–132.

Cheseldine, S., & McConkey, R. (1979). Parental speech to young Down's syndrome children: An intervention study. *American Journal of Mental Deficiency, 83,* 612–620.

Chinn, P. C., Drew, C. J., & Logan, D. R. (1979). *Mental retardation: A life cycle approach* (2nd ed.). St. Louis: C.V. Mosby.

Christoplos, F. (1973). Keeping exceptional children in regular classes. *Exceptional Children, 39,* 569–72.

Cicirelli, V. G. (1969). *The impact of Head Start: An evaluation of the effects of Head Start on children's cognitive and affective development* (Vol. 1). Springfield, VA: Clearinghouse.

A citizen advocate (1978). Personal communication.

Clark, G. M. (1979). *Career education for the handicapped child in the elementary classroom.* Denver: Love Publishing.

Clark, K. E., & Campbell, D. P. (1966). Minnesota Vocational Interest Inventory. New York: Psychological Corporation.

Clarke, A. B., & Clarke, A. M. (1977). Projects for prevention and amelioration of mental retardation: A guest editorial. *American Journal of Mental Deficiency, 81,* 523–33.

Clausen, J. A. (1967). Mental deficiency: Development of a concept. *American Journal of Mental Deficiency, 71,* 727–45.

Clausen, J. A. (1972a). The continuing problem of defining mental deficiency. *Journal of Special Education, 6,* 97–106.

Clausen, J. A. (1972b). Quo Vadis, AAMD? *Journal of Special Education, 6,* 51–60.

Cleland, C. C., & Swartz, J. D. (1972). *Exceptionalities Through the Life Span: An Introduction.* New York: Macmillan.

Cleveland, D., & Miller, N. (1977). Attitudes and life commitments of older siblings of mentally retarded adults: An exploratory study. *Mental Retardation, 15*(3), 38–41.

Clunies-Ross, G. G. (1979). Accelerating the development of Down's syndrome infants and young children. *Journal of Special Education, 13,* 169–77.

Coates, J. F. (1978). Population and education: How demographic trends will shape the U.S. *The Futurist, 12*(1), 35–42.

Cochran, W. E., Sran, P. K., & Varano, G. A. (1977). The relocation syndrome in mentally retarded individuals. *Mental Retardation, 15,*(2), 169–77.

Coffman, T. L., & Harris, M. C. (1980). Transition shock and adjustments of mentally retarded persons. *Mental Retardation, 18,* 28–32.

Cohen, J. S. (1971). Vocational rehabilitation of the mentally retarded: The sheltered workshop. In J. H. Rothstein (Ed.), *Mental retardation: Readings and resources* (2nd ed.). New York: Holt, Rinehart, & Winston.

Cohen, L. (1981). Ethical issues in withholding care from severely handicapped infants. *The Journal of the Association for the Severely Handicapped,* 6(3), 65–67.

Cohen, S. A. (1971). Dyspedagogia as a cause of reading retardation. In B. Bateman (Ed.), *Learning disorders* (Vol. 4). Seattle: Special Child Publications.

Coleman, L. J. (1977). An examination of seven techniques for evaluating the comprehensibility of instructional materials and recommendations for their use. *Education and Training of the Mentally Retarded, 12,* 339–44.

Coleman, R. W., & Provence, S. (1957). Environmental retardation (hospitalism) in infants living in families. *Pediatrics, 19,* 285–92.

Colletti, G., & Harris, S. L. (1977). Behavior modification in the home: Siblings as behavior modifiers, parents as observers. *Journal of Abnormal Child Psychology, 5,* 21–30.

COMTEP. (n.d.). *Community training and employment program.* Honolulu: Hawaii Association for Retarded Citizens.

Connolly, A. (1978). Intelligence levels in Down's syndrome children. *American Journal of Mental Deficiency, 83,* 193–96.

Conroy, J. W. (1977). Trends in deinstitutionalization of the mentally retarded. *Mental Retardation, 15*(4), 44–46.

Cook, P., Dahl, P., & Gale, M. (1977). *Vocational training and placement of the severely handicapped: Vocational opportunities.* Palo Alto, CA: The American Institute for Research in the Behavioral Sciences.

Cooke, N. L., Heron, T. E., Heward, W. L., & Test, D. W. (1982). Integrating a Down's syndrome child in a classwide peer tutoring system: A case report. *Mental Retardation, 20,* 22–25.

Copeland, M. C. (1976). *Occupational therapy for mentally retarded children.* Baltimore: University Park Press.

Cordes, C. (1984). Will Larry P. face the supreme test? *Monitor, 15*(4), 1, 26–27.

Coulter, W. A., & Morrow, H. W. (Eds.). (1978). *Adaptive behavior: Concepts and measurements.* New York: Grune & Stratton.

Crain, E. J. (1980). Socioeconomic status of educable mentally retarded graduates of special education. *Education and Training of the Mentally Retarded,* 90–94.

Cravioto, J., DeLicardie, E. R., & Birch, H. G. (1966). Nutrition, growth, and neuro-integrative development: An experimental and ecological study. *Pediatrics, 38* (Supplement 2), 319.

Crnic, L. S. (1984). Nutrition and mental development. *American Journal of Mental Deficiency, 88,* 526–533.

Crynic, K. A., Friedrich, W. N., & Greenberg, M. T. (1983). Adaptation of families with mentally retarded children: A model of stress, coping, and family ecology. *American Journal of Mental Deficiency.*

Cromwell, Rl L. (1963). A social learning approach to mental retardation. In N. R. Ellis (Ed)., *Handbook of mental deficiency.* New York: McGraw-Hill.

Cronbach, L. J. (1969). Heredity, environment, and educational policy. *Harvard Educational Review, 39,* 338–47.

Cullari, S. (1984). Everybody is talking about the new institution. *Mental Retardation, 22,* 28–29.

Culleton, B. J. (1975). Amniocentesis: HEW backs test for prenatal diagnosis of disease. *Science, 190,* 537–40.

Cummings, S., Bayley, H., & Rie, H. (1966). Effects of the child's deficiency on the mother: A study of mothers of mentally retarded, chronically ill and neurotic children. *American Journal of Orthopsychiatry, 36,* 595–608.

Cummings, T. S. (1976). The impact of the child's deficiency on the father: A study of fathers of mentally retarded and of chronically ill children. *American Journal of Orthopsychiatry, 46,* 246–55.

Daker, M. G., Chidiac, P., Fear, C. N., & Berry, A. C. (1981, April). Fragile X in a normal male: A cautionary tale. *The Lancet, 780.*

Dalton, J., & Epstein, H. (1963). Counseling parents of mentally retarded children. *Social Casework, 44,* 523–30.

Davis, M. R. (1981). A discussion of phenylketonuria and a comparison of behavioral characteristics. Unpublished manuscript, Lynchburg College, Lynchburg, VA.

Delaney, S., & Hayden, A. (1977). Fetal alcohol syndrome: A review. *AAESPH Review, 2,* 164–68.

Dennis, W. (1960). Causes of retardation among institutional children: Iran. *Journal of Genetic Psychology, 96,* 47–59.

Dennis, W., & Najaran, P. (1957). Infant development under environmental handicap. *Psychological Monographs, 71,* No. 7.

Denny, M. (1980). Reducing self-stimulatory behavior of mentally retarded persons by alternative positive practice. *American Journal of Mental Deficiency, 84,* 610–15.

DeSilva, B. (1980, March 24). Retarded persons create a problem in criminal justice. *The Washington Post,* pp. A6–A7.

DeVellis, R. F. (1977). Learned helplessness in institutions. *Mental Retardation, 15(5),* 10–13.

Diana v. State Board of Education, C–70–37 R.F.P. (N.D. California, Jan. 7, 1970 and June 18, 1972).

Dickerson, M., Hamilton, J., Huber, R., & Segal, R. (1974). *The aged mentally retarded: The invisible client—A challenge to the community.* Paper presented at the annual meeting of the American Association on Mental Deficiency, Toronto.

DISTAR Reading (1971). Chicago: Science Research Associates.

Dix, D. (1976). Memorial to the Legislature of Massachusetts, 1843. Speech addressed to the Massachusetts Legislature, Boston, 1843. Reprinted in M. Rosen, G. R. Clark, & M. S. Kivitz (Eds.), *The history of mental retardation: Collected papers.* (Vol. 1). Baltimore: University Park Press.

Dobzhansky, T. (1955). *Evolution, genetics, and man.* New York: John Wiley.

Dobzhansky, T. (1973). *Genetic diversity and human equality.* New York: Basic Books.

Doll, E. A. (1941). The essentials of an inclusive concept of mental deficiency. *American Journal of Mental Deficiency, 46,* 214–19.

Doll, E. A. (1953). *Measurement of social competence: A manual for the Vineland Social Maturity Scale.* Circle Press, MN: American Guidance Service.

Doll, E. A. (1958). Sheltered workshops for the mentally retarded. *Exceptional Children, 25,* 3–4.

Doll, E. A. (1965). *Vineland Social Maturity Scale: Condensed manual of directions* (1965 ed.). Circle Pines, MN: American Guidance Service.

Dorland's Medical Dictionary (1957). (23rd ed.). Philadelphia: W. B. Saunders.

Drew, C. J., & Espeseth, V. K. (1969). Transfer of training in the mentally retarded: A review. *Exceptional Children, 35,* 129–32.

Drew, C. J., Hardman, M. L., & Bluhm, H. P. (Eds.). (1977). *Mental retardation: Social and educational perspectives.* St. Louis: C.V. Mosby.

Drillien, C. M., & Wilkinson, E. M. (1964). Mongolism: When should parents be told? *British Medical Journal, 2,* 1306–7.

Duff, R. S., & Campbell, A. G. M. (1973). Moral and ethical dilemmas in the special-care nursery. *The New England Journal of Medicine, 289,* 890–894. Reprinted in R. F. Weir, (Ed.), *Ethical Issues in Death and Dying.* New York: Columbia Press.

Dugdale, R. L. (1877). *The Jukes, a study in crime, pauperism, disease and heredity.* New York: Putnam.

Duker, P. (1975). Behavior control of self-biting in a Lesch-Nyhan patient. *Journal of Mental Deficiency Research, 19,* 11–19.

Duncan, C. P. (1975). Review of the Science and Politics of IQ. *American Journal of Psychology, 88,* 505–532.

Dunn, L. M. (Ed.) (1963). *Exceptional children in the schools.* New York: Holt, Rinehart, & Winston.

Dunn, L. M. (1968). Special education for the mildly retarded—Is much of it justifiable? *Exceptional Children, 35,* 5–22.

Dunn, L. M. (1973a). Children with mild general learning disabilities. In L. M. Dunn (Ed.), *Exceptional children in the schools: Special education in transition* (2nd ed.). New York: Holt, Rinehart, & Winston.

Dunn, L. M. (Ed.) (1973b). *Exceptional children in the schools: Special education in transition* (2nd ed.). New York: Holt, Rinehart, & Winston.

Dunn, L. M., & Markwardt, F. C. (1970). Peabody Individual Achievement Test. Circle Pines, MN: American Guidance Service.

Ebron, R., & Ebron, H. (1967). Measurement of attitudes toward the retarded and an application with educators. *American Journal of Mental Deficiency, 72,* 100–107.

Edgerton, R. B. (1975). Issues relating to the quality of life among mentally retarded persons. In M. J. Begab & S. A. Richardson (Eds.), *The mentally retarded and society: A social science perspective.* Baltimore: University Park Press.

Edgerton, R. B. (1980). The study of community adaptation: Toward an understanding of lives in process. In E.D. Schulman, *Focus on the retarded adult.* St. Louis: C. V. Mosby.

Edgerton, R. B., & Bercovici, S. M. (1976). The cloak of competence: Years later. *American Journal of Mental Deficiency, 80,* 485–97.

Edgerton, R. B., Bollinger, M., & Herr, B. (1984). The cloak of competence: After two decades. *American Journal of Mental Deficiency, 88*(4), 345–351.

Edgerton, R. M. (1967). *The cloak of competence: Stigma in the lives of the mentally retarded.* Berkeley: University of California Press.

Edwards, A. J., & Scannel, D. P. (1968). *Educational psychology: The teaching-learning process.* New York: International Textbook.

Eller, P., Jordan, H., Parish, A., & Elder, P. (1979). Professional qualification: Mother. In R. York & E. Edgar (Eds.), *Teaching the severely handicapped* (Vol. IV). Seattle: The American Association for the Education of the Severely/Profoundly Handicapped.

Ellis, N. R. (1963). The stimulus trace and behavioral inadequacy. In N. R. Ellis (Ed.), *Handbook of mental deficiency.* New York: McGraw-Hill.

Ellis, N. R. (1969). A behavioral research strategy in mental retardation: Defense and critique. *American Journal of Mental Deficiency, 73,* 557–66.

Ellis, N. R. (1970). Memory processes in retardates and normals. In N. R. Ellis (Ed.), *International review of research in mental retardation* (Vol. 4). New York: Academic Press.

Ellis, N. R., Balla, D., Estes, O., Warren, S. A., Meyers, C. E., Hollis, J., Isaacson, R. L., Palk, B. E., & Siegel, P. S. (1981). Common sense in the habilitation of mentally retarded persons: A reply to Menolascino and McGee. *Mental Retardation, 19,* 221–225.

Emde, R. N., & Brown, C. (1978). Adaptation to the birth of a Down's syndrome infant. *Journal of the American Academy of Child Psychiatry, 17*(2), 299–323.

Engel, E. (1977). One hundred years of cytogenetic studies in health and disease. *American Journal of Mental Deficiency, 82,* 109–17.

Engelmann, S. (1970). The effectiveness of direct verbal instruction on IQ performance and achievement in reading and arithmetic. In J. Hellmuth (Ed.), *The disadvantaged child* (Vol. 3). New York: Bruner/Mazel.

Engelmann, S. (1977). Sequencing cognitive and academic tasks. In R. D. Kneedler & S. G. Traver (Eds.), *Changing perspectives in special education.* Columbus, OH: Charles E. Merrill.

Ensher, G. L., Blatt, B., & Winschell, J. F. (1977). Head Start for the handicapped: Congressional mandate audit. *Exceptional Children, 43,* 202–10.

Erickson, E. H. (1968). *Identity, youth and crisis.* New York: Norton.

Estes, W. K. (1970). *Learning theory and mental development.* New York: Academic Press.

Eyman, R. K., Dingman, H., & Sabagh, G. (1966). Association of characteristics of retarded patients and their families with speed of institutionalization. *American Journal of Mental Deficiency, 71,* 93–99.

Eyman, R. K., O'Connor, G., Tarjan, G., & Justice, R. S. (1972). Factors determining residential placement of mentally retarded children. *American Journal of Mental Deficiency, 76,* 692–98.

Eyman, R. K., & Miller, C. (1978). Introduction: A demographic overview of severe and profound mental retardation. In C. E. Meyers (Ed.), *Quality of life in severely and profoundly mentally retarded people: Research foundations for improvement.* Washington, D.C.: American Association on Mental Deficiency.

Farber, B. (1959). Effects of a severely mentally retarded child on family integration. *Monograph of the Society for Research in Child Development, 24*(2, whole #71).

Farber, B. (1968). *Mental retardation: Its social context and social consequences.* Boston: Houghton Mifflin.

Farber, B. (1970). Notes on sociological knowledge about families with mentally retarded children. In M. Schreiber (Ed.), *Social work and mental retardation.* New York: John Day.

Farber, B. (1975). Family adaptations to severely mentally retarded children. In M. Begab & S. A. Richardson (Eds.), *The mentally retarded and society: A social science perspective.* Baltimore: University Park Press.

Fernald, D. C. (1976). The Lesch-Nyhan syndrome, cerebral palsy, mental retardation and self-mutilation. *Journal of Pediatric Psychology, 1*(3), 51–55.

Feuerstein, R., Miller, R., Hoffman, M. B., Rand, Y., Mintzker, Y., & Mogens, R. J. (1981). Cognitive modifiability in adolescence: Cognitive structure and the effects of intervention. *Journal of Special Education, 15*(2), 269–287.

Feuerstein, R. (1979). Ontogeny of learning in man. In M. A. B. Brazier (Ed.), *Brain mechanisms in memory and learning; From the single neuron to man* (pp. 361–372). New York: Raven Press.

Filler, J. W., Jr. (1976). Modifying maternal teaching style: Effects of task arrangement on the match-to-sample performance of retarded preschool-age children. *American Journal of Mental Deficiency, 80,* 602–612.

Fink, W., & Sandall, S. (1980). A comparison of one-to-one and small group instructional strategies on a word identification task by developmentally disabled preschoolers. *Mental Retardation, 18*(1), 34–35.

Finnie, N. R. (1975). *Handling the young cerebral palsied child at home.* New York: E. P. Dutton.

Fletcher, J. (1974). *The ethics of genetic control: Ending reproductive roulette.* Garden City, NY: Anchor Books.

Fletcher, J. (1975). The "right" to live and the "right" to die. In M. Kohl (Ed.), *Beneficent euthanasia.* Buffalo, NY: Prometheus Books.

Folkman, S., Schaefer, C., & Lazarus, R. S. (1979). Cognitive processes as mediators of stress and coping. In V. Hamilton & D. W. Warburton (Eds.), *Human stress and cognition*. New York: John Wiley.

Folling, A. (1934). Über Ausscheidung von Phenylbrenztraubensaure in den Harn als Stoffweckselanomalie in Verbindung mit Imbezillitat. *Atschrift fur physiolische chemistrie, 227*, 169–76.

Fowle, C. M. (1968). The effect of the severely mentally retarded child on his family. *American Journal of Mental Deficiency, 73*, 468–73.

Fox, R. A., & Rosen, D. L. (1977). A parent administered token program for dietary regulation of phenylketonuria. *Journal of Behavior Therapy and Experimental Psychiatry, 8*, 441–443.

Foxx, R. M. (1982). *Decreasing behaviors of severely retarded and autistic persons*. Champaign, IL: Research Press.

Fraenkel, W. A. (1961). *The mentally retarded and their vocational rehabilitation: A resource handbook*. Arlington, TX: National Association for Retarded Children.

Frankenberger, W. (1984). A survey of state guidelines for identification of mental retardation. *Mental Retardation, 22*(1), 17–20.

Frankenburg, W. K. (1972). *Screening and assessment of young children at developmental risks*. Department of Health, Education, and Welfare Publication No. (05)73–91. Washington, DC: Government Printing Office.

Frankenburg, W. K., & Dodds, J. B. (1967). The Denver Developmental Screening Test. *Journal of Pediatrics, 71*, 181–91.

Fraser, F. C. (1977). Genetic counseling. In A. S. Baer (Ed.), *Heredity and society: Readings in social genetics* (2nd ed.). New York: Macmillan.

Fredericks, H. D. B., Baldwin, V., Moore, W., Templeman, T. P., & Anderson, R. (1980). *The Teaching Research data-based classroom model, JASH, 5*, 211–23.

Fredericks, H. D. B., Riggs, C., Furey, T., Grove, D., Moore, W., McDonnell, J., Jordan, E., Hansen, W., Baldwin, V., & Wadlow, M. (1976). The Teaching Research curriculum for moderately and severely handicapped. Springfield, IL: Charles C. Thomas.

Friedrich, W. N., & Friedrich, W. L. (1981). Psychosocial assets of parents of handicapped and nonhandicapped children. *American Journal of Mental Deficiency, 85*, 551–553.

Fullan, M., & Loubser, J. J. (1972). Education and adaptive capacity. *Sociology of Education, 45*, 271–87.

Gage, N. L. (1972). IQ heritability, race differences, and educational research. *Phi Delta Kappan, 53*, 308–12.

Gallup Organization Report for the President's Committee on Mental Retardation. (1976). Public attitudes regarding mental retardation. In R. Nathan (Ed.), *Mental retardation: Century of decision*. Washington, DC: President's Committee on Mental Retardation.

Gamble, C. J. (1951). The prevention of mental deficiency by sterilization, 1949. *American Journal of Mental Deficiency, 56*, 192–97.

Garber, H., & Heber, R. (1973). *The Milwaukee Project: Early Intervention as a technique to prevent mental retardation.* Storrs: The University of Connecticut Technical Paper.

Garber, H. L., & Heber, R. (1981). The efficacy of early intervention with family rehabilitation. In M. J. Begab, H. C. Haywood, & H. L. Garber (Eds.), *Psychosocial Influences in Retarded Performance: Strategies for Improving Competence,* Vol. II, (p. 71–87). Baltimore: University Park Press.

Garber, H. L., & McIneney, M. (1982). Sociobehavioral factors in mental retardation. In P. T. Cegelka & H. J. Prehm, *Mental retardation: From categories to people.* Columbus, OH: Charles E. Merrill.

Gearheart, B. R. (1980). *Special education for the 80's.* St. Louis: C. V. Mosby.

Gelof, M. (1963). Comparison of systems of classification relating degree of retardation to measured intelligence. *American Journal of Mental Deficiency, 68,* 297–317.

Gilhool, T. K. (1976). The right to community services. In M. Kindred, J. Cohen, D. Penrod, & T. Shaffer (Eds.), *The mentally retarded citizen and the law.* New York: Free Press.

Ginsburg, H. (1972). *The myths of the deprived child: Poor children's intellect and education.* Englewood Cliffs, NJ: Prentice-Hall.

Goddard, J. J. (1912). *The Kallikak family.* New York: Macmillan.

Gold, M. W. (1973). Research on the vocational habilitation of the retarded: The present, the future. In N. R. Ellis (Ed.), *International review of research in mental retardation* (Vol. 6). New York: Academic Press.

Golden, M., & Berns, B. (1976). Social class and infant intelligence. In M. Lewis (Ed.), *Origins of intelligence.* New York: Plenum Press.

Goodman, L. V. (1976). Bill of rights for the handicapped. *American Education, 12*(6), 6–8.

Goodman, N., & Tizard, J. (1962). Prevalence of imbecility and idiocy among children. *British Medical Journal, 1,* 216–19.

Gordon, L. V. (1967). Gordon Occupational Checklist. New York: Harcourt Brace Jovanovich.

Gottesman, I. (1963). Genetic aspects of intelligent behavior. In N. R. Ellis (Ed.), *Handbook of mental deficiency.* New York: McGraw-Hill.

Gottlieb, J. (1975). Public, peer, and professional attitudes toward mentally retarded persons. In M. J. Begab & S. A. Richardson (Eds.), *The mentally retarded in society: A social science perspective.* Baltimore: University Park Press.

Gottlieb, J. (1981). Mainstreaming: Fulfilling the promise? *American Journal of Mental Deficiency, 86,* 115–126.

Gottlieb, J., & Leyser, Y. (1981). Facilitating the social mainstreaming of retarded children. *Exceptional Education Quarterly, 1*(4), 57–69.

Graham, F. K., Ernhart, C. B., Thurston, D., & Craft, M. (1962). Development three years after perinatal anoxia and other potentially damaging experiences. *Psychological Monographs, 76,* (Whole no. 522).

Gray, S. W., & Klaus, R. A. (1965). An experimental preschool program for culturally deprived children. *Child Development, 36,* 887–98.

Gray, S. W., & Klaus, R. A. (1968). The early training project for disadvantaged children: A report after five years. *Monographs for the Society for Research in Child Development, 33* (No. 4).

Gresham, F. M. (1982). Misguided mainstreaming: The case for social skills training with handicapped children. *Exceptional Children, 48,* 422–433.

Griffiths, D. E. (1959). *Administrative theory.* Englewood Cliffs, NJ: Prentice-Hall.

Grossman, F. K. (1972). *Brothers and sisters of retarded children: An exploratory study.* Syracuse, NY: Syracuse University Press.

Grossman, H. J. (Ed.). (1973). *Manual on terminology and classification in mental retardation.* Washington, DC: American Association on Mental Deficiency.

Grossman, H. J. (Ed.). (1977). *Manual on terminology and classification in mental retardation.* Washington, DC: American Association on Mental Deficiency.

Grossman, H. J. (1983). *Classification in Mental Retardation.* Washington, DC: American Association on Mental Deficiency.

Gruber, B., Reeser, R., & Reid, D. H. (1979). Providing a less restrictive environment for profoundly retarded persons by teaching independent walking skills. *Journal of Applied Behavior Analysis, 12,* 285–97.

Guess, D., Horner, R. D., Utley, B., Holvoet, J., Maxon, D., Tucker, D., & Warren, S. (1978). A functional curriculum sequencing model for teaching the severely handicapped. *AAESPH Review, 3,* 202–15.

Gunzburg, H. C. (1958). Psychological assessment in mental deficiency. In A. A. Clarke & A. D. B. Clarke (Eds.), *Mental deficiency—The changing outlook.* London: Methuen and Co.

Guskey, T. R. (1980). Individualizing within the group-centered classroom: The Mastery Learning Model. *Teacher Education and Special Education, 3*(4), 47–54.

Guskin, S. L. (1977). Paradigms for research on attitudes toward the mentally retarded. In P. Mittler (Ed.), *Research to practice in mental retardation.* Baltimore: University Park Press.

Guttmacher, M., & Weihofen, H. (1952). *Psychiatry and the law.* New York: Norton.

Haggard, H. W., & Jellinek, E. M. (1942). *Alcohol explained.* Garden City, NY: Doubleday.

Haldermann v. Pennhurst State School and Hospital, 446 F. Suppl. 1295 (E.D. Pa. 1977), aff'd in part, remanded in part. Nos. 74-1490, 78-1564, 78-1602 (3rd Cir. Dec. 13, 1979).

Hall, R. V., & Hall, M. C. (1980 a). *How to use systematic attention and approval (social reinforcement).* Lawrence, KS: H & H Enterprises.

Hall, R. V., & Hall, M. C. (1980 b). *How to use time out.* Lawrence, KS: H & H Enterprises.

Hallahan, D. P., & Kauffman, J. M. (1976). *Introduction to learning disabilities: A psycho-behavioral approach.* Englewood Cliffs, NJ: Prentice-Hall.

Halle, J. W., Silverman, N. A., & Regan, L. (1983). The effects of a data-based exercise program on physical fitness of retarded children. *Education and Training of the Mentally Retarded, 18*(3), 221–225.

Hamilton, D. L., & Bishop, G. D. (1976). Attitudinal and behavioral effects of initial integration of white suburban neighborhoods. *Journal of Social Issues, 32*, 47–67.

Hamilton, D. L., & Segal, R. M. (Eds.). (1975). Proceedings of a consultation-conference on the gerontological aspects of mental retardation. Ann Arbor: University of Michigan.

Hammill, D., Iano, R., McGettigan, J., & Weiderholt, L. (1972). Retardates' reading achievement in the resource room model: The first year. *Training School Bulletin, 63*, 105–7.

Hansen, J. C., Stevic, R. R. & Warner, R. W. (1972). *Counseling: Theory and process.* Boston: Allyn & Bacon.

Hanson, H. (1978). Decline of Down's syndrome after abortion reform in New York state. *American Journal of Mental Deficiency, 83*, 185–88.

Haring, N. G. (Ed.). (1977). *Developing effective individualized education programs for severely handicapped children and youth.* Washington, DC: Department of Health, Education, and Welfare.

Harth, R. (1977). Attitudes and mental retardation: Review of the literature. In C. J. Drew, M. L. Hardman, & H. P. Bluhm (Eds.), *Mental retardation: Social and educational perspectives.* St. Louis: C. V. Mosby.

Hashem, N., Ebrahim, A., & Nour, A. (1970). Classical and atypical phenylketonuria among Egyptians: Study of 10 families. *American Journal of Mental Deficiency, 75*, 329–35.

Haskins, J. S., & Stifle, J. M. (1978). *He will lift up his head: A report to the developmental disabilities office on the situation of handicapped Navajos and the implications thereof for all native Americans.* Office of Human Development (DHEW), Washington, D.C.

Hawkes, N. (1979). Tracing Burt's descent into scientific fraud. *Science, 205*, 673–75.

Hawkridge, D., Chalupsky, A., & Roberts, A. (1968). *A study of selected programs for the education of disadvantaged children.* Palo Alto, CA: American Institute for Research in the Behavior Sciences.

Hayden, A. H., & McGinness, G. D. (1977). Bases for early intervention. In E. Sontag, J. Smith, & N. Certo (Eds.), *Educational programming for the severely and profoundly handicapped.* Reston, VA: The Council for Exceptional Children.

Hayden, A. H., & Pious, C. G. (1979). The case for early intervention. In R. York & E. Edgar (Eds.), *Teaching the severely handicapped* (Vol. IV). Seattle: The American Association for the Education of the Severely/Profoundly Handicapped.

Haywood, H. C. (1979). What happened to mild and moderate mental retardation? *American Journal of Mental Deficiency, 83*, 429–39.

Heal, L. W., Sigelman, C. K., & Switzky, H. N. (1978). Research on community residential alternatives for the mentally retarded. In N. R. Ellis (Ed.), *International review of research in mental retardation* (Vol. 9, pp. 209–249). New York: Academic Press.

Hearnshaw, L. S. (1979). *Cyril Burt, psychologist.* Ithaca, NY: Cornell University.

Heber, R. F. (1959). A manual on terminology and classification in mental retardation. *Monograph Supplement American Journal of Mental Deficiency, 64.*

Heber, R. F. (1961). A manual on terminology and classification in mental retardation (Rev. ed.). *Monograph Supplement American Journal of Mental Deficiency, 64.*

Heber, R. F. (1964). Personality. In H. A. Stevens & R. F. Heber (Eds.), *Mental retardation: A review of research.* Chicago: University of Chicago Press.

Heber, R. F. & Deyer, R. B. (1970). Research on education and habilitation of the mentally retarded. In H. C. Haywood (Ed.), *Sociocultural aspects of mental retardation.* New York: Appleton-Century-Croft.

Heber, R. F., & Garber, H. (1967). The Milwaukee project: A study of the use of family intervention to prevent cultural-familial mental retardation. In B. Z. Friendlender (Ed.), *The exceptional infant: Assessment and intervention.* New York: Bruner/Mazel.

Heber, R. F., & Garber, H. (1971). An experiment in prevention of cultural-familial mental retardation. In D. A. Primrose (Ed.), *Proceedings of the Second Congress of the International Association for the Scientific Study of Mental Deficiency.* Warsaw: Polish Medical Publishers.

Henderson, N. D. (1982). Human Behavior Genetics. In M. R. Rosenzweig & L. W. Porter (Eds.), *Annual Review of Psychology,* Vol. 33, 403–440.

Hentoff, N. (1977). *Does anybody give a damn?* New York: Knopf.

Hernstein, R. J. (1982, August). IQ Testing and the Media. *The Atlantic Monthly,* 250 (2), 68–74.

Herr, E. L. (1976). *The emerging history of career education: A summary view.* Washington, DC: National Advisory Council on Career Education.

Herr, E. L. (1977). *The emerging history of career education: A summary view.* Washington, DC: National Advisory Council on Career Education.

Herr, S. S. (1984). The Phillip Becker case resolved: A chance for habilitation. *Mental Retardation, 22(1),* 35–39.

Herrnstein, R. (1971, September). I.Q. *Atlantic Monthly, 228,* 43–65.

Hess, R. D., & Shipman, V. C. (1965). Early experience and the socialization of cognitive modes in children. *Child Development, 36,* 869–86.

Heward, W. L., Dardig, J., & Rossett, A. (1979). *Working with parents of handicapped children.* Columbus, OH: Charles E. Merrill.

Heward, W. L., & Orlansky, M. D. (1984). *Exceptional children.* Columbus, OH: Charles E. Merrill.

Hewett, F. M., & Forness, S. (1977). *Education of exceptional learners* (2nd ed.). Boston: Allyn & Bacon.

Hilliard, L. T., & Kirman, B. H. (1965). *Mental deficiency* (2nd ed.). London: Churchill.

Hiskey, M. (1966). Hiskey-Nebraska Test of Learning Aptitude. Lincoln, NE: Union College Press.

Hobbs, N. (1975). *The futures of children.* San Francisco, CA: Jossey-Bass.

Hobson v. Hansen, 269 F. Supp. 401 (D.D.C. 1967, *affirmed sub norm. Smuck v. Hobson,* 408 F. 2d 175 (D.C. Cir 1969).

Hoefnagel, D., Andrew, E. D., Mireault, N. G., & Berndt, W. O. (1965). Hereditary choreathetosis, self-mutilation, and hyperuricemia in young males. *New England Journal of Medicine, 273,* 130–135.

Hollinger, C., & Jones, R. (1970). Community attitudes toward slow learners and mental retardates: What's in a name? *Mental Retardation, 8*(1), 1–23.

Holmes, C. S. (1982). Self monitoring reactivity and a severe feeding problem. *Journal of Clinical Child Psychology, 11,* 66–71.

Holroyd, J., & MacArthur, D. (1976). Mental retardation and stress on the parents: A contrast between Down's Syndrome and childhood autism. *American Journal of Mental Deficiency, 80*(4), 431–436.

Hopkins, G. A. (1982). A comparison of cytogenetic groups of children with Down's syndrome on verbal and nonverbal measures. *Exceptional People Quarterly, 1,* 329–342.

Howard, E. (1971, November 21). Innisfree village to be a haven. *The Daily Progress.*

Howe, S. G. (1848). *On the causes of idiocy;* being the supplement to a report by S. G. Howe and other commissioners appointed by the Governor of Massachusetts to inquire into the conditions of the idiots of the Commonwealth dated February 26, 1848. With an appendix. New York: Arno Press, 1972. Reprint of the 1848 ed.

Hoyt, K. B. (1982). Career education beginning of the end? Or a new beginning? *Career Development for Exceptional Individuals, 5,* 3–13.

Huberty, T. J., Koller, J. R., & Ten Brink, T. D. (1980). Adaptive behavior in the definition of mental retardation. *Exceptional Children, 46,* 256–61.

Hull, J. T., & Thompson, J. C. (1980). Predicting adaptive functioning of mentally retarded persons in community settings. *American Journal of Mental Deficiency, 85*(3), 253–261.

Humphrey, G., & Humphrey, M. (1962). *Wild boy of Aveyron.* New York: Appleton-Century-Crofts.

Hungerford, R. H., DeProspo, C. J., & Rosenzweig, L. E. (1948). The non-academic pupil. *Philosophy of occupational education.* New York: Association of New York City Teachers of Special Education.

Hunt, J. McV. (1961). *Intelligence and experience.* New York: Ronald Press.

Hunt, J. McV. (1969). *The challenge of incompetence and poverty.* Urbana, IL: University of Illinois Press.

Hunter, J., & Bellamy, G. T. (1977). Cable harness construction for severely retarded adults: A demonstration of training techniques. *AAESPH Review, 1*(7), 2–13.

Hurwitz, N. (1975, May). Communications networks and the urban poor. *Equal Opportunity Review*, 1–5.

Hutt, M. L. (1947). A clinical study of "consecutive" and "adaptive" testing with the revised Stanford-Binet. *Journal of Consulting Psychology, 11*, 93–103.

Hutt, M. L., & Gibby, R. G. (1979). The mentally retarded child: Development, training and education. (4th ed.). Boston: Allyn & Bacon.

Huxley, A. (1958). *Brave new world revisited*. New York: Perennial Library.

In re Cavitt, 157 N.W. 2d. 171 (1967).

In re Phillip B., 92 Cal. App. 3rd 796 (May 8, 1979).

In re Phillip B. Amicus, 1979, *4*, 115.

Ingalls, R. P. (1978). *Mental retardation: The changing outlook*. New York: John Wiley.

Ingle, D. J. (1967). Editorial: The need to study biological differences among racial groups: Moral issues. *Perspectives in Biology and Medicine, 10*, 497–99.

Inhelder, B. (1968). *The diagnosis of reasoning in the mentally retarded*. New York: John Day.

Innisfree Village. Brochure, Crozet, Virginia, n.d.

Intagliata, J. C., Willer, B. S., & Cooley, F. B. (1979). Cost comparison of institutional and community-based alternatives for mentally retarded persons. *Mental Retardation, 14*, 154–56.

Intagliata, J., & Willer, B. (1982). Reinstitutionalization of mentally retarded persons successfully placed into family-care and group homes. *American Journal of Mental Deficiency, 87*(1), 34–39.

International League of Societies for the Mentally Handicapped, October 24, 1968. (1969). In R. H. Finch, *MR 69: Toward progress: The story of a decade. Report of the President's Committee on Mental Retardation*. Washington, DC: U.S. Government Printing Office.

Is there a cure for mental retardation? (1980). *ARC News, 29*(3).

Itard, J. M. G. (1932, 1962). *(The wild boy of Aveyron.)* (G. Humphrey & M. Humphrey, eds. and trans.). New York: Appleton-Century-Crofts, (Prentice-Hall). (Originally published in Paris by Gouyon, 1801).

Jackson v. Indiana (1972). 406 U.S. 715.

Jaffe, J. (1966). Attitudes of adolescents toward the mentally retarded. *American Journal of Mental Deficiency, 70*, 907–12.

Janicki, M. P., & Mayeda, T., & Epple, W. A. (1983). Availability of group homes for persons with mental retardation in the United States. *Mental Retardation, 21*, 45–51.

Jastak, J., MacPhee, H., & Whiteman, M. (1963). *Mental retardation: Its nature and incidence*. Newark: University of Delaware Press.

Jencks, C. (1972). *Inequality: A reassessment of the effect of family and schooling in America*. New York: Basic Books.

Jensen, A. R. (1950). The clinical management of the mentally retarded child and the parents. *American Journal of Psychiatry, 106*, 830–33.

Jensen, A. R. (1966). Verbal mediation and educational potential. *Psychology in the Schools, 3,* 99–109.

Jensen, A. R. (1969). How much can we boost IQ and scholastic achievement? *Harvard Educational Review, 39,* 1–123.

Jensen, A. R. (1973). *Educability and group differences.* New York: Harper & Row.

Jensen, A. R. (1980). *Bias in mental testing.* New York: Free Press.

Jensen, A. R. (1981). *Straight talk about mental tests.* New York: Free Press.

Johnson, C. F., Koch, R., Peterson, R. M., & Friedman, E. G. (1978). Congenital and neurological abnormalities in infants with phenylketonuria. *American Journal of Mental Deficiency, 82,* 375–79.

Johnson, G. O. (1959). Here and there the Onondaga census—Fact or artifact. *Exceptional Children, 25,* 226–31.

Johnson, W. R. (1962). Special education for mentally handicapped—A paradox. *Exceptional Children, 19,* 62–69.

Johnson, W. R. (1971). Keynote address given at Planned Parenthood Center of Seattle, December 2–3, 1971. Unpublished manuscript.

Jones, K. L., Smith, D. W., & Hansen, J. W. (1976). The fetal alcohol syndrome: Clinical delineation. *Annals of the New York Academy of Science, 23,* 130–37.

Jones, K. L., Smith D. W., Ulleland, C. N., & Streissguth, A. P. (1973). Pattern of malformation in offspring of chronic alcoholic mothers. *Lancet, 1,* 1267–71.

Jones, Philip R. (1981). *A Practical Guide to Federal Special Education Law: Understanding and Implementing PL 94-142.* New York: Holt, Rinehart, & Winston.

Jordan, T. E. (1976). *The mentally retarded* (4th ed.). Columbus, OH: Charles E. Merrill.

Juel-Nielsen, N. (1965). Individual and environment: A psychiatric-psychological investigation of monozygotic twins reared apart. *Acta Psychiatra et Neurologica Scandanavia,* Monograph Supplement No. 183.

Kagan, J. (1970). On class differences and early development. In V. Denenberg (Ed.), *Education of the infant and young child.* New York: Academic Press.

Kahn, H., & Bruce-Briggs, B. (1972). *Things to come: Thinking about the seventies and eighties.* New York: Macmillan.

Kamin, L. J. (1974). *The science and politics of IQ.* Potomac, MD: Lawrence Erlbaum Associates.

Kanner, L. A. (1964). *A history of the care and study of the mentally retarded.* Springfield, IL: Charles C. Thomas.

Kantner, H. M. (1969). *The identification of elements which contribute to occupational success and failure of adults classified as educable mentally retarded.* Unpublished doctoral dissertation, Arizona State University.

Karan, O., Wehman, P., Renzaglia, A., & Schutz, R. (1976). *Habilitation practices with the severely developmentally disabled.* Madison: University of Wisconsin, Waisman Center on Mental Retardation & Human Development.

Karnes, M. B., Hodgins, A., & Teska, J. A. (1968). An evaluation of two preschool programs for disadvantaged children: A traditional and a highly structured experimental school. *Experimental Children, 34,* 667–76.

Karnes, M. B., & Zehrbach, R. P. (1977). Alternative models for delivering services to young handicapped children. In J. B. Jordan, A. H. Hayden, M. B. Karnes, & M. M. Wood (Eds.), *Early childhood education for exceptional children*. Reston, VA: The Council for Exceptional Children.

Kastner, L. S., Reppucci, N. D., & Pezzoli, J. J. (1979). Assessing community attitudes toward mentally retarded persons. *American Journal of Mental Deficiency, 84*, 137–44.

Katz, E. (Ed.). (1972). *Mental health services for the mentally retarded*. Springfield, IL: Charles C. Thomas.

Katz, S., & Yekutiel, E. (1974). Leisure time problems of mentally retarded graduates of training programs. *Mental Retardation, 12*(3), 54–57.

Kauffman, J. M. (1977). *Characteristics of children's behavior disorders*. Columbus, OH: Charles E. Merrill.

Kauffman, J. M. (1980). Where special education for disturbed children is going: A personal view. *Exceptional Children, 46*, 522–527.

Kauffman, J. M., & Krouse, J. (1981). The cult of educability: Searching for the substance of things hoped for; the evidence of things not seen. *Analysis and Intervention in Developmental Disabilities, 1*, 53–60.

Kauffman, J. M., & Payne, J. S. (1975). *Mental retardation: Introduction and personal perspectives*. Columbus, OH: Charles E. Merrill.

Kaufman, A., & Kaufman, N. (1983). *Kaufman Assessment Battery for Children, interpretive manual*. Circle Pines, MN: American Guidance Service.

Kaufman, M. J., & Morra, L. G. (1978). The least restrictive environment: A major philosophical change. In E. L. Meyen (Ed.), *Exceptional children and youth: An introduction*. Denver: Love Publishing.

Kearsley, R. (1979, September). In B. Rice, Brave new world of intelligence testing. *Psychology Today*, 27–41.

Keirn, W. C. (1971). Shopping parents: Patient problems or professional problem? *Mental Retardation, 9*(4), 6–7.

Keller, O. J., & Alper, B. S. (1970). Halfway houses: Community centered corrections and treatment. Lexington; MA: D.C. Heath.

Kelly, J. A., Wildman, R. G., & Berler, E. S. (1980). Small group behavioral training to improve the job interview skills repertoire of mildly retarded students. *Journal of Applied Behavior Analysis, 13*, 461–71.

Kemp, D. R. (1983). Assessing Human Rights Committees: A mechanism for protecting the rights of institutionalized mentally retarded persons. *Mental Retardation, 21*, 13–16.

Keniston, K., & The Carnegie Council on Children. (1977). *All our children: The American family under pressure*. New York: Carnegie Corporation.

Kennedy, M. M., & Danielson, L. C. (1978). Where are unserved handicapped children? *Education and Training of the Mentally Retarded, 13*, 408–13.

Keogh, B. K., & Daley, S. E. (1983). Early identification: One component of comprehensive services for at-risk children. *Topics in Early Childhood Special Education, 3*(3), 7–16.

Key, W. E. (1915). *Feeble-minded citizens in Pennsylvania.* Philadelphia: The Public Charities Association of Pennsylvania.

Kidd, J. W. (1977). Comments from the executive director: The definitional dilemma. *Education and Training of the Mentally Retarded, 12,* 303–4.

Kidd, J. W. (1979). An open letter to the Committee on Terminology and Classification of AAMD from the Committee on Definition and Terminology of CEC-MR. *Education and Training of the Mentally Retarded, 14,* 74–76.

Kidd, J. W. (1983). The 1983 AAMD definition and classification of mental retardation: The apparent impact of the CEC-MR position. *Education and Training of the Mentally Retarded, 5,* 243–244.

King, F. (1975). Treatment of the mentally retarded character in modern American fiction. *Bulletin of Bibliography, 32*(3), 106–14; 131.

Kirk, S. A. (1958). *Early education of the mentally retarded: An experimental study.* Urbana, IL: University of Illinois Press.

Kirk, S. A. (1962). *Educating exceptional children.* Boston: Houghton Mifflin.

Kirk, S. A. (1964). Research on the education of the mentally retarded. In H. A. Stevens & R. F. Heber (Eds.), *Mental retardation: A review of research.* Chicago: University of Chicago Press.

Kirk, S. A., & Gallagher, J. J. (1979). *Educating Exceptional Children* (3rd ed.). Boston: Houghton Mifflin.

Kleinberg, J., & Galligan, B. (1983). Effects of deinstitutionalization on adaptive behavior of mentally retarded adults. *American Journal of Mental Deficiency, 88*(1), 21–27.

Kneedler, R. D., Hallahan, D. P., & Kauffman, J. M. (1984). *Special education for today.* Englewood Cliffs, NJ: Prentice-Hall.

Koegel, R. L., Glahn, T. J., & Nieminen, G. S. (1978). Generalization of parent training results. *Journal of Applied Behavior Analysis, 11,* 95–109.

Kohlenberg, R. J. (1970). The punishment of persistent vomiting: A case study. *Journal of Applied Behavior Analysis, 11,* 95–109.

Kokaska, C. J. (1968). The occupational status of the educable mentally retarded: A review of follow-up studies. *Journal of Special Education, 2,* 369–77.

Kolstoe, O. P. (1961). An examination of some characteristics which discriminate between employed and not-employed mentally retarded males. *American Journal of Mental Deficiency, 66,* 472–82.

Kolstoe, O. P. (1972). *Mental retardation: An educational viewpoint.* New York: Holt, Rinehart, & Winston.

Kolstoe, O. P. (1975). Secondary programs. In J. M. Kauffman & J. S. Payne (Eds.), *Mental retardation: Introduction and personal perspectives.* Columbus, OH: Charles E. Merrill.

Kolstoe, O. P. (1976). *Teaching educable mentally retarded children.* New York: Holt, Rinehart, & Winston.

Kolstoe, O. P. (1981). Career education for the handicapped: Opportunities for the '80s. *Career Development for Exceptional Individuals, 4,* 3–13.

Kolstoe, O. P., & Frey, R. M. (1965). *A high school work study program for mentally subnormal students.* Carbondale, IL: Southern Illinois University Press.

Konig, K. (1966). The care and education of handicapped children. In C. Pietzner (Ed.), *Aspects of curative education.* Aberdeen, Scotland: Aberdeen University Press.

Krech, D., Rosenzweig, M. R., & Bennett, E. L.(1956). Dimensions of discrimination and level of cholinesterase activity in the cerebral cortex of the rat. *Journal of Comparative and Physiological Psychology, 49,* 261–68.

Kruger, R. (1980). Occupational information systems and their use in rehabilitation. *Rehabilitation Literature, 41,* 229–234.

Kugel, R. B. (1967). Familial mental retardation: Fact or fancy? In J. Hellmuth (Ed.), *Disadvantaged child* (Vol. 1). New York: Bruner/Mazel.

Kugel, R. B., & Parsons, M. H. (1967). *Children of deprivation: Changing the course of familial retardation.* Washington, DC: Children's Bureau.

Kugel, R. B., & Wolfensberger, W. (Eds.). (1969). *Changing patterns in residential services for the mentally retarded.* Washington, DC: U.S. Government Printing Office.

Kuhn, T. S. (1970). *The structure of scientific revolutions* (2nd ed.). Chicago: University of Chicago Press.

Kunzelmann, H. P., & Koenig, C. H. (1980). REFER: Rapid Exam for Early Referral. Columbus, OH: Charles E. Merrill.

Kurtz, D. P., Neisworth, J. T., & Laub, K. W. (1977). Issues concerning the early identification of handicapped children. *Journal of School Psychology, 15,* 136–40.

Kurtz, P. D. (1978). Family approaches. In J. T. Neisworth & R. M. Smith (Eds.), *Retardation: Issues, assessment, and intervention.* New York: McGraw-Hill.

Kurtz, R. A. (1977). *Social aspects of mental retardation.* Lexington, MA: Lexington Books.

LaBov, W. (1970). The logic of nonstandard English. In F. Williams (Ed.), *Language and poverty.* Chicago: Markham Publishing.

Lambert, N. M., & Nicoll, R. C. (1976). Dimensions of adaptive behavior of retarded and nonretarded public school children. *American Journal of Mental Deficiency, 81,* 135–46.

Lambert, N., & Windmiller, M. (1981). *AAMD Adaptive Behavior Scale-School Edition.* Monterey, CA: Publishers Test Service.

Lambert, N. M., Windmiller, M. B., & Cole, L. J. (1975). AAMD Adaptive Behavior Scale, Public School Version. Washington, DC: American Association on Mental Deficiency.

Lambie, D. Z., & Weikart, D. P. (1970). Ypsilanti Carnegie infant education project. In J. Hellmuth (Ed.), *Disadvantaged child* (Vol. 3). New York: Bruner/Mazel.

Landesmann-Dwyer, S. (1978). Behavioral changes in nonambulatory, profoundly mentally retarded individuals. In C. E. Meyers (Ed.), *Quality of life in severely and profoundly retarded people: Research foundations for improvement.* Washington, DC: American Association on Mental Deficiency.

Larry P. v. Riles C–71–2270 (RFP, District Court for Northern California), 1972.

Latkin, K. C., Bruininks, R. H., Hill, R. K., & Hauber, F. A. (1982). Turnover of direct-care staff in a national sample of residential facilities for mentally retarded persons. *American Journal of Mental Deficiency, 87,* 64–72.

Laub, K. W. & Kurtz (1978). Early identification. In J. Neisworth & R. M. Smith (Eds.), *Retardation: Issues, assessment and intervention.* New York: McGraw Hill.

LaVor, M. L. (1976). Federal legislation for exceptional persons: A history. In F. J. Weintraub, A. Abeson, J. Ballard, & M. LaVor (Eds.), *Public policy and the education of exceptional children.* Reston, VA: The Council for Exceptional Children.

LaVor, M. L. (1977). Federal legislation for exceptional children: Implications and a view of the field. In R. D. Kneedler & S. G. Tarver (Eds.), *Changing perspectives in special education.* Columbus, OH: Charles E. Merrill.

LaVor, M. L., & Harvey, J. (1976). Headstart, Economic Opportunity, Community Partnership Act of 1974. *Exceptional Children, 42,* 227–30.

Lawrence, E. A., & Winschel, J. F. (1975). Locus of control: Implications for special education. *Exceptional Children, 41,* 483–90.

Lawry, G. (1972). Matching students with gaps: A real challenge. In *Vocational evaluation and curriculum modification.* Des Moines: Department of Public Instruction.

Lazar, I., & Darlington, R. (1982). Lasting effects of early education: A report from the consortium for longitudinal studies. *Monographs of the Society for Research in Child Development, 47.*

Lehr, D. M., & Brown, F. (1984). Perspectives on the severely handicapped. In E. L. Meyen (Ed.), *Mental retardation: Topics of today and issues of tomorrow.* Reston, VA: CEC-MR.

Lehrke, R. (1972a). A theory of X-linkage of major intellectual traits. *American Journal of Mental Deficiency, 76,* 611–19.

Lehrke, R. (1972b). Response to Dr. Anastasi and to the Drs. Nance and Engel. *American Journal of Mental Deficiency, 76,* 626–31.

Lejeune, J., Gautier, M., & Turpin, R. (1959). Études des chromosomes somatiques de neuf enfants mongoliers. Paris, C. R. *Academy Science, 248,* 1721–22.

Leland, H. (1972). Mental retardation and adaptive behavior. *Journal of Special Education, 6,* 71–80.

Leland, H. (1973). Adaptive behavior and mentally retarded behavior. In R. K. Eymon, C. E. Meyers, & G. Tarjan (Eds.), *Sociobehavioral studies in mental retardation. Monographs of the American Association on Mental Deficiency, 1973* (No. 1), 91–99.

Leland, H. W. (1978). Theoretical considerations of adaptive behavior. In W. A. Coulter & H. W. Morrow (Eds.), *Adaptive behavior: Concepts and measurements.* New York: Grune & Stratton.

Lemkau, P., Tietze, C., & Cooper, M. (1962). Third paper, Mental hygiene problems in an urban district. *Mental Hygiene, 26,* 275–88.

Lenihan, J. (1976–77). Disabled Americans: A history. *Performance, 27*(5, 6, 7), 1–72.

Lerner, J. W. (1981). *Learning Disabilities: Theories, diagnosis and teaching strategies.* (3rd ed.). Boston: Houghton Mifflin.

Lesch, M., & Nyhan, W. L. (1964). A familial disorder of uric acid metabolism and central nervous system function. *American Journal of Medicine, 36,* 561–570.

Levitan, S. A., & Taggart, R. (1977). *Jobs for the disabled.* Washington, DC: John Hopkins University Press.

Levy, E., & McLeod, W. (1977). The effects of environmental design on adolescents in an institution. *Mental Retardation, 15*(2), 28–32.

Lewis, E. O. (1929). *Report of the mental deficiency committee.* Part IV. London: His Majesty's Stationery Office.

Lewis, J. F., & Mercer, J. R. (1978). The System of Multicultural Pluralistic Assessment: SOMPA. In W. A. Coulter & H. W. Morrow (Eds.), *Adaptive Behavior: Concepts and measurements.* New York: Grune & Stratton.

Libby, J. D., Polloway, E. A., & Smith, J. D. (1983). Lesch-Nyhan syndrome: A review. *Education and Training of the Mentally Retarded, 18,* 226–231.

Lillie, D. (1975, April). *Identification and screening.* Paper presented at the Infant Education Conference, San Antonio.

Lindsley, O. R. (1964). Direct measurement and prosthesis of retarded behavior. *Journal of Education, 147,* 62–81.

Lindsley, O. R. (1966). An experiment with parents handling behavior at home. *Johnstone Bulletin, 9,* 27–36.

Linstone, H. A. (1977). *The postindustrial society and mental retardation.* Paper presented for the President's Committee on Mental Retardation.

Litton, F. W. (1978). *Education of trainable mentally retarded: Curriculum, methods, materials.* St. Louis: C. V. Mosby.

Lubin, R. A., Schwartz, A. A., Zigman, W. B., & Janicki, M. P. (1982). Community acceptance of residential programs for developmentally disabled persons. *Applied Research in Mental Retardation, 3,* 191–200.

Luiselli, J. K. (1978). Treatment of an autistic child's fear of riding a school bus through exposure and reinforcement. *Journal of Behavior Therapy and Experimental Psychiatry, 9,* 169–172.

MacAndrew, C., & Edgerton, R. (1964). The everyday life of institutionalized "idiots." *Human Organism, 23,* 312–18.

MacArthur, C. A., Jr., Hagerty, G., & Taymans, J. (1982). Personnel preparation: A catalyst in career education for the handicapped. *Exceptional Education Quarterly, 3*(3), 1–8.

MacMillan, D. L. (1977). *Mental retardation in school and society.* Boston: Little, Brown.

MacMillan, D. L. (1982). *Mental retardation in school and society* (2nd ed.). Boston: Little, Brown.

MacMillan, D. L., & Borthwick, S. (1980). The new educable mentally retarded population: Can they be mainstreamed? *Mental Retardation, 18,* 155–158.

MacMillan, D. L., Jones, R. L., & Aloia, G. F. (1974). The mentally retarded label: A theoretical analysis and review of research. *American Journal of Mental Deficiency, 79,* 241–261.

MacMillan, D. L., Meyers, C. E., & Morrison, G. M. (1980). System-identification of mildly mentally retarded children: Implications for interpreting and conducting research. *American Journal of Mental Deficiency, 85*(2), 108–115.

Mallory, B. M. (1977). The ombudsman in a residential institution: A description of the role and suggested training areas. *Mental Retardation, 15*(5), 14–17.

Maloney, M. P. & Ward, M. P. (1978). *Mental retardation and modern society.* New York: Oxford University Press.

Mandell, C. J., & Gold, V. (1984). *Teaching handicapped students.* St. Paul, MN: West.

Marks, H. E., & Wade, R. (1981). A device for reducing object destruction among institutionalized mentally retarded persons. *Mental Retardation, 19,* 181–182.

Marland, S. P. (1971). Career education now. *The Education Digest, 36,* 9–11.

Marland, S. P. (1972). Career education: Every student headed for a goal. *American Vocational Journal, 47*(3), 34–36.

Marlowe, M., Errera, J., & Jacobs, J. (1983). Increased lead and cadmium disorders among mentally retarded children and children with borderline intelligence. *American Journal of Mental Deficiency, 87,* 477–483.

Marsh, R. L., Friel, C. M., & Eissler, V. (1975). The adult MR in the criminal justice system. *Mental Retardation, 13*(2), 21–25.

Martin, E. W. (1972). Individualism and behaviorism as future trends in educating handicapped children. *Exceptional Children, 38,* 517–25.

Martinson, R. A., (1973). Children with superior cognitive abilities. In L. M. Dunn (Ed.), *Exceptional children in the schools* (2nd ed.). New York: Harper & Row.

Masland, R., Sarason, S., & Gladwin, T. (1958). *Mental subnormality.* New York: Basic Books.

Maslow, A. H. (1954). *Motivation and personality.* New York: Harper & Row.

Massie, W. (1962). Sheltered workshops: A 1962 portrait. *Journal of Rehabilitation, 28*(5), 17–20.

Matthews v. Campbell, Civil Action No. 78–0879–R (Ed. Va. Jul. 16, 1979).

Mayo, L. W. (1962). *A proposed program for national action to combat mental retardation.* Report to the President's Committee on Mental Retardation. Washington, DC: U.S. Government Printing Office.

Mazzullo, M. (1977, April). *The mandate: to identify children with handicapping conditions.* (ERIC Document Reproduction Service No. ED 139-225).

McCarthy, M. M. (1983). The Pennhurst and Rowley decisions: Issues and implications. *Exceptional Children, 49,* 517–522.

McCarver, R. B., & Craig, E. M. (1974). Placement of the retarded in the community: Prognosis and outcome. In N. R. Ellis (Ed.), *International review of research in mental retardation* (Vol. 7). New York: Academic Press.

McLoughlin, J., & Lewis, R. (1981). *Assessing special students*. Columbus, OH: Charles E. Merrill.

Menolascino, F. J. (1974). The mentally retarded offender. *Mental Retardation, 12*(1), 7–11.

Menolascino, F. J., & Egger, M. L. (1978). *Medical dimensions of mental retardation*. Lincoln: University of Nebraska Press.

Menolascino, F. J., & McGee, J. J. (1981). The new institutions: Last ditch arguments. *Mental Retardation, 19*, 215–220.

Mercer, C. D. (1983). *Students with learning disabilities* (2nd ed.). Columbus, OH: Charles E. Merrill.

Mercer, C. D., & Mercer, A. R. (1985). *Teaching students with learning problems* (2nd ed.). Columbus, OH: Charles E. Merrill.

Mercer, C. D., & Payne, J. S. (1975). Learning theories and their implications. In J. M. Kauffman & J. S. Payne (Eds.), *Mental retardation: Introduction and personal perspectives*. Columbus, OH: Charles E. Merrill.

Mercer, C. D., & Snell, M. E. (1977). *Learning theory research in mental retardation: Implications for teaching*. Columbus, OH: Charles E. Merrill.

Mercer, J. R. (1973a). *Labeling the mentally retarded*. Berkeley: University of California Press.

Mercer, J. R. (1973b). The myth of 3% prevalence. In R. K. Eyman, C. E. Meyers, & G. Tarjan (Eds.). *Sociobehavioral studies in mental retardation. Monographs of the American Association on Mental Deficiency* (No. 1).

Mercer, J. R. (1977). *System of Multicultural Pluralistic Assessment: Technical Manual*. New York: Psychological Corporation.

Mercer, J. R., & Lewis, J. F. (1977a). *System of Multicultural Pluralistic Assessment: Parent interview manual*. New York: Psychological Corporation.

Mercer, J. R., & Lewis, J. F. (1977b). *System of Multicultural Pluralistic Assessment: Student assessment manual*. New York: Psychological Corporation.

Mesibov, G. B. (1976). Mentally retarded people: 200 years in America. *Journal of Clinical Child Psychology, 5*(3), 25–29.

Meyen, E. L. (1978). *Exceptional children and youth: An introduction*. Denver: Love Publishing.

Meyers, C. E., & MacMillan, D. L. (1976). Utilization of learning principles in retardation. In R. Koch & J. Dobson (Eds.), *The mentally retarded child and his family: A multidisciplinary handbook* (2nd ed.). New York: Bruner/Mazel.

Meyers, R. (1980). *Like normal people*. New York: McGraw-Hill.

Miller, S. J., & Sloane, H. N. (1976). The generalization effects of parent training across stimulus settings. *Journal of Applied Behavior Analysis, 9*, 355–370.

Mills v. Board of Education of District of Columbia, 348 F. Supp. 866 (D.D.C. 1972).

Mithaug, D. (1979). A comparison of procedures to increase responding in three severely retarded, noncompliant young adults. *AAESPH Review, 4*(1), 66–80.

Mosier, H. D., Grossman, H. J., & Dingman, H. F. (1962). Secondary sex development in mentally deficient individuals. *Child Development, 33,* 273–286.

Mosier, H. D., Grossman, H. J., & Dingman, H. F. (1965). Physical growth in mental defectives. *Pediatrics, 36,* 465–519.

Munro, J. D., Duncan, H. G., & Seymour, L. M. (1983). Effect of frontline staff turnover on the behavior of institutionalized mentally retarded adults. *American Journal of Mental Deficiency, 88,* 328–332.

Naisbitt, J. (1984). *Megatrends: Ten new directions transforming our lives.* New York: Warner Books.

Nance, W. E., & Engel, E. (1972). One x and four hypotheses: Response to Lehrke's "A theory of X-linkage of major intellectual traits." *American Journal of Mental Deficiency, 76,* 623–25.

Nardella, M. T., Sulzbacher, S. I., & Worthington-Roberts, B. S. (1983). Activity levels of persons with Prader-Willi Syndrome. *American Journal of Mental Deficiency, 87,* 498–505.

National Advisory Committee on the Handicapped. (1976). *Annual Report.* Washington, DC: U.S. Office of Education.

National Association for Retarded Children (1971). *Policy statements on the education of mentally retarded children.* Arlington, TX: Author.

National Association for Retarded Citizens (1978). *Mainstreaming mentally retarded students in the public schools: Proposed position statement.* Arlington, TX: Author.

National Association of Sheltered Workshops and Homebound Programs. Publications Committee. (1961). *Planning a workshop: A growing responsibility.* Washington, DC: Author.

National Association of State Directors of Special Education. (1977). *Child find data: A report of feedback information.* Washington, DC: Author. (ERIC Document Reproduction Service No. ED 149 552).

National Association of Superintendents of Public Residential Facilities for the Mentally Retarded (1974). *Contemporary issues in residential programming.* Washington, DC: President's Committee on Mental Retardation.

Neisworth, J. T., Jones, R. T., & Smith, R. M. (1978). Body behavior problems: A conceptualization. *Education and Training of the Mentally Retarded, 13,* 265–71.

Neisworth, J. T., & Smith, R. M. (1975). *Modifying retarded behavior.* Boston: Houghton Mifflin.

Neisworth, J. T., & Smith, R. M. (1978). *Retardation: Issues, assessment and intervention.* New York: McGraw-Hill.

Nelson, C. M. (1977). Alternative education for the mildly and moderately handicapped. In R. D. Kneedler & S. G. Tarver (Eds.), *Changing perspectives in special education.* Columbus, OH: Charles E. Merrill.

New York Association for Retarded Children v. Rockefeller, 357 F. Supp. 752 (E.D.N.Y. 1973). Final consent judgment entered, Civil Nos. 72C 356, 72C 357 (E.D.N.Y. entered May 5, 1975).

Newman, H. H., Freeman, F. N., & Holzinger, K. J. (1937). *Twins: A study of heredity and environment*. Chicago: University of Chicago Press.

Nihira, K. (1969). Factorial dimensions of adaptive behavior in adult retardates. *American Journal of Mental Deficiency, 73*, 868–78.

Nihira, K. (1976). Dimensions of adaptive behavior in institutionalized mentally retarded children and adults. *American Journal of Mental Deficiency, 81*, 215–26.

Nihira, K., Foster, R., Shellhaas, M., & Leland, H. (1969). *Adaptive Behavior Scales: Manual*. Washington, DC: American Association on Mental Deficiency.

Nihira, K., Foster, R., Shellhaas, M., & Leland, H. AAMD Adaptive Behavior Scale (1974 Rev.). Washington, DC: American Association on Mental Deficiency.

Nihira, K., Meyers, E., & Mink, I. T. (1983). Reciprocal relationship between home environment and development of TMR adolescents. *American Journal of Mental Deficiency, 88*, 139–149.

Nirje, B. (1969). The normalization principle and its human management implications. In R. B. Kugel & W. Wolfensberger (Eds.), *Changing patterns in residential services for the mentally retarded*. Washington, DC: U.S. Government Printing Office.

Nolley, D., & Nolley, B. (1984). Microcomputer data analysis at the clinical mental retardation site. *Mental Retardation, 22*, 85–89.

Noonan, M. J., Brown, F., Mulligan, M., & Rettig, M. A. (1982). Educability of severely handicapped persons: Both sides of the issue. *TASH Journal, 7*, 3–12.

Nyhan, W. L. (1976). Behavior in the Lesch-Nyhan syndrome. *Journal of Autism and Childhood Schizophrenia, 6*, 235–252.

Nyhan, W. L., Johnson, H. G., Kaufman, I. A., & Jones, K. (1980). Serotonergic approaches to the modification of behavior in the Lesch-Nyhan syndrome. *Applied Behavior in Mental Retardation, 1*, 25–40.

Oberman, C. E. (1965). *A history of vocational rehabilitation in America*. Minneapolis: T. S. Denison.

O'Connor v. Donaldson, 493 F. 2d 507 (5th Cir. 1974), *vacated and remanded on the issue of immunity*, 95 S. Ct. 258b (1975).

O'Connor, N. (1975). Imbecility and color blindness. *American Journal of Mental Deficiency, 62*, 83–87.

O'Connor, N. (1966). The prevalence of mental defect. In A. M. Clarke & A. D. B. Clarke (Eds.), *Mental deficiency: The changing outlook*. New York: Free Press.

Ogden, C. K. (1934). *The system of basic English*. New York: Harcourt, Brace, Jovanovich.

Olshansky, S. (1962). Chronic sorrow: A response to having a mentally defective child. *Social Casework, 43*, 190–93.

Olshansky, S. (1966). Parent responses to a mentally defective child. *Mental Retardation, 4*(4), 21–23.

O'Neill, C., & Bellamy, G. T. (1978). Evaluation of a procedure for teaching saw chain assembly to a severely retarded woman. *Mental Retardation, 16*, 37–41.

Osgood, C., Gorsuch, L., & McGrew, B. (1966). *Survey of mental retardation services in the Kansas City metropolitan area.* Kansas City, MO: Institute for Community Studies.

Otto, P. L., Sulzbacher, S. I., & Worthington-Roberts, B. S. (1982). Sucrose-induced behavior changes of persons with Prader-Willi syndrome. *American Journal of Mental Deficiency, 86*, 335–41.

Overmier, J. B., & Seligman, M. E. P. (1967). Effects of inescapable shock upon subsequent escape and avoidance learning. *Journal of Comparative and Physiological Psychology, 63*, 22–33.

Page, E. G. (1972). Miracle in Milwaukee: Raising the IQ: *Educational Researcher, 15*, 8–16.

Page, E. P., & Grandon, G. M. (1981). Massive intervention and child intelligence: The Milwaukee Project in Critical Perspective. *Journal of Special Education, 15*, 239–256.

Paige, D. M. (1975). Nutritional deficiency and school performance. In R. A. Haslam & P. J. Valletutti (Eds.), *Medical problems in the classroom.* Baltimore: University Park Press.

Parker, R. M. (1983). *Occupational aptitude survey and interest schedule.* Austin, TX: Pro Ed.

Pasamanick, B. (1959). Influence of sociocultural variables upon organic factors in mental retardation. *American Journal of Mental Deficiency, 64*, 316–20.

Patrick, J. L., & Reschly, D. L. (1982). Relationship of state educational criteria and demographic variables to school-system prevalence of mental retardation. *American Journal of Mental Deficiency, 86*, 351–60.

Patton, J. R., & Payne, J. S. (in press). Mild mental retardation. In N. G. Haring and L. P. McCormick (Eds.), *Exceptional children and youth* (4th ed.). Columbus, OH: Charles E. Merrill.

Patton, J. R., & Polloway, E. A. (1982). The learning disabled: The adult years. *Topics in Learning and Learning Disabilities, 2*(3), 79–88.

Payne, J. S. (1962). A prevalence survey of severely mentally retarded in Wyandotte County, Kansas. Unpublished masters thesis, University of Kansas.

Payne, J. S. (1971). Prevalence survey of severely mentally retarded in Wyandotte County, Kansas. *Training School Bulletin, 67*, 220–27.

Payne, J. S., & Chaffin, J. D. (1968). Developing employer relations in a work-study program for the educable mentally retarded. *Education and Training of the Mentally Retarded, 3.*

Payne, J. S., Miller, A. K., Hazlett, R. L., & Mercer, C. D. (1984). *Rehabilitation techniques: Vocational adjustment for the handicapped.* New York: Human Science Press.

Payne, J. S., Kauffman, J. M., Patton, J. R., Brown, G. B., & DeMott, R. M. (1979). *Exceptional children in focus* (2nd ed.). Columbus, OH: Charles E. Merrill.

Payne, J. S., & Mercer, C. D. (1974). Head Start. In S. E. Goodman (Ed.), *Handbook on contemporary education*. Princeton, NJ: Bowker.

Payne, J. S., Mercer, C. D., & Epstein, M. H. (1974). *Education and rehabilitation techniques*. New York: Behavioral Publications.

Payne, J. S., Patton, J. R., Kauffman, J. M., Brown, G. B., & Payne, R. A. (1983). *Exceptional Children in Focus* (3rd ed.). Columbus, OH: Charles E. Merrill.

Payne, J. S., Polloway, E. A., Smith, J. E., & Payne, R. A. (1977). *Strategies for teaching the mentally retarded*. Columbus, OH: Charles E. Merrill.

Payne, J. S., Polloway, E. A., Smith, J. E., & Payne, R. A. (1981). *Strategies for teaching the mentally retarded* (2nd ed.). Columbus, OH: Charles E. Merrill.

Pearson, P. H. (1972). *Physical therapy services in the developmental disabilities*. Springfield, IL: Charles C. Thomas.

Pennsylvania Association for Retarded Children v. Commonwealth of Pennsylvania, Civil Action No. 71-42, 3-Judge Court, E.D. Pennsylvania, 1971.

Penrose, L. S. (1966). *The biology of mental defect* (2nd rev. ed.). New York: Grune & Stratton.

Penrose, L. S. (1963). *The Biology of Mental Deficiency*. London: Sidgwick & Jackson.

Perkins, S. A. (1977). Malnutrition and mental development. *Exceptional Children, 43*, 214–19.

Perske, R. (1972). The dignity of risk and the mentally retarded. *Mental Retardation, 10*(1), 24–27.

Petzy, V. (1979). A model for employer commitment to job development. *Career Development for Exceptional Individuals, 2*(2), 80–89.

Phelps, L. A., & Lutz, R. J. (1977). *Career exploration and preparation for the special needs learner*. Boston: Allyn & Bacon.

Piaget, J. (1969). *The theory of stages in cognitive development*. New York: McGraw-Hill.

Pietzner, C. (1966). In C. Pietzner (Ed.), *Aspects of curative education*. Aberdeen, Scotland: Aberdeen University Press.

Pines, M. (1966). *Revolution in learning*. New York: Harper & Row.

Pines, M. (1973). *The brain changers: Scientists and the new mind control*. New York: Signet.

Pines, M. (1979, September). A head start in the nursery. *Psychology Today*, 56–68.

Pinneau, S. A. (1955). The infantile disorders of hospitalism and anaclitic depression. *Psychological Bulletin, 52*, 429–52.

Polloway, E. A. (1984). The integration of mildly retarded students in the schools: A historical review. *Remedial and Special Education, 5*(4), 18–28.

Polloway, E. A., Epstein, M. H., & Cullinan, D. (1984). Prevalence of behavior problems among educable mentally retarded students. Manuscript submitted for publication.

Polloway, E. A., & Payne, J. S. (1975). Comparison of the AAMD Heber and Grossman manuals on terminology and classification in mental retardation. *Mental Retardation, 13*(3), 12–14.

Polloway, E. A., Payne, J. S., Patton, J. R., & Payne, R. A. (1985). *Strategies for teaching retarded and special needs learners.* Columbus: Charles E. Merrill.

Polloway, E. A., & Smith, J. D. (1983). Changes in mild mental retardation: Population, programs, and perspectives. *Exceptional Children, 50,* 149–59.

Polloway, E. A., & Smith, J. D. (1984). The right to life: A survey of attitudes among the staff of a residential facility for mentally retarded persons. In J. D. Smith & E. A. Polloway (Eds.), *Special education in transition.* Lynchburg, VA: Vanity Press/Lynchburg College.

Porteus, S. T. (1933). The Porteus Maze Test. New York: The Psychological Corporation.

Powell, T. H., Aiken, J. M., & Smylie, M. A. (1982). Treatment of involuntary euthanasia for severely handicapped newborns: Issues of philosophy and public policy. *The Journal for the Association for the Severely Handicapped, 6*(4), 3–10.

President's Committee on Mental Retardation. (1970). *The six-hour retarded child.* Washington, DC: U.S. Government Printing Office.

President's Committee on Mental Retardation. (1974, April). Gallup poll shows attitudes on MR improving. *President's Committee on Mental Retardation Message.*

President's Committee on Mental Retardation. (1976a). *Mental retardation: Century of decision.* Washington, DC: U.S. Government Printing Office.

President's Committee on Mental Retardation. (1976b). *Mental retardation: The known and the unknown.* Washington, DC: U.S. Government Printing Office.

President's Committee on Mental Retardation. (1977). *Mental retardation: Past and present.* Washington, DC: U.S. Government Printing Office.

President's Committee on Mental Retardation. (1978, March). Washington, DC: PCMR Newsclipping Service.

Pueschel, S. M., Hays, R. M., & Mendoza, T. (1983). Familial X-linked mental retardation syndrome associated with minor congenital anomalies, macroorchidism, and fragile-X chromosome. *American Journal of Mental Deficiency, 87,* 372–376.

Pulliam, J. D. (1968). *History of education in America.* Columbus, OH: Charles E. Merrill.

Raech, H. (1966). A parent discusses initial counseling. *Mental Retardation, 4*(2), 25–26.

Ramey, C. T., & Haskins, R. (1981). The causes and treatment of school failure: Insights from the Carolina Abecedarian Project. In M. J. Begab, H. C. Haywood, & H. L. Garber (Eds.). *Psychosocial Influences in Retarded Performance: Strategies for Improving Competence* Vol. II. (pp. 89–112). Baltimore: University Park Press.

Ramey, C. T., & Campbell, F. A. (1984). Preventive education for high-risk children: Cognitive consequences of the Carolina Abecedarian project. *American Journal of Mental Deficiency, 88*, 515–23.

Rappaport, J. (1977). *Community psychology: Values, research, and action.* New York: Holt, Rinehart, & Winston.

Raven, I. C. (1958). Standard Progressive Matrices, Sets A, B, C, D, and E. London: H. K. Lewis & Co.

Raynes, N. V., Bumstead, D. C., & Pratt, M. W. (1974). Unitization: Its effect on residential care practices. *Mental Retardation, 12*(4), 12–124.

Reed, E. W., & Reed, S. C. (1965). *Mental retardation: A family study.* Philadelphia: W. B. Saunders.

Reger, R., & Koppman, N. (1971). The child-oriented resource room. *Exceptional Children, 37*, 460–62.

Reitan, R. M., & Davison, L. A. (Eds.). (1974). *Clinical neuropsychology: Current status and applications.* Washington, DC: N.H. Winston & Sons.

Report on Education of the Handicapped. (1979). *5*(14), 5.

Repp, A. C., (1983). *Teaching the mentally retarded.* Englewood Cliffs, NJ: Prentice-Hall.

Repp, A. C. & Deitz, D. (1979). Reinforcement-based reductive procedures: Training and monitoring performance of institutional staff. *Mental Retardation, 17*, 221–26.

Reschly, J. D. (1982). Assessing mild retardation: The influence of adaptive behavior, sociocultural status, and prospects for nonbiased assessment. In C. R. Reynolds & T. B. Gutkin (Eds.), *A handbook for school psychology.* New York: John Wiley.

Restak, R. (1975, September). Genetic counseling for defective parents: The danger of knowing too much. *Psychology Today,* 21–23, 92–93.

Rheingold, H. L. (1956). The modification of social responsiveness in institutional babies. *Monograph of the Society for Research in Child Development, 21* (No. 2).

Rheingold, H. L., & Bayley, N. (1959). Later effects of an experimental modification of mothering. *Child Development, 31*, 565–75.

Ribble, M. A. (1944). Infantile experience in relation to personality development. In J. McV. Hunt (Ed.), *Personality and the behavior disorders.* New York: Ronald Press.

Richards, B. W., Sylvester, R. E., & Brooker, C. (1981). Fragile X-linked mental retardation: The Martin-Bell syndrome. *Journal of Mental Deficiency Research, 25*, 253–258.

Richardson, S. A. (1981). Family characteristics associated with mild mental retardation. In M. J. Begab, H. C. Haywood, & H. L. Garber (Eds.), *Psychosocial Influences in Retarded Performance: Strategies for Improving Competence,* Vol. II (pp. 29–43). Baltimore: University Park Press.

Rights Policy Reaffirmed. (1978, December). *The Daily Progress,* p. 1.

Rivera, G. (1972). *Willowbrook.* New York: Random House.

Roberts, R. W. (1965). *Vocational and practical arts education: History, development, and principles* (2nd ed.). New York: Harper & Row.

Robinault, I. P. (Ed.). (1973). *Functional aids for the multiply handicapped.* New York: Harper & Row.

Robinson, H. B., & Robinson, N. M. (1970). Mental retardation. In P. H. Mussen (Ed.), *Carmichael's manual of child psychology* (3rd ed.) (Vol. 2). New York: John Wiley.

Robinson, N. K., & Robinson, H. B. (1976). *The mentally retarded child* (2nd ed.). New York: McGraw-Hill.

Rogers, C. R. (1951). *Client-centered therapy: Its current practice, implications, and theory.* Boston: Houghton Mifflin.

Rogers-Warren, A. K., & Poulson, C. L. (1984). Perspectives on early childhood education. In E. L. Meyen (Ed.), *Mental retardation: Topics of Today—Issues of Tomorrow* (pp. 67–68). Washington, DC: Division of Mental Retardation of the Council for Exceptional Children.

Roistacher, R. C., & Holstrom, E. I., Cantril, A. H., & Chase, J. T. (1982). Toward a comprehensive data system on the demographic and epidemological characteristics of the handicapped population: Final report. National Institute of Handicapped Research. (ERIC Document Reproduction Service No. ED 182 465).

Roos, P. (1975). Parents and families of the mentally retarded. In J. M. Kauffman & J. S. Payne (Eds.), *Mental retardation: Introduction and personal perspectives.* Columbus, OH: Charles E. Merrill.

Rosen, L. (1955). Selected aspects in the development of the mother's understanding of her mentally retarded child. *American Journal of Mental Deficiency, 59,* 522–528.

Rosen, M. (1970). Conditioning appropriate heterosexual behavior in mentally and socially handicapped populations. *Training School Bulletin, 66,* 172–77.

Rosen, M. (1972, October). Psychosexual adjustment of the mentally handicapped. In M. S. Bass (Ed.), *Sexual rights and responsibilities of the mentally retarded.* Proceedings of the conference of the American Association on Mental Deficiency, Region IX, Newark, Delaware.

Rosen, M., Clark, G. R., & Kivitz, M. S. (1977). *Habilitation of the handicapped: New dimensions in programs for the developmentally disabled.* Baltimore: University Park Press.

Ross, A. O. (1976). *Psychological aspects of learning disabilities and reading disorders.* New York: McGraw-Hill.

Rotegard, L. L., Bruininks, R. H., & Krantz, G. C. (1984). State operated residential facilities for people with mental retardation: July 1, 1978–June 30, 1982. *Mental Retardation, 22,* 69–74.

Rotter, J. B. (1954). *Social learning and clinical psychology.* Englewood Cliffs, NJ: Prentice-Hall.

Rowe, P. (1984). Opportunity for the Retarded, Inc. says "Nuts" to Counting Bolts. *Human Development News,* 2–3.

Rubin, R. A., Krus, P., & Balow, B. (1973). Factors in special class placement. *Exceptional Children, 39*, 525–32.

Rusch, F. R. (1979). Toward the validation of social/vocational survival skills. *Mental Retardation, 17*, 143–45.

Rusch, F. R. (1983). Competitive vocational training. In M. E. Snell (Ed.) *Systematic instruction of the moderately and severely handicapped* (2nd ed., pp. 503–523). Columbus, OH: Charles E. Merrill.

Russell, A. T., & Tanguay, P. E. (1981). Mental illness and mental retardation: Cause or coincidence? *American Journal of Mental Deficiency, 85*, 570–574.

Ryan, W. (1976), *Blaming the victim* (Rev. ed.). New York: Vintage Books.

Rynders, J. E., Spiker, D., & Hurrobin, J. M. (1978). Underestimating the educability of Down's syndrome children: Examination of methodological problems in recent literature. *American Journal of Mental Deficiency, 82*, 440–48.

Sabatino, D. A. (1971). An evaluation of resource rooms for children with learning disabilities. *Journal of Learning Disabilities, 4*, 84–93.

Saenger, G. (1957). *The adjustment of severely retarded adults in the community.* Albany, NY: Interdependent Mental Health Resources Board.

Safer, N., Burnette, J., & Hobbs, B. (1977). Exploration 1993: The effects of future trends on services to the handicapped. *Focus on Exceptional Children, 11(3)*, 21–23.

Sagan, C. (1977). *The dragons of Eden: Speculations of the evolution of human intelligence.* New York: Ballantine Books.

Sailor, W. & Mix, B. J. (1975). The TARC Assessment System. Lawrence, KS: H & H Enterprises.

Salend, S. J., & Ehrlich, E. (1983). Involving students in behavior modification programs. *Mental Retardation, 21*, 95–100.

Sali, J., & Amir, M. (1970). Personal factors influencing the retarded person's success at work: A report from Israel. *American Journal of Mental Deficiency, 76*, 42–47.

Salvia, J., & Ysseldyke, J. E. (1981). *Assessment in special and remedial education.* Boston: Houghton Mifflin.

Salvia, J., & Ysseldyke, J. E. (1985). *Assessment in special and remedial education* (3rd ed.). Boston: Houghton Mifflin.

Salzburg, C. L., & Villani, T. V. (1983). Speech training by parents of Down syndrome toddlers. Generalization across settings and instructional contexts. *American Journal of Mental Deficiency, 87*, 403–413.

San Antonio Independent School District v. Rodriquez, 411 U.S. (1973).

Sandgrund, A., Gaines, R. W., & Green, A. H. (1974). Child abuse and mental retardation: A problem of cause and affect. *American Journal of Mental Deficiency, 79*, 327–330.

Sarason, S. B. (1974). *The psychological sense of community.* San Francisco: Jossey-Bass.

Sattler, J. (1974). *Assessment of Children's Intelligence.* Philadelphia: W. B. Saunders.

Sattler, J. (1982). *Assessment of Children's Intelligence and Special Abilities* (2nd ed.). Boston: Allyn & Bacon.

Scarr, S., & Carter-Saltzman, L. (1982). Genetics and Intelligence. In R. J. Sternberg (Ed.), *Handbook of Human Intelligence* (pp. 798–896). Cambridge: Cambridge University Press.

Scarr-Salapatek, S. (1971a). Race, social class and IQ. *Science, 174,* 1285–95.

Scarr-Salapatek, S. (1971b). Unknowns in the IQ equation. *Science, 174,* 1223–28.

Scheerenberger, R. C. (1976a). *Current trends and status of public residential services for the mentally retarded, 1974.* Madison, WI: National Association of Superintendents of Public Residential Facilities.

Scheerenberger, R. C. (1976b). *Deinstitutionalization and institutional reform.* Springfield, IL: Charles C. Thomas.

Scheerenberger, R. C. (1977). A study of public residential facilities, 1976. *Mental Retardation, 15*(5), 58.

Scheerenberger, R. C. (1982). Public residential services, 1981: Status and trends. *Mental Retardation, 20,* 210–215.

Scheiderman, G., Lowden, J. A., & Rae-Grant, Q. (1978). Tay-Sachs and related storage diseases: Family Planning. *Mental Retardation, 16,* 13–15.

Schiefelbusch, R. (1972). Language disabilities of cognitively involved children. In Irwin & M. Marge (Eds.), *Principles of childhood language disabilities.* Englewood Cliffs, NJ: Prentice-Hall.

Schreibman, L., O'Neill, R. E., & Koegel, R. L. (1983). Behavioral training for siblings of autistic children. *Journal of Applied Behavior Analysis, 16,* 129–138.

Schulman, E. D. (1980). *Focus on the retarded adult: Programs and services.* St. Louis: C. V. Mosby.

Schultz, F. R. (1983). Phenylketonuria and other metabolic diseases. In J. A. Blackman (Ed.), *Medical aspects of developmental disabilities in children birth to three.* Iowa City, IA: University of Iowa Press.

Schultz, R., Wehman, P., Renzaglia, A., & Karan, O. (1978). Efficacy of contingent social disapproval on inappropriate verbalizations of two severely retarded males. *Behavior Therapy, 9,* 657–62.

Schutz, R. P., Jostes, K. F., Rusch, F. R., & Lamson, D. S. (1980). Acquisition, transfer, and social validation of two skills in a competitive employment setting. *Education and Training of the Mentally Retarded, 15,* 306–311.

Scientific seer: Rudolf Steiner. (1969). *MD, The Medical News Magazine, 13,* 245–50.

Seguin, E. O. (1846). *Traitement moral, hygiene et education des idiots et des autres enfants arrières.* Paris: Baillier.

Seligman, M. E. P. (1975). *Helplessness: On depression, development, and death.* San Francisco: Freeman.

Sells, C. J., & Bennett, F. C. (1977). Prevention of mental retardation: The role of medicine. *American Journal of Mental Deficiency, 82,* 117–29.

Seltzer, M. M. (1984). Correlates of community opposition to community residences for mentally retarded persons. *American Journal of Mental Deficiency, 89*(1), 1–8.

Seltzer, M., & Seltzer, G. (1978). *Context for competence: A study of retarded adults living and working in the community.* Cambridge, MA: Educational Projects.

Semmel, M., & Dickson, S. (1966). Cognitive reactions of college students to disability labels. *Exceptional Children, 32,* 443–50.

Shearer, M. S., & Shearer, D. E. (1972). The Portage Project: A model for early childhood education. *Exceptional Children, 39,* 210–217.

Shevin, M. (1982). The use of food and drink in classroom management programs for severely handicapped children. *The Journal of the Association for the Severely Handicapped, 7,* 40–46.

Shields, J. (1962). *Monozygotic twins.* London: Oxford University Press.

Shipe, D., Neisman, L. E., Chung, C-Y., Darnell, A., & Kelley, S. (1968). The relationship between cytogenetic constitution, physical stigmata, and intelligence in Down's syndrome. *American Journal of Mental Deficiency, 72,* 789–97.

Shockley, W. B. (1972). Dysgenics, geneticity, raeology: A challenge to the intellectual responsibility of educators. *Phi Delta Kappan, 53,* 297–307.

Shockley, W. B. (1974, November 5). *The moral obligation to diagnose the American Negro tragedy on the basis of statistical evidence.* Paper presented at University of Virginia.

Shuey, A. M. (1966). *Testing of Negro intelligence* (2nd ed.). New York: Social Science Press.

Shusan, R. D. (1974). *Assessment and reduction of deficits in the physical appearance of mentally retarded people.* Unpublished doctoral dissertation, University of California at Los Angeles.

Silverstein, A. B. (1971). Deviation social quotients for the Vineland Social Maturity Scale. *American Journal of Mental Deficiency, 76,* 348–51.

Simeonsson, R. J., Huntington, G. S., & Parse, S. A. (1980). Assessment of children with severe handicaps: Multiple problems—Multivariate goals. *JASH, 5*(1), 55–72.

Singh, N. N. (1980). The effects of facial screening on infant self-injury. *Journal of Behavior Therapy and Experimental Psychiatry, 11,* 131–134.

Skeels, H. M. (1966). Adult status of children with contrasting early life experiences. *Monographs of the Society for Research in Child Development, 31* (No. 3).

Skeels, H. M., & Dye, H. B. (1939). A study of the effects of differential stimulation on mentally retarded children. *Convention Proceedings American Association on Mental Deficiency, 44,* 114–36.

Skeels, H. M. (1942). A study of the effects of differential stimulation on mentally retarded children: A follow-up report. *American Journal of Mental Deficiency, 46,* 340–350.

Sloan, W., & Birch, J. W. (1955). A rationale for degrees of retardation. *American Journal of Mental Deficiency, 60,* 258–64.

Slosson, R. L. (1971). Slosson Intelligence Test. East Aurora, NY: Slosson Educational Publications.

Smith, A. L., Piersel, W. C., Filbeck, R. W., & Gross, E. J. (1983). The elimination of mealtime food stealing and scavenging behavior in an institutionalized severely mentally retarded adult. *Mental Retardation, 21,* 255–259.

Smith, D. D., & Smith, J. O. (1978). Trends. In M. E. Snell (Ed.), *Systematic instruction of the moderately and severely handicapped.* Columbus, Ohio: Charles E. Merrill.

Smith, D. W., Jones, K. L., & Hanson, J. W. (1976). Perspectives on the cause and frequency of the fetal alcohol syndrome. *Annals of the New York Academy of Science, 23,* 138–39.

Smith, D. W., & Wells, M. E. (1983). Use of a microcomputer to assist staff in documenting resident progress. *Mental Retardation, 21,* 111–15.

Smith, J. D. (1981). Down's syndrome, amniocentesis and abortion: Prevention or elimination? *Mental Retardation, 19,* 8–11.

Smith, J. D. (1984, in press). Pediatric euthanasia, handicapped infants, and special education: A challenge to our advocacy. *Exceptional Children.*

Smith, J. D. (1985). *Minds made feeble: the myth and legacy of the Kallikaks.* Rockville, Maryland: Aspen Systems.

Smith, J. D., & Polloway, E. A. (1983). Changes in mild mental retardation: Population, programs and perspectives. *Exceptional Children, 50,* 149–159.

Smith, J. E., & Payne, J. S. (1980). *Teaching exceptional adolescents.* Columbus, OH: Charles E. Merrill.

Smith, J. O., & Arkans, J. R. (1974). Now more than ever: A case for the special class. *Exceptional Children, 40,* 497–502.

Smith, R. M. (1968) *Clinical teaching: Methods of instruction for the retarded.* New York: McGraw-Hill.

Smith, R. M. (1969). Fundamentals of informal educational assessment. In R. M. Smith (Ed.), *Teacher diagnosis of educational difficulties.* Columbus, OH: Charles E. Merrill.

Smith, R. M. (1974). *Clinical teaching: Methods of instruction for the retarded* (2nd ed.). New York: McGraw-Hill.

Smith, R. M., & Neisworth, J. T. (1975). *The exceptional child: A functional approach.* New York: McGraw-Hill.

Smith, R. M., Neisworth, J. T., & Greer, J. C. (1978). Classification and individuality. In J. T. Neisworth, & R. M. Smith (Eds.), *Retardation: Issues, assessment, and intervention.* New York: McGraw-Hill.

Snell, M. E. (Ed.). (1978). *Systematic instruction of the moderately and severely handicapped.* Columbus, OH: Charles E. Merrill.

Snell, M. E., & Beckman-Brindley, S. (1984). Family involvement in intervention with children having severe handicaps.

Sobsey, R., & Bieniek, B. (1983). A family approach to functional sign language. *Behavior Modification, 7,* 488–502.

Soeffing, M. (1975). Abused children are exceptional children. *Exceptional Children, 42*, 126–33.

Solnit, A. J., & Stark, M. H. (1961). Mourning and the birth of a defective child. *Psychoanalytical Study of the Child, 16*, 523–37.

Souder v. Brennan, Civil Action No. 482-73. U.S. District Court, DC, filed March 13, 1973.

Sparrow, S. S., Balla, D. A., & Cicchetti, D. V. (1984). *Vineland Adaptive Behavior Scales.* Circle Pines, MN: American Guidance Service.

Spicker, H. H. (1971). Intellectual development through early childhood education. *Exceptional Children, 37*, 629–40.

Spiker, C. C., & McCandless, B. R. (1954). The concept of intelligence and the philosophy of science. *Psychological Review, 61*, 255–56.

Spitz, H. H. (1966). The role of input organization in the learning and memory of mental retardates. In N. R. Ellis (Ed.), *International review of research in mental retardation* (Vol. 2). New York: Academic Press.

Spitz, H. H. (1973). Consolidating facts into the schematized learning and memory of mental retardates. In N. R. Ellis (Ed.), *International review of research in mental retardation* (Vol. 6). New York: Academic Press.

Spitz, R. A. (1945). Hospitalism: An inquiry into the genesis of psychiatric conditions in early childhood. *Psychoanalytic Study of the Child, 1*, 53–74.

Spitz, R. A. (1946a). A follow-up report. *Psychoanalytic Study of the Child, 2* 113–17.

Spitz, R. A. (1946b). Anaclitic depression. *Psychoanalytic Study of the Child, 2*, 313–42.

Springer, N. S., & Fricke, N. L. (1975). Nutrition and drug therapy for persons with developmental disabilities. *American Journal of Mental Deficiency, 80*, 317–22.

Staats, A. W. (1975). *Social behaviorism.* Homewood, IL: The Dorsey Press.

Staats, A. W., & Burns, G. L. (1981). Intelligence and child development: What intelligence is and how it is learned and functions. *Genetic Psychology Monographs, 104*, 237–301.

Stainback, W., & Stainback, S. (1983, April). A review of research on the educability of profoundly retarded persons. *Education and Training of the Mentally Retarded, 18*(2), 90–100.

Stanfield, J. S. (1973). Graduation: What happens to the retarded child when he grows up? *Exceptional Children, 39*, 548–52.

Stark, J. A. (1983). The search for cures in mental retardation. In F. J. Menolascino, R. Neman, & J. A. Stark (Eds.), *Curative aspects of mental retardation: Biomedical and behavioral advances* (pp. 1–6). Baltimore: Paul H. Brooks.

Stein, Z., & Susser, M. (1975). Public health and mental retardation: New power and new problems. In M. Begab & S. A. Richardson (Eds.), *The mentally retarded and society: A social science perspective.* Baltimore: University Park Press.

Steinmiller, G., & Retish, P. (1980). The employer's role in the transition from school to work. *Career Development for Exceptional Individuals, 3*(2), 87–91.

Stephens, T. M. (1978). *Social skills in the classroom.* Columbus, OH: Cedars Press.

Stephens, T. M., Hartman, A. C., & Lucas, V. H. (1978). *Teaching children basic skills: A curriculum handbook.* Columbus, OH: Charles E. Merrill.

Stephens, W. E. (1966). Category usage of normal and subnormal children on three types of categories. *American Journal of Mental Deficiency, 71,* 266–73.

Stephens, W. E. (1972). Equivalence formation by retarded and nonretarded children at different mental ages. *American Journal of Mental Deficiency, 77,* 311–13.

Stern, W. (1912). The psychological methods of testing intelligence. In G. M. Wipple (Ed.), *Education and Psychological Monographs,* (No. 13).

Stoops, E., Rafferty, M., & Johnson, R. E. (1981). *Handbook of Educational Administration: A Guide for the Practitioner* (2nd ed.). Boston: Allyn & Bacon.

Strauch, J. D. (1970). Social contact as a variable in the expressed attitudes of normal adolescents toward EMR pupils. *Exceptional Children, 36,* 495–500.

Stremel-Campbell, K., Cantreel, D., & Halle, J. (1977). Manual signing as a language system and as a speech initiator for the non-verbal severely handicapped student. In E. Sontag, J. Smith, & N. Certo (Eds.), *Educational programming for the severely and profoundly handicapped.* Reston, VA: The Council for Exceptional Children.

Strichart, S. S., & Gottlieb, J. (1983). Characteristics of mild mental retardation. In T. L. Miller & E. E. Davis (Eds.), *The mildly handicapped student* (pp. 37–65). New York: Grune & Stratton.

Strickland, S. P. (1971). Can slum children learn? *American Education 7*(6), 3–7.

Stump v. Sparkman, 98 S. Ct. 1099 (1978).

Suran, B. G., & Rizzo, J. V. (1983). *Special children: An integrative approach* (2nd ed.). Dallas, TX: Scott, Foresman.

Szymanski, L. S. (1980). Psychiatric diagnosis of retarded persons. In L. S. Szymanski & P. E. Tanguay (Eds.), *Emotional disorders of mentally retarded persons: Assessment, treatment, and consultation* (p. 61–83). Baltimore: University Park Press.

Talkington, L. W. (1971). Outreach: Delivery of services to rural communities. *Mental Retardation, 9*(5), 27–29.

Tarjan, G. (1964, April 9–11). The next decade: Expectations from the biological sciences. *Mental retardation: A handbook for the primary physician.* A Report of the American Medical Association, 123–33.

Tarjan, G., Wright, S. W., Eyman, R. K., & Keeran, D. V. (1973). Natural history of mental retardation: Some aspects of epidemiology. *American Journal of Mental Deficiency, 77,* 369–79.

Tarpley, H. D., & Schroeder, S. R. (1979). Comparison of DRO and DRI on rate of suppression of self-injurious behavior. *American Journal of Mental Deficiency, 84,* 188–94.

Taylor, S. J., & Biklen, D. (1979). *Understanding the law: An advocate's guide to the law and developmental disabilities.* Syracuse, NY: Syracuse University and the Mental Health Law Project.

Taylor, S., & Bogdan, R. (1977). A phenomenological approach to "mental retardation." In B. Blatt, D. Biklen, & R. Bogdan (Eds.), *An alternative textbook in special education: People, schools, and other institutions.* Denver: Love Publishing.

Taylor, S. J., McCord, W., & Stanford, J. S. (1981). Medicaid dollars and community homes: The community ICF/MR controversy. *TASH Journal, 6,* 59–64.

Terman, L. M. (1921). Intelligence and its measurement: A symposium. *Journal of Educational Psychology, 12,* 127–33.

Terman, L. M., & Merrill, M. A. (1960). *The Stanford-Binet Intelligence Scale* (2nd rev.). Boston: Houghton-Mifflin.

Terman, L. M., & Merrill, M. A. (1973). *The Stanford-Binet Intelligence Scale* (3rd rev.). Boston: Houghton-Mifflin.

The Association for Persons with Severe Handicaps. (1984). *Legal, economic, psychological, and moral considerations on the practice of withholding medical treatment from infants with congenital defects* (Monograph No. 1). Seattle: Author.

Thompson, T., & Grabowski, J. (1972). *Behavior modification of the mentally retarded.* New York: Oxford University Press.

Thompson, W. R., & Grusec, J. (1970). Studies of early experience. In P. H. Mussen (Ed.). *Carmichael's manual of child psychology* (Vol. 1). New York: John Wiley.

Thompson, W. R., & Heron, W. (1954). The effects of restrictive early experiences in the problem-solving capacity of dogs. *Canadian Journal of Psychology, 8,* 17–31.

Thorndike, R. L., & Hagen, E. (1969). Measurement and evaluation in psychology and education (3rd ed.). New York: John Wiley.

Time, October 26, 1970, 77–79.

Tredgold, A. F. (1937). *A textbook of mental deficiency.* Baltimore: Wood.

Tucker, S. M. (1978). *Fetal monitoring and fetal assessment in high-risk pregnancy.* St. Louis: C. V. Mosby.

Turnbull, A. (1978). Moving from being a professional to being a parent: A startling experience. In A. Turnbull & H. R. Turnbull (Eds.), *Parents speak out.* Columbus, OH: Charles E. Merrill.

Turnbull, A., & Turnbull, H. R. (Eds.). *Parents speak out.* Columbus, OH: Charles E. Merrill.

Turnbull, H. R. (1975). *Legal aspects of the developmentally disabled.* Topeka, KS: National Organization on Legal Problems of Education.

Turnbull, H. R. (1980, April 18). *Legal issues and challenges in special education.* Address given at Spring Special Education Forum, University of Virginia, Charlottesville.

Turnbull, H. R. (1983). Fundamental rights, Section 504 and Baby Doe. *Mental Retardation, 21,* 218–221.

Turner, R. (1976). *Project: Zero reject. A system for locating and planning for unserved handicapped children.* (ERIC Document Reproduction Service No. ED 144 312).

Turnure, J., & Zigler, E. (1964). Outer-directedness in the problem solving of normal and retarded children. *Journal of Abnormal and Social Psychology, 69,* 427–36.

Ullman, L. P., & Krasner, L. (1969). *A psychological approach to abnormal behavior.* Englewood Cliffs, NJ: Prentice-Hall.

Umbreit, J., & Ostrow, L. S. (1980). The fetal alcohol syndrome. *Mental Retardation, 18,* 109–111.

U.S. Department of Labor. (1970). *Manual for the USES nonreading aptitude test battery.* Washington, D.C.: U.S. Government Printing Office.

Vanderheiden, G., & Grilley, K. (Eds.). (1976). *Non-vocal communication techniques and aids for the severely physically handicapped.* Baltimore: University Park Press.

Van Etten, C., & Van Etten, G. (1976). The measurement of pupil progress and selecting instructional materials. *Journal of Learning Disabilities, 9,* 4.

Van Etten, G., Arkell, C., & Van Etten, C. (1980). *The severely and profoundly handicapped: Programs, methods, and materials.* St. Louis: C. V. Mosby.

Virginia State Department of Education, Division of Special Education. (1977). *Summary of The Education for All Handicapped Children Act of 1975, Public Law 94-142.* Richmond.

Vitello, S. J. (1976). The institutionalization and deinstitutionalization of the mentally retarded in the United States. In L. Mann & D. A. Sabatino (Eds.), *The third review of special education.* New York: Grune & Stratton.

Voeltz, L. M. (1982). Effects of structured interactions with severely handicapped peers on children's attitudes. *American Journal of Mental Deficiency, 86*(4), 380–390.

Waisbren, S. E. (1980). Parents' reactions after the birth of a developmentally disabled child. *American Journal of Mental Deficiency, 84,* 245–51.

Wald, P. M. (1976). Personal and civil rights of mentally retarded citizens. In M. Kindred, J. Cohen, D. Penrod, & T. Shaffer (Eds.), *The mentally retarded citizen and the law.* New York: Free Press.

Walker, J. E., & Shea, T. M. (1980). *Behavior modification: A practical approach for educators.* St. Louis: C. V. Mosby.

Walker, V. S. (1974). The efficacy of the resource room for educating retarded children. *Exceptional Children, 40,* 288–89.

Wallace, G., & Kauffman, J. M. (1978). *Teaching children with learning problems* (2nd ed.). Columbus, OH: Charles E. Merrill.

Wallace, G., & Larsen, S. C. (1978). *Educational assessment of learning problems: Testing for teaching.* Boston: Allyn & Bacon.

Wallace, J., Burger, D., Neal, H. C., Van Breno, M., & Davis, D. E. (1976). Aversive conditioning use in public facilities for the mentally retarded, *Mental Retardation, 14*(2), 17–19.

Waller, J. H. (1971). Achievement and social mobility: Relationships among IQ score, education, and occupation in two generations. *Social Biology, 19,* 252–59.

Wallin, J. W. (1955). *Education of mentally handicapped children.* New York: Harper & Row.

Walls, R. T., Warner, T. J., Bacon, A., & Zane, T. (1977). Behavior checklists. In J. D. Cone & Hawkins (Eds.), *Behavioral assessment: New directions in clinical psychology.* NY: Bruner/Mazel.

Walmsley, S. A. (1978). A life and death issue. *Mental Retardation, 16,* 387–389.

Wannarachue, N., Ruyalcaba, R., & Kelley. (1975). Hypogonadism in Prader-Willi syndrome. *American Journal of Mental Deficiency, 79,* 592–603.

Watson, J. B. (1930). *Behaviorism* (Rev. ed.). Chicago: University of Chicago Press.

Watson, J. S., & Ramey, C. I. (1972). Reactions to response-contingent stimulation in early infancy. *Merrill-Palmer Quarterly, 18,* 219–29.

Wechsler, D. (1981). *Manual for Wechsler adult intelligence scale—revised.* New York: Psychological Corporation.

Wechsler, D. (1939). *The measurement of adult intelligence.* Baltimore: Williams & Wilkins.

Wechsler, D. (1944). *The measurement of adult intelligence* (3rd ed.). Baltimore: Waverly Press.

Wechsler, D. (1949, revised, 1974). *Wechsler Intelligence Scale for Children: Manual.* New York: Psychological Corporation.

Wechsler, D. (1966). *Wechsler preschool and primary scale of intelligence: Manual.* New York: Psychological Corporation.

Wehman, P. (1974). Instructional strategies for improving toy play skills of severely handicapped children. *AAESPH Review, 4,* 125–35.

Wehman, P., Hill, J. W., & Koehler, F. (1979). Helping severely handicapped persons enter competitive employment. *AAESPH, 4*(3), 274–90.

Weikart, D. P., & Lambie, D. Z. (1970). Early enrichment in infants. In V. Denenberg (Ed.), *Education of the infant and young child.* New York: Academic Press.

Wells, C. E. (1973). Will vocational education survive? *Phi Delta Kappan, 54,* 369–80.

Welsch v. Likins, 375 F. Supp. 487 (D. Minn. 1974).

Weurch, B. B. & Voeltz, L. M. (1981). *Ho'onanea program: A leisure curriculum component for severely handicapped children and youth.* Baltimore: Paul H. Brooks.

White, O. R., Edgar, E., & Haring, N. G. (1978). Uniform Performance Assessment System. Seattle: Experimental Education Unit, Child Development and Mental Retardation Center, University of Washington.

White, O. R., & Haring, N. G. (1978). Evaluating educational programs serving the severely and profoundly handicapped. In N. G. Haring & D. D.

Bricker (Eds.), *Teaching the severely handicapped* (Vol. III). Seattle: American Association for the Education of the Severely/Profoundly Handicapped.

Wiener, D., Anderson, R. J., & Nietupski, J. (1982). Impact of community-based residential facilities for mentally retarded adults on surrounding property values using realtor analysis methods. *Education and Training of the Mentally Retarded, 17*(4), 278–282.

Wilbur, H. (1976). Eulogy to Edouard Seguin. Remarks made at Seguin's funeral, Clamecy, France, 1880. Reprinting in M. Rosen, G. R. Clark, & M. S. Kibitz (Eds.), *The history of mental retardation: Collected papers* (Vol. 1). Baltimore: University Park Press.

Willer, B., & Intagliata, J. (1981). Social-environmental factors as predictors of adjustment of deinstitutionalized mentally retarded adults. *American Journal of Mental Deficiency, 86*(3), 252–259.

Williams, H. M. (1963). *Education of the severely retarded child.* Washington, D.C.: U.S. Government Printing Office.

Wilson, G. T. (1974). *Community recreation programming for handicapped children.* Arlington, VA: National Recreation and Park Association.

Wilton, K. M., & Irvine, J. (1983). Nutritional intakes of socioculturally mentally retarded children vs. children of low and average socioeconomic status. *American Journal of Mental Deficiency, 88*(1), 79–85.

Winick, M. (1969). Malnutrition and brain development. *Journal of Pediatrics, 74,* 667.

Wolery, M. R. (1978). Self-stimulatory behavior as a basis for devising reinforcers. *AAESPH Review, 3*(1), 23–29.

Wolfensberger, W. (1967). Counseling parents of the retarded. In A. A. Baumeister (Ed.), *Mental retardation: Appraisal, education, and rehabilitation.* Chicago: Aldine.

Wolfensberger, W. (1969). A new approach to decision-making in human management services. In R. B. Kugel & W. Wolfensberger (Eds.), *Changing patterns in residential services for the mentally retarded.* Washington, DC: President's Committee on Mental Retardation.

Wolfensberger, W. (1972). *The principle of normalization in human services.* Toronto: National Institute on Mental Retardation.

Wolfensberger, W. (1975). *The origin and nature of our institutional models.* Syracuse, NY: Human Policy Press.

Wolfensberger, W. (1983). Social role valorization: A proposed new term for the principle of normalization. *Mental Retardation, 21,* 234–239.

Wolpert, J. (1978). *Group homes for the mentally retarded: An investigation of neighborhood property impacts.* Princeton, NJ: Princeton University.

Wolraich, M. L. (1983). Hydrocephalus. In J. A. Blackman (Ed.), *Medical aspects of developmental disabilities in children birth to three.* Iowa City, IA: University of Iowa Press.

Woodward, W. M. (1963). The application of Piaget's theory to research in mental deficiency. In N. R. Ellis (Ed.), *Handbook of mental deficiency.* New York: McGraw-Hill.

Woodward, W. M. (1979). Piaget's theory and the study of mental retardation. In N. R. Ellis (Ed.), *Handbook of mental deficiency: Psychological theory and research* (2nd ed.). Hillsdale, NJ: Lawrence Erlbaum.

World Health Organization. (1978). *International Classification of Diseases* (9th rev.). Washington, DC: Author.

Wright, L. (1973). Aversive conditioning of self-induced seizures. *Behavior Therapy, 4*, 712–13.

Wyatt v. Aderholt, 368 F. Supp. 1382, 1383 (M.D. Ala. 1974).

Wyatt v. Hardin, Civil Action No. 3195–N (M.D. Ala. Oct. 23, 1978).

Wyatt v. Stickney, 344 F. Supp. 387, 344 F. Supp. 373 (M.D. Ala. 1972), 334 F. Supp. 1341, 325 F. Supp. 781 (M.D. Ala. 1971), *aff'd sub nom. Wyatt v. Aderholt*, 503 F.2d 1305 (5th Cir. 1974).

Youngberg v. Romeo, 50 U.S. Law Week 4681 (1982).

Younie, W. J., & Rusalem, H. (1971). *The world of rehabilitation: An atlas for special education*. New York: John Day.

Ysseldyke, J. E. (1978). Assessment of retardation. In J. T. Neisworth & R. M. Smith (Eds.), *Retardation: Issues, assessment and intervention*. New York: McGraw-Hill.

Zarfas, D. E., & Wolf, L. C. (1979). Maternal age patterns and the incidence of Down's syndrome. *American Journal of Mental Deficiency, 83*, 353–359.

Zeaman, D., & House, B. J. (1979). A review of attention theory. In N. R. Ellis (Ed.), *Handbook of mental deficiency: Psychological theory and research*. Hillsdale, NJ: Lawrence Erlbaum.

Zeaman, D., & House, B. J. (1963). The role of attention in retardate discrimination learning. In N. R. Ellis (Ed.), *Handbook of mental deficiency*. New York: McGraw-Hill.

Zehrbach, R. R. (1975). Determining a preschool handicapped population. *Exceptional Children, 42*, 76–83.

Zigler, E. (1966). Research on personality structure in the retardate. In N. R. Ellis (Ed.), *International review of research in mental retardation* (Vol. 1). New York: Academic Press.

Zigler, E. (1969). Development versus difference theories of mental retardation and problems of motivation. *American Journal of Mental Deficiency, 73*, 536–56.

Zigler, E. (1973). The retarded child as a whole person. In D. K. Routh (Ed.), *The experimental psychology of mental retardation*. Chicago: Aldine.

Zigler, E. (1978). National crisis in mental retardation research. *American Journal of Mental Deficiency, 83*, 1–8.

Zigler, E., & Seitz, V. (1982). Social policy and intelligence. in R. J. Sternberg (Ed.), *Handbook of human intelligence* (pp. 586–641). Cambridge: Cambridge University Press.

Zigler, E., & Balla, D. A. (1977). Impact of institutional experience on the behavior and development of retarded persons. *American Journal of Mental Deficiency, 82*, 1–11.

Zigler, E., & Balla, D. (1981). Issues in personality and motivation in mentally retarded persons. In M. J. Begab, H. C. Haywood, & H. L. Garber (Eds.), *Psychosocial influences in retarded performance: Issues and theories of development* (Vol. 1) (pp. 197–218). Baltimore: University Park Press.

Zigler, E., & Cascione, R. (1977). Head Start has little to do with mental retardation: Reply to Clarke and Clarke. *American Journal of Mental Deficiency, 82,* 246–49.

Zwerling, I. (1954). Initial counseling of parents with mentally retarded children. *Journal of Pediatrics, 44,* 469–79.

ABOUT THE AUTHORS

James R. Patton teaches in the special education mild/moderate program at the University of Hawaii/Manoa. Having experience in secondary, elementary, and adult special education, he is particularly interested in lifelong learning for the mentally retarded, laws concerning the handicapped, and teaching math and science to exceptional students. Currently, he is researching the unique needs of college students with learning problems. Jim earned his M.Ed. and Ed.D. from the University of Virginia.

James S. Payne is Dean of the School of Education of the University of Mississippi. He earned, with honors, the Ed.D. in special education/mental retardation from the University of Kansas. To his teaching, he brings a wealth of information from his experiences in vocational counseling, hiring, and training the retarded in restaurant and custodial services, planning a sheltered workshop, directing a Head Start preschool program, general managing an automobile dealership and consulting attorneys in cases regarding the rights of the handicapped. Jim has been active at the national level with ARC-US since 1975 and has authored many articles and books.

Mary Beirne-Smith is an Assistant Professor of Special Education at the University of Alabama. Her previous experience includes regular and special education classroom teaching, special education public school administration, and adjunct university teaching. She has served on the boards of many professional organizations. Her current interests center around assessment of handicapped individuals, classroom interventions for special education students, and teacher effectiveness. Mary received her B.S. from Longwood College and her M.Ed. and Ed.D. from the University of Virginia.

Diane M. Browder is Assistant Professor of Education at Lehigh University, Bethlehem, Pennsylvania. She taught special education for two years in a rural elementary setting. Diane has consulted with residential programs, group homes, and adult treatment centers. Presently, she is a consultant to programs serving the severely emotionally disturbed. She received her Ph.D. from the University of Virginia in Special Education emphasizing severe/profound in 1981, her M.Ed. in 1976, and a B.A. from Duke University in Psychology in 1975.

Laurence J. Coleman is a professor in the Department of Special Education and Rehabilitation at the University of Tennessee, Knoxville. He has five years experience as a public school teacher. His current interests include career education for the exceptional individual and education of the gifted student. He has published articles and chapters in these areas. Larry was awarded a B.A. from State University of New York at Albany, an M.S. from Southern Connecticut State College, and a Ph.D. from Kent State University.

Jill C. Dardig is a professor of special education at Ohio Dominican College, Columbus, Ohio. She is active in community service and has served as consultant to a number of public school systems. She is particularly interested in educational interventions for exceptional individuals. Her publications include two books, several book chapters, and numerous journal articles. Jill received her A.B. from Mount Holyoke College, her M.Ed. from the University of Massachusetts, and her Ed.D. from the University of Massachusetts.

Robert M. Davis, Jr. is a school psychologist with the Albemarle County, Virginia, Public Schools in the Department of Special Services. His background, training, and years of experience have been in the areas of teaching, counseling, school psychology, and administration. He has also been an adjunct professor on the community college, college, and university level. He publishes in both educational and psychological journals. He was a Doctoral Fellow at East Tennessee State University, from which he received his Ed.D. in Educational Administration.

Keith Hume is Clinical Director of Mountain Wood, a center for the treatment of alcoholism and drug abuse. His previous experience includes consulting with various groups and agencies, including police department units assigned to work with victims of traumatic crimes, outpatient alcoholism clinics and agencies involved in vocational rehabilitation of individuals with multiple handicaps, including the mentally retarded, the emotionally disturbed, and severely physically disabled. Keith received his B.A. from the State University of New York at Buffalo, his M.S. at Niagara University in New York, and his Sc.D. from Boston University.

Eric D. Jones teaches at Bowling Green State University. He has had four years experience teaching bilingual Navajo Indian children with mild learning handicaps. He has also worked with severely retarded persons in residential settings. Eric received an A.B. in experimental psychology from Bucknell University (1973), an MA in special education from the University of Northern Colorado (1974) and an Ed.D. in special education and program evaluation from the University of Virginia. Currently he is conducting research in the areas of teacher training and the acceptability of behavioral interventions.

Jayne-Anne Maresca is a special education teacher (mental retardation) in the Fairfax County Public School District, Fairfax, Virginia. Jayne-Anne was selected as a contributor because of her writing talent and ability that was demonstrated in her special education program while attending the University of Virginia. She received the B.S. degree in special education with a dual endorsement in learning disabilities and mental retardation. While in Charlottesville, Virginia, she became active in Night College, Piedmont Regional Educational Program, and Oakland School for the learning disabled.

Cecil D. Mercer is a professor of education at the University of Florida. He received his Ed.D. in special education from the University of Virginia in 1974. Cecil has authored numerous articles and books on educating exceptional children. Two of his major works are *Students with Learning Disabilities* and *Teaching Students with Learning Problems*. Cecil remains involved in the educational programs of exceptional children through his participation in the learning disabilities program at Shands Teaching Hospital in Gainesville, Florida. He also is Co-Director of the University of Florida Multidisciplinary Diagnostic and Training Program. In addition, he works with children in nonschool settings by coaching Little League baseball.

Allen K. Miller is a teacher of severely disturbed children at Ragged Mountain School, Charlottesville, Virginia. He has five years teaching experience in a rural setting with mild and moderate mentally retarded high school students. Allen received an Ed.D. in special education: mental retardation in 1983 from the University of Virginia. He received a B.S. in animal science from Virginia Polytechnic Institute and State University in 1972, and M.Ed. in special education from the University of Virginia in 1978.

Frances E. Patton received the B.S. degree from the University of Virginia in special education with honors. She was an Isaac L. Carey scholar and was on the Dean's list. She has taught mentally retarded adults for two years and has been active in Special Olympics, ACLD, CEC, and Red Cross. Fran has researched, edited, written, and designed brochures, ads, and pamphlets for many special education organizations. She presently is a production designer for DesignFocus International, Inc., Honolulu, Hawaii.

Ruth Ann Payne was formerly the Vocational Planner for the Charlottesville School System. She has thirteen years of teaching experience, three years of college teaching, and, for two years, was the Academic Advisor for the Athletic Department at the University of Virginia. Ruth Ann has appeared on national television, published in professional journals and co-authored several books in special education, early childhood, and mental retardation. She completed her B.S. at Washburn University and her M.Ed. at the University of Virginia in Counselor Education.

Edward A. Polloway is an associate professor of special education at Lynchburg College, Lynchburg, Virginia where he currently serves as Teacher Certification Officer and Coordinator of Programs in Special Education. His previous experience includes teaching elementary and special education public school classes. He has published numerous books and journal articles and is a member of many professional organizations. He received his B.A. from Dickinson College, and his M.Ed. and Ed.D. from the University of Virginia.

Janis Spiers is director of an ICF-MR faculty and licensed home for adults that serves moderate to profoundly retarded and multiply handicapped individuals. Her previous experience includes work with The Region Ten Community Services Board and supervision of a night education and socialization program for mentally retarded adults. Janis received her B.S. in special education from the University of Virginia.

Carol H. Thomas teaches in the Department of Special Education at the Texas Woman's University, where she also coordinates the doctoral program. Previous professional experiences include several years of classroom teaching with exceptional children and as a school psychologist. She earned a B.A. in psychology and an M.S. in school psychology from Radford University, and an Ed.D. in special education from the University of Virginia. She has published in the area of mental retardation and is presently engaged in compiling the *Directory of College Facilities and Services for the Handicapped* (2nd edition) with her husband.

Thomas J. Zirpoli is coordinator of two training grants at the University of Virginia. As a graduate assistant, Tom is involved in a personnel preparation program that provides training to current and future teachers of individuals with severe handicaps. His duties include classroom instruction at the university and field supervision of teachers in community classrooms. He received his B.S. degree in psychology and his M.Ed. degree in special education from Old Dominion University, and his Ph.D. from the University of Virginia. Before initiating his doctoral studies, he worked at a residential training center for persons with mental and physical handicaps. His current areas of study include the severely handicapped, research, supervision, and child abuse within handicapped populations.

NAME INDEX

SUBJECT INDEX